THE ESSENTIAL FOUCAULT

THE ESSENTIAL WORKS OF FOUCAULT, 1954–1984
PAUL RABINOW, SERIES EDITOR

Ethics
Edited by Paul Rabinow

Aesthetics, Method, and Epistemology
Edited by James D. Faubion

Power
Edited by James D. Faubion

THE ESSENTIAL FOUCAULT

Selections from
The Essential Works of Foucault
1954–1984

EDITED BY PAUL RABINOW
AND NIKOLAS ROSE

THE NEW PRESS

NEW YORK
LONDON

Published in the United States by The New Press, New York, 2003
Distributed by W. W. Norton & Company, Inc., New York
Pages 459–460 constitute an extension of this copyright page.

LIBRARY OF CONGRESS CATALOGING-IN-PUBLICATION DATA
Foucault, Michel.
[Selections. English. 2003]
The essential Foucault : selections from essential works of Foucault, 1954–1984 / edited by
Paul Rabinow and Nikolas Rose.
p.   cm.
Rev. ed of: The essential works of Foucault, 1954–1984. c1997–c2000.
Includes bibliographical references.
ISBN 1-56584-828-4 (hc.)—ISBN 1-56584-801-2 (pbk.)
1. Philosophy, French—20th century.   I. Rabinow, Paul.   II. Rose, Nikolas S.
III. Foucault, Michel. Essential works of Foucault, 1954–1984.   IV. Title.
B2430.F722E5 2003
194—dc21   2003043648

Selections from *Dits et écrits, 1954–1988*, ed. Daniel Defert and François Ewald,
with the assistance of Jacques Lagrange, published by Editions Gallimard, Paris.

The New Press was established in 1990 as a not-for-profit alternative to the large,
commercial publishing houses currently dominating the book publishing industry.
The New Press operates in the public interest rather than for private gain,
and is committed to publishing, in innovative ways, works of educational, cultural,
and community value that are often deemed insufficiently profitable.

The New Press
38 Greene Street, 4th floor
New York, NY 10013
www.thenewpress.com

In the United Kingdom:
6 Salem Road
London W2 4BU

Composition by dix!

Printed in Canada

2   4   6   8   10   9   7   5   3   1

CONTENTS

INTRODUCTION
FOUCAULT TODAY
By Paul Rabinow and Nikolas Rose

> *We do not undertake analyses of works because we want to copy them or because we suspect them. We investigate the methods by which another has created his work, in order to set ourselves in motion.*
>
> PAUL KLEE[1]

> *A critique is not a matter of saying that things are not right as they are. It is a matter of pointing out on what kinds of assumptions, what kinds of familiar, unchallenged, unconsidered modes of thought the practices that we accept rest. . . . We must free ourselves from the sacralization of the social as the only reality and stop regarding as superfluous something so essential in human life and human relations as thought.*
>
> MICHEL FOUCAULT[2]

How should we read Michel Foucault's work today?[3] His writing spans a period from the early 1950s—his *Mental Illness and Psychology* was published in 1954—to his death in 1984. Many biographers and historians of ideas have looked backward and tried to understand his thought in terms of his life and its historical context. But in this introduction to some of Foucault's most important shorter writings—course summaries, interviews, and lectures—we look forward and ask a different question: What does Foucault's thought offer for the analysis of our present and our future? This is not a matter of seeking to define a singular approach or a unique methodology which we can then apply to our current concerns. Foucault would, undoubtedly, have been wryly skeptical about the growth of "Foucault studies" and the related attempt to discipline his thought and turn it into an orthodoxy. The texts collected here certainly do not invite this kind of treatment: they set out to open things up, not close them down; to complicate, not simplify; not to police the boundaries of an oeuvre but to multiply lines of investigation and possibilities for thought. They are not aspects of a single project, but fragmentary—experiments, interventions, provocations, and reflections. Foucault, in these explorations, is constantly asking himself questions about the nature and implications of his work: what I have been doing, where am I going, where have I been, where are "we" today, who is the "we" of whom I write, who might be a future "we," what might be the role of thought or the work of writing and thinking in clarifying and transforming who we are? Thus, the power of these texts does not lie in the illustration of "Foucaultianism," but rather in the way in which they show us the thinking in motion of one of the most innovative intellectuals of the twentieth century. As one reads these texts, one finds that Foucault's thinking is sometimes contradictory, sometimes reinterpreting texts of the past against their apparent nature, sometimes suggesting new and untried investigations, sometimes jumping in completely unexpected ways. Our hope is that, as readers engage with this critical thought on our present, and on ourselves in the present, their own critical thought might be set into a similar and productive motion. That, we think, would be the most fitting legacy to the creativity of Foucault today.

PART ONE: USING FOUCAULT

Field Work in Philosophy

To use a term from Paul Klee, Foucault "rendered visible" certain aspects of our experience *in profoundly new ways* for a whole generation of thinkers. Prisons, schools, and asylums now appeared less than obvious responses to the need of crime control, the treatment of mental illness, or the requirements for mass education, more as strange inventions, apparatuses whose micropowers made possible the creation and disciplining of human capacities in novel ways. The belief that our psyche and our desires lie at the very heart of our existence as experiencing human creatures now turned out to be, not a foundational point that can ground and justify our demands for emancipation, but the fulcrum of a more profound subjectification. Of course, some of these things had long been recognized, but somehow they were obscured by the reigning conceptual grids, in particular the relations that they proposed between truth and power and between power and subjectivity. In identifying power effects with the distortion of truth—notably by means of the concept of ideology—and domination with the suppression or deformation of subjectivity, these grids undoubtedly showed us important things about the working of capitalism, patriarchy, racism, and the like. But they were increasingly unhelpful in visualizing the detailed workings of the forms of thought and practice that shaped our contemporary existence and experience—ways of thinking and acting that worked by producing truth and producing the kinds of human beings who took themselves as subjects.[4] Foucault enabled us to see different kinds of relations between truth and power, in which power was a matter of the production of truth, and truth was itself a thing of this world, intrinsically bound to apparatuses like the prison, the hospital, the school, and the clinic for its production and circulation. And he enabled us to visualize different kind of relations between practices that sought to know and manage human individuals and the emergence of conceptions of ourselves as subjects with certain capacities, rights, and a human nature that can ground all sorts of demands for recognition. This was not achieved by an exercise in philosophy or social theory of the traditional sort, but by a kind of "field work in philosophy"—that is to say, by a meticulous investigation of particular practices, technologies, and sites where power was articulated on bodies, where knowledge of human individuals became possible, and where souls were produced, reformed, and even, sometimes "liberated." In inventing the tools and the insights that made these relations visible, the very words themselves that are now so familiar—truth, knowledge, power, technology, discourse, practice—were given a new sense and made to do conceptual work that they had not done—that had not been done—before. And in anatomizing the detailed ways of thinking and acting that made up our present, and constituted ourselves in that present, Foucault asked us to consider the possibility that we might invent different ways of thinking about and acting on ourselves in relation to our pleasures, our labors, our troubles and those who trouble us, our hopes and aspirations for freedom.

Politics and Power

Today it seems self-evident that sexuality and gender, medicine and illness, the prison and punishment, psychiatry and psychiatric reform, social insurance and social security, are "political" issues: they are aspects of the ways in which we are governed, they involve asymmetrical relations of power, and they are subject to contestation. But it is easy to forget how recently this view of the scope of politics became common sense. A critical work was required—not least on radical politics itself—to recover the sense of the political significance of these issues. It was carried out in different places by many movements and individuals—by feminists, by prison reformers, by the antipsychiatry movement, by welfare activists and many others. In prioritizing these issues for analysis, Foucault was undoubtedly stimulated by the ways in which these movements problematized such practices although his debts to some were sometimes left unacknowledged. However, his empirical work—for example, his studies of the politics of medicine and health in the eighteenth century—showed that no simple lines could be drawn between reformers and reactionaries, between those "on the side of power" and those "on the side of resistance."[5] Even in questions of punishment, as for example in attempts to identify particular dangerous individuals and understand their motives, these studies made it more, rather than less, difficult for the intellectual to make political judgments as, say, among those who sought retributive punishment based on the horror of a criminal act, those who sought to understand and reform the criminal as a sick individual, and those who sought to fictionalize infamy and make transgression the basis of a literary apparatus.[6] No wonder, then, that his analyses did not try to arbitrate on political strategies or radical objectives in any of these areas— his unwillingness to be overtly prescriptive made his work an irritant to much radical thought. His distinctive contribution was different and longer lasting— it was to question the very constitution of these domains—sexuality, criminology, psychiatry, social security—and the ways in which they had come to define the territory and limits of what we must accept and what we could contest and transform. To the extent that these domains had, in part, been constructed through a work of thought, thought could reveal their contingency and fragility—and hence the possibility of their transformation.[7]

Concepts and Creativity

Foucault's concepts create new options for thought and new possibilities for action. Take, for example, governmentality.[8] Of course, the topics of state, government, administration, and citizenship had been the subject of whole libraries of historical investigation, and whole bookshops of radical critique. But when these were viewed from the perspective of governmentality they were placed within a more general field of endeavors by authorities to conduct the conduct of their human charges toward certain ends, some of which become the subject of political argument, the responsibility of political rulers, and the apparatus of state. The growth of the apparatuses of the state, the development of the disciplines of administration and the civil service, and the rise of professionals is intrinsically linked to projects, plans, and practices to conduct the conduct of subjects, whether these be citizens, voters, parishioners, patients, clients, or consumers. This was not a matter of the spread of the tentacles of the state through the spaces of everyday life. Far from it—Foucault initially forged the concept of "governmentality" in an attempt to understand the characteristics of liberalism as a mentality of government that started from the presupposition that society existed external to the state, and constrained itself by limiting the scope of legitimate political power, subjecting it to a range of constraints, and constantly requiring it to justify itself.[9] From this moment on, the play between the inside and the outside of politics, between public and private, between government and freedom, was central to government. And, from this perspective, the analysis of issues of state and politics, of political authority itself, took on a different shape: curiously the key critical dimension now appeared as an ethical one. This was not because these issues now had to be addressed within ethical theory, but because they all involved issues of who should govern us, how should we be governed, what should be governed and to what ends: that is to say, they raised the question of who "we"—the governed—were as the subjects of these kinds of practices and the kinds of lives we have come to lead. We now must investigate the powers of the state and of its apparatus of rule in relation to all those many transactions where our own concerns with our own lives have also become the concern of others—not just explicitly political agencies, but also all those other authorities (religious, medical, commercial, therapeutic) who whisper in our ears and advise us how to act and who to be. Both the demands that led to the "governmentalization of the state" in the twentieth century, and the criticism of this expansion of the scope and role of state powers in the last decades of that century, now appear as linked to strategies, tactics, and contestations over the inculcation of the arts of existence to be exercised by individuals, families, and communities themselves. And, in a way that is disturbing to many, we can now recognize that the precepts, norms, and values disseminated in these practices of government have made us the kinds of persons we take ourselves to be.

Or take, for example, the concept of biopower.[10] So much had been written on health and illness, on statistics, the census, epidemiology and demography, on the science of race, eugenics, population, abortion and dilemmas over new reproductive technology. Yet, strangely, no one had grouped these diverse domains under a common term. Biopower names and groups together these concerns with the management of the phenomena that characterize groups of living human beings. It relates the exercise of this form of power to varying conceptions of the nature of human individuals and collectivities, their apparently biological variability—race, fertility, gender, constitution—and the ways in which these characteristics can be shaped, managed, and selected in order to achieve political objectives. It shows how this problem of the government of living populations produces specific dilemmas for liberalism as a principle for the rationalization and exercise of government based on a conception of autonomous legal subjects endowed with rights and free enterprise of individuals. And it casts new light on the relations between the liberal government of the metropolitan territories and the exercise of colonial government over populations conceived of as naturally, racially, biologically, constitutionally, morally, and ethically distinct. Reframed in the context of biopolitics, each of these issues—the government of racial difference in the colonies, the management of public health, the design of hospitals and sewage systems, concerns about the falling birth rate, female fecundity or the location of cemeteries—morphs. While the empirical detail concerning each stays recognizably the same, the configurations amongst them becomes oddly different. New relations, dangers, promises, apparatuses, stakes, and quandaries come into view and we can see how our present took shape through successive attempts to resolve them. Looking back, how could we not have seen that life itself has been fundamentally at stake in our politics and in our ethics? How could we have avoided recognizing the political consequences of the fact that we humans have come to understand ourselves as living beings whose very vitality, longevity, morbidity, and mortality can be managed, administered, reformed, improved, transformed, and has a political value? From this point on, it will be impossible to pose the question of our existence as political creatures without simultaneously having to think about the ways in which our politics has become a matter of life itself. And, reciprocally, it will be impossible to understand the politics of life without addressing the way in which life itself has entered into knowledge, and the changing ways in which its specificity—as vitality, as organic machine, as code—has been understood.

Knowledge and Objects

This question—of the knowledge of life and the government of life—enables us to stress another key point. To analyze the circuits that link knowledge to practices of normalization, cure, or government is not to reduce truth to a mere effect of such practices—to suggest that truth is merely a legitimation or functional support for power. If Foucault had proposed this, he would not have spent so much time and effort describing the complex circuits and relations between our knowledges of ourselves as living beings and the practices that made those knowledges possible and which they have engendered.[11] Knowledges—even those of the positive sciences which take the human being in its living, acting, desiring, transgressing, sickening, and dying reality as their object—are governed by certain rules that establish what can be said truthfully at any one time, the criteria of evidence, the forms of proof, and even the very object of which they can speak. Life, today, is not what it was for Xavier Bichat writing at the start of the clinical experience in medicine in the late eighteenth century, for Claude Bernard establishing experimental medicine in the nineteenth century, nor even for Kurt Goldstein whose monumental study of the organism was published in the 1930s. Madness today is not what it was for Thomas Willis when he treated the madness of George III, nor for Philippe Pinel when he struck the chains from the inmates of the Salpêtrière, nor even for Jean Delay and Pierre Deniker, the discoverers of the first modern psychiatric drug, chlorpromazine, in the 1950s.[12] In the discourses regulated by the norms of truth—which are those that *primarily* concerned Foucault—it is a matter of investigating the conditions that establish, at any one time, the relation between true and false, which is, on the one hand, intrinsic to the sciences and their history, and, on the other, essential to the ways in which human beings have come to govern themselves and others.

Then and Now

Does that mean that in the texts collected here—or in any others of Foucault's writing—one will find the last word on topics such as biopower, governmentality, or the changing relations between life and knowledge of life. The answer is no. After all, Foucault wrote before the collapse of the Soviet empire, before the "New World Order," before the internet, before the genome project, before global warming, before genetically modified organisms, before preimplantation diagnosis of embryos, before "pharmacogenomics." So it would be futile to search the texts to find his detailed or substantive insights into these configurations. This is not only for the obvious reason that these events postdated his death. Even were he alive today, and although his work was attuned to immediacy and actuality, it was not his practice to deliver evaluations of current affairs. Readers may take *Discipline and Punish* to be a critical history of the prison system at the time it was written—the 1970s—or *Madness and Civilization* as an analysis or critique of the psychiatry of the late 1960s. Undoubtedly, these books are motivated by precisely these conjunctures. But Foucault's diagnosis of the present does not proceed by attempting a comprehensive analysis of these practices as they exist today, but by seeking the conditions that have made these practices possible and have established the grounds on which they depend for their intelligibility—for example, the very idea of the mental patient or of the criminal. *Madness and Civilization* may help us think critically about the psychiatry of the last quarter of the twentieth century, but this "rendering visible" is achieved by a study that terminates in the nineteenth century—a study that hardly mentions that societies in Europe and North America were already dismantling many of the premises of psychiatric systems based upon confinement in the institution of the mental hospital. Similarly, *Discipline and Punish* barely mentions the prison system as it existed in the 1970s, and was written at the very moment when control practices based on the identification, incarceration, and normalization of the deviant individual were already being incorporated within wider circuits for the management of troublesome conduct. Each of these studies started from a point where some of the given-ness of established ways of thinking and acting was already coming into question. But rather than addressing this configuration of problems and solutions directly, Foucault used history to help grasp the way in which this configuration had come into existence and to diagnose some of the fault lines ingrained within it. These works did this by mapping the contingent pathways along which the taken-for-granted possibilities and limits of our present have come into existence.

For example, *Madness and Civilization* is an analysis of the way in which the very territory of twentieth-century psychiatry came into existence—the unification of its subjects, objects, and problems within institutions and practices in which the varieties of madness shared a purely negative ethical value.[13] But from the problem spaces of twenty-first-century psychiatry, we might well trace a different genealogy. We would follow different pathways to diagnose the tangled field where the boundaries are blurred between institution and society and between madness and sanity, where mental disorder is no longer uniquely a question of unreason, where mental ill health is not merely an economic burden on the nation but a vastly profitable market for the enterprise of psychopharmaceuticals. Nevertheless, in addition to their specific historical and ethical insights, the abiding value of texts such as *Madness and Civilization* and *Discipline and Punish* lies in the way they exemplify a certain ethos of investigation. For to do the history of psychiatry or the prison, for Foucault, is not to write a history of what psychiatrists or penal reformers said or did, or even a history of their institutions. Specifically, these studies show that such practices, persons, and institutions gain their sense only from their location within a much wider nexus of relations of knowledge, power, and the production of subjectivities. But more generally, these texts teach us something about the role of history in critical thought. For a certain use of history was central to the critical work of thought that Foucault practiced. Foucault's recourse to history shares something with social history, but he was not, in fact, writing history. This is even more important to recognize, now that categories like archaeology and genealogy have became part of a repertoire of received concepts, and historicizing has become a routine tactic of critical argument. While the displacements of method entailed in this different use of historical materials frequently upset historians, Foucault's studies are not intended to replace conventional ways of practicing the discipline of history. Indeed, some of their power arises out of their tension with these other ways of making use of historical material.[14] While Foucault repeatedly turns to the past to understand the present, this is not an obsession with the past in Nietzsche's sense that Europe was sick from such an historical obsession. Nor is it a relentless presentism, in which all that has gone before is merely put in the service of our own concerns—we do not need George Orwell to remind us that there are dangers in such a motivated rewriting of the past with all the obliterations of the inconvenient that it entails. If Nietzsche's genealogy of morals was an attack on Christendom and European complacency, Foucault's genealogies have a different point of attack and use different techniques. But what they share is the concern to disturb and trouble our own conventions— whether of truth, of politics, or of ethics—through a gray and meticulous labor of detail on the paths that we took—and the paths that were not taken—in putting together the objects, subjects, and values that seem so natural and precious to us.[15]

We cannot assume that this recourse of critical thought to history can simply be repeated in order to address the issues that concern us today and in the future. In his relation to Nietzsche, Foucault demonstrates that genealogy has to be invented anew as situations change. So perhaps the detailed and meticulous labor that needs to be done to unsettle our conventions must find other forms, other points of action on our present. These might be comparative, conjunctural, or ethnographic, or they may take a form that has yet to be invented or named. Thus, the practice of criticism which we might learn from Foucault would not be a methodology. It would be a movement of thought that invents, makes use of, and modifies conceptual tools as they are set into a relation with specific practices and problems that they themselves help to form in new ways. When they have done this work, without regret, they can be recycled or even discarded.

Dispositif

One of the most powerful conceptual tools introduced by Foucault is that of "apparatus" or *dispositif*. Social theory had tended to work in terms of institutions, classes, and cultures and, in a distinct register, in terms of ideas, ideologies, beliefs, and prejudices. But in introducing the concept of apparatus, Foucault cut reality in a different way. In cutting across these categories, new and rather different elements, associations, and relations can be seen. This is not to say that class relations and the like disappear. Rather, Foucault practices a style of research that analyzes the articulations of these grand complexes in the mundane practices of the prison, the hospital, the school, the courtroom, the household, the town planner and colonial governor. The new problems and connections that come into view, precisely because of the level of detail at which they are described, seem to become more amenable to action and transformation.

Foucault's first use of the term, if not exactly the concept, *dispositif* was in 1975 in an interview following the publication of *Surveiller et Punir*. After many years working through the voluminous documentary archives around the prison, the hospital, schools and the like, he had learned, he told his interviewer, that it was not necessary to search for anything hidden when it came to the intentions and projects of the nineteenth-century bourgeoisie. In its classical manifestations, the bourgeoisie was lucid and cynical; they knew what they wanted to accomplish and wrote about their plans with great explicitness. The level of reality that counted was on the surface and it was directly accessible. There was no need to contrive the kinds of sophisticated "symptomatic readings" that were associated with a certain interpretation of Marx's method or the text of *Capital*, to penetrate beneath what was said and written to reveal hidden interests, the structure of sign systems, what was being repressed or projected.[16] "Substitute the logic of strategies for the logic of the unconscious," Foucault calmly advised as if his approach was uncontroversial, "replace the privileged place accorded to the signifier and its semiotic connections with an attention to tactics and their apparatuses."[17] He appears to be taking the term "apparatus" in its ordinary French usage that refers to tools and devices. In the 1976 introduction to a collective work on the *Politics of Health in the Eighteenth Century*, the product of his working seminar at the College de France, Foucault used the

concept as well as the term: "The biological traits of a population became pertinent elements in its economic management, and it was necessary to organize
them through an apparatus that not only assured the constant maximization of
their utility but equally their subjection." [18] Foucault uses the word "apparatus"
to mean a device oriented to produce something—a machinic contraption
whose purpose in this case is control and management of certain characteristics
of a population. In the collective report on the seminar's work, there is a sustained empirical demonstration of what a strategic assemblage looks like. This
shows how, and in what ways, an apparatus composed of a grouping of heterogeneous elements had been deployed for specific purposes at a particular historical conjuncture. The politics of health in the eighteenth century was a politics
of apparatuses. [19] It was a politics of strategically chosen targets. It was an articulation of technologies aimed at first specifying (and to that extent creating)
those targets and then controlling (distributing and regulating) them. [20]

When questioned about his use of the term *dispositif* in 1977, Foucault responded by underscoring that the defining aspect of apparatuses was their
grouping of heterogeneous elements into a common network *(réseau)*. [21] The
apparatus was "a resolutely heterogeneous grouping composing discourses, institutions, architectural arrangements, policy decisions, laws, administrative
measures, scientific statements, philosophic, moral and philanthropic propositions; in sum, the said and the not-said, these are the elements of the apparatus.
The apparatus itself is the network that can be established between these elements." [22] The elements composing or taken up in a network apparently could
be anything. Foucault saw the elements in an apparatus as joined and disjoined
by a strategic logic and a tactical economy of domination operating against a
background of discursive formations. He identified the apparatus as characterized by changes in the position of its elements, the multiplying modifications of
its functions, and an overall articulated strategic intent, albeit an appropriately
flexible one. The apparatus embodied a kind of strategic bricolage articulated
by an identifiable social collectivity. It functioned to define and to regulate targets constituted through a mixed economy of power and knowledge.

As his studies of the birth of social medicine show—and as also spelled out in
Discipline and Punish—these strategic assemblages are initially formed as responses to crises, problems, or perceived challenges to those who govern. [23] The
apparatus is a specific strategic response to a specific historical problem. But
such an initial response to a pressing situation can gradually have a more general
rationality extracted from it, and hence be turned into a technology of power
applicable to other situations. What may have begun, for example, as a rather ad
hoc assemblage of ways of thinking and acting, making use of elements that
were at hand, linking them in new ways and turning them to new ends, in order
to attempt to deal with a problem such as that of urban crime, may turn into a

way of thinking and acting applicable to other problems and populations, at other times and in other places. The apparatus can be rationalized and the techniques turned into a generalizable technology. Further, despite the initial intention that an apparatus will respond in a targeted way to a particular problem to achieve a specific strategic objective, diverse and unplanned effects can and do result. These too can play a role in extending the network of the apparatus. For example, the creation of a delinquent milieu in the city was not planned by prison reformers but arose as an unanticipated effect. It soon became part of the larger problem of urban policing and, as it turned out, not only did this not destroy the strategic utility of the apparatus but to an extent came to be used to extend it. This claim, of course, does not mean it worked "even better," if by that one means it achieved the explicit goals laid out by the forces of order.[24] But it did work if by that one means that an ever wider game of order—that is to say, a whole rationality—and an ever wider set of projects of reform—that is to say, a whole technology—came to be cast within these terms.

Problematization

The term *problématisation* first appears in *Discipline and Punish* and then with increasing frequency in Foucault's later work. During the mid 1970s, Foucault was rethinking the Nietzschean grid of warfare as the basic transhistoric, metaphorics of life, knowledge, and power, developing the concept of governmentality and beginning his analysis of liberalism as a mentality of government that depended upon, created, and constrained free subjects.[25] Foucault here began to take up the question of thinking as an activity, one that similarly involved both constraint and freedom.[26] This crucial reframing of thought and of politics has been lost on many Anglo-American commentators (both favorably and unfavorably disposed to Foucault) who have refused to accept the implications of Foucault's discovery that power was not external to freedom. This interplay of enabling capacities and constraining powers, of the obligation to limit power but also of modes of inflecting it, gained a saliency not only as an analytics but equally as a perpetual practical (political and ethical) problem. It was within the frame of these developments that Foucault began to articulate, albeit in a preliminary fashion, the concept of problematization.

The most direct and explicit presentation of *problématisation* took place in a discussion in Berkeley in 1983, presented in a different form in the second "Preface" that was actually published with *The History of Sexuality, Volume 2: The Use of Pleasure*. Would it be possible, Foucault wondered, "to describe the history of thought as distinct from both the history of ideas (by which I mean the analysis of systems of representation) and from the history of mentalities (by which I mean the analysis of attitudes and types of action [*schémas de comportement*]). It seemed to me that there was one element that was capable of describing the history of thought—this was what one could call the element of problems or, more exactly, problematizations." [27] In part, the concept of problematization was forged in distinction to the traditional sense in which the history of ideas meant the history of philosophic doctrines: as, for example, Foucault's mentor Jean Hyppolite had practiced it in his work on Hegel. In part, the concept distinguishes Foucault's analytics from the analysis of representations as semiotic systems as undertaken, say, by Roland Barthes and taken up by Anglo-American cultural studies. And, in part, it distinguishes his thought from the many French historians and anthropologists, who were seeking the underlying system of codes that shaped a culture's thought and behavior: the object of an analysis of problematizations is not "culture" at all, at least in the sense that had concerned the social sciences.

Problematization, then, named the distinctive dimension on which Foucault's history of thought would operate. A "problematization," Foucault writes, "does not mean the representation of a pre-existent object nor the creation through discourse of an object that did not exist. It is the ensemble of discursive and non-discursive practices that make something enter into the play of true and false and constitute it as an object of thought (whether in the form of moral reflection, scientific knowledge, political analysis, etc.)." [28] For an earlier generation of radical intellectuals, inspired by Marxist conceptions of critique, the role of critical thought was to disturb the naturalness, the taken-for-granted character of everyday life—the nuclear family, the wage form, the commodity was to be revealed as not given and eternal but the contingent product of a set of deep but historically contingent laws and processes. In revealing this contingency, critique hopes to open these givens to political action. Foucault's conception of problematization differs. Like Nietzsche, for Foucault the most profound thought is that which remains on the surface. To analyze problematizations is not to reveal a hidden and suppressed contradiction: it is to address that which has already become problematic. For a problematization to have formed, something prior "must have happened to have made it uncertain, to have made it lose its familiarity, or to have provoked a certain number of difficulties around it." [29] But for Foucault we can always identify several possible ways of responding to the same ensemble of difficulties. For "when thought intervenes, it doesn't assume a unique form that is the direct result or the necessary expression of these difficulties; it is an original or specific response—often taking many forms, sometimes even contradictory in its different aspects—to these difficulties, which are defined for it by a situation or a context, and which hold true as a possible question." [30] The task of the analyst is not to adjudicate between these, but to "rediscover at the root of these diverse solutions the general form of problematization that has made them possible—even in their very opposition . . . what has made possible the transformations of the difficulties and obstacles into a general problem for which one proposes diverse practical solutions."³¹

The specific diacritic of thought is not only to be found in this act of diagnosis. It also rests on the attempt to change the way in which a situation is apprehended: from seeing it as "a given" which generates problems that must be resolved, to seeing it as "a question" whose formation and obviousness must itself be subject to analysis. To enquire into this transformation of difficulties into problems that demand solutions is not to arbitrate between existing responses, but to "free up" possibilities. The act of thinking is an act of modal transformation from the constative to the subjunctive, from the necessary to the contingent.

Critical thought adopts a particular relation to problematization. By definition, the thinker is neither entirely outside of the situation in question nor entirely enmeshed within it without recourse or options. Indeed, thought "is what allows one to step back from this way of acting or reacting, to present it to oneself as an object of thought and to question it as to its meaning, its conditions, and its goals. Thought is freedom in relation to what one does, the motion by which one detaches oneself from it, establishes it as an object, and reflects on it as a problem."³² Thinking is the form given to that motion of detachment, reflection, and reproblematization. For Foucault, this kind of thought is not autonomous in any of the strong senses that it has been given in Western philosophy. Thought is neither transparent, nor is it a passive waiting, nor is it an intentional act of consciousness. Thought is not necessarily coherent, it has no univocal or foundational meaning that is amenable to a complete logical clarification. Thought is not, cannot be, an external evaluation of a situation. "This development of a given into a question, this transformation of a group of obstacles and difficulties into problems to which the diverse solutions will attempt to produce a response, this is what constitutes the point of problematization and the specific work of thought."³³

Subjectification

Many have suggested that in the last phase of his writing, Foucault rethought his relation to a problem that he had previously questioned and sidestepped—the question of "the subject." In part this is true, but in doing so, once again, he transmuted this question into one amenable to a kind of historical investigation:

> After first studying the games of truth [*jeux de vérité*] in their interplay with one another, as exemplified by certain empirical sciences in the seventeenth and eighteenth centuries, and then studying their interaction with power relations, as exemplified by punitive practices—I felt obliged to study the games of truth in the relationship of self with self, and the forming of oneself as a subject.³⁴

Foucault considers his aims in the preface he had originally intended to publish
to the second volume of *The History of Sexuality*, but which was actually published separately.[35] His was not "a history of the self" of the sort that has become familiar in historical sociology—it is not an attempt to write a history of
the transformations of human psychology over time and space. Nor is it a concern with identity, in the way in which that question has beset the social sciences
in recent decades. As one might expect, his was not a romantic or humanist wish
to write the history of *who we are*. Instead, it was an attempt to develop an analytic that could make visible the vectors that shape *our relation to ourselves*. In the
slight gap that opens when one moves from the question "What kinds of selves
have we become?" to "How do we relate to ourselves as selves of a certain
kind?"—in this "epistemology of the relation"—history inserts itself not in
our psyche but in that silent thought that inhabits the most intimate aspects of
our experience of ourselves. As Foucault put it in the version of the introduction that was published with *The Use of Pleasure*, this would be a history of the
"forms and modalities of the relation to the self by which the individual constitutes and recognizes himself *qua* subject"—of "the *problematizations* through
which being offers itself to be, necessarily, thought—and the *practices* on the
basis of which those problematizations are formed."[36] The human being, from
this perspective is not so much an entity—not even an entity with a history—
than the site of a multiplicity of practices or labors. And as for its interiority—
the subjectivity apparently so essential to all theories of the subject and anxieties
about "agency"—perhaps it is best to follow Gilles Deleuze here, and his philosophy of the fold: the apparent depth of the human soul is less a psychological
system than a discontinuous surface, a multiplicity of spaces, cavities, relations,
and divisions established through a kind of infolding of exteriority.[37] Forms of
experience arise, that is to say, on the basis of practices—not necessarily discursive—insofar as they are inhabited by thought: "in every manner of speaking,
doing or behaving in which the individual appears and acts as knowing subject
[*sujet de connaissance*], as ethical or juridical subject, as subject conscious of himself and others."[38]

This approach opens on to specific studies of the problems and problematizations through which human beings have been shaped in a thinkable and man-
ageable form, the sites and locales where these problems are formed, the
techniques and devices invented, the modes of authority and subjectivity engendered, and the telos of these various tactics and strategies.[39] This way of
thinking about subjectification clearly reflects back upon, and reframes, Foucault's earlier analyses of the emergence of the thinking, laboring, living subject as the object of knowledge, and of the individual as the target of practices
of punishment, pedagogy, and cure. In part, these were analyses of language: of
the emergence of new categories of human beings and new explanatory frame-

works within scientific discourse. But if we consider the accounts given of the birth of the subject of psychiatry in *Madness and Civilization,* of the birth of the patient of clinical medical reason in *Birth of the Clinic,* of the birth of the individual in *Discipline and Punish,* we can see that—whatever some careless critics think—these are not discourse analyses in any of the senses given to this term in Anglo-American linguistics or social science. In fact, these investigations, carried out at different times across virtually the whole period of Foucault's work, embody the very ambitions that he makes explicit in his late work on ethics: not analyses of discourse, but of

> the games of truth and error through which being is historically constituted as experience; that is, as something that can and must be thought. What are the games of truth by which man proposes to think his own nature when he considers himself to be ill, when he conceives of himself as a living, speaking, laboring being; when he judges and punishes himself as a criminal? What were the games of truth by which human beings came to see themselves as desiring individuals?[40]

Such "games of truth" have not arisen in some abstract space of thought, but always in relation to specific practices: the places and spaces, the apparatuses, relations, and routines that bind human beings into complex assemblies of vision, action, and judgment, whether these be those of domestic existence, sexual relations, labor, or comportment in public places or consumption. Language—even as discourse—is only one of the heterogeneous and localized intellectual and practical techniques, the "instruments" through which human beings constitute themselves. The games of truth which make up the history of our relation to ourselves should not be studied in terms of ideas, but of *technologies:* the intellectual and practical instruments and devices enjoined upon human beings to shape and guide their ways of "being human."[41]

In Foucault's studies of Greek and Roman texts on the arts of existence from the late 1970s onward, this "technological" aspect of the relation of self to self once more comes to the fore.[42] Ethics, here, is reposed in terms of the aspects of the human being that are singled out as the target of such work, the relations to authority and truth under which that work is constructed, the precise techniques for experiencing and reshaping the self that are employed, and the forms of subject to which one is led to aspire. Each configuration of these relations of self to self implies a certain activity of the subject within a field of constraints—even for the slave or for the mad, under situations where the models of selfhood are imposed from outside, a certain self-crafting is required.[43] And each crafting of a relation with the self arises out of, and entails, a crafting of one's relations to others—be they one's superiors, one's pupils, one's colleagues, one's husband, wife, or mistress, one's family, or one's friends. The central values of our current ethical regimes—the experience of freedom, the necessity for recognition, the inviolable dignity of the human being—do not form the ground of all these ethical configurations or the universal basis for their critique. They are the historical, local, moving, and always troubled resultant of the application of certain arts of existence. And this particular ethic of "the care of the self" is not the only one possible—there have been, and will be, other ways of understanding and relating to oneself and to others.

Pausing, Moving

In what we now know was the last period of his writing, during what turned out to be the end of his life, Foucault had been frustrated by his own inability to gain more clarity about the intellectual, ethical, aesthetic, and political problems that were troubling him. Such a situation of blockage before finding new things to explore, and new means of exploration, was not a unique one for Foucault. These moments of pause and reformulation were typically punctuated by interviews and reflections in which, and through which, Foucault situated his intellectual and autobiographical trajectory. These declarations were often made in sweeping terms and, at times, in a manner that contradicted claims about his work that he had offered on prior occasions. The narrative clarity may well have been a fiction but it was fiction that helped Foucault to begin working and thinking once again. And after his periods of stasis, Foucault usually succeeded in achieving dramatic accelerations in his thinking and his action. Thinking was action, and action was motion—and as a thinker and as a person, Foucault sought to be in motion. Although he had characterized the reasons for his insistence on change and reevaluation in various ways at various moments, the most striking formulation was his quest to "se déprendre de soi." [44] To detach oneself from oneself—such a distance enables motion, and in its turn, motion enables a recurrent activity of self-detachment. In a certain practice of philosophy, as in science, change, reevaluation, and reformulation, is entirely appropriate. For one who searches, such motion lies at the heart of a life devoted to research.

Foucault's later works are neither a final philosophic testament nor the thoughts of a person facing imminent death. Here they contrast, for example, with the last writings of Gilles Deleuze. When Deleuze expresses his surprise in *What is Philosophy?* that it had been remarkably rare for philosophers to take up the question "What is philosophy?"—reserved for a small cohort of thinkers who posed this question for themselves in its brute essentials only at the end of their lives—he could not have known that his friend Felix Guattari would die shortly thereafter, but he was fully aware of his own physical decline, and perhaps of the relationship (of suicide) he would adopt toward his own physical deterioration. Foucault most certainly did not know with any certainty that he was terminally ill until shortly before his death—little was known about AIDS in 1983, and the test for HIV only came on the French market in October 1984, after Foucault's death in June. Even in 1984, in one of his last lectures at the *Collège de France*, Foucault mentioned in passing that he intended to take up a topic under discussion at a future time. Foucault's writings from this period, therefore, do not form a final reflection made as an end approached; they are yet another turning in his life and thought.

Foucault's "detour," as he himself named it, into the climes of the antique world of Greek, Hellenistic, and Roman thought, lasted close to seven years. It culminated with the publication of two books, volumes 2 and 3 of *The History of Sexuality*. It was terminated by Foucault's death in June 1984. On one level, Foucault's frustration turned on the issue of gaining sufficient mastery of the subject matter he was analyzing. The shift to the ancient world was both captivating and troublesome; Foucault knew very well that he had entered into a domain many scholars over the course of many generations had spent their lives exploring. He knew as well that many of these specialists would not welcome the entry of an amateur into their domains, that his work would be received by many as an impertinent intrusion. This reception was especially to be anticipated because Foucault was raising basic questions within this hyper-investigated arena that rather curiously had been underexplored by these men and women of knowledge. The complicated reception by historians—largely negative although not entirely so—of his previous work had prepared Foucault for professional spite but also, much more importantly, for the pleasures of new work that others would be enabled and emboldened to pursue. There was always a price to be paid for detours into new terrains: as a long line of modern thinkers from Nietzsche through Freud and Bourdieu have taught us, there is no *entrée libre* into the commerce of ideas. This time Foucault did not live to experience either the reception of his new books or the fate of the new figures of truth he had "rendered visible."

In the late 1970s and early 1980s, Foucault not only shifted the subject matter of his investigation, he also wrestled with problems about thought itself, about the manner or style of thinking, the form that one gives to thought, and the relation of that mode of thinking to a form of life: what *mode d'assujettissement* was appropriate for the intellectual.[45] Foucault felt bored and trapped in Paris and he was drawn to the existential and intellectual life in the Bay Area: it was here, for example, that one can locate the kinds of experiences that led to his 1981 reflections on "friendship as a way of life."[46] In this period of reexamination and reformulation, in what might be termed his Berkeley and San Francisco years, Foucault posed for himself, in different ways, some questions about the very activity he had been engaging in for so long: "What is thinking?"; "Why think?"; and, perhaps surprisingly, "What is the place of thinking in a good life?" Was it possible to develop a kind of critical thought that would not "judge"—so much criticism has the form of a quasi-judicial tribunal passing down verdicts of guilt or innocence on persons or events—but would create, produce, and intensify the possibilities within existence? And this, perhaps, is the challenge that his work lays down to us today.

PART TWO: AFTER FOUCAULT

The Present and Its History

> *[One of the] most destructive habits of modern thought . . . is that the moment of the present is considered in history as the break, the climax, the fulfillment, the return of youth, etc. . . . One must probably find the humility to admit that the time of one's own life is not the one-time, basic, revolutionary moment of history, from which everything begins and is completed. At the same time, humility is needed to say without solemnity that the present time is rather exciting and demands an analysis. We must ask ourselves the question, What is today? In relation to the Kantian question, "What is Enlightenment?" one can say that it is the task of philosophy to explain what today is and what we are today, but without breast-beating drama and theatricality and maintaining that this moment is the greatest damnation or daybreak of the rising sun. No, it is a day like every other, or much more, a day which is never like another.*[47]

Foucault is famous for a remark that he made in *Discipline and Punish* about the history of the present: his engagement with history, he implied, was not simply because of an interest in the past but was part of a critical project directed toward the present.[48] Of course, he is by no means the only thinker to have explicitly argued that historical investigations should be undertaken in order better to understand the present. But the catch phrase that came to characterize this approach—the history of the present—was to signal neither an historical methodology nor an historical sociology. Perhaps this difference may be understood by addressing it from two directions. The first concerns the present itself as a contemporary problem field, but one which is neither a temporal not a sociological unity. And the second concerns the critical attitude that one might properly adopt towards that present.[49]

For historical sociologists, modernity is accorded the characteristic of an epoch, defined in time, and perhaps now in space as well. It has certain characteristic forms—a type of individualization, certain forms of rationality, typical practices of control and normalization—and a characteristic ethos—an orientation to the future, to progress and the like. For many commentators and crit-ics,—the work of Marx, Weber, and Durkheim is placed within this grid of in-terpretation—whether its essence is capitalism, rationalization, or organic solidarity, modernity defines not only the abstract object of social theory but also the essential features of the real social relations that that theory seeks to grasp in thought. Hence, for this latter concern, debates rage about the geo-graphical span of modernity—is it confined to "the West," is it spreading across the planet under the impulse of globalization? Similar debates rage over the cri-teria for inclusion in modernity—is Islam "premodern"? And, most troubling of all, since its very nature is temporal, what are the chronological limits of modernity—are we, for instance, in "late modernity"? Or, perhaps, we are on the cusp of something new, in which the modern is to be transcended, incorpo-rated in a higher synthesis to which, for a time, many gave the name of post-modernity.

But Foucault's concern with the present does not make him a theorist of "modernity" of this ilk. His earlier work was seen by many to participate in a kind of historical periodization—the very distinction of renaissance, classical, and modern *epistemes* in *The Order of Things* was an analytical strategy that was likely to attract the criticism of "epochalization" and of course it did.[50] Foucault was criticized as a theorist of systems that succeeded one another in radical dis-continuity, and hence his thesis apparently raised—but could not answer—the question of how change between *epistemes* occurred. Whilst it is true that *epis-temes* are not epochs, in the introduction to *The Archaeology of Knowledge*, writ-ten around 1968, Foucault remarks that he found it "mortifying that I was unable to avoid the dangers [of giving the impression that the analyses in his previous books were being conducted in terms of cultural totalities]: I console myself with the thought that they were intrinsic to the enterprise itself, since, in order to carry out its task it first had to free itself from these various methods and forms of history." Indeed he says that it was in answer to questions on this very point that he came to gain a clearer view of the enterprise that he was en-gaged in, and from this time on he sought to distance himself from the residues of structuralism in his mode of criticism.[51] Nonetheless, perhaps the very idea of "systems of thought" imposed a kind of structural obligation on analysis—that is to say, an obligation to identify structures, and to operate through the radical distinction of one structure from another. And whilst his book-length analyses seldom discuss the present in any direct way, the problem of the pres-ent is nonetheless made amenable to thought by means of the distance, and the difference, established between it and that which has preceded it. We can see this in *Madness and Civilization* and its analysis of the relegation of madness to mere mental pathology (there was not always a monologue of reason about mad-ness), in the contrasting spatializations of illness and the body discussed in *Birth of the Clinic* (it was not always the body that was the site of illness and the target of cure), or the changes in regimes of punishment and their targets so dramatically portrayed in *Discipline and Punish* (it was not always the soul that was the origin of infraction and the target of punishment).

In his essay "What Is Enlightenment?"[52] Foucault suggests that, across the local and partial discontinuities that his earlier works had explored, we have remained "beings who are historically determined, to·a certain extent, by the Enlightenment."[53] To this extent, the questions human beings have posed to themselves in these distinct historical configurations are nonetheless recurrent: What is our time, and how does it differ from other times? What kinds of persons have we become? How can we judge good and bad? What can we hope for? Who do we care for and how do we care for them? What must we strive for? But the task of historical investigation of our present is to diagnose the singularity with which each of these questions presents itself at any historical moment, and in doing so to reveal the peculiarity of the dilemmas through which our own world presents itself to us. To make our present itself untimely—or rather, to make our relation to it untimely: for Foucault, as for Nietzsche, what meaning could his studies "have for our time if they were not untimely—that is to say, acting counter to our time and thereby on our time and, let us hope, for the benefit of a time to come."[54] Elsewhere, Foucault thinks of this as an "ethic of discomfort," an ethic that can be seen as the philosophical task bequeathed to us by Maurice Merleau-Ponty:

> Never to consent to being completely comfortable with one's own presuppositions. Never to let them fall peacefully asleep, but also never to believe that a new fact will suffice to overturn them; never to imagine that one can change them like arbitrary axioms, remembering that in order to give them the necessary mobility one must have a distant view, but also to look at what is nearby and all around oneself. To be very mindful that everything one perceives is evident only against a familiar and little known horizon, that every certainty is sure only through the support of a ground that is always unexplored. The most fragile instance has its roots. In that lesson, there is a whole ethic of sleepless evidence that does not rule out, far from it, a rigorous economy of the True and the False; but that is not the whole story.[55]

To act in this way, through history on our present, to show how our seemingly timely and inescapable problems were composed, is not an act of relativization. Our questions, however contingent, remain our questions—historical, yes, but what else could they be? So the effect of this act of thought upon thought is not to relativize thought, let alone minimize or ironize the significance of the questions that haunt our thought, but to establish a certain necessary distance from their apparently implacable immediacy, from the demand they make upon us to provide answers not questions. Such a space is necessary for us to begin to reimagine these problems—it is the space for what might be called freedom in thought: "a virtual break which opens a room, understood as a room of concrete freedom, that is possible transformation."[56]

To speak, here, of transformation—or of possible transformation—is to turn to the second aspect of Foucault's attention to the present—which concerns the critical attitude one might adopt toward it. Some thoughts of Paul Klee are, once again, instructive here: "[The artist] is a philosopher, perhaps without exactly wanting to be one. And while he does not optimistically declare this world to be the best of all possible worlds, or believe it to be so bad that it is unfit to be taken as a model, he nevertheless says to himself: In its present form it is not the only world possible!"[57] And Foucault in a similar vein, in his essay on enlightenment,[58] quotes Baudelaire's precept "You have no right to despise the present."[59] It is true that, at times, some of Foucault's own statements give credence to the view that his work is infused by the same "hermeneutic of suspicion" that activates the repetitive and wearying reflexes of the intellectual left: everything is dangerous, suspect the worst, we know already whose interests this serves—where this covers everything from NATO's actions in former Yugoslavia to the projects to map the human genome. "I do not say everything is bad," Foucault answers to an interviewer who asks if he is doing history in order to find alternative solutions to current problems, "only that everything is dangerous." And when, repeatedly, interviewers suggest that his work is a nihilism that can only lead to stasis, his riposte is to present it as requiring the opposite: a kind of constant activism in relation to the present.[60] But in fact, for Foucault, the critical role of thought is different.

On the one hand, he suggests, it is not the role of thought to say "it is useless to revolt." In extreme situations, even when power appears absolute and despotic "behind all the submissions and coercions, beyond the threats, the violence, and the intimidations, there is the possibility of that moment when life can no longer be bought, when the authorities can no longer do anything, and when, facing the gallows and the machine gun, people revolt."[61] Thought here commingles with something irreducible in life—one needs no ontology to recognize it, no humanism to defend it, no Marxism to evaluate it.

On the other hand, and perhaps this is an even more difficult ethical injunction for intellectuals, neither is it the role of thought—or at least of Foucault's ethic of thought—to demand resistance where it is absent. It is not the role of the intellectual to say "it is imperative to revolt, do you not realize that your world is intolerable?" Nor is it their role to tell all those who play a part in the practices of power—the social workers, the psychiatrists, the doctors, the bioscientists—what to do, what not to do, what to strive for, what to reject. If anything is to discourage the attempts of such practitioners to improve the practices in which they work, it would be this, for such injunctions do not recognize where they are, what they do, the dilemmas and obligations that intersect upon them.[62] "If the social workers . . . don't know where to turn," says Foucault in the 1970s, when questioned about the supposedly anesthetizing effects of *Discipline and Punish* upon those in such roles, "this just goes to show that they're looking, and hence not anesthetized or sterilized at all—on the contrary. And it's because of the need not to tie them down or immobilize them that there can be no question for me of trying to tell 'what is to be done.' If the questions posed by the social workers . . . are going to assume their full amplitude, the most important thing is not to bury them under the weight of prescriptive, prophetic discourse." [63] But, on the other hand, Foucault continues, "The necessity of reform mustn't be allowed to become a form of blackmail serving to limit, reduce or halt the exercise of criticism." To criticize the present without anesthetizing those who must act within it, to make conventional actions problematic without portraying them as acts of bad faith or cowardice, to open a space for movement without slipping into a prophetic posture, to make it possible to act but making it more, not less difficult to "know what to do"—this, it seems, is the ethic of discomfort that Foucault seeks to introduce into our relation to the present and to ourselves in the present.

Biopower

Foucault, in *The Order of Things*, identified three arenas of discourse that in their (unstable and incomplete) coalescence at the end of the classical age constituted the object called "Man" [*l'homme*]. This figure emerges at the intersection of three domains—life, labor, and language—unstably unified around (and constituting) a would-be sovereign subject. The doubling of a transcendental subject and an empirical object and their dynamic and unstable relations defined the form of this being. In 1966, Foucault undoubtedly held an epochal view of Man and of modernity. In his conclusion, Foucault intimated the imminent coming of a new configuration in which the figure of Man would be swept away like "a face drawn in the sand at the edge of the sea." [64] Gilles Deleuze predicted that this meant not so much the disappearance as the transmutation of *l'homme* into a new kind of being.[65] It now appears this presage was miscast. Language (in its modality as *poiesis*) has not been the site of radical transformations through which this being, Man, would either disappear entirely or be transmuted.

Although Foucault did not directly return to his diagnosis of the "end of Man," he did modify his understanding of modernity as an epoch. As we have already suggested, in his essay "What Is Enlightenment?" Foucault sought to invent a new philosophic relationship to the present. Modernity was taken up here, not through the analytic frame of the epoch, but through a practice of inquiry grounded in an ethos of present orientation, of contingency, of form giving. Suppose, then, that we took up recent changes in the *logoi* of life, labor, and language not in terms of an epochal shift with a totalizing coherence for Man, but rather as fragmented and sectorial changes that pose problems, both in and of themselves as well as for attempts to make sense of what form(s) *anthropos* is currently being given. And we might get some clue to these transformations in *anthropos* from a different reflection offered by Foucault upon *l'homme moderne*—as a being "whose politics puts its existence in question." [67] This suggests that an analysis of changing forms of power over life—of biopower— might provide a perspective from which we might address this larger question of the transformations in *l'homme moderne*. [68]

The concept of biopower is introduced in a few pages in the *History of Sexuality, Volume 1*. It seems to incorporate both the individualizing pole of discipline and the collectivizing pole of the politics of population, to embrace all the historical processes that have brought human life and its mechanisms into the realm of knowledge-power, and hence amenable to calculated transformation. [69] But the most substantive discussion of the concept is in the course at the *Collège de France* in 1975–1976 that Foucault called *"Il faut défendre la société"* ("Society Must Be Defended"). [70] Biopower is a distinct regime of power: its objects and its method are given shape within a particular type of rationality. Foucault contrasts that rationality (and its associated practices) to the one it superseded, that of sovereign power: "On top of the older right of the sovereign to *take* life or to *let* live, was substituted the power to *foster* life or to *disallow* it to the point of death." [71] In *Discipline and Punish,* Foucault had presented memorably vivid exemplifications of the terrible corporal theater of the sovereign's imperative to wage war on those that threaten his body politic. Foucault proposes a reversal of object and agency: in the rationality of biopolitics the new object is life and its regulation, to be achieved through the continuous regulation of its mechanisms. This imperative implies knowing those mechanisms and forging technologies and institutions to achieve that regulation: "What was demanded and what served as an objective was life, understood as the basic needs, man's concrete essence, the realization of his potential, a plentitude of the possible." [72] If fostering life is an active agenda, so, too, is disallowing it. In one of those striking amplifications for which he was infamous, Foucault writes: "If genocide is indeed the dream of modern powers, this is not because of a recent return of the ancient right to kill; it is because power is situated and exercised at the level of life, the species, the race, and the large-scale phenomena of population." [73]

It is evident that systematic exterminations of the population have continued into our present in the name of one or other authoritarian discourse. However, few of the recent examples, ghastly as they have been, have called upon the truth discourse of modern bioscience or the technologies of modern knowledge-power to support them. These have been wars of sovereignty: however

powerful and in some ways comforting is the rhetoric that sees them as the culmination and hence the hidden truth of modern power, we would argue that
much qualification is demanded. If biopower sutures together the management
of life and the management of death, today "the dream of power" focuses on
the pole of life. The place of death in these ways of thinking and acting is more
modest, more enigmatic and more troublesome—decisions as to selective abortion, selective fetal implantation, euthanasia, brain death, and the end of life.
Even for the twentieth century, a period which saw the culmination of scientific
thanato-politics, the dream of modern powers can with equal plausibility be
presented as the universalization of the well-run welfare state, the spread of liberal democracy, the vast expansion of NGOs bearing witness to the abuse of
human rights, and the maximization of well-being, or more elementally the
progressive containment of many infectious diseases. One of the most compelling intellectual challenges for our present is certainly to develop an analytics
that brings questions of the administration of life and death into a relationship.
But this must be done, not by claiming there is some deep hidden secret of
modernity to be revealed, but through that labor of gray, meticulous attention
to the details of the practices of life and death that we, in our present have constructed, inhabit, and contest.

Any initial survey of our contemporary problematization of life itself would
begin by recognizing that, at the turn of the twenty-first century, the practices
and dilemmas of life politics are not monopolized by states or even by doctors.
There are a multitude of other actors in this new field of biosociality, not least
amongst them being the patients, their families, their communities themselves,
not to mention the transnational pharmaceutical companies, biotech industry,
massively funded science faculties, ethics commissions, regulatory agencies—
and the vociferous social critics of bioscience and genomics themselves. Further, one would need to address these issues in a manner that was informed by
Foucault's own reflections on the mentalities of liberal government. For over
the twentieth century, in liberalism and, more especially, in neoliberalism, one
saw the emergence of formulae of power that not only postulated, but also
sought to create, certain forms and spaces of self government, self-regulation,
and self-responsibility. These were not illusory, but were the quid pro quo for
limiting the scope of the central administration, which, for such political rationalities, neither could nor should know and control all those forces upon which it
depended. In part through imitation and exemplarity, in part through the efforts
of quite specific and identifiable agencies such as the International Monetary
Fund and the World Bank, this formula for politics has proved extremely mobile. It has penetrated way beyond the confines of a particular political doctrine
or body of political philosophical texts to become the premise for the operation
of political power on a transnational—we are tempted even to say global—

scale. And it has proved translatable into the reshaping of practices in a range of microlocales including all those where health and life, illness and death, are governed. This is not to say there is anything automatic or inevitable about its functioning, still less to take it on its own terms, or to pronounce it "a success." Indeed, the role of critical thought is precisely to address the problem space in which life and health have become so central to our contemporary relations to ourselves and others and the relations of expectation and obligation we have with our authorities, to reproblematize the emergence of the living body as perhaps the key ethical substance upon which we must ourselves work in order to fashion ourselves and fulfill our potential as human beings.

And, in these processes, the ways in which we understand and relate to ourselves as human beings is under transformation. In the twentieth century, we came to ground our ethical practices in an understanding of ourselves as creatures inhabited by a deep interior, the font of all our desires and the place where we might discover the secret source of all our troubles. But these relations to ourselves are being transformed in the new games of truth that we are caught up in. New sciences of brain and behavior forge direct links between what we do—how we conduct ourselves—and what we are. These games of truth work at a molecular level—the level of neurons, receptor sites, neurotransmitters, and the precise sequences of base pairs at particular locations in what we now think of as the human genome. At the same time, these molecular phenomena, rendered visible and transformed into the determinants of our moods, desires, personalities, and pathologies, become the target of new pharmaceutical techniques that promise not merely coping, nor even cure, but correction and enhancement of the kinds of persons we are or want to be. Such developments are not primarily mobilized by the kinds of actors we have come to think of as political—biopolitics today is a matter of the meticulous work of the laboratory in its attempts to create new phenomena, the massive computing power of the apparatus that seeks to link medical histories and family genealogies with genomic sequences, the marketing powers of the pharmaceutical companies, the regulatory strategies of research ethics, drug licensing bodies, committees and bioethics commissions, and, of course, the search for the profits and shareholder value that truth here promises. It is here, in the practices of contemporary biopower, that the figure of *l'homme* is mutating: the human, here, is not erased but transformed from ontological to artificial—in the sense of open to artifice. This is not a matter, as some prophesy, of our becoming "post-human." More mundanely, and yet more profoundly, it is merely another move in the games of truth, power, and ethics within which we have, historically, come to understand and act upon ourselves as humans of particular kinds.

Forward

And what, in the end, is the gain for critical thought achieved by such a work of thought? For Foucault, this work is a mode of critique he terms historical ontology. Thus, toward the end of his essay on "What Is Enlightenment?," following his attempt to distinguish the theme of humanism from that of Enlightenment, he writes:

> . . . we must obviously give a more positive content to what may be a philosophical ethos [of Enlightenment] consisting in a critique of what we are saying, thinking, and doing through a historical ontology of ourselves . . . criticism is no longer going to be practiced in the search from formal structures with universal value but, rather, as a historical investigation into the events that have led us to constitute ourselves, and to recognize ourselves as subjects of what we are doing, thinking, saying.[74]

And, as significantly, it is not a method of critique that seeks to reinvent ourselves anew "the historical ontology of ourselves must turn away from all projects that claim to be global or radical" for we know from our history the fate of such attempts to escape from the constraints of the present:

> I prefer the very specific transformations that have proved to be possible in the last twenty years in a certain number of areas which concern our ways of being and thinking, relations to authority, relations between the sexes, the way in which we perceive insanity or illness; I prefer even these partial transformations, which have been made in the correlation of historical analysis and the practical attitude, to the programs for a new man that the worst political systems have repeated throughout the twentieth century.[75]

What faces us, then, if we are to take historical ontology seriously, is not a grand gesture of transgression or liberation, but a certain modest philosophical and pragmatic work on ourselves: "a historical-practical test of the limits we may go beyond, and thus as work carried out by ourselves on ourselves as free beings." A work, that is to say, which is both banal and profound, which we carry out upon ourselves in the very real practices within which we are constituted as beings of a certain type, as beings simultaneously constrained and obligated to be free, in our own present.

Notes

1. Paul Klee, *Notebooks, Volume 1: The Thinking Eye*, trans. Ralph Mannheim (London: Lund Humphries, 1961), from "The Concept of Analysis," p. 99.

2. Foucault, "Practicing Criticism" or "Is It Really Important to Think?" interview by Didier Eribon, May 30–31, 1981, in Foucault, *Politics, Philosophy, Culture*, ed. Lawrence Kriztman (New York and London: Routledge, 1988), p. 155.

3. We would like to thank James Faubion, Thomas Osborne, Tobias Rees, and Mariana Valverde for helpful comments on earlier drafts of this introduction.

4. See "Truth and Power" and "The Subject and Power," this volume.

5. See "The Birth of Social Medicine" and "The Politics of Health in the Eighteenth Century," this volume.

6. See "Lives of Infamous Men" and "Dangerous Individual," this volume.

7. See "So Is It Important to Think?" this volume.

8. See "Governmentality" and "Omnes et Singulatim," this volume.

9. See "The Birth of Biopolitics," this volume.

10. See "Society Must Be Defended," "Security, Territory, and Population," and "The Birth of Biopolitics," this volume.

11. See "Questions of Method," this volume.

12. See "On the Archaeology of the Sciences" and "Life, Experience, and Science," this volume.

13. See "Madness and Society," this volume.

14. See "Nietzsche, Genealogy, History," this volume.

15. See "Questions of Method" and "On the Genealogy of Ethics," this volume.

16. Louis Althusser et al., *Lire le Capital, Lire Marx* (New York: Patheon, 1970).

17. Foucault, *Dits et écrits, Vol. 2*, p. 720.

18. Foucault, *Dits et écrits, Vol. 3*, p. 18.

19. See "The Politics of Health in the Eighteenth Century," this volume.

20. There are selections in volume 3 of *The Essential Works of Foucault: Power*, ed. James Faubion (New York: The New Press, 2000).

21. "Quel est pour toi le sens et la fonction méthodologique de ce terme: 'dispositif'?" (*Dits et écrits, Vol. 3*, p. 298).

22. Michel Foucault, "Le Jeu de Michel Foucault," in *Dits et écrits, Vol. 3*, p. 298.

23. See "The Birth of Social Medicine" and "The Politics of Health in the Eighteenth Century," this volume.

24. "The Confession of the Flesh" in *Power/Knowledge*, ed. Colin Gordon (New York: Pantheon, 1980) p. 195.

25. Arpad Szakolczai details this fact and provides an explanation for it, in his *Max Weber and Michel Foucault: Parallel Life Worlds*, (London and New York: Routledge Ltd., 1998).

26. "The Ethics of the Concern of the Self as a Practice of Freedom," this volume.

27. "Polemics, Politics, and Problematization," in volume 1 of *The Essential Works of Foucault: Ethics*, ed. Paul Rabinow (New York: The New Press, 1997), p. 117.

28. Foucault, *Dits et écrits, Vol. 4*, p. 670.

29. "Polemics, Politics, and Problematization," in volume 1 of *The Essential Works of Foucault: Ethics*, p. 117.

30. Ibid., p. 118.

31. Ibid., p. 118.

32. Ibid., p. 117.

33. Ibid., p. 118.

34. *The History of Sexuality, Vol. 2: The Use of Pleasure*, trans. R. Hurley (New York: Vintage Books, 1986, 1990), p. 6.

35. "Preface to *The History of Sexuality*, Volume 2," this volume.

36. *The History of Sexuality, Vol. 2*, pp. 6, 11.

37. Gilles Deleuze, *Foucault*, trans. Sean Hand (Minneapolis: University of Minnesota Press, 1988), pp. 94–123.

38. "Preface to *The History of Sexuality, Vol. 2*," this volume.

39. "On the Genealogy of Ethics," this volume.

40. *The History of Sexuality, Vol. 2*, pp. 6–7.

41. See "Technologies of the Self," this volume.

42. See "On the Genealogy of Ethics," this volume.

43. See "The Ethics of the Concern of the Self as a Practice of Freedom," this volume.

44. "Introduction," volume 1 of *The Essential Works of Foucault: Ethics*.

45. See "The Masked Philosopher," this volume.

46. "Friendship as a Way of Life," in volume 1 of *The Essential Works of Foucault: Ethics*, p. 135.

47. "How Much Does It Cost to Tell the Truth," in *Foucault Live* ed. Sylvère Lotringer, (New York: Semiotext(e), 1996), pp. 348–62, at p. 359.

48. Foucault, *Discipline and Punish*, trans. Alan Sheridan (London: Allen Lane, 1977), p. 31.

49. The argument in this section rehearses that in the introduction to Andrew Barry, Thomas Osborne, and Nikolas Rose, *Foucault and Political Reason*, (London: UCL Press, 1996), pp. 1–18.

50. Foucault discusses these issues in "Structuralism and Post-Structuralism," this volume.

51. Introduction to *The Archaeology of Knowledge*, trans. Alan Sheridan Smith (London: Tavistock, 1972), pp. 16–17. Foucault refers here in particular to his reply to questions posed by the *Cercle de Epistémologie* of the E.N.S, published in *Cahiers pour l'analyse*, 9 (1968), which was published in English translation in *Theoretical Practice*, 3/4 (1971), and to his "Réponse à une question" put to him about *The Order of Things* by the editors of *Esprit* and published in *Esprit* in 1968, translated as "Politics and the Study of Discourse," *Ideology and Consciousness*, 3, (1978), pp. 7–26.

52. "What Is Enlightenment?," this volume.

53. Ibid.

54. F. W. Nietzsche, "On the Uses and Disadvantages of History for Life," in *Untimely Meditations*, trans. R. J. Hollingdale (Cambridge: Cambridge University Press, [1874] 1893), p. 60.

55. "For an Ethic of Discomfort" in volume 3 of *The Essential Works of Foucault: Power*, p. 448.

56. Quoted in Barry et al., *Foucault and Political Reason*, p. 5.

57. Klee, *Notebooks*, p. 92.

58. "What Is Enlightenment?," this volume.

59. Ibid.

60. "On the Genealogy of Ethics: An Overview of Work in Progress," a 1983 interview with Michel Foucault, volume 1 of *The Essential Works of Foucault: Ethics*, p. 256 (also included in this volume).

61. "Useless to Revolt?," volume 3 of *The Essential Works of Foucault: Power*, pp. 459–50.

62. "Questions of Method," this volume.

63. Ibid.

64. Michel Foucault, *Les Mots et les choses* (Paris: Editions Gallimard, 1966), p. 398.

65. Deleuze, "Appendix: On the Death of Man and Superman," in *Foucault* (Minneapolis: University of Minnesota Press, 1988) [original, *Foucault*, (Editions de Minuit, 1986)].

66. Ibid.

67. "L'homme moderne est un animal dans la politique duquel sa vie d'être vivant est en question" [La Volonté de savoir (Paris: Editions Gallimard, 1976), p. 188].

68. Foucault identified *l'homme moderne* as "that being whose politics puts its existence in question" (ibid.).

69. *History of Sexuality, Volume 1: An Introduction* (London: Allen Lane, 1979), pp. 139–43.

70. The summary of the course is included in volume 1 of *The Essential Works of Foucault: Ethics*.

71. *History of Sexuality, Volume 1*, p. 137.

72. Ibid., p. 145.

73. Ibid., p. 137.

74. "What Is Enlightenment?," this volume.

75. Ibid.

FOUCAULT

Maurice Florence

*T*o the extent that Foucault fits into the philosophical tradition, it is the critical tradition of Kant, and his project could be called a *Critical History of Thought*.[1] This should not be taken to mean a history of ideas that would be at the same time an analysis of errors that might be gauged after the fact; or a decipherment of the misinterpretations linked to them and on which what we think today might depend. If what is meant by thought is the act that posits a subject and an object, along with their various possible relations, a critical history of thought would be an analysis of the conditions under which certain relations of subject to object are formed or modified, insofar as those relations constitute a possible knowledge [*savoir*]. It is not a matter of defining the formal conditions of a relationship to the object; nor is it a matter of isolating the empirical conditions that may, at a given moment, have enabled the subject in general to become acquainted with an object already given in reality. The problem is to determine what the subject must be, to what condition he is subject, what status he must have, what position he must occupy in reality or in the imaginary, in order to become a legitimate subject of this or that type of knowledge [*connaissance*]. In short, it is a matter of determining its mode of "subjectivation," for the latter is obviously not the same, according to whether the knowledge involved has the form of an exegesis of a sacred text, a natural history observation, or the analysis of a mental patient's behavior. But it is also and at the same time a question of determining under what conditions something can become an object for a possible knowledge [*connaissance*], how it may have been problematized as an object to be known, to what selective procedure [*procédure de découpage*] it may have been subjected, the part of it that is regarded as pertinent. So it is a matter of de-

In the early eighties, Denis Huisman asked François Ewald, Foucault's assistant at the Collège de France, to reedit the entry on Foucault for a new edition of the *Dictionnaire des philosophes*. The text submitted to Huisman was written almost entirely by Foucault himself, and signed pseudonymously "Maurice Florence." Robert Hurley's translation.

termining its mode of objectivation, which is not the same either, depending on the type of knowledge [*savoir*] that is involved.

This objectivation and this subjectivation are not independent of each other. From their mutual development and their interconnection, what could be called the "games of truth" come into being—that is, not the discovery of true things but the rules according to which what a subject can say about certain things depends on the question of true and false. In sum, the critical history of thought is neither a history of acquisitions nor a history of concealments of truth; it is the history of "veridictions," understood as the forms according to which discourses capable of being declared true or false are articulated concerning a domain of things. What the conditions of this emergence were, the price that was paid for it, so to speak, its effects on reality and the way in which, linking a certain type of object to certain modalities of the subject, it constituted the historical a priori of a possible experience for a period of time, an area and for given individuals.

Now, Michel Foucault did not pose this question—or this series of questions, which are those of an "archaeology of knowledge"—and does not wish to pose it concerning just any game of truth, but concerning only those in which the subject himself is posited as an object of possible knowledge: What are the processes of subjectivation and objectivation that make it possible for the subject qua subject to become an object of knowledge [*connaissance*], as a subject? Of course, it is a matter not of ascertaining how a "psychological knowledge" was constituted in the course of history but of discovering how various truth games were formed through which the subject became an object of knowledge. Michel Foucault attempted to conduct his analysis in two ways. First, in connection with the appearance and insertion of the question of the speaking, laboring, and living subject, in domains and according to the form of a scientific type of knowledge. This had to do with the formation of certain "human sciences," studied in reference to the practice of the empirical sciences, and of their characteristic discourse in the seventeenth and eighteenth centuries (*The Order of Things*). Foucault also tried to analyze the formation of the subject as he may appear on the other side of a normative division, becoming an object of knowledge—as a madman, a patient, or a delinquent, through practices such as those of psychiatry, clinical medicine, and penality (*Madness and Civilization, Birth of the Clinic, Discipline and Punish*).

Foucault has now undertaken, still within the same general project, to study the constitution of the subject as an object for himself: the formation of procedures by which the subject is led to observe himself, analyze himself, interpret himself, recognize himself as a domain of possible knowledge. In short, this concerns the history of "subjectivity," if what is meant by the term is the way in which the subject experiences himself in a game of truth where he relates to himself. The question of sex and sexuality appeared, in Foucault's view, to constitute not the only possible example, certainly, but at least a rather privileged case. Indeed, it was in this connection that through the whole of Christianity, and perhaps beyond, individuals were all called on to recognize themselves as subjects of pleasure, of desire, of lust, of temptation and were urged to deploy, by various means (self-examination, spiritual exercises, admission, confession), the game of true and false in regard to themselves and what constitutes the most secret, the most individual part of their subjectivity.

In sum, this history of sexuality is meant to constitute a third segment, added to the analyses of relations between the subject and truth or, to be exact, to the study of the modes according to which the subject was able to be inserted as an object in the games of truth.

Taking the question of relations between the subject and truth as the guiding thread for all these analyses implies certain choices of method. And, first, a systematic skepticism toward all anthropological universals—which does not mean rejecting them all from the start, outright and once and for all, but that nothing of that order must be accepted that is not strictly indispensable. In regard to human nature or the categories that may be applied to the subject, everything in our knowledge which is suggested to us as being universally valid must be tested and analyzed. Refusing the universal of "madness," "delinquency," or "sexuality" does not imply that what these notions refer to is nothing, or that they are only chimeras invented for the sake of a dubious cause. Something more is involved, however, than the simple observation that their content varies with time and circumstances: It means that one must investigate the conditions that enable people, according to the rules of true and false statements, to recognize a subject as mentally ill or to arrange that a subject recognize the most essential part of himself in the modality of his sexual desire. So the first rule of method for this kind of work is this: Insofar as possible, circumvent the anthropological universals (and, of course, those of a humanism that would assert the rights, the privileges, and the nature of a human being as an immediate and timeless truth of the subject) in order to examine them as historical constructs. One must also reverse the philosophical way of proceeding upward to the constituent subject which is asked to account for every possible object of knowledge in general. On the contrary, it is a matter of proceeding back down to the study of the concrete practices by which the subject is constituted in the immanence of a domain of knowledge. There too, one must be careful: Refusing the philosophical recourse to a constituent subject does not amount to acting as if the subject did not exist, making an abstraction of it on behalf of a pure objectivity. This refusal has the aim of eliciting the processes that are peculiar to an experience in which the subject and the object "are formed and transformed" in relation to and in terms of one another. The discourses of mental illness, delinquency, or sexuality say what the subject is only in a certain, quite particular game of truth; but these games are not imposed on the subject from the outside according to a necessary causality or structural determination. They open up a field of experience in which the subject and the object are both constituted only under certain simultaneous conditions, but in which they are constantly modified in relation to each other, and so they modify this field of experience itself.

Hence a third principle of method: Address "practices" as a domain of analysis, approach the study from the angle of what "was done." For example, what was done with madmen, delinquents, or sick people? On course, one can try to infer the institutions in which they were placed and the treatments to which they were subjected from the ideas that people had about them, or knowledge that people believed they had about them. One can also look for the form of "true" mental illnesses and the modalities of real delinquency in a given period in order to explain what was thought about them at the time. Michel Foucault approaches things in an altogether different way. He first studies the ensemble of more or less regulated, more or less deliberate, more or less finalized ways of doing things, through which can be seen both what was constituted as real for those who sought to think it and manage it and the way in which the latter constituted themselves as subjects capable of knowing, analyzing, and ultimately altering reality. These are the "practices," understood as a way of acting and thinking at once, that provide the intelligibility key for the correlative constitution of the subject and the object.

Now, since it is a matter of studying the different modes of objectivation of the subject that appear through these practices, one understands how important it is to analyze power relations. But it is essential to clearly define what such an analysis can be and can hope to accomplish. Obviously, it is a matter not of examining "power" with regard to its origin, its principles, or its legitimate limits, but of studying the methods and techniques used in different institutional contexts to act upon the behavior of individuals taken separately or in a group, so as to shape, direct, modify their way of conducting themselves, to impose ends on their inaction or fit it into overall strategies, these being multiple consequently, in their form and their place of exercise; diverse, too, in the procedures and techniques they bring into play. These power relations characterize the manner in which men are "governed" by one another; and their analysis shows how, through certain forms of "government," of madmen, sick people, criminals, and so on, the mad, the sick, the delinquent subject is objectified. So an analysis of this kind implies not that the abuse of this or that power has created madmen, sick people, or criminals, there where there was nothing, but that the various and particular forms of "government" of individuals were determinant in the different modes of objectivation of the subject.

One sees how the theme of a "history of sexuality" can fit within Michel Foucault's general project. It is a matter of analyzing "sexuality" as a historically singular mode of experience in which the subject is objectified for himself and for others through certain specific procedures of "government."

Notes

1. The italicized phrase is by François Ewald, who wrote the first part of this statement.—Ed.

LIFE: EXPERIENCE AND SCIENCE

Everyone knows that there are few logicians in France, but that there have been a fair number of historians of science. We also know that they have occupied a considerable place in the philosophic institution, in teaching and re-search. But people may be less aware of the significance and impact of a work like that of Georges Canguilhem, extending as it has over the past twenty or thirty years, and to the very boundaries of the institution. There have been noisier arenas no doubt—psychoanalysis, Marxism, linguistics, ethnology. But let us not overlook this fact, which pertains, as one prefers, to the sociology of French intellectual milieus, the operation of our university institutions, or our system of cultural values: the role of philosophy—I do not just mean of those who received their university training in philosophy departments—was impor-tant in all the political and scientific discussions of those strange years, the six-ties. Too important perhaps, in the opinion of some. Now, it so happens that all these philosophers, or nearly all, were affected directly or indirectly by the teaching or the books of Canguilhem.

Whence a paradox: this man, whose work is austere, deliberately delimited and carefully tailored to a particular domain in a history of science that in any case is not regarded as a spectacular discipline, was in some way present in the debates in which he took care never to appear. But, take away Canguilhem, and you will no longer understand very much about a whole series of discussions that took place among French Marxists; nor will you grasp what is specific about sociologists such as Pierre Bourdieu, Robert Castel, Jean-Claude Passeron, what makes them so distinctive in the field of sociology; you will miss a whole aspect of the theoretical work done by psychoanalyists and, in particular, by the Lacanians. Furthermore, in the whole debate of ideas that preceded or followed

This essay originally appeared in the *Revue de métaphysique et de morale* 90:1 (Jan.–March 1985), pp. 3–14. It is a modi-fied version of Foucault's introduction to the English translation of Georges Canguilhem's *The Normal and the Patho-logical*, trans. Carolyn Fawcett with Robert Cohen (New York: Zone, 1989). Robert Hurley's translation.

the movement of 1968, it is easy to find the place of those who were shaped in one way or another by Canguilhem.

Without ignoring the cleavages that in recent years and since the end of the war have set Marxists against non-Marxists, Freudians against non-Freudians, specialists in a discipline against philosophers, academics against nonacademics, theoreticians against politicians, it seems to me that one could find another dividing line that runs through all these oppositions. It is the one that separates a philosophy of experience, of meaning, of the subject, and a philosophy of knowledge, of rationality, and of the concept. On one side, a filiation which is that of Jean-Paul Sartre and Maurice Merleau-Ponty; and then another, which is that of Jean Cavaillès, Gaston Bachelard, Alexandre Koyré, and Canguilhem. Doubtless this cleavage comes from afar, and one could trace it back through the nineteenth century: Henri Bergson and Henri Poincaré, Jules Lachelier and Louis Couturat, Pierre Maine de Biran and Auguste Comte. And, in any case, it was so well established in the twentieth century that, through it, phenomenology was admitted into France. Delivered in 1929, modified, translated and published shortly afterward, the *Cartesian Meditations*[1] soon became the contested object of two possible readings: one that sought to radicalize Husserl in the direction of a philosophy of the subject, and before long was to encounter the questions of *Being and Time*[2]: I have in mind Sartre's article on the "Transcendence of the Ego"[3] in 1935; and the other, that would go back to the founding problems of Husserl's thought, the problems of formalism and intuitionalism; this would be, in 1938, the two theses of Cavaillès on the *Méthode axiomatique* and on *La Formation de la théorie des ensembles*.[4] Whatever the ramifications, the interferences, even the rapprochements may have been in the years that followed, these two forms of thought constituted in France two strains that remained, for a time at least, rather deeply heterogeneous.

On the surface, the second one remained the most theoretical, the most geared to speculative tasks, and the farthest removed from immediate political inquiries. And yet, it was this one that during the war participated, in a very direct way, in the combat, as if the question of the basis of rationality could not be dissociated from an interrogation concerning the current conditions of its existence. It was this one, too, that in the sixties played a crucial part in a crisis that was not just that of the university, but also that of the status and role of knowledge [*savoir*]. One may wonder why this type of reflection turned out to be, in accordance with its own logic, so deeply involved in the present.

One of the main reasons appears to lie in this: the history of the sciences owes its philosophical standing to the fact that it employs one of the themes that entered, somewhat surreptitiously and as if by accident, the philosophy of the seventeenth century. During that era, rational thought was questioned for the first time not only as to its nature, its basis, its powers and its rights, but as to its history and its geography, its immediate past and its conditions of exercise, its time, its place, and its current status. One can take as a symbol of this question, through which philosophy has constructed an essential enquiry concerning its present form and its connection to its context, the debate that was begun in the *Berlinische Monatsschrift* on the theme: *Was ist Aufklärung?* [What is enlightenment?] Moses Mendelssohn, then Immanuel Kant, each on his own account, wrote a reply to this question.[5]

At first it was understood no doubt as a relatively minor query: philosophy was questioned concerning the form it might assume, the shape it had at the moment, and the results that should be expected of it. But it soon became apparent that the reply given risked going far beyond. *Aufklärung* was made into the moment when philosophy found the possibility of establishing itself as the determining figure of an epoch, and when that epoch became the form of that philosophy's fulfilment. Philosophy could also be read as being nothing else than the composition of the particular traits of the period in which it appeared, it was that period's coherent figure, its systematization, or its conceptualized form; but, from another standpoint, the epoch appeared as being nothing less than the emergence and manifestation, in its fundamental traits, of what philosophy was in its essence. Philosophy appears then both as a more or less revealing element of the significations of an epoch, and, on the contrary, as the general law that determined the figure that it was to have for each epoch. Reading philosophy in the context of a general history and interpreting it as the principle of decipherment of any historical sequence became simultaneously possible. So the question of the "present moment" becomes for philosophy an inquiry it can longer leave aside: to what extent does this "moment" belong to a general historical process, and to what extent is philosophy the point where history itself must be deciphered in its conditions?

In that period, history became one of the major problems of philosophy. It would be necessary no doubt to try and determine why this question of *Aufklärung* has had, without ever disappearing, such a different destiny in the traditions of Germany, France, and the Anglo-Saxon countries; why has it taken hold here and there in so many and—according to the chronologies—such varied domains? Let us say, in any case, that German philosophy shaped it into a historical and political reflection on society, above all (with one central problem, the religious experience as it related to the economy and the state). From the post-Hegelians to the Frankfurt School and to Georg Lukács, going by way of Ludwig Feuerbach, Karl Marx, Friedrich Nietzsche and Max Weber, all these thinkers give evidence of the same concern. In France, it is the history of science in particular that has served as a medium for the philosophical question of historical *Aufklärung;* in a sense, the critiques of Claude-Henri Saint-Simon, the positivism of Auguste Comte and his successors were in fact a way of resuming the inquiry of Mendelssohn and of Kant on the scale of a general history of societies. Knowledge [*savoir*] and belief, the scientific form of knowledge [*connaissance*] and the religious contents of representation, or the transition from the prescientific to the scientific, the formation of a rational power against a background of traditional experience, the emergence, in the midst of a history of ideas and beliefs, of a type of history peculiar to scientific knowledge, origin and threshold of rationality: these were the themes through which, via positivism and those who opposed it, via the rowdy debates on scientism and the discussions on medieval science, the question of *Aufklärung* was conveyed into France. And if phenomenology, after a long period in which it was kept on the fringe, finally joined in, this was no doubt from the day that Husserl, in the *Cartesian Meditations* and the *Crisis,* raised the question of the relations between the Western project of a universal deployment of reason, the positivity of the sciences and the radicality of philosophy.[6]

For a century and a half the history of the sciences has been a bearer of philosophical issues that are easily recognized. Though works like those of Koyré, Bachelard, Cavaillès, or Canguilhem may indeed have had specific, "regional," chronologically well defined areas of the history of the sciences as their centers of reference, they have functioned as hotbeds of philosophical elaboration insofar as they have focused on the different facets of this question of *Aufklärung,* essential to contemporary philosophy.

If one had to look outside France for something corresponding to the work of Koyré, Bachelard, Cavaillès, and Canguilhem, it would be in the vicinity of the Frankfurt School, no doubt, that one would find it. And yet the styles are very different, as are the methods and the areas treated. But both groups ultimately raise the same kind of questions, even if they are haunted, here, by the memory of Descartes and, there, by the ghost of Luther. These are the questions that must be addressed to a rationality that aspires to the universal while developing within contingency, that asserts its unity and yet proceeds only through partial modifications, that validates itself by its own supremacy but that cannot be dissociated in its history from the inertias, the dullnesses, or the coercions that subjugate it. In the history of the sciences in France, as in German Critical Theory, what is to be examined, basically, is a reason whose structural autonomy carries the history of dogmatisms and despotisms along with it—a reason, therefore, that has a liberating effect only provided it manages to liberate itself.

Several processes that mark the second half of the twentieth century have brought the question of enlightenment back to the center of contemporary concerns. The first one is the importance assumed by scientific and technical rationality in the development of the productive forces and the making of political decisions. The second is the very history of a "revolution" for which the hope had been borne, since the end of the eighteenth century, by a whole rationalism of which we are entitled to ask what part it may have played in the effects of despotism where that hope got lost. The third and last is the movement that caused people in the West to ask it what basis there could be in its culture, its science, its social organization, and finally its very rationality for it to claim a universal validity: is it anything more than a mirage tied to a domination and a political hegemony? Two centuries after its appearance, *Aufklärung* makes a comeback—as a way for the West to become aware of its present possibilities and of the freedoms it may have access to, but also as a way to question oneself about its limits and the powers it has utilized. Reason as both despotism and enlightenment.

We should not be surprised that the history of the sciences, and especially in the particular form that Georges Canguilhem gave it, was able to occupy such a central place in contemporary debates in France.

To put things very roughly, for a long time the history of the sciences concerned itself (by preference if not exclusively) with a few "noble" disciplines that took their prestige from the antiquity of their founding, their high degree of formalization, their capacity for being mathematized, and the privileged place they occupied in the positivist hierarchy of the sciences. By thus remaining fastened to that knowledge [*connaissance*] which, from the Greeks to Leibniz, had in effect been integral with philosophy, the history of the sciences avoided the question that was central for it and concerned its relation with philosophy. Georges Canguilhem reversed the problem: he centered the main part of his work on the history of biology and on that of medicine, knowing very well that the theoretical importance of the problems raised by the development of a science is not necessarily in direct proportion with the degree of formalization it has attained. So he brought the history of the sciences down from the heights (mathematics, astronomy, Galilean mechanics, Newtonian physics, relativity theory) to regions where the knowledge is much less deductive, where it remained connected, for a much longer time, to the wonders of the imagination, and where it posed a series of questions that were much more foreign to philosophical habits.

But in effecting this displacement, Canguilhem did far more than ensure the revalorization of a relatively neglected domain. He did not just broaden the field of the history of the sciences; he reshaped the discipline itself on a number of essential points.

1. First, he took up the theme of "discontinuity." An old theme that emerged early on, to the point of being contemporaneous, or nearly so, with the birth of a history of the sciences. What marks such a history, as Fontenelle already said, is the sudden formation of certain sciences "out of nothing," the extreme rapid-

ity of certain advances that were unexpected, the distance separating scientific knowledge from "common custom," and the motifs that stirred up the scientists. The polemical form of this history is responsible for endless accounts of battles against "preconceptions," "resistances" and "obstacles."[7] Taking up this same theme, developed by Koyré and Bachelard, Canguilhem stresses the fact that for him identifying discontinuities does not have to do with postulates or results; it is more a "way of proceeding," a procedure that is integral with the history of the sciences because it is called for by the very object that the latter must deal with. The history of the sciences is not the history of the true, of its slow epiphany; it cannot hope to recount the gradual discovery of a truth that has always been inscribed in things or in the intellect, except by imagining that today's knowledge finally possesses it in such a complete and definitive way that it can use that truth as a standard for measuring the past. And yet the history of the sciences is not a pure and simple history of ideas and of the conditions under which they appeared before they faded away. In the history of the sciences one cannot grant oneself the truth as an assumption, but neither can one dispense with a relation to truth and to the opposition of the true and the untrue. It is this reference to the order of the true and the false that gives this history its specificity and its importance. In what way? By considering that one is dealing with the history of "truthful discourses," that is, with discourses that rectify and correct themselves, and that carry out a whole labor of self-development governed by the task of "truth-telling." The historical connections that the different moments of a science may have with each other necessarily have that form of discontinuity which is constituted by the reformulations, the recastings, the revealing of new foundations, the changes in scale, the transition to a new type of objects—"the perpetual revision of contents by deeper investigation and by erasure," as Cavaillès expressed it. Error is eliminated not by the blunt force of a truth that would gradually emerge from the shadows but by the formation of a new way of "truth-telling."[8] Indeed, one of the conditions of possibility for a history of the sciences to take form at the beginning of the eighteenth century was, as Canguilhem points out, the awareness that people had of the recent "scientific revolutions"—that of algebraic geometry and infinitesimal calculus, that of Copernican and Newtonian cosmology.[9]

2. Whoever says "history of truthful discourse" is also saying recursive method. Not in the sense in which the history of the sciences would say, "Given the truth, finally recognized now, when did people get an inkling of it, what paths did it have to take, what groups did it have to coax into discovering and demonstrating it?" but in the sense in which the successive transformations of this truthful discourse constantly produce reworkings in their own history. What had long remained a dead end one day became a way out; a lateral essay becomes a central problem around which all the others begin to gravitate; a

slightly divergent step becomes a fundamental break: the discovery of noncellular fermentation—a side phenomenon in the reign of Pasteurian microbiology—did not mark an essential break until the day when the physiology of enzymes developed.[10] In short, the history of discontinuities is not acquired once and for all; it is "impermanent" by its nature; it is discontinuous; it must constantly be resumed at a new cost.

Must we conclude that science is always making and remaking its own history in a spontaneous way, to the extent that a science's only authorized historian would have to be the scientist himself, reconstructing the past of what he is doing now? For Canguilhem the problem is not of a professional kind; it is a problem of viewpoint. The history of the sciences cannot merely collect what the scientists of the past may have thought or demonstrated; one does not write a history of plant physiology by going back over "everything that people called botanists, physicians, chemists, horticulturalists, agronomists, or economists might have written in regard to conjectures, observations, or experiments with a bearing on the relation between structure and function in objects variously termed herbs, plants, or vegetables."[11] But neither does one do a history of the sciences by refiltering the past through the set of statements or theories that are currently validated, thus detecting the future true in what was "false" and the subsequently manifest error in what was true. This is one of the basic points of Canguilhem's method.

The history of the sciences can be constituted in its specific form only by considering, between the pure historian and the scientist himself, the point of view of the epistemologist. This point of view is that which elicits a "latent orderly progression" from the various episodes of a scientific knowledge [savoir]—which means that the processes of elimination and selection of statements, theories, and objects always occur in terms of a certain norm. The latter cannot be identified with a theoretical structure or a current paradigm, for today's scientific truth is itself only an episode of it—let us say, at most, its temporary outcome. One cannot go back to the past and validly trace its history by starting from a "normal science"; it can only be done by rediscovering the "normal" process of which current knowledge is but a moment, and there is no way, short of prophecy, to predict the future. The history of the sciences, Canguilhem says, citing Suzanne Bachelard, cannot construct its object anywhere but in "an ideal space-time."[12] And this space-time is given to it neither by the "realistic" time accumulated by the historians' erudition nor by the space of ideality that partitions science today in an authoritative way but by the viewpoint of epistemology. The latter is not the general theory of every science and of every possible scientific statement; it is the search for the normativity internal to the different scientific activities, as they have actually been carried out. So it involves an indispensable theoretical reflection that enables the history of the sciences to be constituted in a different mode from history in general; and, conversely, the history of the sciences opens up a domain of analysis that is indispensable if epistemology is to be anything else but the simple reproduction of the internal schemas of a science at a given time.[13] In the method employed by Canguilhem, the formulation of "discontinuistic" analyses and the elucidation of the historical relation between the sciences and epistemology go hand in hand.

3. Now, by putting sciences of life back into this historico-epistemological perspective, Canguilhem brings to light a certain number of essential traits that make their development different from that of the other sciences and present their historians with specific problems. At the end of the eighteenth century, it was thought that one could find the common element between a physiology studying the phenomena of life and a pathology devoted to the analysis of diseases, and that this element would enable one to consider the normal processes and the disease processes as a unit. From Xavier Bichat to Claude Bernard, from the analysis of fevers to the pathology of the liver and its functions, there had opened up an immense domain that seemed to promise the unity of a physiopathology and access to an understanding of disease phenomena based on the analysis of normal processes. People expected the healthy organism to provide the general framework in which these pathological phenomena took hold and assumed, for a time, their own form. It seems that this pathology, grounded in normality, characterized the whole of medical thought for a long time.

But there are phenomena in the study of life which keep it separate from any knowledge that may refer to the physicochemical domains; the fact is that it has been able to find the principle of its development only in the investigation of pathological phenomena. It has not been possible to constitute a science of the living without taking into account, as something essential to its object, the possibility of disease, death, monstrosity, anomaly, and error. Although one may come to know, with increasing exactness, the physicochemical mechanisms that cause them, they have their place nonetheless in a specificity that the life sciences must take into account, lest they obliterate the very thing that forms their object and their particular domain.

There results a paradoxical fact in the sciences of life. While their establishment did come about through the elucidation of physical and chemical mechanisms, through the constituting of domains like the chemistry of cells and molecules, through the use of mathematical models and so on, this process, on the other hand, could unfold only to the extent that the problem of the specificity of disease and the threshold it marks among natural beings was constantly revisited.[14] This does not mean that vitalism, which put so many images in circulation and perpetuated so many myths, is true. Nor does it mean that that notion, which so often became deeply rooted in the least rigorous philosophies, must constitute the unsurpassable philosophy of biologists. But it does mean that it had and no doubt still has an essential role as an "indicator" in the history of biology. And in two ways: as a theoretical indicator of problems to be solved (that is, in a general way, what constitutes the originality of life without the latter's constituting under any circumstances an independent empire in nature); and as a critical indicator of the reductions to be avoided (namely, all those which tend to conceal the fact that the sciences of life cannot do without a certain value assertion that emphasizes conservation, regulation, adaptation, reproduction, and so on); "an exigency rather than a method, an ethic more than a theory." [15]

4. The life sciences call for a certain way of doing their history. They also raise, in a peculiar way, the philosophical question of knowledge [*connaissance*].

Life and death are never problems of physics in themselves, even though the physicist in his work may risk his own life or that of others; for him it is a question of ethics or politics, not a scientific question. As André Lwoff puts it, lethal or not, as far as the physicist is concerned a genetic mutation is neither more nor less than the replacement of one nucleic base by another. But in this difference the biologist recognizes the mark of his own object—and of a type of object to which he himself belongs, since he lives and since he reveals, manipulates, and develops this nature of the living in an activity of knowledge that must be understood as "a general method for the direct or indirect relieving of the tensions between man and the environment." The biologist has to grasp what makes life a specific object of knowledge and, thus, what accounts for the fact that among the living, and because they are living, there are beings capable of knowing, and of knowing, finally, life itself.

Phenomenology expected "lived experience" to supply the originary meaning of every act of knowledge. But can we not or must we not look for it in the "living" itself?

Through an elucidation of knowledge about life and of the concepts that articulate that knowledge, Canguilhem wishes to determine the situation of the *concept in life*. That is, of the concept insofar as it is one of the modes of that information which every living being takes from its environment and by which conversely it structures its environment. The fact that man lives in a conceptually structured environment does not prove that he has turned away from life, or that a historical drama has separated him from it—just that he lives in a certain way, that he has a relationship with his environment such that he has no set point of view toward it, that he is mobile on an undefined or a rather broadly defined territory, that he has to move around in order to gather information, that he has to move things relative to one another in order to make them useful. Forming concepts is a way of living and not a way of killing life; it is a way to live in a relative mobility and not a way to immobilize life; it is to show, among those billions of living beings that inform their environment and inform themselves on the basis of it, an innovation that can be judged as one likes, tiny or substantial: a very special type of information.

Hence the importance that Canguilhem attributes to the encounter, in the life sciences, of the old question of the normal and the pathological with the set of notions that biology, during these last decades, has borrowed from information theory—codes, messages, messengers, and so on. From this viewpoint, *The Normal and the Pathological*, a part of which was written in 1943 and the other part during the period 1963–1966, undoubtedly constitutes Canguilhem's most significant work. It shows how the problem of the specific nature of life has recently been inflected in a direction where one meets with some of the problems that were thought to belong strictly to the most developed forms of evolution.

At the center of these problems one finds that of error. For, at the most basic level of life, the processes of coding and decoding give way to a chance occurrence that, before becoming a disease, a deficiency, or a monstrosity, is something like a disturbance in the informative system, something like a "mistake." In this sense, life—and this is its radical feature—is that which is capable of error. And perhaps it is this datum or rather this contingency which must be asked to account for the fact that the question of anomaly permeates the whole of biology. And it must also be asked to account for the mutations and evolutive processes to which they lead. Further, it must be questioned in regard to that singular but hereditary error which explains the fact that, with man, life has led to a living being that is never completely in the right place, that is destined to "err" and to be "wrong."

And if one grants that the concept is the reply that life itself has given to that chance process, one must agree that error is the root of what produces human thought and its history. The opposition of the true and the false, the values that are attributed to the one and the other, the power effects that different societies and different institutions link to that division—all this may be nothing but the most belated response to that possibility of error inherent in life. If the history of the sciences is discontinuous—that is, if it can be analyzed only as a series of "corrections," as a new distribution that never sets free, finally and forever, the terminal moment of truth—the reason, again, is that "error" constitutes not a neglect or a delay of the promised fulfillment but the dimension peculiar to the life of human beings and indispensable to the duration [*temps*] of the species.

Nietzsche said that truth was the greatest lie. Canguilhem, who is far from and near to Nietzsche at the same time, would perhaps say that on the huge calendar of life it is the most recent error; or, more exactly, he would say that the true/false dichotomy and the value accorded to truth constitute the most singular way of living that has been invented by a life that, from the depths of its origin, bore the potential for error within itself. For Canguilhem, error is the

permanent contingency [*aléa*] around which the history of life and the development of human beings are coiled. It is this notion of error that enables him to
connect what he knows about biology and the manner in which he does history,
without ever intending to deduce the latter from the former, as was done in the
time of evolutionism. It is what allows him to bring out the relationship between
life and knowledge [*connaissance*] and to follow, like a red thread, the presence of
value and the norm within it.

This historian of rationalities, himself so "rationalistic," is a philosopher of
error—I mean that error provides him with the basis for posing philosophical
problems; or, let us say more exactly, the problem of truth and life. Here we
touch on one of the fundamental events, no doubt, in the history of modern philosophy: if the great Cartesian break raised the question of the relations between truth and subjectivity, the eighteenth century introduced a series of
questions concerning truth and life, *The Critique of Judgment* and the *Phenomenology of Spirit* being the first great formulations of these.[16] And since that time
this has been one of the issues of philosophical discussion. Should life be considered as nothing more than one of the areas that raises the general question of
truth, the subject, and knowledge? Or does it oblige us to pose the question in a
different way? Should not the whole theory of the subject be reformulated, seeing that knowledge, rather than opening onto the truth of the world, is deeply
rooted in the "errors" of life?

One understands why Georges Canguilhem's thought, his work as a historian and a philosopher, has had such a decisive importance in France for all those
who, from very different points of view, have tried to rethink the question of
the subject. Although phenomenology brought the body, sexuality, death, and
the perceived world into the field of analysis, the *cogito* remained central to it;
neither the rationality of science nor the specificity of the life sciences could
compromise its founding role. In opposition to this philosophy of meaning, the
subject, and lived experience, Canguilhem has proposed a philosophy of error,
of the concept of the living, as a different way of approaching the notion of life.

Notes

1. Edmund Husserl, *Cartesianishe Meditationen: Eine Einleitung in die Phänomenologie* [1931], in *Gesam-
    melte Werke* (The Hague: Nijhoff, 1950), vol. 1 [*Cartesian Meditations: An Introduction to Phenomenol-
    ogy*, trans. Dorion Cairns (The Hague: Martinus Nijhoff, 1960)].

2. Martin Heidegger, *Sein und Zeit* (Tübingen: Niemeyer, 1927) [*Being and Time*, trans. Joan Stambaugh
    (Albany: State University of New York Press, 1996)].

3. Jean-Paul Sartre, "La Transcendance de l'ego: esquisse d'une description phénoménologique,"
    Recherches philosophiques 6 (1935), republished (Paris: Vrin, 1988) [*The Transcendence of the Ego: An*

Existentialist Theory of Consciousness, trans. Forrest Williams and Robert Kirkpatrick (New York: Noonday Press, 1957)].

4. Jean Cavaillès, *Méthode axiomatique et formalisme: essai sur le problème du fondement des mathématiques* (Paris: Hermann, 1957); *Remarques sur la formation de la théorie abstraite des ensembles: étude historique et critique* (Paris: Hermann, 1937).

5. Moses Mendelssohn, "Über die Frage: Was heisst Aufklären?," *Berlinische Monatsschrift* 4:3 (Sept. 1784), pp. 193–200; Immanuel Kant, "Beantwortung der Frage: Was ist Aufklärung?" *Berlinische Monatsschrift* 4:6 (Dec. 1784), pp. 491–94 [*Réponse à la question: Qu'est-ce que les Lumières?* trans. S. Piobetta, in Kant, *La Philosophie de l'histoire* [*Opuscules*] (Paris: Aubier, 1947), pp. 81–92].

6. Husserl, *Die Krisis der europäischen Wissenschaft und die transzendentale Phänomenologie: Einleitung in die Phänomenologie* (Belgrade: Philosophia, 1936), vol. 1, pp. 77–176 [*The Crisis of European Sciences and Transcendental Phenomenology: An Introduction to Phenomenological Philosophy,* trans. David Carr (Evanston, IL: Northwestern University Press, 1970)].

7. B. Le Bovier de Fontenelle, *Préface à l'histoire de l'Académie,* in *Oeuvres,* edition of 1790, vol. 6, pp. 73–74. Georges Canguilhem cites this text in the *Introduction à l'histoire des sciences* (Paris, 1970), vol. 1: *Elements et instruments,* pp. 7–8.

8. On this theme, see Canguilhem, *Idéologie et rationalité dans l'histoire des sciences de la vie* (Paris: Vrin, 1977), p. 21. [*Ideology and Rationality in the History of the Life Sciences,* trans. Arthur Goldhammer (Cambridge, Mass.: MIT Press, 1988), pp. 10–11].

9. *Etudes d'histoire et de philosophie des sciences* (Paris: Vrin, 1968), p. 17.

10. Canguilhem takes up the example discussed by M. Florkin in *A History of Biochemistry* (Amsterdam: Elsevier, 1972–75); cf. Canguilhem, *Idéologie et Rationalité,* p. 15 [*Ideology and Rationality,* p. 5].

11. Canguilhem, *Idéologie et rationalité,* p. 14 [*Ideology and Rationality,* p. 4].

12. Suzanne Bachelard, "Epistémologie et histoire des sciences," in Twelfth International History of the Sciences Conference (Paris: 1968), *Revue de synthèse,* 3rd ser., 49–52 (Jan.–Dec. 1968), p. 51.

13. On the relationship between epistemology and history, see especially the introduction to Canguilhem, *Idéologie et rationalité,* pp. 11–29 [*Ideology and Rationality,* pp. 1–23].

14. Canguilhem, *Études d'histoire et de philosophie des sciences,* p. 239.

15. Canguilhem, *La Connaissance de la vie* [1952] (2d ed., Paris: Vrin, 1965), p. 88.

16. Immanuel Kant, *Kritik der Urteilskraft* [1790], in *Gesammelte Schriften* (Berlin: Königlich Preussischen Akademie der Wissenschaften, 1902), vol. 5, pp. 165–486 [*Critique of Judgment,* trans. Werner S. Pluhar (Indianapolis: Hackett, 1987)]; G. W. F. Hegel, *Phänomenologie des Geistes* (Würzburg: Goebhardt, 1807) [*The Phenomenology of Spirit,* trans. A. V. Miller (New York: Oxford University Press, 1977)].

POLEMICS, POLITICS, AND PROBLEMATIZATIONS: AN INTERVIEW WITH MICHEL FOUCAULT

P.R. Why is it that you don't engage in polemics?

M.F. I like discussions, and when I am asked questions, I try to answer them. It's true that I don't like to get involved in polemics. If I open a book and see that the author is accusing an adversary of "infantile leftism," I shut it again right away. That's not my way of doing things; I don't belong to the world of people who do things that way. I insist on this difference as something essential: a whole morality is at stake, the morality that concerns the search for the truth and the relation to the other.

In the serious play of questions and answers, in the work of reciprocal elucidation, the rights of each person are in some sense immanent in the discussion. They depend only on the dialogue situation. The person asking the questions is merely exercising the right that has been given him: to remain unconvinced, to perceive a contradiction, to require more information, to emphasize different postulates, to point out faulty reasoning, and so on. As for the person answering the questions, he too exercises a right that does not go beyond the discussion itself; by the logic of his own discourse, he is tied to what he has said earlier, and by the acceptance of dialogue he is tied to the questioning of the other. Questions and answers depend on a game—a game that is at once pleasant and difficult—in which each of the two partners takes pains to use only the rights given him by the other and by the accepted form of the dialogue.

The polemicist, on the other hand, proceeds encased in privileges that he

This interview was conducted by Paul Rabinow in May 1984, just before Foucault's death, to answer questions frequently asked by American audiences. It was translated by Lydia Davis. Special thanks are due Thomas Zummer for his help in preparing it.

possesses in advance and will never agree to question. On principle, he possesses rights authorizing him to wage war and making that struggle a just undertaking; the person he confronts is not a partner in the search for the truth but an adversary, an enemy who is wrong, who is harmful, and whose very existence constitutes a threat. For him, then, the game consists not of recognizing this person as a subject having the right to speak but of abolishing him, as interlocutor, from any possible dialogue; and his final objective will be not to come as close as possible to a difficult truth but to bring about the triumph of the just cause he has been manifestly upholding from the beginning. The polemicist relies on a legitimacy that his adversary is by definition denied.

Perhaps, someday, a long history will have to be written of polemics, polemics as a parasitic figure on discussion and an obstacle to the search for the truth. Very schematically, it seems to me that today we can recognize the presence in polemics of three models: the religious model, the judiciary model, and the political model. As in heresiology, polemics sets itself the task of determining the intangible point of dogma, the fundamental and necessary principle that the adversary has neglected, ignored, or transgressed; and it denounces this negligence as a moral failing; at the root of the error, it finds passion, desire, interest, a whole series of weaknesses and inadmissible attachments that establish it as culpable. As in judiciary practice, polemics allows for no possibility of an equal discussion: it examines a case; it isn't dealing with an interlocutor, it is processing a suspect; it collects the proofs of his guilt, designates the infraction he has committed, and pronounces the verdict and sentences him. In any case, what we have here is not on the order of a shared investigation; the polemicist tells the truth in the form of his judgment and by virtue of the authority he has conferred on himself. But it is the political model that is the most powerful today. Polemics defines alliances, recruits partisans, unites interests or opinions, represents a party; it establishes the other as an enemy, an upholder of opposed interests against which one must fight until the moment this enemy is defeated and either surrenders or disappears.

Of course, the reactivation, in polemics, of these political, judiciary, or religious practices is nothing more than theater. One gesticulates: anathemas, excommunications, condemnations, battles, victories, and defeats are no more than ways of speaking, after all. And yet, in the order of discourse, they are also ways of acting which are not without consequence. There are the sterilizing effects. Has anyone ever seen a new idea come out of a polemic? And how could it be otherwise, given that here the interlocutors are incited not to advance, not to take more and more risks in what they say, but to fall back continually on the rights that they claim, on their legitimacy, which they must defend, and on the affirmation of their innocence? There is something even more serious here: in this comedy, one mimics war, battles, annihilations, or unconditional surrenders, putting forward as much of one's killer instinct as possible. But it is really dangerous to make anyone believe that he can gain access to the truth by such paths and thus to validate, even if in a merely symbolic form, the real political practices that could be warranted by it. Let us imagine, for a moment, that a magic wand is waved and one of the two adversaries in a polemic is given the ability to exercise all the power he likes over the other. One doesn't even have to imagine it: one has only to look at what happened during the debates in the USSR over linguistics or genetics not long ago. Were these merely aberrant deviations from what was supposed to be the correct discussion? Not at all—they were the real consequences of a polemic attitude whose effects ordinarily remain suspended.

P.R. You have been read as an idealist, as a nihilist, as a "new philosopher," an anti-Marxist, a new conservative, and so on . . . Where *do* you stand?

M.F. I think I have in fact been situated in most of the squares on the political checkerboard, one after another and sometimes simultaneously: as anarchist, leftist, ostentatious or disguised Marxist, nihilist, explicit or secret anti-Marxist, technocrat in the service of Gaullism, new liberal, and so on. An American professor complained that a crypto-Marxist like me was invited to the USA, and I was denounced by the press in Eastern European countries for being an accomplice of the dissidents. None of these descriptions is important by itself; taken together, on the other hand, they mean something. And I must admit that I rather like what they mean.

It's true that I prefer not to identify myself, and that I'm amused by the diversity of the ways I've been judged and classified. Something tells me that by now a more or less approximate place should have been found for me, after so many efforts in such various directions; and since I obviously can't suspect the competence of the people who are getting muddled up in their divergent judgments, since it isn't possible to challenge their inattention or their prejudices, I have to be convinced that their inability to situate me has something to do with me.

And no doubt fundamentally it concerns my way of approaching political questions. It is true that my attitude isn't a result of the form of critique that claims to be a methodical examination in order to reject all possible solutions except for the one valid one. It is more on the order of "problematization"— which is to say, the development of a domain of acts, practices, and thoughts that seem to me to pose problems for politics. For example, I don't think that in regard to madness and mental illness there is any "politics" that can contain the just and definitive solution. But I think that in madness, in derangement, in behavior problems, there are reasons for questioning politics; and politics must answer these questions, but it never answers them completely. The same is true for crime and punishment: naturally, it would be wrong to imagine that politics has nothing to do with the prevention and punishment of crime, and therefore nothing to do with a certain number of elements that modify its form, its meaning, its frequency; but it would be just as wrong to think that there is a political formula likely to resolve the question of crime and put an end to it. The same is true of sexuality: it doesn't exist apart from a relationship to political structures, requirements, laws, and regulations that have a primary importance for it; and yet one can't expect politics to provide the forms in which sexuality would cease to be a problem.

It is a question, then, of thinking about the relations of these different experiences to politics, which doesn't mean that one will seek in politics the main constituent of these experiences or the solution that will definitively settle their fate. The problems that experiences like these pose to politics have to be elaborated. But it is also necessary to determine what "posing a problem" to politics really means. Richard Rorty points out that in these analyses I do not appeal to any "we"—to any of those "*wes*" whose consensus, whose values, whose traditions constitute the framework for a thought and define the conditions in which it can be validated. But the problem is, precisely, to decide if it is actually suitable to place oneself within a "we" in order to assert the principles one recognizes and the values one accepts; or if it is not, rather, necessary to make the future formation of a "we" possible by elaborating the question. Because it seems to me that the "we" must not be previous to the question; it can only be the result—and the necessarily temporary result—of the question as it is posed in the new terms in which one formulates it. For example, I'm not sure that at the time when I wrote the history of madness, there was a preexisting and receptive "we" to which I would only have had to refer in order to write my book, and of which this book would have been the spontaneous expression. Laing, Cooper, Basaglia, and I had no community, nor any relationship; but the problem posed itself to those who had read us, as it also posed itself to some of us, of seeing if it were possible to establish a "we" on the basis of the work that had been done, a "we" that would also be likely to form a community of action.

I have never tried to analyze anything whatsoever from the point of view of politics, but always to ask politics what it had to say about the problems with which it was confronted. I question it about the positions it takes and the reasons it gives for this; I don't ask it to determine the theory of what I do. I am neither an adversary nor a partisan of Marxism; I question it about what it has to say about experiences that ask questions of it.

As for the events of May 1968, it seems to me they depend on another problematic. I wasn't in France at that time; I only returned several months later. And it seemed to me one could recognize completely contradictory elements in it: on the one hand, an effort, which was very widely asserted, to ask politics a whole series of questions that were not traditionally a part of its statutory domain (questions about women, about relations between the sexes, about medicine, about mental illness, about the environment, about minorities, about delinquency); and, on the other hand, a desire to rewrite all these problems in the vocabulary of a theory that was derived more or less directly from Marxism. But the process that was evident at that time led not to taking over the problems posed by the Marxist doctrine but, on the contrary, to a more and more manifest powerlessness on the part of Marxism to confront these problems. So that one found oneself faced with interrogations that were addressed to politics but had not themselves sprung from a political doctrine. From this point of view, such a liberation of the act of questioning seemed to me to have played a positive role: now there was a plurality of questions posed to politics rather than the reinscription of the act of questioning in the framework of a political doctrine.

P.R. Would you say that your work centers on the relations among ethics, politics, and the genealogy of truth?

M.F. No doubt one could say that in some sense I try to analyze the relations among science, politics, and ethics; but I don't think that would be an entirely accurate representation of the work I set out to do. I don't want to remain at that level; rather, I am trying to see how these processes may have interfered with one another in the formation of a scientific domain, a political structure, a moral practice. Let's take psychiatry as an example: no doubt, one can analyze it today in its epistemological structure—even if that is still rather loose; one can also analyze it within the framework of the political institutions in which it operates; one can also study it in its ethical implications, as regards the person who is the object of the psychiatry as much as the psychiatrist himself. But my goal hasn't been to do this; rather, I have tried to see how the formation of psychiatry as a science, the limitation of its field, and the definition of its object implicated a political structure and a moral practice: in the twofold sense that they were presupposed by the progressive organization of psychiatry as a science, and that they were also changed by this development. Psychiatry as we know it couldn't have existed without a whole interplay of political structures and without a set of ethical attitudes; but inversely, the establishment of madness as a domain of knowledge [savoir] changed the political practices and the ethical attitudes that concerned it. It was a matter of determining the role of politics and ethics in the establishment of madness as a particular domain of scientific knowledge [connaissance], and also of analyzing the effects of the latter on political and ethical practices.

The same is true in relation to delinquency. It was a question of seeing which political strategy had, by giving its status to criminality, been able to appeal to certain forms of knowledge [savoir] and certain moral attitudes; it was also a question of seeing how these modalities of knowledge [connaissance] and these forms of morality could have been reflected in, and changed by, these disciplinary techniques. In the case of sexuality it was the development of a moral attitude that I wanted to isolate; but I tried to reconstruct it through the play it engaged in with political structures (essentially in the relation between self-control [*maîtrise de soi*] and domination of others) and with the modalities of knowledge [*connaissance*] (self-knowledge and knowledge of different areas of activity).

So that in these three areas—madness, delinquency, and sexuality—I emphasized a particular aspect each time: the establishment of a certain objectivity, the development of a politics and a government of the self, and the elaboration of an ethics and a practice in regard to oneself. But each time I also tried to point out the place occupied here by the other two components necessary for constituting a field of experience. It is basically a matter of different examples in which the three fundamental elements of any experience are implicated: a game of truth, relations of power, and forms of relation to oneself and to others. And if each of these examples emphasizes, in a certain way, one of these three aspects—since the experience of madness was recently organized as primarily a field of knowledge [*savoir*], that of crime as an area of political intervention, while that of sexuality was defined as an ethical position—each time I have tried to show how the two other elements were present, what roles they played, and how each one was affected by the transformations in the other two.

P.R. You have recently been talking about a "history of problematics." What is a history of problematics?

M.F. For a long time, I have been trying to see if it would be possible to describe the history of thought as distinct both from the history of ideas (by which I mean the analysis of systems of representation) and from the history of mentalities (by which I mean the analysis of attitudes and types of action [*schémas de comportement*]). It seemed to me there was one element that was capable of describing the history of thought—this was what one could call the element of problems or, more exactly, problematizations. What distinguishes thought is that it is something quite different from the set of representations that underlies a certain behavior; it is also something quite different from the domain of attitudes that can determine this behavior. Thought is not what inhabits a certain conduct and gives it its meaning; rather, it is what allows one to step back from this way of acting or reacting, to present it to oneself as an object of thought and to question it as to its meaning, its conditions, and its goals. Thought is freedom in relation to what one does, the motion by which one detaches oneself from it, establishes it as an object, and reflects on it as a problem.

To say that the study of thought is the analysis of a freedom does not mean one is dealing with a formal system that has reference only to itself. Actually, for a domain of action, a behavior, to enter the field of thought, it is necessary for a certain number of factors to have made it uncertain, to have made it lose its familiarity, or to have provoked a certain number of difficulties around it. These elements result from social, economic, or political processes. But here their only role is that of instigation. They can exist and perform their action for a very long time, before there is effective problematization by thought. And when thought intervenes, it doesn't assume a unique form that is the direct result or the necessary expression of these difficulties; it is an original or specific response—often taking many forms, sometimes even contradictory in its different aspects—to these difficulties, which are defined for it by a situation or a context, and which hold true as a possible question.

To one single set of difficulties, several responses can be made. And most of the time different responses actually are proposed. But what must be understood is what makes them simultaneously possible: it is the point in which their simultaneity is rooted; it is the soil that can nourish them all in their diversity and sometimes in spite of their contradictions. To the different difficulties encountered by the practice regarding mental illness in the eighteenth century, diverse solutions were proposed: Tuke's and Pinel's are examples. In the same way, a whole group of solutions was proposed for the difficulties encountered in the second half of the eighteenth century by penal practice. Or again, to take a very remote example, the diverse schools of philosophy of the Hellenistic period proposed different solutions to the difficulties of traditional sexual ethics.

But the work of a history of thought would be to rediscover at the root of these diverse solutions the general form of problematization that has made them possible—even in their very opposition; or what has made possible the transformations of the difficulties and obstacles of a practice into a general problem for which one proposes diverse practical solutions. It is problematization that responds to these difficulties, but by doing something quite other than expressing them or manifesting them: in connection with them, it develops the conditions in which possible responses can be given; it defines the elements that will constitute what the different solutions attempt to respond to. This development of a given into a question, this transformation of a group of obstacles and difficulties into problems to which the diverse solutions will attempt to produce a response, this is what constitutes the point of problematization and the specific work of thought.

It is clear how far one is from an analysis in terms of deconstruction (any confusion between these two methods would be unwise). Rather, it is a question of a movement of critical analysis in which one tries to see how the different solutions to a problem have been constructed; but also how these different solutions result from a specific form of problematization. And it then appears that any new solution which might be added to the others would arise from current problematization, modifying only several of the postulates or principles on which one bases the responses that one gives. The work of philosophical and historical reflection is put back into the field of the work of thought only on condition that one clearly grasps problematization not as an arrangement of representations but as a work of thought.

THE ETHICS OF THE CONCERN
OF THE SELF AS A PRACTICE
OF FREEDOM

Q. First of all, I would like to ask what is the focus of your current thinking. Having followed the latest developments in your thought, particularly your lectures at the Collège de France in 1981–82 on the hermeneutics of the subject, I would like to know if your current philosophical approach is still determined by the poles of subjectivity and truth.

M.F. In actual fact, I have always been interested in this problem, even if I framed it somewhat differently. I have tried to find out how the human subject fits into certain games of truth, whether they were truth games that take the form of a science or refer to a scientific model, or truth games such as those one may encounter in institutions or practices of control. This is the theme of my book *The Order of Things,* in which I attempted to see how, in scientific discourses, the human subject defines itself as a speaking, living, working individual. In my courses at the Collège de France, I brought out this problematic in its generality.

Q. Isn't there a "break" between your former problematic and that of subjectivity/truth, particularly starting with the concept of the "care of the self"?

M.F. Up to that point I had conceived the problem of the relationship between the subject and games of truth in terms either of coercive practices—such as those of psychiatry and the prison system—or of theoretical or scientific games—such as the analysis of wealth, of language, and of living beings. In my lectures at the Collège de France, I tried to grasp it in terms of what may be called a practice of the self; although this phenomenon has not been

This interview was conducted by H. Becker, R. Fornet-Betancourt, and A. Gomez-Müller on January 20, 1984. It appeared in *Concordia: Revista internacional de filosophia* 6 (July–December 1984), pp. 96–116. The translation, by P. Aranov and D. McGrawth, has been amended and the footnotes of the French text added.

studied very much, I believe it has been fairly important in our societies ever since the Greco-Roman period. In the Greek and Roman civilizations, such practices of the self were much more important and especially more autonomous than they were later, after they were taken over to a certain extent by religious, pedagogical, medical, or psychiatric institutions.

Q. Thus there has been a sort of shift: these games of truth no longer involve a coercive practice, but a practice of self-formation of the subject.

M.F. That's right. It is what one could call an ascetic practice, taking asceticism in a very general sense—in other words, not in the sense of a morality of renunciation but as an exercise of the self on the self by which one attempts to develop and transform oneself, and to attain to a certain mode of being. Here I am taking asceticism in a more general sense than that attributed to it by Max Weber, for example, but along the same lines.

Q. A work of the self on the self that may be understood as a certain liberation, as a process of liberation?

M.F. I would be more careful on that score. I have always been somewhat suspicious of the notion of liberation, because if it is not treated with precautions and within certain limits, one runs the risk of falling back on the idea that there exists a human nature or base that, as a consequence of certain historical, economic, and social processes, has been concealed, alienated, or imprisoned in and by mechanisms of repression. According to this hypothesis, all that is required is to break these repressive deadlocks and man will be reconciled with himself, rediscover his nature or regain contact with his origin, and reestablish a full and positive relationship with himself. I think this idea should not be accepted without scrutiny. I am not trying to say that liberation as such, or this or that form of liberation, does not exist: when a colonized people attempts to liberate itself from its colonizers, this is indeed a practice of liberation in the strict sense. But we know very well, and moreover in this specific case, that this practice of liberation is not in itself sufficient to define the practices of freedom that will still be needed if this people, this society, and these individuals are to be able to define admissible and acceptable forms of existence or political society. This is why I emphasize practices of freedom over processes of liberation; again, the latter indeed have their place, but they do not seem to me to be capable by themselves of defining all the practical forms of freedom. This is precisely the problem I encountered with regard to sexuality: does it make any sense to say, "Let's liberate our sexuality"? Isn't the problem rather that of defining the practices of freedom by which one could define what is sexual pleasure and erotic, amorous and passionate relationships with others? This ethical problem of the definition of practices of freedom, it seems to me, is much more important than the rather repetitive affirmation that sexuality or desire must be liberated.

Q. But doesn't the exercise of practices of freedom require a certain degree of liberation?

M.F. Yes, absolutely. And this is where we must introduce the concept of domination. The analyses I am trying to make bear essentially on relations of power. By this I mean something different from states of domination. Power relations are extremely widespread in human relationships. Now, this means not that political power is everywhere, but that there is in human relationships a whole range of power relations that may come into play among individuals, within families, in pedagogical relationships, political life, and so on. The analysis of power relations is an extremely complex area; one sometimes encounters what may be called situations or states of domination in which the power relations, instead of being mobile, allowing the various participants to adopt strategies modifying them, remain blocked, frozen. When an individual or social group succeeds in blocking a field of power relations, immobilizing them and preventing any reversibility of movement by economic, political, or military means, one is faced with what may be called a state of domination. In such a state, it is certain that practices of freedom do not exist or exist only unilaterally or are extremely constrained and limited. Thus, I agree with you that liberation is sometimes the political or historical condition for a practice of freedom. Taking sexuality as an example, it is clear that a number of liberations were required vis-à-vis male power, that liberation was necessary from an oppressive morality concerning heterosexuality as well as homosexuality. But this liberation does not give rise to the happy human being imbued with a sexuality to which the subject could achieve a complete and satisfying relationship. Liberation paves the way for new power relationships, which must be controlled by practices of freedom.

Q. Can't liberation itself be a mode or form of practice of freedom?

M.F. Yes, in some cases. You have situations where liberation and the struggle for liberation are indispensable for the practice of freedom. With respect to sexuality, for example—and I am not indulging in polemics, because I don't like polemics, I think they are usually futile—there is a Reichian model derived from a certain reading of Freud. Now, in Reich's view the problem was entirely one of liberation. To put it somewhat schematically, according to him there is desire, drive, prohibition, repression, internalization, and it is by getting rid of these prohibitions, in other words, by liberating oneself, that the problem gets resolved. I think—and I know I am vastly oversimplifying much more interesting and refined positions of many authors—this completely misses the ethical problem of the practice of freedom: How can one practice freedom? With regard to sexuality, it is obvious that it is by liberating our desire that we will learn to conduct ourselves ethically in pleasure relationships with others.

Q. You say that freedom must be practiced ethically . . .

M.F. Yes, for what is ethics, if not the practice of freedom, the conscious [*réfléchie*] practice of freedom?

Q. In other words, you understand freedom as a reality that is already ethical in itself.

M.F. Freedom is the ontological condition of ethics. But ethics is the considered form that freedom takes when it is informed by reflection.

Q. Ethics is what is achieved in the search for or the care of the self?

M.F. In the Greco-Roman world, the care of the self was the mode in which individual freedom—or civic liberty, up to a point—was reflected [*se réfléchie*] as an ethics. If you take a whole series of texts going from the first Platonic dialogues up to the major texts of late Stoicism—Epictetus, Marcus Aurelius, and so on—you will see that the theme of the care of the self thoroughly permeated moral reflection. It is interesting to see that, in our societies on the other hand, at a time that is very difficult to pinpoint, the care of the self became somewhat suspect. Starting at a certain point, being concerned with oneself was readily denounced as a form of self-love, a form of selfishness or self-interest in contradiction with the interest to be shown in others or the self-sacrifice required. All this happened during Christianity; however, I am not simply saying that Christianity is responsible for it. The question is much more complex, for, with Christianity, achieving one's salvation is also a way of caring for oneself. But in Christianity, salvation is attained through the renunciation of the self. There is a paradox in the care of the self in Christianity—but that is another problem. To come back to the question you were talking about, I believe that among the Greeks and Romans—especially the Greeks—concern with the self and care of the self were required for right conduct and the proper practice of freedom, in order to know oneself [*se connaître*]—the familiar aspect of the *gnōthi seauton*— as well as to form oneself, to surpass oneself, to master the appetites that threaten to overwhelm one. Individual freedom was very important for the Greeks—contrary to the common-place derived more or less from Hegel that sees it as being of no importance when placed against the imposing totality of the city. Not to be a slave (of another city, of the people around you, of those governing you, of your own passions) was an absolutely fundamental theme. The concern with freedom was an essential and permanent problem for eight full centuries of ancient culture. What we have here is an entire ethics revolving around the care of the self; this is what gives ancient ethics its particular form. I am not saying that ethics is synonymous with the care of the self, but that, in antiquity, ethics as the conscious practice of freedom has revolved around this fundamental imperative: "Take care of yourself" [*soucie-toi de toi-même*].

Q. An imperative that implies the assimilation of the *logoi*, truths.

M.F. Certainly. Taking care of oneself requires knowing [*connaître*] oneself.

Care of the self is, of course, knowledge [*connaissance*] of the self—this is the Socratic-Platonic aspect—but also knowledge of a number of rules of acceptable conduct or of principles that are both truths and prescriptions. To take care of the self is to equip oneself with these truths: this is where ethics is linked to the game of truth.

Q. You are saying that it involves making this truth that is learned, memorized, and progressively applied into a quasi subject that reigns supreme in yourself. What is the status of this quasi subject?

M.F. In the Platonic current of thought, at least at the end of the *Alcibiades*, the problem for the subject or the individual soul is to turn its gaze upon itself, to recognize itself in what it is and, recognizing itself in what it is, to recall the truths that issue from it and that it has been able to contemplate,[1] on the other hand, in the current of thinking we can broadly call Stoicism, the problem is to learn through the teaching of a number of truths and doctrines, some of which are fundamental principles while others are rules of conduct. You must proceed in such a way that these principles tell you in each situation and, as it were, spontaneously, how to conduct yourself. It is here that one encounters a metaphor that comes not from the Stoics but from Plutarch: "You must learn the principles in such a constant way that whenever your desires, appetites, and fears awake like barking dogs, the *logos* will speak like the voice of the master who silences his dogs with a single cry."[2] Here we have the idea of a *logos* functioning, as it were, without any intervention on your part; you have become the *logos*, or the *logos* has become you.

Q. I would like to come back to the question of the relationship between freedom and ethics. When you say that ethics is the reflective part [*la partie réfléchie*] of freedom, does that mean that freedom can become aware of itself as ethical practice? Is it first and always a freedom that is, so to speak, "moralized," or must one work on oneself to discover the ethical dimension of freedom?

M.F. The Greeks problematized their freedom, and the freedom of the individual, as an ethical problem. But ethical in the sense in which the Greeks understood it: *ēthos* was a way of being and of behavior. It was a mode of being for the subject, along with a certain way of acting, a way visible to others. A person's *ēthos* was evident in his clothing, appearance, gait, in the calm with which he responded to every event, and so on. For the Greeks, this was the concrete form of freedom; this was the way they problematized their freedom. A man possessed of a splendid *ēthos*, who could be admired and put forward as an example, was someone who practiced freedom in a certain way. I don't think that a shift is needed for freedom to be conceived as *ēthos*; it is immediately problematized as *ēthos*. But extensive work by the self on the self is required for this practice of freedom to take shape in an *ēthos* that is good, beautiful, honorable, estimable, memorable, and exemplary.

Q. Is this where you situate the analysis of power?

M.F. I think that insofar as freedom for the Greeks signifies non-slavery—which is quite a different definition of freedom from our own—the problem is already entirely political. It is political in that nonslavery to others is a condition: a slave has no ethics. Freedom is thus inherently political. And it also has a political model insofar as being free means not being a slave to oneself and one's appetites, which means that with respect to oneself one establishes a certain relationship of domination, of mastery, which was called *arkhē*, or power, command.

Q. As you have stated, care of the self is in a certain sense care for others. In this sense, the care of the self is also always ethical, and ethical in itself.

M.F. What makes it ethical for the Greeks is not that it is care for others. The care of the self is ethical in itself; but it implies complex relationships with others insofar as this *ēthos* of freedom is also a way of caring for others. This is why it is important for a free man who conducts himself as he should to be able to govern his wife, his children, his household; it is also the art of governing. *Ēthos* also implies a relationship with others, insofar as the care of the self enables one to occupy his rightful position in the city, the community, or interpersonal relationships, whether as a magistrate or a friend. And the care of the self also implies a relationship with the other insofar as proper care of the self requires listening to the lessons of a master. One needs a guide, a counselor, a friend, someone who will be truthful with you. Thus, the problem of relationships with others is present throughout the development of the care of the self.

Q. The care of the self always aims for the well-being of others; it aims to manage the space of power that exists in all relationships, but to manage it in a nonauthoritarian manner. What role could a philosopher play in this context, as a person who is concerned with care for others?

M.F. Let's take Socrates as an example. He would greet people in the street or adolescents in the gymnasium with the question: Are you caring for yourself? For he has been entrusted with this mission by a god and he will not abandon it even when threatened with death. He is the man who cares about the care of others; this is the particular position of the philosopher. But let me simply say that in the case of the free man, I think the postulate of this whole morality was that a person who took proper care of himself would, by the same token, be able to conduct himself properly in relation to others and for others. A city in which everybody took proper care of himself would be a city that functioned well and found in this the ethical principle of its permanence. But I don't think we can say that the Greek who cares for himself must first care for others. To my mind, this view only came later. Care for others should not be put before the care of oneself. The care of the self is ethically prior in that the relationship with oneself is ontologically prior.

Q. Can this care of the self, which possesses a positive ethical meaning, be understood as a sort of conversion of power?

M.F. A conversion, yes. In fact, it is a way of limiting and controlling power. For if it is true that slavery is the great risk that Greek freedom resists, there is also another danger that initially appears to be the opposite of slavery: the abuse of power. In the abuse of power, one exceeds the legitimate exercise of one's power and imposes one's fantasies, appetites, and desires on others. Here we have the image of the tyrant, or simply of the rich and powerful man who uses his wealth and power to abuse others, to impose an unwarranted power on them. But one can see—in any case, this is what the Greek philosophers say—that such a man is the slave of his appetites. And the good ruler is precisely the one who exercises his power as it ought to be exercised, that is, simultaneously exercising his power over himself. And it is the power over oneself that thus regulates one's power over others.

Q. Doesn't the care of the self, when separated from care for others, run the risk of becoming an absolute? And couldn't this "absolutization" of the care of the self become a way of exercising power over others, in the sense of dominating others?

M.F. No, because the risk of dominating others and exercising a tyrannical power over them arises precisely only when one has not taken care of the self and has become the slave of one's desires. But if you take proper care of yourself, that is, if you know ontologically what you are, if you know what you are capable of, if you know what it means for you to be a citizen of a city, to be the master of a household in an *oikos,* if you know what things you should and should not fear, if you know what you can reasonably hope for and, on the other hand, what things should not matter to you, if you know, finally, that you should not be afraid of death—if you know all this, you cannot abuse your power over others. Thus, there is no danger. That idea will appear much later, when love of self becomes suspect and comes to be perceived as one of the roots of various moral offenses. In this new context, renunciation of self will be the prime form of care of the self. All this is evident in Gregory of Nyssa's *Treatise on Virginity,* which defines the care of the self, the *epimeleia heautou,* as the renunciation of all earthly attachments. It is the renunciation of all that may be love of self, of attachment to an earthly self.[3] But I think that in Greek and Roman thought the care of the self cannot in itself tend toward so exaggerated a form of self-love as to neglect others or, worse still, to abuse one's power over them.

Q. Thus it is a care of the self that, in thinking of itself, thinks of others?

M.F. Yes, absolutely. He who takes care of himself to the point of knowing exactly what duties he has as master of a household and as a husband and father will find that he enjoys a proper relationship with his wife and children.

Q. But doesn't the human condition, in terms of its finitude, play a very important role here? You have talked about death: if you are not afraid of death, then you cannot abuse your power over others. It seems to me that this problem of finitude is very important; the fear of death, of finitude, of being hurt, is at the heart of the care of the self.

M.F. Of course. And this is where Christianity, by presenting salvation as oc-curring beyond life, in a way upsets or at least disturbs the balance of the care of the self. Although, let me say it again, to seek one's salvation definitely means to take care of oneself. But the condition required for attaining salvation is pre-cisely renunciation. Among the Greeks and Romans, however, given that one takes care of oneself in one's own life, and that the reputation one leaves behind is the only afterlife one can expect, the care of the self can be centered entirely on oneself, on what one does, on the place one occupies among others. It can be centered totally on the acceptance of death—this will become quite evident in late Stoicism—and can even, up to a point, become almost a desire for death. At the same time, it can be, if not a care for others, at least a care of the self which will be beneficial to others. In Seneca, for example, it is interesting to note the importance of the theme, let us hurry and get old, let us hasten toward the end, so that we may thereby come back to ourselves. This type of moment before death, when nothing more can happen, is different from the desire for death one finds among the Christians, who expect salvation through death. It is like a movement to rush through life to the point where there is no longer anything ahead but the possibility of death.

Q. I would now like to turn to another topic. In your lectures at the Collège de France you spoke about the relationship between power and knowledge [savoir]. Now you are talking about the relationship between subject and truth. Are these pairs of concepts—power-knowledge and subject-truth—complementary in some way?

M.F. As I said when we started, I have always been interested in the problem of the relationship between subject and truth. I mean, how does the subject fit into a certain game of truth? The first problem I examined was why madness was problematized, starting at a certain time and following certain processes, as an illness falling under a certain model of medicine. How was the mad subject placed in this game of truth defined by a medical model or a knowledge? And it was while working on this analysis that I realized that, contrary to what was rather common practice at that time (around the early sixties), this phenomenon could not be properly accounted for simply by talking about ideology. In fact, there were practices—essentially the widespread use of incarceration which had been developed starting at the beginning of the seventeenth century, and had been the condition for the insertion of the mad subject in this type of truth game—that sent me back to the problem of institutions of power much more than to the problem of ideology. This is what led me to pose the problem of knowledge and power, which for me is not the fundamental problem but an instrument that makes it possible to analyze the problem of the relationship between subject and truth in what seems to me the most precise way.

Q. But you have always "forbidden" people to talk to you about the subject in general?

M.F. No, I have not "forbidden" them. Perhaps I did not explain myself adequately. What I rejected was the idea of starting out with a theory of the subject—as is done, for example, in phenomenology or existentialism—and, on the basis of this theory, asking how a given form of knowledge [*connaissance*] was possible. What I wanted to try to show was how the subject constituted itself, in one specific form or another, as a mad or a healthy subject, as a delinquent or nondelinquent subject, through certain practices that were also games of truth, practices of power, and so on. I had to reject a priori theories of the subject in order to analyze the relationships that may exist between the constitution of the subject or different forms of the subject and games of truth, practices of power, and so on.

Q. That means that the subject is not a substance.

M.F. It is not a substance. It is a form, and this form is not primarily or always identical to itself. You do not have the same type of relationship to yourself when you constitute yourself as a political subject who goes to vote or speaks at a meeting and when you are seeking to fulfill your desires in a sexual relationship. Undoubtedly there are relationships and interferences between these different forms of the subject; but we are not dealing with the same type of subject. In each case, one plays, one establishes a different type of relationship to oneself. And it is precisely the historical constitution of these various forms of the subject in relation to the games of truth which interests me.

Q. But the mad, the ill, the delinquent subject—and perhaps even the sexual subject—was a subject that was the object of a theoretical discourse, let us say a "passive" subject, while the subject you have been speaking about over the past two years in your lectures at the Collège de France is an "active," a politically active subject. The care of the self concerns all the problems of political practice and government, and so on. It would seem, then, that there has been a change for you, a change not of perspective but of problematic.

M.F. If it is indeed true that the constitution of the mad subject may be considered the consequence of a system of coercion—this is the passive subject—you know very well that the mad subject is not an unfree subject, and that the mentally ill person is constituted as a mad subject precisely in relation to and over against the one who declares him mad. Hysteria, which was so important in the history of psychiatry and in the asylums of the nineteenth century, seems to me to be the very picture of how the subject is constituted as a mad subject. And it is certainly no accident that the major phenomena of hysteria were observed precisely in those situations where there was a maximum of coercion to force individuals to constitute themselves as mad. On the other hand, I would say that if I am now interested in how the subject constitutes itself in an active fashion through practices of the self, these practices are nevertheless not something invented by the individual himself. They are models that he finds in his culture and are proposed, suggested, imposed upon him by his culture, his society, and his social group.

Q. It would seem that there is something of a deficiency in your problematic, namely, in the notion of resistance against power. Which presupposes a very active subject, very concerned with the care of itself and of others and, therefore, competent politically and philosophically.

M.F. This brings us back to the problem of what I mean by power. I scarcely use the word *power,* and if I use it on occasion it is simply as shorthand for the expression I generally use: *relations of power.* But there are readymade models: when one speaks of *power,* people immediately think of a political structure, a government, a dominant social class, the master and the slave, and so on. I am not thinking of this at all when I speak of *relations of power.* I mean that in human relationships, whether they involve verbal communication such as we are engaged in at this moment, or amorous, institutional, or economic relationships, power is always present: I mean a relationship in which one person tries to control the conduct of the other. So I am speaking of relations that exist at different levels, in different forms; these power relations are mobile, they can be modified, they are not fixed once and for all. For example, the fact that I may be older than you, and that you may initially have been intimidated, may be turned around during the course of our conversation, and I may end up being intimidated before someone precisely because he is younger than I am. These power relations are thus mobile, reversible, and unstable. It should also be noted that power relations are possible only insofar as the subjects are free. If one of them were completely at the other's disposal and became his thing, an object on which he could wreak boundless and limitless violence, there wouldn't be any relations of power. Thus, in order for power relations to come into play, there must be at least a certain degree of freedom on both sides. Even when the power relation is completely out of balance, when it can truly be claimed that one side has "total power" over the other, a power can be exercised over the other only insofar as the other still has the option of killing himself, of leaping out the window, or of killing the other person. This means that in power relations there is necessarily the possibility of resistance because if there were no possibility of resistance (of violent resistance, flight, deception, strategies capable of reversing the situation), there would be no power relations at all. This being the general form, I refuse to reply to the question I am sometimes asked: "But if power is everywhere, there is no freedom." I answer that if there are relations of power in every social field, this is because there is freedom everywhere. Of course, states of domination do indeed exist. In a great many cases, power relations are fixed in such a way that they are perpetually asymmetrical and allow an extremely limited margin of freedom. To take what is undoubtedly a very simplified example, one cannot say that it was only men who wielded power in the conventional marital structure of the eighteenth and nineteenth centuries; women had quite a few options: they could deceive their husbands, pilfer money from them, refuse them sex. Yet they were still in a state of domination insofar as these options were ultimately only stratagems that never succeeded in reversing the situation. In such cases of domination, be they economic, social, institutional, or sexual, the problem is knowing where resistance will develop. For example, in a working class that will resist domination, will this be in unions or political parties; and what form will it take—a strike, a general strike, revolution, or parliamentary opposition? In such a situation of domination, all of these questions demand specific answers that take account of the kind and precise form of domination in question. But the claim that "you see power everywhere, thus there is no room for freedom" seems to me absolutely inadequate. The idea that power is a system of domination that controls everything and leaves no room for freedom cannot be attributed to me.

Q. You were talking before about the free man and the philosopher as two different modes of the care of the self. The care of the self of the philosopher would have a specificity that cannot be confused with that of the free man.

M.F. I would say that these figures represent two different places in the care of the self, rather than two forms of care of the self. I believe that the form of such care remains the same, but in terms of intensity, in the degree of zeal for the self, and, consequently, also for others, the place of the philosopher is not that of just any free man.

Q. Is there a fundamental link we can make at this point between philosophy and politics?

M.F. Yes, certainly. I believe that the relationship between philosophy and politics is permanent and fundamental. It is certain that if one takes the history of the care of the self in Greek philosophy, the relationship with politics is obvious. And it takes a very complex form: on the one hand, you have, for example, Socrates as well as Plato in the *Alcibiades*[4] and Xenophon in the *Memorabilia*[5]—greeting young men, saying to them: "You want to become a politician, to govern a city, to care for others, and you haven't even taken care of yourself. If you do not care for yourself you will make a poor ruler." From this perspective, the care of the self appears a pedagogical, ethical, and also ontological condition for the development of a good ruler. To constitute oneself as a governing subject implies that one has constituted oneself as a subject who cares for oneself. Yet, on the other hand, we have Socrates saying in the *Apology* that he approaches everyone because everyone has to take care of himself;[6] but he also adds, "In doing so, I am performing the highest service for the city, and instead of punishing me, you should reward me even more than you reward a winner in the Olympic Games."[7] Thus we see a very strong connection between philosophy and politics, which was to develop further when the philosopher would care not only for the soul of the citizen but for that of the prince. The philosopher becomes the prince's counselor, teacher, and spiritual adviser.

Q. Could the problematic of the care of the self be at the heart of a new way of thinking about politics, of a form of politics different from what we know today?

M.F. I admit that I have not got very far in this direction, and I would very much like to come back to more contemporary questions to try to see what can be made of all this in the context of the current political problematic. But I have the impression that in the political thought of the nineteenth century—and perhaps one should go back even farther, to Rousseau and Hobbes—the political subject was conceived of essentially as a subject of law, whether natural or positive. On the other hand, it seems to me that contemporary political thought allows very little room for the question of the ethical subject. I don't like to reply to questions I haven't studied. However, I would very much like to come back to the questions I examined through ancient culture.

Q. What is the relationship between the path of philosophy, which leads to knowledge of the self, and the path of spirituality?

M.F. By spirituality I mean—but I'm not sure this definition can hold for very long—the subject's attainment of a certain mode of being and the transformations that the subject must carry out on itself to attain this mode of being. I believe that spirituality and philosophy were identical or nearly identical in ancient spirituality. In any case, philosophy's most important preoccupation centered around the self, with knowledge [connaissance] of the world coming after and serving, most often, to support the care of the self. Reading Descartes, it is remarkable to find in the Meditations this same spiritual concern with the attainment of a mode of being where doubt was no longer possible, and where one could finally know [connaît][8]. But by thus defining the mode of being to which philosophy gives access, one realizes that this mode of being is defined entirely in terms of knowledge, and that philosophy in turn is defined in terms of the development of the knowing [connaissant] subject, or of what qualifies the subject as such. From this perspective, it seems to me that philosophy superimposes the functions of spirituality upon the ideal of a grounding for scientificity.

Q. Should the concept of the care of the self in the classical sense be updated to confront this modern thought?

M.F. Absolutely, but I would certainly not do so just to say, "We have unfortunately forgotten about the care of the self; so here, here it is, the key to everything." Nothing is more foreign to me than the idea that, at a certain moment, philosophy went astray and forgot something, that somewhere in its history there is a principle, a foundation that must be rediscovered. I feel that all such forms of analysis, whether they take a radical form and claim that philosophy has from the outset been a forgetting, or whether they take a much more historical viewpoint and say, "Such and such a philosopher forgot something"—neither of these approaches is particularly interesting or useful. Which does not mean that contact with such and such a philosopher may not produce something, but it must be emphasized that it would be something new.

Q. This leads me to ask: Why should one have access to the truth today, to *truth* in the political sense, in other words, in the sense of a political strategy directed against the various "blockages" of power in the system of relations?

M.F. This is indeed a problem. After all, why truth? Why are we concerned with truth, and more so than with the care of the self? And why must the care of the self occur only through the concern for truth? I think we are touching on a fundamental question here, what I would call *the* question for the West: How did it come about that all of Western culture began to revolve around this obligation of truth which has taken a lot of different forms? Things being as they are, nothing so far has shown that it is possible to define a strategy outside of this concern. It is within the field of the obligation to truth that it is possible to move about in one way or another, sometimes against effects of domination which may be linked to structures of truth or institutions entrusted with truth. To greatly simplify matters, there are numerous examples: there has been a whole so-called ecological movement—a very ancient one, by the way, that did not just start in the twentieth century—that was often in opposition, as it were, to a science or, at least, to a technology underwritten by claims to truth. But this same ecology articulated its own discourse of truth: criticism was authorized in the name of a knowledge [*connaissance*] of nature, the balance of life processes, and so on. Thus, one escaped from a domination of truth not by playing a game that was totally different from the game of truth but by playing the same game differently, or playing another game, another hand, with other trump cards. I believe that the same holds true in the order of politics; here one can criticize on the basis, for example, of the consequences of the state of domination caused by an unjustified political situation, but one can only do so by playing a certain game of truth, by showing its consequences, by pointing out that there are other reasonable options, by teaching people what they don't know about their own situation, their working conditions, and their exploitation.

Q. With regard to the question of games of truth and games of power, don't you think that there can be found in history evidence of a particular kind of these games of truth, one that has a particular status in relation to all other possible games of truth and power, and is marked by its essential openness, its opposition to all blockages of power—power here meaning domination/subjugation?

M.F. Yes, absolutely. But when I talk about power relations and games of truth, I am absolutely not saying that games of truth are just concealed power relations—that would be a horrible exaggeration. My problem, as I have already said, is in understanding how truth games are set up and how they are connected with power relations. One can show, for example, that the medicalization of madness, in other words, the organization of medical knowledge [*savoir*] around individuals designated as mad, was connected with a whole series of social and economic processes at a given time, but also with institutions and practices of power. This fact in no way impugns the scientific validity or the therapeutic effectiveness of psychiatry: it does not endorse psychiatry, but neither does it invalidate it. It is also true that mathematics, for example, is linked, albeit in a completely different manner than psychiatry, to power structures, if only in the way it is taught, the way in which consensus among mathematicians is organized, functions in a closed circuit, has its values, determines what is good (true) or bad (false) in mathematics. This in no way means that mathematics is only a game of power, but that the game of truth of mathematics is linked in a certain way—without thereby being invalidated in any way—to games and institutions of power. It is clear that in some cases these connections are such that one could write the entire history of mathematics without taking them into account, although this problematic is always interesting and even historians of mathematics are now beginning to study the history of their institutions. Finally, it is clear that the connection that may exist between power relations and games of truth in mathematics is totally different from what it is in psychiatry; in any case, one simply cannot say that games of truth are nothing but games of power.

Q. This question takes us back to the problem of the subject because, with games of truth, it is a question of knowing *who* is speaking the truth, how he speaks it, and why he speaks it. For, in games of truth, one can play at speaking the truth: there is a game, one plays at truth or truth is a game.

M.F. The word "game" can lead you astray: when I say "game," I mean a set of rules by which truth is produced. It is not a game in the sense of an amusement; it is a set of procedures that lead to a certain result, which, on the basis of its principles and rules of procedure, may be considered valid or invalid, winning or losing.

Q. There remains the problem of "who": Is it a group, a body?

M.F. It may be a group or an individual. Indeed, there is a problem here. With regard to these multiple games of truth, one can see that ever since the age of the Greeks our society has been marked by the lack of a precise and imperative definition of the games of truth which are permitted to the exclusion of all others. In a given game of truth, it is always possible to discover something different and to more or less modify this or that rule, and sometimes even the entire game of truth. This has undoubtedly given the West possibilities for development not found in other societies. Who speaks the truth? Free individuals who establish a certain consensus, and who find themselves within a certain network of practices of power and constraining institutions.

Q. So truth is not a construction?

M.F. That depends. There are games of truth in which truth is a construction and others in which it is not. One can have, for example, a game of truth that consists of describing things in such and such a way: a person giving an anthropological description of a society supplies not a construction but a description, which itself has a certain number of historically changing rules, so that one can say that it is to a certain extent a construction with respect to another description. This does not mean that there's just a void, that everything is a figment of the imagination. On the basis of what can be said, for example, about this transformation of games of truth, some people conclude that I have said that nothing exists—I have been seen as saying that madness does not exist, whereas the problem is absolutely the converse: it was a question of knowing how madness, under the various definitions that have been given, was at a particular time integrated into an institutional field that constituted it as a mental illness occupying a specific place alongside other illnesses.

Q. At the heart of the problem of truth there is ultimately a problem of communication, of the transparency of the words of a discourse. The person who has the capacity to formulate truths also has a power, the power of being able to speak the truth and to express it in the way he wants.

M.F. Yes, and yet this does not mean that what the person says is not true, which is what most people believe. When you tell people that there may be a relationship between truth and power, they say: "So it isn't truth after all!"

Q. This is tied up with the problem of communication because, in a society where communication has reached a high level of transparency, games of truth are perhaps more independent of structures of power.

M.F. This is indeed an important problem; I imagine you are thinking a little about Habermas when you say that. I am quite interested in his work, although I know he completely disagrees with my views. While I, for my part, tend to be a little more in agreement with what he says, I have always had a problem insofar as he gives communicative relations this place which is so important and, above all, a function that I would call "utopian." The idea that there could exist a state of communication that would allow games of truth to circulate freely, without any constraints or coercive effects, seems utopian to me. This is precisely a failure to see that power relations are not something that is bad in itself, that we have to break free of. I do not think that a society can exist without power relations, if by that one means the strategies by which individuals try to direct and control the conduct of others. The problem, then, is not to try to dissolve them in the utopia of completely transparent communication but to acquire the rules of law, the management techniques, and also the morality, the *ēthos*, the practice of the self, that will allow us to play these games of power with as little domination as possible.

Q. You are very far from Sartre, who told us power is evil.

M.F. Yes, and that idea, which is very far from my way of thinking, has often been attributed to me. Power is not evil. Power is games of strategy. We all know that power is not evil! For example, let us take sexual or amorous relationships: to wield power over the other in a sort of open-ended strategic game where the situation may be reversed is not evil; it's a part of love, of passion and sexual pleasure. And let us take, as another example, something that has often been rightly criticized—the pedagogical institution. I see nothing wrong in the practice of a person who, knowing more than others in a specific game of truth, tells those others what to do, teaches them, and transmits knowledge and techniques to them. The problem in such practices where power—which is not in itself a bad thing—must inevitably come into play is knowing how to avoid the kind of domination effects where a kid is subjected to the arbitrary and unnecessary authority of a teacher, or a student put under the thumb of a professor who abuses his authority. I believe that this problem must be framed in terms of rules of law, rational techniques of government and *ēthos*, practices of the self and of freedom.

Q. Are we to take what you have just said as the fundamental criteria of what you have called a new ethics? It is a question of playing with as little domination as possible . . .

M.F. I believe that this is, in fact, the hinge point of ethical concerns and the political struggle for respect of rights, of critical thought against abusive techniques of government and research in ethics that seeks to ground individual freedom.

Q. When Sartre speaks of power as the supreme evil, he seems to be alluding to the reality of power as domination. On this point you are probably in agreement with Sartre.

M.F. Yes, I believe that all these concepts have been ill defined, so that one hardly knows what one is talking about. I am not even sure if I made myself clear, or used the right words, when I first became interested in the problem of power. Now I have a clearer sense of the problem. It seems to me that we must distinguish between power relations understood as strategic games between liberties—in which some try to control the conduct of others, who in turn try to avoid allowing their conduct to be controlled or try to control the conduct of the others—and the states of domination that people ordinarily call "power."

And between the two, between games of power and states of domination, you have technologies of government—understood, of course, in a very broad sense that includes not only the way institutions are governed but also the way one governs one's wife and children. The analysis of these techniques is necessary because it is very often through such techniques that states of domination are established and maintained. There are three levels to my analysis of power: strategic relations, techniques of government, and states of domination.

Q. In your lectures on the hermeneutics of the subject there is a passage in which you say that the first and only useful point of resistance to political power is in the relationship of the self to the self.

M.F. I do not believe that the only possible point of resistance to political power—understood, of course, as a state of domination—lies in the relationship of the self to the self. I am saying that "governmentality" implies the relationship of the self to itself, and I intend this concept of "governmentality" to cover the whole range of practices that constitute, define, organize, and instrumentalize the strategies that individuals in their freedom can use in dealing with each other. Those who try to control, determine, and limit the freedom of others are themselves free individuals who have at their disposal certain instruments they can use to govern others. Thus, the basis for all this is freedom, the relationship of the self to itself and the relationship to the other. Whereas, if you try to analyze power not on the basis of freedom, strategies, and governmentality, but on the basis of the political institution, you can only conceive of the subject as a subject of law. One then has a subject who has or does not have rights, who has had these rights either granted or removed by the institution of political society; and all this brings us back to a legal concept of the subject. On the other hand, I believe that the concept of governmentality makes it possible to bring out the freedom of the subject and its relationship to others—which constitutes the very stuff [*matière*] of ethics.

Q. Do you think that philosophy has anything to say about why there is this tendency to try to control the conduct of others?

M.F. The way the conduct of others is controlled takes very different forms and arouses desires and appetites that vary greatly in intensity depending on the society. I don't know anything about anthropology, but I can well imagine societies in which the control of the conduct of others is so well regulated in advance that, in a sense, the game is already over. On the other hand, in a society like our own, games can be very numerous, and the desire to control the conduct of others is all the greater—as we see in family relationships, for example, or emotional or sexual relationships. However, the freer people are with respect to each other, the more they want to control each other's conduct. The more open the game, the more appealing and fascinating it becomes.

Q. Do you think the role of philosophy is to warn of the dangers of power?

M.F. This has always been an important function of philosophy. In its critical aspect—and I mean critical in a broad sense—philosophy is that which calls into question domination at every level and in every form in which it exists, whether political, economic, sexual, institutional, or what have you. To a certain extent, this critical function of philosophy derives from the Socratic injunction "Take care of yourself," in other words, "Make freedom your foundation, through the mastery of yourself."

Notes

1. Plato, *Alcibiade*, trans. M. Croiset (Paris: Belles Lettres, 1925), pp. 109–110 [*Alcibiades*, trans. W. R. M. Lamb, in *Plato* (Cambridge, Mass.: Harvard University, 1967), vol. 12, pp. 210–13].

2. Plutarch, *De la tranquillité de l'âme*, trans. J. Dumortier and J. Defradas, in *Oeuvres Morales* (Paris: Belles Lettres, 1975), vol. 3, pt. 1, 465c, p. 99 [*Tranquillity of Mind*, in *The Complete Works of Plutarch: Essays and Miscellanies*, ed. W. L. Bevan (New York: Thomas Y. Crowell, 1909), vol. 2, pp. 283–84]. The citation is an inexact paraphrase.

3. Gregory of Nyssa, *Traité de la virginité*, trans. M. Aubineau (Paris: Cerf, 1966), ch. 13, 303c–305c, pp. 411–17 [*Treatise on Virginity*, in *Saint Gregory of Nyssa: Ascetical Works*, trans. V. W. Callahan (Washington, D.C.: Catholic Universities of America Press, 1966), pp. 46–48].

4. Plato, *Alcibiade*, 124b, p. 92; 127d–e, p. 99 [*Alcibiades*, pp. 173–75; p. 189].

5. Xenophon, *Mémorables*, trans. E. Chambry (Paris: Garnier, 1935), bk. 3, ch. 7, §9, p. 412 [*Memorabilia*, trans. A. L. Bonnette (Ithaca: Cornell University Press, 1994), bk. 3, ch. 7, §9, p. 91].

6. Plato, *Apologie de Socrate*, trans. M. Croiset (Paris: Belles Lettres, 1925), 30b, p. 157 [*Socrates' Defense (Apology)*, trans. H. Tredennick, in *Plato: The Collected Dialogues*, ed. E. Hamilton and H. Cairns (Princeton: Princeton University Press, 1961), 30b, p. 16].

7. Plato, *Apologie de Socrate*, 36c–d, p. 166 [*Socrates' Defense (Apology)*, 36c–d, pp. 21–22].

8. R. Descartes, *Méditations sur la philosophie première*, in *Oeuvres* (Paris: Gallimard, 1952), pp. 253–334 [*Meditations on First Philosophy*, trans. and ed. J. Cottingham (Cambridge: Cambridge University Press, 1996)].

WHAT IS ENLIGHTENMENT?

I

Today when a periodical asks its readers a question, it does so in order to collect opinions on some subject about which everyone has an opinion already; there is not much likelihood of learning anything new. In the eighteenth century, editors preferred to question the public on programs that did not yet have solutions. I do not know whether or not that practice was more effective; it was unquestionably more entertaining.

In any event, in line with this custom, in November 1784 a German periodical, *Berlinische Monatschrift*, published a response to the question: *Was ist Aufklärung?* And the respondent was Kant.

A minor text, perhaps. But it seems to me that it marks the discreet entrance into the history of thought of a question that modern philosophy has not been capable of answering but has never managed to get rid of either. And one that has been repeated in various forms for two centuries now. From Hegel through Nietzsche or Max Weber to Horkheimer or Habermas, hardly any philosophy has failed to confront this same question, directly or indirectly. What, then, is this event that is called the *Aufklärung* and that has determined, at least in part, what we are, what we think, and what we do today? Let us imagine that the *Berlinische Monatschrift* still exists and that it is asking its readers the question: What is modern philosophy? Perhaps we could respond with an echo: modern philosophy is the philosophy that is attempting to answer the question raised so imprudently two centuries ago: *Was ist Aufklärung?*

Let us linger a few moments over Kant's text. It merits attention for several reasons.

1. To this same question, Moses Mendelssohn had also replied in the same

---

This translation, by Catherine Porter, has been amended.

journal, just two months earlier. But Kant had not seen Mendelssohn's text when he wrote his. To be sure, the encounter of the German philosophical movement with the new development of Jewish culture does not date from this precise moment. Mendelssohn had been at that crossroads for thirty years or so, in company with Lessing. But up to this point it had been a matter of making a place for Jewish culture within German thought—which Lessing had tried to do in *Die Juden*—or else of identifying problems common to Jewish thought and to German philosophy; this is what Mendelssohn had done in his *Phädon; oder, über die Unsterblichkeit der Seele*. With the two texts published in the *Berlinische Monatschrift*, the German *Aufklärung* and the Jewish *Haskala* recognize that they belong to the same history; they are seeking to identify the common processes from which they stem. And it is perhaps a way of announcing the acceptance of a common destiny—we now know to what drama that was to lead.

2. But there is more. In itself and within the Christian tradition, Kant's text poses a new problem.

It was certainly not the first time that philosophical thought had sought to reflect on its own present. But, speaking schematically, we may say that this reflection had until then taken three main forms.

- The present may be represented as belonging to a certain era of the world, distinct from the others through some inherent characteristics, or separated from the others by some dramatic event. Thus, in Plato's *The Statesman* the interlocutors recognize that they belong to one of those revolutions of the world in which the world is turning backward, with all the negative consequences that may ensue.
- The present may be interrogated in an attempt to decipher in it the heralding signs of a forthcoming event. Here we have the principle of a kind of historical hermeneutics of which Augustine might provide an example.
- The present may also be analyzed as a point of transition toward the dawning of a new world. That is what Vico describes in the last chapter of *La Scienza nuova;* what he sees "today" is "a complete humanity . . . spread abroad through all nations, for a few great monarchs rule over this world of peoples"; it is also "Europe . . . radiant with such humanity that it abounds in all the good things that make for the happiness of human life." [1]

Now, the way Kant poses the question of *Aufklärung* is entirely different: it is neither a world era to which one belongs, nor an event whose signs are perceived, nor the dawning of an accomplishment. Kant defines *Aufklärung* in an almost entirely negative way, as an *Ausgang*, an "exit," a "way out." In his other texts on history, Kant occasionally raises questions of origin or defines the internal teleology of a historical process. In the text on *Aufklärung*, he deals with the question of contemporary reality alone. He is not seeking to understand the present on the basis of a totality or of a future achievement. He is looking for a difference: What difference does today introduce with respect to yesterday?

3. I shall not go into detail here concerning this text, which is not always very clear despite its brevity. I should simply like to point out three or four features that seem to me important if we are to understand how Kant raised the philosophical question of the present day [*du présent*].

Kant indicates right away that the "way out" which characterizes Enlightenment is a process that releases us from the status of "immaturity." And by "immaturity," he means a certain state of our will which makes us accept someone else's authority to lead us in areas where the use of reason is called for. Kant gives three examples: we are in a state of "immaturity" when a book takes the place of our understanding, when a spiritual director takes the place of our conscience, when a doctor decides for us what our diet is to be. (Let us note in passing that the register of these three critiques is easy to recognize, even though the text does not make it explicit.) In any case, Enlightenment is defined by a modification of the preexisting relation linking will, authority, and the use of reason.

We must also note that this way out is presented by Kant in a rather ambiguous manner. He characterizes it as a phenomenon, an ongoing process; but he also presents it as a task and an obligation. From the very first paragraph, he notes that man himself is responsible for his immature status. Thus, it has to be supposed that he will be able to escape from it only by a change that he himself will bring about in himself. Significantly, Kant says that this Enlightenment has a *Wahlspruch*: now, a *Wahlspruch* is a heraldic device, that is, a distinctive feature by which one can be recognized, and it is also a motto, an instruction that one gives oneself and proposes to others. What, then, is this instruction? *Aude sapere:* "dare to know," "have the courage, the audacity, to know." Thus, Enlightenment must be considered both as a process in which men participate collectively and as an act of courage to be accomplished personally. Men are at once elements and agents of a single process. They may be actors in the process to the extent that they participate in it; and the process occurs to the extent that men decide to be its voluntary actors.

A third difficulty appears here in Kant's text, in his use of the word "mankind," *Menschheit*. The importance of this word in the Kantian conception of history is well known. Are we to understand that the entire human race is caught up in the process of Enlightenment? In that case, we must imagine Enlightenment as a historical change that affects the political and social existence of all people on the face of the earth. Or are we to understand that it involves a change affecting what constitutes the humanity of human beings? But the question then arises of knowing what this change is. Here again, Kant's answer is not without a certain ambiguity. In any case, beneath its appearance of simplicity, it is rather complex.

Kant defines two essential conditions under which mankind can escape from its immaturity. And these two conditions are at once spiritual and institutional, ethical and political.

The first of these conditions is that the realm of obedience and the realm of the use of reason be clearly distinguished. Briefly characterizing the immature status, Kant invokes the familiar expression: "Don't think, just follow orders"; such is, according to him, the form in which military discipline, political power, and religious authority are usually exercised. Humanity will reach maturity when it is no longer required to obey, but when men are told: "Obey, and you will be able to reason as much as you like." We must note that the German word used here is *räsonieren;* this word, which is also used in the *Critiques,* refers not to just any use of reason but to a use of reason in which reason has no other end but itself: *räsonieren* is to reason for reasoning's sake. And Kant gives examples, these too being perfectly trivial in appearance: paying one's taxes while being able to argue as much as one likes about the system of taxation, would be characteristic of the mature state; or again, taking responsibility for parish service, if one is a pastor, while reasoning freely about religious dogmas.

We might think that there is nothing very different here from what has been meant, since the sixteenth century, by freedom of conscience: the right to think as one pleases so long as one obeys as one must. Yet it is here that Kant brings into play another distinction, and in a rather surprising way. The distinction he introduces is between the private and public uses of reason. Yet he adds at once that reason must be free in its public use and must be submissive in its private use. Which is, term for term, the opposite of what is ordinarily called freedom of conscience.

But we must be somewhat more precise. What constitutes, for Kant, this private use of reason? In what area is it exercised? Man, Kant says, makes a private use of reason when he is "a cog in a machine," that is, when he has a role to play in society and jobs to do: to be a soldier, to have taxes to pay, to be in charge of a parish, to be a civil servant, all this makes the human being a particular segment of society; he finds himself thereby placed in a circumscribed position, where he has to apply particular rules and pursue particular ends. Kant asks not that people practice a blind and foolish obedience but that they adapt the use they make of their reason to these determined circumstances; and reason must then be subjected to the particular ends in view. Thus, there cannot be, here, any free use of reason.

On the other hand, when one is reasoning only in order to use one's reason, when one is reasoning as a reasonable being (and not as a cog in a machine), when one is reasoning as a member of reasonable humanity, then the use of reason must be free and public. Enlightenment is thus not merely the process by which individuals would see their own personal freedom of thought guaranteed. There is Enlightenment when the universal, the free, and the public uses of reason are superimposed on one another.

Now this leads us to a fourth question that must be put to Kant's text. We can readily see how the universal use of reason (apart from any private end) is the business of the subject himself as an individual; we can readily see, too, how the freedom of this use may be assured in a purely negative manner through the absence of any challenge to it; but how is a public use of that reason to be assured? Enlightenment, as we see, must not be conceived simply as a general process affecting all humanity; it must not be conceived only as an obligation prescribed to individuals: it now appears as a political problem. The question, in any event, is that of knowing how the use of reason can take the public form that it requires, how the audacity to know can be exercised in broad daylight, while individuals are obeying as scrupulously as possible. And Kant, in conclusion, proposes to Frederick II, in scarcely veiled terms, a sort of contract—what might be called the contract of rational despotism with free reason: the public and free use of autonomous reason will be the best guarantee of obedience, on condition, however, that the political principle which must be obeyed itself be in conformity with universal reason.

Let us leave Kant's text here. I do not by any means propose to consider it as capable of constituting an adequate description of Enlightenment; and no historian, I think, could be satisfied with it for an analysis of the social, political, and cultural transformations that occurred at the end of the eighteenth century.

Nevertheless, notwithstanding its circumstantial nature, and without intending to give it an exaggerated place in Kant's work, I believe that it is necessary to stress the connection that exists between this brief article and the three *Critiques*. Kant, in fact, describes Enlightenment as the moment when humanity is going to put its own reason to use, without subjecting itself to any authority; now, it is precisely at this moment that the critique[2] is necessary, since its role is that of defining the conditions under which the use of reason is legitimate in order to determine what can be known [*connaître*], what must be done, and what may be hoped. Illegitimate uses of reason are what give rise to dogmatism and heteronomy, along with illusion; on the other hand, it is when the legitimate use of reason has been clearly defined in its principles that its autonomy can be assured. The critique is, in a sense, the handbook of reason that has grown up in Enlightenment; and, conversely, the Enlightenment is the age of the critique.

It is also necessary, I think, to underline the relation between this text of Kant's and the other texts he devoted to history. These latter, for the most part, seek to define the internal teleology of time and the point toward which history of humanity is moving. Now, the analysis of Enlightenment, defining this history as humanity's passage to its adult status, situates contemporary reality with respect to the overall movement and its basic directions. But at the same time, it shows how, at this very moment, each individual is responsible in a certain way for that overall process.

The hypothesis I should like to propose is that this little text is located, in a sense, at the crossroads of critical reflection and reflection on history. It is a reflection by Kant on the contemporary status of his own enterprise. No doubt, it is not the first time that a philosopher has given his reasons for undertaking his work at a particular moment. But it seems to me that it is the first time that a philosopher has connected in this way, closely and from the inside, the significance of his work with respect to knowledge [*connaissance*], a reflection on history and a particular analysis of the specific moment at which he is writing and because of which he is writing. It is in the reflection on "today" as difference in history and as motive for a particular philosophical task that the novelty of this text appears to me to lie.

And, by looking at it in this way, it seems to me we may recognize a point of departure: the outline of what one might call the attitude of modernity.

II

I know that modernity is often spoken of as an epoch, or at least as a set of features characteristic of an epoch; situated on a calendar, it would be preceded by a more or less naive or archaic premodernity, and followed by an enigmatic and troubling "postmodernity." And then we find ourselves asking whether modernity constitutes the sequel to the Enlightenment and its development, or whether we are to see it as a rupture or a deviation with respect to the basic principles of the eighteenth century.

Thinking back on Kant's text, I wonder whether we may not envisage modernity as an attitude rather than as a period of history. And by "attitude," I mean a mode of relating to contemporary reality; a voluntary choice made by certain people; in the end, a way of thinking and feeling; a way, too, of acting and behaving that at one and the same time marks a relation of belonging and presents itself as a task. No doubt, a bit like what the Greeks called an *ēthos*. And consequently, rather than seeking to distinguish the "modern era" from the "premodern" or "postmodern," I think it would be more useful to try to find out how the attitude of modernity, ever since its formation, has found itself struggling with attitudes of "countermodernity."

To characterize briefly this attitude of modernity, I shall take an almost-indispensable example, namely, Baudelaire; for his consciousness of modernity is widely recognized as one of the most acute in the nineteenth century.

1. Modernity is often characterized in terms of consciousness of the discontinuity of time: a break with tradition, a feeling of novelty, a vertigo in the face of the passing moment. And this is indeed what Baudelaire seems to be saying when he defines modernity as "the ephemeral, the fleeting, the contingent." [3] But, for him, being modern does not lie in recognizing and accepting this perpetual movement; on the contrary, it lies in adopting a certain attitude with respect to this movement; and this deliberate, difficult attitude consists in recapturing something eternal that is not beyond the present instant, nor behind it, but within it. Modernity is distinct from fashion, which does no more than call into question the course of time; modernity is the attitude that makes it possible to grasp the "heroic" aspect of the present moment. Modernity is not a phenomenon of sensitivity to the fleeting present; it is the will to "heroize" the present.

I shall restrict myself to what Baudelaire says about the painting of his contemporaries. Baudelaire makes fun of those painters who, finding nineteenth-century dress excessively ugly, want to depict nothing but ancient togas. But modernity in painting does not consist, for Baudelaire, in introducing black clothing onto the canvas. The modern painter is the one who can show the dark frock-coat as "the necessary costume of our time," the one who knows how to make manifest, in the fashion of the day, the essential, permanent, obsessive relation that our age entertains with death. "The dress-coat and frock-coat not only possess their political beauty, which is an expression of universal equality, but also their poetic beauty, which is an expression of the public soul—an immense cortège of undertaker's mutes (mutes in love, political mutes, bourgeois mutes . . .). We are each of us celebrating some funeral." [4] To designate this attitude of modernity, Baudelaire sometimes employs a litotes that is highly significant because it is presented in the form of a precept: "You have no right to despise the present."

2. This heroization is ironic, needless to say. The attitude of modernity does not treat the passing moment as sacred in order to try to maintain or perpetuate it. It certainly does not involve harvesting it as a fleeting and interesting curiosity. That would be what Baudelaire would call the spectator's posture. The *flâneur*, the idle, strolling spectator, is satisfied to keep his eyes open, to pay attention and to build up a storehouse of memories. In opposition to the *flâneur*, Baudelaire describes the man of modernity: "Away he goes, hurrying, searching. . . . Be very sure that this man . . . this solitary, gifted with an active imagination, ceaselessly journeying across the great human desert—has an aim loftier than that of a mere *flâneur*, an aim more general, something other than

the fugitive pleasure of circumstance. He is looking for that quality which you must allow me to call 'modernity.' . . . He makes it his business to extract from fashion whatever element it may contain of poetry, within history." As an example of modernity, Baudelaire cites the artist Constantin Guys. In appearance a spectator, a collector of curiosities, he remains "the last to linger wherever there can be a glow of light, an echo of poetry, a quiver of life or a chord of music; wherever a passion can *pose* before him, wherever natural man and conventional man display themselves in a strange beauty, wherever the sun lights up the swift joys of the *depraved animal.*"[5]

But let us make no mistake. Constantin Guys is not a *flâneur;* what makes him the modern painter par excellence in Baudelaire's eyes is that, just when the whole world is falling asleep, he begins to work, and he transfigures that world. His transfiguration entails not an annulling of reality but a difficult interplay between the truth of what is real and the exercise of freedom; "natural" things become "more than natural," "beautiful" things become "more than beautiful," and individual objects appear "endowed with an impulsive life like the soul of [their] creator."[6] For the attitude of modernity, the high value of the present is indissociable from a desperate eagerness to imagine it, to imagine it otherwise than it is, and to transform it not by destroying it but by grasping it in what it is. Baudelairean modernity is an exercise in which extreme attention to what is real is confronted with the practice of a liberty that simultaneously respects this reality and violates it.

3. However, modernity for Baudelaire is not simply a form of relationship to the present; it is also a mode of relationship that must be established with oneself. The deliberate attitude of modernity is tied to an indispensable asceticism. To be modern is not to accept oneself as one is in the flux of the passing moments; it is to take oneself as object of a complex and difficult elaboration: what Baudelaire, in the vocabulary of his day, calls *dandysme.* Here I shall not recall in detail the well-known passages on "vulgar, earthy, vile nature"; on man's indispensable revolt against himself; on the "doctrine of elegance" which imposes "upon its ambitious and humble disciples" a discipline more despotic than the most terrible religions; the pages, finally, on the asceticism of the dandy who makes of his body, his behavior, his feelings and passions, his very existence, a work of art. Modern man, for Baudelaire, is not the man who goes off to discover himself, his secrets and his hidden truth; he is the man who tries to invent himself. This modernity does not "liberate man in his own being"; it compels him to face the task of producing himself.

4. Let me add just one final word. This ironic heroization of the present, this transfiguring play of freedom with reality, this ascetic elaboration of the self— Baudelaire does not imagine that these have any place in society itself or in the

body politic. They can only be produced in another, a different place, which Baudelaire calls art.

I do not pretend to be summarizing in these few lines either the complex historical event that was the Enlightenment, at the end of the eighteenth century, or the attitude of modernity in the various guises it may have taken on during the last two centuries.

I have been seeking, on the one hand, to emphasize the extent to which a type of philosophical interrogation—one that simultaneously problematizes man's relation to the present, man's historical mode of being, and the constitution of the self as an autonomous subject—is rooted in the Enlightenment. On the other hand, I have been seeking to stress that the thread which may connect us with the Enlightenment is not faithfulness to doctrinal elements but, rather, the permanent reactivation of an attitude—that is, of a philosophical ethos that could be described as a permanent critique of our historical era. I should like to characterize this ethos very briefly.

Negatively

1. This ethos implies, first, the refusal of what I like to call the "blackmail" of the Enlightenment. I think that the Enlightenment, as a set of political, economic, social, institutional, and cultural events on which we still depend in large part, constitutes a privileged domain for analysis. I also think that, as an enterprise for linking the progress of truth and the history of liberty in a bond of direct relation, it formulated a philosophical question that remains for us to consider. I think, finally, as I have tried to show with reference to Kant's text, that it defined a certain manner of philosophizing.

Yet that does not mean that one has to be "for" or "against" the Enlightenment. It even means precisely that one must refuse everything that might present itself in the form of a simplistic and authoritarian alternative: you either accept the Enlightenment and remain within the tradition of its rationalism (this is considered a positive term by some and used by others, on the contrary, as a reproach), or else you criticize the Enlightenment and then try to escape from its principles of rationality (which may be seen once again as good or bad). And we do not break free of this blackmail by introducing "dialectical" nuances while seeking to determine what good and bad elements there may have been in the Enlightenment.

We must try to proceed with the analysis of ourselves as beings who are historically determined, to a certain extent, by the Enlightenment. Such an analysis implies a series of historical inquiries that are as precise as possible; and these inquiries will not be oriented retrospectively toward the "essential kernel of rationality" that can be found in the Enlightenment, which would have to be preserved in any event; they will be oriented toward the "contemporary limits of the necessary," that is, toward what is not or is no longer indispensable for the constitution of ourselves as autonomous subjects.

2. This permanent critique of ourselves must avoid the always too facile confusions between humanism and Enlightenment.

We must never forget that the Enlightenment is an event, or a set of events and complex historical processes, that is located at a certain point in the development of European societies. As such, it includes elements of social transformation, types of political institution, forms of knowledge, projects of rationalization of knowledge and practices, technological mutations that are very difficult to sum up in a word, even if many of these phenomena remain important today. The one I have pointed out, which seems to me to have been at the basis of an entire form of philosophical reflection, concerns only the mode of reflective relation to the present.

Humanism is something entirely different. It is a theme or, rather, a set of themes that have reappeared on several occasions, over time, in European societies; these themes, always tied to value judgments, have obviously varied greatly in their content as well as in the values they have preserved. Furthermore, they have served as a critical principle of differentiation. In the seventeenth century, there was a humanism that presented itself as a critique of Christianity or of religion in general; there was a Christian humanism opposed to an ascetic and much more theocentric humanism. In the nineteenth century, there was a suspicious humanism, hostile and critical toward science, and another that, to the contrary, placed its hope in that same science. Marxism has been a humanism; so have existentialism and personalism; there was a time when people supported the humanistic values represented by National Socialism, and when the Stalinists themselves said they were humanists.

From this, we must not conclude that everything which has ever been linked with humanism is to be rejected, but that the humanistic thematic is in itself too supple, too diverse, too inconsistent to serve as an axis for reflection. And it is a fact that, at least since the seventeenth century, what is called "humanism" has always been obliged to lean on certain conceptions of man borrowed from religion, science, or politics. Humanism serves to color and to justify the conceptions of man to which it is, after all, obliged to take recourse.

Now, in this connection, I believe that this thematic, which so often recurs, and always depends on humanism, can be opposed by the principle of a critique and a permanent creation of ourselves in our autonomy: that is, a principle at the heart of the historical consciousness that the Enlightenment has of itself. From this standpoint, I am inclined to see Enlightenment and humanism in a state of tension rather than identity.

In any case, it seems to me dangerous to confuse them; and further, it seems historically inaccurate. If the question of man, of the human species, of the humanist, was important throughout the eighteenth century, this is very rarely, I believe, because the Enlightenment considered itself a humanism. It is worthwhile, too, to note that throughout the nineteenth century, the historiography of sixteenth-century humanism, which was so important for people like Saint-Beuve or Burckhardt, was always distinct from, and sometimes explicitly opposed to, the Enlightenment and the eighteenth century. The nineteenth century had a tendency to oppose the two, at least as much as to confuse them.

In any case, I think that, just as we must free ourselves from the intellectual blackmail of "being for or against the Enlightenment," we must escape from the historical and moral confusionism that mixes the theme of humanism with the question of the Enlightenment. An analysis of their complex relations in the course of the last two centuries would be a worthwhile project, an important one if we are to bring some measure of clarity to the consciousness that we have of ourselves and of our past.

Positively

Yet while taking these precautions into account, we must obviously give a more positive content to what may be a philosophical ethos consisting in a critique of what we are saying, thinking, and doing, through a historical ontology of ourselves.

1. This philosophical ethos may be characterized as a *limit-attitude*. We are not talking about a gesture of rejection. We have to move beyond the outside-inside alternative; we have to be at the frontiers. Criticism indeed consists of analyzing and reflecting upon limits. But if the Kantian question was that of knowing [*savoir*] what limits knowledge [*connaissance*] must renounce exceeding, it seems to me that the critical question today must be turned back into a positive one: In what is given to us as universal, necessary, obligatory, what place is occupied by whatever is singular, contingent, and the product of arbitrary constraints? The point, in brief, is to transform the critique conducted in the form of necessary limitation into a practical critique that takes the form of a possible crossing-over [*franchissement*].

This entails an obvious consequence: that criticism is no longer going to be practiced in the search for formal structures with universal value but, rather, as a historical investigation into the events that have led us to constitute ourselves and to recognize ourselves as subjects of what we are doing, thinking, saying. In that sense, this criticism is not transcendental, and its goal is not that of making a metaphysics possible: it is genealogical in its design and archaeological in its method. Archaeological—and not transcendental—in the sense that it will not seek to identify the universal structures of all knowledge [*connaissance*] or of all

possible moral action, but will seek to treat the instances of discourse that articulate what we think, say, and do as so many historical events. And this critique
will be genealogical in the sense that it will not deduce from the form of what we
are what it is impossible for us to do and to know; but it will separate out, from
the contingency that has made us what we are, the possibility of no longer
being, doing, or thinking what we are, do, or think. It is not seeking to make possible a metaphysics that has finally become a science; it is seeking to give new
impetus, as far and wide as possible, to the undefined work of freedom.

2. Yet if we are not to settle for the affirmation or the empty dream of freedom, it seems to me that this historico-critical attitude must also be an experimental one. I mean that this work done at the limits of ourselves must, on the
one hand, open up a realm of historical inquiry and, on the other, put itself to
the test of reality, of contemporary reality, both to grasp the points where
change is possible and desirable, and to determine the precise form this change
should take. This means that the historical ontology of ourselves must turn
away from all projects that claim to be global or radical. In fact, we know from
experience that the claim to escape from the system of contemporary reality so
as to produce the overall programs of another society, of another way of thinking, another culture, another vision of the world, has led only to the return of
the most dangerous traditions.

I prefer the very specific transformations that have proved to be possible in
the last twenty years in a certain number of areas which concern our ways of
being and thinking, relations to authority, relations between the sexes, the way
in which we perceive insanity or illness; I prefer even these partial transformations, which have been made in the correlation of historical analysis and the
practical attitude, to the programs for a new man that the worst political systems
have repeated throughout the twentieth century.

I shall thus characterize the philosophical ethos appropriate to the critical ontology of ourselves as a historico-practical test of the limits we may go beyond,
and thus as work carried out by ourselves upon ourselves as free beings.

3. Still, the following objection would no doubt be entirely legitimate: If we
limit ourselves to this type of always partial and local inquiry or test, do we not
run the risk of letting ourselves be determined by more general structures of
which we may well not be conscious and over which we may have no control?

To this, two responses. It is true that we have to give up hope of ever acceding to a point of view that could give us access to any complete and definitive
knowledge [connaissance] of what may constitute our historical limits. And,
from this point of view, the theoretical and practical experience we have of our
limits, and of the possibility of moving beyond them, is always limited and determined; thus, we are always in the position of beginning again.

But that does not mean that no work can be done except in disorder and contingency. The work in question has its generality, its systematicity, its homogeneity, and its stakes.

ITS STAKES. These are indicated by what might be called "the paradox of the relations of capacity and power." We know that the great promise or the great hope of the eighteenth century, or a part of the eighteenth century, lay in the simultaneous and proportional growth of individuals with respect to one another. And, moreover, we can see that throughout the entire history of Western societies (it is perhaps here that the root of their singular historical destiny is located—such a peculiar destiny, so different from the others in its trajectory and so universalizing, so dominant with respect to the others), the acquisition of capabilities and the struggle for freedom have constituted permanent elements. Now, the relations between the growth of capabilities and the growth of autonomy are not as simple as the eighteenth century may have believed. And we have been able to see what forms of power relation were conveyed by various technologies (whether we are speaking of productions with economic aims, or institutions whose goal is social regulation, or of techniques of communication): disciplines, both collective and individual, procedures of normalization exercised in the name of the power of the state, demands of society or of population zones, are examples. What is at stake, then, is this: how can the growth of capabilities [*capacités*] be disconnected from the intensification of power relations?

HOMOGENEITY. This leads to the study of what could be called "practical systems." Here we are taking as a homogeneous domain of reference not the representations that men give of themselves, not the conditions that determine them without their knowledge, but rather what they do and the way they do it. That is, the forms of rationality that organize their ways of doing things (this might be called the technological aspect) and the freedom with which they act within these practical systems, reacting to what others do, modifying the rules of the game, up to a certain point (this might be called the strategic side of these practices). The homogeneity of these historico-critical analyses is thus ensured by this realm of practices, with their technological side and their strategic side.

SYSTEMATICITY. These practical systems stem from three broad areas: relations of control over things, relations of action upon others, relations with oneself. This does not mean that each of these three areas is completely foreign to the others. It is well known that control over things is mediated by relations with others; and relations with others in turn always entail relations with oneself, and vice versa. But we have three axes whose specificity and whose interconnections have to be analyzed: the axis of knowledge, the axis of power, the axis of ethics. In other words, the historical ontology of ourselves must answer an open series of questions; it must make an indefinite number of inquiries which may be multiplied and specified as much as we like, but which will all address the questions

systematized as follows: How are we constituted as subjects of our own knowledge? How are we constituted as subjects who exercise or submit to power relations? How are we constituted as moral subjects of our own actions?

GENERALITY. Finally, these historico-critical investigations are quite specific
in the sense that they always bear upon a material, an epoch, a body of determined practices and discourses. And yet, at least at the level of the Western societies from which we derive, they have their generality, in the sense that they
have continued to recur up to our time: for example, the problem of the relationship between sanity and insanity, or sickness and health, or crime and the
law; the problem of the role of sexual relations; and so on.

Yet by evoking this generality, I do not mean to suggest that it has to be retraced in its metahistorical continuity over time, nor that its variations have to
be pursued. What must be grasped is the extent to which what we know of it, the
forms of power that are exercised in it, and the experience that we have in it of
ourselves constitute nothing but determined historical figures, through a certain
form of problematization that defines objects, rules of action, modes of relation
to oneself. The study of (modes of) problematization [*(modes de) problématisa-
tions*] (that is, of what is neither an anthropological constant nor a chronological
variation) is thus the way to analyze questions of general import in their historically unique form.

A brief summary, to conclude and to come back to Kant.

I do not know whether we will ever reach mature adulthood. Many things in
our experience convince us that the historical event of the Enlightenment did
not make us mature adults, and we have not reached that stage yet. However, it
seems to me that a meaning can be attributed to that critical interrogation on the
present and on ourselves which Kant formulated by reflecting on the Enlightenment. It seems to me that Kant's reflection is even a way of philosophizing
which has not been without its importance or effectiveness during the last two
centuries. The critical ontology of ourselves must be considered not, certainly,
as a theory, a doctrine, nor even as a permanent body of knowledge that is accu-
mulating; it must be conceived as an attitude, an ethos, a philosophical life in
which the critique of what we are is at one and the same time the historical
analysis of the limits imposed on us and an experiment with the possibility of
going beyond them [*de leur franchissement possible*].

This philosophical attitude must be translated into the labor of diverse inquiries. These inquiries have their methodological coherence in the at once archaeological and genealogical study of practices envisaged simultaneously as a
technological type of rationality and as strategic games of liberties; they have
their theoretical coherence in the definition of the historically unique forms in
which the generalities of our relations to things, to others, to themselves, have

been problematized. They have their practical coherence in the care brought to the process of putting historico-critical reflection to the test of concrete practices. I do not know whether it must be said today that the critical task still entails faith in Enlightenment; I continue to think that this task requires work on our limits, that is, a patient labor giving form to our impatience for liberty.

Notes

1. Giambattista Vico, *The New Science of Giambattista Vico* (1744), abridged trans. T. G. Bergin and M. H. Fisch (Ithaca and London: Cornell University Press, 1970), pp. 370, 372.

2. In this paragraph, occurrences of the phrase "the critique" are glosses of *"la Critique"* (capitalized in the French); it should probably be understood as referring not to critique in general but, rather, to Kant's own works, or perhaps particularly to his "First Critique," *The Critique of Pure Reason.*

3. Charles Baudelaire, *The Painter of Modern Life and Other Essays,* trans. Jonathan Mayne (London: Phaidon, 1964), p. 13.

4. Charles Baudelaire, "On the Heroism of Modern Life," in *The Mirror of Art: Critical Studies by Charles Baudelaire,* trans. Jonathan Mayne (London: Phaidon, 1955), p. 127.

5. Baudelaire, *Painter,* pp. 11, 12.

6. Ibid., p. 12.

PREFACE TO *THE HISTORY OF SEXUALITY*, VOLUME TWO

In this series of researches on sexuality, it was not my aim to reconstitute the history of sexual behavior—by studying its successive forms, their respective models, how they spread, how they conflicted or agreed with laws, rules, customs, or conventions. Nor did I intend to analyze religious, moral, medical, or biological ideas about sexuality. Not that such inquiries should be considered illegitimate, impossible, or sterile; plenty of work has proved otherwise. But I wanted to confront this very everyday notion of sexuality, step away from it, monitor [*éprouver*] its familiar evidence, and analyze the theoretical and practical content in which it made its appearance and with which it is still associated.

I wanted to undertake a history in which sexuality would not be conceived as a general type of behavior whose particular elements might vary according to demographic, economic, social, or ideological conditions, any more than it would be seen as a collection of representations (scientific, religious, moral) which, though diverse and changeable, are joined to an invariant reality. My object was to analyze sexuality as a historically singular form of experience. Taking this historical singularity into account does not mean overinterpreting the recent emergence of the term *sexuality*, or taking it for granted that the word has brought in its trail the reality to which it refers. Rather, it means an effort to treat sexuality as the correlation of a domain of knowledge [*savoir*], a type of normativity, and a mode of relation to the self; it means trying to decipher how, in Western societies, a complex experience is constituted from and around certain forms of behavior: an experience that conjoins a field of knowledge [*con-*

The first paragraph of the French text, omitted here, reads: "This volume appears later than I had foreseen and in a quite different form." In fact, the text does not serve as the preface to the second volume of *The History of Sexuality*. Foucault replaced it with a much longer version, and chose to publish it separately. It initially appeared in English translation in *The Foucault Reader*, ed. P. Rabinow (New York: Pantheon Books, 1984), pp. 333–39. The translation, by William Smock, is reproduced here slightly amended.

naissance] (with its own concepts, theories, diverse disciplines), a collection of rules (which differentiate the permissible from the forbidden, natural from monstrous, normal from pathological, what is decent from what is not, and so on), and a mode of relation between the individual and himself (which enables him to recognize himself as a sexual subject amid others).

To study forms of experience in this way—in their history—is an idea that originated with an earlier project, in which I made use of the methods of existential analysis in the field of psychiatry and in the domain of "mental illness." For two reasons, not unrelated to each other, this project left me unsatisfied: its theoretical weakness in elaborating the notion of experience, and its ambiguous link with a psychiatric practice, which it simultaneously ignored and took for granted. One could deal with the first problem by referring to a general theory of the human being, and treat the second altogether differently by turning, as is so often done, to the "economic and social context"; one could choose, by doing so, to accept the resulting dilemma of a philosophical anthropology and a social history. But I wondered whether, rather than playing on this alternative, it would not be possible to consider the very historicity of forms of experience. This entailed two negative tasks: first, a "nominalist" reduction of philosophical anthropology and the notions that could rest upon it, and second, a shift of domain to the concepts and methods of the history of societies. On the positive side, the task was to bring to light the domain where the formation, development, and transformation of forms of experience can situate themselves—that is, a history of thought. By "thought," I mean what establishes, in a variety of possible forms, the play of true and false, and consequently constitutes the human being as a knowing subject [*sujet de connaissance*]; in other words, it is the basis for accepting or refusing rules, and constitutes human beings as social and juridical subjects; it is what establishes the relation with oneself and with others, and constitutes the human being as ethical subject.

"Thought," understood in this way, then, is not to be sought only in theoretical formulations such as those of philosophy or science; it can and must be analyzed in every manner of speaking, doing, or behaving in which the individual appears and acts as knowing subject [*sujet de connaissance*], as ethical or juridical subject, as subject conscious of himself and others. In this sense, thought is understood as the very form of action—as action insofar as it implies the play of true and false, the acceptance or refusal of rules, the relation to oneself and others. The study of forms of experience can thus proceed from an analysis of "practices"—discursive or not—as long as one qualifies that word to mean the different systems of action *insofar as* they are inhabited by thought as I have characterized it here.

Posing the question in this way brings into play certain altogether general principles. Singular forms of experience may perfectly well harbor universal structures; they may well not be independent of the concrete determinations of social existence. However, neither those determinations nor those structures can allow for experiences (that is, for understandings of a certain type, for rules of a certain form, for certain modes of consciousness of oneself and of others) except through thought. There is no experience that is not a way of thinking and cannot be analyzed from the viewpoint of the history of thought; this is what might be called the principle of irreducibility of thought. According to a second principle, this thought has a historicity which is proper to it. That it should have this historicity does not mean it is deprived of all universal form but, rather, that the putting into play of these universal forms is itself historical. And that this historicity should be proper to it means not that it is independent of all the other historical determinations (of an economic, social, or political order) but that it has complex relations with them, which always leave their specificity to the forms, transformations, and events of thought. This is what could be called the principle of singularity of the history of thought: there are events of thought. There is a third and final principle implied by this enterprise: an awareness that criticism—understood as analysis of the historical conditions that bear on the creation of links to truth, to rules, and to the self—does not mark out impassable boundaries or describe closed systems; it brings to light transformable singularities. These transformations could not take place except by means of a working of thought upon itself; that is the principle of the history of thought as critical activity. All of this bears upon the work and teaching I have labeled "the history of systems of thought"; it infers a double reference—to philosophy, which must be asked to explain how thought could have a history, and to history, which must be asked to produce the various forms of thought in whatever concrete forms they may assume (system of representations, institutions, practices). What is the price to philosophy of a history of thought? What is the effect, within history, of thought and the events that are proper to it? In what way do individual or collective experiences arise from singular forms of thought—that is, from what constitutes the subject in its relations to the true, to rules, to itself? It is easy to see how the reading of Nietzsche in the early fifties has given access to these kinds of questions, by breaking with the double tradition of phenomenology and Marxism.

I know this rereading is schematic: things did not really unfold so neatly, and there were many obscurities and hesitations along the way. But in *Madness and Civilization* I was trying, after all, to describe a locus of experience from the viewpoint of the history of thought, even if my usage of the word "experience" was very floating. Looking at practices of internment, on the one hand, and medical procedures, on the other, I tried to analyze the genesis, during the seventeenth and eighteenth centuries, of a system of thought as the matter of possible experiences: first, the formation of a domain of recognitions [*connais-sances*] that constitute themselves as specific knowledge [*savoir*] of "mental illness"; second, the organization of a normative system built on a whole technical, administrative, juridical, and medical apparatus whose purpose was to isolate and take custody of the insane; and finally, the definition of a relation to oneself and to others as possible subjects of madness. It is also these three axes and the play between types of understanding [*savoir*], forms of normality, and modes of relation to oneself and others which seemed to me to give individual cases the status of significant experiences—cases such as those of Pierre Rivière or Alexina B.—and to assign a like importance to that permanent dramatization of family affairs which one finds in the *lettres de cachet* (whereby people committed their relatives to asylums) in the eighteenth century.

Yet the relative importance of these three axes is not always the same for all forms of experience. And, moreover, it was necessary to elaborate the analysis of each a little more precisely, starting with the problem of the formation of domains of knowledge [*savoir*]. The work was directed along two lines: first, in the "vertical" dimension, taking the example of sickness, and studying how an institutional organization for therapy, instruction, and research is related to the constitution of a clinical medicine articulated on the development of pathological anatomy. The object was to bring out the complex causalities and reciprocal determinations affecting, on the one hand, the development of a certain kind of medical knowledge [*savoir*] and, on the other, the transformations of an institutional field linked directly to social and political changes. Then, once scientific knowledge [*savoir*] was endowed with its own rules for which external determinations could not account—its own structure as discursive practice—I tried to show what common, but transformable, criteria—what epistemes [*épistèmes*]—governed those bodies of knowledge which, from the seventeenth to the early nineteenth centuries, had been charged with explaining certain aspects of human activity or existence: the wealth men produce, exchange, and circulate; the linguistic signs they use to communicate; and the collectivity of living things to which they belong.

It is the second axis—the relation to rules—that I wanted to explore using the example of punitive practices. It was a matter not of studying the theory of penal law itself, or the evolution of such and such penal institution, but of analyzing the formation of a certain "punitive rationality" whose appearance might seem that much more surprising in that it offered, as its principal means of action, a practice of imprisonment which had long been and still was criticized at the time. Instead of seeking the explanation in a general conception of the law, or in the evolving modes of industrial production (as Rusche and Kirchheimer did), it seemed to me far wiser to look at the workings of power. I was concerned not with some omnipresent power, almighty and above all clairvoyant, diffusing itself throughout the social body in order to control it down to the tiniest detail, but with the refinement, the elaboration, and the installation since the seventeenth century of techniques for "governing" individuals—that is, for "guiding their conduct"—in domains as different as the school, the army, and the workshop. The new punitive rationality must be relocated in the context of this technology, itself linked to the demographic, economic, and political changes that accompany the development of industrial states. Accordingly, the analysis does not revolve around the general principle of the law or the myth of power, but concerns itself with the complex and multiple practices of a "governmentality" that presupposes, on the one hand, rational forms, technical procedures, instrumentations through which to operate, and, on the other, strategic games that subject the power relations they are supposed to guarantee to instability and reversal. Starting from an analysis of these forms of "government," one can see how criminality was constituted as an object of knowledge [*savoir*], and how a certain "consciousness" of criminality could be formed (including the image that criminals might have of themselves, and the representation of criminals which the rest of us might entertain).

The project of a history of sexuality was linked to a desire on my part to analyze more closely the third of the axes that constitute any matrix of experience: the modality of relation to the self. Not that sexuality cannot and should not—like madness, sickness, or criminality—be envisaged as a locus of experience, one that includes a domain of knowledge [*savoir*], a system of rules, and a model for relations to the self. However, the relative importance of the last element recommends it as a guiding thread for the very history of this experience and its formation; my planned study of children, women, and "perverts" as sexual subjects was to have followed those lines.

    I found myself confronted with a choice that was a long time in unraveling: a choice between fidelity to the chronological outline I had originally imagined, and a different line of inquiry in which the modes of relation to the self took precedence. The period when this singular form of experience, sexuality, took shape is particularly complex: the very important role played at the end of the eighteenth and in the nineteenth centuries by the formation of domains of knowledge [*savoir*] about sexuality from the points of view of biology, medicine, psychopathology, sociology, and ethnology; the determining role also played by the normative systems imposed on sexual behavior through the intermediary of education, medicine, and justice made it hard to distinguish the form and effects of the relation to the self as particular elements in the constitution of this experience. There was always the risk of reproducing, with regard to sexuality, forms of analysis focused on the organization of a domain of learning [*connaissance*], or on the techniques of control and coercion, as in my previous work on sickness or criminality. In order better to analyze the forms of relation to the self, in and of themselves, I found myself spanning eras in a way that took me farther and farther from the chronological outline I had first decided on, both in order to address myself to periods when the effect of scientific knowledges and the complexity of normative systems were less, and in order eventually to make out forms of relation to the self different from those characterizing the experience of sexuality. And that is how, little by little, I ended up placing the work's emphasis on what was to have been simply the point of departure or historical background; rather than placing myself at the threshold of the formation of the experience of sexuality, I tried to analyze the formation of a certain mode of relation to the self in the experience of the flesh. This called for a marked chronological displacement because it became obvious that I should study the period in late antiquity when the principal elements of the Christian ethic of the flesh were being formulated. And it led in turn to a rearrangement of my original plan, a considerable delay in publication, and the hazards of studying material I had barely heard of six or seven years ago. But I reflected that, after all, it was best to sacrifice a definite program to a promising line of approach. I also reminded myself that it would probably not be worth the trouble of making books if they failed to teach the author something he had not known before, if they did not lead to unforeseen places, and if they did not disperse one toward a strange and new relation with himself. The pain and pleasure of the book is to be an experience.

CONFRONTING GOVERNMENTS: HUMAN RIGHTS

We are just private individuals here, with no other grounds for speaking, or for speaking together, than a certain shared difficulty in enduring what is taking place.

Of course, we accept the obvious fact that there's not much that we can do about the reasons why some men and women would rather leave their country than live in it. The fact is beyond our reach.

Who appointed us, then? No one. And that is precisely what constitutes our right. It seems to me that we need to bear in mind three principles that, I believe, guide this initiative, and many others that have preceded it: the *Île-de-Lumière*, Cape Anamour, the Airplane for El Salvador, Terre des Hommes, Amnesty International.

1. There exists an international citizenship that has its rights and its duties, and that obliges one to speak out against every abuse of power, whoever its author, whoever its victims. After all, we are all members of the community of the governed, and thereby obliged to show mutual solidarity.
2. Because they claim to be concerned with the welfare of societies, governments arrogate to themselves the right to pass off as profit or loss the human unhappiness that their decisions provoke or their negligence permits. It is a duty of this international citizenship to always bring the testimony of people's suffering to the eyes and ears of governments, suffering for which it's untrue that they are not responsible. The suffering of men must never be a silent residue of policy. It grounds an absolute right to stand up and speak to those who hold power.

The occasion for this statement, published in *Libération* in June 1984, was the announcement in Geneva of the creation of an International Committee against Piracy.—Eds.

3. We must reject the division of labor so often proposed to us: individuals can get indignant and talk; governments will reflect and act. It's true that good governments appreciate the holy indignation of the governed, provided it remains lyrical. I think we need to be aware that very often it is those who govern who talk, are capable only of talking, and want only to talk. Experience shows that one can and must refuse the theatrical role of pure and simple indignation that is proposed to us. Amnesty International, Terre des Hommes, and Médecins du Monde are initiatives that have created this new right—that of private individuals to effectively intervene in the sphere of international policy and strategy. The will of individuals must make a place for itself in a reality of which governments have attempted to reserve a monopoly for themselves, that monopoly which we need to wrest from them little by little and day by day.

THE RISKS OF SECURITY

SECURITY AND DEPENDENCY: A DIABOLICAL PAIR?

Q: *Traditionally, social security protects individuals against a certain number of risks in connection with sickness, family structure, and old age. Clearly, it must continue to fulfill this function.*

However, between 1946 and today, things have changed. New needs have appeared. Thus we are witnessing a growing desire for independence among individuals and groups: the aspirations of children vis-à-vis their parents, of women vis-à-vis men, of the sick vis-à-vis doctors, and of the handicapped vis-à-vis all sorts of institutions. It is becoming equally clear that we need to put an end to the phenomenon of marginalization, attributable in large part to unemployment, but also, in certain cases, to the deficiencies of our system of social protection.

We believe that at least these two needs must be taken into account by the next social security administration, in order that the system take on newly defined functions that entail a remodeling of its system of allocations. Do you believe that these needs really exist in our society? Would you call attention to others? And how, in your opinion, can social security respond to them?

A: I believe that it is necessary to emphasize three things right at the beginning.

First of all, our system of social guarantees, as it was established in 1946, has now reached its economic limits.

Second, this system, elaborated during the interwar years—that is, during a period when one of the goals was to attenuate or to minimize a certain number of social conflicts, and when the conceptual model was informed by a rationality born around World War I—today reaches its limits as it stumbles against the political, economic, and social rationality of modern societies.

This interview, conducted by Robert Bono, first appeared in *Sécurité sociale: l'enjeu* (Paris: Syros, 1983) under the title "Un Système fini face à une demande infinie." The English translation has been edited slightly.

Third, social security, whatever its positive effects, has also had some "perverse effects": the growing rigidity of certain mechanisms and the creation of situations of dependency. This is inherent in the functioning of the system: on the one hand, we give people greater security and, on the other, we increase their dependency. Instead, we should expect our system of social security to free us from dangers and from situations that tend to debase or to subjugate us.

Q: If indeed people seem willing to give up some liberty and independence provided that the system extend and reinforce their security, how can we manage this "diabolical pair" of security and dependency?
A: We have before us a problem the terms of which are negotiable. We must try to appreciate the capacity of people who undertake such negotiation and the level of compromise they are able to attain.

The way in which we look at these things has changed. In the thirties and after the war, the problem of security was so acute and so immediate that the question of dependency was practically ignored. From the fifties on, in contrast, and even more from the sixties on, the notion of security began to be associated with the question of independence. This inflection was an extremely important cultural, political, and social phenomenon. We cannot ignore it.

It seems to me that certain proponents of antisecurity arguments reject, in a somewhat simplistic manner, everything that might be dangerous in "security and liberty" law. We must be more prudent in considering this opposition.

There is indeed a positive demand: a demand for a security that opens the way to richer, more numerous, more diverse, and more flexible relationships with ourselves and others, all the while assuring each of us real autonomy. This is a new fact that should weigh on present-day conceptions of social protection.

Very schematically, that is how I would situate the question of the demand for independence.

Q: The negotiation of which you speak can be conducted only along a narrow line. On one side we can see that certain rigidities in our apparatus of social protection, combined with its interventionist nature, threaten the independence of groups and individuals, enclosing them in an administrative yoke that (if one goes by the Swedish experience) becomes intolerable in the end. On the other side, the form of liberalism described by Jules Guesde when he spoke of "free foxes in free chicken coops" is no more desirable—one has only to look at the United States to be convinced of this.
A: It is precisely the difficulty of establishing a compromise along this narrow line that calls for as subtle an analysis as possible of the actual situation. By "actual situation" I do not mean the system of economic and social mechanisms, which others describe better than I could. Rather, I speak of this interface between, on the one hand, people's sensibilities, their moral choices, their rela-

tions to themselves and, on the other, the institutions that surround them. It is here that dysfunctions, malaise, and, perhaps, crises arise in the social system.

Considering what one might call the "negative effects" of the system, it is necessary, it seems to me, to distinguish two tendencies. We can see that dependency results not only from integration, but also from marginalization and exclusion. We need to respond to both threats.

I believe that there are instances when it is necessary to resist the phenomenon of integration. An entire mechanism of social protection, in fact, does not fully benefit the individual unless he finds himself integrated into a family milieu, a work milieu, or a geographic milieu.

Q: *Could we also pose the question of integration in the context of the relationship of the individual to the state?*
A: In this regard, too, we are witnessing an important phenomenon: before the "crisis," or more precisely, before the emergence of the problems that we now encounter, it is my impression that the individual never questioned his relationship to the state, insofar as this relationship (keeping in mind the way in which the great centralizing institutions worked) was based on an "input"—the dues he paid—and an "output"—the benefits that accrued to him.

Today a problem of limits intervenes. What is at stake is no longer the equal access of all to security but, rather, the infinite access of each to a certain number of possible benefits. We tell people: "You cannot consume indefinitely." And when the authorities claim, "You no longer have a right to that," or "You will no longer be covered for such operations," or yet again, "You will pay a part of the hospital fees," or in the extreme case, "It would be useless to prolong your life by three months, we are going to let you die"—then the individual begins to question the nature of his relationship to the state and starts to feel his dependency on institutions whose power of decision he had heretofore misapprehended.

Q: *Doesn't this problem of dependency perpetuate the ambivalence that reigned, even before the establishment of a mechanism of social protection, at the creation of the first health institutions? Was it not the objective of the Hôtel-Dieu both to relieve misery and to withdraw the poor and the sick from society's view, at the same time reducing their threat to the public order?*

And can we not, in the twentieth century, leave behind a logic that links charity to isolation in order to conceive of less alienating systems, which the people could—let us use the word—"appropriate"?
A: It is true, in a sense, that in the long run certain problems manifest themselves as permanent.

That said, I am very suspicious of two intellectual attitudes, the persistence of which over the last two decades is to be deplored. One consists in presupposing the repetition and extension of the same mechanisms throughout the history of our societies. From this, one derives the notion of a kind of cancer that spreads in the social body. It is an unacceptable theory. The way in which we used to confine certain segments of the population in the seventeenth century, to return to this example, is very different from the hospitalization we know from the nineteenth century, and even more from the security mechanisms of the present.

Another attitude, every bit as frequent, maintains the fiction of "the good old days" when the social body was alive and warm, when families were united, and individuals independent. This happy interlude was cut short by the advent of capitalism, the bourgeoisie, and industrialization. Here we have a historical absurdity.

The linear reading of history as well as the nostalgic reference to a golden age of social life still haunts a great deal of thinking, and informs a number of political and sociological analyses. We must flush these attitudes out.

Q: *With this remark, we come perhaps to the question of marginality. It seems that our society is divided into a "protected" sector and an exposed or precarious sector. Even though social security alone cannot remedy this situation, it remains the case that a system of social protection can contribute to a decline in marginalization and segregation through adequate measures directed toward the handicapped, immigrants, and all categories of precarious status. At least this is our analysis. Is it also yours?*

A: No doubt, we can say that certain phenomena of marginalization are linked to factors of separation between an "insured" population and an "exposed" population. Moreover, this sort of cleavage was foreseen explicitly by a certain number of economists during the seventies, who thought that in postindustrial societies the exposed sector would, on the whole, have to grow considerably. Such "programming" of society, however, was not often realized, and we cannot accept this as the sole explanation of the process of marginalization.

There are in certain forms of marginalization what I would call another aspect of the phenomenon of dependency. Our systems of social coverage impose a determined way of life that subjugates [*assujettit*] individuals. As a result, all persons or groups who, for one reason or another, cannot or do not want to accede to this way of life find themselves marginalized by the very game of the institutions.

Q: *There is a difference between marginality which one chooses and marginality to which one is subjected.*

A: True, and it would be necessary to distinguish them in a more detailed analysis. In any case, it is important to shed light on the relationship between the working of social security and ways of life, the ways of life that we began to observe about ten years ago. But this is a study that demands more thorough investigation, at the same time that it needs to be disengaged from a too strict "sociologism" that neglects ethical problems of paramount importance.

A CERTAIN CONCEPTUAL DEFICIENCY

Q: *Our goal is to give people security as well as autonomy. Perhaps we can come closer to this goal by two means: on the one hand, by rejecting the absurd juridicism of which we are so fond in France, which raises mountains of paperwork in everyone's way (so as to discriminate yet a bit more against the marginals) in favor of an experiment with a posteriori legislation that would facilitate access to social benefits and amenities; and, on the other hand, by achieving real decentralization with a staff and appropriate places for welcoming people.*

What do you think? Do you subscribe to the objectives I just stated?

A: Yes, certainly. And the objective of an optimal social coverage joined to a maximum of independence is clear enough. As for reaching this goal . . .

I think that such an aim requires two kinds of means. On the one hand, it requires a certain empiricism. We must transform the field of social institutions into a field of experimentation, in order to determine which levers to turn and which bolts to loosen in order to bring about the desired effects. It is indeed important to undertake a campaign of decentralization, for example, in order to bring the users closer to the decision-making centers on which they depend, and to tie them into the decision-making process, avoiding the type of great, globalizing integration that leaves people in complete ignorance about the conditions of particular judgments. We must then multiply these experiments wherever possible on the particularly important and interesting terrain of the social, considering that an entire institutional system, now fragile, will probably undergo a restructuring from top to bottom.

On the other hand—and it is a nodal point—there would be a considerable amount of work to do in order to renovate the conceptual categories that inspire our way of approaching all of these problems of social guarantees and of security. We are still thinking inside a mental framework formed between 1920 and 1940, essentially under the influence of Beveridge,[1] a man who would be over one hundred years old today.

For the moment, we lack completely the intellectual instruments to envisage in new terms the framework within which we could achieve our goals.

Q: *To illustrate the obsolescence of the mental frameworks of which you speak, don't we need a linguistic study of the sense of the word "subject" in the language of social security?*

A: Absolutely! And the question is what to do so that the person would no longer be a "subject" in the sense of subjugation.

As for the intellectual deficiency that I have just outlined, one may well wonder from where new forms of analysis, new conceptual frameworks, will spring.

What stands out in my mind, to be schematic, is that at the end of the eighteenth century in England, and in the nineteenth century in certain European countries, the parliamentary life was able to constitute a place to work out and discuss new projects (such as the fiscal and customs laws in Great Britain). That is where great campaigns of reflection and exchange were ignited. In the second half of the nineteenth century, many problems, many projects, were born from what was then a new associative life, that of labor unions, of political parties, of various associations. In the first half of the twentieth century, a very important task—a conceptual effort—was carried out in the political, economic, and social domains by people such as Keynes or Beveridge, as well as by a certain number of intellectuals, academics, and administrators.

But let us admit, the crisis that we are undergoing, which soon will be ten years old, has not elicited anything interesting or new from these intellectual milieus. It seems that in those quarters there has been a sort of sterilization: one cannot find any significant innovation there.

Q: *Can the unions be those "loci of illumination"?*
A: If it is true that the current malaise brings into question everything on the side of state institutional authority, it is a fact that the answers will not come from those who exercise this authority: rather, they should be raised by those who intend to counterbalance the state prerogative and to constitute counterpowers. What comes out of union activity might then eventually, in fact, open up a space for innovation.

Q: *Does this need to renovate the conceptual framework of social protection give a chance to "civil society"—of which the unions are a part—in relation to the state?*
A: If this opposition between civil society and the state could, with good reason, be used at the end of the eighteenth century and in the nineteenth century, I am not sure that it is still operative today. The Polish example in this case is very interesting: when one likens the powerful social movement that has swept across that country to a revolt of civil society against the state, one underestimates the complexity and the multiplicity of confrontations. It was not only against the state that the Solidarity movement had to fight.

The relationship between the political power, the systems of dependency that it generates, and individuals is too complex to be captured by this schema. In fact, the idea of an opposition between civil society and the state was formulated in a given context in response to a precise intention: some liberal economists proposed it at the end of the eighteenth century to limit the sphere of action of the state, civil society being conceived of as the locus of an autonomous economic process. This was a quasi-polemical concept, opposed to administrative options of states of that era, so that a certain liberalism could flourish.

But something bothers me even more: the reference to this antagonistic pair is never exempt from a sort of Manicheism, afflicting the notion of state with a pejorative connotation at the same time as it idealizes society as something good, lively, and warm.

What I am attentive to is the fact that all human relationships are to a certain degree relationships of power. We evolve in a world of perpetual strategic relations. All power relations are not bad in and of themselves, but it is a fact that they always entail certain risks.

Let's take the example of penal justice, which is more familiar to me than that of social security. An entire movement is now developing in Europe and in the United States in favor of an "informal justice," or even of certain forms of arbitration conducted by the groups themselves. It requires a very optimistic view of society to think it capable, by simple internal regulation, of resolving the problems it faces.

In short, returning to our topic, I remain quite circumspect about playing with the opposition between state and civil society. As for the project of transferring to civil society a power of initiative and action annexed by the state and exercised in an authoritarian manner: whatever the scenario, a relationship of power would be operating and the question would be to know how to limit the effects of this relationship, this relationship being in itself neither good nor bad but dangerous, so that it would be necessary to think, on all levels, about the way in which to channel its efficacy in the best possible direction.

Q: *What we have very much on our minds at this time is the fact that social security, in its present form, is perceived as a remote institution, with a statist character—even if this is not the case—because it is a big centralized machine. Our problem, then, is the following: in order to open up the channel of participation to the users, it is necessary to bring them closer to the centers of decision. How?*

A: This problem is empirical more than a matter of the opposition between civil society and the state: it is what I would call a matter of "decisional distance." In other words, the problem is to estimate an optimal distance between a decision taken and the individual concerned, so that the individual has a voice in the matter and so that the decision is intelligible to him. At the same time, it is important to be able to adapt to his situation without having to pass through an inextricable maze of regulations.

WHAT RIGHT TO HEALTH?

Q: *What is your position regarding the idea of the "right to health," which plays a part in the claims of the CFDT?*[2]

A: Here we find ourselves at the heart of an extremely interesting problem.

When the system of social security that we know today was put in place on a large scale, there was a more or less explicit consensus on what could be called "the needs of health." It was, in sum, the need to deal with "accidents"—that is, with invalidating deviations linked to sickness and to congenital or acquired handicaps.

From that point on, two processes unfolded. On the one hand, there was a technical acceleration of medicine that increased its therapeutic power but increased many times faster its capacity for examination and analysis. On the other hand, there was a growth in the demand for health, which demonstrates that the need for health (at least as far as it is felt) has no internal principle of limitation.

Consequently, it is not possible to set objectively a theoretical and practical threshold, valid for all, from which one could say that the needs of health are entirely and definitively satisfied.

The question of rights appears particularly thorny in this context. I would like to make a few simple remarks.

It is clear that there is no sense in talking about a "right to health." Health—good health—cannot arise from a right. Good and bad health, however rough or fine the criteria used, are facts—states of things and also states of consciousness. And even if we correct for this by pointing out that the border separating health from sickness is in part defined by the capacity of doctors to diagnose a sickness, by the sort of life or activity of the subject, and by what in a given culture is recognized as health or sickness, this relativity does not preclude the fact that there is no right to be on this side or that of the dividing line.

On the other hand, one can have a right to working conditions that do not increase in a significant manner the risk of sickness or various handicaps. One can also have a right to compensation, care, and damages when a health accident is, in one way or another, the responsibility of an authority.

But that is not the current problem. It is, I believe, this: must a society endeavor to satisfy by collective means the need for health of individuals? And can individuals legitimately demand satisfaction of health needs?

It appears—if these needs are liable to grow indefinitely—that an affirmative answer to this question would be without an acceptable or even conceivable translation into practice. On the other hand, one can speak of "means of health"—and by that I mean not just hospital installations and medications but everything that is at society's disposal at a given moment for effecting those corrections and adjustments of health that are technically possible. These means of health define a mobile line—which results from the technical capacity of medicine, from the economic capacity of the collectivity, and from what society wishes to devote as resources and means to health. And we can define the right to have access to these means of health, a right that presents itself under different aspects. There is the problem of equality of access—a problem that is easy to answer in principle, though it is not always easy to assure this access in practice. There is the problem of indefinite access to the means of health; here we must not delude ourselves: the problem undoubtedly does not have a theoretical solution. The important thing is to know by what arbitration, always flexible, always provisional, the limits of access will be defined. It is necessary to keep in mind the fact that these limits cannot be established once and for all by a medical definition of health, nor by the idea of "needs of health" expressed as an absolute.

Q: *That poses a certain number of problems, among which is this, a rather mundane problem of inequality: the life expectancy of a manual laborer is much lower than that of an ecclesiastic or a teacher; how would we proceed so that the arbitration from which a "norm of health" will result takes this situation into account?*

Besides, the expenditures on health care today represent 8.6 percent of the gross national product. That was not planned. The cost of health—this is the tragedy—is fed by a multiplicity of individual decisions and by a process of renewal of those decisions. Are we not, therefore, even while we demand equality of access to health, in a situation of "rationed" health?

A: I believe that our concern is the same: it is a question of knowing, and this is a formidable political, economic, as well as cultural problem, how to select the criteria according to which we could establish a norm which would serve to define, at any given moment, the right to health.

The question of costs, which intrudes in a familiar manner, adds a new dimension to this interrogation.

I do not see, and nobody can explain to me, how technically it would be possible to satisfy all the needs of health along the infinite line on which they develop. And even though I do not know what would limit them, it would be impossible in any case to let expenditures grow under this rubric at the pace of recent years.

An apparatus made to assure the security of people in the domain of health has thus reached the point in its development at which it will be necessary to decide that such an illness, such a suffering, will no longer benefit from any coverage—a point at which even life, in certain cases, will no longer enjoy any protection. And that poses a political and moral problem somewhat related, observing due proportion, to the question of the right of the state to ask an individual to die in a war. This question, without having lost any of its acuteness, has been integrated perfectly, through long historical developments, into the consciousness of people, so that soldiers have in effect agreed to be killed—thus placing their lives outside of protection. The question today is to know how the people will accept being exposed to certain risks without preserving the benefit of coverage by the welfare state.

Q: *Does this mean that we will call into question incubators, consider euthanasia, and thus return to what social security fought, namely certain forms of eliminating the most biologically fragile individuals? Will the prevailing word of order be: "It is necessary to choose; let us choose the strongest"? Who will choose among unrelenting therapy, development of neonatal medicine, and the improvement of working conditions (every year, in French companies, twenty out of every one hundred women suffer nervous breakdowns)?*

A: Such choices are being made at every instant, even if left unsaid. They are made according to the logic of a certain rationality which certain discourses are made to justify.

The question that I pose is to know whether a "strategy of health"—this problematic of choice—must remain mute. Here we touch upon a paradox: this strategy is acceptable, in the current state of things, insofar as it is left unsaid. If it is explicit, even in the form of a more or less acceptable rationality, it becomes morally intolerable. Take the example of dialysis: how many patients are undergoing dialysis, how many others are unable to benefit from it? Suppose we expose the choices that culminated in this sort of inequality of treatment—this would bring to light scandalous rules! It is here that a certain rationality itself becomes a scandal.

I have no solution to propose. But I believe that it is futile to cover our eyes—we must try to go to the bottom of things and to face up to them.

Q: *Would there not be room, moreover, to do a fairly detailed analysis of costs in order to pinpoint some possibilities of economizing before making more painful and indeed "scandalous" choices? I am thinking in particular of iatrogenic ailments, which currently represent (if one believes certain figures) 8 percent of all health problems. Is this not an example of a "perverse effect" precisely attributable to some defect in rationality?*

A: To reexamine the rationality that presides over our choices in the matter of health—this is indeed a task to which we should apply ourselves resolutely.

Thus we can point out that certain troubles like dyslexia, because we view them as benign, are but minimally covered by social security, whereas their social cost can be tremendous. For example, have we evaluated all that dyslexia can entail in educational investment beyond simply considering the treatments available? This is the type of situation to be reconsidered when we reexamine what could be called "normality" in matters of health. There is an enormous amount of work in the way of investigation, experimentation, measure-taking, and intellectual and moral reformulation to be done on this score.

Clearly, we have come upon a turning point that must be negotiated.

A MATTER OF CONSCIENCE
AND CULTURE

Q: *The definition of a norm in health, and the search for a consensus about a certain level of expenditure or about the modes of allocation of these expenditures, consti-tute an extraordinary opportunity for people to take responsibility for matters that concern them fundamentally, matters of life and well-being. But it is also a task of such magnitude as to inspire some hesitation, is it not?*

How can we bring the debate to all levels of public opinion?

A: It is true that certain contributions to this debate have aroused an outcry.[3] What is significant is that the protests address proposals that touch on matters that are by nature controversial: life and death. By evoking these health prob-lems, we enter into a system of values that allows for an absolute and infinite de-mand. The problem raised is therefore that of reconciling an infinite demand with a finite system.

This is not the first time that mankind has encountered this problem. After all, was religion not made to solve it? But today, we must find a solution to it in technical terms.

Q: *Does the proposal to make the individual responsible for his or her own choices contain an element of the answer? When we ask a smoker to pay a surcharge, for ex-ample, does this not amount to obliging him financially to assume the risk that he runs? Can we not, in the same way, bring home to people the meaning and implication of their individual decisions instead of marking out boundaries beyond which life would no longer have the same price?*

A: I totally agree. When I speak of arbitration and normativity, I do not have in mind a sort of committee of wise men who can proclaim each year: "Given the circumstances and state of our finances, such a risk will be covered and such an-other will not." I picture, in a more global sense, something like a cloud of deci-sions arranging themselves around an axis that would roughly define the retained norm. It remains to be seen how to ensure that this normative axis is as representative as possible of a certain state of consciousness of the people—that is, of the nature of their demand and of that which can be the object of con-sent on their part. I believe that results of arbitration should be the effect of a kind of ethical consensus, so that the individual can recognize himself in the decisions made and in the values behind the decisions. It is under this condition that the decisions will be acceptable, even if someone protests and rebels.

Given this, if it is true that people who smoke and those who drink must know that they are running a risk, it is also true that to have a salty diet when one has arteriosclerosis is dangerous, just as it is dangerous to have a sugar-laden diet when one is diabetic. I point this out to indicate just how complex the problems are, and to suggest that arbitration, or a "decisional cloud," should never assume the form of a univocal rule. All uniform, rational models arrive very quickly at paradoxes!

It is quite obvious, for all that, that the cost of diabetes and of arteriosclerosis are minuscule compared to the expenses incurred by tobacco addiction and alcoholism.

Q: *Which rank as veritable plagues, and the cost of which is also a social cost. I am thinking of a certain delinquency, of martyred children, of battered wives . . .*
A: Let us also remember that alcoholism was literally implanted in the French working-class, in the nineteenth century, by the authority's opening of bars. Let us also remember that neither the problem of home distillers nor that of viticulture have ever been solved. One can speak of a veritable politics of organized alcoholism in France. Perhaps we are at a point at which it becomes possible to take the bull by the horns and to move toward a reduced coverage of the risks linked to alcoholism.

Whatever the case, it goes without saying that I do not advocate that savage liberalism that would lead to individual coverage for those who have the means to pay for it, and to a lack of coverage for the others.

I am merely emphasizing that the fact of "health" is a cultural fact in the broadest sense of the word, a fact that is political, economic, and social as well, a fact that is tied to a certain state of individual and collective consciousness. Every era outlines a "normal" profile of health. Perhaps we should direct ourselves toward a system that defines, in the domain of the *abnormal*, the pathological, the sicknesses *normally* covered by society.

Q: *Do you not think, in order to clarify the debate, it would also behoove us to distinguish, in attempting to define a norm of health, between that which arises from the medical sphere and that which arises from social relationships? Have we not witnessed, in the last thirty years, a kind of "medicalization" of what could be called society's problems? We have, for example, brought a type of medical response to the problem of absenteeism on the job, when we should have instead improved working conditions. This type of "displacement" puts a strain on the health budget.*
A: A thousand things, in fact, have been "medicalized" or even "over-medicalized," things that arise from phenomena other than medicine. It so hap-

pened that, faced with certain problems, we judged the medical solution to be the most useful and the most economical. This was the case for certain scholastic problems, for sexual problems, for detention problems . . . Clearly, we should revise many of the options of this kind.

A HAPPIER OLD AGE—UNTIL THE NON-EVENT?

Q: *We have not touched upon the problem of old age. Doesn't our society tend to relegate its old people to rest homes, as if to forget about them?*
A: I confess that I am somewhat reserved and taken aback by all that is being said about older people, about their isolation and misery in our society.

It's true that the rest homes of Nanterre and of Ivry offer a rather sordid image. But the fact that we are scandalized by this sordidness is indicative of a new sensibility, which is itself linked to a new situation. Before the war, families shoved the elderly into a corner of the house, complaining of the burden they placed on them, making them pay for their presence in the household with a thousand humiliations, a thousand hatreds. Today, the older people receive a pension on which they can live, and in cities all over France there are "senior citizens' clubs" frequented by people who meet each other, who travel, who shop, and who constitute an increasingly important sector of the population. Even if a certain number of individuals are still marginalized, the overall condition of the senior citizen has improved considerably within a few decades. That is why we are so sensitive—and it is an excellent thing—to what is still happening in certain establishments.

Q: *How, when all is said and done, can social security contribute to an ethic of the human person?*
A: Without recounting all of the elements of the answer to this question brought out in the course of this interview, I would say that social security contributes to an ethic of the human person at least by posing a certain number of problems, and especially by posing the question about the value of life and the way in which we face up to death.

The idea of bringing individuals and decision centers closer together should imply, at least as a consequence, the recognized right of each individual to kill himself when he wants to under decent conditions . . . If I won a few billion in the lottery, I would create an institute where people who would like to die would come spend a weekend, a week, or a month in pleasure, under drugs perhaps, in order to disappear afterward, as if erased.

Q: *A right to suicide?*
A: Yes.

Q: *What is there to say about the way in which we die today? What are we to think of this sterilized death, often in a hospital, without the company of family?*
A: Death becomes a non-event. Most of the time, people die in a cloud of medication, if it is not by accident, so that they entirely lose consciousness in a few hours, a few days, or a few weeks: they fade away. We live in a world in which the medical and pharmaceutical accompaniment to death removes much of the suffering and drama.

I do not really subscribe to all that is being said about the "sterilization" of death, which makes reference to something like a great integrative and dramatic ritual. Loud crying around the coffin was not always exempt from a certain cynicism: the joy of inheritance could be mixed in. I prefer the quiet sadness of disappearance to this sort of ceremony.

The way we die now seems to me indicative of a sensibility, of a system of values, which prevails today. There would be something chimerical in wanting to reinstate, in a fit of nostalgia, practices that no longer make any sense.

Let us, rather, try to give sense and beauty to an effacing death.

Notes

1. Lord William Henry Beveridge (1879–1963), English economist and administrator, author of a social security plan in 1942.

2. CFDT: Confédération Française du Travail. With Pierre Bourdieu, Foucault published a protest against the French Minister of Foreign Affairs' classification of the establishment of a military dictatorship in Poland as "a matter of Poland's internal politics." The protest won the support of some hundred or so intellectuals, whom the CFDT invited to participate in a common appeal "in the spirit of the Solidarity movement" (in Poland). The CFDT subsequently organized a committee of support for the Solidarity movement, in which Foucault took an active and, indeed, actively bureaucratic part. (See vol. 1 of *Dits et écrits*, "Chronologie," compiled by Daniel Defert, pp. 59–60.)

3. Foucault refers here to the polemics following the publication of *L'Ordre cannibale: vie et mort de la médecine* by Jacques Attali (Paris: B. Grasset, 1979).

STRUCTURALISM AND POST-STRUCTURALISM

G.R. How should we begin? I have had two questions in mind. First, what is the origin of this global term, "post-structuralism"?

M.F. First, none of the protagonists in the structuralist movement—and none of those who, willingly or otherwise, were dubbed structuralists—knew very clearly what it was all about. Certainly, those who were applying structural methods in very precise disciplines such as linguistics and comparative mythology knew what structuralism was, but as soon as one strayed from these very precise disciplines, nobody knew exactly what it was. I am not sure how interesting it would be to attempt a redefinition of what was known, at the time, as structuralism. It would be interesting, though, to study formal thought and the different kinds of formalism that ran through Western culture during the twentieth century—and if I had the time, I would like to. When we consider the extraordinary destiny of formalism in painting or formal research in music, or the importance of formalism in the analysis of folklore and legend, in architecture, or its application to theoretical thought, it is clear that formalism in general has probably been one of the strongest and at the same time one of the most varied currents in twentieth-century Europe. And it is worth pointing out that formalism has very often been associated at once precisely and in each case interestingly with political situations and even political movements. It would certainly be worth examining more closely the relation of Russian formalism to the Russian Revolution. The role of formalist art and formalist thought at the beginning of the twentieth century, their ideological value, their links with different political movements—all of this would be very interesting.

This interview, conducted by Gérard Raulet, originally appeared in *Telos* 16:55 (1983), pp. 195–211. The translation, by Jeremy Harding, has been amended.

I am struck by how far the structuralist movements in France and Western Europe during the sixties echoed the efforts of certain Eastern countries—notably Czechoslovakia—to free themselves of dogmatic Marxism; and toward the mid-fifties and early sixties, while countries like Czechoslovakia were seeing a renaissance of the old tradition of prewar European formalism, we also witnessed the birth in Western Europe of what was known as structuralism—which is to say, I suppose, a new modality of this formalist thought and investigation. That is how I would situate the structuralist phenomenon—by relocating it within the broad current of formal thought.

G.R.   In Western Europe, Germany was particularly inclined to conceive the student movement, which began earlier there than it did in France (from '64 or '65, there was definite agitation in the universities), in terms of Critical Theory.

M.F.   Yes.

G.R.   Clearly, there is no necessary relation between Critical Theory and the student movement. If anything, the student movement instrumentalized Critical Theory, or made use of it. In the same way, there is no direct connection either between structuralism and '68.

M.F.   That is correct.

G.R.   But were you not saying, in a way, that structuralism was a necessary preamble?

M.F.   No. There is nothing necessary in this order of ideas. But to put it very, very crudely, formalist culture, thought and art in the first third of the twentieth century were generally associated with political, or shall we say, critical—even in some cases revolutionary—movements of the left; and Marxism concealed all that. It was fiercely critical of formalism in art and theory, most clearly from the thirties onward. Thirty years later, you saw people in certain Eastern bloc countries and even in France beginning to circumscribe Marxist dogmatism with types of analysis obviously inspired by formalism. What happened in France in 1968, and in other countries as well, is at once extremely interesting and highly ambiguous—and ambiguous because interesting. It is a case of movements that, very often, have endowed themselves with a strong reference to Marxism and, at the same time, have insisted on a violent critique vis-à-vis the dogmatic Marxism of parties and institutions. Indeed, the range of interplay between a certain kind of non-Marxist thinking and these Marxist references was the space in which the student movements developed—movements that sometimes carried revolutionary Marxist discourse to the height of exaggeration but were often inspired at the same time by an antidogmatic violence that ran counter to this type of discourse.

G.R.   An antidogmatic violence in search of references . . .

M.F.   And looking for them, on occasion, in an exasperated dogmatism.

G.R.   Via Freud or via structuralism.

M.F. Correct. So, once again, I would like to reassess the history of formalism and relocate this minor structuralist episode in France—relatively short,
with diffuse forms—within the larger phenomenon of formalism in twentieth
century, as important in its way as romanticism or even positivism was during
the nineteenth century.

G.R. We will return later to positivism. For now, I want to follow the thread
of this French evolution you are almost retracing: a thread of references (both
very dogmatic and inspired by a will to antidogmatism) to Marx, Freud, and
structuralism, in the hope of discovering in people like Jacques Lacan a figure
who would put an end to syncretism and would manage to unify all these
strands. This approach, moreover, drew a magisterial response from Lacan to
the students at Vincennes, running roughly as follows: "You want to combine
Marx and Freud. Psychoanalysis can teach you that you are looking for a master; and you will have this master"—an extremely violent kind of disengagement from this attempt at a combination.[1] I read in Vincent Descombes's book,
Le même et l'autre, with which you are no doubt familiar . . . [2]

M.F. No. I know it exists but I have not read it.

G.R. . . . that fundamentally, it was necessary to wait until 1972 in order to
emerge from this vain effort to combine Marxism and Freudianism; and that this
emergence was achieved by Gilles Deleuze and Felix Guattari, who came from
the Lacanian school. Somewhere, I took the liberty of writing that we had certainly emerged from this fruitless attempt at a combination, but in a way that
Hegel would have criticized.[3] In other words, we went in pursuit of the third
man—Nietzsche—to bring him into the site of the impossible synthesis, referring to him rather than to the impossible combination of Marx and Freud. In any
case, according to Descombes, it seems that this tendency to resort to Nietzsche
began in 1972. What do you think?

M.F. No, I do not think that is quite right. First, you know how I am. I am always a bit suspicious of these forms of synthesis which present French thought
as Freudian-Marxist at one stage and then as having discovered Nietzsche at another. Since 1945, for a whole range of political and cultural reasons, Marxism in
France was a kind of horizon that Sartre thought for a time was impossible to
surpass. At that time, it was definitely a very closed horizon, and a very imposing one. Also, we should not forget that throughout the period from 1945 to
1955 in France, the entire French University—the young French University, as
opposed to what had been the traditional university—was very much preoccupied, even occupied, with the task of building something that was not Freudian-
Marxist but Husserlian-Marxist—the phenomenology-Marxism relation. That
is what was at stake in the debates and efforts of a whole series of people. Maurice Merleau-Ponty and Jean-Paul Sartre, in moving from phenomenology to
Marxism, were definitely operating on that axis. Jean Desanti too . . .

G.R.   Mikel Dufrenne, even Jean-François Lyotard.

M.F.   And Paul Ricoeur, who was certainly not a Marxist, but a phenomenologist in no way oblivious to Marxism. So, at first they tried to wed Marxism and phenomenology; and it was later, once a certain kind of structural thinking—structural method—had begun to develop, that we saw structuralism replace phenomenology and become coupled with Marxism. It was a movement from phenomenology toward structuralism, and essentially it concerned the problem of language. That, I think, was a fairly critical point—Merleau-Ponty's encounter with language. And, as you know, Merleau-Ponty's later efforts addressed that question. I remember clearly some lectures in which Merleau-Ponty began speaking of Saussure who, even if he had been dead for fifty years, was quite unknown, not so much to French linguists and philologists but to the cultured public. So the problem of language appeared, and it was clear that phenomenology was no match for structural analysis in accounting for the effects of meaning that could be produced by a structure of the linguistic type, in which the subject (in the phenomenological sense) did not intervene to confer meaning. And quite naturally, with the phenomenological spouse finding herself disqualified by her inability to address language, structuralism became the new bride. That is how I would look at it. Even so, psychoanalysis—in large part under the influence of Lacan—also raised a problem which, though very different, was not unanalogous. For the unconscious could not feature in any discussion of a phenomenological kind; of which the most conclusive proof, as the French saw it anyhow, was the fact that Sartre and Merleau-Ponty—I am not talking about the other—were always trying to break down what they saw as positivism, or mechanism, or Freudian "concretism" in order to affirm a constituting subject. And when Lacan, around the time that questions of language were beginning to be posed, remarked, "Whatever you do, the unconscious as such can never be reduced to the effects of a conferral of meaning to which the phenomenological subject is susceptible," he was posing a problem absolutely symmetrical with that of the linguists. Once again, the phenomenological subject was disqualified by psychoanalysis, as it had been by linguistic theory. And it is quite understandable at that point that Lacan could say the unconscious was structured like a language. For one and all, it was the same type of problem. So we had a Freudian-structuralist-Marxism. And with phenomenology disqualified for the reasons I have just outlined, there was simply a succession of fiancées, each flirting with Marx in turn. Only, all was not exactly going well. Of course, I am describing it as though I were talking about a very general movement. What I describe did undoubtedly take place, and it involved a certain number of individuals; but there were also people who did not follow the movement. I am thinking of those who were interested in the history of science—an important tradition in France, probably since the time of Auguste Comte. Particularly around Georges Canguilhem, an extremely influential figure in the French University—the young French University. Many of his students were neither Marxists nor Freudians nor structuralists. And here I am speaking of myself.

G.R. You were one of those people, then?

M.F. I have never been a Freudian, I have never been a Marxist, and I have never been a structuralist.

G.R. Yes, here too, as a formality and just so the reader is under no misapprehensions, we only need to look at the dates. You began . . .

M.F. My first book was written toward the end of my student days. It was *Madness and Civilization,* written between '55 and '60. This book is neither Freudian nor Marxist nor structuralist. Now, as it happened, I had read Nietzsche in '53 and curious as it may seem, from a perspective of inquiry into the history of knowledge—the history of reason: how does one elaborate a history of rationality? This was the problem of the nineteenth century.

G.R. Knowledge, reason, rationality.

M.F. Knowledge, reason, rationality, the possibility of elaborating a history of rationality. I would say that here again, we run across phenomenology, in someone like Koyré, a historian of science, with his German background, who came to France between 1930 and 1935, I believe, and developed a historical analysis of the forms of rationality and knowledge in a phenomenological perspective. For me, the problem was framed in terms not unlike those we mentioned earlier. Is the phenomenological, transhistorical subject able to provide an account of the historicity of reason? Here, reading Nietzsche was the point of rupture for me. There is a history of the subject just as there is a history of reason; but we can never demand that the history of reason unfold as a first and founding act of the rationalist subject. I read Nietzsche by chance, and I was surprised to see that Canguilhem, the most influential historian of science in France at the time, was also very interested in Nietzsche and was thoroughly receptive to what I was trying to do.

G.R. On the other hand, there are no perceptible traces of Nietzsche in his work . . .

M.F. But there are; and they are very clear. There are even explicit references; more explicit in his later texts than in his earlier ones. The relation of the French to Nietzsche and even the relation of all twentieth-century thought to Nietzsche was difficult, for understandable reasons . . . But I am talking about myself. We should also talk about Deleuze. Deleuze wrote his book on Nietzsche in the sixties. He was interested in empiricism, in Hume, and again in the question: Is the theory of the subject we have in phenomenology a satisfactory one? He could elude this question by means of the slant of Hume's empiricism. I am convinced that he encountered Nietzsche under the same conditions. So I would say everything that took place in the sixties arose from a dissatisfaction with the phenomenological theory of the subject, and involved different escapades, subterfuges, breakthroughs, according to whether we use a negative or a positive term, in the direction of linguistics, psychoanalysis or Nietzsche.

G.R. At any rate, Nietzsche represented a determining experience for the abolition of the founding act of the subject.

M.F. Exactly. And this is where French writers like Bataille and Blanchot were important for us. I said earlier that I wondered why I had read Nietzsche. But I know very well. I read him because of Bataille, and Bataille because of Blanchot. So, it is not at all true that Nietzsche appeared in 1972. He appeared in 1972 for people who were Marxists during the sixties and who emerged from Marxism by way of Nietzsche. But the first people who had recourse to Nietzsche were not looking for a way out of Marxism. They wanted a way out of phenomenology.

G.R. You have spoken about historians of science, of writing a history of knowledge, a history of rationality and a history of reason. Before returning to Nietzsche, could we briefly define these four terms, which might well be taken—in the light of what you have said—to be synonymous?

M.F. No, no. I was describing a movement that involved many factors and many different problems. I am not saying that these problems are identical. I am speaking about the kinship between the lines of inquiry and the proximity of those who undertook them.

G.R. All the same, could we try to specify their relationships? It is true that this can definitely be found in your books, particularly *The Archaeology of Knowledge*. Nonetheless, could we try to specify these relations between science, knowledge, and reason?

M.F. It is not very easy in an interview. I would say that the history of science has played an important role in philosophy in France. I would say that perhaps if modern philosophy (that of the nineteenth and twentieth centuries) derives in great part from the Kantian question, *"Was ist Aufklärung?"* or, in other words, if we admit that one of the main functions of modern philosophy has been an inquiry into the historical point at which reason could appear in its "adult" form, "unchaperoned," then the function of nineteenth-century philosophy consisted in asking, "What is this moment when reason accedes to autonomy? What is the meaning of a history of reason, and what value can be ascribed to the ascendancy of reason in the modern world, through these three great forms: scientific thought, technical apparatus, and political organization?" I think one of philosophy's great functions was to inquire into these three domains, in some sense, to take stock of things or smuggle an anxious question into the rule of reason. To continue then . . . to pursue the Kantian question, *"Was ist Aufklärung?"* This reprise, this reiteration of the Kantian question in France assumed a precise and perhaps, moreover, an inadequate form: "What is the history of science? What happened, between Greek mathematics and modern physics, as this universe of science was built?" From Comte right through the sixties, I think the philosophical function of the history of science has been to pursue this question. Now, in Germany, this question "What is the history of reason, of rational forms in Europe?" did not appear so much in the history of science but in the current of thought which runs roughly from Max Weber to Critical Theory.

G.R. Yes, the meditations on norms, on values.

M.F. From Max Weber to Jürgen Habermas. And the same question arises here. How do matters stand with the history of reason, with the ascendancy of reason, and with the different forms in which this ascendancy operates? Now, the striking thing is that France knew absolutely nothing—or only vaguely, only very indirectly—about the current of Weberian thought. Critical Theory was hardly known in France, and the Frankfurt School was practically unheard of. This, by the way, raises a minor historical problem that fascinates me, and I have not been able to resolve at all. It is common knowledge that many representatives of the Frankfurt School came to Paris in 1935, seeking refuge, and left very hastily, sickened presumably—some even said as much—but saddened anyhow not to have found more of an echo. Then came 1940, but they had already left for England and the U.S. where they were actually much better received. The understanding that might have been established between the Frankfurt School and French philosophical thought—by way of the history of science and, therefore, the question of the history of rationality—never occurred. And when I was a student, I can assure you that I never once heard the name of the Frankfurt School mentioned by any of my professors.

G.R. It is really quite astonishing.

M.F. Now, obviously, if I had been familiar with the Frankfurt School, if I had been aware of it at the time, I would not have said a number of stupid things that I did say, and I would have avoided many of the detours I made while trying to pursue my own humble path—when, meanwhile, avenues had been opened up by the Frankfurt School. It is a strange case of nonpenetration between two very similar types of thinking which is explained, perhaps, by that very similarity. Nothing hides the fact of a problem in common better than two similar ways of approaching it.

G.R. What you have just said about the Frankfurt School—about Critical Theory, if you like—which might, under different circumstances, have spared you some fumblings, is even more interesting in view of the fact that one finds an Oskar Negt or a Habermas doffing his hat to you. In an interview I did with Habermas, he praised your "masterly description of the bifurcation of reason": reason had bifurcated at a given moment. But I have still wondered whether you would agree with this bifurcation of reason as conceived by Critical Theory—with the dialectic of reason, in other words, whereby reason becomes perverse under the effects of its own strength, transformed and reduced to instrumental knowledge. The prevailing idea in Critical Theory is the dialectical continuity of reason, and of a perversion that completely transformed it at a certain stage—which it now becomes a question of rectifying. That is what seemed to be at issue in the struggle for emancipation. Basically, to judge from your work, the will to knowledge has never ceased to bifurcate in some way or another—bifurcating hundreds of times in the course of history. Perhaps "bifurcate" is not even the right word. Reason has split knowledge again and again.

M.F. Yes, yes. I think the blackmail that has very often been at work in every critique of reason or every critical inquiry into the history of rationality (either you accept rationality or you fall prey to the irrational) operates as though a rational critique of rationality were impossible, or as though a rational history of all the ramifications and all the bifurcations, a contingent history of reason, were impossible. I think that since Weber, in the Frankfurt School and anyhow for many historians of science such as Canguilhem, it was a question of isolating the form of rationality presented as dominant and endowed with the status of the one-and-only reason, in order to show that it is only *one* possible form among others. In this French history of science—I consider it quite important—the role of Gaston Bachelard, whom I have not mentioned so far, is also crucial.

G.R. Even so, this praise from Habermas is a little barbed. According to Habermas, you provided a masterly description of the "moment reason bifurcated." This bifurcation was unique. It happened once. At a certain point, reason took a turn that led it toward an instrumental rationality, an autoreduction, a self-limitation. This bifurcation, if it is also a division, happened once and once only in history, separating the two realms with which we have been acquainted since Kant. This analysis of bifurcation is Kantian. There is the knowledge of understanding and the knowledge of reason, there is instrumental reason and there is moral reason. To assess this bifurcation, we clearly situate ourselves at the vantage point of practical reason, or moral practical reason. Whence a unique bifurcation, a separation of technique and practice which continues to dominate the entire German history of ideas. And, as you said earlier, this tradition arises from the question, *"Was ist Aufklärung?"* Now, in my view, this praise reduces your own approach to the history of ideas.

M.F. True, I would not speak about *one* bifurcation of reason but more about an endless, multiple bifurcation—a kind of abundant ramification. I do not speak of the point at which reason became instrumental. At present, for example, I am studying the problem of techniques of the self in Greek and Roman antiquity; how man, human life, and the self were all objects of a certain number of *tekhnai* that, with their exacting rationality, could well be compared to any technique of production.

G.R. Without comprising the whole of society.

M.F. Right. And what led the *tekhnē* of self to develop. Everything propitious to the development of a technology of the self can very well be analyzed, I think, and situated as a historical phenomenon—which does not constitute *the* bifurcation of reason. In this abundance of branchings, ramifications, breaks, and ruptures, it was an important event, or episode; it had considerable consequences, but it was not a *unique* phenomenon.

G.R. But directly we cease to view the self-perversion of reason as a unique phenomenon, occurring only once in history, at a moment when reason would seem to have lost something essential, something substantial—as we would have to say after Weber—would you not agree that your work aims to rehabilitate a fuller version of reason? Can we find, for example, another conception of reason implicit in your approach; a project of rationality that differs from the one we have nowadays?

M.F. Yes, but here, once more, I would try to take my distance from phenomenology, which was my point of departure. I do not believe in a kind of founding act whereby reason, in its essence, was discovered or established and from which it was subsequently diverted by such-and-such an event. I think, in fact, that reason is self-created, which is why I have tried to analyze forms of rationality: different foundations, different creations, different modifications in which rationalities engender one another, oppose and pursue one another. Even so, you cannot assign a point at which reason would have lost sight of its fundamental project, or even a point at which the rational becomes the irrational. During the sixties, to put it very, very schematically, I wanted to depart as much from the phenomenological account (with its foundational and essential project of reason, from which we have shifted away on account of some forgetfulness and to which we must return) as from the Marxist account, or the account of Georg Lukács. A rationality existed, and it was the form par excellence of Reason itself, but a certain number of social conditions (capitalism, or rather, the shift from one form of capitalism to another) precipitated this rationality into a crisis, that is, a forgetting of reason, a fall into irrationalism. I tired to take my bearings in relation to these two major models, presented very schematically and unfairly.

G.R. In these models, we see either a unique bifurcation or a forgetfulness, at a given moment, following the confiscation of reason by a class. Thus, the movement across history toward emancipation consists not only in reappropriating what was confiscated (to confiscate it again) but—on the contrary—in giving reason back its truth, intact, investing it with the status of an absolutely universal science. For you, clearly—you have made it plain in your writing—there is no project of a new science, of a broader science.

M.F. Definitely not.

G.R. But you show that each time a type of rationality asserts itself, it does so by a kind of cut-out—by exclusion or by self-demarcation, drawing a boundary between self and other. Does your project include any effort to rehabilitate this other? Do you think, for example, in the silence of the mad person you might discover language that would have much to say about the conditions in which works are brought into existence?

M.F. Yes, what interested me, starting out from the general frame of reference we mentioned earlier, were precisely the forms of rationality applied by the human subject to itself. While historians of science in France were interested essentially in the problem of how a scientific object is constituted, the question I asked myself was this: How is it that the human subject took itself as the object of possible knowledge? Through what forms of rationality and historical conditions? And, finally, at what price? This is my question: At what price can subjects speak the truth about themselves? At what price can subjects speak the truth about themselves as mad persons? At the price of constituting the mad person as absolutely other, paying not only the theoretical price but also an institutional and even an economic price, as determined by the organization of psychiatry. An ensemble of complex, staggered elements where you find that institutional game-playing, class relations, professional conflicts, modalities of knowledge and, finally, a whole history of the subject and of reason are involved. That is what I have tried to piece back together. Perhaps the project is utterly mad, very complex—and I have only brought a few moments to light, a few specific points such as the problem of the mad subject and what it is. How can the truth of the sick subject ever be told? How can one speak the truth about the mad subject? This is the substance of my first two books. *The Order of Things* asked the price of problematizing and analyzing the speaking subject, the working subject, the living subject. Which is why I attempted to analyze the birth of grammar, general grammar, natural history, and economics. I went on to pose the same kind of question in the case of the criminal and systems of punishment: How to state the truth of oneself, insofar as one might be a criminal subject. I will be doing the same thing with sexuality, only going back much farther: How does the subject speak truthfully about itself, inasmuch as it is the subject of sexual pleasure? And at what price?

G.R. According to the relation of subjects to whatever they are, in each case, through the constitution of language or knowledge.

M.F. It is an analysis of the relation between forms of reflexivity—a relation of self to self—and, hence, of relations between forms of reflexivity and the discourse of truth, forms of rationality and effects of knowledge [*connaissance*].

G.R. In any event, it is not a case of exhuming some prehistorical "archaic" by means of archaeology. (You shall see why I ask this question. It directly concerns certain readings of the so-called French Nietzschean current in Germany.)

M.F. No, absolutely not. I meant this word "archaeology," which I no longer use, to suggest that the kind of analysis I was using was out-of-phase, not in terms of time but by virtue of the level at which it was situated. Studying the history of ideas, as they evolve, is not my problem so much as trying to discern beneath them how one or another object could take shape as a possible object of knowledge. Why, for instance, did madness become, at a given moment, an object of knowledge corresponding to a certain type of knowledge? By using the word "archaeology" rather than "history," I tried to designate this desynchronization between ideas about madness and the constitution of madness as an object.

G.R. I asked this question because nowadays there is a tendency—its pretext being the appropriation of Nietzsche by the New German Right—to lump everything together; to imagine that French Nietzscheanism, if Nietzscheanism it is—it seems to me that you just confirmed that Nietzsche played a determinant role—is in the same vein. All these elements are associated in order to recreate what are fundamentally the fronts of theoretical class struggle, so hard to find nowadays.

M.F. I do not believe there is a single Nietzscheanism. There are no grounds for believing that there is a true Nietzscheanism, or that ours is any truer than others. But those who found in Nietzsche, more than twenty-five years ago, a means of displacing themselves in terms of a philosophical horizon dominated by phenomenology and Marxism have nothing to do with those who use Nietzsche nowadays. In any case, even if Deleuze has written a superb book about Nietzsche, and although the presence of Nietzsche in his other works is clearly apparent, there is no deafening reference to Nietzsche, nor any attempt to wave the Nietzschean flag for rhetorical or political ends. It is striking that someone like Deleuze has simply taken Nietzsche seriously, which indeed he has. That is what I wanted to do. What serious use can Nietzsche be put to? I have lectured on Nietzsche but written very little about him. The only rather extravagant homage I have rendered Nietzsche was to call the first volume of my *History of Sexuality* "The Will to Know."

G.R. Certainly, as regards the will to know, I think we have been able to see in what you have just said that it was always a *relation*. I suppose you will detest this word with its Hegelian ring. Perhaps we should say "evaluation," as Nietzsche would—a way of evaluating truth. At any rate, a way in which force, neither an archaic instance nor an originary or original resource, is actualized; and so too, a relation of forces and perhaps already a relation of power in the constituting act of all knowledge.

M.F. I would not say so. That is too involved. My problem is the relation of self to self and of telling the truth. My relation to Nietzsche, or what I owe Nietzsche, derives mostly from the texts of around 1880, where the question of truth, the history of truth and the will to truth were central to his work. Did you know that Sartre's first text—written when he was a young student—was Nietzschean? "The History of Truth," a little paper first published in a *Lycée* review around 1925.[4] He began with the same problem. And it is very odd that his approach should have shifted from the history of truth to phenomenology, while for the next generation—ours—the reverse was true.

G.R. I think we are now in the process of clarifying what you mean by "will to know"—this reference to Nietzsche. You concede a certain kinship with Deleuze, but only up to a point. Would this kinship extend as far as the Deleuzian notion of desire?

M.F. No, definitely not.

G.R. I am asking this question because Deleuzian desire—productive desire—becomes precisely this kind of originary resource which then begins to generate forms.

M.F. I do not want to take up a position on this, or say what Deleuze may have had in mind. People say what they want or what they can say. The moment a kind of thought is constituted, fixed, or identified within a cultural tradition, it is quite normal that this cultural tradition should take hold of it, make what it wants of it and have it say what it did not mean, by implying that this is merely another form of what it was actually trying to say. Which is all a part of cultural play. But my relation to Deleuze is evidently not that; so I will not say what I think he meant. All the same, I think his task was, at least for a long time, to formulate the problem of desire. And, evidently, the effects of the relation to Nietzsche are visible in his theory of desire, whereas my own problem has always been the question of truth, of telling the truth, the *Wahr-sagen*—what it is to tell the truth—and the relation between telling the truth and forms of reflexivity, of self upon self.

G.R. Yes, but I think Nietzsche makes no fundamental distinction between will to know and will to power.

M.F. I think there is a perceptible displacement in Nietzsche's texts between those which are broadly preoccupied with the question of will to know and those which are preoccupied with will to power. But I do not want to get into this argument for the very simple reason that it is years since I have read Nietzsche.

G.R. It is important to try to clarify this point, I think, precisely because of the hold-all approach that characterizes the way this question is received abroad, and in France for that matter.

M.F. I would say, in any case, that my relation to Nietzsche has not been historical. The actual history of Nietzsche's thought interests me less than the kind of challenge I felt one day, a long time ago, reading Nietzsche for the first time. When you open *The Gay Science* after you have been trained in the great, time-honored university traditions—Descartes, Kant, Hegel, Husserl—and you come across those rather strange, witty, cheeky texts, you say: Well, I won't do what my contemporaries, colleagues or professors are doing; I won't just dismiss this. What is the maximum of philosophical intensity, and what are the current philosophical effects to be found in these texts? That, for me, was the challenge of Nietzsche.

G.R. In the way all this is received at the moment, I think there is a second hold-all concept, that is, postmodernity, which quite a few people refer to and which also plays a role in Germany, since Habermas has taken up the term in order to criticize this trend in all its aspects . . .

M.F. What are we calling postmodernity? I'm not up to date.

G.R. . . . the current of North American sociology (Daniel Bell) as much as what is known as postmodernity in art, which would require another definition (perhaps a return to a certain formalism). Anyway, Habermas attributes the term "postmodernity" to the French current, the tradition, as he says in his text on postmodernity, "running from Bataille to Derrida by way of Foucault." This is an important question in Germany, because reflections on modernity have existed for a long time—ever since Weber. What is postmodernity, as regards the aspect that interests us here? Mainly, it is the idea of modernity, of reason, we find in Lyotard: a "grand narrative" from which we have finally been freed by a kind of salutary awakening. Postmodernity is a breaking apart of reason; Deleuzian schizophrenia. Postmodernity reveals, at least, that reason has only been one narrative among others in history; a grand narrative, certainly, but one of many, which can now be followed by other narratives. In your vocabulary, reason was *one* form of the will to know. Would you agree that this has to do with a certain current? Do you situate yourself within this current; and, if so, how?

M.F. I must say that I have trouble answering this. First, because I've never clearly understood what was meant in France by the word "modernity." In the case of Bauderlaire, yes, but thereafter I think the sense begins to get lost. I do not know what Germans mean by modernity. The Americans were planning a kind of seminar with Habermas and myself. Habermas had suggested the theme of "modernity" for the seminar. I feel troubled here because I do not grasp clearly what that might mean, though the word itself is unimportant; we can always use any arbitrary label. But neither do I grasp the kind of problems intended by this term—or how they would be common to people thought of as being "postmodern." While I see clearly that behind what was known as structuralism, there was a certain problem—broadly speaking, that of the subject and the recasting of the subject—do not understand what kind of problem is common to the people we call "post modern" or "poststructuralist."

G.R. Obviously, reference or opposition to modernity is not only ambiguous, it actually confines modernity. Modernity also has several definitions: the historian's definition, Weber's definition, Theodor Adorno's definition, and Walter Benjamin's of Baudelaire, as you've mentioned. So there are at least some references. Habermas, in opposition to Adorno, seems to privilege the tradition of reason, that is, the Weberian definition of modernity. It is in relation to this that he sees in postmodernity the crumbling-away or the breakup of reason, and allows himself to declare that one of the forms of postmodernity—the one that is in relation with the Weberian definition—is the current that envisages reason as *one* form among others of will to know—a grand narrative, but *one* narrative among others.

M.F. That is not my problem, insofar as I am not prepared to identify reason entirely with the totality of rational forms which have come to dominate—at any given moment, in our own era and even very recently—in types of knowledge, forms of technique, and modalities of government or domination; realms where we can see all the major applications of rationality. I am leaving the problem of art to one side; it is complicated. For me, no given form of rationality is actually reason. So I do not see how we can say that the forms of rationality which have been dominant in the three sectors I have mentioned are in the process of collapsing and disappearing. I cannot see any disappearance of that kind. I can see multiple transformations, but I cannot see why we should call this transformation a "collapse of reason." Other forms of rationality are created endlessly. So there is no sense at all to the proposition that reason is a long narrative that is now finished, and that another narrative is under way.

G.R. Let us just say that the field is open to many forms of narrative.

M.F. Here, I think, we are touching on one of the forms—perhaps we should call them "habits"—one of the most harmful habits in contemporary thought, in modern thought even; at any rate, in post-Hegelian thought: the analysis of the present as being precisely, in history, a present of rupture, or of high point, or of completion or of a returning dawn, and so on. The solemnity with which everyone who engages in philosophical discourse reflects on his own time strikes me as a flaw. I can say so all the more firmly, since it is something I have done myself; and since, in someone like Nietzsche, we find this incessantly—or, at least, insistently enough. I think we should have the modesty to say to ourselves that, on the one hand, the time we live in is not *the* unique or fundamental or irruptive point in history where everything is completed and begun again. We must also have the modesty to say, on the other hand, that—even without this solemnity—the time we live in is very interesting; it needs to be analyzed and broken down, and that we would do well to ask ourselves, "What is today?" I wonder if one of the great roles of philosophical thought since the Kantian *"Was ist Aufklärung?"* might not be characterized by saying that the task of philosophy is to describe the nature of today, and of "ourselves today." With the proviso that we do not allow ourselves the facile, rather theatrical declaration that this moment in which we exist is one of total perdition, in the abyss of darkness, or a triumphant daybreak, and so on. It is a time like any other, or rather, a time that is never quite like any other.

G.R. This poses dozens of questions; ones that you have posed yourself in any case. What is the nature of today? Is the era characterized more than others, in spite of everything, by a greater fragmentation, by "deterritorialization" and "schizophrenia"—no need to take a position on these terms?

M.F. I would like to say something about the function of any diagnosis concerning what today is. It does not consist in a simple characterization of what we are but, instead—by following lines of fragility in the present—in managing to grasp why and how that which is might no longer be that which is. In this sense, any description must always be made in accordance with these kinds of virtual fracture which open up the space of freedom understood as a space of concrete freedom, that is, of possible transformation.

G.R. It is here, along the fractures, that the work of the intellectual—practical work, quite clearly—is situated?

M.F. That is my own belief. I would say also, about the work of the intellectual, that it is fruitful in a certain way to describe that which is, while making it appear as something that might not be, or that might not be as it is. Which is why this designation or description of the real never has a prescriptive value of the kind, "because this is, that will be." It is also why, in my opinion, recourse to history—one of the great facts in French philosophical thought for at least twenty years—is meaningful to the extent that history serves to show how that which is has not always been; that is, the things which seem most evident to us are always formed in the confluence of encounters and chances, during the course of a precarious and fragile history. What reason perceives as *its* necessity or, rather, what different forms of rationality offer as their necessary being, can perfectly well be shown to have a history; and the network of contingencies from which it emerges can be traced. Which is not to say, however, that these forms of rationality were irrational; it means that they reside on a base of human practice and human history—and that since these things have been made, they can be unmade, as long as we know how it was that they were made.

G.R. This work on the fractures, both descriptive and practical, is fieldwork.

M.F. Perhaps it is fieldwork and perhaps it is a work which can go farther back in terms of historical analysis, starting with questions posed in the field.

G.R. Would you describe the work on these fracture areas, work in the field, as the microphysics of power, the analytics of power?

M.F. Yes, it is something like that. It has struck me that these forms of rationality—put to work in the process of domination—deserve analysis in themselves, provided we recognize from the outset that they are not foreign to other forms of power which are put to work, for instance, in knowledge [*connaissance*] or technique. On the contrary, there is exchange; there are transmissions, transferences, interferences. But I wish to emphasize that I do not think it is possible to point to a unique form of rationality in these three realms. We come across the same types, but displaced. At the same time, there is multiple, compact interconnection, but no isomorphism.

G.R. In all eras or specifically?

M.F. There is no general law indicating the types of relation between rationalities and the procedures of domination which are put to work.

G.R. I ask this question because there is a scheme at work in a certain number of criticisms made about you. Jean Baudrillard's criticism, for instance, is that you speak at a very precise moment and conceive a moment in which power has become "unidentifiable through dissemination."[5] This unidentifiable dissemination, this necessary multiplication, is reflected in the microphysical approach. Or, again, in the opinion of Alexander Schubert,[6] you address a point where capitalism has dissolved the subject in a way that makes it possible to admit that the subject has only ever been a multiplicity of positions.

M.F. I would like to return to this question in a moment, because I had already begun to talk about two or three things. The first is that, in studying the rationality of dominations, I try to establish interconnections that are not isomorphisms. Second, when I speak of power relations, of the forms of rationality which can rule and regulate them, I am not referring to Power—with a capital P—dominating and imposing its rationality upon the totality of the social body. In fact, there are power relations. They are multiple; they have different forms, they can be in play in family relations, or within an institution, or an administration—or, between a dominating and a dominated class, power relations having specific forms of rationality, forms that are common to them, and so on. It is a field of analysis and not at all a reference to any unique instance. Third, in studying these power relations, I in no way construct a theory of power. But I wish to know how the reflexivity of the subject and the discourse of truth are linked—"How can the subject tell the truth about itself?"—and I think that relations of power exerting themselves upon one another constitute one of the determining elements in this relation I am trying to analyze. This is clear, for example, in the first case I examined, that of madness. It was indeed through a certain mode of domination, exercised by certain people upon certain other people, that the subject could undertake to tell the truth about its madness presented in the form of the other. Thus I am far from being a theoretician of power. At the limit, I would say that power, as an autonomous question, does not interest me. In many instances, I have been led to address the question of power only to the extent that the political analysis of power which was offered did not seem to me to account for the finer, more detailed phenomena I wish to evoke when I pose the question of telling the truth about oneself. If I tell the truth about myself, as I am now doing, it is in part that I am constituted as a subject across a number of power relations that are exerted over me and I exert over others. I say this in order to situate what for me is the question of power. To return to the question you raised earlier, I must admit that I see no grounds for the objection. I am not developing a theory of power. I am working on the history, at a given moment, of the way reflexivity of self upon self established, and the discourse of truth linked to it. When I speak about institutions of confinement in the eighteenth century, I am speaking about power relations as they existed at the time. So I fail utterly to see the objection, unless one imputes to me a project altogether different from my own—either that of developing a general theory of power or, again, that of developing an analysis of power as it exists now. Not at all! I take psychiatry, of course, as it is now. In it, I look at the appearance of certain problems, in the very workings of the institution, which refer us, in my view, to a history—and a relatively long one, involving several centuries. I try to work on the history or archaeology, if you like, of the way people undertook to speak truthfully about madness in the seventeenth and eighteenth centuries. And I would like to bring it to light as it existed at the time. On the subject of criminals, for example, and the system of punishment established in the eighteenth century, which characterizes our own penal system, I have not gone into detail on *all* kinds of power exercised in the eighteenth century. Instead, I have examined, in a certain number of model eighteenth-century institutions, the forms of power exercised and how they were put into play. So I can see no relevance whatever in saying that power is no longer what it used to be.

G.R.   Two more rather disconnected questions, which nonetheless strike me as important. Let us begin with the status of the intellectual. We have broadly defined how you conceive of the work, the practice even, of the intellectual. Would you be prepared to discuss here the philosophical situation in France along the following general lines? The function of the intellectual is no longer either to oppose the state with a universal reason or to provide it with its legitimation. Is there a connection with this rather strange, disconcerting situation we see today—a tacit kind of consensus among intellectuals with regard to the Left, and at the same time, the complete silence of thought on the Left—something one is tempted to see as forcing the powers of the Left to invoke very archaic themes of legitimation? The Socialist Party Congress at Valence with its rhetorical excesses, the class struggle . . . [7]

M.F.   The recent remarks of the president of the National Assembly to the effect that we must replace the egoist, individualist, bourgeois cultural model with a new cultural model of solidarity and sacrifice . . . I was not very old when Pétain came to power in France, but this year I recognized in the words of this socialist the very tones that lulled my childhood.

G.R. Yes. Basically, we are witnessing the astonishing spectacle of a power, divested of intellectual logistics, invoking pretty obsolete themes of legitimation. As for intellectual logistics, it seems that as soon as the Left comes to power, no one on the Left has anything to say.

M.F. It is a good question. First, we should remember that if the Left exists in France—the Left in a general sense—and if there are people who have the sentiment of being on the Left, people who vote Left, and if there can be a substantial party of the Left (as the Socialist Party has become), I think an important factor has been the existence of a Left thought and a Left reflection, of an analysis, a multiplicity of analyses, developed on the Left, of political choices made on the Left since at least 1960, which have been made outside the parties. No thanks to the Communist Party, though, or to the old S.F.I.O.—which was not dead until '72 (it took a long time to die)—that the Left is alive and well in France.[8] It is because, through the Algerian war, for example, in a whole sector of intellectual life also, in sectors dealing with the problems of daily life, sectors such as those of political and economic analysis, there was an extraordinarily lively Left thought. And it did not die, even at the moment when the parties of the Left disqualified themselves for different reasons. On the contrary.

G.R. No, at the time, certainly not.

M.F. And we can say that the Left survived for fifteen years—the first fifteen years of Gaullism and then the regime that followed—because of that effort. Second, it should be noted that the Socialist Party was greeted so responsively in large part because it was reasonably open to these new attitudes, new questions, and new problems. It was open to questions concerning daily life, sexual life, couples, women's issues. It was sensitive to the problems of self-management, for example. All these are themes of Left thought—a Left thought that is not encrusted in the political parties and is not traditional in its approach to Marxism. New problems, new thinking—these have been crucial. I think that one day, when we look back at this episode in French history, we will see in it the growth of a new kind of Left thought that—in multiple and nonunified forms (perhaps one of its positive aspects)—has completely transformed the horizon of contemporary Left movements. We might well imagine this particular form of Left culture as being allergic to any party organization, incapable of finding its real expression in anything but *groupuscules* and individualities. But apparently not. Finally, there has been—as I said earlier—a kind of symbiosis which has meant that the new Socialist Party is now fairly saturated with these ideas. In any case—something sufficiently interesting and attractive to be worthy of note—we have seen a number of intellectuals keeping company with the Socialist Party. Of course, the Socialist Party's very astute political tactics and strategy—and this is not pejorative—account for their coming to power. But here again, the Socialist Party came to power after having absorbed a certain number of Left cultural forms. However, since the Congress of Metz[9] and a fortiori, the Congress of Valence—where we heard things such as we discussed earlier—it is clear that this Left thought is asking itself questions.

G.R. Does this thought itself exist any more?

M.F. I do not know. We have to bear several complex factors in mind. We have to see, for example, that in the Socialist Party, this new Left thought was most active in the circle of someone like Michel Rocard—that Rocard and his group, and of the Rocard current in the Socialist Party, are now hidden under a chimney-flue tile, has had a major effect. The situation is very complex; but I think that the rather wooden pronouncements of many Socialist Party leaders at present are a betrayal of the earlier hopes expressed by a large part of this Left thought. They also betray the recent history of the Socialist Party, and they silence, in a fairly authoritarian manner, certain currents within the party itself. Undoubtedly, confronted with this phenomenon, intellectuals are tending to keep quiet. I say tending, because it is a journalistic error to say that the intellectuals are keeping quiet. Personally, I know several intellectuals who have reacted, who have given their opinion on some measure or on some problem. And I think that if we drew up an exact balance sheet of interventions by intellectuals over the last few months, there would certainly not be any less than before. Anyway, for my part, I have never written as many articles in the press as I have since word went out that I was keeping quiet. Still, let's not worry about me personally. It is true that these reactions are not a kind of fundamental choice. They are finely nuanced interventions—hesitant, slightly doubtful, slightly encouraging, and so on. But they correspond to the present state of affairs—and, instead of complaining about the silence of intellectuals, we should recognize much more clearly their thoughtful reserve in response to a recent event, a recent process, whose outcome we do not yet know for certain.

G.R. No necessary relation, then, between *this* political situation, *this* type of discourse and the thesis, nonetheless very widespread, that reason is power and so we are to divest ourselves of the one and the other?

M.F. No. You must understand that is part of the destiny common to all problems once they are posed: they degenerate into slogans. Nobody has said, "Reason is power." I do not think anyone has said knowledge is power.

G.R. It has been said.

M.F. It has been said, but you have to understand when I read—and I know it was being attributed to me—the thesis "Knowledge is power" or "Power is knowledge," I begin to laugh, since studying their *relation* is precisely my problem. If they were identical, I would not have to study them and I would be spared a lot of fatigue as a result. The very fact that I pose the question of their relation proves clearly that I do not *identify* them.

G.R. Last question. The view that Marxism is doing rather badly today because it drank from the springs of the Enlightenment has dominated thought, whether we like it or not, since the seventies, if only because a number of individuals—intellectuals—known as the New Philosophers have vulgarized the theme. So, Marxism, we are told, is doing fairly badly.

M.F. I do not know if it is doing well or badly. It is an idea that has dominated thought, or philosophy; that is the formula I stop at, if you like. I think you are quite right to put the question, and to put it in that way. I would be inclined to say—I nearly stopped you there—that this view has not dominated thought so much as the "lower depths" of thought. But that would be facile. Uselessly polemical. And it is not really fair. I think we should recognize that in France, toward the fifties, there were two circuits of thought which, if not foreign to one another, were practically independent of one another. There was what I would call the "university circuit"—a circuit of scholarly thought—and then there was the circuit of open thought, or mainstream thought. When I say "mainstream," I do not necessarily mean poor quality. But a university book, a thesis, a course, and so on, were things you found in the academic presses, available to university readers. They scarcely had any influence except in universities. There was the special case of Bergson, that was exceptional. But from the end of the war onward—and no doubt existentialism played a part in this—we have seen ideas of profoundly academic origins, or roots (and the roots of Sartre, after all, are Husserl and Heidegger, who were hardly public dancers) addressed to a much broader public than that of the universities. Now, even though there is nobody of Sartre's stature to continue it, this phenomenon has become democratized. Only Sartre—or perhaps Sartre and Merleau-Ponty—could do it. But then it tended to become something within everybody's range, more or less, and for a certain number of reasons. First, there was the dislocation of the university, the growing number of students and professors, and so on, who came to constitute a kind of social mass; the dislocation of internal structures and a broadening of the university public; also the diffusion of culture (by no means a negative thing). The public's cultural level, on average, has really risen considerably; and, whatever one says, television has played a major role. People come to see that there is a new history, and so forth. Add to this all the political phenomena—the groups and movements half inside and half outside the universities. It all gave university activity an echo that reverberated widely beyond academic institutions or even groups of specialist, professional intellectuals. One remarkable phenomenon in France at the moment is the almost complete absence of specialized philosophy journals. Or they are more or less worthless. So when you want to write something, where do you publish? Where *can* you publish? In the end, you can only manage to slip something into one of the wide-circulation weeklies and general interest magazines. That is very significant. And so what happens—and what is fatal in such situations—is that a fairly evolved discourse, instead of being relayed by additional work which perfects it (either with criticism or amplification), rendering it more difficult and even finer, nowadays undergoes a process of amplification from the bottom up. Little by little, from the book to the review, to the newspaper article, and from the newspaper article to television, we come to summarize a work, or a problem, in terms of slogans. This passage of the philosophical question into the realm of the slogan, this transformation of the Marxist question, which becomes "Marxism is dead," is not the responsibility of any one person in particular, but we can see the slide whereby philosophical thought, or a philosophical issue, becomes a consumer item. In the past, there were two different circuits. Even if it could not avoid all the pitfalls, the institutional circuit, which had its drawbacks—it was closed, dogmatic, academic—nevertheless managed to sustain less heavy losses. The tendency to entropy was less, while nowadays entropy sets in at an alarming rate. I could give personal examples. It took fifteen years to convert my book about madness into a slogan: all mad people were confined in the eighteenth century. But it did not even take fifteen months—it only took three weeks—to convert my book on the will to know into a slogan "Sexuality has never been repressed." In my own experience, I have seen this entropy accelerate in a detestable way for philosophical thought. But it should be remembered that this means added responsibility for people who write.

G.R. I was tempted for a moment to say in conclusion—in the form of a question—not wanting to substitute one slogan for another: Is Marxism not finished, then? In the sense that you say in *The Archaeology of Knowledge* that a "nonfalsified Marxism would help us to formulate a general theory of discontinuity, series, limits, unities, specific orders, autonomies and differentiated dependencies."

M.F. Yes. I am reluctant to make assessments about the type of culture that may be in store. Everything is present, you see, at least as a virtual object, inside a given culture. Or everything that has already featured once. The problem of objects that have never featured in the culture is another matter. But it is part of the function of memory and culture to be able to reactualize any objects whatever that have already been featured. Repetition is always possible, repetition with application, transformation. God knows in 1945 Nietzsche appeared to be completely disqualified. It is clear, even if one admits that Marx will disappear for now, that he will reappear one day. What I wish for—and it is here that my formulation has changed in relation to the one you cited—is not so much the defalsification and restitution of a true Marx but the unburdening and liberation of Marx in relation to party dogma, which has constrained it, touted it, and brandished it for so long. The phrase "Marx is dead" can be given a conjunctural sense. One can say it is relatively true, but to say that Marx will disappear like that . . .

G.R.   But does this reference in *The Archaeology of Knowledge* mean that, in a certain way, Marx is at work in your own methodology?

M.F.   Yes, absolutely. You see, given the period in which I wrote those books, it was good form (in order to be viewed favorably by the institutional Left) to cite Marx in the footnotes. So I was careful to steer clear of that. But I could dredge up—which is of no interest—quite a few passages I wrote referring to Marx, and Marx would not have been that author, functioning that way in French culture, with such a political surcharge. That is the Marx I would have cited at the bottom of the page. I didn't do it: to have some fun, and to set a trap for those among the Marxists who have tacked me to those sentences. That was part of the game.

Notes

1.   The exact quotation can be found in transcript of the proceedings at Vincennes, December 1969, published in *Le Magazine littéraire* 121 (Feb. 1977): "What you as a revolutionary aspire to is a master. You will have one." [See "Impromptu at Vincennes," *October* 40 (Spring 1987); p. 121.—Ed.]

2.   See Vincent Descombes, *Le Même et l'Autre: quarante-cinq ans de philosophie française* (Paris: Minuit, 1979); "In fact, when one looks at things a bit more closely, one turns out to be in a plural world, in which phenomena appear out of alignment and produce somewhat unforeseen encounters. Take Freudianism-Marxism."

3.   See Gérard Raulet, *Materiellen zur Kritischen Theorie* (Frankfurt: Suhrkamp Verlag, 1982).

4.   Jean-Paul Sartre, *La Légende de la vérité* [1929], a fragment of which was first published in *Bifur* 8 (June 1931), pp. 77–96.

5.   Jean Baudrillard, *Oublier Foucault* (Paris: Galilée, 1977) [*Forget Foucault*, trans. N. Defresne (New York: Semiotext[e], 1987), pp. 7–64].

6.   See Alexander Schubert, *Die Decodierung des Menschen* (Frankfurt: Focus, 1981).

7.   This took place in 1981.–Ed.

8.   *Section française de l'internationale ouvrière.*–Ed.

9.   This took place in 1979.–Ed.

ON THE GENEALOGY OF ETHICS: AN OVERVIEW OF WORK IN PROGRESS

HISTORY OF THE PROJECT

Q. The first volume of *The History of Sexuality* was published in 1976, and none has appeared since. Do you still think that understanding sexuality is central for understanding who we are?

M.F. I must confess that I am much more interested in problems about techniques of the self and things like that than sex . . . sex is boring.

Q. It sounds like the Greeks were not too interested either.

M.F. No, they were not much interested in sex. It was not a great issue. Compare, for instance, what they say about the place of food and diet. I think it is very, very interesting to see the move, the very slow move, from the privileging of food, which was overwhelming in Greece, to interest in sex. Food was still much more important during the early Christian days than sex. For instance, in the rules for monks, the problem was food, food, food. Then you can see a very slow shift during the Middle Ages, when they were in a kind of equilibrium . . . and after the seventeenth century it was sex.

Q. Yet Volume Two of *The History of Sexuality*, *L'Usage des plaisirs* [*The Uses of Pleasure*], is concerned almost exclusively with, not to put too fine a point on it, sex.

M.F. Yes. One of the numerous reasons I had so much trouble with that book was that I first wrote a book about sex, which I put aside. Then I wrote a book about the self and the techniques of the self; sex disappeared, and for the third

The following is the result of a series of working sessions with Michel Foucault conducted by Paul Rabinow and Hubert Dreyfus at Berkeley in April 1983. Although we have retained the interview form, the material was jointly reedited. Foucault generously allowed the interviewers to publish these preliminary formulations, which were the product of oral interviews and free conversations in English and therefore lack the precision and supporting scholarship found in Foucault's written texts.

time I was obliged to rewrite a book in which I tried to keep the equilibrium between one and the other.

You see, what I wanted to do in Volume Two of *The History of Sexuality* was to show that you have nearly the same restrictive, the same prohibitive code in the fourth century B.C. and in the moralists and doctors at the beginning of the empire. But I think that the way they integrate those prohibitions in relation to oneself is completely different. I don't think one can find any normalization in, for instance, the Stoic ethics. The reason is, I think, that the principal aim, the principal target of this kind of ethics, was an aesthetic one. First, this kind of ethics was only a problem of personal choice. Second, it was reserved for a few people in the population; it was not a question of giving a pattern of behavior for everybody. It was a personal choice for a small elite. The reason for making this choice was the will to live a beautiful life, and to leave to others memories of a beautiful existence. I don't think that we can say that this kind of ethics was an attempt to normalize the population.

The continuity of the themes of this ethics is something very striking, but I think that behind, below this continuity, there were some changes, which I have tried to acknowledge.

Q. So the equilibrium in your work has shifted from sex to techniques of the self?

M.F. I wondered what the technology of the self before Christianity was, or where the Christian technology of the self came from, and what kind of sexual ethics was characteristic of the ancient culture. And then I was obliged after I finished *Les Aveux de la chair* ["Confessions of the Flesh," as yet unpublished], the book about Christianity, to reexamine what I said in the introduction to *L'Usage des plaisirs* about the supposed pagan ethics, because what I had said about pagan ethics were only clichés borrowed from secondary texts. And then I discovered, first, that this pagan ethics was not at all liberal, tolerant, and so on, as it was supposed to be; second, that most of the themes of Christian austerity were very clearly present nearly from the beginning, but that also in pagan culture the main problem was not the rules for austerity but much more the techniques of the self.

Reading Seneca, Plutarch, and all those people, I discovered that there were a very great number of problems or themes about the self, the ethics of the self, the technology of the self, and I had the idea of writing a book composed of a set of separate studies, papers about such and such aspects of ancient, pagan technologies of the self.

Q. What is the title?

M.F. *Le Souci de soi* [*The Care of the Self*]. So in the series about sexuality: the first one is *L'Usage des plaisirs,* and in this book there is a chapter about the technology of the self, since I think it's not possible to understand clearly what Greek sexual ethics was without relating it to this technology of the self. Then, a second volume in the same sex series, *Les Aveux de la chair,* deals with Christian technologies of the self. And then, *Le Souci de soi,* a book separate from the sex series, is composed of different papers about the self—for instance, a commentary on Plato's *Alcibiades* in which you find the first elaboration of the notion of *epimeleia heautou,* "care of the self," about the role of reading and writing in constituting the self, maybe the problem of the medical experience of the self, and so on. . . .

Q. And what will come next? Will there be more on the Christians when you finish these three?

M.F. Well, I am going to take care of myself! . . . I have more than a draft of a book about sexual ethics in the sixteenth century, in which also the problem of the techniques of the self, self-examination, the cure of souls, is very important, both in the Protestant and Catholic churches.

What strikes me is that in Greek ethics people were concerned with their moral conduct, their ethics, their relations to themselves and to others much more than with religious problems. For instance, what happens to us after death? What are the gods? Do they intervene or not?—these are very, very unimportant problems for them, and they are not directly related to ethics, to conduct. The second thing is that ethics was not related to any social—or at least to any legal—institutional system. For instance, the laws against sexual misbehavior were very few and not very compelling. The third thing is that what they were worried about, their theme was to constitute a kind of ethics which was an aesthetics of existence.

Well, I wonder if our problem nowadays is not, in a way, similar to this one, since most of us no longer believe that ethics is founded in religion, nor do we want a legal system to intervene in our moral, personal, private life. Recent liberation movements suffer from the fact that they cannot find any principle on which to base the elaboration of a new ethics. They need an ethics, but they cannot find any other ethics than an ethics founded on so-called scientific knowledge of what the self is, what desire is, what the unconscious is, and so on. I am struck by this similarity of problems.

Q. Do you think that the Greeks offer an attractive and plausible alternative?

M.F. No! I am not looking for an alternative; you can't find the solution of a problem in the solution of another problem raised at another moment by other people. You see, what I want to do is not the history of solutions—and that's the reason why I don't accept the word *alternative.* I would like to do the genealogy of problems, of *problématiques.* My point is not that everything is bad, but that everything is dangerous, which is not exactly the same as bad. If everything is dangerous, then we always have something to do. So my position leads not to apathy but to a hyper- and pessimistic activism.

I think that the ethico-political choice we have to make every day is to determine which is the main danger. Take as an example Robert Castel's analysis of the history of the antipsychiatry movement [*La Gestion des risques*]. I agree completely with what Castel says, but that does not mean, as some people suppose, that the mental hospitals were better than antipsychiatry; that does not mean that we were not right to criticize those mental hospitals. I think it was good to do that, because *they* were the danger. And now it's quite clear that the danger has changed. For instance, in Italy they have closed all the mental hospitals, and there are more free clinics, and so on—and they have new problems.

Q. Isn't it logical, given these concerns, that you should be writing a genealogy of biopower?

M.F. I have no time for that now, but it could be done. In fact, I have to do it.

WHY THE ANCIENT WORLD WAS NOT A GOLDEN AGE, BUT WHAT WE CAN LEARN FROM IT ANYWAY

Q. So Greek life may not have been altogether perfect; still, it seems an attractive alternative to endless Christian self-analysis.

M.F. The Greek ethics were linked to a purely virile society with slaves, in which the women were underdogs whose pleasure had no importance, whose sexual life had only to be oriented toward, determined by, their status as wives, and so on.

Q. So the women were dominated, but surely homosexual love was better than now?

M.F. It might look that way. Since there is an important and large literature about loving boys in Greek culture, some historians say, "Well, that's the proof that they loved boys." But I say that proves that loving boys was a problem. Because if there were no problem, they would speak of this kind of love in the same terms as love between men and women. The problem was that they couldn't accept that a young boy who was supposed to become a free citizen could be dominated and used as an object for someone's pleasure. A woman, a slave, could be passive: such was their nature, their status. All this reflection, philosophizing about the love of boys—with always the same conclusion: please, don't treat a boy as a woman—is proof that they could not integrate this real practice in the framework of their social selves.

You can see through a reading of Plutarch how they couldn't even imagine reciprocity of pleasure between a boy and a man. If Plutarch finds problems in loving boys, it is not at all in the sense that loving boys was antinatural or something like that. He says, "It's not possible that there could be any reciprocity in the physical relations between a boy and a man."

Q. There seems to be an aspect of Greek culture that we are told about in Aristotle, that you don't talk about, but that seems very important—friendship. In classical literature, friendship is the locus of mutual recognition. It's not traditionally seen as the highest virtue, but both in Aristotle and in Cicero, you could read it as really being the highest virtue because it's selfless and enduring, it's not easily bought, it doesn't deny the utility and pleasure of the world, but yet it seeks something more.

M.F. But don't forget *L'Usage des plaisirs* is a book about sexual ethics; it's not a book about love, or about friendship, or about reciprocity. And it's very significant that when Plato tries to integrate love for boys and friendship, he is obliged to put aside sexual relations. Friendship is reciprocal, and sexual relations are not reciprocal: in sexual relations, you can penetrate or you are penetrated. I agree completely with what you say about friendship, but I think it confirms what I say about Greek sexual ethics: if you have friendship, it is difficult to have sexual relations. If you look at Plato, reciprocity is very important in a friendship, but you can't find it on the physical level; one of the reasons why they needed a philosophical elaboration in order to justify this kind of love was that they could not accept a physical reciprocity. You find in Xenophon, in the *Banquet,* Socrates saying that between a man and a boy it is obvious that the boy is only the spectator of the man's pleasure. What they say about this beautiful love of boys implies that the pleasure of the boy was not to be taken into account; moreover, that it was dishonorable for the boy to feel any kind of physical pleasure in a relation with a man.

What I want to ask is: Are we able to have an ethics of acts and their pleasures which would be able to take into account the pleasure of the other? Is the pleasure of the other something that can be integrated in our pleasure, without reference either to law, to marriage, to I don't know what?

Q. It looks like nonreciprocity was a problem for the Greeks all right, but it seems to be the kind of problem that one could straighten out. Why does sex have to be virile? Why couldn't women's pleasure and boys' pleasure be taken account of without any big change to the general framework? Or is it that it's not just a little problem, because if you try to bring in the pleasure of the other, the whole hierarchical, ethical system would break down?

M.F. That's right. The Greek ethics of pleasure is linked to a virile society, to dissymmetry, exclusion of the other, an obsession with penetration, and a kind of threat of being dispossessed of your own energy, and so on. All that is quite disgusting!

Q. OK, granted that sexual relations were both nonreciprocal and a cause of worry for the Greeks, at least pleasure itself seems unproblematic for them.

M.F. Well, in *L'Usage des plaisirs* I try to show, for instance, that there is a growing tension between pleasure and health. When you take the physicians and all the concern with diet, you see first that the main themes are very similar during several centuries. But the idea that sex has its dangers is much stronger in the second century A.D. than in the fourth century B.C. I think that you can show that, for Hippocrates, the sexual act was already dangerous, so you had to be very careful with it and not have sex all the time, only in certain seasons and so on. But in the first and second centuries it seems that, for a physician, the sexual act is much closer to *pathos*. And I think the main shift is this one: that in the fourth century B.C., the sexual act was an activity, and for the Christians it is a passivity. You have a very interesting analysis by Augustine which is, I think, quite typical concerning the problem of erection. The erection was, for the Greek of the fourth century, the sign of activity, the main activity. But since, for Augustine and the Christians, the erection is not something voluntary, it is a sign of a passivity—it is a punishment for the first sin.

Q. So the Greeks were more concerned with health than with pleasure?

M.F. Yes, about what the Greeks had to eat in order to be in good health, we have thousands of pages. And there are comparatively few things about what to do when you have sex with someone. Concerning food, it was the relation between the climate, the seasons, the humidity or dryness of the air and the dryness of the food, and so on. There are very few things about the way they had to cook it; much more about these qualities. It's not a cooking art; it's a matter of choosing.

Q. So, despite the German Hellenists, classical Greece was not a golden age. Yet surely we can learn something from it?

M.F. I think there is no exemplary value in a period that is not our period . . . it is not anything to get back to. But we do have an example of an ethical experience which implied a very strong connection between pleasure and desire. If we compare that to our experience now, where everybody—the philosopher or the psychoanalyst—explains that what is important is desire, and pleasure is nothing at all, we can wonder whether this disconnection wasn't a historical event, one that was not at all necessary, not linked to human nature, or to any anthropological necessity.

Q. But you already illustrated that in *The History of Sexuality* by contrasting our science of sexuality with the oriental *ars erotica*.

M.F. One of the numerous points where I was wrong in that book was what I said about this *ars erotica*. I should have opposed our science of sex to a contrasting practice in our own culture. The Greeks and Romans did not have any *ars erotica* to be compared with the Chinese *ars erotica* (or at least it was not something very important in their culture). They had a *tekhnē tou biou* in which the economy of pleasure played a very large role. In this "art of life," the notion of exercising a perfect mastery over oneself soon became the main issue. And the Christian hermeneutics of the self constituted a new elaboration of this *tekhnē*.

Q. But, after all you have told us about nonreciprocity and obsession with health, what can we learn from this third possibility?

M.F. What I want to show is that the general Greek problem was not the *tekhnē* of the self, it was the *tekhnē* of life, the *tekhnē tou biou*, how to live. It's quite clear from Socrates to Seneca or Pliny, for instance, that they didn't worry about the afterlife, what happened after death, or whether God exists or not. That was not really a great problem for them; the problem was: Which *tekhnē* do I have to use in order to live well as I ought to live? And I think that one of the main evolutions in ancient culture has been that this *tekhnē tou biou* became more and more a *tekhnē* of the self. A Greek citizen of the fifth or fourth century would have felt that his *tekhnē* for life was to take care of the city, of his companions. But for Seneca, for instance, the problem is to take care of himself.

With Plato's *Alcibiades*, it's very clear: you have to take care of yourself because you have to rule the city. But taking care of yourself for its own sake starts with the Epicureans—it becomes something very general with Seneca, Pliny, and so on: everybody has to take care of himself. Greek ethics is centered on a problem of personal choice, of the aesthetics of existence.

The idea of the *bios* as a material for an aesthetic piece of art is something that fascinates me. The idea also that ethics can be a very strong structure of existence, without any relation with the juridical per se, with an authoritarian system, with a disciplinary structure. All that is very interesting.

Q. How, then, did the Greeks deal with deviance?

M.F. The great difference in sexual ethics for the Greeks was not between people who prefer women or boys or have sex in this way or another, but was a question of quantity and of activity and passivity. Are you a slave of your own desires or their master?

Q. What about someone who had sex so much he damaged his health?

M.F. That's hubris, that's excess. The problem is not one of deviancy but of excess or moderation.

Q. What did they do with these people?

M.F. They were considered ugly; they had a bad reputation.

Q. They didn't try to cure or reform such people?

M.F. There were exercises in order to make one master of oneself. For Epictetus, you had to be able to look at a beautiful girl or a beautiful boy without having any desire for her or him. You have to master yourself completely.

Sexual austerity in Greek society was a trend or movement, a philosophical movement coming from very cultivated people in order to give to their life much more intensity, much more beauty. In a way, it's the same in the twentieth century when people, in order to get a more beautiful life, tried to get rid of all the sexual repression of their society, of their childhood. Gide in Greece would have been an austere philosopher.

Q. In the name of a beautiful life they were austere, and now in the name of psychological science we seek self-fulfillment.

M.F. Exactly. My idea is that it's not at all necessary to relate ethical problems to scientific knowledge. Among the cultural inventions of mankind there is a treasury of devices, techniques, ideas, procedures, and so on, that cannot exactly be reactivated but at least constitute, or help to constitute, a certain point of view which can be very useful as a tool for analyzing what's going on now—and to change it.

We don't have to choose between our world and the Greek world. But since we can see very well that some of the main principles of our ethics have been related at a certain moment to an aesthetics of existence, I think that this kind of historical analysis can be useful. For centuries we have been convinced that between our ethics, our personal ethics, our everyday life, and the great political and social and economic structures, there were analytical relations, and that we couldn't change anything, for instance, in our sex life or our family life, without ruining our economy, our democracy, and so on. I think we have to get rid of this idea of an analytical or necessary link between ethics and other social or economic or political structures.

Q. So what kind of ethics can we build now, when we know that between ethics and other structures there are only historical coagulations and not a necessary relation?

M.F. What strikes me is the fact that, in our society, art has become something that is related only to objects and not to individuals or to life. That art is something which is specialized or done by experts who are artists. But couldn't everyone's life become a work of art? Why should the lamp or the house be an art object but not our life?

Q. Of course, that kind of project is very common in places like Berkeley where people think that everything from the way they eat breakfast, to the way they have sex, to the way they spend their day, should itself be perfected.

M.F. But I am afraid in most of those cases, most of the people think if they do what they do, if they live as they live, the reason is that they know the truth about desire, life, nature, body, and so on.

Q. But if one is to create oneself without recourse to knowledge or universal rules, how does your view differ from Sartrean existentialism?

M.F. I think that from the theoretical point of view, Sartre avoids the idea of the self as something that is given to us, but through the moral notion of authenticity, he turns back to the idea that we have to be ourselves—to be truly our true self. I think that the only acceptable practical consequence of what

Sartre has said is to link his theoretical insight to the practice of creativity—and not that of authenticity. From the idea that the self is not given to us, I think that there is only one practical consequence: we have to create ourselves as a work of art. In his analyses of Baudelaire, Flaubert, and so on, it is interesting to see that Sartre refers the work of creation to a certain relation to oneself—the author to himself—which has the form of authenticity or inauthenticity. I would like to say exactly the contrary: we should not have to refer the creative activity of somebody to the kind of relation he has to himself, but should relate the kind of relation one has to oneself to a creative activity.

Q. That sounds like Nietzsche's observation in *The Gay Science* that one should create one's life by giving style to it through long practice and daily work [no. 290].

M.F. Yes. My view is much closer to Nietzsche's than to Sartre's.

THE STRUCTURE OF GENEALOGICAL INTERPRETATION

Q. How do the next two books after *The History of Sexuality*, Volume One, *L'Usage des plaisirs* and *Les Aveux de la chair*, fit into the structure of your genealogy project?

M.F. Three domains of genealogy are possible. First, a historical ontology of ourselves in relation to truth through which we constitute ourselves as subjects of knowledge; second, a historical ontology of ourselves in relation to a field of power through which we constitute ourselves as subjects acting on others; third, a historical ontology in relation to ethics through which we constitute ourselves as moral agents.

So, three axes are possible for genealogy. All three were present, albeit in a somewhat confused fashion, in *Madness and Civilization*. The truth axis was studied in *The Birth of the Clinic* and *The Order of Things*. The power axis was studied in *Discipline and Punish*, and the ethical axis in *The History of Sexuality*.

The general framework of the book about sex is a history of morals. I think, in general, we have to distinguish, where the history of morals is concerned, acts and moral code. The acts [*conduites*] are the real behavior of people in relation to the moral code [*prescriptions*] imposed on them. I think we have to distinguish between the code that determines which acts are permitted or forbidden and the code that determines the positive or negative value of the different possible behaviors—you're not allowed to have sex with anyone but your wife, that's an element of the code. And there is another side to the moral prescriptions, which most of the time is not isolated as such but is, I think, very important: the kind of relationship you ought to have with yourself, *rapport à soi,* which I call ethics, and which determines how the individual is supposed to constitute himself as a moral subject of his own actions.

This relationship to oneself has four major aspects. The first aspect answers the question: Which is the aspect or the part of myself or my behavior which is concerned with moral conduct? For instance, you can say, in general, that in our society the main field of morality, the part of ourselves which is most relevant for morality, is our feelings. (You can have a girl in the street or anywhere, if you have very good feelings toward your wife.) Well, it's quite clear that from the Kantian point of view, intention is much more important than feelings. And from the Christian point of view, it is desire—well, we could discuss that, because in the Middle Ages it was not the same as the seventeenth century. . . .

Q. But, roughly, for the Christians it was desire, for Kant it was intentions, and for us now it's feelings?

M.F. Well, you can say something like that. It's not always the same part of ourselves, or of our behavior, which is relevant for ethical judgment. That's the aspect I call the ethical substance [*substance éthique*].

Q. The ethical substance is like the material that's going to be worked over by ethics?

M.F. Yes, that's it. And, for instance, when I describe the *aphrodisia* in *L'Usage des plaisirs,* it is to show that the part of sexual behavior which is relevant in Greek ethics is something different from concupiscence, from flesh. For the Greeks, the ethical substance was acts linked to pleasure and desire in their unity. And it is very different from flesh, Christian flesh. Sexuality is a third kind of ethical substance.

Q. What is the difference ethically between flesh and sexuality?

M.F. I cannot answer because all that can only be analyzed through a precise inquiry. Before I studied Greek or Greco-Roman ethics, I couldn't answer the question: What exactly is the ethical substance of Greco-Roman ethics? Now I think that I know, through the analysis of what they mean by *aphrodisia*, what the Greek ethical substance was.

For the Greeks, when a philosopher was in love with a boy, but did not touch him, his behavior was valued. The problem was: Does he touch the boy or not? That's the ethical substance: the act linked with pleasure and desire. For Augustine, it's very clear that when he remembers his relationship to his young friend when he was eighteen years old, what bothers him is what exactly was the kind of desire he had for him. So you see that the ethical substance has changed.

The second aspect is what I call the mode of subjectivation [*mode d'assujettissement*], that is, the way in which people are invited or incited to recognize their moral obligations. Is it, for instance, divine law that has been revealed in a text? Is it natural law, a cosmological order, in each case the same for every living being? Is it a rational rule? Is it the attempt to give your existence the most beautiful form possible?

Q. When you say "rational," do you mean scientific?

M.F. No, Kantian, universal. You can see, for instance, in the Stoics, how they move slowly from an idea of an aesthetics of existence to the idea that we must do such and such things because we are rational beings—as members of the human community, we must do them. For example, you find in Isocrates a very interesting discourse, which is supposed to be held with Nicocles, who was the ruler of Cyprus. There he explains why he has always been faithful to his wife: "Because I am the king, and because as somebody who commands others, who rules others, I have to show that I am able to rule myself." And you can see that this rule of faithfulness has nothing to do with the universal and Stoic formulation: "I have to be faithful to my wife because I am a human and rational being." In the former case, it is because I am the king! And you can see that the way the same rule is accepted by Nicocles and by a Stoic is quite different. And that's what I call the *mode d'assujettissement*, the second aspect of ethics.

Q. When the king says, "because I am the king," is that a form of the beautiful life?

M.F. Both aesthetic and political, which were directly linked. Because if I want people to accept me as a king, I must have a kind of glory which will survive me, and this glory cannot be dissociated from aesthetic value. So political power, glory, immortality, and beauty are all linked at a certain moment. That's the *mode d'assujettissement*, the second aspect of ethics.

The third one is: What are the means by which we can change ourselves in order to become ethical subjects?

Q. How we work on this ethical substance?

M.F. Yes. What are we to do, either to moderate our acts, or to decipher what we are, or to eradicate our desires, or to use our sexual desire in order to obtain certain aims such as having children, and so on—all this elaboration of ourselves in order to behave ethically? In order to be faithful to your wife, you can do different things to the self. That's the third aspect, which I call the self-forming activity [*pratique de soi*] or *l'ascétisme*—asceticism in a very broad sense.

The fourth aspect is: Which is the kind of being to which we aspire when we behave in a moral way? For instance, shall we become pure, or immortal, or free, or masters of ourselves, and so on? So that's what I call the telos [*téléologie*]. In what we call morals, there is the effective behavior of people, there are the codes, and there is this kind of relationship to oneself with the above four aspects.

Q. Which are all independent?

M.F. There are both relationships between them and a certain kind of independence. For instance, you can very well understand why, if the goal is an absolute purity of being, then the type of techniques of self-forming activity, the techniques of asceticism you are to use, are not exactly the same as when you try to be master of your own behavior. In the first place, you are inclined to a kind of deciphering technique, or purification technique.

Now, if we apply this general framework to pagan or early Christian ethics, what would we say? First, if we take the code—what is forbidden and what is not—you see that, at least in the philosophical code of behavior, you find three main prohibitions or prescriptions. One about the body—that is, you have to be very careful with your sexual behavior since it is very costly, so do it as infrequently as possible. The second is: When you are married, please don't have sex with anybody else but your wife. And with boys—please don't touch boys. And you find this in Plato, in Isocrates, in Hippocrates, in late Stoics, and so on—and you find it also in Christianity, and even in our own society. So I think you can say that the codes in themselves didn't change a great deal. Some of those interdictions changed; some of the prohibitions are much stricter and much more rigorous in Christianity than in the Greek period. But the themes are the same. So I think that the great changes that occurred between Greek society, Greek ethics, Greek morality, and how the Christians viewed themselves are not in the code but in what I call the "ethics," which is the relation to oneself. In *L'Usage des plaisirs,* I analyze those four aspects of the relation to oneself, through the three austerity themes of the code: health, wives or women, and boys.

Q. Would it be fair to say that you're not doing the genealogy of morals because you think the moral codes are relatively stable, but that what you're doing is a genealogy of ethics?

M.F. Yes, I'm writing a genealogy of ethics. The genealogy of the subject as a subject of ethical actions, or the genealogy of desire as an ethical problem. So, if we take ethics in classical Greek philosophy or medicine, what is the ethical substance? It is the *aphrodisia,* which are at the same time acts, desire, and pleasure. What is the *mode d'assujettissement?* It is that we have to build our existence as a beautiful existence; it is an aesthetic mode. You see, what I tried to show is that nobody is obliged in classical ethics to behave in such a way as to be truthful to their wives, to not touch boys, and so on. But if they want to have a beautiful existence, if they want to have a good reputation, if they want to be able to rule others, they have to do this. So they accept those obligations in a conscious way for the beauty or glory of existence. The choice, the aesthetic choice or the political choice, for which they decide to accept this kind of existence—that's the *mode d'assujettissement.* It's a choice, it's a personal choice.

In late Stoicism, when they start saying, "Well, you are obliged to do that because you are a human being," something changes. It's not a problem of choice; you have to do it because you are a rational being. The *mode d'assujettissement* is changing.

In Christianity, what is very interesting is that the sexual rules for behavior were, of course, justified through religion. The institutions by which they were imposed were religious institutions. But the form of the obligation was a legal form. There was a kind of the internal juridification of religious law inside Christianity. For instance, all the casuistic practice was typically a juridical practice.

Q. After the Enlightenment, though, when the religious drops out, is the juridical what's left?

M.F. Yes, after the eighteenth century, the religious framework of those rules disappears in part, and then between a medical or scientific approach and a juridical framework there was competition, with no resolution.

Q. Could you sum this up?

M.F. Well, the *substance éthique* for the Greeks was the *aphrodisia;* the *mode d'assujettissement* was a politico-aesthetic choice; the *form d'ascèse* was the *tekhnē* that was used—and there we find, for example, the *tekhnē* about the body, or economics as the rules by which you define your role as husband, or the erotic as a kind of asceticism toward oneself in loving boys, and so on—and the *téléologie* was the mastery of oneself. So that's the situation I describe in the two first parts of *L'Usage des plaisirs.*

Then there is a shift within this ethics. The reason for the shift is the change of the role of men within society, both in their homes toward their wives and also in the political field, since the city disappears. So, for those reasons, the way they can recognize themselves as subjects of political, economic behavior changes. We can say roughly that along with these sociological changes something is changing also in classical ethics—that is, in the elaboration of the relationship to oneself. But I think that the change doesn't affect the ethical substance: it is still *aphrodisia*. There are some changes in the *mode d'assujettissement*, for instance, when the Stoics recognize themselves as universal beings. And there are also very important changes in the *asceticism*, the kind of techniques you use in order to recognize, to constitute yourself as a subject of ethics. And also a change in the goal. I think that the difference is that in the classical perspective, to be master of oneself meant, first, taking into account only oneself and not the other, because to be master of oneself meant that you were able to rule others. So the mastery of oneself was directly related to a dissymmetrical relation to others. You should be master of yourself in a sense of activity, dissymmetry, and nonreciprocity.

Later on, due to the changes in marriage, society, and so on, mastery of oneself is something that is not primarily related to power over others: you have to be master of yourself not only in order to rule others, as it was in the case of Alcibiades or Nicocles, but you have to be master of yourself because you are a rational being. And in this mastery of yourself, you are related to other people, who are also masters of themselves. And this new kind of relation to the other is much less nonreciprocal than before.

So those are the changes, and I try to show those changes in the three last chapters, the fourth part of *L'Usage des plaisirs*. I take the same themes—the body, wives or women, and boys—and I show that these same three austerity themes are linked to a partially new ethics. I say "partially" because some of the parts of this ethics do not change: for instance, the *aphrodisia*. On the other hand, others do: for instance, the techniques. According to Xenophon, the way to become a good husband is to know exactly what your role is inside your home or outside, what kind of authority you have to exercise on your wife, what are your expectations of your wife's behavior, and so on. All this calculation gives you the rules for behavior, and defines the way you have to be toward yourself. But for Epictetus, or for Seneca, for instance, in order to be really master of yourself, you don't have to know what your role in society or in your home is, but you do have to do some exercises like depriving yourself of eating for two or three days, in order to be sure that you can control yourself. If one day you are in prison, you won't suffer from being deprived of food, and so on. And you have to do that for all the pleasures—that's a kind of asceticism you can't find in Plato or Socrates or Aristotle.

There is no complete and identical relation between the techniques and the *telē*. You can find the same techniques in different *telē*, but there are privileged relations, some privileged techniques related to each telos.

In the Christian book—I mean the book about Christianity!—I try to show that all this ethics has changed. Because the telos has changed: the telos is immortality, purity, and so on. The asceticism has changed, because now self-examination takes the form of self-deciphering. The *mode d'assujettissement* is now divine law. And I think that even the ethical substance has changed, because it is not *aphrodisia*, but desire, concupiscence, flesh, and so on.

Q. It seems, then, that we have a grid of intelligibility for desire as an ethical problem?

M.F. Yes, we now have this scheme. If, by sexual behavior, we understand the three poles—acts, pleasure, and desire—we have the Greek "formula," which is the same at the first and at the second stage. In this Greek formula what is underscored is "acts," with pleasure and desire as subsidiary: *acte*—*plaisir*—[*désir*]. I have put desire in brackets because I think that in the Stoic ethics you start a kind of elision of desire; desire begins to be condemned.

The Chinese "formula" would be *plaisir*—*désir*—[*acte*]. Acts are put aside because you have to restrain acts in order to get the maximum duration and intensity of pleasure.

The Christian "formula" puts an accent on desire and tries to eradicate it. Acts have to become something neutral; you have to act only to produce chil-

dren or to fulfill your conjugal duty. And pleasure is both practically and theoretically excluded: [*désir*]—*acte*—[*plaisir*]. Desire is practically excluded—you
have to eradicate your desire—but theoretically very important.

And I could say that the modern "formula" is desire, which is theoretically
underlined and practically accepted, since you have to liberate your own desire.
Acts are not very important, and pleasure—nobody knows what it is!

FROM THE CLASSICAL SELF TO THE MODERN SUBJECT

Q. What is the care of the self which you have decided to treat separately in *Le
Souci de soi?*

M.F. What interests me in the Hellenistic culture, in the Greco-Roman culture, starting from about the third century B.C. and continuing until the second
or third century after Christ, is a precept for which the Greeks had a specific
word, *epimeleia heautou*, which means taking care of one's self. It does not mean
simply being interested in oneself, nor does it mean having a certain tendency to
self-attachment or self-fascination. *Epimeleia heautou* is a very powerful word
in Greek which means "working on" or "being concerned with" something. For
example, Xenophon used *epimeleia heautou* to describe agricultural management. The responsibility of a monarch for his fellow citizens was also *epimeleia
heautou*. That which a doctor does in the course of caring for a patient is
epimeleia heautou. It is therefore a very powerful word; it describes a sort of
work, an activity; it implies attention, knowledge, technique.

Q. But isn't the application of knowledge and technology to the self a modern invention?

M.F. Knowledge played a different role in the classical care of the self. There
are very interesting things to analyze about relations between scientific knowledge and the *epimeleia heautou*. The one who cared for himself had to choose
among all the things that you can know through scientific knowledge only those
kinds of things which were relative to him and important to life.

Q. So theoretical understanding, scientific understanding, was secondary to,
and guided by, ethical and aesthetic concerns?

M.F. Their problem and their discussion concerned what limited sorts of
knowledge were useful for *epimeleia*. For instance, for the Epicureans, the general knowledge of what is the world, of what is the necessity of the world, the
relation between world, necessity, and the gods—all that was very important
for the care of the self. Because it was first a matter of meditation: if you were
able exactly to understand the necessity of the world, then you could master

passions in a much better way, and so on. So, for the Epicureans, there was a kind of adequation between all possible knowledge and the care of the self. The reason that one had to become familiar with physics or cosmology was that one had to take care of the self. For the Stoics, the true self is defined only by what I can be master of.

Q. So knowledge is subordinated to the practical end of mastery?

M.F. Epictetus is very clear on that. He gives as an exercise to walk every morning in the streets looking, watching. And if you meet a consular figure you say, "Is the consul something I can master?" No, so I have nothing to do. If I meet a beautiful girl or beautiful boy, is their beauty, their desirability, something that depends on me, and so on? For the Christians, things are quite different; for Christians, the possibility that Satan can get inside your soul and give you thoughts you cannot recognize as satanic, but might interpret as coming from God, leads to uncertainty about what is going on inside your soul. You are unable to know what the real root of your desire is, at least without hermeneutic work.

Q. So, to what extent did the Christians develop new techniques of self-mastery?

M.F. What interests me about the classical concept of care of the self is that we see here the birth and development of a certain number of ascetic themes ordinarily attributed to Christianity. Christianity is usually given credit for replacing the generally tolerant Greco-Roman lifestyle with an austere lifestyle marked by a series of renunciations, interdictions, or prohibitions. Now, we can see that in this activity of the self on itself, the ancients developed a whole series of austerity practices that the Christians later directly borrowed from them. So we see that this activity became linked to a certain sexual austerity that was subsumed directly into the Christian ethic. We are not talking about a moral rupture between tolerant antiquity and austere Christianity.

Q. In the name of what does one choose to impose this lifestyle upon oneself?

M.F. In antiquity, this work on the self with its attendant austerity is not imposed on the individual by means of civil law or religious obligation, but is a choice about existence made by the individual. People decide for themselves whether or not to care for themselves.

I don't think it is to attain eternal life after death, because they were not particularly concerned with that. Rather, they acted so as to give to their life certain values (reproduce certain examples, leave behind them an exalted reputation, give the maximum possible brilliance to their lives). It was a question of making one's life into an object for a sort of knowledge, for a *tekhnē*—for an art.

We have hardly any remnant of the idea in our society that the principal work of art which one must take care of, the main area to which one must apply aesthetic values, is oneself, one's life, one's existence. We find this in the Renaissance, but in a slightly academic form, and yet again in nineteenth-century dandyism, but those were only episodes.

Q. But isn't the Greek concern with the self just an early version of our self-absorption, which many consider a central problem in our society?

M.F. You have a certain number of themes—and I don't say that you have to reutilize them in this way—which indicate to you that in a culture to which we owe a certain number of our most important constant moral elements, there was a practice of the self, a conception of the self, very different from our present culture of the self. In the Californian cult of the self, one is supposed to discover one's true self, to separate it from that which might obscure or alienate it, to decipher its truth thanks to psychological or psychoanalytic science, which is supposed to be able to tell you what your true self is. Therefore, not only do I not identify this ancient culture of the self with what you might call the Californian cult of the self, I think they are diametrically opposed.

What happened in between is precisely an overtuning of the classical culture of the self. This took place when Christianity substituted the idea of a self that one had to renounce, because clinging to the self was opposed to God's will, for the idea of a self that had to be created as a work of art.

Q. We know that one of the studies for *Le Souci de soi* concerns the role of writing in the formation of the self. How is the question of the relation of writing and the self posed by Plato?

M.F. First, to bring out a certain number of historical facts that are often glossed over when posing this problem of writing, we must look into the famous question of the *hupomnēmata*. Current interpreters see in the critique of the *hupomnēmata* in the *Phaedrus* a critique of writing as a material support for memory. Now, in fact, *hupomnēmata* has a very precise meaning: it is a copybook, a notebook. Precisely this type of notebook was coming into vogue in Plato's time for personal and administrative use. This new technology was as disrupting as the introduction of the computer into private life today. It seems to me the question of writing and the self must be posed in terms of the technical and material framework in which it arose.

Second, there are problems of interpretation concerning the famous critique of writing as opposed to the culture of memory in the *Phaedrus*. If you read the *Phaedrus*, you will see that this passage is secondary with respect to another one, which is fundamental and in line with the theme that runs throughout the end of the text. It does not matter whether a text is written or oral—the problem is whether or not the discourse in question gives access to truth. Thus, the written/oral question is altogether secondary with respect to the question of truth.

Third, what seems remarkable to me is that these new instruments were immediately used for the constitution of a permanent relationship to oneself—one must manage oneself as a governor manages the governed, as a head of an enterprise manages his enterprise, a head of household manages his household. This new idea that virtue consists essentially in perfectly governing oneself, that is, in exercising upon oneself as exact a mastery as that of a sovereign against whom there would no longer be revolts, is something very important that we will find, for centuries—practically until Christianity. So, if you will, the point at which the question of the *hupomnēmata* and the culture of the self come together in a remarkable fashion is the pont at which the culture of the self takes as its goal the perfect government of the self—a sort of permanent political relationship between self and self. The ancients carried on this politics of themselves with these notebooks just as governments and those who manage enterprises administered by keeping registers. This is how writing seems to me to be linked to the problem of the culture of the self.

Q. Can you tell us more about the *hupomnēmata?*

M.F. In the technical sense, the *hupomnēmata* could be account books, public registers, individual notebooks serving as memoranda. Their use as books of life, guides for conduct, seems to have become a current thing among a whole cultivated public. Into them one entered quotations, fragments of works, examples, and actions to which one had been witness or of which one had read the account, reflections or reasonings one had heard or had come to mind. They constituted a material memory of things read, heard, or thought, thus offering these as an accumulated treasure for rereading and later meditation. They also formed a raw material for the writing of more systematic treatises in which were given arguments and means by which to struggle against some defect (such as anger, envy, gossip, flattery) or to overcome some difficult circumstance (a mourning, an exile, downfall, disgrace).

Q. But how does writing connect up with ethics and the self?

M.F. No technique, no professional skill can be acquired without exercise; neither can one learn the art of living, the *tekhnē tou biou,* without an *askēsis* which must be taken as a training of oneself by oneself: this was one of the traditional principles to which the Pythagoreans, the Socratics, the Cynics had for a long time attributed great importance. Among all the forms this training took (which included abstinences, memorizations, examinations of conscience, meditations, silence, and listening to others), it seems that writing—the fact of writing for oneself and for others—came quite late to play a sizable role.

Q. What specific role did the notebooks play when they finally became influential in late antiquity?

M.F. As personal as they were, the *hupomnēmata* must nevertheless not be taken for intimate diaries or for those accounts of spiritual experience (temptations, struggles, falls, and victories) which can be found in later Christian literature. They do not constitute an "account of oneself"; their objective is not to bring the *arcana conscientiae* to light, the confession of which—be it oral or written—has a purifying value. The movement that they seek to effect is the inverse of this last one: the point is not to pursue the indescribable, not to reveal the hidden, not to say the nonsaid, but, on the contrary, to collect the already-said, to reassemble that which one could hear or read, and this to an end which is nothing less than the constitution of oneself.

The *hupomnēmata* are to be resituated in the context of a very sensitive tension of that period. Within a culture very affected by traditionality, by the recognized value of the already-said, by the recurrence of discourse, by the "citational" practice under the seal of age and authority, an ethic was developing that was very explicitly oriented to the care of oneself, toward definite objectives such as retiring into oneself, reaching oneself, living with oneself, being sufficient to oneself, profiting by and enjoying oneself. Such is the objective of the *hupomnēmata:* to make of the recollection of the fragmentary *logos* transmitted by teaching, listening, or reading a means to establish as adequate and as perfect a relationship of oneself to oneself as possible.

Q. Before we turn to the role of these notebooks in early Christianity, could you tell us something about how Greco-Roman austerity differs from Christian austerity?

M.F. One thing that has been very important is that in Stoic ethics the question of purity was nearly nonexistent or, rather, marginal. It was important in Pythagorean circles and also in the Neoplatonic schools and became more and more important through their influence and also through religious influences. At a certain moment, the problem of an aesthetics of existence is covered over by the problem of purity, which is something else, and requires another kind of technique. In Christian asceticism, the question of purity becomes more and more important; the reason why you have to take control of yourself is to keep yourself pure. The problem of virginity, this model of feminine integrity, becomes much more important in Christianity. The theme of virginity has nearly nothing to do with sexual ethics in Greco-Roman asceticism; there the problem is a problem of self-domination. It was a virile model of self-domination, and a woman who was temperate was as virile to herself as a man. The paradigm of sexual self-restraint becomes a feminine paradigm through the theme of purity and virginity, based on the model of physical integrity. Physical integrity rather than self-regulation became important. So the problem of ethics as an aesthetics of existence is covered over by the problem of purification.

This new Christian self had to be constantly examined because in this self were lodged concupiscence and desires of the flesh. From that moment on, the self was no longer something to be made but something to be renounced and deciphered. Consequently, between paganism and Christianity, the opposition is not between tolerance and austerity but between a form of austerity linked to an aesthetics of existence and other forms of austerity linked to the necessity of renouncing the self and deciphering its truth.

Q. So Nietzsche, then, must be wrong, in *The Genealogy of Morals*, when he credits Christian asceticism for making us the kind of creatures that can make promises?

M.F. Yes, I think he has given mistaken credit to Christianity, given what we know about the evolution of pagan ethics from the fourth century B.C. to the fourth century after.

Q. How was the role of the notebooks transformed when the technique of using them to relate oneself to oneself was taken over by the Christians?

M.F. One important change is that the writing down of inner movements appears, according to Athanasius's text on the life of Saint Anthony, as an arm in spiritual combat: while the demon is a force that deceives and makes one be deceived about oneself (one great half of the *Vita Antonii* is devoted to these ploys), writing constitutes a test and something like a touchstone: in bringing to light the movements of thought, it dissipates the inner shadow where the enemy's plots are woven.

Q. How could such a radical transformation take place?

M.F. There is indeed a dramatic change between the *hupomnēmata* evoked by Xenophon, where it was only a question of remembering the elements of a diet, and the description of the nocturnal temptations of Saint Anthony. An interesting place to look for a transitional set of techniques seems to be the description of dreams. Almost from the beginning, one had to have a notebook beside one's bed upon which to write one's dreams in order either to interpret them oneself the next morning or to show them to someone who would interpret them. By means of this nightly description, an important step is taken toward the description of the self.

Q. But surely the idea that the contemplation of the self allows the self to dissipate shadows and arrive at truth is already present in Plato?

M.F. Yes, but this is an ontological and not a psychological form of contemplation. This ontological knowledge of the self takes shape, at least in certain texts and in particular in the *Alcibiades,* in the form of the contemplation of the soul by itself in terms of the famous metaphor of the eye. Plato asks, "How can the eye see itself?" The answer is apparently very simple, but in fact it is very complicated. For Plato, one cannot simply look at oneself in a mirror; one has to look into another eye, that is, one *in* oneself, however in oneself in the shape of the eye of the other. And there, in the other pupil, one will see oneself: the pupil serves as a mirror. And, in the same manner, the soul contemplating itself in another soul (or in the divine element of the other soul), which is like its pupil, will recognize its divine element.

You see that this idea that one must know oneself—that is, gain ontological knowledge of the soul's mode of being—is independent of what one could call an exercise of the self upon the self. When grasping the mode of being of your soul, there is no need to ask yourself what you have done, what you are thinking, what the movements of your ideas or your representations are, to what you are attached. That's why you can perform this technique of contemplation using as your object the soul of an other. Plato never speaks of the examination of conscience—never!

Q. It is a commonplace in literary studies that Montaigne was the first great autobiographer, yet you seem to trace writing about the self to much earlier sources.

M.F. It seems to me that in the religious crisis of the sixteenth century—the great rejection of the Catholic confessional practices—new modes of relationship to the self were being developed. We can see the reactivation of a certain number of ancient Stoic practices. The notion, for example, of proofs of oneself seems to me thematically close to what we find among the Stoics, where the experience of the self is not a discovering of a truth hidden inside the self but an attempt to determine what one can and cannot do with one's available freedom. Among both the Catholics and Protestants, the reactivation of these ancient techniques in the form of Christian spiritual practices is quite marked.

Let me take as an example the walking exercise recommended by Epictetus. Each morning, while taking a walk in the city, one should try to determine with respect to each thing (a public official or an attractive woman), one's motives, whether one is impressed by or drawn to it, or whether one has sufficient self-mastery so as to be indifferent.

In Christianity one has the same sort of exercises, but they serve to test one's dependence on God. I remember having found in a seventeenth-century text an exercise reminiscent of Epictetus, where a young seminarist, when he is walking, does certain exercises that show in what way each thing shows his dependence vis-à-vis God—which permit him to decipher the presence of divine providence. These two walks correspond to the extent that you have a case with Epictetus of a walk during which the individual assures himself of his own sovereignty over himself and shows that he is dependent on nothing, while in the Christian case the seminarist walks and before each thing he sees, says, "Oh, how God's goodness is great! He who made this, holds all things in his power, and me, in particular"—thus reminding himself that he is nothing.

Q. So discourse plays an important role but always serves other practices, even in the constitution of the self.

M.F. It seems to me, that all the so-called literature of the self—private diaries, narratives of the self, and so on—cannot be understood unless it is put into the general and very rich framework of these practices of the self. People have been writing about themselves for two thousand years, but not in the same way. I have the impression—I may be wrong—that there is a certain tendency to present the relationship between writing and the narrative of the self as a phenomenon particular to European modernity. Now, I would not deny it is modern, but it was also one of the first uses of writing.

So it is not enough to say that the subject is constituted in a symbolic system. It is not just in the play of symbols that the subject is constituted. It is constituted in real practices—historically analyzable practices. There is a technology of the constitution of the self which cuts across symbolic systems while using them.

Q. If self-analysis is a cultural invention, why does it seem so natural and pleasurable to us?

M.F. It may have been an extremely painful exercise at first and required many cultural valorizations before ending up transformed into a positive activity. Techniques of the self, I believe, can be found in all cultures in different forms. Just as it is necessary to study and compare the different techniques of the production of objects and the direction of men by men through government, one must also question techniques of the self. What makes the analysis of the techniques of the self difficult is two things. First, the techniques of the self do not require the same material apparatus as the production of objects; therefore they are often invisible techniques. Second, they are frequently linked to the techniques for the direction of others. For example, if we take educational institutions, we realize that one is managing others and teaching them to manage themselves.

Q. Let's move on to the history of the modern subject. To begin with, was the classical culture of the self completely lost, or was it, rather, incorporated and transformed by Christian techniques?

M.F. I do not think that the culture of the self disappeared or was covered up. You find many elements that have simply been integrated, displaced, reutilized in Christianity. From the moment that the culture of the self was taken up by Christianity, it was, in a way, put to work for the exercise of a pastoral power to the extent that the *epimeleia heautou* became, essentially, *epimeleia tōn allōn*—the care of others—which was the pastor's job. But insofar as individual salvation is channeled—to a certain extent, at least—through a pastoral institution that has the care of souls as its object, the classical care of the self disappeared, that is, was integrated and lost a large part of its autonomy.

What is interesting is that during the Renaissance you see a whole series of religious groups (whose existence is, moreover, already attested to in the Middle Ages) that resist this pastoral power and claim the right to make their own statutes for themselves. According to these groups, the individual should take care of his own salvation independently of the ecclesiastical institution and of the ecclesiastical pastorate. We can see, therefore, a reappearance, up to a certain point, not of the culture of the self, which had never disappeared, but a reaffirmation of its autonomy.

In the Renaissance, you also see—and here I refer to Burckhardt's text on the famous aesthetics of existence—the hero as his own work of art. The idea that from one's own life one can make a work of art is an idea that was undoubtedly foreign to the Middle Ages, and reappears at the moment of the Renaissance.

Q. So far you have been treating various degrees of appropriation of ancient techniques of self-mastery. In your own writing, you always show a big break between the Renaissance and the classical age. Was there an equally significant change in the way self-mastery was related to other social practices?

M.F. That is very interesting, but I won't answer you immediately. Let us start by saying that the relationship between Montaigne, Pascal, and Descartes could be rethought in terms of this question. First, Pascal was still in a tradition in which practices of the self, the practice of asceticism, were tied up with the knowledge of the world. Second, we must not forget that Descartes wrote "meditations"—and meditations are a practice of the self. But the extraordinary thing in Descartes's texts is that he succeeded in substituting a subject as founder of practices of knowledge for a subject constituted through practices of the self.

This is very important. Even if it is true that Greek philosophy founded rationality, it always held that a subject could not have access to the truth if he did not first operate upon himself a certain work that would make him susceptible to knowing the truth—a work of purification, conversion of the soul by contemplation of the soul itself. You also have the theme of the Stoic exercise by which a subject first ensures his autonomy and independence—and he ensures it in a rather complex relationship to the knowledge of the world, since it is this knowledge which allows him to ensure his independence, and it is only once he has ensured it that he is able to recognize the order of the world as it stands. In European culture up to the sixteenth century, the problem remains: What is the work I must effect upon myself so as to be capable and worthy of acceding to the truth? To put it another way: truth always has a price; no access to truth without ascesis. In Western culture up to the sixteenth century, asceticism and access to truth are always more or less obscurely linked.

Descartes, I think, broke with this when he said, "To accede to truth, it suffices that I be *any* subject that can see what is evident." Evidence is substituted for ascesis at the point where the relationship to the self intersects the relationship to others and the world. The relationship to the self no longer needs to be ascetic to get into relation to the truth. It suffices that the relationship to the self reveals to me the obvious truth of what I see for me to apprehend the truth definitively. Thus, I can be immoral and know the truth. I believe this is an idea that, more or less explicitly, was rejected by all previous culture. Before

Descartes, one could not be impure, immoral, and know the truth. With Descartes, direct evidence is enough. After Descartes, we have a nonascetic subject of knowledge. This change makes possible the institutionalization of modern science.

I am obviously schematizing a very long history, which is, however, fundamental. After Descartes, we have a subject of knowledge which poses for Kant the problem of knowing the relationship between the subject of ethics and that of knowledge. There was much debate in the Enlightenment as to whether these two subjects were completely different or not. Kant's solution was to find a universal subject that, to the extent it was universal, could be the subject of knowledge, but which demanded, nonetheless, an ethical attitude—precisely the relationship to the self which Kant proposes in *The Critique of Practical Reason.*

Q. You mean that once Descartes had cut scientific rationality loose from ethics, Kant reintroduced ethics as an applied form of procedural rationality?

M.F. Right. Kant says, "I must recognize myself as universal subject, that is, I must constitute myself in each of my actions as a universal subject by conforming to universal rules." The old questions were reinterpreted: How can I constitute myself as a subject of ethics? Recognize myself as such? Are ascetic exercises needed? Or simply this Kantian relationship to the universal which makes me ethical by conformity to practical reason? Thus Kant introduces one more way in our tradition whereby the self is not merely given but is constituted in relationship to itself as subject.

THE SUBJECT AND POWER

WHY STUDY POWER: THE QUESTION OF THE SUBJECT

The ideas I would like to discuss here represent neither a theory nor a methodology.

I would like to say, first of all, what has been the goal of my work during the last twenty years. It has not been to analyze the phenomena of power, nor to elaborate the foundations of such an analysis.

My objective, instead, has been to create a history of the different modes by which, in our culture, human beings are made subjects. My work has dealt with three modes of objectification that transform human beings into subjects.

The first is the modes of inquiry that try to give themselves the status of sciences; for example, the objectivizing of the speaking subject in *grammaire générale*, philology, and linguistics. Or again, in this first mode, the objectivizing of the productive subject, the subject who labors, in the analysis of wealth and of economics. Or, a third example, the objectivizing of the sheer fact of being alive in natural history or biology.

In the second part of my work, I have studied the objectivizing of the subject in what I shall call "dividing practices." The subject is either divided inside himself or divided from others. This process objectivizes him. Examples are the mad and the sane, the sick and the healthy, the criminals and the "good boys."

Finally, I have sought to study—it is my current work—the way a human being turns him- or herself into a subject. For example, I have chosen the domain of sexuality—how men have learned to recognize themselves as subjects of "sexuality."

This text first appeared in English in 1982 as an appendix to Hubert Dryfus and Paul Rabinow's *Michel Foucault: Beyond Structuralism and Hermeneutics.*—Eds.

Thus, it is not power, but the subject, that is the general theme of my research.

It is true that I became quite involved with the question of power. It soon appeared to me that, while the human subject is placed in relations of production and of signification, he is equally placed in power relations that are very complex. Now, it seemed to me that economic history and theory provided a good instrument for relations of production, and that linguistics and semiotics offered instruments for studying relations of signification—but for power relations we had no tools of study. We had recourse only to ways of thinking about power based on legal models, that is: What legitimates power? Or we had recourse to ways of thinking about power based on institutional models, that is: What is the state?

It was therefore necessary to expand the dimensions of a definition of power if one wanted to use this definition in studying the objectivizing of the subject.

Do we need a theory of power? Since a theory assumes a prior objectification, it cannot be asserted as a basis for analytical work. But this analytical work cannot proceed without an ongoing conceptualization. And this conceptualization implies critical thought—a constant checking.

The first thing to check is what I should call the "conceptual needs." I mean that the conceptualization should not be founded on a theory of the object—the conceptualized object is not the single criterion of a good conceptualization. We have to know the historical conditions that motivate our conceptualization. We need a historical awareness of our present circumstance.

The second thing to check is the type of reality with which we are dealing.

A writer in a well-known French newspaper once expressed his surprise: "Why is the notion of power raised by so many people today? Is it such an important subject? Is it so independent that it can be discussed without taking into account other problems?"

This writer's surprise amazes me. I feel skeptical about the assumption that this question has been raised for the first time in the twentieth century. Anyway, for us it is not only a theoretical question but a part of our experience. I'd like to mention only two "pathological forms"—those two "diseases of power"—fascism and Stalinism. One of the numerous reasons why they are so puzzling for us is that, in spite of their historical uniqueness, they are not quite original. They used and extended mechanisms already present in most other societies. More than that: in spite of their own internal madness, they used, to a large extent, the ideas and the devices of our political rationality.

What we need is a new economy of power relations—the word "economy" being used in its theoretical and practical sense. To put it in other words: since

Kant, the role of philosophy is to prevent reason from going beyond the limits of what is given in experience. But from the same moment—that is, since the development of the modern state and the political management of society—the role of philosophy is also to keep watch over the excessive powers of political rationality. This is a rather high expectation.

Everybody is aware of such banal facts. But the fact that they're banal does not mean they don't exist. What we have to do with banal facts is to discover—or try to discover—which specific and perhaps original problem is connected with them.

The relationship between rationalization and excesses of political power is evident. And we should not need to wait for bureaucracy or concentration camps to recognize the existence of such relations. But the problem is: What to do with such an evident fact?

Shall we try reason? To my mind, nothing would be more sterile. First, because the field has nothing to do with guilt or innocence. Second, because it is senseless to refer to reason as the contrary entity to nonreason. Lastly, because such a trial would trap us into playing the arbitrary and boring part of either the rationalist or the irrationalist.

Shall we investigate this kind of rationalism which seems to be specific to our modern culture and which originates in Enlightenment? I think that was the approach of some of the members of the Frankfurt School. My purpose, however, is not to start a discussion of their works, although they are most important and valuable. Rather, I would suggest another way of investigating the links between rationalization and power.

It may be wise not to take as a whole the rationalization of society or of culture but to analyze such a process in several fields, each with reference to a fundamental experience: madness, illness, death, crime, sexuality, and so forth.

I think that the word "rationalization" is dangerous. What we have to do is analyze specific rationalities rather than always invoking the progress of rationalization in general.

Even if the Enlightenment has been a very important phase in our history and in the development of political technology, I think we have to refer to much more remote processes if we want to understand how we have been trapped in our own history.

I would like to suggest another way to go further toward a new economy of power relations, a way that is more empirical, more directly related to our present situation, and one that implies more relations between theory and practice. It consists in taking the forms of resistance against different forms of power as a starting point. To use another metaphor, it consists in using this resistance as a chemical catalyst so as to bring to light power relations, locate their position, find out their point of application and the methods used. Rather than analyzing power from the point of view of its internal rationality, it consists of analyzing power relations through the antagonism of strategies.

For example, to find out what our society means by "sanity," perhaps we should investigate what is happening in the field of insanity.

And what we mean by "legality" in the field of illegality.

And, in order to understand what power relations are about, perhaps we should investigate the forms of resistance and attempts made to dissociate these relations.

As a starting point, let us take a series of oppositions that have developed over the last few years: opposition to the power of men over women, of parents over children, of psychiatry over the mentally ill, of medicine over the population, of administration over the ways people live.

It is not enough to say that these are anti-authority struggles; we must try to define more precisely what they have in common.

1. They are "transversal" struggles, that is, they are not limited to one country. Of course, they develop more easily and to a greater extent in certain countries, but they are not confined to a particular political or economic form of government.

2. The targets of these struggles are power effects as such. For example, the medical profession is criticized not primarily because it is a profit-making concern but because it exercises an uncontrolled power over people's bodies, their health and their life and death.

3. These are "immediate" struggles for two reasons. In such struggles, people criticize instances of power that are the closest to them, those which exercise their action on individuals. They look not for the "chief enemy" but for the immediate enemy. Nor do they expect to find a solution to their problem at a future date (that is, liberations, revolutions, end of class struggle). In comparison with a theoretical scale of explanations or a revolutionary order that polarizes the historian, they are anarchistic struggles.

    But these are not their most original points. The following seem to me to be more specific.

4. They are struggles that question the status of the individual. On the one hand, they assert the right to be different and underline everything that makes individuals truly individual. On the other hand, they attack everything that separates the individual, breaks his links with others, splits up community life, forces the individual back on himself, and ties him to his own identity in a constraining way.

    These struggles are not exactly for or against the "individual"; rather, they are struggles against the "government of individualization."

5. They are an opposition to the effects of power linked with knowledge, com-

petence, and qualification—struggles against the privileges of knowledge. But they are also an opposition against secrecy, deformation, and mystifying representations imposed on people.

There is nothing "scientistic" in this (that is, a dogmatic belief in the value of scientific knowledge), but neither is it a skeptical or relativistic refusal of all verified truth. What is questioned is the way in which knowledge circulates and functions, its relations to power. In short, the regime of knowledge [*savoir*].

6. Finally, all these present struggles revolve around the question: Who are we? They are a refusal of these abstractions, of economic and ideological state violence, which ignore who we are individually, and also a refusal of a scientific or administrative inquisition that determines who one is.

To sum up, the main objective of these struggles is to attack not so much such-or-such institution of power, or group, or elite, or class but, rather, a technique, a form of power.

This form of power that applies itself to immediate everyday life categorizes the individual, marks him by his own individuality, attaches him to his own identity, imposes a law of truth on him that he must recognize and others have to recognize in him. It is a form of power that makes individuals subjects. There are two meanings of the word "subject": subject to someone else by control and dependence, and tied to his own identity by a conscience or self-knowledge. Both meanings suggest a form of power that subjugates and makes subject to.

Generally, it can be said that there are three types of struggles: against forms of domination (ethnic, social, and religious); against forms of exploitation that separate individuals from what they produce; or against that which ties the individual to himself and submits him to others in this way (struggles against subjection [*assujettissement*], against forms of subjectivity and submission).

I think that in history you can find a lot of examples of these three kinds of social struggles, either isolated from each other, or mixed together. But even when they are mixed, one of them, most of the time, prevails. For instance, in feudal societies, the struggles against the forms of ethnic or social domination were prevalent, even though economic exploitation could have been very important among the causes of revolt.

In the nineteenth century, the struggle against exploitation came into the foreground.

And nowadays, the struggle against the forms of subjection—against the submission of subjectivity—is becoming more and more important, even though the struggles against forms of domination and exploitation have not disappeared. Quite the contrary.

I suspect that it is not the first time that our society has been confronted with this kind of struggle. All those movements that took place in the fifteenth and sixteenth centuries, which had the Reformation as their main expression and result, should be analyzed as a great crisis of the Western experience of subjectivity and a revolt against the kind of religious and moral power that gave form, during the Middle Ages, to this subjectivity. The need to take a direct part in spiritual life, in the work of salvation, in the truth that lies in the Book—all that was a struggle for a new subjectivity.

I know what objections can be made. We can say that all types of subjection are derived phenomena, that they are merely the consequences of other economic and social processes: forces of production, class struggle, and ideological structures that determine the form of subjectivity.

It is certain that the mechanisms of subjection cannot be studied outside their relation to the mechanisms of exploitation and domination. But they do not merely constitute the "terminal" of more fundamental mechanisms. They entertain complex and circular relations with other forms.

The reason this kind of struggle tends to prevail in our society is due to the fact that, since the sixteenth century, a new political form of power has been continuously developing. This new political structure, as everybody knows, is the state. But most of the time, the state is envisioned as a kind of political power that ignores individuals, looking only at the interests of the totality or, I should say, of a class or a group among the citizens.

That's quite true. But I'd like to underline the fact that the state's power (and that's one of the reasons for its strength) is both an individualizing and a totalizing form of power. Never, I think, in the history of human societies—even in the old Chinese society—has there been such a tricky combination in the same political structures of individualization techniques and of totalization procedures.

This is due to the fact that the modern Western state has integrated into a new political shape an old power technique that originated in Christian institutions. We can call this power technique "pastoral power."

First of all, a few words about this pastoral power.

It has often been said that Christianity brought into being a code of ethics fundamentally different from that of the ancient world. Less emphasis is usually placed on the fact that it proposed and spread new power relations throughout the ancient world.

Christianity is the only religion that has organized itself as a Church. As such, it postulates in principle that certain individuals can, by their religious quality, serve others not as princes, magistrates, prophets, fortune-tellers, benefactors, educationalists, and so on, but as pastors. However, this word designates a very special form of power.

1. It is a form of power whose ultimate aim is to assure individual salvation in the next world.

2. Pastoral power is not merely a form of power that commands; it must also be prepared to sacrifice itself for the life and salvation of the flock. Therefore, it is different from royal power, which demands a sacrifice from its subjects to save the throne.

3. It is a form of power that looks after not just the whole community but each individual in particular, during his entire life.

4. Finally, this form of power cannot be exercised without knowing the inside of people's minds, without exploring their souls, without making them reveal their innermost secrets. It implies a knowledge of the conscience and an ability to direct it.

This form of power is salvation-oriented (as opposed to political power). It is oblative (as opposed to the principle of sovereignty); it is individualizing (as opposed to legal power); it is coextensive and continuous with life; it is linked with a production of truth—the truth of the individual himself.

But all this is part of history, you will say; the pastorate has, if not disappeared, at least lost the main part of its efficacy.

This is true, but I think we should distinguish between two aspects of pastoral power—between the ecclesiastical institutionalization that has ceased or at least lost its vitality since the eighteenth century, and its function, which has spread and multiplied outside the ecclesiastical institution.

An important phenomenon took place around the eighteenth century—it was a new distribution, a new organization of this kind of individualizing power.

I don't think that we should consider the "modern state" as an entity that was developed above individuals, ignoring what they are and even their very existence, but, on the contrary, as a very sophisticated structure in which individuals can be integrated, under one condition: that this individuality would be shaped in a new form, and submitted to a set of very specific patterns.

In a way, we can see the state as a modern matrix of individualization, or a new form of pastoral power.

A few more words about this new pastoral power.

1. We may observe a change in its objective. It was a question no longer of leading people to their salvation in the next world but, rather, ensuring it in this world. And in this context, the word "salvation" takes on different meanings: health, well-being (that is, sufficient wealth, standard of living), security, protection against accidents. A series of "worldly" aims took the place of the religious aims of the traditional pastorate, all the more easily because the lat-

ter, for various reasons, had followed in an accessory way a certain number of these aims; we only have to think of the role of medicine and its welfare function assured for a long time by the Catholic and Protestant churches.

2. Concurrently, the officials of pastoral power increased. Sometimes this form of power was exerted by state apparatus or, in any case, by a public institution such as the police. (We should not forget that in the eighteenth century the police force was invented not only for maintaining law and order, nor for assisting governments in their struggle against their enemies, but also for assuring urban supplies, hygiene, health and standards considered necessary for handicrafts and commerce.) Sometimes the power was exercised by private ventures, welfare societies, benefactors, and generally by philanthropists. But ancient institutions, for example the family, were also mobilized at this time to take on pastoral functions. It was also exercised by complex structures such as medicine, which included private initiatives with the sale of services on market economy principles but also included public institutions such as hospitals.

3. Finally, the multiplication of the aims and agents of pastoral power focused the development of knowledge of man around two roles: one, globalizing and quantitative, concerning the population; the other, analytical, concerning the individual.

And this implies that power of a pastoral type, which over centuries—for more than a millennium—had been linked to a defined religious institution, suddenly spread out into the whole social body. It found support in a multitude of institutions. And, instead of a pastoral power and a political power, more or less linked to each other, more or less in rivalry, there was an individualizing "tactic" that characterized a series of powers: those of the family, medicine, psychiatry, education, and employers.

At the end of the eighteenth century, Kant wrote in a German newspaper—the *Berlinischer Monatschrift*—a short text. The title was *Was ist Aufklärung?* [*What Is Enlightenment?*]. It was for a long time, and it is still, considered a work of relatively little importance.

But I can't help finding it very interesting and puzzling because it was the first time a philosopher proposed as a philosophical task to investigate not only the metaphysical system or the foundations of scientific knowledge but a historical event—a recent, even a contemporary event.

When in 1784 Kant asked "What is Enlightenment?" he meant, "What's going on just now? What's happening to us? What is this world, this period, this precise moment in which we are living?"

Or in other words: What are we, as *Aufklärer*, as part of the Enlightenment? Compare this with the Cartesian question: Who am I? I, as a unique but universal and unhistorical subject? I, for Descartes, is everyone, anywhere at any moment.

But Kant asks something else: What are we? in a very precise moment of history. Kant's question appears as an analysis of both us and our present.

I think that this aspect of philosophy took on more and more importance. Hegel, Nietzsche . . .

The other aspect of "universal philosophy" didn't disappear. But the task of philosophy as a critical analysis of our world is something that is more and more important. Maybe the most certain of all philosophical problems is the problem of the present time, and of what we are, in this very moment.

Maybe the target nowadays is not to discover what we are but to refuse what we are. We have to imagine and to build up what we could be to get rid of this kind of political "double bind," which is the simultaneous individualization and totalization of modern power structures.

The conclusion would be that the political, ethical, social, philosophical problem of our days is not to try to liberate the individual from the state, and from the state's institutions, but to liberate us both from the state and from the type of individualization linked to the state. We have to promote new forms of subjectivity through the refusal of this kind of individuality that has been imposed on us for several centuries.

HOW IS POWER EXERCISED?

For some people, asking questions about the "how" of power means limiting oneself to describing its effects without ever relating those effects either to causes or to a basic nature. It would make this power a mysterious substance that one avoids interrogating in itself, no doubt because one prefers *not* to call it into question. By proceeding this way, which is never explicitly justified, these people seem to suspect the presence of a kind of fatalism. But does not their very distrust indicate a presupposition that power is something that exists with its own distinct origin, basic nature, and manifestations?

If, for the time being, I grant a certain privileged position to the question of "how," it is not because I would wish to eliminate the questions of "what" and "why." Rather, it is that I wish to present these questions in a different way— better still, to know if it is legitimate to imagine a power that unites in itself a what, a why, and a how. To put it bluntly, I would say that to begin the analysis with a "how" is to introduce the suspicion that power as such does not exist. It is, in any case, to ask oneself what contents one has in mind when using this grand, all-embracing, and reifying term; it is to suspect that an extremely complex configuration of realities is allowed to escape while one endlessly marks time before the double question: what is power, and where does power come from? The flat and empirical little question, "What happens?" is not designed to introduce by stealth a metaphysics or an ontology of power but, rather, to undertake a critical investigation of the thematics of power.

"How?" not in the sense of "How does it manifest itself?" but "How is it exercised?" and "What happens when individuals exert (as we say) power over others?"

As far as this power is concerned, it is first necessary to distinguish that which is exerted over things and gives the ability to modify, use, consume, or destroy them—a power that stems from aptitudes directly inherent in the body or relayed by external instruments. Let us say that here it is a question of "capacity." On the other hand, what characterizes the power we are analyzing is that it brings into play relations between individuals (or between groups). For let us not deceive ourselves: if we speak of the power of laws, institutions, and ideologies, if we speak of structures or mechanisms of power, it is only insofar as we suppose that certain persons exercise power over others. The term "power" designates relationships between "partners" (and by that I am not thinking of a game with fixed rules but simply, and for the moment staying in the most general terms, of an ensemble of actions that induce others and follow from one another).

It is necessary also to distinguish power relations from relationships of communication that transmit information by means of a language, a system of signs, or any other symbolic medium. No doubt, communicating is always a certain way of acting upon another person or persons. But the production and circulation of elements of meaning can have as their objective or as their consequence certain results in the realm of power; the latter are not simply an aspect of the former. Whether or not they pass through systems of communication, power relations have a specific nature.

Power relations, relationships of communication, objective capacities should not therefore be confused. This is not to say that there is a question of three separate domains. Nor that there is, on the one hand, the field of things, of perfected technique, work, and the transformation of the real, and, on the other, that of signs, communication, reciprocity, and the production of meaning; finally that of the domination of the means of constraint, of inequality and the action of men upon other men.[1] It is a question of three types of relationships that in fact always overlap one another, support one another reciprocally, and use each other mutually as means to an end. The application of objective capacities in their most elementary forms implies relationships of communication (whether in the form of previously acquired information or of shared work); it is tied also to power relations (whether they consist of obligatory tasks, of gestures imposed by tradition or apprenticeship, of subdivisions or the more or less obligatory distribution of labor). Relationships of communication imply goal-directed activities (even if only the correct putting into operation of directed el-

ements of meaning) and, by modifying the field of information between partners, produce effects of power. Power relations are exercised, to an exceedingly
important extent, through the production and exchange of signs; and they are
scarcely separable from goal-directed activities that permit the exercise of a
power (such as training techniques, processes of domination, the means by
which obedience is obtained), or that, to enable them to operate, call on relations of power (the division of labor and the hierarchy of tasks).

Of course, the coordination between these three types of relationships is neither uniform nor constant. In a given society, there is no general type of equilibrium between goal-directed activities, systems of communication, and power
relations; rather, there are diverse forms, diverse places, diverse circumstances
or occasions in which these interrelationships establish themselves according to
a specific model. But there are also "blocks" in which the adjustment of abilities,
the resources of communication, and power relations constitute regulated and
concerted systems. Take, for example, an educational institution: the disposal of
its space, the meticulous regulations that govern its internal life, the different activities that are organized there, the diverse persons who live there or meet one
another, each with his own function, his well-defined character—all these
things constitute a block of capacity-communication—power. Activity to ensure learning and the acquisition of aptitudes or types of behavior works via a
whole ensemble of regulated communications (lessons, questions and answers,
orders, exhortations, coded signs of obedience, differential marks of the
"value" of each person and of the levels of knowledge) and by means of a
whole series of power processes (enclosure, surveillance, reward and punishment, the pyramidal hierarchy).

These blocks, in which the deployment of technical capacities, the game of
communications, and the relationships of power are adjusted to one another according to considered formulae, constitute what one might call, enlarging a little the sense of the word, "disciplines." The empirical analysis of certain
disciplines as they have been historically constituted presents for this very reason a certain interest. This is so because the disciplines show, first, according to
artificially clear and decanted systems, the way in which systems of objective finality and systems of communication and power can be welded together. They
also display different models of articulation, sometimes giving preeminence to
power relations and obedience (as in those disciplines of a monastic or penitential type), sometimes to goal-directed activities (as in the disciplines of workshops or hospitals), sometimes to relationships of communication (as in the
disciplines of apprenticeship), sometimes also to a saturation of the three types
of relationship (as perhaps in military discipline, where a plethora of signs indicates, to the point of redundancy, tightly knit power relations calculated with
care to produce a certain number of technical effects).

What is to be understood by the disciplining of societies in Europe since the eighteenth century is not, of course, that the individuals who are part of them become more and more obedient, nor that all societies become like barracks, schools, or prisons; rather, it is that an increasingly controlled, more rational, and economic process of adjustment has been sought between productive activities, communications networks, and the play of power relations.

To approach the theme of power by an analysis of "how" is therefore to introduce several critical shifts in relation to the supposition of a fundamental power. It is to give oneself as the object of analysis *power relations* and not power itself—power relations that are distinct from objective capacities as well as from relations of communication, power relations that can be grasped in the diversity of their linkages to these capacities and relations.

WHAT CONSTITUTES THE SPECIFICITY OF POWER RELATIONS?

The exercise of power is not simply a relationship between "partners," individual or collective; it is a way in which some act on others. Which is to say, of course, that there is no such entity as power, with or without a capital letter; global, massive, or diffused; concentrated or distributed. Power exists only as exercised by some on others, only when it is put into action, even though, of course, it is inscribed in a field of sparse available possibilities underpinned by permanent structures. This also means that power is not a matter of consent. In itself, it is not the renunciation of freedom, a transfer of rights, or power of each and all delegated to a few (which does not prevent the possibility that consent may be a condition for the existence or the maintenance of a power relation); the relationship of power may be an effect of a prior or permanent consent, but it is not by nature the manifestation of a consensus.

Is this to say that one must seek the character proper to power relations in the violence that must have been its primitive form, its permanent secret, and last resort, that which in the final analysis appears as its real nature when it is forced to throw aside its mask and to show itself as it really is? In effect, what defines a relationship of power is that it is a mode of action that does not act directly and immediately on others. Instead, it acts upon their actions: an action upon an action, on possible or actual future or present actions. A relationship of violence acts upon a body or upon things; it forces, it bends, it breaks, it destroys, or it closes off all possibilities. Its opposite pole can only be passivity, and if it comes up against any resistance it has no other option but to try to break it down. A power relationship, on the other hand, can only be articulated on the basis of two elements that are indispensable if it is really to be a power relationship: that "the other" (the one over whom power is exercised) is recognized and maintained to the very end as a subject who acts; and that, faced with a relationship of power, a whole field of responses, reactions, results, and possible inventions may open up.

Obviously the establishing of power relations does not exclude the use of violence any more than it does the obtaining of consent; no doubt, the exercise of power can never do without one or the other, often both at the same time. But even though consent and violence are instruments or results, they do not constitute the principle or basic nature of power. The exercise of power can produce as much acceptance as may be wished for: it can pile up the dead and shelter itself behind whatever threats it can imagine. In itself, the exercise of power is not a violence that sometimes hides, or an implicitly renewed consent. It operates on the field of possibilities in which the behavior of active subjects is able to inscribe itself. It is a set of actions on possible actions; it incites, it induces, it seduces, it makes easier or more difficult; it releases or contrives, makes more probable or less; in the extreme, it constrains or forbids absolutely, but it is always a way of acting upon one or more acting subjects by virtue of their acting or being capable of action. A set of actions upon other actions.

Perhaps the equivocal nature of the term "conduct" is one of the best aids for coming to terms with the specificity of power relations. To "conduct" is at the same time to "lead" others (according to mechanisms of coercion that are, to varying degrees, strict) and a way of behaving within a more or less open field of possibilities.[2] The exercise of power is a "conduct of conducts" and a management of possibilities. Basically, power is less a confrontation between two adversaries or their mutual engagement than a question of "government." This word must be allowed the very broad meaning it had in the sixteenth century. "Government" did not refer only to political structures or to the management of states; rather, it designated the way in which the conduct of individuals or of groups might be directed—the government of children, of souls, of communities, of families, of the sick. It covered not only the legitimately constituted forms of political or economic subjection but also modes of action, more or less considered and calculated, that were destined to act upon the possibilities of action of other people. To govern, in this sense, is to structure the possible field of action of others. The relationship proper to power would therefore be sought not on the side of violence or of struggle, nor on that of voluntary contracts (all of which can, at best, only be the instruments of power) but, rather, in the area of that singular mode of action, neither warlike nor juridical, which is government.

When one defines the exercise of power as a mode of action upon the actions of others, when one characterizes these actions as the government of men by other men—in the broadest sense of the term—one includes an important element: freedom. Power is exercised only over free subjects, and only insofar as they are "free." By this we mean individual or collective subjects who are faced with a field of possibilities in which several kinds of conduct, several ways of reacting and modes of behavior are available. Where the determining factors are exhaustive, there is no relationship of power: slavery is not a power relationship when a man is in chains, only when he has some possible mobility, even a chance of escape. (In this case it is a question of a physical relationship of constraint.) Consequently, there is not a face-to-face confrontation of power and freedom as mutually exclusive facts (freedom disappearing everywhere power is exercised) but a much more complicated interplay. In this game, freedom may well appear as the condition for the exercise of power (at the same time its precondition, since freedom must exist for power to be exerted, and also its permanent support, since without the possibility of recalcitrance power would be equivalent to a physical determination).

The power relationship and freedom's refusal to submit cannot therefore be separated. The crucial problem of power is not that of voluntary servitude (how could we seek to be slaves?). At the very heart of the power relationship, and constantly provoking it, are the recalcitrance of the will and the intransigence of freedom. Rather than speaking of an essential antagonism, it would be better to speak of an "agonism" [3]—of a relationship that is at the same time mutual incitement and struggle; less of a face-to-face confrontation that paralyzes both sides than a permanent provocation.

HOW IS ONE TO ANALYZE THE POWER RELATIONSHIP?

One can analyze such relationships or, rather, I should say that it is perfectly legitimate to do so by focusing on carefully defined institutions. The latter constitute a privileged point of observation, diversified, concentrated, put in order, and carried through to the highest point of their efficacy. It is here that, as a first approximation, one might expect to see the appearance of the form and logic of their elementary mechanisms. However, the analysis of power relations as one finds them in certain closed institutions presents a certain number of problems. First, the fact that an important part of the mechanisms put into operation by an institution are designed to ensure its own preservation brings with it the risk of deciphering functions that are essentially reproductive, especially in power relations within institutions. Second, in analyzing power relations from the standpoint of institutions, one lays oneself open to seeking the explanation and the origin of the former in the latter, that is to say in sum, to explain power by power. Finally, insofar as institutions act essentially by bringing into play two elements, explicit or tacit regulations and an apparatus, one risks giving to one or the other an exaggerated privilege in the relations of power and, hence, seeing in the latter only modulations of law and coercion.

This is not to deny the importance of institutions in the establishment of power relations but, rather, to suggest that one must analyze institutions from the standpoint of power relations, rather than vice versa, and that the fundamental point of anchorage of the relationships, even if they are embodied and crystallized in an institution, is to be found outside the institution.

Let us come back to the definition of the exercise of power as a way in which certain actions may structure the field of other possible actions. What would be proper to a relationship of power, then, is that it be a mode of action on actions. That is, power relations are rooted deep in the social nexus, not a supplementary structure over and above "society" whose radical effacement one could perhaps dream of. To live in society is, in any event, to live in such a way that some can act on the actions of others. A society without power relations can only be an abstraction. Which, be it said in passing, makes all the more politically necessary the analysis of power relations in a given society, their historical formation, the source of their strength or fragility, the conditions that are necessary to transform some or to abolish others. For to say that there cannot be a society without power relations is not to say either that those which are established are necessary, or that power in any event, constitutes an inescapable fatality at the heart of societies, such that it cannot be undermined. Instead, I would say that the analysis, elaboration, and bringing into question of power relations and the "agonism" between power relations and the intransitivity of freedom is an increasingly political task—even, the political task that is inherent in all social existence.

Concretely, the analysis of power relations demands that a certain number of points be established:

1. *The system of differentiations* that permits one to act upon the actions of others: juridical and traditional differences of status or privilege; economic differences in the appropriation of wealth and goods, differing positions within the processes of production, linguistic or cultural differences, differences in know-how and competence, and so forth. Every relationship of power puts into operation differences that are, at the same time, its conditions and its results.

2. *The types of objectives* pursued by those who act upon the actions of others: maintenance of privileges, accumulation of profits, the exercise of statutory authority, the exercise of a function or a trade.

3. *Instrumental modes:* whether power is exercised by the threat of arms, by the effects of speech, through economic disparities, by more or less complex

means of control, by systems of surveillance, with or without archives, by rules, explicit or not, fixed or modifiable, with or without the material means of enforcement.

4. *Forms of institutionalization:* these may mix traditional conditions, legal structures, matters of habit or fashion (such as one sees in the institution of the family); they can also take the form of an apparatus closed in upon itself, with its specific loci, its own regulations, its hierarchical structures that are carefully defined, a relative autonomy in its functioning (such as scholastic or military institutions); they can also form very complex systems endowed with multiple apparatuses, as in the case of the state, whose function is the taking of everything under its wing, to be the global overseer, the principle of regulation and, to a certain extent also, the distributor of all power relations in a given social ensemble.

5. *The degrees of rationalization:* the bringing into play of power relations as action in a field of possibilities may be more or less elaborate in terms of the effectiveness of its instruments and the certainty of its results (greater or lesser technological refinements employed in the exercise of power) or, again, in proportion to the possible cost (economic cost of the means used, or the cost in terms of the resistance encountered). The exercise of power is not a naked fact, an institutional given, nor is it a structure that holds out or is smashed: it is something that is elaborated, transformed, organized; it endows itself with processes that are more or less adjusted to the situation.

One sees why the analysis of power relations within a society cannot be reduced to the study of a series of institutions or even to the study of all those institutions that would merit the name "political." Power relations are rooted in the whole network of the social. This is not to say, however, that there is a primary and fundamental principle of power which dominates society down to the smallest detail; but, based on this possibility of action on the action of others that is coextensive with every social relationship, various kinds of individual disparity, of objectives, of the given application of power over ourselves or others, of more or less partial or universal institutionalization and more or less deliberate organization, will define different forms of power. The forms and the specific situations of the government of some by others in a given society are multiple; they are superimposed, they cross over, limit and in some cases annul, in others reinforce, one another. It is certain that, in contemporary societies, the state is not simply one of the forms of specific situations of the exercise of power—even if it is the most important—but that, in a certain way, all other forms of power relation must refer to it. But this is not because they are derived from it; rather, it is because power relations have come more and more under state control (although this state control has not taken the same form in peda-

gogical, judicial, economic, or family systems). Using here the restricted meaning of the word "government," one could say that power relations have been
progressively governmentalized, that is to say, elaborated, rationalized, and
centralized in the form of, or under the auspices of, state institutions.

RELATIONS OF POWER AND RELATIONS
OF STRATEGY

The word "strategy" is currently employed in three ways. First, to designate the
means employed to attain a certain end; it is a question of rationality functioning
to arrive at an objective. Second, to designate the way in which a partner in a certain game acts with regard to what he thinks should be the action of the others
and what he considers the others think to be his own; it is the way in which one
seeks to have the advantage over others. Third, to designate the procedures used
in a situation of confrontation to deprive the opponent of his means of combat
and to reduce him to giving up the struggle; it is a question, therefore, of the
means destined to obtain victory. These three meanings come together in situations of confrontation—war or games—where the objective is to act on an adversary in such a way as to render the struggle impossible for him. So strategy is
defined by the choice of winning solutions. But it must be borne in mind that this
is a very special type of situation, and that there are others in which the distinctions between the different senses of the word "strategy" must be maintained.

Referring to the first sense I have indicated, one may call some systems of
power strategy the totality of the means put into operation to implement power
effectively or to maintain it. One may also speak of a strategy proper to power
relations insofar as they constitute modes of action on possible action, the action of others. Thus, one can interpret the mechanisms brought into play in
power relations in terms of strategies. Obviously, though, most important is the
relationship between power relations and confrontation strategies. For, if it is
true that at the heart of power relations and as a permanent condition of their
existence there is an insubordination and a certain essential obstinacy on the part
of the principles of freedom, then there is no relationship of power without the
means of escape or possible flight. Every power relationship implies, at least in
potentia, a strategy of struggle, in which the two forces are not superimposed,
do not lose their specific nature, or do not finally become confused. Each constitutes for the other a kind of permanent limit, a point of possible reversal. A relationship of confrontation reaches its term, its final moment (and the victory of
one of the two adversaries) when stable mechanisms replace the free play of antagonistic reactions. Through such mechanisms one can direct, in a fairly con-

stant manner and with reasonable certainty, the conduct of others. For a relationship of confrontation, from the moment it is not a struggle to the death, the fixing of a power relationship becomes a target—at one and the same time its fulfillment and its suspension. And, in return, the strategy of struggle also constitutes a frontier for the relationship of power, the line at which, instead of manipulating and inducing actions in a calculated manner, one must be content with reacting to them after the event. It would not be possible for power relations to exist without points of insubordination that, by definition, are means of escape. Accordingly, every intensification or extension of power relations intended to wholly suppress these points of insubordination can only bring the exercise of power up against its outer limits. It reaches its final term either in a type of action that reduces the other to total impotence (in which case victory over the adversary replaces the exercise of power) or by a confrontation with those whom one governs and their transformation into adversaries. Which is to say, that every strategy of confrontation dreams of becoming a relationship of power and every relationship of power tends, both through its intrinsic course of development and when frontally encountering resistances, to become a winning strategy.

In fact, between a relationship of power and a strategy of struggle there is a reciprocal appeal, a perpetual linking and a perpetual reversal. At every moment, the relationship of power may become a confrontation between two adversaries. Equally, the relationship between adversaries in society may, at every moment, give place to the putting into operation of mechanisms of power. The consequence of this instability is the ability to decipher the same events and the same transformations either from inside the history of struggle or from the standpoint of the power relationships. The resulting interpretations will not consist of the same elements of meaning or the same links or the same types of intelligibility, though they refer to the same historical fabric, and each of the two analyses must have reference to the other. In fact, it is precisely the disparities between the two readings that make visible those fundamental phenomena of "domination" that are present in a large number of human societies.

Domination is, in fact, a general structure of power whose ramifications and consequences can sometimes be found reaching down into the fine fabric of society. But, at the same time, it is a strategic situation, more or less taken for granted and consolidated, within a long-term confrontation between adversaries. It can certainly happen that the fact of domination may only be the transcription of a mechanism of power resulting from confrontation and its consequences (a political structure stemming from invasion); it may also be that a relationship of struggle between two adversaries is the result of power relations with the conflicts and cleavages they engender. But what makes the domination of a group, a caste, or a class, together with the resistance and revolts that domination comes up against, a central phenomenon in the history of societies is that they manifest in a massive and global form, at the level of the whole social body, the locking-together of power relations with relations of strategy and the results proceeding from their interaction.

Notes

1. When Jürgen Habermas distinguishes between domination, communication, and finalized activity, I think that he sees in them not three separate domains but, rather, three "transcendentals."

2. Foucault is playing on the double meaning in French of the verb *conduire* (to lead or to drive) and *se conduire* (to behave or conduct oneself)—whence *la conduite,* conduct or behavior.—Trans.

3. Foucault's neologism is based on the Greek *agōnisma* meaning "a combat." The term would hence imply a physical contest in which the opponents develop a strategy of reaction and of mutual taunting, as in a wrestling match.—Trans.

TECHNOLOGIES OF THE SELF

I

Technologies of the Self

When I began to study the rules, duties, and prohibitions of sexuality, the interdictions and restrictions associated with it, I was concerned not simply with the acts that were permitted and forbidden but with the feelings represented, the thoughts, the desires one might experience, the inclination to seek within the self any hidden feeling, any movement of the soul, any desire disguised under illusory forms. There is a very significant difference between interdictions about sexuality and other forms of interdiction. Unlike other interdictions, sexual interdictions are constantly connected with the obligation to tell the truth about oneself.

Two facts may be raised against me: first, that confession played an important part in penal and religious institutions for all offenses, not only in sex. But the task of analyzing one's sexual desire is always more important than analyzing any other kind of sin.

I am also aware of the second objection: that sexual behavior more than any other was submitted to very strict rules of secrecy, decency, and modesty so that sexuality is related in a strange and complex way both to verbal prohibition and to the obligation to tell the truth, of hiding what one does and of deciphering who one is.

The association of a prohibition and a strong injunction to speak is a constant feature of our culture. The theme of the renunciation of the flesh was linked to the confession of the monk to the abbot, to the monk confiding to the abbot everything that was on his mind.

This text derives from a seminar Foucault gave at the University of Vermont in October 1982. It appears here amended for style and clarity; it has been supplemented with notes to correspond to the text in *Dits et écrits*.

I conceived of a rather odd project: not the study of the evolution of sexual behavior but of the historical study of the link between the obligation to tell the truth and the prohibitions weighing on sexuality. I asked: How had the subject been compelled to decipher himself in regard to what was forbidden? It is a question that interrogates the relation between asceticism and truth.

Max Weber posed the question: If one wants to behave rationally and regulate one's action according to true principles, what part of one's self should one renounce? What is the ascetic price of reason? To what kind of asceticism should one submit? I posed the opposite question: How have certain kinds of interdictions required the price of certain kinds of knowledge about oneself? What must one know about oneself in order to be willing to renounce anything?

Thus, I arrived at the hermeneutics of technologies of the self in pagan and early Christian practice. I encountered certain difficulties in this study because these practices are not well known. First, Christianity has always been more interested in the history of its beliefs than in the history of real practices. Second, such a hermeneutics was never organized into a body of doctrine like textual hermeneutics. Third, the hermeneutics of the self has been confused with theologies of the soul—concupiscence, sin, and the fall from grace. Fourth, a hermeneutics of the self has been diffused across Western culture through numerous channels and integrated with various types of attitudes and experience, so that it is difficult to isolate and separate it from our own spontaneous experiences.

Context of Study

My objective for more than twenty-five years has been to sketch out a history of the different ways in our culture that humans develop knowledge about themselves: economics, biology, psychiatry, medicine, and penology. The main point is not to accept this knowledge at face value but to analyze these so-called sciences as very specific "truth games" related to specific techniques that human beings use to understand themselves.

As a context, we must understand that there are four major types of these "technologies," each a matrix of practical reason: (1) technologies of production, which permit us to produce, transform, or manipulate things; (2) technologies of sign systems, which permit us to use signs, meanings, symbols, or signification; (3) technologies of power, which determine the conduct of individuals and submit them to certain ends or domination, an objectivizing of the subject; (4) technologies of the self, which permit individuals to effect by their own means, or with the help of others, a certain number of operations on their own bodies and souls, thoughts, conduct, and way of being, so as to transform themselves in order to attain a certain state of happiness, purity, wisdom, perfection, or immortality.

These four types of technologies hardly ever function separately, although each one of them is associated with a certain type of domination. Each implies certain modes of training and modification of individuals, not only in the obvious sense of acquiring certain skills but also in the sense of acquiring certain attitudes. I wanted to show both their specific nature and their constant interaction. For instance, the relation between manipulating things and domination appears clearly in Karl Marx's *Capital*, where every technique of production requires modification of individual conduct—not only skills but also attitudes.

Usually, the first two technologies are used in the study of the sciences and linguistics. It is the last two, the technologies of domination and self, which have most kept my attention. I have attempted a history of the organization of knowledge with respect to both domination and the self. For example, I studied madness not in terms of the criteria of formal sciences but to show what type of management of individuals inside and outside of asylums was made possible by this strange discourse. This encounter between the technologies of domination of others and those of the self I call "governmentality."

Perhaps I've insisted too much on the technology of domination and power. I am more and more interested in the interaction between oneself and others, and in the technologies of individual domination, in the mode of action that an individual exercises upon himself by means of the technologies of the self.

The Development of Technologies of the Self

I wish to sketch out the evolution of the hermeneutics of the self in two different contexts that are historically contiguous: (1) Greco-Roman philosophy in the first two centuries A.D. of the early Roman Empire, and (2) Christian spirituality and the monastic principles developed in the fourth and fifth centuries of the late Roman Empire.

Moreover, I wish to take up the subject not only in theory but in relation to a set of practices in late antiquity. Among the Greeks, these practices took the form of a precept: *epimeleisthai seautou*, "to take care of yourself," to take "care of the self," "to be concerned, to take care of yourself."

The precept of the "care of the self" [*souci de soi*] was, for the Greeks, one of the main principles of cities, one of the main rules for social and personal conduct and for the art of life. For us now, this notion is rather obscure and faded. When one is asked "What is the most important moral principle in ancient philosophy?" the immediate answer is not "Take care of oneself" but the Delphic principle, *gnōthi seauton* ("Know yourself").

Without doubt, our philosophical tradition has overemphasized the latter and forgotten the former. The Delphic principle was not an abstract one concerning life; it was technical advice, a rule to be observed for the consultation of the oracle. "Know yourself" meant "Do not suppose yourself to be a god."

Other commentators suggest that it meant "Be aware of what you really ask when you come to consult the oracle."

In Greek and Roman texts, the injunction of having to know oneself was always associated with the other principle of the care of the self, and it was that need to care for oneself that brought the Delphic maxim into operation. It is implicit in all Greek and Roman culture and has been explicit since Plato's *Alcibiades I.*[1] In the Socratic dialogues, in Xenophon, Hippocrates, and in the Neoplatonist tradition from Albinus on, one had to be concerned with oneself. One had to occupy oneself with oneself before the Delphic principle was brought into action. There was a subordination of the second principle to the former. I have three or four examples of this.

In Plato's *Apology,* 29e, Socrates presents himself before his judges as a master of *epimeleia heautou.*[2] You "preoccupy yourselves without shame in acquiring wealth and reputation and honors," he tells them, but you do not concern yourselves with yourselves, that is, with "wisdom, truth and the perfection of the soul." He, on the other hand, watches over the citizens to make sure they concern themselves with themselves.

Socrates says three important things with regard to his invitation to others to occupy themselves with themselves: (1) His mission was conferred on him by the gods, and he won't abandon it except with his last breath. (2) For this task he demands no reward; he is disinterested; he performs it out of benevolence. (3) His mission is useful for the city—more useful than the Athenians' military victory at Olympia—because, in teaching people to occupy themselves with themselves, he teaches them to occupy themselves with the city.

Eight centuries later, one finds the same notion and the same phrase in Gregory of Nyssa's treatise, *On Virginity,* but with an entirely different meaning. Gregory did not mean the movement by which one takes care of oneself and the city; he meant the movement by which one renounces the world and marriage as well as detaches oneself from the flesh and, with virginity of heart and body, recovers the immortality of which one has been deprived. In commenting on the parable of the drachma (Luke 15.8–10), Gregory exhorts man to light his lamp and turn the house over and search, until gleaming in the shadow he sees the drachma within. In order to recover the efficacy that God has printed on the human soul and the body has tarnished, man must take care of himself and search every corner of his soul.[3]

We see that Christian asceticism and ancient philosophy are placed under the same sign: that of the care of the self. The obligation to know oneself is one of the central elements of Christian asceticism. Between these two extremes— Socrates and Gregory of Nyssa—taking care of oneself constituted not only a principle but also a constant practice.

I have two more examples. The first Epicurean text to serve as a manual of morals was the *Letter to Menoeceus*.[4] Epicurus writes that it is never too early, never too late, to occupy oneself with one's soul. One should philosophize when one is young and also when one is old. It is a task to be carried on throughout life. Precepts governing everyday life are organized around the care of the self in order to help every member of the group with the common task of salvation.

Another example comes from an Alexandrian text, *On the Contemplative Life*, by Philo of Alexandria. He describes an obscure, enigmatic group on the periphery of Hellenistic and Hebraic culture called the *Therapeutae*, marked by its religiosity. It is an austere community, devoted to reading, to healing meditation, to individual and collective prayer, and to meeting for a spiritual banquet (*agapē*, "feast"). These practices stem from the principal task, the care of the self.[5]

This is the point of departure for a possible analysis of the care of the self in ancient culture. I would like to analyze the relation between the care of the self and knowledge of the self, the relation found in Greco-Roman and Christian traditions between the preoccupation an individual has with himself and the too-well-known principle "Know yourself." Just as there are different forms of care, there are different forms of self.

Summary

There are several reasons why "Know yourself" has obscured "Take care of yourself." First, there has been a profound transformation in the moral principles of Western society. We find it difficult to base rigorous morality and austere principles on the precept that we should give more care to ourselves than to anything else in the world. We are more inclined to see taking care of ourselves as an immorality, as a means of escape from all possible rules. We inherit the tradition of Christian morality which makes self-renunciation the condition for salvation. To know oneself was, paradoxically, a means of self-renunciation.

We also inherit a secular tradition that sees in external law the basis for morality. How then can respect for the self be the basis for morality? We are the inheritors of a social morality that seeks the rules for acceptable behavior in relations with others. Since the sixteenth century, criticism of established morality has been undertaken in the name of the importance of recognizing and knowing the self. Therefore, it is difficult to see the care of the self as compatible with morality. "Know thyself" has obscured "Take care of yourself" because our morality, a morality of asceticism, insists that the self is that which one can reject.

The second reason is that, in theoretical philosophy from Descartes to Husserl, knowledge of the self (the thinking subject) takes on an ever-increasing importance as the first step in the theory of knowledge.

To summarize: There has been an inversion in the hierarchy of the two principles of antiquity, "Take care of yourself" and "Know yourself." In Greco-Roman culture, knowledge of oneself appeared as the consequence of the care of the self. In the modern world, knowledge of oneself constitutes the fundamental principle.

II

The first philosophical elaboration of the concern with taking care of oneself that I wish to consider is found in Plato's *Alcibiades I.* The date of its writing is uncertain, and it may be a spurious Platonic dialogue. It is not my intention to study dates but to point out the principal features of the care of the self which is the center of the dialogue.

The Neoplatonists in the third or fourth century A.D. show the significance given to this dialogue and the importance it assumed in the classical tradition. They wanted to transform Plato's dialogues into a pedagogical tool, to make them the matrix for encyclopedic knowledge. They considered *Alcibiades* to be the first dialogue of Plato—the first to be read, the first to be studied. It was the *arkhē.* In the second century, Albinus said that every gifted young man who wanted to stand apart from politics and practice virtue should study the *Alcibiades.*[6] It provided the point of departure and a program for all Platonic philosophy. "Taking care of oneself" is its first principle. I would like to analyze the care of self in the *Alcibiades I* in terms of three aspects.

1. How is this question introduced into the dialogue? What are the reasons Alcibiades and Socrates are brought to the notion of the care of the self?

Alcibiades is about to begin his public and political life. He wishes to speak before the people and be all-powerful in the city. He is not satisfied with his traditional status, with the privileges of his birth and heritage. He wishes to gain personal power over all others both inside and outside the city. At this point of intersection and transformation, Socrates intervenes and declares his love for Alcibiades. Alcibiades can no longer be the beloved; he must become a lover. He must become active in the political and the love game. Thus, there is a dialectic between political and erotic discourse. Alcibiades makes his transition in specific ways in both politics and love.

An ambivalence is evident in Alcibiades' political and erotic vocabulary. During his adolescence, Alcibiades was desirable and had many admirers, but now that his beard is growing, his suitors are disappearing. Earlier, he had rejected them all in the bloom of his beauty because he wanted to be dominant, not dominated. He refused to let himself be dominated in youth, but now he wants to dominate others. This is the moment Socrates appears, and he succeeds where the others have failed: he will make Alcibiades submit, but in a different sense. They make a pact—Alcibiades will submit to his lover, Socrates, not in a physical but in a spiritual sense. The intersection of political ambition and philosophical love is "the care of the self."

2. In such a relationship, why should Alcibiades be concerned with himself, and why is Socrates preoccupied with that concern of Alcibiades? Socrates asks Alcibiades about his personal capacities and the nature of his ambition. Does he know the meaning of the rule of law, of justice or concord? Alcibiades clearly knows nothing. Socrates calls upon him to compare his education with that of the Persian and Spartan kings, his rivals. Spartan and Persian princes have teachers in wisdom, justice, temperance, and courage. By comparison, Alcibiades' education is like that of an old, ignorant slave: he doesn't know these things, so he can't apply himself to knowledge. But, says Socrates, it is not too late. To help him gain the upper hand—to acquire *tekhnē*—Alcibiades must apply himself, he must take care of himself. But Alcibiades does not know to what he must apply himself. What is this knowledge he seeks? He is embarrassed and confused. Socrates calls upon him not to lose heart.

In 127d of the *Alcibiades* we find the first appearance of the phrase *epimeleisthai seautou*. Concern for self always refers to an active political and erotic state. *Epimeleisthai* expresses something much more serious than the simple fact of paying attention. It involves various things: taking pains with one's holdings and one's health. It is always a real activity and not just an attitude. It is used in reference to the activity of a farmer tending his fields, his cattle, and his house, or to the job of the king in taking care of his city and citizens, or to the worship of ancestors or gods, or as a medical term to signify the fact of caring. It is highly significant that the concern for self in *Alcibiades I* is directly related to a defective pedagogy, one that concerns political ambition and a specific moment of life.

3. The rest of the text is devoted to an analysis of this notion of *epimeleisthai*, "taking pains with oneself." It is divided into two questions: What is this self of which one has to take care, and of what does that care consist?

First, what is the self (129b)? *Self* is a reflexive pronoun, and it has two meanings. *Auto* means "the same," but it also conveys the notion of identity. The latter meaning shifts the question from "What is this self?" to "Departing from what ground shall I find my identity?" Alcibiades tries to find the self in a dialectical movement. When you take care of the body, you do not take care of the self. The self is not clothing, tools, or possessions; it is to be found in the principle that uses these tools, a principle not of the body but of the soul. You have to worry about your soul—that is the principal activity of caring for yourself. The care of the self is the care of the activity and not the care of the soul-as-substance.

The second question is: How must we take care of this principle of activity, the soul? Of what does this care consist? One must know of what the soul consists. The soul cannot know itself except by looking at itself in a similar element, a mirror. Thus, it must contemplate the divine element. In this divine contemplation, the soul will be able to discover rules to serve as a basis for just behavior and political action. The effort of the soul to know itself is the principle on which just political action can be founded, and Alcibiades will be a good politician insofar as he contemplates his soul in the divine element.

Often the discussion gravitates around and is phrased in terms of the Delphic principle "Know yourself." To take care of oneself consists of knowing oneself. Knowing oneself becomes the object of the quest of concern for self. Being occupied with oneself and political activities are linked. The dialogue ends when Alcibiades knows he must take care of himself by examining his soul.

This text, one of Plato's first, illuminates the historical background of the precept "taking care of oneself" and sets out four main problems that endure throughout antiquity, although the solutions offered often differ from those in Plato's *Alcibiades*.

First, there is the problem of the relation between the care of the self and political activity. In the later Hellenistic and imperial periods, the question is presented in an alternative way: When is it better to turn away from political activity to concern oneself with oneself?

Second, there is the problem of the relationship between the care of the self and pedagogy. For Socrates, occupying oneself with oneself is the duty of a young man, but later in the Hellenistic period it is seen as the permanent duty of one's whole life.

Third, there is the problem of the relationship between the care of the self and the knowledge of oneself. Plato gave priority to the Delphic maxim "Know yourself." The privileged position of "Know yourself" is characteristic of all Platonists. Later, in the Hellenistic and Greco-Roman periods, this is reversed: the accent was not on the knowledge of self but on the concern with oneself. The latter was given an autonomy and even a preeminence as a philosophical issue.

Fourth, there is the problem of the relationship between the care of self and philosophical love, or the relation to a master.

In the Hellenistic and imperial periods, the Socratic notion of "the care of the self" became a common, universal philosophical theme. "Care of the self" was accepted by Epicurus and his followers, by the Cynics, and by such Stoics as Seneca, Rufus, and Galen. The Pythagoreans gave attention to the notion of an ordered life in common. This theme of the care of the self was not abstract advice but a widespread activity, a network of obligations and services to the soul. Following Epicurus himself, the Epicureans believed that it is never too late to occupy oneself with oneself. The Stoics say you must attend to the self, "retire into the self and stay there." Lucian parodied the notion.[7] It was an extremely widespread activity, and it brought about competition between the rhetoricians and those who turned toward themselves, particularly over the question of the role of the master.

There were charlatans, of course, but certain individuals took it seriously. It was generally acknowledged that it was good to be reflective, at least briefly. Pliny advises a friend to set aside a few moments a day, or several weeks or months, for a retreat into himself. This was an active leisure—to study, to read, to prepare for misfortune or death. It was a meditation and a preparation.

Writing was also important in the culture of the care of the self. One of the tasks that defines the care of the self is that of taking notes on oneself to be reread, writing treatises and letters to friends to help them, and keeping notebooks in order to reactivate for oneself the truths one needed. Seneca's letters are an example of this self-exercise.

In traditional political life, oral culture was largely dominant, and therefore rhetoric was important. Yet the development of the administrative structures and the bureaucracy of the imperial period increased the amount and role of writing in the political sphere. In Plato's writings, dialogue gave way to the literary pseudodialogue. By the Hellenistic age, though, writing prevailed, and real dialectic passed to correspondence. Taking care of oneself became linked to constant writing activity. The self is something to write about, a theme or object (subject) of writing activity. That is not a modern trait born of the Reformation or of Romanticism; it is one of the most ancient Western traditions. It was well established and deeply rooted when Augustine started his *Confessions.*[8]

The new care of the self involved a new experience of self. The new form of the experience of the self is to be seen in the first and second centuries, when introspection becomes more and more detailed. A relation developed between writing and vigilance. Attention was paid to nuances of life, mood, and reading, and the experience of self was intensified and widened by virtue of this act of writing. A whole field of experience opened which earlier was absent.

One can compare Cicero to the later Seneca or Marcus Aurelius. We see, for example, Seneca's and Marcus's meticulous concern with the details of daily life, with the movements of the spirit, with self-analysis. Everything in the imperial period is present in Marcus Aurelius's letter of 144–45 A.D. to Fronto:

Hail, my sweetest of masters.

We are well. I slept somewhat late owing to my slight cold, which seems now to have subsided. So from five A.M. till nine I spent the time partly in reading some of Cato's *Agriculture* and partly in writing not quite such wretched stuff, by heavens, as yesterday. Then, after paying my respects to my father, I relieved my throat, I will not say by gargling—though the word *gargarisso* is, I believe, found in Novius and elsewhere—but by swallowing honey water as far as the gullet and ejecting it again. After easing my throat I went off to my

father and attended him at a sacrifice. Then we went to luncheon. What do you
think I ate? A wee bit of bread, though I saw others devouring beans, onions,
and herrings full of roe. We then worked hard at grape-gathering, and had a
good sweat, and were merry and, as the poet says, "still left some clusters
hanging high as gleanings of the vintage." After six o'clock we came home.

I did but little work and that to no purpose. Then I had a long chat with my
little mother as she sat on the bed. My talk was this: "What do you think my
Fronto is now doing?" Then she: "And what do you think my Gratia is
doing?" Then I: "And what do you think our little sparrow, the wee Gratia, is
doing?" Whilst we were chattering in this way and disputing which of us two
loved the one or other of you two the better, the gong sounded, an intimation
that my father had gone to his bath. So we had supper after we had bathed in
the oil-press room; I do not mean bathed in the oil-press room, but when we
had bathed, had supper there, and we enjoyed hearing the yokels chaffing one
another. After coming back, before I turn over and snore, I get my task done
and give my dearest of masters an account of the day's doings, and if I could
miss him more, I would not grudge wasting away a little more. Farewell, my
Fronto, wherever you are, most honeysweet, my love, my delight. How is it
between you and me? I love you and you are away.[9]

This letter presents a description of everyday life. All the details of taking care
of oneself are here, all the unimportant things he has done. Cicero tells only important things, but in Aurelius's letter these details are important because they
are you—what you thought, what you felt.

The relation between the body and the soul is interesting too. For the Stoics,
the body was not so important, but Marcus Aurelius speaks of himself, his
health, what he has eaten, his sore throat. That is quite characteristic of the ambiguity about the body in this cultivation of the self. Theoretically, the cultivation of the self is soul-oriented, but all the concerns of the body take on a
considerable importance. In Pliny and Seneca, hypochondria is an essential
trait. They retreat to a house in the countryside. They have intellectual activities but rural activities as well. They eat and participate in the activities of peasants. The importance of the rural retreat in this letter is that nature helps put one
in contact with oneself.

There is also a love relationship between Aurelius and Fronto, one between a
twenty-four-year-old and a forty-year-old man. *Ars erotica* is a theme of discussion. Homosexual love was important in this period and carried over into Christian monasticism.

Finally, in the last lines, there is an allusion to the examination of conscience
at the end of the day. Aurelius goes to bed and looks in the notebook to see what
he was going to do and how it corresponds to what he did. The letter is the tran-

scription of that examination of conscience. It stresses what the individual did, not what he thought. That is the difference between practice in the Hellenistic and imperial periods and later monastic practice. In Seneca, too, there are only deeds, not thoughts; but it does prefigure Christian confession.

This genre of epistles shows a side apart from the philosophy of the era. The examination of conscience begins with this letter-writing. Diary-writing comes later. It dates from the Christian era and focuses on the notion of the struggle of the soul.

III

In my discussion of Plato's *Alcibiades*, I have isolated three major themes: (1) the relation between care of the self and care for the political life; (2) the relation between the care of the self and defective education; and (3) the relation between the care of the self and knowing oneself. Whereas we saw in the *Alcibiades* the close relation between "Take care of yourself" and "Know yourself," taking care of yourself eventually was absorbed in knowing yourself.

We can see these three themes in Plato, also in the Hellenistic period, and four to five centuries later in Seneca, Plutarch, Epictetus, and the like. If the problems are the same, the solutions and themes are quite different and, in some cases, the opposite of the Platonic meanings.

First, to be concerned with self in the Hellenistic and Roman periods is not exclusively a preparation for political life. Care of the self has become a universal principle. One must leave politics to take better care of the self.

Second, the concern with oneself is not just obligatory for young people concerned with their education; it is a way of living for everybody throughout their lives.

Third, even if self-knowledge plays an important role in the care of the self, it involves other relationships as well.

I want to discuss briefly the first two points: the universality of the care of the self independent of political life, and the care of the self throughout one's life.

1. A medical model was substituted for Plato's pedagogical model. The care of the self isn't another kind of pedagogy; it has to become permanent medical care. Permanent medical care is one of the central features of the care of the self. One must become the doctor of oneself.

2. Since we have to take care throughout life, the objective is no longer to get prepared for adult life, or for another life, but to get prepared for a certain complete achievement of life. This achievement is complete at the moment just prior to death. This notion of a happy proximity to death—of old age as completion—is an inversion of the traditional Greek values on youth.

3. Lastly, we have the various practices to which cultivation of self has given rise and the relation of self-knowledge to these.

In *Alcibiades I*, the soul had a mirror relation to itself, which relates to the concept of memory and justifies dialogue as a method of discovering truth in the soul. Yet from the time of Plato to the Hellenistic age, the relationship between care of the self and knowledge of the self changed. We may note two perspectives.

In the philosophical movements of Stoicism in the imperial period, there is a different conception of truth and memory, and another method of examining the self. First, we see the disappearance of dialogue and the increasing importance of a new pedagogical relationship—a new pedagogical game where the master-teacher speaks and does not ask questions, and the disciple does not answer but must listen and keep silent. A cultivation of silence becomes more and more important. In Pythagorean cultivation, disciples kept silent for five years as a pedagogical rule. They did not ask questions or speak up during the lesson, but they developed the art of listening. This is the positive condition for acquiring truth. The tradition is picked up during the imperial period, where we see the beginning of the cultivation of silence and the art of listening rather than the cultivation of dialogue as in Plato.

To learn the art of listening, we have to read Plutarch's treatise on the art of listening to lectures, *Peri tou akouein*.[10] At the beginning of this treatise, Plutarch says that, following schooling, we must learn to listen to *logos* throughout our adult life. The art of listening is crucial so that you can tell what is true and what is dissimulation, what is rhetorical truth and what is falsehood in the discourse of the rhetoricians. Listening is linked to the fact that the disciple is not under the control of the masters but must listen to *logos*. One keeps silent at the lecture; one thinks about it afterward. This is the art of listening to the voice of the master and the voice of reason in the self.

The advice may seem banal, but I think it is important. In his treatise *On the Contemplative Life*, Philo of Alexandria describes banquets of silence, not debauched banquets with wine, boys, revelry, and dialogue. There is instead a teacher who gives a monologue on the interpretation of the Bible and a very precise indication of the way people must listen.[11] For example, they must always assume the same posture when listening. The morphology of this notion is an interesting theme in monasticism and pedagogy henceforth.

In Plato, the themes of contemplation of self and care of self are related dialectically through dialogue. Now in the imperial period, we have the theories of, on one side, the obligation of listening to the truth and, on the other side, of looking and listening to the self for the truth within. The difference between the one era and the other is one of the great signs of the disappearance of the dialectical structure.

What was an examination of conscience in this culture, and how does one look at oneself? For the Pythagoreans, the examination of conscience had to do with purification. Since sleep was related to death as a kind of encounter with the gods, one had to purify oneself before going to sleep. Remembering the dead was an exercise for the memory. But in the Hellenistic and the early imperial periods, you see this practice acquiring new values and signification. There are several relevant texts: Seneca's *De Ira* and *De Tranquillitae*,[12] and the beginning of Marcus Aurelius's fourth book of *Meditations*.[13]

Seneca's *De Ira* (Book Three) contains some traces of the old tradition.[14] He describes an examination of conscience. The same thing was recommended by the Epicureans, and the practice was rooted in the Pythagorean tradition. The goal was the purification of the conscience using a mnemonic device. Do good things, have a good examination of the self, and a good sleep follows together with good dreams, which is contact with the gods.

Seneca seems to use juridical language, and it seems that the self is both the judge and the accused. Seneca is the judge and prosecutes the self so that the examination is a kind of trial. Yet if you look closer, it is rather different from a court: Seneca uses terms related not to juridical but to administrative practices, as when a comptroller looks at the books or when a building inspector examines a building. Self-examination is taking stock. Faults are simply good intentions left undone. The rule is a means of doing something correctly, not judging what has happened in the past. Later, Christian confession will look for bad intentions.

It is this administrative view of his own life much more than the juridical model that is important. Seneca is not a judge who has to punish but a stock-taking administrator. He is a permanent administrator of himself, not a judge of his past. He sees that everything has been done correctly following the rule but not the law. It is not real faults for which he reproaches himself but, rather, his lack of success. His errors are of strategy, not of moral character. He wants to make adjustments between what he wanted to do and what he had done, and to reactivate the rules of conduct, not excavate his guilt. In Christian confession, the penitent is obliged to memorize laws but does so in order to discover his sins.

For Seneca, the problem is not that of discovering truth in the subject but of remembering truth, recovering a truth that has been forgotten. Second, the subject does not forget himself, his nature, origin, or his supernatural affinity, but the rules of conduct, what he ought to have done. Third, the recollection of errors committed in the day measures the distinction between what has been done and what should have been done. Fourth, the subject is not the operating ground for the process of deciphering but the point where rules of conduct come together in memory. The subject constitutes the intersection between acts that have to be regulated and rules for what ought to be done. This is quite different from the Platonic conception and from the Christian conception of conscience.

The Stoics spiritualized the notion of *anakhōrēsis,* the retreat of an army, the hiding of an escaped slave from his master, or the retreat into the country away from the towns, as in Marcus Aurelius's country retreat. A retreat into the country becomes a spiritual retreat into oneself. It is a general attitude and also a precise act every day; you retire into the self to discover—but not to discover faults and deep feelings, only to remember rules of action, the main laws of behavior. It is a mnemotechnical formula.

IV

I have spoken of three Stoic technologies of the self: letters to friends and disclosure of self; examination of self and conscience, including a review of what was done, of what should have been done, and comparison of the two. Now I want to consider the third Stoic technique, *askēsis,* not a disclosure of the secret self but a remembering.

For Plato, one must discover the truth that is within one. For the Stoics, truth is not in oneself but in the *logoi,* the teachings of the masters. One memorizes what one has heard, converting the statement one hears into rules of conduct. The subjectivation of truth is the aim of these techniques. During the imperial period, one could not assimilate ethical principles without a theoretical framework such as science, as for example in Lucretius's *De Rerum natura.*[15] There are structural questions underlying the practice of the examination of the self every night. I want to underscore the fact that in Stoicism it is not the deciphering of the self, not the means to disclose secrecy, which is important; it is the memory of what one has done and what one has had to do.

In Christianity, asceticism always refers to a certain renunciation of the self and of reality because most of the time the self is a part of that reality that must be renounced in order to gain access to another level of reality. This move to attain the renunciation of the self distinguishes Christian asceticism.

In the philosophical tradition inaugurated by Stoicism, *askēsis* means not renunciation but the progressive consideration of self, or mastery over oneself, obtained not through the renunciation of reality but through the acquisition and assimilation of truth. It has as its final aim not preparation for another reality but access to the reality of this world. The Greek word for this is *paraskeuazō* ("to get prepared"). It is a set of practices by which one can acquire, assimilate, and transform truth into a permanent principle of action. *Alētheia* becomes *ēthos.* It is a process of the intensification of subjectivity.

What are the principal features of *askēsis?* They include exercises in which the subject puts himself in a situation in which he can verify whether he can confront events and use the discourses with which he is armed. It is a question of

testing the preparation. Is this truth assimilated enough to become ethics so that
we can behave as we must when an event presents itself?

The Greeks characterized the two poles of those exercises by the terms
meletē and *gymnasia*. *Meletē* means "meditation," according to the Latin
translation, *meditatio*. It has the same root as *epimeleisthai*. It is a rather vague
term, a technical term borrowed from rhetoric. *Meletē* is the work one undertakes in order to prepare a discourse or an improvisation by thinking over useful
terms and arguments. It is a matter of anticipating the real situation through dialogue in one's thoughts. The philosophical meditation is this kind of meditation: it is composed of memorizing responses and reactivating those memories
by placing oneself in a situation where one can imagine how one would react.
One judges the reasoning one should use in an imaginary exercise ("Let us suppose . . .") in order to test an action or event (for example, "How would I
react?"). Imagining the articulation of possible events to test how one would
react—that is meditation.

The most famous exercise of meditation is the *praemeditatio malorum* as practiced by the Stoics. It is an ethical, imaginary experience. In appearance, it is a
rather dark and pessimistic vision of the future. You can compare it to what
Husserl says about eidetic reduction.

The Stoics developed three eidetic reductions of future misfortune. First, it is
not a question of imagining the future as it is likely to turn out but to imagine the
worst that can happen, even if there is little chance that it will turn out that way—
the worst as certainty, as actualizing what could happen, not as calculation of
probability. Second, one should not envisage things as possibly taking place in the
distant future but as already actual and in the process of taking place. For example, imagining not that one might be exiled but rather that one is already exiled,
subjected to torture, and dying. Third, one does this not in order to experience
inarticulate sufferings but in order to convince oneself that they are not real ills.
The reduction of all that is possible, of all the duration and of all the misfortunes,
reveals not something bad but what we must accept. It consists of having at the
same time the future and the present event. The Epicureans were hostile to it because they thought it was useless: they thought it was better to recollect and memorize past pleasures in order to derive pleasure from present events.

At the opposite pole is *gymnasia* ("to train oneself"). While *meditatio* is an
imaginary experience that trains thought, *gymnasia* is training in a real situation, even if it has been artificially induced. There is a long tradition behind this:
sexual abstinence, physical privation, and other rituals of purification.

Those practices of abstinence have other meanings than purification or witnessing demonic force, as in Pythagoras and Socrates. In the culture of the Stoics, their function is to establish and test the independence of the individual with
regard to the external world. For example, in Plutarch's *On the Daemon of*

Socrates, one gives oneself over to very hard sporting activities. Or one tempts oneself by placing oneself in front of many tantalizing dishes and then renouncing them; then one calls his slaves and gives them the dishes, and takes the meal prepared for the slaves.[16] Another example is Seneca's Letter 18 to Lucilius: he prepares for a great feast day by acts of mortification of the flesh in order to convince himself that poverty is not an evil, and that he can endure it.[17]

Between these poles of training in thought and training in reality, *melete* and *gymnasia,* there are a whole series of intermediate possibilities. Epictetus provides the best example of the middle ground between these poles. He wants to watch perpetually over representations, a technique that will find its apogee in Freud. There are two metaphors important from his point of view: the night watchman, who will not admit anyone into town if that person cannot prove who he is (we must be "watchmen" over the flux of thought),[18] and the moneychanger, who verifies the authenticity of currency, looks at it, weighs and assures himself of its worth. We have to be moneychangers of our own representations, of our thoughts, vigilantly testing them, verifying them, their metal, weight, effigy.[19]

The same metaphor of the moneychanger is found in the Stoics and in early Christian literature, but with different meanings. When Epictetus says you must be a moneychanger, he means as soon as an idea comes to mind you have to think of the rules you must apply to evaluate it. For Cassian, being a moneychanger and looking at your thoughts means something very different: it means you must try to decipher if, at the root of the movement that brings you the representations, there is or is not concupiscence or desire—if your innocent thought has evil origins; if you have something underlying which is the great Seducer, which is perhaps hidden, the money of your thought.[20]

In Epictetus there are two exercises—sophistical and ethical. The first are exercises borrowed from school, question-and-answer games. This must be an ethical game; that is, it must teach a moral lesson.[21] The second are ambulatory exercises. In the morning you go for a walk, and you test your reactions to that walk. The purpose of both exercises is control of representations, not the deciphering of truth. They are reminders about conforming to the rules in the face of adversity. A pre-Freudian machine of censorship is described word for word in the tests of Epictetus and Cassian. For Epictetus, the control of representations means not deciphering but recalling principles of acting, and thus seeing, through self-examination, if they govern one's life. It is a kind of permanent self-examination. One must be one's own censor. The meditation on death is the culmination of all these exercises.

In addition to letters, examination, and *askēsis,* we must now evoke a fourth technique in the examination of the self, the interpretation of dreams. It was to have an important destiny in the nineteenth century, but it occupied a relatively marginal position in the ancient world. Philosophers had an ambivalent attitude toward the interpretation of dreams. Most Stoics are critical and skeptical about such interpretation; but there is still the popular and general practice of it. There were experts who were able to interpret dreams, including Pythagoras and some of the Stoics, and some experts who wrote books to teach people to interpret their own dreams. There were huge amounts of literature on how to do it, but the only surviving dream manual is *The Interpretation of Dreams* by Artemidorus (second century A.D.).[22] Dream interpretation was important because, in antiquity, the meaning of a dream was an announcement of a future event.

I should mention two other documents dealing with the importance of dream interpretation for everyday life. The first is by Synesius of Cyrene in the fourth century A.D.[23] He was well known and cultivated. Even though he was not a Christian, he asked to be a bishop. His remarks on dreams are interesting, for public divination was forbidden in order to spare the emperor bad news. Therefore, one had to interpret one's own dreams; one had to be a self-interpreter. To do it, one had to remember not only one's own dreams but the events before and after. One had to record what happened every day, both the life of the day and the life of the night.

Aelius Aristides' *Sacred Discourses,*[24] written in the second century, records his dreams and explains how to interpret them. He believed that in the interpretation of dreams we receive advice from the gods about remedies for illness. With this work, we are at the crossing point of two kinds of discourses. It is not the writing of the self's daily activities that is the matrix of the *Sacred Discourses* but the ritual inscription of praises to the gods that have healed you.

V

I wish to examine the scheme of one of the main techniques of the self in early Christianity and what it was as a truth game. To do so, I must look at the transition from pagan to Christian culture, in which it is possible to see clear-cut continuities and discontinuities.

Christianity belongs to the salvation religions. It is one of those religions which is supposed to lead the individual from one reality to another, from death to life, from time to eternity. In order to achieve that, Christianity imposed a set of conditions and rules of behavior for a certain transformation of the self.

Christianity is not only a salvation religion, it is a confessional religion; it imposes very strict obligations of truth, dogma, and canon, more so than do the pagan religions. Truth obligations to believe this or that were and are still very numerous. The duty to accept a set of obligations, to hold certain books as permanent truth, to accept authoritarian decisions in matters of truth, not only to believe certain things but to show that one believes, and to accept institutional authority are all characteristic of Christianity.

Christianity requires another form of truth obligation different from faith. Each person has the duty to know who he is, that is, to try to know what is happening inside him, to acknowledge faults, to recognize temptations, to locate desires; and everyone is obliged to disclose these things either to God or to others in the community and, hence, to bear public or private witness against oneself. The truth obligations of faith and the self are linked together. This link permits a purification of the soul impossible without self-knowledge.

It is not the same in the Catholic as in the Reform tradition. But the main features of both are an ensemble of truth obligations dealing with faith, books, dogma, and one dealing with truth, heart, and soul. Access to truth cannot be conceived of without purity of the soul. Purity of the soul is the consequence of self-knowledge and a condition for understanding the text: *quis facit veritatem* (to make truth in oneself, to get access to the light), in Augustine.

I would like to analyze the ways by which, in order to get access to the light, the Church conceived of illumination: the disclosure of the self. The sacrament of penance and the confession of sins are rather late innovations. Christians of the first centuries had different forms for discovering and deciphering truth about themselves. One of the two main forms of these discourses can be characterized by the word *exomologēsis*, or "recognition of fact." Even the Latin fathers used this Greek term with no exact translation. For Christians, it meant to recognize publicly the truth of their faith or to recognize publicly that they were Christians.

The word also had a penitential meaning. When a sinner seeks penance, he must visit the bishop and ask for it. In early Christianity, penitence was not an act or a ritual but a status imposed on somebody who had committed very serious sins.

Exomologesis was a ritual of recognizing oneself as a sinner and penitent. It had several characteristics. First, you were a penitent for four to ten years, and this status affected your life. There was fasting, and there were rules about clothing and prohibitions about sex; the individual was marked so he could not live the same life as others. Even after his reconciliation, he suffered from a number of prohibitions; for example, he could not marry or become a priest.

Within this status you find the obligation of exomologesis. The sinner seeks his penance. He visits the bishop and asks the bishop to impose on him the status of a penitent. He must explain why he wants the status, and he must explain his faults. This was not a confession; it was a condition of the status. Later, in the medieval period, exomologesis became a ritual that took place at the end of the period of penance, just before reconciliation. This ceremony placed him among the other Christians. Of this recognition ceremony, Tertullian says that wearing a hair shirt and ashes, wretchedly dressed, the sinner stands humbled before the church. Then he prostrates himself and kisses the brethren's knees.[25] Exomologesis is not a verbal behavior but the dramatic recognition of one's status as a penitent. Much later, in the *Epistles* of Jerome, there is a description of the penitence of Fabiola, a Roman lady.[26] During these days, Fabiola was in the ranks of penitents. People wept with her, lending drama to her public chastisement.

Recognition also designates the entire process that the penitent experiences in this status over the years. He is the aggregate of manifested penitential behavior, of self-punishment as well as of self-revelation. The acts by which he punishes himself are indistinguishable from the acts by which he reveals himself: self-punishment and the voluntary expression of the self are bound together. This link is evident in many writings; Cyprian, for example, talks of exhibitions of shame and modesty. Penance is not nominal but theatrical.[27]

To prove suffering, to show shame, to make visible humility and exhibit modesty—these are the main features of punishment. Penitence in early Christianity is a way of life acted out at all times by accepting the obligation to disclose oneself. It must be visibly represented and accompanied by others who recognize the ritual. This approach endured until the fifteenth and sixteenth centuries.

Tertullian uses the term *publicatio sui* to characterize exomologesis. *Publicatio sui* is related to Seneca's daily self-examination, which was, however, completely private. For Seneca, exomologesis or *publicatio sui* does not imply verbal analysis of deeds or thoughts; it is only a somatic and symbolic expression. What was private for the Stoics was public for the Christians.

What were its functions? First, this publication was a way to rub out sin and to restore the purity acquired by baptism. Second, it was also to show a sinner as he is. That is the paradox at the heart of exomologesis: it rubs out the sin and yet reveals the sinner. The greater part of the act of penitence was not in telling the truth of sin but in showing the true sinful being of the sinner; it was not a way for the sinner to explain his sins but a way to present himself as a sinner.

Why should showing forth efface the sins? Exposé is the heart of exomologesis. In the Christianity of the first centuries, Christian authors had recourse to three models to explain the relation between the paradox of rubbing out sins and disclosing oneself.

The first is the medical model: one must show one's wounds in order to be cured. Another model, which was less frequent, was the tribunal model of judgment: one always appeases one's judge by confessing faults. The sinner plays devil's advocate, as will the devil on the Day of Judgment.

The most important model used to explain exomologesis was the model of death, of torture, or of martyrdom. The theories and practices of penance were elaborated around the problem of the man who prefers to die rather than to compromise or abandon the faith; the way the martyr faces death is the model for the penitent. For the relapsed to be reintegrated into the Church, he must expose himself voluntarily to ritual martyrdom. Penance is the affect of change, of rupture with self, past, and world. It is a way to show that you are able to renounce life and self, to show that you can face and accept death. Penitence of sin does not have as its target the establishing of an identity but, instead, serves to mark the refusal of the self, the breaking away from self: *ego non sum, ego*. This formula is at the heart of *publicatio sui*. It represents a break with one's past identity. These ostentatious gestures have the function of showing the truth of the state of being of the sinner. Self-revelation is at the same time self-destruction.

The difference between the Stoic and Christian traditions is that in the Stoic tradition examination of self, judgment, and discipline show the way to self-knowledge by superimposing truth about self through memory, that is, by memorizing the rules. In exomologesis, the penitent superimposes truth about self by violent rupture and dissociation. It is important to emphasize that this exomologesis is not verbal. It is symbolic, ritual, and theatrical.

VI

During the fourth century, we find a very different technology for the disclosure of the self, *exagoreusis*, much less famous than exomologesis but more important. This one is reminiscent of the verbalizing exercises in relation to a teacher-master of the pagan philosophical schools. We can see the transfer of several Stoic techniques of the self to Christian spiritual techniques.

At least one example of self-examination, proposed by Chrysostom, was exactly the same form and the same administrative character as that described by Seneca in *De Ira*. In the morning, we must take account of our expenses, and in the evening we must ask ourselves to render account of our conduct of ourselves, to examine what is to our advantage and what is prejudicial against us, with prayers instead of indiscreet words.[28] That is exactly the Senecan style of self-examination. It is also important to note that this self-examination is rare in Christian literature.

The well-developed and elaborated practice of the self-examination in monastic Christianity is different from the Senecan self-examination and very different from Chrysostom and from exomologesis. This new kind of practice must be understood from the viewpoint of two principles of Christian spirituality: obedience and contemplation.

In Seneca, the relationship of the disciple with the master was important, but it was instrumental and professional. It was founded on the capacity of the master to lead the disciple to a happy and autonomous life through good advice. The relationship would end when the disciple gained access to that life.

For a long series of reasons, obedience has a very different character in monastic life. It differs from the Greco-Roman type of relation to the master in the sense that obedience is not based just upon a need for self-improvement but must bear on all aspects of a monk's life. There is no element in the life of the monk which may escape from this fundamental and permanent relation of total obedience to the master. Cassian repeats an old principle from the oriental tradition: "Everything the monk does without permission of his master constitutes a theft." [29] Here, obedience is complete control of behavior by the master, not a final autonomous state. It is a sacrifice of the self, of the subject's own will. This is the new technology of the self.

The monk must have the permission of his director to do anything, even die. Everything he does without permission is stealing; there is not a single moment when the monk can be autonomous. Even when he becomes a director himself, he must retain the spirit of obedience. He must keep the spirit of obedience as a permanent sacrifice of the complete control of behavior by the master. The self must constitute itself through obedience.

The second feature of monastic life is that contemplation is considered the supreme good. It is the obligation of the monk to turn his thoughts continuously to that point which is God and to make sure that his heart is pure enough to see God. The goal is permanent contemplation of God.

This new technology of the self, which developed from obedience and contemplation in the monastery, presents some peculiar characteristics. Cassian gives a rather clear exposition of this technology of the self, a principle of self-examination which he borrowed from the Syrian and Egyptian monastic traditions.

This technology of self-examination of oriental origins, dominated by obedience and contemplation, is much more concerned with thought than with action. Seneca had placed his stress on action. With Cassian, the object is not past actions of the day—it is the present thoughts. Since the monk must continuously turn his thoughts toward God, he must scrutinize the actual course of this thought. This scrutiny thus has as its object the permanent discrimination between thoughts which lead toward God and those which don't. This continual concern with the present is different from the Senecan memorization of deeds and their correspondence with rules. It is what the Greeks referred to with a pejorative word: *logismoi*, "cogitations, reasoning, calculating thought." There is an etymology of *logismoi* in Cassian, but I do not know if it is sound: *co-agitationes*. The spirit is *polukinētos*, "perpetually moving." [30] In Cassian, perpetual mobility of spirit is the spirit's weakness. It distracts one from contemplation of God. [31]

The scrutiny of conscience consists of trying to immobilize consciousness, to eliminate movements of the spirit which divert one from God. That means we must examine any thought that presents itself to consciousness to see the relation between act and thought, truth and reality, to see if there is anything in this thought which will move our spirit, provoke our desire, turn our spirit away from God. The scrutiny is based on the idea of a secret concupiscence.

There are three major types of self-examination: (1) self-examination with respect to thoughts in correspondence to reality (Cartesian); (2) self-examination with respect to the way our thoughts relate to rules (Senecan); (3) the examination of self with respect to the relation between the hidden thought and an inner impurity. At this moment begins the Christian hermeneutics of the self with its deciphering of inner thoughts. It implies that there is something hidden in ourselves and that we are always in a self-illusion that hides the secret.

In order to make this kind of scrutiny, Cassian says we must care for ourselves, to attest to our thoughts directly. He gives three analogies. First is the analogy of the mill.[32] Thoughts are like grains, and consciousness is the mill store: it is our role as the miller to sort out among the grains those which are bad and those which can be admitted to the mill store to give the good flour and good bread of our salvation.

Second, Cassian makes military analogies.[33] He uses an analogy of the officer who orders the good soldiers to march to the right, the bad to the left. We must act like officers who divide soldiers into two files, the good and the bad.

Third, he uses the analogy of a moneychanger.[34] Conscience is the moneychanger of the self. It must examine coins, their effigy, their metal, where they came from. It must weigh them to see if they have been ill used. As there is the image of the emperor on money, so must the image of God be on our thoughts. We must verify the quality of the thought: This effigy of God, is it real? What is its degree of purity? Is it mixed with desire or concupiscence? Thus, we find the same image as in Seneca, but with a different meaning.

Since we have as our role to be a permanent moneychanger of ourselves, how is it possible to make this discrimination and recognize if a thought is of good quality? How can this "discrimination" actively be done? There is only one way: to tell all thoughts to our director, to be obedient to our master in all things, to engage in the permanent verbalization of all our thoughts. In Cassian, self-examination is subordinated to obedience and the permanent verbalization of thoughts. Neither is true of Stoicism. By telling himself not only his thoughts but also the smallest movements of consciousness, his intentions, the monk stands in a hermeneutic relation not only to the master but to himself. This verbalization is the touchstone or the money of thought.

Why is confession able to assume this hermeneutic role? How can we be the hermeneuts of ourselves in speaking and transcribing all of our thoughts? Confession permits the master to know because of his greater experience and wisdom and therefore to give better advice. Even if the master, in his role as a discriminating power, does not say anything, the fact that the thought has been expressed will have an effect of discrimination.

Cassian gives an example of the monk who stole bread. At first he cannot tell. The difference between good and evil thoughts is that evil thoughts cannot be expressed without difficulty, for evil is hidden and unstated. Because evil thoughts cannot be expressed without difficulty and shame, the cosmological difference between light and dark, between verbalization and sin, secrecy and silence, between God and the Devil, may not emerge. Then the monk prostrates himself and confesses. Only when he confesses verbally does the Devil go out of him. The verbal expression is the crucial moment.[35] Confession is a mark of truth. This idea of the permanent verbal is only an ideal: it is never completely possible. But the price of the permanent verbal was to make everything that could not be expressed into a sin.

In conclusion, in the Christianity of the first centuries, there are two main forms of disclosing self, of showing the truth about oneself. The first is exomologesis, or a dramatic expression of the situation of the penitent as sinner which makes manifest his status as sinner. The second is what was called in the spiritual literature exagoreusis. This is an analytical and continual verbalization of thoughts carried on in the relation of complete obedience to someone else; this relation is modeled on the renunciation of one's own will and of one's own self.

There is a great difference between exomologesis and exagoreusis; yet we have to underscore the fact that there is one important element in common: you cannot disclose without renouncing. In exomologesis, the sinner must "kill" himself through ascetic macerations. Whether through martyrdom or through obedience to a master, disclosure of self is the renunciation of one's own self. In exagoreusis, on the other hand, you show that, in permanently verbalizing your thoughts and permanently obeying the master, you are renouncing your will and yourself. This practice continues from the beginning of Christianity to the seventeenth century. The inauguration of penance in the thirteenth century is an important step in its rise.

This theme of self-renunciation is very important. Throughout Christianity there is a correlation between disclosure of the self, dramatic or verbalized, and the renunciation of self. My hypothesis, from looking at these two techniques, is that it is the second one, verbalization, that becomes the more important. From the eighteenth century to the present, the techniques of verbalization have been reinserted in a different context by the so-called human sciences in order to use them without renunciation of the self but to constitute, positively, a new self. To use these techniques without renouncing oneself constitutes a decisive break.

Notes

1. Plato, *Alcibiade,* trans. M. Croiset (Paris: Belles Lettres, 1925) [Plato, *Alcibiades,* trans. W. R. M. Lamb, in *Plato* (Cambridge, Mass.: Harvard, 1967), vol. 12].

2. Plato, *Apologie de Socrate,* trans. M. Croiset (Paris: Belles Lettres, 1925), p. 157 [*Socrates' Defense (Apology),* trans. H. Tredennick, in *Plato: The Collected Dialogues,* ed. E. Hamilton and H. Cairns (Princeton: Princeton University Press, 1961), p. 16].

3. Gregory of Nyssa, *Traité de la virginité,* trans. M. Aubineau (Paris: Cerf, 1966), ch. 13, §3, pp. 411–17 [*Treatise on Virginity,* trans. V. W. Callahan, in *Saint Gregory of Nyssa: Ascetical Works* (Washington, D.C.: Catholic University of America Press, 1966), pp. 46–48].

4. Epicurus, *Lettre à Ménécée,* in *Lettres et Maximes,* trans. M. Conche (Villiers-sur-Mer: Mégare, 1977), pp. 215–27 [*Letter to Menoeceus,* in *The Philosophy of Epicurus,* trans. and ed. G. K. Strodach (Evanston, Ill.: Northwestern University Press, 1963), pp. 122–35].

5. Philo of Alexandria, *La Vie contemplative,* trans. P. Miquel (Paris: Cerf, 1963), §36, p. 105 [*The Contemplative Life,* in *Philo of Alexandria,* trans. D. Winston (New York: Paulist Press, 1981), pp. 42–43].

6. Albinus, *Prologos,* §5 (cited in A. S. Festugière, *Etudes de philosophie grecque* [Paris: Vrin, 1971], p. 536).

7. Lucian, *Hermotine Works,* trans. K. Kiburn (Cambridge, Mass.: Harvard, 1959), vol. 4, p. 65.

8. Augustine composes his *Confessions* between 397 and 401. In *Oeuvres complètes,* trans. G. Bouissou and E. Tréhorel (Paris: Desclée de Brouwer, 1962), vols. 13–14 [Saint Augustine, *Confessions,* trans. R. S. Pine-Coffin (London: Penguin, 1961)].

9. Marcus Aurelius, *Lettres à Fronton,* in *Pensées,* trans. A. Cassan (Paris: Charpentier et Fasquelle, n.d.), let. 29, pp. 391–93 [*Letter to Fronto,* in *The Correspondence of Marcus Cornelius Fronto,* ed. and trans. C. R. Haines (New York: G. Putnam's Sons, 1919), pp. 181–83].

10. Plutarch, *Comment écouter,* in *Oeuvres Complètes,* trans. R. Klaerr, A. Philippon, and J. Sirinelli (Paris: Belles Lettres, 1989), vol. 1, 2d part, ch. 3, pp. 39–40 [*Concerning Hearing,* in *The Complete Works of Plutarch,* ed. W. Lloyd Bevan (New York: Thomas Y. Crowell, 1909), vol. 2, p. 393].

11. Philo of Alexandria, *La Vie contemplative,* p. 77 [*The Contemplative Life,* p. 47].

12. Seneca, *De Ira (De la colère),* trans. A. Bourgery, in *Dialogues* (Paris: Belles Lettres, 1922) [*On Anger,* trans. J. W. Basore, in *Seneca: Moral Essays* (New York: G. Putnam's Sons, 1928)]; *De la tranquillité de l'âme,* trans. R. Waltz, in *Dialogues,* vol. 4, bk. 6, §§1–8, pp. 84–86 [*De Tranquillitate Animi,* in *Seneca: Four Dialogues,* ed. and trans. C. D. N. Costa (Warminster, Eng.: Aris and Phillips Ltd., 1994), pp. 54–56].

13. Marcus Aurelius Antoninus, *Pensées,* trans. A. Trannoy (Paris: Belles Lettres, 1925), bk. 4, §3, pp. 27–29 [*To Himself,* in *The Communings with Himself of Marcus Aurelius Antoninus, Emperor of Rome,* trans. C. R. Haines (New York: G. Putnam's Sons, 1930), bk. 4, §3, pp. 67–71].

14. Seneca, *De Ira (De la colère),* bk. 3, §36, pp. 102–103 [*On Anger,* pp. 339–41].

15. Lucretius, *De la nature des choses,* trans. A. Ernout, 5th ed. (Paris: Belles Lettres, 1984–85) [*On the Nature of Things,* ed. and trans. A. M. Esolen (Baltimore: Johns Hopkins, 1995)].

16. Plutarch, *Le Démon de Socrate,* trans. J. Hani, in *Oeuvres Complètes,* vol. 8 (1980), §586a, p. 95 [*A Discourse Concerning the Demon of Socrates,* in *The Complete Works of Plutarch,* vol. 1, pp. 643–44].

17. Seneca, *Lettres à Lucilius,* trans. H. Noblot (Paris: Belles Lettres, 1945), let. 18, §§1–8, pp. 71–76 [*Ad Lucilium Epistulae Morales,* trans. R. M. Gummere (New York: G. Putnam's Sons, 1917), vol. 1, let. 18, §§1–8, pp. 116–21].

18. Epictetus, *Entretiens,* trans. J. Souilhé (Paris: Belles Lettres, 1963), bk. 3, ch. 12, §15, p. 45 [*The Discourses of Epictetus,* trans. and ed. G. Lond (New York: A. L. Burt, n.d.), bk. 3, ch. 12, pp. 252–54].

19. Epictetus, *Entretiens,* pp. 76–77 [*The Discourses of Epictetus,* bk. 3, ch. 22, pp. 283–85].

20. John Cassian, *Première conférence de l'abbé Moïse,* in *Conférences,* trans. Dom E. Pichery (Paris: Cerf, 1955), vol. 1, ch. 20, pp. 101–105 ["The Goal or Objective of the Monk," in *Conferences,* trans. C. Luibheid (New York: Paulist Press, 1985), pp. 54–57].

21. Epictetus, *Entretiens,* pp. 32–33 [*The Discourses of Epictetus,* bk. 3, ch. 8, pp. 243–44].

22. Artemidorus, *La Clef des songes: Onirocriticon,* trans. A. J. Festugière (Paris: Vrin, 1975) [*The Interpretation of Dreams,* trans. R. J. White (Park Ridge, N.J.: Noyes, 1975)].

23. Synesius of Cyrene, *Sur les rêves,* in *Oeuvres,* trans. H. Druon (Paris: Hachette, 1878), pp. 346–76 [*Concerning Dreams,* in *The Essays and Hymns of Synesius of Cyrene,* trans. and ed. A. Fitzgerald (Oxford University, 1930), vol. 2, pp. 326–59].

24. Aelius Aristides, *Discours sacrés,* trans. A. J. Festugière (Paris: Macula, 1986) [see C. A. Behr, *Aelius Aristides and the Sacred Tales* (Amsterdam: A. M. Hakkert, 1968)].

25. Tertullian, *La Pénitence,* trans. C. Munier (Paris: Cerf, 1984), ch. 9, p. 181 [*On Penitence,* in *Tertullian: Treatises on Penance,* trans. W. P. Le Saint (Westminster, Md.: Newman, 1959), pp. 28–33].

26. Saint Jerome *Corréspondance,* trans. J. Labourt (Paris: Belles Lettres, 1954), vol. 4, let. 78, pp. 42–44.

27. Cyprian of Carthage, *De ceux qui ont failli,* in *Textes,* trans. D. Gorce (Namur: Soleil levant, 1958), pp. 89–92 [*The Lapsed,* in *Saint Cyprian: Treatises,* trans. and ed. R. J. Deferrari (New York: Fathers of the Church, Inc., 1961), pp. 81–86].

28. John Chrysostom, *Homélie:* "Qu'il est dangereux pour l'orateur et l'auditeur de parler pour plaire, qu'il est de la plus grande utilité comme de la plus rigoureuse justice d'accuser ses pechés" [Just as it is dangerous for the speaker and auditor to speak in order to please, so it is of the greatest utility and the most rigorous justice to denounce his sins], in *Oeuvres Complètes,* trans. M. Jeannin (Nancy: Thomas et Pieron, 1864), vol. 3, p. 401.

29. Cassian, *Institutions cénobitiques,* trans. J. A. Guy (Paris: Cerf, 1965), bk. 4, chs. 10–12, pp. 133–37; chs. 23–32, pp. 153–71.

30. Cassian, *Première Conférences de l'abbé Serenus,* "De la mobilité de l'âme et des esprits du mal," in *Conférences,* trans. Dom E. Pichery (Paris: Cerf, 1955), p. 248.

31. Cassian, *Première Conférence de l'abbé Nesterus,* in *Conférences,* vol. 2 (1958), pp. 199–201.

32. Cassian, *Première Conférence de l'abbé Moïse,* in *Conférences,* p. 99 ["The Goal or Objective of the Monk," in *Conferences,* p. 52].

33. Cassian, *Première Conférence de l'abbé Serenus,* in *Conférences,* pp. 249–52.

34. Cassian, *Première Conférence de l'abbé Moïse,* in *Conférences,* pp. 101–107 ["The Goal or Objective of the Monk," in *Conferences,* pp. 54–57].

35. Cassian, *Deuxième Conférence de l'abbé Moïse,* in *Conférences,* pp. 121–23 ["On Discernment," in *Conferences,* p. 52].

SO IS IT IMPORTANT TO THINK?

Q: *The evening of the elections,[1] we asked you what your first reactions were, and you didn't wish to say. But today you feel more comfortable talking . . .*
A: Yes, I was thinking that voting was itself a way of acting, and it was up to the government to act in turn. Now the time has come to react to what is beginning to be done.

In any case, I believe we have to consider that people are mature enough to make their own decisions in the voting booth, and to be glad about the result if that's what's called for. Moreover, it seems to me that they managed very well in this instance.

Q: *So what are your reactions today?*
A: I'm struck by three things. For a good twenty years, a series of questions have been raised in society itself. And, for a long time these questions weren't accepted in "serious," institutional politics. The Socialists seem to have been the only ones to grasp the reality of these problems, to echo them back—which no doubt had something to do with their victory.

Second, with respect to these problems (I'm thinking in particular of the judicial system or the question of immigrants), the first measures or the first statements are completely consistent with what might be called a "logic of the Left," the one for which Mitterrand was elected.

Third, the most remarkable thing is that the measures don't follow the majority opinion. On both the death penalty issue and the question of immigrants, the choices don't go along with the most common opinion.

This is something that gives the lie to what was said about the inanity of all these questions raised in the course of the past ten or fifteen years: what was said about the nonexistence of a logic of the Left in the manner of governing; what was said about the demagogic facility of the first measures that would be taken. On the nuclear question, immigrants, the judicial system, the government has anchored its decisions in actual problems that have been raised, by referring to a logic that did not accord with the majority opinion. And I am sure that the majority approves of this way of doing things, if not with the measures themselves. In saying that, I'm not saying that it's taken care of and we can go take a rest. These measures are not a charter, but they *are* more than symbolic gestures.

Compare with what Giscard did right after his election: a handshake with prisoners. That was a purely symbolic gesture directed to an electorate that wasn't his. Today we have a first set of real measures that may not suit a portion of the electorate, but that mark a style of government.

Q: *It does seem to be a completely different way of governing that is being set in place.*
A: Yes, that's an important point and one that appeared as soon as Mitterrand's electoral victory was declared. It seems to me that this election was experienced by many people as a kind of victory event—that is, a modification of the relation between governors and governed. After all, it involved a shift in the political class. France is entering a party government with all the dangers that entails, and one mustn't ever forget the fact.

But what is at stake with this modification is the possibility of establishing a relation between governor and governed that is not a relation of obedience but a relation in which work will have an important role.

Q: *Are you saying that it is going to be possible to work with this government?*
A: We need to escape the dilemma of being either for or against. One can, after all, be face to face, and upright. Working with a government doesn't imply either a subjection or a blanket acceptance. One can work and be intransigent at the same time. I would even say that the two things go together.

Q: *After Michel Foucault the critic, are we going to see Michel Foucault the reformist? All the same, this was a reproach that was often made: the criticism carried out by intellectuals doesn't lead to anything.*
A: I'll reply first to the point about not having "produced any results." There are hundreds and thousands of people who have worked for the emergence of a certain number of problems that are now actually before us. Saying that such efforts have not produced any results is completely false. Do you think that twenty years ago the problems of the relation between mental illness and psychological normality, the problem of imprisonment, the problem of the relation between the sexes, and so on, were raised as they are today?

Furthermore, there are no reforms in themselves. Reforms do not come about in empty space, independently of those who make them. One cannot avoid considering those who will have to administer this transformation.

And then, above all, I don't think that criticism can be set against transformation, "ideal" criticism against "real" transformation.

A critique does not consist in saying that things aren't good the way they are. It consists in seeing on what type of assumptions, of familiar notions, of established, unexamined ways of thinking the accepted practices are based.

We need to free ourselves of the sacralization of the social as the only instance of the real and stop regarding that essential element in human life and human relations—I mean thought—as so much wind. Thought does exist, both beyond and before systems and edifices of discourse. It is something that is often hidden but always drives everyday behaviors. There is always a little thought occurring even in the most stupid institutions; there is always thought even in silent habits.

Criticism consists in uncovering that thought and trying to change it: showing that things are not as obvious as people believe, making it so that what is taken for granted is no longer taken for granted. To do criticism is to make harder those acts which are now too easy.

Understood in these terms, criticism (and radical criticism) is utterly indispensable for any transformation. For a transformation that would remain within the same mode of thought, a transformation that would only be a certain way of better adjusting the same thought to the reality of things, would only be a superficial transformation.

On the other hand, as soon as people begin to have trouble thinking things the way they have been thought, transformation becomes at the same time very urgent, very difficult, and entirely possible.

So there is not a time for criticism and a time for transformation; there are not those who have to do criticism and those who have to transform, those who are confined within an inaccessible radicality and those who are obliged to make the necessary concessions to reality. As a matter of fact, I believe that the work of deep transformation can be done in the open and always turbulent atmosphere of a continuous criticism.

Q: *But do you think that the intellectual should have a programming role in such a transformation?*

A: A reform is never anything but the outcome of a process in which there is conflict, confrontation, struggle, resistance . . .

To say to oneself from the start, "What is the reform that I will be able to make?"—that's not a goal for the intellectual to pursue, I think. His role, since he works precisely in the sphere of thought, is to see how far the liberation of thought can go toward making these transformations urgent enough for people to want to carry them out, and sufficiently difficult to carry out for them to be deeply inscribed in reality.

It is a matter of making conflicts more visible, of making them more essential than mere clashes of interest or mere institutional blockages. From these conflicts and clashes a new relation of forces must emerge whose temporary profile will be a reform.

Whatever the project of reform, if its basis has not been thought working in itself; and if ways of thinking—which is to say, ways of acting—have not actually been modified, we know that it will be phagocyted and digested by behavioral and institutional modes that will always be the same.

Q: *After having participated in numerous movements, you have placed yourself a bit in retreat. Are you going to enter into such movements once again?*
A: Every time I have tried to do a piece of theoretical work it has been on the basis of elements of my own experience: always in connection with processes I saw unfolding around me. It was always because I thought I identified cracks, silent tremors, and dysfunctions in things I saw, institutions I was dealing with, or my relations with others, that I set out to do a piece of work, and each time was partly a fragment of autobiography.

I am not a retired activist who would now like to go back on duty. My way of working hasn't changed much; but what I expect from it is that it will continue to change me.

Q: *You are said to be rather pessimistic. Listening to you, though, I get the impression that you are something of an optimist instead.*
A: There is an optimism that consists in saying, "In any case, it couldn't be any better." My optimism would consist rather in saying, "So many things can be changed, being as fragile as they are, tied more to contingencies than to necessities, more to what is arbitrary than to what is rationally established, more to complex but transitory historical contingencies than to inevitable anthropological constants . . ." You know, to say that we are more recent than we thought is not a way of bringing the whole weight of our history down on our shoulders. Rather, it is to make available for the work that we can do on ourselves the largest possible share of what is presented to us as inaccessible.

Note

1. The elections in question brought the left to power, with François Mitterrand winning the presidency. This interview, conducted by Didier Erihon, appeared several weeks later in *Libération* (30–31 May 1981).—Eds.

THE MASKED PHILOSOPHER

C.D. Allow me to ask you first why you have chosen anonymity?

M.F. You know the story of the psychologists who went to make a little film test in a village in darkest Africa. They then asked the spectators to tell the story in their own words. Well, only one thing interested them in this story involving three characters: the movement of the light and shadow through the trees.

In our societies, characters dominate our perceptions. Our attention tends to be arrested by the activities of faces that come and go, emerge and disappear.

Why did I suggest that we use anonymity? Out of nostalgia for a time when, being quite unknown, what I said had some chance of being heard. With the potential reader, the surface of contact was unrippled. The effects of the book might land in unexpected places and form shapes that I had never thought of. A name makes reading too easy.

I shall propose a game: that of the "year without a name." For a year, books would be published without their authors' names. The critics would have to cope with a mass of entirely anonymous books. But, now that I come to think of it, it's possible they would have nothing to do: all the authors would wait until the following year before publishing their books . . .

C.D. Do you think intellectuals today talk too much? That they encumber us with their discourses at every occasion, and more often than not independent of any occasion?

M.F. The word *intellectual* strikes me as odd. Personally, I've never met any intellectuals. I've met people who write novels, others who treat the sick; people who work in economics and others who compose electronic music. I've met

Between 1979 and 1984 the newspaper *Le Monde* published a weekly series of interviews with leading European intellectuals. On April 6–7, 1980, an interview between Christian Delacampagne and Michel Foucault was published in which the latter opted for the mask of anonymity—the philosopher declined to reveal his name—in order to demystify the power society ascribes to the "name" of the intellectual. Foucault set out to liberate the consumer of culture from a critical discourse that is overdetermined by the characters that dominate our perceptions. This interview was reprinted in *Entretiens avec Le Monde*, vol. 1: *Philosophies* (Paris: Découverte, 1984), pp. 21–30. The translation, by Alan Sheridan, has been amended.

people who teach, people who paint, and people of whom I have never really understood what they do. But intellectuals? Never.

On the other hand, I've met a lot of people who talk about "the intellectual." And, listening to them, I've got some idea of what such an animal could be. It's not difficult—he's quite personified. He's guilty of pretty well everything: of speaking out and of keeping silent, of doing nothing and of getting involved in everything. . . . In short, the intellectual is raw material for a verdict, a sentence, a condemnation, an exclusion . . .

I don't find that intellectuals talk too much, since for me they don't exist. But I do find that more and more is being said about intellectuals, and I don't find it very reassuring.

I have an unfortunate habit. When people speak about this or that, I try to imagine what the result would be if translated into reality. When they "criticize" someone, when they "denounce" his ideas, when they "condemn" what he writes, I imagine them in the ideal situation in which they would have complete power over him. I take the words they use—*demolish, destroy, reduce to silence, bury*—and see what the effect would be if they were taken literally. And I catch a glimpse of the radiant city in which the intellectual would be in prison or, if he were also a theoretician, hanged, of course. We don't, it's true, live under a regime in which intellectuals are sent to the ricefields. But have you heard of a certain Toni Negri?[1] Isn't he in prison simply for being an intellectual?

C.D. So what has led you to hide behind anonymity? Is it the way in which philosophers, nowadays, exploit the publicity surrounding their names?

M.F. That doesn't shock me in the least. In the corridors of my old *lycée* I used to see plaster busts of great men. And now at the bottom of the front pages of newspapers I see the photograph of some thinker or other. I don't know whether things have improved, from an aesthetic point of view. Economic rationality, certainly . . .

I'm very moved by a letter that Kant wrote when he was already very old: he was in a hurry, he says, against old age and declining sight, and confused ideas, to finish one of his books for the Leipzig Fair. I mention this to show that it isn't of the slightest importance. With or without publicity, with or without a fair, a book is something quite special. I shall never be convinced that a book is bad because its author has been seen on television. But, of course, it isn't good for that reason alone either.

If I have chosen anonymity, it is not, therefore, to criticize this or that individual, which I never do. It's a way of addressing the potential reader, the only individual here who is of interest to me, more directly: "Since you don't know who I am, you will be more inclined to find out why I say what you read; just allow yourself to say, quite simply, it's true, it's false. I like it or I don't like it. Period."

c.d. But doesn't the public expect the critic to provide him with precise assessments as to the value of a work?

m.f. I don't know whether the public does or does not expect the critic to judge works or authors. Judges were there, I think, before he was able to say what he wanted.

It seems that Courbet had a friend who used to wake up in the night yelling: "I want to judge, I want to judge." It's amazing how people like judging. Judgment is being passed everywhere, all the time. Perhaps it's one of the simplest things mankind has been given to do. And you know very well that the last man, when radiation has finally reduced his last enemy to ashes, will sit down behind some rickety table and begin the trial of the individual responsible.

I can't help but dream about a kind of criticism that would try not to judge but to bring an oeuvre, a book, a sentence, an idea to life; it would light fires, watch the grass grow, listen to the wind, and catch the sea foam in the breeze and scatter it. It would multiply not judgments but signs of existence; it would summon them, drag them from their sleep. Perhaps it would invent them sometimes—all the better. All the better. Criticism that hands down sentences sends me to sleep; I'd like a criticism of scintillating leaps of the imagination. It would not be sovereign or dressed in red. It would bear the lightning of possible storms.

c.d. So there are so many things to tell people about, so much interesting work being done, that the mass media ought to talk about philosophy all the time . . .

m.f. It's true that there is a traditional discomfort between the "critics" and those who write books. The first feel misunderstood, and the second think the first are trying to bring them to heel. But that's the game.

It seems to me that today the situation is rather special. We have institutions administering shortages, whereas we are in a situation of superabundance.

Everybody has noticed the overexcitement that often accompanies the publication (or reprinting) of some work that may in fact be quite interesting. But it is never presented as being anything less than the "subversion of all the codes," the "antithesis of contemporary culture," the "radical questioning of all our ways of thinking." One would be justified in thinking that its author must be some unknown fellow living on the fringes of society.

On the other hand, others must be banished into total oblivion, from which they must never be allowed to reemerge; they were only the froth of "mere fashion," a mere product of the cultural institution, and so forth.

A superficial, very Parisian phenomenon, it will be said. I see it, rather, as the effect of a deep-seated anxiety. The feeling of "no room," "him or me," "it's my turn now." We have to walk in line because of the extreme narrowness of the place where one can listen and make oneself heard.

Hence a sort of anxiety that finds expression in innumerable symptoms, some funny, some less so. Hence, too, on the part of those who write, a sense of impotence when confronted by the mass media, which they criticize for running the world of books and creating or destroying reputations at will. Hence, too, the feeling among the critics that they will not be heard unless they shout louder and pull a rabbit out of the hat each week. Hence, too, a pseudopoliticization that masks, beneath the need to wage an "ideological struggle" or to root out "dangerous thoughts," a deep-seated anxiety that one will not be heard or read. Hence, too, the fantastic phobia for power: anybody who writes exerts a disturbing power upon which one must try to place limitations, if not actually to put an end to it. Hence, too, the declaration, repeated over and over, that everything nowadays is empty, desolate, uninteresting, unimportant: a declaration that obviously comes from those who, not doing anything themselves, consider that there are too many others who are.

c.d. But don't you think that our period is really lacking in great writers and in minds capable of dealing with its problems?

m.f. No, I don't subscribe to the notion of a decadence, of a lack of writers, of the sterility of thought, of a gloomy future lacking in prospects.

On the contrary, I believe that there is a plethora. What we are suffering from is not a void but inadequate means for thinking about everything that is happening. There is an overabundance of things to be known: fundamental, terrible, wonderful, funny, insignificant, and crucial at the same time. And there is an enormous curiosity, a need, a desire to know. People are always complaining that the mass media stuff one's head with people. There is a certain misanthropy in this idea. On the contrary, I believe that people react; the more one convinces them, the more they question things. The mind isn't made of soft wax. It's a reactive substance. And the desire to know [*savoir*] more, and to know it more deeply and to know other things increases as one tries to stuff peoples' heads.

If you accept that, and if you add that there's a whole host of people being trained in the universities and elsewhere who could act as intermediaries between this mass of things and this thirst for knowledge, you will soon come to the conclusion that student unemployment is the most absurd thing imaginable. The problem is to multiply the channels, the bridges, the means of information, the radio and television networks, the newspapers.

Curiosity is a vice that has been stigmatized in turn by Christianity, by philosophy, and even by a certain conception of science. Curiosity is seen as futility. However, I like the word; it suggests something quite different to me. It evokes "care"; it evokes the care one takes of what exists and what might exist; a sharpened sense of reality, but one that is never immobilized before it; a readiness to find what surrounds us strange and odd; a certain determination to throw off familiar ways of thought and to look at the same things in a different way; a passion for seizing what is happening now and what is disappearing; a lack of respect for the traditional hierarchies of what is important and fundamental.

I dream of a new age of curiosity. We have the technical means; the desire is there; there is an infinity of things to know; the people capable of doing such work exist. So what is our problem? Too little: channels of communication that are too narrow, almost monopolistic, inadequate. We mustn't adopt a protectionist attitude, to stop "bad" information from invading and stifling the "good." Rather, we must increase the possibility for movement backward and forward. This would not lead, as people often fear, to uniformity and leveling-down, but, on the contrary, to the simultaneous existence and differentiation of these various networks.

c.d. I imagine that, at this level, the mass media and the universities, instead of continuing to oppose one another, might play complementary roles.

m.f. You remember Sylvain Lévi's wonderful saying: when you have one listener, it's teaching; when you have two, it's popularization. Books, universities, learned journals are also information media. One should refrain from calling every channel of information to which one cannot or does not wish to gain access a "mass medium." The problem is to know how to exploit the differences, whether we ought to set up a reserve, a "cultural park," for delicate species of scholars threatened by the rapacious inroads of mass information, while the rest of the space would be a huge market for shoddy products. Such a division does not seem to me to correspond to reality. What's more, it isn't at all desirable. If useful differentiations are to be brought into play, there must not be any such division.

c.d. Let's risk a few concrete propositions. If everything is going badly, where do we make a start?

m.f. But everything *isn't* going badly. In any case, I believe we shouldn't confuse useful criticism of things with repetitive jeremiads against people. As for concrete propositions, they can't just make an appearance like gadgets, unless certain general principles are accepted first. And the first of such general principles should be that the right to knowledge [*droit au savoir*] must not be reserved to a particular age group or to certain categories of people, but that one must be able to exercise it constantly and in many different ways.

c.d. Isn't this desire for knowledge [*envie de savoir*] somewhat ambiguous? What, in fact, are people to do with all that knowledge that they are going to acquire? What use will it be to them?

m.f. One of the main functions of teaching was that the training of the individual should be accompanied by his being situated in society. We should now see teaching in such a way that it allows the individual to change at will, which is possible only on condition that teaching is a possibility always being offered.

c.d. Are you in fact for a society of scholars [*société savante*]?

m.f. I'm saying that people must be constantly able to plug into culture and

in as many ways as possible. There ought not to be, on the one hand, this education to which one is subjected and, on the other, this information one is fed.

C.D. What becomes of the eternal questions of philosophy in this learned
society [*société savante*]? . . . Do we still need them, these unanswerable questions, these silences before the unknowable?

M.F. What is philosophy if not a way of reflecting, not so much on what is
true and what is false, as on our relationship to truth? People sometimes complain that there is no dominant philosophy in France. So much the better for
that! There is no sovereign philosophy, it's true, but a philosophy or rather philosophy in activity. The movement by which, not without effort and uncertainty, dreams and illusions, one detaches oneself from what is accepted as true
and seeks other rules—that is philosophy. The displacement and transformation of frameworks of thinking, the changing of received values and all the
work that has been done to think otherwise, to do something else, to become
other than what one is—that, too, is philosophy. From this point of view, the
last thirty years or so have been a period of intense philosophical activity. The
interaction between analysis, research, "learned" or "theoretical" criticism, and
changes in behavior, in people's real conduct, their way of being, their relation
to themselves and to others has been constant and considerable.

I was saying just now that philosophy was a way of reflecting on our relationship to truth. It should also be added that it is a way of interrogating ourselves: If this is the relationship that we have with truth, how must we behave? I
believe that a considerable and varied amount of work has been done and is still
being done that alters both our relation to truth and our way of behaving. And
this has taken place in a complex situation, between a whole series of investigations and a whole set of social movements. It's the very life of philosophy.

It is understandable that some people should weep over the present void and
hanker instead, in the world of ideas, after a little monarchy. But those who, for
once in their lives, have found a new tone, a new way of looking, a new way of
doing, those people, I believe, will never feel the need to lament that the world is
error, that history is filled with people of no consequence, and that it is time for
others to keep quiet so that at last the sound of their disapproval may be heard . . .

Note

1. Italian philosopher, ex-professor at the University of Padua; a leading intellectual influence in the ex-
   treme-left movement Workers' Autonomy, he underwent four years and three months preventative
   detention for armed insurrection against the state, subversive association, and the formation of armed
   gangs. He was freed on July 8, 1983, after being elected a Radical deputy during his imprisonment. His
   parliamentary immunity was lifted by the Chamber of Deputies, new warrants for his arrest were is-
   sued, and he took refuge in France.

"*OMNES ET SINGULATIM*": TOWARD A CRITIQUE OF POLITICAL REASON

I

The title sounds pretentious, I know. But the reason for that is precisely its own excuse. Since the nineteenth century, Western thought has never stopped laboring at the task of criticizing the role of reason—or the lack of reason—in political structures. It's therefore perfectly unfitting to undertake such a vast project once again. However, so many previous attempts are a warrant that every new venture will be just about as successful as the former ones—and in any case, probably just as fortunate.

Under such a banner, mine is the embarrassment of one who has only sketches and incompletable drafts to propose. Philosophy gave up trying to offset the impotence of scientific reason long ago; it no longer tries to complete its edifice.

One of the Enlightenment's tasks was to multiply reason's political powers. But the men of the nineteenth century soon started wondering whether reason wasn't getting too powerful in our societies. They began to worry about a relationship they confusedly suspected between a rationalization-prone society and certain threats to the individual and his liberties, to the species and its survival.

In other words, since Kant, the role of philosophy has been to prevent reason from going beyond the limits of what is given in experience; but from the same moment—that is, from the development of modern states and political management of society—the role of philosophy has also been to keep watch over the excessive powers of political rationality, which is rather a promising life expectancy.

This is the text of the two Tanner lectures that Foucault delivered at Stanford University on October 10 and 16, 1979.—Eds.

Everybody is aware of such banal facts. But that they are banal does not mean they don't exist. What we have to do with banal facts is to discover, to try to discover, which specific and perhaps original problems are connected with them.

The relationship between rationalization and the excesses of political power is evident. And we should not need to wait for bureaucracy or concentration camps to recognize the existence of such relations. But the problem is what to do with such an evident fact.

Shall we "try" reason? To my mind, nothing would be more sterile. First, because the field has nothing to do with guilt or innocence. Second, because it's senseless to refer to "reason" as the contrary entity to nonreason. Last, because such a trial would trap us into playing the arbitrary and boring part of either the rationalist or the irrationalist.

Shall we investigate this kind of rationalism that seems to be specific to our modern culture and originates in Enlightenment? I think that that was the way of some of the members of the Frankfurt School. My purpose is not to begin a discussion of their works—they are most important and valuable. I would suggest another way of investigating the links between rationalization and power:

1. It may be wise not to take as a whole the rationalization of society or of culture, but to analyze this process in several fields, each of them grounded in a fundamental experience: madness, illness, death, crime, sexuality, and so on.
2. I think that the word "rationalization" is a dangerous one. The main problem when people try to rationalize something is not to investigate whether or not they conform to principles of rationality but to discover which kind of rationality they are using.
3. Even if the Enlightenment has been a very important phase in our history, and in the development of political technology, I think we have to refer to much more remote processes if we want to understand how we have been trapped in our own history.

This was my modus operandi in my previous work—to analyze the relations between experiences like madness, death, crime, sexuality, and several technologies of power. What I am working on now is the problem of individuality—or, I should say, self-identity in relation to the problem of "individualizing power."

Everyone knows that in European societies political power has evolved toward more and more centralized forms. Historians have been studying this organization of the state, with its administration and bureaucracy, for dozens of years.

I'd like to suggest in these two lectures the possibility of analyzing another

kind of transformation in such power relationships. This transformation is, perhaps, less celebrated. But I think that it is also important, mainly for modern societies. Apparently, this evolution seems antagonistic to the evolution toward a
centralized state. What I mean in fact is the development of power techniques
oriented toward individuals and intended to rule them in a continuous and permanent way. If the state is the political form of a centralized and centralizing
power, let us call pastorship the individualizing power.

My purpose this evening is to outline the origin of this pastoral modality of
power, or at least some aspects of its ancient history. And in the next lecture, I'll
try to show how this pastorship happened to combine with its opposite, the
state.

The idea of the deity, or the king, or the leader, as a shepherd followed by a flock
of sheep wasn't familiar to the Greeks and Romans. There were exceptions, I
know—early ones in Homeric literature, later ones in certain texts of the Lower
Empire. I'll come back to them later. Roughly speaking, we can say that the
metaphor of the flock didn't occur in great Greek or Roman political literature.

This is not the case in ancient Oriental societies—Egypt, Assyria, Judaea.
Pharaoh was an Egyptian shepherd. Indeed, he ritually received the herdsman's
crook on his coronation day; and the term "shepherd of men" was one of the
Babylonian monarch's titles. But God was also a shepherd leading men to their
grazing ground and ensuring them food. An Egyptian hymn invoked Ra this
way: "O Ra that keepest watch when all men sleep, Thou who seekest what is
good for thy cattle . . ." The association between God and king is easily made,
since both assume the same role: the flock they watch over is the same; the shep-
herd-king is entrusted with the great divine shepherd's creatures. An Assyrian
invocation to the king ran like this: "Illustrious companion of pastures, Thou
who carest for thy land and feedest it, shepherd of all abundance."

But, as we know, it was the Hebrews who developed and intensified the pastoral theme—with nevertheless a highly peculiar characteristic: God, and God
only, is his people's shepherd. With just one positive exception: David, as the
founder of the monarchy, is the only one to be referred to as a shepherd. God
gave him the task of assembling a flock.

There are negative exceptions, too. Wicked kings are consistently compared
to bad shepherds; they disperse the flock, let it die of thirst, shear it solely for
profit's sake. Yahweh is the one and only true shepherd. He guides his own people in person, aided only by his prophets. As the Psalms say: "Like a flock / hast
Thou led Thy people, by Moses' and by Aaron's hand." Of course, I can treat
neither the historical problems pertaining to the origin of this comparison nor
its evolution throughout Jewish thought. I just want to show a few themes typical of pastoral power. I'd like to point out the contrast with Greek political

thought, and to show how important these themes became in Christian thought and institutions later on.

1. The shepherd wields power over a flock rather than over a land. It's probably much more complex than that, but, broadly speaking, the relation between the deity, the land, and men differs from that of the Greeks. Their gods owned the land, and this primary possession determined the relationship between men and gods. On the contrary, it's the Shepherd-God's relationship with his flock that is primary and fundamental here. God gives, or promises, his flock a land.

2. The shepherd gathers together, guides, and leads his flock. The idea that the political leader was to quiet any hostilities within the city and make unity reign over conflict is undoubtedly present in Greek thought. But what the shepherd gathers together is dispersed individuals. They gather together on hearing his voice: "I'll whistle and will gather them together." Conversely, the shepherd only has to disappear for the flock to be scattered. In other words, the shepherd's immediate presence and direct action cause the flock to exist. Once the good Greek lawgiver, like Solon, has resolved any conflicts, what he leaves behind him is a strong city with laws enabling it to endure without him.

3. The shepherd's role is to ensure the salvation of his flock. The Greeks said also that the deity saved the city; they never stopped declaring that the competent leader is a helmsman warding his ship away from the rocks. But the way the shepherd saves his flock is quite different. It's not only a matter of saving them all, all together, when danger comes nigh. It's a matter of constant, individualized, and final kindness. Constant kindness, for the shepherd ensures his flock's food; every day he attends to their thirst and hunger. The Greek god was asked to provide a fruitful land and abundant crops. He wasn't asked to foster a flock day by day. And individualized kindness, too, for the shepherd sees that all the sheep, each and every one of them, is fed and saved. Later Hebrew literature, especially, laid the emphasis on such individually kindly power: a rabbinical commentary on Exodus explains why Yahweh chose Moses to shepherd his people: he had left his flock to go and search for one lost sheep.

    Last and not least, it's final kindness. The shepherd has a target for his flock. It must either be led to good grazing ground or brought back to the fold.

4. Yet another difference lies in the idea that wielding power is a "duty." The Greek leader, naturally, had to make decisions in the interest of all; he would have been a bad leader had he preferred his personal interest. But his duty was a glorious one: even if in war he had to give up his life, such a sacrifice

was offset by something extremely precious—immortality. He never lost. By way of contrast, shepherdly kindness is much closer to "devotedness." Everything the shepherd does is geared to the good of his flock. That's his constant concern. When they sleep, *he* keeps watch.

The theme of keeping watch is important. It brings out two aspects of the shepherd's devotedness. First, he acts, he works, he puts himself out, for those he nourishes and who are asleep. Second, he watches over them. He pays attention to them all and scans each one of them. He's got to know his flock as a whole, and in detail. Not only must he know where good pastures are, the seasons' laws, and the order of things; he must also know each one's particular needs. Once again, a rabbinical commentary on Exodus describes Moses' qualities as a shepherd in this way: he would send each sheep in turn to graze—first, the youngest, for them to browse on the tenderest sward; then the older ones; and last the oldest, who were capable of browsing on the roughest grass. The shepherd's power implies individual attention paid to each member of the flock.

These are just themes that Hebraic texts associate with the metaphors of the Shepherd-God and his flock of people. In no way do I claim that that is effectively how political power was wielded in Hebrew society before the fall of Jerusalem. I do not even claim that such a conception of political power is in any way coherent.

They're just themes. Paradoxical, even contradictory, ones. Christianity was to give them considerable importance, both in the Middle Ages and in modern times. Among all the societies in history, ours—I mean, those that came into being at the end of Antiquity on the Western side of the European continent—have perhaps been the most aggressive and the most conquering; they have been capable of the most stupefying violence, against themselves as well as against others. They invented a great many different political forms. They profoundly altered their legal structures several times. It must be kept in mind that they alone evolved a strange technology of power treating the vast majority of men as a flock with a few as shepherds. Thus, they established between them a series of complex, continuous, and paradoxical relationships.

This is undoubtedly something singular in the course of history. Clearly, the development of "pastoral technology" in the management of men profoundly disrupted the structures of ancient society.

So as to better explain the importance of this disruption, I'd like to briefly return to what I was saying about the Greeks. I can see the objections liable to be made.

One is that the Homeric poems use the shepherd metaphor to refer to the kings. In the *Iliad* and the *Odyssey*, the expression *poimēn laon* crops up several times. It qualifies the leaders, highlighting the grandeur of their power. Moreover, it's a ritual title, common in even late Indo-European literature. In *Beowulf*, the king is still regarded as a shepherd. But there is nothing really surprising in the fact that the same title, as in the Assyrian texts, is to be found in archaic epic poems.

The problem arises, rather, as to Greek thought: there is at least one category of texts where references to shepherd models are made—the Pythagorean ones. The metaphor of the herdsman appears in the *Fragments* of Archytas, quoted by Stobeus. The word *nomos* (the law) is connected with the word *nomeus* (shepherd): the shepherd shares out, the law apportions. Then Zeus is called *Nomios* and *Nemeios* because he gives his sheep food. And, finally, the magistrate must be *philanthrōpos*, that is, devoid of selfishness. He must be full of zeal and solicitude, like a shepherd.

B. Grube, the German editor of Archytas' *Fragments*, says that this proves a Hebrew influence unique in Greek literature. Other commentators, such as Armand Delatte, say that the comparison between gods, magistrates, and shepherds was common in Greece; it is therefore not to be dwelt upon.

I shall restrict myself to political literature. The results of the inquiry are clear: the political metaphor of the shepherd occurs neither in Isocrates, nor in Demosthenes, nor in Aristotle. This is rather surprising when one reflects that in his *Areopagiticus*, Isocrates insists on the magistrates' duties; he stresses the need for them to be devoted and to show concern for young people. Yet not a word as to any shepherd.

By contrast, Plato often speaks of the shepherd-magistrate. He mentions the idea in *Critias*, *The Republic*, and *Laws*. He thrashes it out in *The Statesman*. In the former, the shepherd theme is rather subordinate. Sometimes, those happy days when mankind was governed directly by the gods and grazed on abundant pastures are evoked (*Critias*). Sometimes, the magistrates' necessary virtue—as contrasted with Thrasymachos' vice, is what is insisted upon (*The Republic*). And sometimes, the problem is to define the subordinate magistrates' role: indeed, they, just as the watchdogs, have to obey "those at the top of the scale" (*Laws*).

But in *The Statesman*, pastoral power is the central problem and it is treated at length. Can the city's decision-maker, can the commander, be defined as a sort of shepherd?

Plato's analysis is well known. To solve this question he uses the division method. A distinction is drawn between the man who conveys orders to inanimate things (for example, the architect) and the man who gives orders to animals; between the man who gives orders to isolated animals (like a yoke of oxen) and he who gives orders to flocks; and he who gives orders to animal flocks, and he who commands human flocks. And there we have the political leader—a shepherd of men.

But this first division remains unsatisfactory. It has to be pushed further. The method of opposing *men* to all the other animals isn't a good one. And so the dialogue starts all over again. A whole series of distinctions is established: between wild animals and tame ones; those which live in water and those which live on land; those with horns and those without; between cleft- and plain-hoofed animals; between those capable and incapable of mutual reproduction. And the dialogue wanders astray with these never-ending subdivisions.

So, what do the initial development of the dialogue and its subsequent failure show? That the division method can prove nothing at all when it isn't managed correctly. It also shows that the idea of analyzing political power as the relationship between a shepherd and his animals was probably a rather controversial one at the time. Indeed, it's the first assumption to cross the interlocutors' minds when seeking to discover the essence of the politician. Was it a commonplace at the time? Or, rather, was Plato discussing one of the Pythagorean themes? The absence of the shepherd metaphor in other contemporary political texts seems to tip the scale toward the second hypothesis. But we can probably leave the discussion open.

My personal inquiry bears upon how Plato impugns the theme in the rest of the dialogue. He does so first by means of methodological arguments, then by means of the celebrated myth of the world revolving around its spindle.

The methodological arguments are extremely interesting. Whether the king is a sort of shepherd or not can be told not by deciding which different species can form a flock but, rather, by analyzing what the shepherd does.

What is characteristic of his task? First, the shepherd is alone at the head of his flock. Second, his job is to supply his cattle with food; to care for them when they are sick; to play them music to get them together, and guide them; to arrange their intercourse with a view to the finest offspring. So we *do* find the typical shepherd metaphor themes of Oriental texts.

And what's the king's task in regard to all this? Like the shepherd, he is alone at the head of the city. But, for the rest, who provides mankind with food? The king? No. The farmer, the baker do. Who looks after men when they are sick? The king? No. The physician. And who guides them with music? The gymnasiarch—not the king. And so, many citizens could quite legitimately claim the title "shepherd of men." Just as the human flock's shepherd has many rivals, so has the politician. Consequently, if we want to find out what the politician really and essentially is, we must sift it out from "the surrounding flood," thereby demonstrating in what ways he *isn't* a shepherd.

Plato therefore resorts to the myth of the world revolving around its axis in two successive and contrary motions.

In a first phase, each animal species belonged to a flock led by a Genius-shepherd. The human flock was led by the deity itself. It could lavishly avail itself of the fruits of the earth; it needed no abode; and, after Death, men came back to life. A crucial sentence adds: "The deity being their shepherd, mankind needed no political constitution."

In a second phase, the world turned in the opposite direction. The gods were no longer men's shepherds; men had to look after themselves, for they had been given fire. What would the politician's role then be? Would *he* become the shepherd in the gods' stead? Not at all. His job was to weave a strong fabric for the city. Being a politician didn't mean feeding, nursing, and breeding offspring but, rather, binding: binding different virtues; binding contrary temperaments (either impetuous or moderate), using the "shuttle" of popular opinion. The royal art of ruling consisted in gathering lives together "into a community based upon concord and friendship," and so he wove "the finest of fabrics." The entire population, "slaves and free men alike, were mantled in its folds."

The Statesman therefore seems to be classical Antiquity's most systematic reflection on the theme of the pastorate that was later to become so important in the Christian West. That we are discussing it seems to prove that a perhaps initially Oriental theme was important enough in Plato's day to deserve investigation, but I stress the fact that it was impugned.

Not impugned entirely, however. Plato did admit that the physician, the farmer, the gymnasiarch, and the pedagogue acted as shepherds. But he refused to get them involved with the politician's activity. He said so explicitly: How would the politician ever find the time to come and sit by each person, feed him, give him concerts, and care for him when sick? Only a god in a golden age could ever act like that; or again, like a physician or pedagogue, be responsible for the lives and development of a few individuals. But, situated between the two—the gods and the swains—the men who hold political power are not to be shepherds. Their task doesn't consist in fostering the life of a group of individuals. It consists in forming and assuring the city's unity. In short, the political problem is that of the relation between the one and the many in the framework of the city and its citizens. The pastoral problem concerns the lives of individuals.

All this seems very remote, perhaps. The reason for my insisting on these ancient texts is that they show us how early this problem—or rather, this series of problems—arose. They span the entirety of Western history. They are still quite important for contemporary society. They deal with the relations between political power at work within the state as a legal framework of unity, and a power we can call "pastoral," whose role is to constantly ensure, sustain, and improve the lives of each and every one.

The well-known "welfare state problem" does not only bring the needs or the new governmental techniques of today's world to light. It must be recognized for what it is: one of the extremely numerous reappearances of the tricky adjustment between political power wielded over legal subjects and pastoral power wielded over live individuals.

Obviously, I have no intention whatsoever of recounting the evolution of pastoral power throughout Christianity. The immense problems this would raise can easily be imagined: from doctrinal problems, such as Christ's denomination as "the good shepherd," right up to institutional ones such as parochial organization or the way pastoral responsibilities were shared between priests and bishops.

All I want to do is bring to light two or three aspects I regard as important for the evolution of pastorship, that is, the technology of power.

First of all, let us examine the theoretical elaboration of the theme in ancient Christian literature: Chyrsostom, Cyprian, Ambrose, Jerome, and, for monastic life, Cassian or Benedict. The Hebrew themes are considerably altered in at least four ways:

1. First, with regard to responsibility. We saw that the shepherd was to assume responsibility for the destiny of the whole flock and of each and every sheep. In the Christian conception, the shepherd must render an account—not only of each sheep, but of all their actions, all the good or evil they are liable to do, all that happens to them.

   Moreover, between each sheep and its shepherd Christianity conceives a complex exchange and circulation of sins and merits. The sheep's sin is also imputable to the shepherd. He'll have to render an account of it at the Final Judgment. Conversely, by helping his flock to find salvation, the shepherd will also find his own. But by saving his sheep, he lays himself open to getting lost; so if he wants to save himself, he must run the risk of losing himself for others. If he does get lost, it is the flock that will incur the greatest danger. But let's leave all these paradoxes aside. My aim was just to underline the force and complexity of the moral ties binding the shepherd to each member of his flock. And what I especially wanted to underline was that such ties not only concerned individuals' lives but the details of their actions as well.

2. The second important alteration concerns the problem of obedience. In the Hebrew conception, God being a shepherd, the flock following him complies to his will, to his law.

   Christianity, on the other hand, conceived the shepherd-sheep relationship as one of individual and complete dependence. This is undoubtedly one of the points at which Christian pastorship radically diverged from Greek thought. If a Greek had to obey, he did so because it was the law, or the will of the city. If he did happen to follow the will of someone in particular (a physician, an orator, a pedagogue), then that person had rationally persuaded him to do so. And it had to be for a strictly determined aim: to be cured, to acquire a skill, to make the best choice.

In Christianity, the tie with the shepherd is an individual one. It is personal submission to him. His will is done, not because it is consistent with the law, and not just as far as it is consistent with it, but, principally, because it is his *will*. In Cassian's *Cenobitical Institutions*, there are many edifying anecdotes in which the monk finds salvation by carrying out the absurdest of his superior's orders. Obedience is a virtue. This means that it is not, as for the Greeks, a provisional means to an end but, rather, an end in itself. It is a permanent state; the sheep must permanently submit to their pastors—*subditi*. As Saint Benedict says, monks do not live according to their own free will; their wish is to be under the abbot's command—*ambulantes alieno judicio et imperio*. Greek Christianity named this state of obedience apatheia. The evolution of the word's meaning is significant. In Greek philosophy, apatheia denotes the control that the individual, thanks to the exercise of reason, can exert over his passions. In Christian thought, pathos is willpower exerted over oneself, for oneself. Apatheia delivers us from such willfulness.

3. Christian pastorship implies a peculiar type of knowledge between the pastor and each of his sheep.

    This knowledge is particular. It individualizes. It isn't enough to know the state of the flock. That of each sheep must also be known. The theme existed long before there was Christian pastorship, but it was considerably amplified in three different ways. The shepherd must be informed as to the material needs of each member of the flock and provide for them when necessary. He must know what is going on, what each of them does—his public sins. Last but not least, he must know what goes on in the soul of each one, that is, his secret sins, his progress on the road to sanctity.

    In order to ensure this individual knowledge, Christianity appropriated two essential instruments at work in the Hellenistic world—self-examination and the guidance of conscience. It took them over, but not without altering them considerably.

    It is well known that self-examination was widespread among the Pythagoreans, the Stoics, and the Epicureans as a means of daily taking stock of the good or evil performed in regard to one's duties. One's progress on the way to perfection, (that is, self-mastery) and the domination of one's passions could thus be measured. The guidance of conscience was also predominant in certain cultured circles, but as advice given—and sometimes paid for—in particularly difficult circumstances: in mourning, or when one was suffering a setback.

Christian pastorship closely associated these two practices. On one hand, conscience-guiding constituted a constant bind: the sheep didn't let itself be led only to come through any rough passage victoriously, it let itself be led every second. Being guided was a state and you were fatally lost if you tried to escape it. The ever-quoted phrase runs like this: He who suffers not guidance withers away like a dead leaf. As for self-examination, its aim was not to close self-awareness in upon itself but, rather, to enable it to open up entirely to its director—to unveil to him the depths of the soul.

There are a great many first-century ascetic and monastic texts concerning the link between guidance and self-examination which show how crucial these techniques were for Christianity and how complex they had already become. What I would like to emphasize is that they delineate the emergence of a very strange phenomenon in Greco-Roman civilization, that is, the organization of a link between total obedience, knowledge of oneself, and confession to someone else.

4. There is another transformation—maybe the most important. All those Christian techniques of examination, confession, guidance, obedience, have an aim: to get individuals to work at their own "mortification" in this world. Mortification is not death, of course, but it is a renunciation of this world and of oneself, a kind of everyday death—a death that is supposed to provide life in another world. This is not the first time we see the shepherd theme associated with death; but here it is different than in the Greek idea of political power. It is not a sacrifice for the city: Christian mortification is a kind of relation of oneself to oneself. It is a part, a constitutive part of Christian self-identity.

We can say that Christian pastorship has introduced a game that neither the Greeks nor the Hebrews imagined. It is a strange game whose elements are life, death, truth, obedience, individuals, self-identity—a game that seems to have nothing to do with the game of the city surviving through the sacrifice of the citizens. Our societies proved to be really demonic since they happened to combine those two games—the city-citizen game and the shepherd-flock game—in what we call the modern states.

As you may notice, what I have been trying to do this evening is not to solve a problem but to suggest a way to approach a problem. This problem is similar to those I have been working on since my first book about insanity and mental illness. As I told you previously, this problem deals with the relations between experiences (like madness, illness, transgression of laws, sexuality, self-identity), knowledge (like psychiatry, medicine, criminology, sexology, psy-

chology), and power (such as the power wielded in psychiatric and penal institutions, and in all other institutions that deal with individual control).

Our civilization has developed the most complex system of knowledge, the
most sophisticated structures of power. What has this kind of knowledge, this
type of power made of us? In what way are those fundamental experiences of
madness, suffering, death, crime, desire, individuality connected—even if we
are not aware of it—with knowledge and power? I am sure I'll never get the answer; but that does not mean that we don't have to ask the question.

II

I have tried to show how primitive Christianity shaped the idea of a pastoral influence continuously exerting itself on individuals and through the demonstration of their particular truth. And I have tried to show how this idea of pastoral
power was foreign to Greek thought despite a certain number of borrowings
such as practical self-examination and the guidance of conscience.

I would like at this time, leaping across many centuries, to describe another
episode that has been in itself particularly important in the history of this government of individuals by their own verity.

This instance concerns the formation of the state in the modern sense of the
word. If I make this historical connection, it is obviously not in order to suggest
that the aspect of pastoral power disappeared during the ten great centuries of
Christian Europe, Catholic and Roman, but it seems to me that this period, contrary to what one might expect, has not been that of the triumphant pastorate.
And that is true for several reasons: some are of an economic nature—the pastorate of souls is an especially urban experience, difficult to reconcile with the
poor and extensive rural economy at the beginning of the Middle Ages. The
other reasons are of a cultural nature: the pastorate is a complicated technique
that demands a certain level of culture, not only on the part of the pastor but
also among his flock. Other reasons relate to the sociopolitical structure. Feu-
dality developed between individuals a tissue of personal bonds of an altogether different type than the pastorate.

I do not wish to say that the idea of a pastoral government of men disappeared entirely in the medieval Church. It has, indeed, remained and one can
even say that it has shown great vitality. Two series of facts tend to prove this.
First, the reforms that had been made in the Church itself, especially in the
monastic orders—the different reforms operating successively inside existing
monasteries—had the goal of restoring the rigor of pastoral order among the
monks themselves. As for the newly created orders—Dominican and Francis-
can—essentially they proposed to perform pastoral work among the faithful.

The Church tried ceaselessly during successive crises to regain its pastoral functions. But there is more. In the population itself one sees all during the Middle Ages the development of a long series of struggles whose object was pastoral power. Critics of the Church that fails in its obligations reject its hierarchical structure, look for the more or less spontaneous forms of community in which the flock could find the shepherd it needed. This search for pastoral expression took on numerous aspects, at times extremely violent struggles, as was the case for the Vaudois, sometimes peaceful quests as among the Frères de la Vie community. Sometimes it stirred very extensive movements such as the Hussites, sometimes it fermented limited groups like the Amis de Dieu de l'Oberland. Some of these movements were close to heresy, as among the Beghards; others were at times stirring orthodox movements that dwelled within the bosom of the Church (like that of the Italian Oratorians in the fifteenth century).

I raise all of this in a very allusive manner in order to emphasize that if the pastorate was not instituted as an effective, practical government of men during the Middle Ages, it has been a permanent concern and a stake in constant struggles. There was, across the entire period of the Middle Ages, a yearning to arrange pastoral relations among men, and this aspiration affected both the mystical tide and the great millenarian dreams.

Of course, I don't intend to treat here the problem of how states are formed. Nor do I intend to go into the different economic, social, and political processes from which they stem. Neither do I want to analyze the different institutions or mechanisms with which states equipped themselves in order to ensure their survival. I'd just like to give some fragmentary indications as to something midway between the state as a type of political organization and its mechanisms, namely, the type of rationality implemented in the exercise of state power.

I mentioned this in my first lecture. Rather than wonder whether aberrant state power is due to excessive rationalism or irrationalism, I think it would be more appropriate to pin down the specific type of political rationality the state produced.

After all, at least in this respect, political practices resemble scientific ones: it's not "reason in general" that is implemented but always a very specific type of rationality.

The striking thing is that the rationality of state power was reflective and perfectly aware of its specificity. It was not tucked away in spontaneous, blind practices. It was not brought to light by some retrospective analysis. It was formulated especially in two sets of doctrine: the *reason of state* and the *theory of police*. These two phrases soon acquired narrow and pejorative meanings, I know. But for the 150 or 200 years during which modern states were formed, their meaning was much broader than now.

The doctrine of reason of state attempted to define how the principles and methods of state government differed, say, from the way God governed the world, the father his family, or a superior his community.

The doctrine of the police defines the nature of the objects of the state's rational activity; it defines the nature of the aims it pursues, the general form of the instruments involved.

So, what I'd like to speak about today is the system of rationality. But first, there are two preliminaries: First, Friedrich Meinecke having published a most important book on reason of state, I'll speak mainly of the policing theory. Second, Germany and Italy underwent the greatest difficulties in getting established as states, and they produced the greatest number of reflections on reason of state and the police. I'll often refer to the Italian and German texts.

Let's begin with *reason of state.* Here are a few definitions:

Botero: "A perfect knowledge of the means through which states form, strengthen themselves, endure, and grow."

Palazzo (*Discourse on Government and True Reason of State,* 1606): "A rule or art enabling us to discover how to establish peace and order within the Republic."

Chemnitz (*De Ratione status,* 1647): "A certain political consideration required for all public matters, councils, and projects, whose only aim is the state's preservation, expansion, and felicity; to which end, the easiest and promptest means are to be employed."

Let me consider certain features these definitions have in common.

1. Reason of state is regarded as an "art," that is, a technique conforming to certain rules. These rules do not simply pertain to customs or traditions, but to knowledge—rational knowledge. Nowadays, the expression "reason of state" evokes "arbitrariness" or "violence." But at the time, what people had in mind was a rationality specific to the art of governing states.

2. From where does this specific art of government draw its rationale? The answer to this question provokes the scandal of nascent political thought. And yet it's very simple: the art of governing is rational, if reflection causes it to observe the nature of what is governed—here, the *state.*

   Now, to state such a platitude is to break with a simultaneously Christian and judiciary tradition, a tradition that claimed that government was essentially just. It respected a whole system of laws: human laws, the law of nature, divine law.

   There is a quite significant text by Aquinas on these points. He recalls that "art, in its field, must imitate what nature carries out in its own"; it is only reasonable under that condition. The king's government of his kingdom must imitate God's government of nature or, again, the soul's government of the body. The king must found cities just as God created the world, just as the soul gives form to the body. The king must also lead men toward their finality, just as God does for natural beings, or as the soul does when directing the body. And what is man's finality? What's good for the body? No; he'd need only a physician, not a king. Wealth? No; a steward would suffice. Truth? Not even that, for only a teacher would be needed. Man needs someone capable of opening up the way to heavenly bliss through his conformity, here on earth, to what is *honestum*.

As we can see, the model for the art of government is that of God imposing his laws upon his creatures. Aquinas's model for rational government is not a political one, whereas what the sixteenth and seventeenth centuries seek under the denomination "reason of state" are principles capable of guiding an actual government. They aren't concerned with nature and its laws in general—they're concerned with what the state is; what its exigencies are.

And so we can understand the religious scandal aroused by such a type of research. It explains why reason of state was assimilated to atheism. In France, in particular, the expression generated in a political context was commonly associated with "atheist."

3. Reason of state is also opposed to another tradition. In *The Prince*, Machiavelli's problem is to decide how a province or territory acquired through inheritance or by conquest can be held against its internal or external rivals. Machiavelli's entire analysis is aimed at defining what keeps up or reinforces the link between prince and state, whereas the problem posed by reason of state is that of the very existence and nature of the state itself. This is why the theoreticians of reason of state tried to stay aloof from Machiavelli; he had a bad reputation, and they couldn't recognize their own problem in his. Conversely, those opposed to reason of state tried to impair this new art of governing, denouncing it as Machiavelli's legacy. However, despite these confused quarrels a century after *The Prince* had been written, *reason of state* marks the emergence of an extremely—albeit only partly—different type of rationality from Machiavelli's.

The aim of such an art of governing is precisely not to reinforce the power a prince can wield over his domain: its aim is to reinforce the state itself. This is one of the most characteristic features of all the definitions that the sixteenth and seventeenth centuries put forward. Rational government is this, so to speak: given the nature of the state, it can hold down its enemies for an indeterminate length of time. It can do so only if it increases its own strength. And its enemies do likewise. The state whose only concern would be to hold out would most certainly come to disaster. This idea is a very important one. It is bound up with a new historical outlook; indeed, it implies that states are realities that must hold out for an indefinite length of historical time—and in a disputed geographical area.

4. Finally, we can see that reason of state, understood as rational government able to increase the state's strength in accordance with itself, presupposes the constitution of a certain type of knowledge. Government is only possible if the strength of the state is known; it can thus be sustained. The state's capacity, and the means to enlarge it, must be known. The strength and capacities of the other states must also be known. Indeed, the governed state must hold out against the others. Government therefore entails more than just implementing general principles of reason, wisdom, and prudence. Knowledge is necessary—concrete, precise, and measured knowledge as to the state's strength. The art of governing, characteristic of reason of state, is intimately bound up with the development of what was then called either political "statistics" or "arithmetic," that is, the knowledge of different states' respective forces. Such knowledge was indispensable for correct government.

Briefly speaking, then: reason of state is not an art of government according to divine, natural, or human laws. It doesn't have to respect the general order of the world. It's government in accordance with the state's strength. It's government whose aim is to increase this strength within an extensive and competitive framework.

So what the seventeenth- and eighteenth-century authors understand by "the police" is very different from what we put under the term. It would be worth studying why these authors are mostly Italians and Germans, but whatever! What they understand by "police" is not an institution or mechanism functioning within the state but a governmental technology peculiar to the state—domains, techniques, targets where the state intervenes.

To be clear and simple, I will exemplify what I'm saying with a text that is both utopian and a project. It's one of the first utopia programs for a policed state. Louis Turquet de Mayerne drew it up and presented it in 1611 to the Dutch States General. In his book *Science and Rationalism in the Government of Louis XIV*, J. King draws attention to the importance of this strange work. Its title is *Aristo-democratic Monarchy*. That's enough to show what is important in the author's eyes—not so much choosing between these different types of constitution as their mixture in view to a vital end, namely, the state. Turquet also calls it the City, the Republic, or yet again, the Police.

Here is the organization Turquet proposes. Four grand officials rank beside the king. One is in charge of Justice; another, of the Army; the third, of the Exchequer, that is, the king's taxes and revenues; the fourth is in charge of the *police*.

It seems that this officer's role was to have been mainly a moral one. According to Turquet, he was to foster among the people "modesty, charity, loyalty, industriousness, friendly cooperation, honesty." [1] We recognize the traditional idea that the subject's virtue ensures the kingdom's good management. But, when we come down to the details, the outlook is somewhat different.

Turquet suggests that in each province, there should be boards keeping law and order. There should be two that see to people; the other two see to things. The first board pertaining to people was to see to the positive, active, productive aspects of life. In other words, it was concerned with education; determining each one's tastes and aptitudes; the choosing of occupations—useful ones (each person over the age of twenty-five had to be enrolled on a register noting his occupation). Those not usefully employed were regarded as the dregs of society.

The second board was to see to the negative aspects of life: the poor (widows, orphans, the aged) requiring help; the unemployed; those whose activities required financial aid (no interest was to be charged); public health (disease, epidemics); and accidents such as fire and flood.

One of the boards concerned with things was to specialize in commodities and manufactured goods. It was to indicate what was to be produced and how; it was also to control markets and trading. The fourth board would see to the "demesne," that is, the territory, space: private property, legacies, donations, sales were to be controlled; manorial rights were to be reformed; roads, rivers, public buildings, and forests would also be seen to.

In many features, the text is akin to the political utopias that were so numerous at the time. But it is also contemporary with the great theoretical discussions on reason of state and the administrative organization of monarchies. It is highly representative of what the epoch considered a traditionally governed state's tasks to be.

What does this text demonstrate?

1. The "police" appears as an administration heading the state, together with the judiciary, the army, and the exchequer. True. Yet in fact, it embraces everything else. Turquet says so: "It branches out into all of the people's conditions, everything they do or undertake. Its field comprises justice, finance, and the army."

2. The *police* includes everything. But from an extremely particular point of view. Men and things are envisioned as to their relationships: men's coexistence on a territory; their relationships as to property; what they produce; what is exchanged on the market. It also considers how they live, the diseases and accidents that can befall them. What the police sees to is a live, active, productive man. Turquet employs a remarkable expression: "The police's true object is man."

3. Such intervention in men's activities could well be qualified as totalitarian. What are the aims pursued? They fall into two categories. First, the police has to do with everything providing the city with adornment, form, and splendor. Splendor denotes not only the beauty of a state ordered to perfection but also its strength, its vigor. The police therefore ensures and highlights the state's vigor. Second, the police's other purpose is to foster working and trading relations between men, as well as aid and mutual help. There again, the word Turquet uses is important: the police must ensure "communication" among men, in the broad sense of the word—otherwise, men wouldn't be able to live, or their lives would be precarious, poverty-stricken, and perpetually threatened.

And here, we can make out what is, I think, an important idea. As a form of rational intervention wielding political power over men, the role of the police is to supply them with a little extra life—and, by so doing, supply the state with a little extra strength. This is done by controlling "communication," that is, the common activities of individuals (work, production, exchange, accommodation).

You'll object: "But that's only the utopia of some obscure author. You can hardly deduce any significant consequences from it!" But *I* say: Turquet's book is but one example of a huge literature circulating in most European countries of the day. The fact that it is over-simple and yet very detailed brings out all the better the characteristics that could be recognized elsewhere. Above all, I'd say that such ideas were not stillborn. They spread all through the seventeenth and eighteenth centuries, either as applied policies (such as Cameralism or mercantilism), or as subjects to be taught (the German *Polizeiwissenschaft;* let us not forget that this was the title under which the science of administration was taught in Germany).

These are the two perspectives that I'd like, not to study, but at least to suggest. First I'll refer to a French administrative compendium, then to a German textbook.

1. Every historian knows N. De Lamare's compendium, *Treaty on the Police.* At the beginning of the eighteenth century, this administrator undertook the compilation of the whole kingdom's police regulations. It's an infinite source of very valuable information. The general conception of the police that such a quantity of rules and regulations could convey to an administrator like De Lamare is what I'd like to emphasize.

De Lamare says that the police must see to eleven things within the state: (1) religion; (2) morals; (3) health; (4) supplies; (5) roads, highways, town buildings; (6) public safety; (7) the liberal arts (roughly speaking, arts and science); (8) trade; (9) factories; (10) manservants and laborers; (11) the poor.

The same classification features in every treatise concerning the police. As in Turquet's utopia program, apart from the army, justice properly speaking, and direct taxes, the police apparently sees to everything. The same thing can be said differently: royal power had asserted itself against feudalism, thanks to the support of an armed force and by developing a judicial system and establishing a tax system. These were the ways in which royal power was traditionally wielded. Now, "the police" is the term covering the whole new field in which centralized political and administrative power can intervene.

Now, what is the logic behind intervention in cultural rites, small-scale production techniques, intellectual life, and the road network?

De Lamare's answer seems a bit hesitant. Here he says, "The police sees to everything pertaining to men's *happiness*"; there he says, "The police sees to everything regulating '*society*' (social relations) carried on between men"; elsewhere he says that the police sees to *living*. This is the definition I will dwell upon. It's the most original and it clarifies the other two, and De Lamare himself dwells upon it. He makes the following remarks as to the police's eleven objects. The police deals with religion, not, of course, from the viewpoint of dogmatic truth but from that of the moral quality of life. In seeing to health and supplies, it deals with the preservation of life; concerning trade, factories, workers, the poor, and public order—it deals with the conveniences of life. In seeing to the theater, literature, entertainment, its object is life's pleasures. In short, life is the object of the police: the indispensable, the useful, and the superfluous. That people survive, live, and even do better than just that: this is what the police has to ensure.

And so we link up with the other definitions De Lamare proposes: "The sole purpose of the police is to lead man to the utmost happiness to be enjoyed in this life." Or, again, the police cares for the good of the soul (thanks to religion and morality), the good of the body (food, health, clothing, housing), wealth (industry, trade, labor). Or, again, the police sees to the benefits that can be derived only from living in society.

2. Now let us have a look at the German textbooks. They were used to teach the science of administration somewhat later on. It was taught in various universities, especially in Göttingen, and was extremely important for continental Europe. Here it was that the Prussian, Austrian, and Russian civil servants—those who were to carry out Joseph II's and Catherine the Great's reforms—were trained. Certain Frenchmen, especially in Napoleon's entourage, knew the teachings of *Polizeiwissenschaft* very well.

What was to be found in these textbooks?

Huhenthal's *Liber de politia* featured the following items: the number of citizens; religion and morals; health; food; the safety of persons and of goods (particularly in reference to fires and floods); the administration of justice; citizens' conveniences and pleasures (how to obtain them, how to restrict them). Then comes a series of chapters about rivers, forests, mines, brine pits, housing, and, finally, several chapters on how to acquire goods either through farming, industry, or trade.

In his *Précis for the Police*, J. P. Willebrand speaks successively of morals, trades and crafts, health, safety, and last of all, town building and planning. Considering the subjects at least, there isn't a great deal of difference from De Lamare's.

But the most important of these texts is Johann Heinrich Gottlob von Justi's *Elements of Police*. The police's specific purpose is still defined as live individuals living in society. Nevertheless, the way von Justi organizes his book is somewhat different. He studies first what he calls the "state's landed property," that is, its territory. He considers it in two different aspects: how it is inhabited (town versus country), and then who inhabit these territories (the number of people, their growth, health, mortality, immigration). Von Justi then analyzes the "goods and chattels," that is, the commodities, manufactured goods, and their circulation, which involve problems pertaining to cost, credit, and currency. Finally, the last part is devoted to the conduct of individuals: their morals, their occupational capabilities, their honesty, and how they respect the law.

In my opinion, von Justi's work is a much more advanced demonstration of how the police problem evolved than De Lamare's introduction to his compendium of statutes. There are four reasons for this.

First, von Justi defines much more clearly what the central paradox of *police* is. The police, he says, is what enables the state to increase its power and exert its strength to the full. On the other hand, the police has to keep the citizens happy—happiness being understood as survival, life, and improved living. He perfectly defines what I feel to be the aim of the modern art of government, or state rationality, namely, to develop those elements constitutive of individuals' lives in such a way that their development also fosters the strength of the state.

Von Justi then draws a distinction between this task, which he calls *Polizei*, as do his contemporaries, and *Politik, Die Politik. Die Politik* is basically a negative task: it consists in the state's fighting against its internal and external enemies. *Polizei*, however, is a positive task: it has to foster both citizens' lives *and* the state's strength.

And here is the important point: von Justi insists much more than does De Lamare on a notion that became increasingly important during the eighteenth century—population. Population was understood as a group of live individuals. Their characteristics were those of all the individuals belonging to the same species, living side by side. (Thus, they presented mortality and fecundity rates; they were subject to epidemics, overpopulation; they presented a certain type of territorial distribution.) True, De Lamare did use the term "life" to characterize the concern of the police, but the emphasis he gave it wasn't very pronounced. Proceeding through the eighteenth century, and especially in Germany, we see that what is defined as the object of the police is population, that is, a group of beings living in a given area.

And last, one only has to read von Justi to see that it is not only a utopia, as with Turquet, or a compendium of systematically filed regulations. Von Justi claims to draw up a *Polizeiwissenschaft*. His book isn't simply a list of prescriptions: it's also a grid through which the state—that is, territory, resources, population, towns, and so on—can be observed. Von Justi combines "statistics" (the description of states) with the art of government. *Polizeiwissenschaft* is at once an art of government and a method for the analysis of a population living on a territory.

Such historical considerations must appear to be very remote; they must seem useless in regard to present-day concerns. I wouldn't go as far as Hermann Hesse, who says that only the "constant reference to history, the past, and antiquity" is fecund. But experience has taught me that the history of various forms of rationality is sometimes more effective in unsettling our certitudes and dogmatism than is abstract criticism. For centuries, religion couldn't bear having its history told. Today, our schools of rationality balk at having their history written, which is no doubt significant.

What I've wanted to show is a direction for research. These are only the rudiments of something I've been working at for the last two years. It's the historical analysis of what we could call, using an obsolete term, the "art of government."

This study rests upon several basic assumptions. I'd sum them up like this:

1. Power is not a substance. Neither is it a mysterious property whose origin must be delved into. Power is only a certain type of relation between individuals. Such relations are specific, that is, they have nothing to do with exchange, production, communication, even though they combine with them. The characteristic feature of power is that some men can more or less entirely determine other men's conduct—but never exhaustively or coercively. A man who is chained up and beaten is subject to force being exerted over him, not power. But if he can be induced to speak, when his ultimate recourse could have been to hold his tongue, preferring death, then he has been caused to behave in a certain way. His freedom has been subjected to power. He has

How is power constituted?

been submitted to government. If an individual can remain free, however little his freedom may be, power can subject him to government. There is no power without potential refusal or revolt.

2. As for all relations among men, many factors determine power. Yet rationalization is also constantly working away at it. There are specific forms to such rationalization. It differs from the rationalization peculiar to economic processes, or to production and communication techniques; it differs from that of scientific discourse. The government of men by men—whether they form small or large groups, whether it is power exerted by men over women, or by adults over children, or by one class over another, or by a bureaucracy over a population—involves a certain type of rationality. It doesn't involve instrumental violence.

3. Consequently, those who resist or rebel against a form of power cannot merely be content to denounce violence or criticize an institution. Nor is it enough to cast the blame on reason in general. What has to be questioned is the form of rationality at stake. The criticism of power wielded over the mentally sick or mad cannot be restricted to psychiatric institutions; nor can those questioning the power to punish be content with denouncing prisons as total institutions. The question is: How are such relations of power rationalized? Asking it is the only way to avoid other institutions, with the same objectives and the same effects, from taking their stead.

4. For several centuries, the state has been one of the most remarkable, one of the most redoubtable, forms of human government.

Very significantly, political criticism has reproached the state with being simultaneously a factor for individualization and a totalitarian principle. Just to look at nascent state rationality, just to see what its first policing project was, makes it clear that, right from the start, the state is both individualizing and totalitarian. Opposing the individual and his interests to it is just as hazardous as opposing it with the community and its requirements.

Political rationality has grown and imposed itself all throughout the history of Western societies. It first took its stand on the idea of pastoral power, then on that of reason of state. Its inevitable effects are both individualization and totalization. Liberation can come only from attacking not just one of these two effects but political rationality's very roots.

Note

1. J. King, *Science and Rationalism in the Government of Louis XIV* (Baltimore: Johns Hopkins, 1949).

THE BIRTH OF BIOPOLITICS

As it turned out, this year's course was devoted in its entirety to what was to have formed only its introduction. The theme addressed was "biopolitics." By that I meant the endeavor, begun in the eighteenth century, to rationalize the problems presented to governmental practice by the phenomena characteristic of a group of living human beings constituted as a population: health, sanitation, birthrate, longevity, race . . . We are aware of the expanding place these problems have occupied since the nineteenth century, and of the political and economic issues they have constituted up to the present day.

It seemed to me that these problems could not be dissociated from the framework of political rationality within which they appeared and developed their urgency. "Liberalism" enters the picture here, because it was in connection with liberalism that they began to have the look of a challenge. In a system anxious to have the respect of legal subjects and to ensure the free enterprise of individuals, how can the "population" phenomenon, with its specific effects and problems, be taken into account? On behalf of what, and according to what rules, can it be managed? The debate that took place in England in the middle of the nineteenth century concerning public health legislation can serve as an example.

What should we understand by "liberalism"? I relied on Paul Veyne's reflections concerning historical universals and the need to test a nominalist method in history. And taking up a number of choices of method already made, I tried to analyze "liberalism" not as a theory or an ideology—and even less, certainly, as a way for "society" to "represent itself"—but, rather, as a practice, which is to say, as a "way of doing things" oriented toward objectives and regulating itself by means of a sustained reflection. Liberalism is to be analyzed, then, as a principle and a method of rationalizing the exercise of government, a rationalization that obeys—and this is its specificity—the internal rule of maximum economy. While any rationalization of the exercise of government aims at maximizing its effects while diminishing, as far as possible, its cost (understood in the political as well as the economic sense), liberal rationalization starts from the assumption that government (meaning not the institution "government," of course, but the activity that consists in governing human behavior in the framework of, and by means of, state institutions) cannot be its own end. It does not have its reason for being in itself, and its maximization, even under the best possible conditions, should not be its regulative principle. On this point, liberalism breaks with that "reason of state" which, since the end of the nineteenth century, had sought, in the existence and strengthening of the state, the end capable both of justifying a growing governmentality and of regulating its development. The *Polizeiwissenschaft* developed by the Germans in the eighteenth century—either because they lacked a large state form, or also because the narrowness of their territorial partitions gave them access to much more easily observable units, given the technical and conceptual tools of the time—always subscribed to the principle: One is not paying enough attention, too many things escape one's control, too many areas lack regulation and supervision, there's not enough order and administration. In short, one is governing too little. *Polizeiwissenschaft* is the form taken by a governmental technology dominated by the principle of the reason of state, and it is in a "completely natural way," as it were, that it attends to the problems of population, which ought to be the largest and most active possible—for the strength of the state. Health, birthrate, sanitation find an important place in it, therefore, without any problem.

For its part, liberalism resonates with the principle: "One always governs too much"—or, at any rate, one always must suspect that one governs too much. Governmentality should not be exercised without a "critique" far more radical than a test of optimization. It should inquire not just as to the best (or least costly) means of achieving its effects but also concerning the possibility and even the lawfulness of its scheme for achieving effects. The suspicion that one always risks governing too much is inhabited by the question: Why, in fact, must one govern? This explains why the liberal critique barely detaches itself from a problematic, new at the time, of "society": it is on the latter's behalf that one will try to determine why there has to be a government, to what extent it can be done without, and in which cases it is needless or harmful for it to intervene. The rationalization of governmental practice, in terms of a reason of state, implied its maximization in optimal circumstances insofar as the existence of the state immediately assumes the exercise of government. Liberal thought starts not from the existence of the state, seeing in the government the means for attaining that end it would be for itself, but rather from society, which is in a complex relation of exteriority and interiority with respect to the state. Society, as both a precondition and a final end, is what enables one to no longer ask the question: How can one govern as much as possible and at the least possible cost? Instead, the question becomes: Why must one govern? In other words, what makes it necessary for there to be a government, and what ends should it pursue with regard to society in order to justify its existence? The idea of society enables a technology of government to be developed based on the principle that it itself is already "too much," "in excess"—or at least that it is added on as a supplement which can and must always be questioned as to its necessity and its usefulness.

Instead of making the distinction between state and civil society into a historical universal that allows us to examine all the concrete systems, we can try to see it as a form of schematization characteristic of a particular technology of government.

It cannot be said, then, that liberalism is a utopia never realized—unless the core of liberalism is taken to be the projections it has been led to formulate out of its analyses and criticisms. It is not a dream that comes up against a reality and fails to find a place within it. It constitutes—and this is the reason for both its polymorphism and its recurrences—a tool for criticizing the reality: (1) of a previous governmentality that one tries to shed; (2) of a current governmentality that one attempts to reform and rationalize by stripping it down; (3) of a governmentality that one opposes and whose abuses one tries to limit. So that we will be able to find liberalism, in different but simultaneous forms, as a regulative scheme of governmental practice and as the theme of a sometimes-radical opposition. English political thought, at the end of the eighteenth century and in the first half of the nineteenth, is highly characteristic of these multiple uses of liberalism. And even more specifically, the developments and ambiguities of Bentham and the Benthamites.

There is no doubt that the market as a reality and political economy as a theory played an important role in the liberal critique. But, as P. Rosanvallon's important book has confirmed, liberalism is neither the consequence nor the development of these,[1] rather, the market played, in the liberal critique, the role of a "test," a locus of privileged experience where one can identify the effects of excessive governmentality and even weigh their significance: the analysis of the mechanisms of "dearth" or more generally, of the grain trade in the middle of the eighteenth century, was meant to show the point at which governing was always governing too much. And whether it is a question of the physiocrats' Table or Smith's "invisible hand"; whether it is a question, therefore, of an analysis aiming to make visible (in the form of "evidence") the formation of the value and circulation of wealth—or, on the contrary, an analysis presupposing the intrinsic invisibility of the connection between individual profit-seeking and the growth of collective wealth—economics, in any case, shows a basic incompatibility between the optimal development of the economic process and a maximization of governmental procedures. It is by this, more than by the play of ideas, that the French or English economists broke away from mercantilism and cameralism; they freed reflection on economic practice from the hegemony of the "reason of state" and from the saturation of governmental intervention. By using it as a measure of "governing too much," they placed it "at the limit" of governmental action.

Liberalism does not derive from juridical thought any more than it does from an economic analysis. It is not the idea of a political society founded on a contractual tie that gave birth to it; but in the search for a liberal technology of government, it appeared that regulation through the juridical form constituted a far more effective tool than the wisdom or moderation of the governors. (Rather, the physiocrats tended, out of a distrust of law and the juridical institution, to look for that regulation in the recognition, by a despot with institutionally limited power, of the economy's "natural" laws, impressing themselves upon him as an evident truth.) Liberalism sought that regulation in "the law," not through a legalism that would be natural to it but because the law defines forms of general intervention excluding particular, individual, or exceptional measures; and because the participation of the governed in the formulation of the law, in a parliamentary system, constitutes the most effective system of governmental economy. The "state of right," the *Rechtsstaat*, the rule of law, the organization of a "truly representative" parliamentary system was, therefore, during the whole beginning of the nineteenth century, closely connected with liberalism, but just as political economy—used at first as a test of excessive governmentality—was not liberal either by nature or by virtue, and soon even led to antiliberal attitudes (whether in the *Nationaloekonomie* of the nineteenth century or in the planning economies of the twentieth), so the democracies of the state of right were not necessarily liberal, nor was liberalism necessarily democratic or devoted to the forms of law.

Rather than a relatively coherent doctrine, rather than a politics pursuing a certain number of more or less clearly defined goals, I would be tempted to see in liberalism a form of critical reflection on governmental practice. That criticism can come from within or without, it can rely on this or that economic theory, or refer to this or that juridical system without any necessary and one-to-one connection. The question of liberalism, understood as a question of "too much government," was one of the constant dimensions of that recent European phenomenon, having appeared first in England, it seems—namely, "political life." Indeed, it is one of the constituent elements of it, if it is the case that political life exists when governmental practice is limited in its possible excess by the fact that it is the object of public debate as to its "good or bad," its "too much or too little."

Of course, the above reflections constitute not an "interpretation" of liberalism which would claim to be exhaustive but, rather, a plan of possible analysis—of "governmental reason," that is, of those types of rationality which are brought into play in the methods by which human behavior is directed via a state admin-istration. I have tried to carry out such an analysis concerning two contempo-rary examples: German liberalism of the years 1948–62, and American liberalism of the Chicago school. In both cases, liberalism presented itself, in a definite context, as a critique of the irrationality peculiar to "excessive govern-ment" and as a return to a technology of "frugal government," as Franklin would have said.

In Germany, that excess was the regime of war, Nazism, but, beyond that, a type of directed and planned economy developing out of the 1914–18 period and the general mobilization of resources and men; it was also "state socialism." In point of fact, German liberalism of the second postwar period was defined, programmed, and even to a certain extent put into practice by men who, starting in the years 1928–1930, had belonged to the Freiburg school (or at least had been inspired by it) and who had later expressed themselves in the journal *Ordo*. At the intersection of neo-Kantian philosophy, Husserl's phenomenology, and Weber's sociology, on certain points close to the Viennese economists, con-cerned about the historical correlation between economic processes and juridi-cal structures, men like Eucken, W. Roepke, Franz Böhm, and Von Rustow had conducted their critiques on three different political fronts: Soviet socialism, National Socialism, and interventionist policies inspired by Keynes. But they addressed what they considered as a single adversary: a type of economic gov-ernment systematically ignorant of the market mechanisms that were the only thing capable of price-forming regulation. Ordo-liberalism, working on the basic themes of the liberal technology of government, tried to define what a market economy could be, organized (but not planned or directed) within an in-stitutional and juridical framework that, on the one hand, would offer the guar-antees and limitations of law, and, on the other, would make sure that the freedom of economic processes did not cause any social distortion. The first part of this course was devoted to the study of this Ordo-liberalism, which had inspired the economic choice of the general policy of the German Federal Re-public during the time of Adenauer and Ludwig Erhard.

The second part was devoted to a few aspects of what is called "American neoliberalism": that liberalism which is generally associated with the Chicago school and which also developed in reaction against the "excessive govern-ment" exhibited in its eyes, starting with Simons, by the New Deal, war-planning, and the great economic and social programs generally supported by postwar Democratic administrations. As in the case of the German Ordo-liberals, the critique carried out in the name of economic liberalism cited the danger represented by the inevitable sequence: economic interventionism, inflation of governmental apparatuses, overadministration, bureaucracy, and rigidification of all the power mechanisms, accompanied by the production of new economic distortions that would lead to new interventions. But what was striking in this American neoliberalism was a movement completely contrary to what is found in the social economy of the market in Germany: where the latter considers regulation of prices by the market—the only basis for a rational economy—to be in itself so fragile that it must be supported, managed, and "ordered" by a vigilant internal policy of social interventions (involving assistance to the unemployed, health care coverage, a housing policy, and so on), American neoliberalism seeks rather to extend the rationality of the market, the schemes of analysis it proposes, and the decisionmaking criteria it suggests to areas that are not exclusively or not primarily economic. For example, the family and birth policy, or delinquency and penal policy.

What would need to be studied now, therefore, is the way in which the specific problems of life and population were raised within a technology of government which, without always having been liberal—far from it—was always haunted since the end of the eighteenth century by liberalism's question.

The seminar was devoted this year to the crisis of juridical thought in the last years of the nineteenth century. Papers were read by François Ewald (on civil law), Catherine Mevel (on public and administrative law), Eliane Allo (on the right to life in legislation concerning children), Nathalie Coppinger and Pasquale Pasquino (on penal law), Alexandre Fontana (on security measures), François Delaporte and Anne-Marie Moulin (on health policy and health politics).

Note

1. P. Rosanvallon, *Le Capitalisme utopique: critique de l'idéologie économique* (Paris: Seuil, 1979).

ABOUT THE CONCEPT OF THE "DANGEROUS INDIVIDUAL" IN NINETEENTH-CENTURY LEGAL PSYCHIATRY

I would like to begin by relating a brief exchange which took place the other day in the Paris criminal courts. A man who was accused of five rapes and six attempted rapes, between February and June 1975, was being tried. The accused hardly spoke at all. Questions from the presiding judge:

"Have you tried to reflect upon your case?"

Silence.

"Why, at twenty-two years of age, do such violent urges overtake you? You must make an effort to analyze yourself. You are the one who has the keys to your own actions. Explain yourself."

Silence.

"Why would you do it again?"

Silence.

Then a juror took over and cried out, "For heaven's sake, defend yourself!"

Such a dialogue or, rather, such an interrogatory monologue, is not in the least exceptional. It could doubtlessly be heard in many courts in many countries. But, seen in another light, it can only arouse the amazement of the historian. Here we have a judicial system designed to establish misdemeanors, to determine who committed them, and to sanction these acts by imposing the penalties prescribed by the law. In this case, we have facts that have been established, an individual who admits to them—one who, consequently, accepts the punishment he will receive. All should be for the best in the best of all possible judicial worlds. The legislators, the authors of the legal codes in the late eigh-

---

This essay was first published in English in the *Journal of Law and Psychiatry* in 1978.—Eds.

teenth and early nineteenth centuries, could not have dreamed of a clearer situation. And yet it happens that the machinery jams, the gears seize up. Why? Because the accused remains silent. Remains silent about what? About the facts? About circumstances? About the way in which they occurred? About the immediate cause of the events? Not at all. The accused evades a question that is essential in the eyes of a modern tribunal but would have had a strange ring to it 150 years ago: "Who are you?"

And the dialogue I just quoted shows that it is not enough for the accused to say in reply to that question, "I am the author of the crimes before you, period. Judge since you must, condemn if you will." Much more is expected of him. Beyond admission, there must be confession, self-examination, explanation of oneself, revelation of what one is. The penal machine can no longer function simply with a law, a violation, and a responsible party—it needs something else, supplementary material. The magistrates and the jurors, the lawyers too, and the department of the public prosecutor cannot really play their roles unless they are provided with another type of discourse, the one given by the accused about himself, or the one he makes possible for others, through his confessions, memories, intimate disclosures, and so on. If it happens that this discourse is missing, the presiding judge is relentless, the jury is upset. They urge, they push the accused, he does not play the game. He is not unlike those condemned persons who have to be carried to the guillotine or the electric chair because they drag their feet. They really ought to walk a little by themselves, if indeed they want to be executed. They really ought to speak a little about themselves, if they want to be judged. The following argument used recently by a French lawyer in the case of the kidnapping and murder of a child clearly indicates that the judicial stage cannot do without this added element, that no judgment, no condemnation is possible without it being provided, in one way or another.

For a number of reasons, this case created a great stir, not only because of the seriousness of the crime but also because the question of the retention or the abolition of the death penalty was at stake in the case. In his plea, which was directed against the death penalty more than in favor of the accused, the lawyer stressed the point that very little was known about him, and that the nature of the man had only barely been glimpsed at in the interrogations and in the psychiatric examinations. And he made this amazing remark (I quote approximately): "Can one condemn to death a person one does not know?"

This is probably no more than one illustration of a well-known fact, which could be called the "law of the third element," or the "Garofalo principle," since Garofalo was the one who formulated it with complete clarity: "Criminal law knew only two terms, the offense and the penalty. The new criminology recognizes three, the crime, the criminal and the means of repression." In large part, the evolution—if not of the penal systems then at least of the day-to-day penal practice of many countries—is determined by the gradual emergence in the course of the nineteenth century of this additional character. At first a pale phantom, used to adjust the penalty determined by the judge for the crime, this character becomes gradually more substantial, more solid, and more real, until finally it is the crime that seems nothing but a shadow hovering about the criminal, a shadow that must be drawn aside in order to reveal the only thing that is now of importance, the criminal.

Legal justice today has at least as much to do with criminals as with crimes. Or, more precisely, though for a long time the criminal had been no more than the person to whom a crime could be attributed and who could therefore be punished, today the crime tends to be no more than the event that signals the existence of a dangerous element—that is, more or less dangerous—in the social body.

From the very beginning of this development, resorting to the criminal over and above the crime was justified by a double concern: to introduce more rationality into penal practice, and to adjust the general provisions of laws and legal codes more closely to social reality. Probably, it was not realized, at least at first, that to add the notion of psychological symptomatology of a danger to the notion of legal imputability of a crime was not only to enter an extremely obscure labyrinth but also to come slowly out of a legal system that had gradually developed since its birth during the medieval inquisition. It could be said that hardly had the great eighteenth-century legal reformers completed the systematic codification of the results of the preceding evolution, hardly had they developed all its possibilities, when a new crisis began to appear in the rules and regulations of legal punishment. "What must be punished, and how?" That was the question to which, it was believed, a rational answer had finally been found. And now a further question arose to confuse the issue: "Whom do you think you are punishing?"

In this development, psychiatry and psychiatrists, as well as the notion of "danger," played a permanent role. I would like to draw attention to two stages in what one might call the "psychiatrization" of criminal danger.

The intervention of psychiatry in the field of law occurred in the beginning of the nineteenth century, in connection with a series of cases that took place between 1800 and 1835 whose pattern was about the same.

Case reported by Metzger: A retired officer who lives a solitary life becomes attached to his landlady's child. One day, "with absolutely no motive, in the absence of any passion, such as anger, pride, or vengeance," he attacks the child and hits him twice with a hammer, though not fatally.

Sélestat case: In Alsace, during the extremely hard winter of 1817, when famine threatens, a peasant woman takes advantage of her husband's being away at work to kill their little daughter, cuts off her leg, and cooks it in the soup.

In Paris in 1827, Henriette Cornier, a servant, goes to the neighbor of her employers and insists that the neighbor leave her daughter with her for a time. The neighbor hesitates, agrees; when she returns for the child, Henriette Cornier has just killed her and has cut off her head, which she has thrown out the window.

In Vienna, Catherine Ziegler kills her illegitimate child. On the stand, she explains that her act was the result of an irresistible force. She is acquitted on grounds of insanity. She is released from prison. But she declares that it would be better if she were kept there, for she will do it again. Ten months later, she gives birth to a child, which she kills immediately, and she declares at the trial that she became pregnant for the sole purpose of killing her child. She is condemned to death and executed.

In Scotland, a certain John Howison enters a house where he kills an old woman whom he hardly knows, leaves without stealing anything, and does not go into hiding. Arrested, he denies the fact against all evidence; but the defense argues that it is the crime of a madman since it is a crime without material motive. Howison is executed, and his comment to an official at the execution, that he felt like killing him, was considered in retrospect as supplementary evidence of madness.

In New England, out in the open fields, Abraham Prescott kills his foster mother, with whom he had always gotten along very well. He goes home and breaks into tears in front of his foster father, who questions him. Prescott willingly confesses his crime. He explains later that he was overcome by a sudden and acute toothache, and that he remembers nothing. The inquiry will establish that he had already attacked his foster parents during the night, an act that had been believed to be the result of a fit of sleepwalking. Prescott is condemned to death, but the jury also recommends a commutation. He is nevertheless executed.

The psychiatrists of the period, Metzger, Hoffbauer, Esquirol and Georget, William Ellis and Andrew Combe refer tirelessly to these cases and to others of the same type.

Out of all the crimes committed, why did these particular ones seem important? Why were they at issue in the discussions between doctors and jurists? First, it must be noted that they present a picture very different from what had hitherto constituted the jurisprudence of criminal insanity. In general terms, until the end of the eighteenth century, the question of insanity was raised under penal law only in cases where it was also raised in the civil code or in canon law, that is when it appeared either in the form of *dementia* and of imbecility, or in the form of *furor*. In both cases, whether it was a matter of a permanent state or a passing outburst, insanity manifested itself through numerous signs that were easy enough to recognize, to the extent that it was debated whether a doctor was really necessary to authenticate it. The important thing is that criminal psychiatry did not develop from a subtle redefining of the traditional question of *dementia* (for example, by discussing its gradual evolution, its global or partial character, its relationship to congenital disabilities of individuals), nor through a closer analysis of the symptomatology of *furor* (its remissions, it recurrences, its rhythm). All these problems, along with the discussions that had gone on for years, were replaced by a new problem, that of crimes that are not preceded, accompanied, nor followed by any of the traditional, recognized, visible symptoms of insanity. It is stressed in each case that there was no previous history, no earlier disturbance in thought or behavior, no delirium; neither was there any agitation, nor visible disorder as in *furor*. Indeed, the crime would arise out of a state one might call the zero degree of insanity.

The second common feature is too obvious to be dealt with at any length. The crimes in question are not minor offenses but serious crimes, almost all murders, sometimes accompanied by strange cruelties (cannibalism in the case of the woman from Sélestat). It is important to note that the psychiatrization of delinquency occurred in a sense "from above." This is also a departure from the fundamental tendency of previous jurisprudence. The more serious the crime, the less usual it was to raise the question of insanity (for a long period, it was not taken into consideration in cases involving sacrilege or lèse majesté). That there is a considerable area of overlap between insanity and illegality was readily admitted in the case of minor offenses—little acts of violence, vagrancy—and these were dealt with, at least in some countries (such as France), by the ambiguous measure of internment. But it was not through the ill-defined zone of day-to-day disorders that psychiatry was able to penetrate penal justice in full force. Rather, it was by tackling the great criminal event of the most violent and rarest sort.

Another common feature of these great murders is that they take place in a domestic setting. They are family crimes, household crimes, and, at most, neighborhood crimes—parents who kill their progeny, children who kill their parents or guardians, servants who kill their employers' or their neighbors' child, and so on. As we can see, these are crimes that bring together partners from different generations. The child-adult or adolescent-adult couple is almost always present. In those days, such relationships of age, of place, of kinship were held to be at the same time the most sacred and the most natural, and also the most innocent. Of all relationships, they were the ones that ought to have been the least charged with material motive or passion. Rather than crimes against society and its rules, they are crimes against nature, against those laws perceived to be inscribed directly on the human heart and to link families and generations. At the beginning of the nineteenth century, the form of crime about which it appeared that the question of insanity could properly be raised was thus the crime against nature. The individual in whom insanity and criminality met in such a way as to cause specialists to raise the question of their relationship was not the man of the little everyday disorder, the pale silhouette moving about on the edges of law and normality but, rather, the great monster. Criminal psychiatry first proclaimed itself a pathology of the monstrous.

Finally, all these crimes were committed without reason—I mean without profit, without passion, without motive, not even based on disordered illusions. In all the cases I have mentioned, the psychiatrists justify their intervention by insisting that there existed between the two actors in the drama no relationship that would help to make the crime intelligible. In the case of Henriette Cornier, who had decapitated her neighbor's daughter, it was carefully established that she had not been the father's mistress, and that she had not acted out of vengeance. In the case of the woman from Sélestat who had boiled her daughter's thigh, an important element of the discussion had been, "Was there or was there not famine at the time? Was the accused poor or not, starving or not?" The public prosecutor had said, "If she had been rich, she could have been considered deranged, but she was poverty-stricken; she was hungry; to cook the leg with the cabbage was interested behavior; she was therefore not insane."

At the time when the new psychiatry was being established, and when the principles of penal reform were being applied nearly everywhere in Europe and in North America, the great and monstrous murder, without reason, without preliminaries, the sudden eruption of the unnatural in nature, was the singular and paradoxical form taken by criminal insanity or pathological crime. I say paradoxical because there was an attempt to grasp a type of derangement that manifested itself only in the moment and in the guise of the crime, a derangement that would have no symptom other than the crime itself and could disappear once the crime had been committed. And, conversely, it entailed identifying crimes whose reason, whose author—whose "legally responsible agent" so to speak—is that part of the subject beyond his responsibility; that is, the insanity that hides in him, which he cannot even control because he is frequently not even aware of it. Nineteenth-century psychiatry invented an entirely fictitious entity, a crime that is insanity, a crime that is nothing but insanity, an insanity that is nothing but a crime. For more than half a century, this entity was called "homicidal monomania." I do not intend to go over the theoretical background of the notion or to follow up the innumerable discussions it prompted between men of the law and doctors, lawyers and magistrates. I simply want to underline this strange fact: psychiatrists have tried very stubbornly to take their place in the legal machinery. They justified their right to intervene not by searching out the thousand little visible signs of madness that may accompany the most ordinary crimes but by insisting—a preposterous stance—that there were kinds of insanity which manifested themselves only in outrageous crimes and in no other way. And I would also like to underline the fact that, in spite of all their reservations about accepting this notion of monomania, when the magistrates of the time finally accepted the psychiatric analysis of crime, they did so on the basis of this same notion, so foreign and so unacceptable to them.

Why was the great fiction of homicidal mania the key notion in the protohistory of criminal psychiatry? The first set of questions to be asked is probably the following: At the beginning of the nineteenth century, when the task of psychiatry was to define its specificity in the field of medicine and to assure that its scientific character was recognized among other medical practices—at the point, that is, when psychiatry was establishing itself as a medical specialization (previously it had been an aspect rather than a field of medicine)—why then did it want to meddle in an area where so far it had intervened very discretely? Why did doctors want so badly to describe as insane, and thus to claim, people whose status as mere criminals had up to that point been unquestioned? Why can they be found in so many countries, denouncing the medical ignorance of judges and jurors, requesting pardons or the commutation of punishment for certain convicts, demanding the right to be heard as experts by the tribunals, publishing hundreds of reports and studies to show that this criminal or that one was a madman? Why this crusade in favor of the "pathologification" of crime and under the banner, no less, of homicidal mania? This is all the more paradoxical in that, shortly before, at the end of the eighteenth century, the very first students of insanity (especially Philippe Pinel) protested against the practice followed in many detention centers of mixing delinquents and the mentally ill. Why would one want to renew a kinship one had taken such trouble to break down?

It is not enough to invoke some sort of imperialism on the part of psychiatrists seeking a new domain for themselves, or even the internal dynamics of medical knowledge attempting to rationalize the confused area where madness and crime mix. Crime, then, became an important issue for psychiatrists, because what was involved was less a field of knowledge to be conquered than a modality of power to be secured and justified. If psychiatry became so important in the nineteenth century, it was not simply because it applied a new medical rationality to mental or behavioral disorders; it was also because it functioned as a sort of public hygiene.

In the eighteenth century, the development of demography, of urban structures, of the problem of industrial labor, had raised in biological and medical terms the question of human "populations," with their conditions of existence, of habitation, of nutrition, with their birth and mortality rates, with their pathological phenomena (epidemics, endemic diseases, infant mortality). The social "body" ceased to be a simple juridico-political metaphor (like the one in the *Leviathan*) and became, instead, a biological reality and a field for medical intervention. The doctor must therefore be the technician of this social body, and medicine a public hygiene. At the turn of the nineteenth century, psychiatry became an autonomous discipline and assumed such prestige precisely because it had been able to develop within the framework of a medical discipline conceived of as a reaction to the dangers inherent in the social body. The alienists of the period may well have had endless discussions about the organic or psychic origin of mental illnesses; they may well have proposed physical or psychic therapies. Nonetheless, through all their differences, they were all conscious that they were treating a social "danger," either because insanity seemed to them to be linked to living conditions (overpopulation, overcrowding, urban life, alcoholism, debauchery), or because it was perceived as a source of danger for oneself, for others, for one's contemporaries, and also for one's descendants through heredity. Nineteenth-century psychiatry was a medical science as much for the societal body as for the individual soul.

One can see why it was important for psychiatry to prove the existence of something as extravagant as homicidal mania. One can see why for half a century there were continuous attempts to make that notion work, in spite of its meager scientific justification. Indeed, if it exists, homicidal mania shows:

First, that in some of its pure, extreme, intense manifestations, insanity is entirely crime, nothing but crime—that is, at least at the ultimate boundaries of insanity, there is crime.

Second, that insanity can produce not just behavioral disorders but absolute crime, the crime that transgresses all the laws of nature and of society.

And third, that even though this insanity may be extraordinarily intense, it remains invisible until it explodes; that for this reason no one can forecast it, unless he has considerable experience and a trained eye. In short, only a specialist can spot monomania. The contradiction is more apparent than real when the alienists eventually define monomania as an illness that manifests itself only in crime while, at the same time, they reserve the right to know how to determine its premonitory signs, its predisposing conditions.

So homicidal mania is the danger of insanity in its most harmful form: a maximum of consequences, a minimum of warning. The most effects and fewest signs. Homicidal mania thus necessitates the intervention of a medical eye, which must take into account not only the obvious manifestations of madness but also the barely perceptible traces, appearing randomly where they are the least expected, and foretelling the worst explosions. Such an interest in the great crimes "without reason," I think, indicates on the part of psychiatry not a desire to take over criminality but a desire to justify its functions—the control of the dangers hidden in human behavior. What is at stake in this great issue of homicidal mania is the function of psychiatry. It must not be forgotten that, in most Western countries, psychiatry was then striving to establish its right to impose upon the mentally ill a therapeutic confinement. After all, it had to be shown that madness, by its nature, and even in its most discrete manifestations, was haunted by the absolute danger, death. The functioning of modern psychiatry is linked to this kinship between madness and death, which was not scientifically established but, rather, symbolically represented in the figure of homicidal mania.

However, there is another question to be asked, this time from the point of view of the judges and the judicial apparatus. Why indeed did they accept if not the notion of monomania then at least the problems it entailed? It will probably be said that the great majority of magistrates refused to recognize this notion which made it possible to transform a criminal into a madman whose only illness was to commit crimes. With a great deal of tenacity—and, one might add, with a certain degree of good sense—they did everything they could to dismiss this notion the doctors proposed to them and lawyers used spontaneously to defend their clients. And yet, through this controversy about monstrous crimes, about crimes "without reason," the idea of a possible kinship between madness and delinquency became acclimatized even within the judicial institution. Why was this accomplished, and relatively easily at that? In other words, why did the penal institution, which had been able to do without medical intervention for so many centuries, which had been able to judge and condemn without the problem of madness being raised except in a few obvious cases, why did this penal institution so willingly have recourse to medical knowledge from the 1820s on? For there is no mistaking the fact that English, German, Italian, and French judges of the time quite often refused to accept the conclusions of the doctors. They rejected many of the notions the doctors proposed to them. After all, the doctors did not take them by force. They themselves solicited—following the laws, the rules, the jurisprudence that vary from country to country—the duly formulated advice of psychiatrists, and they solicited it especially in connection with those famous crimes "without reason." Why? Was it because the new codes written and applied at the beginning of the nineteenth century took into account psychiatric expertise or gave a new emphasis to the problem of pathological irresponsibility? Not at all. Surprisingly enough, these new laws hardly modified the previous situation. Most of the codes based on the Napoleonic model incorporated the old principle that the state of mental disorder is incompatible with legal responsibility and thus is immune from the usual legal consequences. Most of the codes also incorporate the traditional notions of *dementia* and *furor* used in the older legal systems. Neither the great theoreticians Cesare de Beccaria and Jeremy Bentham, nor those who actually wrote up the new penal laws, tried to elaborate upon these traditional notions, or to establish new relationships between punishment and criminal medicine, except to affirm in a very general way that penal justice must cure this illness of societies, that is, crime. It was not "from above," by way of legal codes or theoretical principles, that psychiatric medicine penetrated the penal system. Rather, it was "from below," through the mechanics of punishment and through the interpretation given to them. Among all the new techniques for controlling and transforming individuals, punishment had become a system of procedures designed to reform lawbreakers. The terrifying example of torture or exile by banishment could no longer suffice in a society in which exercise of power implied a reasoned technology applied to individuals. The forms of punishment to which all the late eighteenth-century reformers and all the early nineteenth-century legislators rallied—that is, imprisonment, forced labor, constant surveillance, partial or total isolation, moral reform—all this implies that punishment bears on the criminal himself rather than on the crime, that is, on what makes him a criminal, on his reasons, his motives, his inner will, his tendencies, his instincts. In the older systems, the horror of the punishment had to reflect the enormity of the crime; henceforth, the attempt was made to adapt the modalities of punishment to the nature of the criminal.

In these circumstances, one sees why the great unmotivated crimes posed a difficult problem for the judges. In the past, to impose a punishment for a crime one had only to find the author of the crime, and it was enough that he had no excuse and that he had not been in a state of *furor* or *dementia*. But how can one punish someone whose reasons are unknown, who keeps silent before his judges, except to admit the facts and to agree that he had been perfectly conscious of what he was doing? What is to be done when a woman like Henriette Cornier appears in court, a woman who has killed a child whom she hardly knew, the daughter of people whom she could neither have hated nor loved, who decapitates the girl but is unable to give the slightest explanation, who does not try for a moment to hide her crime, and who had nonetheless prepared for her act, had chosen the moment, had procured a knife, had eagerly sought an opportunity to be alone for a moment with her victim? Thus, in a person who had given no sign of madness, there arises an act at once voluntary, conscious, and reasoned—that is, all that is necessary for a condemnation according to the terms of the law—and yet nothing, no reason, no motive, no evil tendencies that would have made it possible to determine what should be punished in the guilty woman. It is clear that there should be a condemnation, but it is hard to understand why there should be a punishment, except of course for the external but insufficient reason of setting an example. Now that the reason for the crime had become the reason for the punishment, how could one punish if the crime was without reason? In order to punish, one needs to know the nature of the guilty person, his obduracy, the degree of his evilness, what his interests or his leanings are. But if one has nothing more than the crime, on the one hand, and the author, on the other, pure and simple judicial responsibility formally authorizes punishment but does not allow one to make sense of it.

One can see why these great unmotivated crimes, which the psychiatrists had good reason to emphasize, were also, but for very different reasons, such important problems for the judicial apparatus. The public prosecutors obstinately referred to the law: no *dementia,* no *furor,* no recognized evidence of derangement; on the contrary, perfectly organized acts; therefore, the law must be applied. But no matter how hard they tried, they could not avoid the question of motivation, for they knew very well that from now on, in practice, the judges would link punishment, at least in part, to the determination of motives. Perhaps Henriette Cornier had been the mistress of the girl's father, and sought revenge; perhaps, having had to abandon her own children, she was jealous of the happy family living near her. All the indictments prove that in order for the punitive mechanism to work, the reality of an offense and a person to whom it can be attributed are not sufficient: the motive must also be established, that is, a psychologically intelligible link between the act and the author. The Sélestat case, in which a cannibalistic woman was executed because she *could* have been hungry, seems to me to be very significant.

The doctors who were normally called in only to certify cases of *dementia* or of *furor* began now to be called upon as "specialists in motivation"; they had to evaluate not only the subject's reason but also the rationality of the act, the whole system of relationships that link the act to the interests, the plans, the character, the inclinations, and the habits of the subject. And even though the judges were often reluctant to accept the diagnosis of monomania so relished by the doctors, they were obliged to entertain willingly the set of problems raised by the notion—that is, in slightly more modern terms, the integration of the act into the global behavior of the subject. The more clearly visible this integration, the more clearly punishable the subject. The less obvious the integration, the more it seems as if the act has erupted in the subject, like a sudden and irrepressible mechanism, and the less punishable the responsible party appears. And justice will then agree that it cannot proceed with the case, since the subject is insane, and will commit him to psychiatric confinement.

Several conclusions can be drawn from this:

First: The intervention of psychiatric medicine in the penal system starting in the nineteenth century is neither the consequence nor the simple development of the traditional theory of the irresponsibility of those suffering from *dementia* or *furor.*

Second: It is due to the regulating of two phenomena arising necessarily— one from the functioning of medicine as a public hygiene, the other from the functioning of legal punishment as a technique for transforming the individual.

Third: These two new demands are both bound up with the transformation of the mechanism of power through which the control of the social body has been attempted in industrial societies since the eighteenth century. In spite of their common origin, though, the reasons for the intervention of medicine in the criminal field and the reasons for the recourse of penal justice to psychiatry are essentially different.

Fourth: The monstrous crime, both antinatural and irrational, is the meeting point of the medical demonstration that insanity is ultimately always dangerous, and of the court's inability to determine the punishment of a crime without having determined the motives for the crime. The bizarre symptomatology of homicidal mania was delineated at the point of convergence of these two mechanisms.

Fifth: In this way, the theme of the dangerous man is inscribed in the institutions of psychiatry as well as of justice. Increasingly in the nineteenth and twentieth centuries, penal practice and then penal theory will tend to make of the dangerous individual the principal target of punitive intervention. Increasingly, nineteenth-century psychiatry will also tend to seek out pathological stigmata that may mark dangerous individuals: moral insanity, instinctive insanity, and degeneration. This theme of the dangerous individual will give rise, on the one hand, to the anthropology of criminal man as in the Italian school, and, on the other, to the theory of social defense first represented by the Belgian school.

Sixth: Another important consequence is that there will be a considerable transformation of the old notion of penal responsibility. This notion, at least in certain aspects, was still close to civil law. It was necessary, for instance, in order to impute a violation to someone, that he be free, conscious, unafflicted by *dementia*, untouched by any crisis of *furor*. Now, however, responsibility would be limited no longer only to this form of consciousness but also to the intelligibility of the act with reference to the conduct, the character, the antecedents of the individual. The more psychologically determined an act is found to be, the more its author can be considered legally responsible. The more the act is, so to speak, gratuitous and undetermined, the more it will tend to be excused. A paradox, then: the legal freedom of a subject is proven by the fact that his act is seen to be necessary, determined; his lack of responsibility proven by the fact that his act is seen to be unnecessary. With this untenable paradox of monomania and of the monstrous act, psychiatry and penal justice entered a phase of uncertainty from which we have yet to emerge; the play between penal responsibility and psychological determinism has become the cross of legal and medical thought.

I would now like to turn to another moment that was particularly fertile for the relationship between psychiatry and penal law: the last years of the nineteenth century and the first few of the twentieth from the first congress on Criminal Anthropology (1885) to A. Prinz's publication of his *Social Defense* (1910).

Between the period I was recalling previously and the one I would like to speak about now, what happened? First of all, within the discipline of psychiatry in the strict sense of the term, the notion of monomania was abandoned, not without some hesitations and reversions, shortly before 1870. Abandoned for two reasons. First, because the essentially negative idea of a partial insanity, bearing on only one point and unleashed only at certain moments, was gradually replaced by the idea that a mental illness is not necessarily an affliction of thought or of consciousness, but that it may attack the emotions, the instincts, spontaneous behavior, leaving the forms of thought virtually intact. (What was called "moral insanity," instinctive insanity, aberration of the instincts, and finally perversion, corresponds to this elaboration, whose favored example since about the 1840s has been the deviations in sexual conduct.) But there was another reason for abandoning monomania; that is, the idea of mental illness—its evolution is complex and polymorphous—which may present one particular symptom or another at one stage or another of its development, not only at the level of the individual but also at the level of several generations; in short, the idea of degeneration.

Because of the fact that these great evolutive ramifications can be defined, it is no longer necessary to make a distinction between the great monstrous and mysterious crimes that could be ascribed to the incomprehensible violence of *insanity* and minor delinquency, which is too frequent, too familiar to necessitate a recourse to the pathological. From then on, whether one had to deal with incomprehensible massacres or minor offenses (having to do with property or sexuality), in every case one might suspect a more or less serious perturbation of instincts or the stages in an uninterruped process. Thus, there appear in the field of legal psychiatry new categories—such as necrophilia around 1840, kleptomania around 1860, exhibitionism in 1876—and also legal psychiatry's annexation of behavior like pederasty and sadism. There now exists, at least in principle, a psychiatric and criminological continuum that permits one to pose questions in medical terms at any level of the penal scale. The psychiatric question is no longer confined to some great crimes; even if it must receive a negative answer, it is to be posed across the whole range of infractions.

Now, this has important consequences for the legal theory of responsibility. In the conception of monomania, suspicions of pathology were aroused precisely when there was no reason for an act; insanity was seen as the cause of that which made no sense, and legal nonresponsibility was established in view of this inconsistency. But with this new analysis of instinct and emotions, it would be possible to provide a casual analysis for all kinds of conduct, whether delinquent or not, and whatever their degree of criminality. Hence the infinite labyrinth in which the legal and psychiatric problem of crime found itself. If an act is determined by a causal nexus, can it be considered to be free? Does it not imply responsibility? And is it necessary, in order to be able to condemn someone, that it be impossible to reconstruct the causal intelligibility of his act?

Now, as background for this new way of posing the problem, I must mention several transformations that were, at least in part, the conditions of its being possible. First, the intensive development of the police network, which led to a new mapping and closer surveillance of urban space and also to a much more systematic and efficient prosecution of minor delinquency. It must be added that social conflicts, class struggles and political confrontations, armed revolts—from the machine-smashers of the beginning of the century to the anarchists of the last few years of the century, including the violent strikes, the revolutions of 1848, and the Commune of 1870—prompted those in power to treat political misdemeanors in the same way as ordinary crimes in order to discredit them. Little by little, an image was built up of an enemy of society who can equally well be a revolutionary or a murderer—since, after all, revolutionaries do sometimes kill. Corresponding to this, throughout the whole second half of the century there developed a "literature of criminality," and I use the word in its largest sense, including miscellaneous news items (and even popular newspapers) as well as detective novels and all the romanticized writings that developed around crime—the transformation of the criminal into a hero, perhaps, but equally the affirmation that ever-present criminality is a constant menace to the social body as a whole. The collective fear of crime, and the obsession with this danger which seems to be an inseparable part of society itself, are thus perpetually inscribed in each individual consciousness.

Referring to the 9,000 murders then recorded annually in Europe, not counting Russia, B. R. Garofalo said in the preface to the first edition of his *Criminology* (1887): "Who is the enemy who has devastated this land? It is a mysterious enemy, unknown to history; his name is: the criminal."

To this must be added another element—the continuing failure of the penitentiary system, which is very frequently reported. It was the dream of the eighteenth-century reformers, then of the philanthropists of the following period, that incarceration, provided that it be rationally directed, might serve as a true penal therapy. The result was meant to be the reform of the prisoners. It soon became clear that prison had exactly the opposite result, that it was on the whole a school for delinquency and that the more refined methods of the police system and the legal apparatus, far from ensuring better protection against crime, brought about a strengthening of the criminal milieu, through the medium of prison itself.

For all sorts of reasons, a situation existed such that there was a very strong social and political demand for a reaction to, and for repression of, crime. This demand had to do with a criminality, which in its totality had to be thought of in judicial and medical terms; and yet, the key notion of the penal institution since the Middle Ages—that is, legal responsibility—seems utterly inadequate for the conceptualization of this broad and dense domain of medico-legal criminality.

This inadequacy became apparent, both at the conceptual and at the institutional level, in the conflict between the so-called school of Criminal Anthropology and the International Association of Penal Law around the 1890s. In attempting to cope with the traditional principles of criminal legislation, the Italian School (the Criminal Anthropologists) called for nothing less than a putting-aside of legality—a true "depenalization" of crime, by setting up an apparatus of an entirely different type from the one provided for by the Codes.

For the Criminal Anthropologists, this meant totally abandoning the judicial notion of responsibility, and posing as the fundamental question not the degree of freedom of the individual but the level of danger he represents for society. Moreover, it meant noting that the accused, whom the law recognized as not responsible because he was ill, insane, a victim of irresistible impulses, was precisely the most seriously and immediately dangerous. The Criminal Anthropologists emphasized that what is called "penalty" need not be a punishment but, rather, a mechanism for the defense of society; they therefore noted that the relevant difference is not between legally responsible subjects who are found guilty, and legally irresponsible subjects who are released, but between absolutely and definitively dangerous subjects and those who can cease to be dangerous provided they receive certain treatment. They concluded that there should be three main types of social reaction to crime or, rather, to the danger represented by the criminal: definitive elimination (by death or by incarceration in an institution), temporary elimination (with treatment), and more or less relative and partial elimination (sterilization and castration).

One can see the series of shifts required by the anthropological school: from the crime to the criminal; from the act as it was actually committed to the danger potentially inherent in the individual; from the modulated punishment of the guilty party to the absolute protection of others. All these shifts implied quite clearly an escape from a universe of penal law revolving around the act, its imputability to a de jure subject, the legal responsibility of the latter and a punishment proportionate to the gravity of this act as defined by law. Neither the "criminality" of an individual nor the index of his dangerousness, neither his potential or future behavior nor the protection of society at large from these possible perils—none of these are or can be juridical notions in the classical sense of the term. They can be made to function in a rational way only within a technical knowledge-system, a knowledge-system capable of characterizing a criminal individual in himself and, in a sense, beneath his acts; a knowledge-system able to measure the index of danger present in an individual; a knowledge-system that might establish the protection necessary in the face of such a danger. Hence the idea that crime ought to be the responsibility not of judges but of experts in psychiatry, criminology, psychology, and so on. Actually, that extreme conclusion was not often formulated in such an explicit and radical way, no doubt through practical prudence. But it followed implicitly from all the theses of Criminal Anthropology. And at the second meeting of this Association (1889), Pugliese expressed it straightforwardly. We must, he said, turn around the old adage "the judge is the expert of experts." Rather, it is up to the expert to be the judge of judges. "The commission of medical experts to whom the judgment ought to be referred should not limit itself to expressing its wishes: on the contrary it should render a real decision."

It can be said that a point of breakdown was being reached. Criminology, which had developed out of the old notion of monomania, maintaining a frequently stormy relationship with penal law, was in danger of being excluded from it as excessively radical. This would have led to a situation similar to the original one: a technical knowledge-system incompatible with law, besieging it from without and unable to make itself heard. As the notion of monomania could be used to overlay with madness a crime with no apparent reasons, so, to some extent, the notion of degeneration made it possible to link the most insignificant of criminals to a peril of pathological dimensions for society, and, eventually, for the whole human species. The whole field of infractions could be held together in terms of danger and thus of protection to be provided. The law had only to hold its tongue. Or to plug its ears and refuse to listen.

It is usual to say that the fundamental propositions of criminal anthropology were fairly rapidly disqualified for a number of reasons: because they were linked to a form of scientism, to a certain positivist naiveté which the very development of the sciences in the twentieth century has taken upon itself to cure; because they were related to historical and social evolutionism, which was itself quickly discredited; because they found support in a neuropsychiatric theory of degeneration that both neurology and psychoanalysis have quickly dismantled; and because they were unable to become operational within the format of penal legislation and within legal practice. The age of criminal anthropology, with its radical naivetés, seems to have disappeared with the nineteenth century; and a much more subtle psychosociology of delinquency, much more acceptable to penal law, seems to have taken up the fight.

It seems to me that, at least in its general outlines, criminal anthropology has not disappeared as completely as some people say, and that a number of its most fundamental theses—often those most foreign to traditional law—have gradually taken root in penal thought and practice. But this could not have happened solely by virtue of the truth of this psychiatric theory of crime or, rather, solely through its persuasive force. In fact, there had been a significant mutation within the law. When I say "within the law," I probably say too much, for, with a few exceptions (such as the Norwegian code, but it was written for a new state, after all), and aside from some projects left in limbo (such as the Swiss plan for a penal code), penal legislation remained pretty well unchanged. The laws relating to suspension of sentence, recidivism, or relegation were the principal mod-

ifications somewhat hesitantly made in French legislation. This is not where I
see the significant mutations; rather, I see them in connection with an element at
the same time theoretical and essential, namely, the notion of responsibility.
And it was possible to modify this notion not so much because of the pressure of
some internal shock but mainly because considerable evolution had taken place
in the area of civil law during the same period. My hypothesis would be that it
was civil law, not criminology, that made it possible for penal thought to change
on two or three major points. It was civil law that made it possible to graft onto
criminal law the essential elements of the criminological theses of the period. It
may well be that, without the reformulation that occurred first in civil law, the
jurists would have turned a deaf ear to the fundamental propositions of criminal
anthropology, or at least would never have possessed the proper tool for integrating them into the legal system. In a way that may at first seem strange, it was
civil law that made possible the articulation of the legal code and of science in
penal law.

   This transformation in civil law revolves around the notion of accident and
legal responsibility. In a very general way, it is worth emphasizing the significance that the problem of accidents had, not only for law but also for economics
and politics, especially in the second half of the nineteenth century. One could
object that, since the sixteenth century, insurance plans had shown how important the idea of risk had already become. But, on the one hand, insurance dealt
only with more or less individual risks and, on the other, it entirely excluded the
legal responsibility of the interested party. In the nineteenth century, the development of wage-earning, of industrial techniques, of mechanization, of trans-
portation, of urban structures, brought two important things. First, risks were
incurred by third parties (the employer exposed his employees to work-related
accidents; transport companies exposed not only their passengers to accidents
but also people who just happened to be there). Then, these accidents could
often be linked to a sort of error—but a minor error (inattention, lack of pre-
caution, negligence)—committed, moreover, by someone who could not carry
the civil responsibility for it or pay the ensuing damages. The problem was to
establish in law the concept of no-fault responsibility. It was the effort of Western civil legislators and especially German jurists, influenced as they were by
the demands of Bismarckian society—a society characterized not only by discipline but also by security-consciousness. In this search for a no-fault responsibility, the civil legislators emphasized a certain number of important principles:

   First: This responsibility must be established not according to the series of
errors committed but according to the chain of causes and effects. Responsibility is on the side of cause, rather than on the side of fault. This is what German
jurists meant by *Causalhaftung*.

   Second: These causes are of two orders that are not mutually exclusive: the chain of precise and individual facts, each of which has been induced by the preceding one; and the creation of risks inherent in a type of action, of equipment, of enterprise.

Third: Granted, these risks are to be reduced in the most systematic and rigorous way possible. But they will certainly never be made to disappear; none of the characteristic undertakings of modern society will be without risk. As Raymond Saleilles said, "a causal relationship linked to a purely material fact which in itself appears as hazardous fact, not in itself irregular, nor contrary to the customs of modern life, but contemptuous of that extreme caution which paralyzes action, in harmony with the activity which is imperative today and therefore defying hatreds and accepting risks, that is the law of life today, that is the common rule, and law is made to reflect this contemporary conception of the soul, in the course of its successive evolution."

Fourth: Since this no-fault liability is linked to a risk that can never entirely be eliminated, indemnity is not meant to sanction it as a sort of punishment but, rather, to repair its effects and also to tend, in an asymptotic way, toward an eventual reduction of its risks. By eliminating the element of fault within the system of liability, the civil legislators introduced into law the notion of causal probability and of risk, and they brought forward the idea of a sanction whose function would be to defend, to protect, to exert pressure on inevitable risks.

In a rather strange way, this depenalization of civil liability would constitute a model for penal law, on the basis of the fundamental propositions formulated by criminal anthropology. After all, what is a "born criminal" or a degenerate, or a criminal personality, if not someone who, according to a causal chain that is difficult to reconstruct, carries a particularly high index of criminal probability and is in himself a criminal risk? Well, just as one can determine civil liability without establishing fault—but solely by estimating the risk created and against which it is necessary to build up a defense (although it can never be eliminated)—in the same way, one can render an individual responsible under law without having to determine whether he was acting freely and, therefore, whether there was fault but, rather, by linking the act committed to the risk of criminality his very personality constitutes. He is responsible since, by his very existence, he is a creator of risk, even if he is not at fault, since he has not of his own free will chosen evil rather than good. Thus, the purpose of the sanction will not be to punish a legal subject who has voluntarily broken the law; its role will be to reduce as much as possible—either by elimination, or by exclusion or by various restrictions, or by therapeutic measures—the risk of criminality represented by the individual in question.

The general idea of the *Social Defense*, as it was put forward by Prinz at the beginning of the twentieth century, was developed by transferring to criminal justice formulations proper to the new civil law. The history of the conferences on Criminal Anthropology and conferences on penal law at the turn of the century, the chronicle of the conflicts between positivist scholars and traditional jurists, and the sudden détente that occurred at the time of Liszt, of Saleilles, of Prinz, the rapid eclipse of the Italian School after that, but also the reduction of the jurists' resistance to the psychological approach to the criminal, the establishment of a relative consensus around a criminology that would be accessible to the law, and of a system of sanctions that would take into account criminological knowledge—all of these seem indeed to indicate that at that moment the required "shunting switch" had just been found. This "switch" is the key notion of *risk* which the law assimilates through the idea of a no-fault liability, and which anthropology, or psychology, or psychiatry can assimilate through the idea of imputability without freedom. The term, henceforth central, of "dangerous being" was probably introduced by Prinz at the September 1905 session of the International Union of Penal Law.

I will not list here the innumerable legal codes, rules, and memoranda that carried into effect, in one way or another, this notion of the *dangerous state* of an individual in penal institutions throughout the world. Let me simply underline a couple of things.

First, since the great crimes without reason of the early nineteenth century, the debate did not in fact revolve so much around freedom, even though the question was always there. The real problem, the one in effect throughout, was the problem of the dangerous individual. Are there individuals who are intrinsically dangerous? By what signs can they be recognized, and how can one react to their presence? In the course of the past century, penal law did not evolve from an ethic of freedom to a science of psychic determinism; rather, it enlarged, organized, and codified the suspicion and the locating of dangerous individuals, from the rare and monstrous figure of the monomaniac to the common everyday figure of the degenerate, of the pervert, of the constitutionally unbalanced, of the immature, and so on.

It must also be noted that this transformation took place not only from medicine toward law, as through the pressure of rational knowledge on older prescriptive systems; it also operated through a perpetual mechanism of summoning and of interacting between medical or psychological knowledge and the judicial institution. It was not the latter that yielded. A set of objects and of concepts was born at their boundaries and from their interchanges.

This is the point I would like to stress, for it seems that most of the notions thus formed are operational for legal medicine or for psychiatric expertise in criminal matters. But has not something more been introduced into the law than the uncertainties of a problematic knowledge—to wit, the rudiments of another type of law? For the modern system of sanctions—most strikingly since Beccaria—gives society a claim to individuals only because of what they do.

Only an act, defined by law as an infraction, can result in a sanction, modifiable of course according to the circumstances or the intentions. But by bringing increasingly to the fore not only the criminal as author of the act, but also the dangerous individual as potential source of acts, does not one give society rights over the individual based on what he is? No longer, of course, based on what he is by statute (as was the case in the societies under the Ancien Régime), but on what he is by nature, according to his constitution, character traits, or his pathological variables. A form of justice that tends to be applied to what one is—this is what is so outrageous when one thinks of the penal law of which the eighteenth-century reformers had dreamed, which was intended to sanction, in a completely egalitarian way, offenses explicitly defined beforehand by the law.

It could be objected that, in spite of this general principle, even in the nineteenth century the right to punish was applied and varied on the basis not only of what men do but also of what they are, or of what it is supposed that they are. Hardly had the great modern codes been established when attempts were made to mitigate them by legislation such as the laws dealing with extenuating circumstances, with recidivism, and with conditional release. It was a matter of taking into account the author behind the acts that had been committed. And a complete and comparative study of the legal decisions would no doubt easily show that on the penal stage the offenders were at least as present as their offenses. A form of justice applied only to what one does is probably purely utopian and not necessarily desirable. But, since the eighteenth century at least, it has constituted the guiding principle, the juridico-moral principle that governs the modern system of sanctions. There was, therefore, no question—there can still be no question—of suddenly putting it aside. Only insidiously, slowly, and, as it were, from below and fragmentally, has a system of sanctions based on what one *is* been taking shape. It has taken nearly one hundred years for the notion of "dangerous individual," which was potentially present in the monomania of the first alienists, to be accepted in judicial thought. After one hundred years, although this notion may have become a central theme in psychiatric expertise (in France, psychiatrists appointed as experts speak about the dangerousness of an individual much more than about his responsibility), the law and the codes seem reluctant to give it a place. The revision of the penal code presently under way in France has just barely succeeded in replacing the older notion of *dementia* (which made the author of an act not responsible) with the notions of discernment and control, which in effect are only another version of the same thing, hardly modernized at all. Perhaps this indicates a foreboding of the dreadful dangers inherent in authorizing the law to intervene against individuals because of what they are: a horrifying society could emerge from that.

Nonetheless, on the functional level, judges more and more need to believe that they are judging a man as he is and according to what he is. The scene I described at the beginning bears witness to this. When a man comes before his judges with nothing but his crimes, when he has nothing else to say but "this is what I have done," when he has nothing to say about himself, when he does not do the tribunal the favor of confiding to them something like the secret of his own being, then the judicial machine ceases to function.

GOVERNMENTALITY

In a previous lecture on "apparatuses of security," I tried to explain the emergence of a set of problems specific to the issue of population; on closer inspection, it turned out that we would also need to take into account the problematic of government. In short, one needed to analyze the series: security, population, government. I would now like to try to begin making an inventory of this question of government.

Throughout the Middle Ages and classical Antiquity, we find a multitude of treatises presented as "advice to the prince," concerning his proper conduct, the exercise of power, the means of securing the acceptance and respect of his subjects, the love of God and obedience to him, the application of divine law to the cities of men, and so on. But a more striking fact is that, from the middle of the sixteenth century to the end of the eighteenth, there develops and flourishes a notable series of political treatises that are no longer exactly "advice to the prince," and not yet treatises of political science, but instead are presented as works on the "art of government." Government as a general problem seems to me to explode in the sixteenth century, posed by discussions of quite diverse questions. One has, for example, the question of the government of oneself, that ritualization of the problem of personal conduct characteristic of the sixteenth century Stoic revival. There is the problem too of the government of souls and lives, the entire theme of Catholic and Protestant pastoral doctrine. There is government of children and the great problematic of pedagogy that emerges and develops during the sixteenth century. And, perhaps only as the last of these questions to be taken up, there is the government of the state by the prince. How to govern oneself, how to be governed, how to govern others, by whom the people will accept being governed, how to become the best possible

This essay was presented as part of a course on "Security, Territory, and Population" (see summary in *Essential Works*, vol. 1, pp. 67–71) that Foucault gave at the Collège de France in the 1977–78 academic year. It was first published in 1978. —Eds.

governor—all these problems, in their multiplicity and intensity, seem to me to be characteristic of the sixteenth century, which lies, to put it schematically, at the crossroads of two processes: the one that, shattering the structures of feudalism, leads to the establishment of the great territorial, administrative, and colonial states; and a totally different movement that, with the Reformation and Counter-reformation, raises the issue of how one must be spiritually ruled and led on this earth in order to achieve eternal salvation.

There is a double movement, then, of state centralization, on the one hand, and of dispersion and religious dissidence, on the other. It is, I believe, at the intersection of these two tendencies that the problem comes to pose itself with this peculiar intensity, of how to be ruled, how strictly, by whom, to what end, by what methods, and so on. There is a problematic of government in general.

Out of all this immense and monotonous literature on government which extends to the end of the eighteenth century, with the transformations I will try to identify in a moment, I would like to underline some points that are worthy of notice because they relate to the actual definition of what is meant by the government of the state, of what we would today call the political form of government. The simplest way to do this is to compare all of this literature with a single text that, from the sixteenth to the eighteenth century, never ceased to function as the object of explicit or implicit opposition and rejection, and relative to which the whole literature on government established its standpoint—Machiavelli's *The Prince*. It would be interesting to trace the relationship of this text to all those works that succeeded, criticized, and rebutted it.

We must first of all remember that Machiavelli's *The Prince* was not immediately made an object of execration; on the contrary, it was honored by its immediate contemporaries and immediate successors, and once again at the end of the eighteenth century (or perhaps rather at the very beginning of the nineteenth century), at the very moment when all this literature on the art of government was about to come to an end. *The Prince* reemerges at the beginning of the nineteenth century, especially in Germany, where it is translated, prefaced, and commented upon by writers such as A. W. Rehberg, H. Leo, Leopold von Ranke, and Kellerman. In Italy as well, it makes its appearance in context that is worth analyzing, one that is partly Napoleonic but also partly created by the Revolution and the problems of revolution in the United States, of how and under what conditions a ruler's sovereignty over the state can be maintained. But this is also the context in which there emerges, with Clausewitz, the problem (whose political importance was evident at the Congress of Vienna in 1815) of the relationship between politics and strategy, and the problem of relations of force and the calculation of these relations as a principle of intelligibility and rationalization in international relations; and finally, in addition, it connects with the problem of Italian and German territorial unity, since Machiavelli had been one of those who tried to define the conditions under which Italian territorial unity could be restored.

This is the context in which Machiavelli reemerges. But it is clear that, between the initial honor accorded him in the sixteenth century and his rediscovery at the start of the nineteenth, there was a whole "affair" around his work, one that was complex and took various forms: some explicit praise of Machiavelli (Naudé, Machon), numerous frontal attacks (from Catholic sources: Ambrozio Politi, *Disputationes de Libris a Christiano detestandis;* and from Protestant sources: Innocent Gentillet, *Discours sur les moyens de bien gouverner contre Nicolas Machiavel,* 1576), and also a number of implicit critiques (Guillaume de La Perrière, *Miroir Politique,* 1567; Th. Elyott, *The Governor,* 1580; P. Paruta, *Della Perfezione della Vita politica,* 1579).

This whole debate should not be viewed solely in terms of its relation to Machiavelli's text and what were felt to be its scandalous or radically unacceptable aspects. It needs to be seen in terms of something it was trying to define in its specificity, namely, an art of government. Some authors rejected the idea of a new art of government centered on the state and reason of state, which they stigmatized with the name of Machiavellianism; others rejected Machiavelli by showing that there existed an art of government that was both rational and legitimate, and of which Machiavelli's *The Prince* was only an imperfect approximation or caricature; finally, there were others who, in order to prove the legitimacy of a particular art of government, were willing to justify some at least of Machiavelli's writings (this was what Naudé did to the *Discourses* on Livy; Machon went so far as to attempt to show that nothing was more Machiavellian than the way in which, according to the Bible, God himself and his prophets had guided the Jewish people).

All these authors shared a common concern to distance themselves from a certain conception of the art of government which, once shorn of its theological foundations and religious justifications, took the sole interest of the prince as its object and principle of rationality. Let us leave aside the question of whether the interpretation of Machiavelli in these debates was accurate or not. The essential thing is that they attempted to articulate a kind of rationality that was intrinsic to the art of government, without subordinating it to the problematic of the prince and of his relationship to the principality of which he is lord and master.

Thus, the art of government is defined in a way that differentiates it from a certain capacity of the prince, which some think they can find expounded in Machiavelli's writings but others are unable to find; others still will criticize this art of government as a new form of Machiavellianism.

This politics of *The Prince,* fictitious or otherwise, from which people sought to distance themselves, was characterized by one principle: for Machiavelli, it was alleged, the prince stood in a relation of singularity and externality, and thus

of transcendence, to his principality. The prince acquires his principality by inheritance or conquest, but in any case he does not form part of it, he remains external to it. The link that binds him to his principality may have been established
through violence, through family heritage, or by treaty, with the complicity or
the alliance of other princes; this makes no difference—the link remains, in any
event, a purely synthetic one, and there is no fundamental, essential, natural, and
juridical connection between the prince and his principality. As a corollary of
this, given that this link is external, it will be fragile and continually under
threat—from outside by the prince's enemies who seek to conquer or recapture
his principality, and from within by subjects who have no a priori reason to accept his rule. Finally, this principle and its corollary lead to a conclusion, deduced as an imperative: that the objective of the exercise of power is to reinforce,
strengthen, and protect the principality, but with this last understood to mean not
the objective ensemble of its subjects and the territory but, rather, the prince's
relation with what he owns, with the territory he has inherited or acquired, and
with his subjects. This fragile link is what the art of governing or of being prince,
as espoused by Machiavelli, has as its object. Consequently, the mode of analysis
of Machiavelli's text will be twofold: to identify dangers (where they come from,
what they consist in, their severity: which are the greater, which the slighter),
and second, to develop the art of manipulating the relations of forces that will
allow the prince to ensure the protection of his principality, understood as the
link that binds him to his territory and his subjects.

Schematically, one can say that Machiavelli's *The Prince*, as profiled in all
these implicitly or explicitly anti-Machiavellian treatises, is essentially a treatise
about the prince's ability to keep his principality. And it is this savoir-faire that
the anti-Machiavellian literature wants to replace with something else that's
new, namely, the art of government. Having the ability to retain one's principality is not at all the same thing as possessing the art of governing. But what
does this latter ability comprise? To get a view of this problem, which is still at a
raw and early stage, let us consider one of the earliest texts of this great anti-
Machiavellian literature—Guillaume de La Perrière's *Miroir Politique*.

This text, disappointingly thin in comparison with Machiavelli, prefigures a
number of important ideas. First of all, what does La Perrière mean by "to govern" and "governor"? What definition does he give of these terms? He writes:
"governor can signify monarch, emperor, king, prince, lord, magistrate,
prelate, judge and the like." Like La Perrière, others who write on the art of
government constantly recall that one speaks also of "governing" a household,
souls, children, a province, a convent, a religious order, a family.

These points of simple vocabulary actually have important political implications: Machiavelli's prince, at least as these authors interpret him, is by definition
unique in his principality and occupies a position of externality and transcen-

dence. We have seen, however, that practices of government are, on the one hand, multifarious and concern many kinds of people—the head of a family, the superior of a convent, the teacher or tutor of a child or pupil—so that there are several forms of government among which the prince's relation to his state is only one particular mode; on the other hand, though, all these other kinds of government are internal to the state or society. It is within the state that the father will rule the family, the superior the convent, and so on. Thus, we find at once a plurality of forms of government and their immanence to the state: the multiplicity and immanence of these activities distinguish them radically from the transcendent singularity of Machiavelli's prince.

To be sure, among all these forms of government that interweave within the state and society, there remains one special and precise form: there is the question of defining the particular form of governing that can be applied to the state as a whole. Thus, seeking to produce a topology of forms of the art of government, La Mothe Le Vayer, in a text from the following century (consisting of educational writings intended for the French Dauphin), says that there are three fundamental types of government, each of which relates to a particular science or discipline: the art of self-government, connected with morality; the art of properly governing a family, which belongs to economy; and, finally, the science of ruling the state, which concerns politics. In comparison with morality and economy, politics evidently has its own specific nature, which La Mothe Le Vayer states clearly. What matters, notwithstanding this topology, is that the art of government is always characterized by the essential continuity of one type with the other, and of a second type with a third.

This means that, whereas the doctrine of the prince and the juridical theory of sovereignty are constantly attempting to draw the line between the power of the prince and any other form of power—because its task is to explain and justify this essential discontinuity between them—in the art of government the task is to establish a continuity, in both an upward and a downward direction.

Upward continuity means that a person who wishes to govern the state well must first learn how to govern himself, his goods, and his patrimony, after which he will be successful in governing the state. This ascending line characterizes the pedagogies of the prince, which are an important issue at this time, as the example of La Mothe Le Vayer shows: he wrote for the Dauphin first a treatise of morality, then a book of economics, and, finally, a political treatise. It is the pedagogical formation of the prince, then, that will assure this upward continuity. On the other hand, we also have a downward continuity in the sense that, when a state is well run, the head of the family will know how to look after his family, his goods, and his patrimony, which means that individuals will, in turn, behave as they should. This downward line, which transmits to individual behavior and the running of the family the same principles as the good government of the state, is just at this time beginning to be called "police." The prince's pedagogical formation ensures the upward continuity of the forms of government, and police the downward one. The central term of this continuity is the government of the family, termed "economy."

The art of government, as becomes apparent in this literature, is essentially concerned with answering the question of how to introduce economy—that is to say, the correct way of managing individuals, goods, and wealth within the family (which a good father is expected to do in relation to his wife, children, and servants) and of making the family fortunes prosper—how to introduce this meticulous attention of the father toward his family into the management of the state.

This, I believe, is the essential issue in the establishment of the art of government—introduction of economy into political practice. And if this is the case in the sixteenth century, it remains so in the eighteenth. In Rousseau's *Encyclopedia* article on "Political Economy," the problem is still posed in the same terms. What he says here, roughly, is that the word "economy" can only properly be used to signify the wise government of the family for the common welfare of all, and this is its actual original use; the problem, writes Rousseau, is how to introduce it, mutatis mutandis, and with all the discontinuities that we will observe below, into the general running of the state. To govern a state will mean, therefore, to apply economy, to set up an economy at the level of the entire state, which means exercising toward its inhabitants, and the wealth and behavior of each and all, a form of surveillance and control as attentive as that of the head of a family over his household and his goods.

An expression that was important in the eighteenth century captures this very well: François Quesnay speaks of good government as "economic government." This latter notion becomes tautological, given that the art of government is just the art of exercising power in the form, and according to the model, of the economy. But the reason why Quesnay speaks of "economic government" is that the word "economy," for reasons I will explain later, is in the process of acquiring a modern meaning, and it is at this moment becoming apparent that the very essence of government—that is, the art of exercising power in the form of economy—is to have as its main objective that which we are today accustomed to call "the economy."

The word "economy," which in the sixteenth century signified a form of government, comes in the eighteenth century to designate a level of reality, a field of intervention, through a series of complex processes that I regard as absolutely fundamental to our history.

The second point I should like to discuss in Guillaume de La Perrière's book consists of the following statement: "government is the right disposition of things, arranged so as to lead to a convenient end."

I would like to link this sentence with another series of observations. Government is the right disposition of things. I would like to pause over this word "things" because, if we consider what characterizes the ensemble of objects of the prince's power in Machiavelli, we will see that for Machiavelli the object and, in a sense, the target of power are two things—on the one hand, the territory, and, on the other, its inhabitants. In this respect, Machiavelli simply adapted to his particular aims a juridical principle that from the Middle Ages to the sixteenth century defined sovereignty in public law: sovereignty is exercised not on things but, above all, on a territory and consequently on the subjects who inhabit it. In this sense, we can say that the territory is the fundamental element both in Machiavellian principality and in juridical sovereignty as defined by the theoreticians and philosophers of right. Obviously enough, these territories can be fertile or infertile, the population dense or sparse, the inhabitants rich or poor, active or lazy, but all these elements are mere variables by comparison with territory itself, which is the very foundation of principality and sovereignty. On the contrary, in La Perrière's text, you will notice that the definition of government in no way refers to territory: one governs *things*. But what does this mean? I think this is not a matter of opposing things to men but, rather, of showing that what government has to do with is not territory but, rather, a sort of complex composed of men and things. The things, in this sense, with which government is to be concerned are in fact men, but men in their relations, their links, their imbrication with those things that are wealth, resources, means of subsistence, the territory with its specific qualities, climate, irrigation, fertility, and so on; men in their relation to those other things that are customs, habits, ways of acting and thinking, and so on; and finally men in their relation to those still other things that might be accidents and misfortunes such as famine, epidemics, death, and so on. The fact that government concerns things understood in this way, this imbrication of men and things, is, I believe, readily confirmed by the metaphor that is inevitably invoked in these treatises on government, namely, that of the ship. What does it mean to govern a ship? It means clearly to take charge of the sailors, but also of the boat and its cargo; to take care of a ship means also to reckon with winds, rocks, and storms; and it consists in that activity of establishing a relation between the sailors, who are to be taken care of, and the ship, which is to be taken care of, and the cargo, which is to be brought safely to port, and all those eventualities like winds, rocks, storms, and so on. This is what characterizes the government of a ship. The same goes for the running of a household. Governing a household, a family, does not essentially mean safeguarding the family property; what it concerns is the individuals who compose the family, their wealth and prosperity. It means reckoning with all the possible events that may intervene, such as births and deaths, and with all the things that can be done, such as possible alliances with other families; it is this general form of management that is characteristic of government. By comparison, the question of landed property for the family, and the question of the acquisition of sovereignty over a territory for a prince, are only relatively secondary matters. What counts essentially is this complex of men and things; property and territory are merely one of its variables.

This theme of the government of things as we find it in La Perrière can also be met with in the seventeenth and eighteenth centuries. Frederick the Great has some notable pages on it in his *Anti-Machiavel*. He says, for instance, let us compare Holland with Russia: Russia may have the largest territory of any European state, but it is mostly made up of swamps, forests, and deserts, and is inhabited by miserable groups of people totally destitute of activity and industry; if one takes Holland, on the other hand, with its tiny territory, again mostly marshland, we find that it nevertheless possesses such a population, such wealth, such commercial activity, and such a fleet as to make it an important European state, something that Russia is only just beginning to become.

To govern, then, means to govern things. Let us consider once more the sentence I quoted earlier, where La Perrière says: "government is the right disposition of things, arranged so as to lead to a convenient end." Government, that is to say, has a finality of its own, and in this respect again, I believe, it can be clearly distinguished from sovereignty. Of course, I do not mean that sovereignty is presented in philosophical and juridical texts as a pure and simple right; no jurist or, a fortiori, theologian ever said that the legitimate sovereign is purely and simply entitled to exercise his power regardless of its ends. The sovereign must always, if he is to be a good sovereign, have as his aim "the common welfare and the salvation of all." Take for instance a late seventeenth-century author. Pufendorf says: "Sovereign authority is conferred upon them [the rulers] only in order to allow them to use it to attain or conserve what is of public utility." The ruler may not have consideration for anything advantageous for himself, unless it also be so for the state. What does this common good or general salvation consist of, which the jurists talk about as being the end of sovereignty? If we look closely at the real content that jurists and theologians give to it, we can see that "the common good" refers to a state of affairs where all the subjects without exception obey the laws, accomplish the tasks expected of them, practice the trade to which they are assigned, and respect the established order insofar as this order conforms to the laws imposed by God on nature and men: in other words, "the common good" means essentially obedience to the law, either that of their earthly sovereign or that of God, the absolute sovereign. In every case, what characterizes the end of sovereignty, this common and general good, is in sum nothing other than submission to sovereignty. This means that the end of sovereignty is the exercise of sovereignty. The good is obedience to the law, hence the good for sovereignty is that people should obey it. This is

an essential circularity; whatever its theoretical structure, moral justification, or practical effects, it comes very close to what Machiavelli said when he stated that the primary aim of the prince was to retain his principality. We always come back to this self-referring circularity of sovereignty or principality.

Now, with the new definition given by La Perrière, with his attempt at a definition of government, I believe we can see a new kind of finality emerging. Government is defined as a right manner of disposing things so as to lead not to the form of the common good, as the jurists' texts would have said, but to an end that is "convenient" for each of the things that are to be governed. This implies a plurality of specific aims: for instance, government will have to ensure that the greatest possible quantity of wealth is produced, that the people are provided with sufficient means of subsistence, that the population is enabled to multiply, and so on. Thus, there is a whole series of specific finalities that become the objective of government as such. In order to achieve these various finalities, things must be disposed—and this term, "dispose," is important because, with sovereignty, the instrument that allowed it to achieve its aim—that is, obedience to the laws—was the law itself: law and sovereignty were absolutely inseparable. On the contrary, with government it is a question not of imposing law on men but of disposing things: that is, of employing tactics rather than laws, and even of using laws themselves as tactics—to arrange things in such a way that, through a certain number of means, such-and-such ends may be achieved.

I believe we are at an important turning point here: whereas the end of sovereignty is internal to itself and possesses its own intrinsic instruments in the shape of its laws, the finality of government resides in the things it manages and in the pursuit of the perfection and intensification of the processes it directs; and the instruments of government, instead of being laws, now come to be a range of multiform tactics. Within the perspective of government, law is not what is important: this is a frequent theme throughout the seventeenth century, and it is made explicit in the eighteenth-century texts of the Physiocrats, which explain that it is not through law that the aims of government are to be reached.

Finally, a fourth remark, still concerning this text from La Perrière. He says that a good ruler must have patience, wisdom, and diligence. What does he mean by patience? To explain it, he gives the example of the king of bees, the bumblebee, who, he says, rules the beehive without needing a sting; through this example, God has sought to show us in a mystical way that the good governor does not have to have a sting—that is to say, a weapon of killing, a sword—in order to exercise his power; he must have patience rather than wrath, and it is not the right to kill, to employ force, that forms the essence of the figure of the governor. And what positive content accompanies this absence of sting? Wisdom and diligence. Wisdom, understood no longer in the traditional sense as knowledge of divine and human laws, of justice and equality, but, rather, as the knowledge of things, of the objectives that can and should be attained, and the disposition of things required to reach them: it is this knowledge that is to constitute the wisdom of the sovereign. As for his diligence, this is the principle that a governor should only govern in such a way that he thinks and acts as though he were in the service of those who are governed. And here, once again, La Perrière cites the example of the head of the family who rises first in the morning and goes to bed last, who concerns himself with everything in the household because he considers himself as being in its service. We can see at once how far this characterization of government differs from the idea of the prince as found in or attributed to Machiavelli. To be sure, this notion of governing, for all its novelty, is still very crude here.

This schematic presentation of the notion and theory of the art of government did not remain a purely abstract question in the sixteenth century, and it was of concern not only to political theoreticians. I think we can identify its connections with political reality. The theory of the art of government was linked, from the sixteenth century, to the whole development of the administrative apparatus of the territorial monarchies, the emergence of governmental apparatuses; it was also connected to a set of analyses and forms of knowledge that began to develop in the late sixteenth century and grew in importance during the seventeenth. These were essentially to do with knowledge of the state, in all its different elements, dimensions, and factors of power, questions that were termed precisely "statistics," meaning the science of the state. Finally, as a third vector of connections, I do not think one can fail to relate this search for an art of government to mercantilism and the Cameralists' science of police.

To put it very schematically, in the late sixteenth century and early seventeenth century, the art of government finds its first form of crystallization, organized around the theme of reason of state, understood not in the negative and pejorative sense we give to it today (as that which infringes on the principles of law, equity, and humanity in the sole interests of the state) but in a full and positive sense: the state is governed according to rational principles that are intrinsic to it and cannot be derived solely from natural or divine laws or the principles of wisdom and prudence. The state, like nature, has its own proper form of rationality, albeit of a different sort. Conversely, the art of government, instead of seeking to found itself in transcendental rules, a cosmological model, or a philosophicomoral ideal, must find the principles of its rationality in that which constitutes the specific reality of the state. In my subsequent lectures, I will be examining the elements of this first form of state rationality. But we can say here that, right until the early eighteenth century, this form of "reason of state" acted as a sort of obstacle to the development of the art of government.

This is for a number of reasons. First, there are the strictly historical ones, the series of great crises of the seventeenth century: first the Thirty Years' War

with its ruin and devastation; then, in the midcentury, the peasant and urban rebellions; and finally the financial crisis, the crisis of revenues that affected all
Western monarchies at the end of the century. The art of government could
only spread and develop in subtlety in an age of expansion, free from the great
military, political, and economic tensions that afflicted the seventeenth century
from beginning to end. Massive and elementary historical causes thus blocked
the propagation of the art of government. I think also that the doctrine formulated during the sixteenth century was impeded in the seventeenth by a series of
other factors I might term, to use expressions I do not much care for, "mental"
and "institutional" structures. The preeminence of the problem of the exercise
of sovereignty—both as a theoretical question and as a principle of political organization—was the fundamental factor here so long as sovereignty remained
the central question. So long as the institutions of sovereignty were the basic
political institutions and the exercise of power was conceived as an exercise of
sovereignty, the art of government could not be developed in a specific and autonomous way. I think we have a good example of this in mercantilism. Mercantilism might be described as the first sanctioned effort to apply this art of
government at the level of political practices and knowledge of the state; in this
sense one can in fact say that mercantilism represents a first threshold of rationality in this art of government which La Perrière's text had defined in terms
more moral than real. Mercantilism is the first rationalization of exercise of
power as a practice of government; for the first time with mercantilism we see
the development of knowledge [*savoir*] of state that can be used as a tactic of
government. All this may be true, but mercantilism was blocked and arrested, I
believe, precisely by the fact that it took as its essential objective the might of
the sovereign: it sought a way not so much to increase the wealth of the country
as to allow the ruler to accumulate wealth, build up his treasury, and create the
army with which he could carry out his policies. And the instruments mercantilism used were laws, decrees, regulations—that is, the traditional weapons of
sovereignty. The objective was the sovereign's might, the instruments those of
sovereignty: mercantilism sought to reinsert the possibilities opened up by a
consciously conceived art of government within a mental and institutional
structure, that of sovereignty, which by its very nature stifled them.

Thus, throughout the seventeenth century up to the liquidation of the
themes of mercantilism at the beginning of the eighteenth, the art of government remained in a certain sense immobilized. It was trapped within the inordi-
nately vast, abstract, rigid framework of the problem and institution of
sovereignty. This art of government tried, so to speak, to reconcile itself with
the theory of sovereignty by attempting to derive the ruling principles of an art
of government from a renewed version of the theory of sovereignty—and this
is where those seventeenth-century jurists come into the picture who formalize

or ritualize the theory of the contract. Contract theory enables the founding contract, the mutual pledge of ruler and subjects, to function as a sort of theoretical matrix for deriving the general principles of an art of government. But although contract theory, with its reflection on the relationship between ruler and subjects, played a very important role in theories of public law, in practice, as is evidenced by the case of Hobbes (even though what Hobbes was aiming to discover was the ruling principles of an art of government), it remained at the stage of the formulation of general principles of public law.

On the one hand, there was this framework of sovereignty, which was too large, too abstract, and too rigid; and, on the other, the theory of government suffered from its reliance on a model that was too thin, too weak, and too insubstantial, that of the family—an economy of enrichment still based on a model of the family was unlikely to be able to respond adequately to the importance of territorial possessions and royal finance.

How, then, was the art of government able to outflank these obstacles? Here again a number of general processes played their part: the demographic expansion of the eighteenth century, connected with an increasing abundance of money, which in turn was linked to the expansion of agricultural production through a series of circular processes with which the historians are familiar. If this is the general picture, then we can say more precisely that the art of government found fresh outlets through the emergence of the problem of population; or let us say, rather, that a subtle process took place, which we must seek to reconstruct in its particulars, through which the science of government, the recentering of the theme of economy on a different plane from that of the family, and the problem of population are all interconnected.

It was through the development of the science of government that the notion of economy came to be recentered onto that different plane of reality we characterize today as the "economic," and it was also through this science that it became possible to identify problems specific to the population. But, conversely, we can say as well that it was thanks to the perception of the specific problems of the population, and thanks to the isolation of that area of reality we call the economy, that the problem of government finally came to be thought, considered, and calculated outside of the juridical framework of sovereignty. And, further, that "statistics"—which in mercantilist tradition only ever worked within and for the benefit of a monarchical administration that functioned according to the form of sovereignty—now becomes the major technical factor, or one of the major technical factors, of the unfreezing [*déblocage*] of the art of government.

In what way did the problem of population make possible the unfreezing of the art of government? The perspective of population, the reality accorded to specific phenomena of population, render possible the final elimination of the model of the family and the recentering of the notion of economy. Whereas statistics had previously worked within the administrative frame and thus in terms of the functioning of sovereignty, it now gradually reveals that population has its own regularities, its own rate of deaths and diseases, its cycles of scarcity, and so on; statistics shows also that the domain of population involves a range of intrinsic, aggregate effects, phenomena that are irreducible to those of the family, such as epidemics, endemic levels of mortality, ascending spirals of labor and wealth; finally, it shows that, through its shifts, customs, activities, and so on, population has specific economic effects. Statistics, by making it possible to quantify these specific phenomena of population, also shows that this specificity is irreducible to the dimension of the family. The latter now disappears as the model of government, except for a certain number of residual themes of a religious or moral nature. On the other hand, what now emerges into prominence is the family considered as an element internal to population, and as a fundamental instrument in its government.

In other words, prior to the emergence of population, it was impossible to conceive the art of government except on the model of the family, in terms of economy conceived as the management of a family. From the moment when, on the contrary, population appears absolutely irreducible to the family, the latter becomes of secondary importance compared to population as an element internal to population: that is, no longer a model but a segment. Nevertheless, it remains a privileged segment, because whenever information is required concerning the population (sexual behavior, demography, consumption, and so on), it must be obtained through the family. But the family becomes an instrument rather than a model—the privileged instrument for the government of the population and not the chimerical model of good government. This shift from the level of the model to that of an instrument is, I believe, absolutely fundamental, and it is from the middle of the eighteenth century that the family appears in this dimension of instrumentality relative to the population, with the institution of campaigns to reduce mortality, and to promote marriages, vaccinations, and so on. Thus, what makes it possible for the theme of population to unblock the field of the art of government is this elimination of the family as model.

In the second place, population comes to appear above all else as the ultimate end of government. In contrast to sovereignty, government has as its purpose not the act of government itself, but the welfare of the population, the improvement of its condition, the increase of its wealth, longevity, health, and so on; and the means the government uses to attain these ends are themselves all, in some sense, immanent to the population; it is the population itself on which government will act either directly, through large-scale campaigns, or indirectly, through techniques that will make possible, without the full awareness of the people, the stimulation of birth rates, the directing of the flow of population into certain regions or activities, and so on. The population now represents more the end of government than the power of the sovereign; the population is the subject of needs, of aspirations, but it is also the object in the hands of the government, aware, vis-à-vis the government, of what it wants, but ignorant of what is being done to it. Interest as the consciousness of each individual who makes up the population, and interest considered as the interest of the population regardless of what the particular interests and aspirations may be of the individuals who compose it: this is the new target and the fundamental instrument of the government of population. This is the birth of a new art, or at any rate of a range of absolutely new tactics and techniques.

Finally, population is the point around which is organized what in sixteenth-century texts came to be called the "patience" of the sovereign, in the sense that the population is the object that government must take into account in all its observations and knowledge [savoir], in order to be able to govern effectively in a rational and conscious manner. The constitution of knowledge [savoir] of government is absolutely inseparable from that of a knowledge of all the processes related to population in its larger sense—that is, what we now call the economy. I said in my last lecture that the constitution of political economy depended upon the emergence, from among all the various elements of wealth, a new subject—population. The new science called "political economy" arises out of the perception of new networks of continuous and multiple relations between population, territory, and wealth; and this is accompanied by the formation of a type of intervention characteristic of government, namely, intervention in the field of economy and population. In other words, the transition that takes place in the eighteenth century from an art of government to a political science, from a regime dominated by structures of sovereignty to one ruled by techniques of government, turns on the theme of population, hence also on the birth of political economy.

This is not to say that sovereignty ceases to play a role from the moment when the art of government begins to become a political science. On the contrary, I would say that the problem of sovereignty was never posed with greater force than at this time, because it no longer involved—as it had in the sixteenth and seventeenth centuries—an attempt to derive an art of government from a theory of sovereignty; instead, given that such an art now existed and was spreading, it involved an attempt to see what juridical and institutional form, what foundation in the law, could be given to the sovereignty that characterizes a state. It suffices to read in chronological succession two different texts by Rousseau. In his *Encyclopedia* article on "Political Economy," we can see the way in which Rousseau sets up the problem of the art of government by pointing out (and the text is very characteristic from this point of view) that the word "economy" essentially signifies the management of family property by the father, but that this model can no longer be accepted, even if it had been valid in the past; today, says Rousseau, we know that political economy is not the economy of the family. And even without making explicit reference to the Physiocrats, to statistics, or to the general problem of the population, he sees quite clearly this turning point consisting in the fact that the economy of "political economy" has a totally new sense that cannot be reduced to the old model of the family. He undertakes in this article the task of giving a new definition of the art of government. Later he writes *The Social Contract*, where he poses the problem of how it is possible, using concepts such as nature, contract, and general will, to provide a general principle of government that allows room both for a juridical principle of sovereignty and for the elements through which an art of government can be defined and characterized. Consequently, sovereignty is far from being eliminated by the emergence of a new art of government, even by one that has passed the threshold of political science; on the contrary, the problem of sovereignty is made more acute than ever.

As for discipline, this is not eliminated either; clearly, its modes of organization, all the institutions within which it had developed in the seventeenth and eighteenth centuries—schools, manufactories, armies, and so on—all this can only be understood on the basis of the development of the great administrative monarchies. Nevertheless, though, discipline was never more important or more valorized than at the moment when it became important to manage a population: the managing of a population not only concerns the collective mass of phenomena, the level of its aggregate effects, but it also implies the management of population in its depths and its details. The notion of a government of population renders all the more acute the problem of the foundation of sovereignty (consider Rousseau) and all the more acute equally the necessity for the development of discipline (consider all the history of the disciplines, which I have attempted to analyze elsewhere).

Accordingly, we need to see things not in terms of the replacement of a society of sovereignty by a disciplinary society and the subsequent replacement of a disciplinary society by a society of government; in reality one has a triangle, sovereignty-discipline-government, which has as its primary target the population and as its essential mechanism the apparatuses of security. In any case, I wanted to demonstrate the deep historical link between the movement that overturns the constants of sovereignty in consequence of the problem of choices of government; the movement that brings about the emergence of population as a datum, as a field of intervention, and as an objective of governmental techniques; the process that isolates the economy as a specific sector of reality; and political economy as the science and the technique of intervention of the government in that field of reality. Three movements—government, population, political economy—that constitute from the eighteenth century onward a solid series, one that even today has assuredly not been dissolved.

In conclusion, I would like to say that, on second thought, the more exact title I would like to have given to the course of lectures I have begun this year is not the one I originally chose, "Security, Territory, and Population": what I would like to undertake is something I would term a history of "governmentality." By this word I mean three things:

1. The ensemble formed by the institutions, procedures, analyses, and reflections, the calculations and tactics that allow the exercise of this very specific albeit complex form of power, which has as its target population, as its principal form of knowledge political economy, and as its essential technical means apparatuses of security.
2. The tendency that, over a long period and throughout the West, has steadily led toward the preeminence over all other forms (sovereignty, discipline, and so on) of this type of power—which may be termed "government"—resulting, on the one hand, in the formation of a whole series of specific governmental apparatuses, and, on the other, in the development of a whole complex of knowledges [*savoirs*].
3. The process or, rather, the result of the process through which the state of justice of the Middle Ages transformed into the administrative state during the fifteenth and sixteenth centuries and gradually becomes "governmentalized."

We all know the fascination that the love, or horror, of the state exercises today; we know how much attention is paid to the genesis of the state, its history, its advance, its power, abuses, and so on. The excessive value attributed to the problem of the state is expressed, basically, in two ways: the one form, immediate, affective, and tragic, is the lyricism of the cold monster we see confronting us. But there is a second way of overvaluing the problem of the state, one that is paradoxical because it is apparently reductionist: it is the form of analysis that consists in reducing the state to a certain number of functions, such as the development of productive forces and the reproduction of relations of production, and yet this reductionist vision of the relative importance of the state's role nevertheless invariably renders it absolutely essential as a target needing to be attacked and a privileged position needing to be occupied. But the state, no more probably today than at any other time in its history, does not have this unity, this individuality, this rigorous functionality, nor, to speak frankly, this importance. Maybe, after all, the state is no more than a composite reality and a mythicized abstraction, whose importance is a lot more limited than many of us think. Maybe what is really important for our modernity—that is, for our present—is not so much the statization [*étatisation*] of society, as the "governmentalization" of the state.

We live in the era of a "governmentality" first discovered in the eighteenth century. This governmentalization of the state is a singularly paradoxical phenomenon: if in fact the problems of governmentality and the techniques of government have become the only political issue, the only real space for political struggle and contestation, this is because the governmentalization of the state is, at the same time, what has permitted the state to survive. It is possible to suppose that if the state is what it is today, this is so precisely thanks to this governmentality, which is at once internal and external to the state—since it is the tactics of government that make possible the continual definition and redefinition of what is within the competence of the state and what is not, the public versus the private, and so on. Thus, the state can only be understood in its survival and its limits on the basis of the general tactics of governmentality.

And maybe we could even, albeit in a very global, rough, and inexact fashion, reconstitute the great forms, the great economies of power in the West in the following way. First came the state of justice, born in a territoriality of feudal type and corresponding in large part to a society of the law—customary laws and written laws—with a whole game of engagements and litigations. Second, the administrative state, born in the fifteenth and sixteenth centuries in a frontier and no longer feudal territoriality, an administrative state that corresponds to a society of regulations and disciplines. Finally, the state of government, which is no longer essentially defined by its territoriality, by the surface it occupies, but by a mass: the mass of the population, with its volume, its density, with the territory that it covers, to be sure, but only in a sense as one of its components. And this state of government, which is grounded in its population and which refers and has resort to the instrumentality of economic knowledge, would correspond to a society controlled by apparatuses of security.

There, if you like, are certain pointers [*propos*] for positioning this phenomenon—which I believe to be important—of governmentality. I will try further to show how such governmentality is born, in one part, out of an archaic model, that of the Christian pastoral, and secondly, while drawing support from a diplomatico-military model, or better, technics, and finally, thirdly, how governmentality could not have assumed the dimensions it has except thanks to a series of quite particular instruments, whose formation is precisely contemporary with the art of government, and which one could call, in the old sense of the term, that of the twelfth and thirteenth centuries, the police. The pastoral, the new diplomatico-military technics, and finally the police, I believe, were the three elements from which the phenomenon of the governmentalization of the state, so fundamental in the history of the West, could be produced.

QUESTIONS OF METHOD

WHY THE PRISON?

Q: *Why do you see the birth of the prison—and, in particular, this process you call "hurried substitution," which in the early years of the nineteenth century establishes the prison at the center of the new penal system—as being so important?*

Aren't you inclined to overstate the importance of the prison in penal history, given that other quite distinct modes of punishment (the death penalty, the penal colonies, deportation) remained in effect too? At the level of historical methods, you seem to scorn explanations in terms of causality or structure, and sometimes to prioritize a description of a process that is purely one of events. No doubt, it's true that the preoccupation with "social history" has invaded historians' work in an uncontrolled manner; but even if one does not accept the "social" as the only valid level of historical explanation, is it right for you to throw out social history altogether from your "interpretative diagram"?

A: I wouldn't want what I may have said or written to be seen as laying any claims to totality. I don't try to universalize what I say; conversely, what I don't say isn't meant to be thereby disqualified as being of no importance. My work takes place between unfinished abutments and anticipatory strings of dots. I like to open up a space of research, try it out, and then if it doesn't work, try again somewhere else. On many points—I am thinking especially of the relations between dialectics, genealogy, and strategy—I am still working and don't yet know whether I am going to get anywhere. What I say ought to be taken as "propositions," "game openings" where those who may be interested are invited to join in—they are not meant as dogmatic assertions that have to be taken or left en bloc. My books aren't treatises in philosophy or studies of history; at

Originally titled "Round Table of 20 May 1978," this interview was published in 1980. The French editors have condensed the questions posed to Foucault by various interlocutors into those of a "collective historian." We preserve their amendation.—Eds.

most, they are philosophical fragments put to work in a historical field of problems.

I will attempt to answer the questions that have been posed. First, about the prison. You wonder whether it was as important as I have claimed, or whether it acted as the real focus of the penal system. I don't mean to suggest that the prison was the essential core of the entire penal system; nor am I saying that it would be impossible to approach the problems of penal history—not to speak of the history of crime in general—by other routes than the history of the prison. But it seemed to me legitimate to take the prison as my object, for two reasons. First, because it had been rather neglected in previous analyses; when people had set out to study the problems of "the penal order" [*pénalité*]—a confused enough term, in any case—they usually opted to prioritize one of two directions: either the sociological problem of the criminal population, or the juridical problem of the penal system and its basis. The actual practice of punishment was scarcely studied except, in the line of the Frankfurt School, by Georg Rusche and Otto Kircheimer. There have indeed been studies of prisons as institutions, but very few of imprisonment as a general punitive practice in our societies.

My second reason for wanting to study the prison was the idea of reactivating the project of a "genealogy of morals," one that worked by tracing the lines of transformation of what one might call "moral technologies." In order to get a better understanding of what is punished and why, I wanted to ask the question *how* does one punish? This was the same procedure as I had used when dealing with madness: rather than asking *what*, in a given period, is regarded as sanity or insanity, as mental illness or normal behavior, I wanted to ask *how* these divisions are effected. It's a method that seems to me to yield—I wouldn't say the maximum of possible illumination—at least a fairly fruitful kind of intelligibility.

There was also, while I was writing this book, a contemporary issue relating to the prison and, more generally, to the numerous aspects of penal practice being brought into question. This development was noticeable not only in France but also in the United States, Britain, and Italy. Incidentally, it would be interesting to consider why all these problems about confinement, internment, the penal dressage of individuals and their distribution, classification, and objectification through forms of knowledge came to be posed so urgently at this time, well in advance of May 1968: the themes of antipsychiatry were formulated around 1958 to 1960. The connection with the matter of the concentration camps is evident—look at Bruno Bettelheim.[1] But one would need to analyze more closely what took place around 1960.

In this piece of research on the prisons, as in my other earlier work, the target of analysis wasn't "institutions," "theories," or "ideology" but *practices*—with the aim of grasping the conditions that make these acceptable at a given moment; the hypothesis being that these types of practice are not just governed by institutions, prescribed by ideologies, guided by pragmatic circumstances—whatever role these elements may actually play—but, up to a point, possess their own specific regularities, logic, strategy, self-evidence, and "reason." It is a question of analyzing a "regime of practices"—practices being understood here as places where what is said and what is done, rules imposed and reasons given, the planned and the taken-for-granted meet and interconnect.

To analyze "regimes of practices" means to analyze programs of conduct that have both prescriptive effects regarding what is to be done (effects of "jurisdiction") and codifying effects regarding what is to be known (effects of "veridiction").

So I was aiming to write a history not of the prison as an institution, but of the *practice of imprisonment:* to show its origin or, more exactly, to show how this way of doing things—ancient enough in itself—was capable of being accepted at a certain moment as a principal component of the penal system, thus coming to seem an altogether natural, self-evident, and indispensable part of it.

It's a matter of shaking this false self-evidence, of demonstrating its precariousness, of making visible not its arbitrariness but its complex interconnection with a multiplicity of historical processes, many of them of recent date. From this point of view, I can say that the history of penal imprisonment exceeded my wildest hopes. All the early nineteenth-century texts and discussions testify to the astonishment at finding the prison being used as a general means of punishment—something that had not at all been what the eighteenth-century reformers had had in mind. I did not at all take this sudden change—which was what its contemporaries recognized it as being—as marking a result at which one's analysis could stop. I took this discontinuity, this—in a sense—"phenomenal" set of mutations, as my starting point and tried, without eradicating it, to account for it. It was a matter not of digging down to a buried stratum of continuity, but of identifying the transformation that made this hurried transition possible.

As you know, no one is more of a continuist than I am: to recognize a discontinuity is never anything more than to register a problem that needs to be solved.

EVENTALIZATION

Q: *What you have just said clears up a number of things. All the same, historians have been troubled by a sort of equivocation in your analyses, a sort of oscillation between "hyperrationalism" and "infrarationality."*

A: I am trying to work in the direction of what one might call "eventalization." Even though the "event" has been for some while now a category little esteemed by historians, I wonder whether, understood in a certain sense, "eventalization" may not be a useful procedure of analysis. What do I mean by this term? First of all, a breach of self-evidence. It means making visible a *singularity* at places where there is a temptation to invoke a historical constant, an immediate anthropological trait, or an obviousness that imposes itself uniformly on all. To show that things "weren't as necessary as all that"; it wasn't as a matter of course that mad people came to be regarded as mentally ill; it wasn't self-evident that the only thing to be done with a criminal was to lock him up; it wasn't self-evident that the causes of illness were to be sought through the individual examination of bodies; and so on. A breach of self-evidence, of those self-evidences on which our knowledges, acquiescences, and practices rest: this is the first theoretico-political function of "eventalization."

Second, eventalization means rediscovering the connections, encounters, supports, blockages, plays of forces, strategies, and so on, that at a given moment establish what subsequently counts as being self-evident, universal, and necessary. In this sense, one is indeed effecting a sort of multiplication or pluralization of causes.

Does this mean that one regards the singularity one is analyzing simply as a fact to be registered, a reasonless break in an inert continuum? Clearly not, since that would amount to treating continuity as a self-sufficient reality that carries its own raison d'être within itself.

This procedure of causal multiplication means analyzing an event according to the multiple processes that constitute it. So, to analyze the practice of penal incarceration as an "event" (not as an institutional fact or ideological effect) means to determine the processes of "penalization" (that is, progressive insertion into the forms of legal punishment) of already existing practices of internment; the processes of "carceralization" of practices of penal justice (that is, the movement by which imprisonment as a form of punishment and technique of correction becomes a central component of the penal order). And these vast processes need themselves to be further broken down: the penalization of internment comprises a multiplicity of processes such as the formation of closed pedagogical spaces functioning through rewards, punishments, and so on.

As a way of lightening the weight of causality, "eventalization" thus works by constructing around the singular event analyzed as process a "polygon" or, rather, "polyhedron" of intelligibility, the number of whose faces is not given in advance and can never properly be taken as finite. One has to proceed by progressive, necessarily incomplete saturation. And one has to bear in mind that the further one breaks down the processes under analysis, the more one is enabled and indeed obliged to construct their external relations of intelligibility. (In concrete terms: the more one analyzes the process of "carceralization" of penal practice down to its smallest details, the more one is led to relate them to such practices as schooling, military discipline, and so on.) The internal analysis of processes goes hand in hand with a multiplication of analytical "salients."

This operation thus leads to an increasing polymorphism as the analysis progresses:

1. A polymorphism of the elements brought into relation: starting from the prison, one introduces the history of pedagogical practices, the formation of professional armies, British empirical philosophy, techniques of use of firearms, new methods of division of labor.
2. A polymorphism of relations described: these may concern the transposition of technical models (such as architectures of surveillance), tactics calculated in response to a particular situation (such as the growth of banditry, the disorder provoked by public tortures and executions, the defects of the practice of penal banishment), or the application of theoretical schemas (such as those representing the genesis of ideas and the formation of signs, the utilitarian conception of behavior, and so on).
3. A polymorphism of domains of reference (varying in their nature, generality, and so on), ranging from technical mutations in matters of detail to the attempted emplacement in a capitalist economy of new techniques of power designed in response to the exigencies of that economy.

Forgive this long detour, but it enables me to better reply to your question about hyper- and hyporationalism, one that is often put to me.

It has been some time since historians lost their love of events and made "deeventalization" their principle of historical intelligibility. The way they work is by ascribing the object they analyze to the most unitary, necessary, inevitable, and (ultimately) extrahistorical mechanism or structure available. An economic mechanism, an anthropological structure, or a demographic process that figures the climactic stage in the investigation—these are the goals of deeventalized history. (Of course, these remarks are only intended as a crude specification of a certain broad tendency.)

Clearly, viewed from the standpoint of this style of analysis, what I am proposing is at once too much and too little. There are too many diverse kinds of relations, too many lines of analysis, yet at the same time there is too little necessary unity. A plethora of intelligibilities, a deficit of necessities.

But for me this is precisely the point at issue, both in historical analysis and in political critique. We aren't, nor do we have to put ourselves, under the sign of a unitary necessity.

THE PROBLEM OF RATIONALITIES

Q: *I would like to pause for a moment on this question of eventalization, because it lies at the center of a certain number of misunderstandings about your work. (I am not talking about the misguided portrayal of you as a "thinker of discontinuity.") Behind the identifying of breaks and the careful, detailed charting of these networks of relations that engender a reality and a history, there persists from one book to the next something amounting to one of those historical constants or anthropologico-cultural traits you were objecting to just now: this version of a general history of rationalization spanning three or four centuries, or at any rate of a history of one particular kind of rationalization as it progressively takes effect in our society. It's not by chance that your first book was a history of reason as well as of madness, and I believe that the themes of all your other books, the analysis of different techniques of isolation, the social taxonomies, and so on—all this boils down to one and the same meta-anthropological or meta-historical process of rationalization. In this sense, the "eventalization" you define here as central to your work seems to me to constitute only one of its extremes.*

A: If one calls "Weberians" those who set out to trade off [*relayer*] the Marxist analysis of the contradictions of capital for that of the irrational rationality of capitalist society, then I don't think I am a Weberian, since my basic preoccupation isn't rationality considered as an athropological invariant. I don't believe one can speak of an intrinsic notion of "rationalization" without, on the one hand, positing an absolute value inherent in reason, and, on the other, taking the risk of applying the term empirically in a completely arbitrary way. I think one must restrict one's use of this word to an instrumental and relative meaning. The ceremony of public torture isn't in itself more irrational than imprisonment in a cell; but it's irrational in terms of a type of penal practice that involves new ways of envisaging the effects to be produced by the penalty imposed, new ways of calculating its utility, justifying it, fixing its degrees and so on. One isn't assessing things in terms of an absolute against which they could be evaluated as constituting more or less perfect forms of rationality but, rather, examining how forms of rationality inscribe themselves in practices or systems of practices, and what role they play within them—because it's true that "practices" don't exist without a certain regime of rationality. But, rather than measuring this regime against a value of reason, I would prefer to analyze it according to two axes: on the one hand, that of codification/prescription (how it forms an ensemble of rules, procedures, means to an end, and so on), and, on the other, that of true or false formulation (how it determines a domain of objects about which it is possible to articulate true or false propositions).

If I have studied "practices" such as those of the sequestration of the insane,

or clinical medicine, or the organization of the empirical sciences, or legal punishment, it was in order to study this interplay between a "code" that governs
ways of doing things (how people are to be graded and examined, things and
signs classified, individuals trained [*trier*], and so on) and a production of true
discourses that served to found, justify, and provide reasons and principles for
these ways of doing things. To put the matter clearly: my problem is to see how
men govern (themselves and others) by the production of truth (I repeat once
again that by production of truth I mean not the production of true utterances
but the establishment of domains in which the practice of true and false can be
made at once ordered and pertinent).

Eventalizing singular ensembles of practices, so as to make them graspable as
different regimes of "jurisdiction" and "veridiction": that, to put it in exceedingly barbarous terms, is what I would like to do. You see that this is neither a
history of knowledge [*connaissances*] nor an analysis of the advancing rationalities that rule our society, nor an anthropology of the codifications that, without
our knowledge, rule our behavior. I would like, in short, to resituate the production of true and false at the heart of historical analysis and political critique.

Q: *It's not an accident that you speak of Max Weber. There is in your work—no
doubt, in a sense you wouldn't want to accept—a sort of "ideal type" that paralyzes
and mutes analysis when one tries to account for reality. Isn't this what led you to ab-
stain from all commentary when you published the memoir of Pierre Rivère?*
A: I don't think your comparison with Max Weber is exact. Schematically, one
can say that the "ideal type" is a category of historical interpretation: it's a
structure of understanding for the historian who seeks to integrate, after the
fact, a certain set of data—it allows him to recapture an "essence" (Calvinism,
the state, the capitalist enterprise), working from general principles that are not
at all present in the thought of the individuals whose concrete behavior is nevertheless to be understood on their basis.

When I try to analyze the rationalities proper of penal imprisonment, the
psychiatrization of madness, or the organization of the domain of sexuality, and
when I lay stress on the fact that the real functioning of institutions isn't confined to the unfolding of this rational schema in its pure form, is this an analysis
in terms of "ideal types"? I don't think so, for a number of reasons.

The rational schemas of the prison, the hospital, or the asylum are not general
principles that can be rediscovered only through the historian's retrospective interpretation. They are explicit *programs;* we are dealing with sets of calculated,
reasoned prescriptions in terms of which institutions are meant to be recognized,
spaces arranged, behaviors regulated. If they have an ideality, it is that of a programming left in abeyance, not that of a general but hidden meaning.

Of course, this programming depends on forms of rationality much more general than those they directly implement. I tried to show that the rationality envisaged in penal imprisonment wasn't the outcome of a straightforward calculation of immediate interest (internment turning out to be, in the last analysis, the simplest and cheapest solution), but that it arose out of a whole technology of human training, surveillance of behavior, individualization of the elements of a social body. "Discipline" isn't the expression of an "ideal type" (that of "disciplined man"); it's the generalization and interconnection of different techniques themselves designed in response to localized requirements (schooling, training troops to handle rifles).

These programs don't take effect in the institutions in an integral way; they are simplified, or some are chosen and not others; and things never work out as planned. But what I wanted to show is that this difference is not one between the purity of the ideal and the disorderly impurity of the real, but that in fact there are different strategies that are mutually opposed, composed, and superposed so as to produce permanent and solid effects that can perfectly well be understood in terms of their rationality, even though they don't conform to the initial programming: this is what gives the resulting apparatus its solidity and suppleness.

Programs, technologies, apparatuses—none of these is an "ideal type." I try to study the play and development of a set of diverse realities articulated onto each other; a program, the connection that explains it, the law that gives it its coercive power, and so on, are all just as much realities—albeit in a different mode—as the institutions that embody them or the behaviors that more or less faithfully conform to them.

You say to me: Nothing happens as laid down in these "programs," they are no more than dreams, utopias, a sort of imaginary production that you aren't entitled to substitute for reality. Jeremy Bentham's *Panopticon* isn't a very good description of "real life" in nineteenth-century prisons.

To this I would reply: If I had wanted to describe "real life" in the prisons, I indeed wouldn't have gone to Bentham. But the fact that this real life isn't the same thing as the theoreticians' schemes doesn't entail that these schemes are therefore utopian, imaginary, and so on. One could only think this if one had a very impoverished notion of the real. For one thing, the elaboration of these schemas corresponds to a whole series of diverse practices and strategies: the search for effective, measured, unified penal mechanism is unquestionably a response to the disalignment of the institutions of judicial power with the new economic forms, urbanization, and so on; again, there is the attempt—very noticeable in a country like France—to reduce the autonomy and insularity of judicial practice and personnel within the overall workings of the state. There is the wish to respond to emerging new forms of criminality, and so on. For another thing, these programs induce a whole series of effects in the real (which isn't of course the same as saying that they take the place of the real): they crystallize into institutions, they inform individual behavior, they act as grids for the perception and evaluation of things. It is absolutely true that criminals stubbornly resisted the new disciplinary mechanism in the prison; it is absolutely correct that the actual functioning of the prisons, in the inherited buildings where they were established and with the governors and guards who administered them, was a witches' brew compared to the beautiful Benthamite machine. But if the prisons were seen to have failed, if criminals were perceived as incorrigible, and a whole new criminal "race" emerged into the field of vision of public opinion and "justice," if the resistance of the prisoners and the pattern of recidivism took the forms we know they did, it's precisely because this type of programming didn't just remain a utopia in the heads of a few contrivers.

These programmings of behavior, these regimes of jurisdiction and veridiction aren't abortive schemas for the creation of a reality. They are fragments of reality that induce such particular effects in the real as the distinction between true and false implicit in the ways men "direct," "govern," and "conduct" themselves and others. To grasp these effects as historical events—with what this implies for the question of truth (which is the question of philosophy itself)—this is more or less my theme. You see that this has nothing to do with the project—an admirable one in itself—of grasping a "whole society" in its "living reality."

The question I won't succeed in answering here but have been asking myself from the beginning is roughly the following: What is history, given that there is continually being produced within it a separation of true and false? By that I mean four things. First, in what sense is the production and transformation of the true/false division characteristic and decisive for our historicity? Second, in what specific ways has this relation operated in Western societies, which produce scientific knowledge whose forms are perpetually changing and whose values are posited as universal? Third, what historical knowledge is possible of a history that itself produces the true/false distinction on which such knowledge depends? Fourth, isn't the most general of political problems the problem of truth? How can one analyze the connection between ways of distinguishing true and false and ways of governing oneself and others? The search for a new foundation for each of these practices, in itself and relative to the other, the will to discover a different way of governing oneself through a different way of dividing up true and false—this is what I would call "political spirituality."

THE ANESTHETIC EFFECT

Q: *There is a question here about the way your analyses have been transmitted and received. For instance, if one talks to social workers in the prisons, one finds that the arrival of* Discipline and Punish *had an absolutely sterilizing or, rather, anesthetiz-*

ing effect on them, because they felt your critique had an implacable logic that left them no possible room for initiative. You said just now, talking about eventalization, that you want to work toward breaking up existing self-evidences to show both how they are produced and how they are nevertheless always unstable. It seems to me that the second half of the picture—the aspect of instability—isn't clear.

A: You're quite right to pose this problem of anesthesia, one that is of capital importance. It's quite true that I don't feel myself capable of effecting the "subversion of all codes," "dislocation of all orders of knowledge," "revolutionary affirmation of violence," "overturning of all contemporary culture"—these hopes and prospectuses that currently underpin all those brilliant intellectual ventures I admire all the more because the worth and previous achievements of those who undertake them guarantees an appropriate outcome. My project is far from being of comparable scope. To give some assistance in wearing away certain self-evidences and commonplaces about madness, normality, illness, crime, and punishment; to bring it about, together with many others, that certain phrases can no longer be spoken so lightly, certain acts no longer—or at least no longer so unhesitatingly—performed; to contribute to changing certain things in people's ways of perceiving and doing things; to participate in this difficult displacement of forms of sensibility and thresholds of tolerance—I hardly feel capable of attempting much more than that. If only what I have tried to say might somehow, to some degree, not remain altogether foreign to some such real effects. . . . And yet I realize how much all this can remain precarious, how easily it can all lapse back into somnolence.

But you are right, one has to be more suspicious. Perhaps what I have written has had an anaesthetic effect. But one still needs to distinguish on whom.

To judge by what the psychiatric authorities have had to say, the cohorts on the right who charge me with being against any form of power, those on the left who call me the "last bulwark of the bourgeoisie" (this isn't a pronouncement of Kanapa's[2]—on the contrary), the worthy psychoanalyst who likened me to the Hitler of *Mein Kampf,* the number of times I've been "autopsied" and "buried" during the past fifteen years—well, I have the impression of having had an irritant rather than anesthetic effect on a good many people. The epidermises bristle with a constancy I find encouraging. A journal recently warned its readers in deliciously Pétainist style against accepting as a credo what I had had to say about sexuality ("the importance of the subject," "the personality of the author" rendered my enterprise "dangerous"). No risk of anesthesis in that direction. But I agree with you, these are trifles, amusing to note but tedious to collect. The only important problem is what happens on the ground.

We have known at least since the nineteenth century the difference between anaesthesis and paralysis. Let's talk about paralysis first. Who has been paralyzed? Do you think what I wrote on the history of psychiatry paralyzed those people who had already been concerned for some time about what was happening in psychiatric institutions? And, seeing what has been happening in and around the prisons, I don't think the effect of paralysis is very evident there, either. As far as the people in prison are concerned, things aren't doing too badly. On the other hand, it's true that certain people, such as those who work in the institutional setting of the prison—which is not quite the same as being in prison—are not likely to find advice or instructions in my books that tell them "what is to be done." But my project is precisely to bring it about that they "no longer know what to do," so that the acts, gestures, discourses that up until then had seemed to go without saying become problematic, difficult, dangerous. This effect is intentional. And then I have some news for you: for me, the problem of the prisons isn't one for the "social workers" but one for the prisoners. And on that aside, I'm not so sure what's been said over the last fifteen years has been quite so—how shall put it?—demobilizing.

But paralysis isn't the same thing as anesthesia—on the contrary. It's insofar as there's been an awakening to a whole series of problems that the difficulty of doing anything comes to be felt. Not that this effect is an end in itself. But it seems to me that "what is to be done" ought not to be determined from above by reformers, be they prophetic or legislative, but by a long work of comings and goings, of exchanges, reflections, trials, different analyses. If the social workers you are talking about don't know which way to turn, this just goes to show that they're looking and, hence, are not anesthetized or sterilized at all—on the contrary. And it's because of the need not to tie them down or immobilize them that there can be no question of trying to dictate "what is to be done." If the questions posed by the social workers you spoke of are going to assume their full amplitude, the most important thing is not to bury them under the weight of prescriptive, prophetic discourse. The necessity of reform mustn't be allowed to become a form of blackmail serving to limit, reduce, or halt the exercise of criticism. Under no circumstances should one pay attention to those who tell one: "Don't criticize, since you're not capable of carrying out a reform." That's ministerial cabinet talk. Critique doesn't have to be the premise of a deduction that concludes, "this, then, is what needs to be done." It should be an instrument for those who fight, those who resist and refuse what is. Its use should be in processes of conflict and confrontation, essays in refusal. It doesn't have to lay down the law for the law. It isn't a stage in a programming. It is a challenge directed to what is.

The problem, you see, is one for the subject who acts—the subject of action through which the real is transformed. If prisons and punitive mechanisms are transformed, it won't be because a plan of reform has found its way into the heads of the social workers; it will be when those who have a stake in that reality, all those people, have come into collision with each other and with themselves, run into dead ends, problems, and impossibilities, been through conflicts and confrontations—when critique has been played out in the real, not when reformers have realized their ideas.

Q: *This anesthetic effect has operated on the historians. If they haven't responded to your work it's because, for them, the "Foucauldean schema" was becoming as much of an encumbrance as the Marxist one. I don't know if the "effect" you produce interests you. But the explanations you have given here weren't so clear in* Discipline and Punish.

A: I really wonder whether we are using this word "anesthetize" in the same sense. These historians seemed to me more to be "anasthetized," "irritated" (in Broussais's sense of the term, of course). Irritated by what? By a schema? I don't believe so, because there is no schema. If there is an "irritation" (and I seem to recall that in a certain journal a few signs of this irritation may have been discreetly manifested), it's more because of the absence of a schema. No infra- or superstructure, no Malthusian cycle, no opposition between state and civil society: none of these schemas that have bolstered historians' operations, explicitly or implicitly, for the past hundred or hundred and fifty years.

Hence, no doubt, the sense of malaise and the questions enjoining me to situate myself within some such schema: "How do you deal with the state? What theory do you offer us of the state?" Some say I neglect its role, others that I see it everywhere, imagining it capable of minutely controlling individuals' everyday lives. Or that my descriptions leave out all reference to an infrastructure—while others say that I make an infrastructure out of sexuality. The totally contradictory nature of these objections proves that what I am doing doesn't correspond to any of these schemas.

Perhaps the reason why my work irritates people is precisely the fact that I'm not interested in constructing a new schema or in validating one that already exists. Perhaps it's because my objective isn't to propose a global principle for analyzing society. And it's here that my project has differed since the outset from that of the historians. They—rightly or wrongly, that's another question—take "society" as the general horizon of their analysis, the instance relative to which they set out to situate this or that particular object ("society, economy, civilization," as the *Annales* have it). My general theme isn't society but the discourse of true and false, by which I mean the correlative formation of domains and objects and of the verifiable, falsifiable discourses that bear on them; and it's not just their formation that interests me, but the effects in the real to which they are linked.

I realize I'm not being clear. I'll take an example. It's perfectly legitimate for the historian to ask whether sexual behaviors in a given period were supervised and controlled, and to ask which among them were heavily disapproved of. (It would of course be frivolous to suppose that one had explained a certain intensity of "repression" by the delaying of the age of marriage. Here one has scarcely even begun to outline a problem: why is it that the delay in the age of marriage takes effect thus and not otherwise?) But the problem I pose myself is a quite different one: it's a matter of how the rendering of sexual behavior into discourse comes to be transformed, what types of jurisdiction and "veridiction" it's subject to, and how the constitutive elements are formed of the domain that comes—and only at a very late stage—to be termed "sexuality" are formed. Among the numerous effects the organization of this domain has undoubtedly had, one is that of having provided historians with a category so "self-evident" that they believe they can write a history of sexuality and its repression.

The history of the "objectification" of those elements historians consider as objectively given (if I dare put it thus: of the objectification of objectivities), this is the sort of sphere I would like to traverse. A "tangle," in sum, that is difficult to sort out. This, not the presence of some easily reproducible schema, is what doubtless troubles and irritates people. Of course, this is a problem of philosophy to which the historian is entitled to remain indifferent. But if I am posing it as a problem within historical analysis, I'm not demanding that history answer it. I would just like to find out what effects the question produces within historical knowledge. Paul Veyne saw this very clearly:[3] it's a matter of the effect on historical knowledge of a nominalist critique itself arrived at by way of a historical analysis.

Notes

1. Foucault is referring to Bettelheim's studies of concentration camp survivors; see Bettelheim, *Individual and Mass Behavior in Extreme Situations* (Indianapolis: Bobbs-Merrill, 1943) and *The Informed Heart: Autonomy in a Mass Age* (New York: The Free Press), 1960. —Eds.

2. Jean Kanapa is a leading Marxist and director of *La Nouvelle Critique*.

3. Cf. "Foucault révolutionne l'histoire," in Paul Veyne, *Comment on écrit l'histoire* (2nd ed., Paris: Seuil, 1978).

SECURITY, TERRITORY,
AND POPULATION

The course dealt with the genesis of a political knowledge that was to place at the center of its concerns the notion of population and the mechanisms capable of ensuring its regulation. A transition from a "territorial state" to a "population state"? No, one would have to say, because what occurred was not a replacement but, rather, a shift of accent and the appearance of new objectives, and hence of new problems and new techniques.

To follow that genesis, we took up the notion of government as our leading thread.

1. One would need to do an in-depth inquiry concerning the history not merely of the notion but even of the procedures and means employed to ensure, in a given society, the "government of men." In a very first approach, it seems that for the Greek and Roman societies the exercise of political power did not involve the right or the possibilities of a "government" understood as an activity that undertakes to conduct individuals throughout their lives by placing them under the authority of a guide responsible for what they do and for what happens to them. Following the indications furnished by Paul Veyne, it seems that the idea of a pastor-sovereign, a king or judge-shepherd of the human flock, is rarely found outside the archaic Greek texts or except in certain authors of the imperial epoch. On the other hand, the metaphor of the shepherd watching over the sheep is accepted when it comes to characterizing the activity of the educator, the doctor, the gymnastics teacher. An analysis of the *Politics* would confirm this hypothesis.

It was in the East that the theme of pastoral power was fully developed— above all, in Hebrew society. A certain number of traits mark this theme: the shepherd's power is exercised not so much over a fixed territory as over a multitude in movement toward a goal; it has the role of providing the flock with its sustenance, watching over it on a daily basis, and ensuring its salvation; lastly, it is a matter of a power that individualizes by granting, through an essential paradox, as much value to a single one of the sheep as to the entire flock. It is this type of power that was introduced into the West by Christianity and took an institutional form in the ecclesiastical pastorate: the government of souls was constituted in the Christian Church as a central, knowledge-based activity indispensable for the salvation of each and every one.

Now, the fifteenth and sixteenth centuries saw a general crisis of the pastorate open up and develop, but in a much more complex fashion: a search for other modes (and not necessarily less strict ones) of spiritual direction and new types of relations between pastor and flock; but also inquiries concerning the right way to "govern" children, a family, a domain, a principality. The general questioning of government and self-government, of guidance and self-guidance, accompanies, at the end of feudalism, the birth of new forms of economic and social relations and new political structurations.

2. We next analyzed some aspects of the formation of a political "governmentality": that is, the way in which the behavior of a set of individuals became involved, more and more markedly, in the exercise of sovereign power. This important transformation is expressed in the different "arts of governing" that were written at the end of the sixteenth century and the first half of the seventeenth. No doubt, it is linked to the emergence of the "reason of state." One goes from an art of governing whose principles were borrowed from the traditional virtues (wisdom, justice, liberality, respect for divine laws and human customs) or from the common abilities (prudence, thoughtful decisions, taking care to surround oneself with the best adviser) to an art of governing whose rationality has its principles and its specific domain of application in the state. The "reason of state" is not the imperative in the name of which one can or must upset all the other rules; it is the new matrix of rationality according to which the prince must exercise his sovereignty in governing men. One is far from the virtue of the sovereign of justice—far, too, from that virtue which is proper to Machiavelli's hero.

The development of the reason of state is correlative with the fading away of the imperial theme. Rome finally disappears. A new historical perception takes form; it is no longer polarized around the end of time and the consolidation of all the particular sovereignties into the empire of the last days; it is open to an indefinite time in which the states have to struggle against one another to ensure their own survival. And more than the problems of a sovereign's legitimate dominion over a territory, what will appear important is the knowledge and development of a state's forces: in a space (European and global at once) of competition between states, very different from that in which dynastic rivals confront each other, the major problem is that of a dynamic of the forces and the rational techniques which enable one to intervene in those forces.

Thus, the reason of state, apart from the theories that formulated and justified it, takes shape in two great ensembles of political knowledge and technology: a diplomatico-military technology that consists in ensuring and
developing the forces of a state through a system of alliances, and the organizing of an armed apparatus. The search for a European equilibrium, which was
one of the guiding principles of the treaties of Westphalia, is a consequence of
this political technology. The second is constituted by "policy" [*police*], in the
sense given to the word then: that is, the set of means necessary to make the
forces of the state increase from within. At the junction point of these two great
technologies, and as a shared instrument, one must place commerce and monetary circulation between the states: enrichment through commerce offers the
possibility of increasing the population, the manpower, production, and export,
and of endowing oneself with large, powerful armies. During the period of
mercantilism and cameralistics, the population-wealth pair was the privileged
object of the new governmental reason.

3. The working-out of this population-wealth problem (in its different
concrete aspects: taxation [*fiscalité*], scarcity, depopulation, idleness-beggary-
vagabondage) constitutes one of the conditions of formation of political economy. The latter develops when it is realized that the resources-population
relationship can no longer be fully managed through a coercive regulatory
system that would tend to raise the population in order to augment the resources. The physiocrats are not antipopulationist in opposition to the mercantilists of the preceding epoch; they frame the population problem in a different
way. For them, the population is not simply the sum of subjects who inhabit a
territory, a sum that would be the result of each person's desire to have children or of laws that would promote or discourage births—it is a variable dependent on a number of factors. These are not all natural by any means (the tax
system, the activity of circulation, and the distribution of profit are essential
determinants of the population rate). But this dependence can be rationally analyzed, in such a way that the population appears as "naturally" dependent on
multiple factors that may be artificially alterable. So there begins to appear,
branching off from the technology of "policy" and in correlation with the
birth of economic thought, the political problem of population. The latter is
not conceived as a collection of legal subjects, nor as a mass of human arms intended for labor; it is analyzed as a set of elements that, first, is connected with
the general system of living beings (population in this sense falls in the category of "the human race" [*l'espèce humaine*]; the notion, new at the time, is to
be distinguished from "mankind" [*le genre humain*]) and, second, may offer a
purchase for concerted interventions (through laws, but also through changes
of attitude, of ways of acting and living that can be obtained through "campaigns").

S

Sok

SEMINAR

The seminar was devoted to a few aspects of what the Germans, in the eighteenth century, called *Polizeiwissenschaft*—that is, the theory and analysis of everything "that tends to affirm and increase the power of the state to make good use of its forces, to obtain the welfare of its subjects," and, above all, "the maintenance of order and discipline, the regulations that tend to make their lives comfortable and to provide them with the things they need for their livelihood."

We tried to show what problems this "policy" was meant to address; how the role it was assigned was different from the one that would later devolve upon the police institution; what results were expected of it in order to bring about the growth of the state, and this in terms of two objectives—enable it to mark out and improve its position in the game of rivalry and competition between European states, and to guarantee internal order by ensuring the "welfare" of individuals. Development of the competitive state (economically and militarily), development of the *Wohlfahrt* state (wealth-tranquility-happiness): it is these two principles that "policy," understood as a rational art of governing, must be able to coordinate. It was conceived during this period as a sort of "technology of state forces." Among the main objects with which this technology needed to be concerned was population, in which the mercantilists saw a principle of enrichment and in which everyone recognized an essential component of the strength of states. And the management of this population required, among other things, a health policy capable of diminishing infant mortality, preventing epidemics, and bringing down the rates of endemic diseases, of intervening in living conditions in order to alter them and impose standards on them (whether this involved nutrition, housing, or urban planning), and of ensuring adequate medical facilities and services. The development, starting in the second half of the eighteenth century, of what was called *medizinische Polizei*, public health, or social medicine, must be written back into the general framework of a "biopolitics"; the latter tends to treat the "population" as a mass of living and coexisting beings who present particular biological and pathological traits and who thus come under specific knowledge and technologies. And this "biopolitics" itself must be understood in terms of a theme developed as early as the seventeenth century: the management of state forces.

Papers were read on the notion of *Polizeiwissenschaft* (Pasquale Pasquino), on the antismallpox campaigns in the eighteenth century (Anne-Marie Moulin), on the Paris cholera epidemic in 1832 (François Delaporte), on the legislation dealing with work-related accidents, and the development of insurance in the nineteenth century (François Ewald).

WHAT IS CRITIQUE?

Actually, the question about which I wanted to speak and about which I still want to speak is: *What is critique?* It might be worth trying out a few ideas on this project that keeps taking shape, being extended and reborn on the outer limits of philosophy, very close to it, up against it, at its expense, in the direction of a future philosophy and in lieu, perhaps, of all possible philosophy. And it seems that between the high Kantian enterprise and the little polemical professional activities that are called critique, it seems to me that there has been in the modern Western world (dating, more or less, empirically from the fifteenth to the sixteenth centuries) a certain way of thinking, speaking and acting, a certain relationship to what exists, to what one knows, to what one does, a relationship to society, to culture and also a relationship to others that we could call, let's say, the critical attitude. Of course, you will be surprised to hear that there is something like a critical attitude that would be specific to modern civilization, since there have been so many critiques, polemics, etc., and since even Kant's problems presumably have origins which go back way before the fifteenth and sixteenth centuries. One will be surprised to see that one tries to find a unity in this critique, although by its very nature, by its function, I was going to say, by its profession, it seems to be condemned to dispersion, dependency and pure heteronomy. After all, critique only exists in relation to something other than itself: it is an instrument, a means for a future or a truth that it will not know nor happen to be, it oversees a domain it would want to police and is unable to regulate. All this means that it is a function which is subordinated in relation to what philosophy, science, politics, ethics, law, literature, etc., positively constitute. And at the same time, whatever the pleasures or compensations accompanying this curious activity of critique, it seems that it rather regularly, almost always, brings not only some stiff bit of utility it claims to have, but also that it is sup-

From *The Politics of Truth* by Michel Foucault, edited by Sylvère Lotringer and Lysa Hochroth (New York: Semiotext(e), 1997).

ported by some kind of more general imperative—more general still than that of eradicating errors. There is something in critique which is akin to virtue. And in a certain way, what I wanted to speak to you about is this critical attitude as virtue in general.

There are several routes one could take to discuss the history of this critical attitude. I would simply like to suggest this one to you, which is one possible route, again, among many others. I will suggest the following variation: the Christian pastoral, or the Christian church inasmuch as it acted in a precisely and specifically pastoral way, developed this idea—singular and, I believe, quite foreign to ancient culture—that each individual, whatever his age or status, from the beginning to the end of his life and in his every action, had to be governed and had to let himself be governed, that is to say directed towards his salvation, by someone to whom he was bound by a total, meticulous, detailed relationship of obedience. And this salvation-oriented operation in a relationship of obedience to someone, has to be made in a triple relationship to the truth: truth understood as dogma, truth also to the degree where this orientation implies a special and individualizing knowledge of individuals; and finally, in that this direction is deployed like a reflective technique comprising general rules, particular knowledge, precepts, methods of examination, confessions, interviews, etc. After all, we must not forget what, for centuries, the Greek church called *technè technôn* and what the Latin Roman church called *ars artium*. It was precisely the direction of conscience; the art of governing men. Of course, this art of governing for a long time was linked to relatively limited practices, even in medieval society, to monastic life and especially to the practice of relatively restricted spiritual groups. But I believe that from the fifteenth century on and before the Reformation, one can say that there was a veritable explosion of the art of governing men. There was an explosion in two ways: first, by displacement in relation to the religious center, let's say if you will, secularization, the expansion in civil society of this theme of the art of governing men and the methods of doing it; and then, second, the proliferation of this art of governing into a variety of areas—how to govern children, how to govern the poor and beggars, how to govern a family, a house, how to govern armies, different groups, cities, states and also how to govern one's own body and mind. *How to govern* was, I believe, one of the fundamental questions about what was happening in the fifteenth or sixteenth centuries. It is a fundamental question which was answered by the multiplication of all the arts of governing—the art of pedagogy, the art of politics, the art of economics, if you will—and of all the institutions of government, in the wider sense the term government had at the time.

So, this governmentalization, which seems to me to be rather characteristic of these societies in Western Europe in the sixteenth century, cannot apparently be dissociated from the question "how not to be governed?" I do not mean by that

that governmentalization would be opposed in a kind of face-off by the opposite affirmation, "we do not want to be governed, and we do not want to be governed *at all*." I mean that, in this great preoccupation about the way to govern and the search for the ways to govern, we identify a perpetual question which would be: "how not to be governed *like that*, by that, in the name of those principles, with such and such an objective in mind and by means of such procedures, not like that, not for that, not by them." And if we accord this movement of governmentalization of both society and individuals the historic dimension and breadth which I believe it has had, it seems that one could approximately locate therein what we could call the critical attitude. Facing them head on and as compensation, or rather, as both partner and adversary to the arts of governing, as an act of defiance, as a challenge, as a way of limiting these arts of governing and sizing them up, transforming them, of finding a way to escape from them or, in any case, a way to displace them, with a basic distrust, but also and by the same token, as a line of development of the arts of governing, there would have been something born in Europe at that time, a kind of general cultural form, both a political and moral attitude, a way of thinking, etc., and which I would very simply call the art of not being governed or better, the art of not being governed like that and at that cost. I would therefore propose, as a very first definition of critique, this general characterization: the art of not being governed quite so much.

You will tell me that this definition is both very general and very vague or fluid. Well, of course it is! But I still believe that it may allow us to identify some precise points inherent to what I try to call the critical attitude. These are historical anchoring points, of course, which we can determine as follows:

1. First anchoring point: during a period of time when governing men was essentially a spiritual art, or an essentially religious practice linked to the authority of a Church, to the prescription of a Scripture, not to want to be governed like that essentially meant finding another function for the Scriptures unrelated to the teaching of God. Not wanting to be governed was a certain way of refusing, challenging, limiting (say it as you like) ecclesiastical rule. It meant returning to the Scriptures, seeking out what was authentic in them, what was really written in the Scriptures. It meant questioning what sort of truth the Scriptures told, gaining access to this truth of the Scriptures in the Scriptures and maybe in spite of what was written, to the point of finally raising the very simple question: were the Scriptures true? And, in short, from Wycliffe to Pierre Bayle, critique developed in part, for the most part, but not exclusively, of course, in relation to the Scriptures. Let us say that critique is biblical, historically.

2. Not to want to be governed, this is the second anchoring point. Not to want to be governed like that also means not wanting to accept these laws because they are unjust because, by virtue of their antiquity or the more or less

threatening ascendancy given them by today's sovereign, they hide a fundamental illegitimacy. Therefore, from this perspective, confronted with government and the obedience it stipulates, critique means putting forth universal and indefeasible rights to which every government, whatever it may be, whether a monarch, a magistrate, an educator or a pater familias, will have to submit. In brief, if you like, we find here again the problem of natural law.

Natural law is certainly not an invention of the Renaissance, but from the sixteenth century on, it took on a critical function that it still maintains to this day. To the question "how not to be governed?" it answers by saying: "What are the limits of the right to govern?" Let us say that here critique is basically a legal issue.

3. And finally "to not to want to be governed" is of course not accepting as true, here I will move along quickly, what an authority tells you is true, or at least not accepting it because an authority tells you that it is true, but rather accepting it only if one considers valid the reasons for doing so. And this time, critique finds its anchoring point in the problem of certainty in its confrontation with authority.

The Bible, jurisprudence, science, writing, nature, the relationship to oneself; the sovereign, the law, the authority of dogmatism. One sees how the interplay of governmentalization and critique has brought about phenomena which are, I believe, of capital importance in the history of Western culture whether in the development of philological sciences, philosophical thought, legal analysis or methodological reflections. However, above all, one sees that the core of critique is basically made of the bundle of relationships that are tied to one another, or one to the two others, power, truth and the subject. And if governmentalization is indeed this movement through which individuals are subjugated in the reality of a social practice through mechanisms of power that adhere to a truth, well, then! I will say that critique is the movement by which the subject gives himself the right to question truth on its effects of power and question power on its discourses of truth. Well, then!: critique will be the art of voluntary insubordination, that of reflected intractability. Critique would essentially insure the desubjugation of the subject in the context of what we could call, in a word, the politics of truth.

I would have the arrogance to think that this definition, however empirical, approximate and deliciously distant its character in relation to the history it encompasses, is not very different from the one Kant provided: not to define critique, but precisely to define something else. It is not very far off in fact from the definition he was giving of the *Aufklärung*. It is indeed characteristic that, in his text from 1784, *What is the Aufklärung?*, he defined the *Aufklärung* in relation to a certain minority condition in which humanity was maintained and maintained in an authoritative way. Second, he defined this minority as characterized by a certain incapacity in which humanity was maintained, an incapacity to use its own understanding precisely without something which would be someone else's direction, and he uses *leiten,* which has a religious meaning, well-defined historically. Third, I think that it is telling that Kant defined this incapacity by a certain correlation between the exercise of an authority which maintains humanity in this minority condition, the correlation between this excess of authority and, on the other hand, something that he considers, that he calls a lack of decision and courage. And consequently, this definition of the *Aufklärung* is not simply going to be a kind of historical and speculative definition. In this definition of the *Aufklärung,* there will be something which no doubt it may be a little ridiculous to call a sermon, and yet it is very much a call for courage that he sounds in this description of the *Aufklärung.* One should not forget that it was a newspaper article. There is much work to be done on the relationship between philosophy and journalism from the end of the 18th century on, a study . . . Unless it has already been done, but I am not sure of that . . . It is very interesting to see from what point on philosophers intervene in newspapers in order to say something that is for them philosophically interesting and which, nevertheless, is inscribed in a certain relationship to the public which they intend to mobilize. And finally, it is characteristic that, in this text on the *Aufklärung,* Kant precisely gives religion, law and knowledge as examples of maintaining humanity in the minority condition and consequently as examples of points where the *Aufklärung* must lift this minority condition and in some way majoritize men. What Kant was describing as the *Aufklärung* is very much what I was trying before to describe as critique, this critical attitude which appears as a specific attitude in the Western world starting with what was historically, I believe, the great process of society's governmentalization. And in relation to this *Aufklärung* (whose motto you know and Kant reminds us is *sapere aude,* to which Frederick II countered: "Let them reason all they want to as long as they obey") in any case, in relation to this *Aufklärung,* how will Kant define critique? Or, in any case, since I am not attempting to recoup Kant's entire critical project in all its philosophical rigor . . . I would not allow myself to do so before such an audience of philosophers, since I myself am not a philosopher and barely a critic . . . in terms of this *Aufklärung,* how is one going to situate what is understood by *critique?* If Kant actually calls in this whole critical movement which preceded the *Aufklärung,* how is one going to situate what *he* understands as critique. I will say, and these are completely childish things, that in relation to the *Aufklärung,* in Kant's eyes, critique will be what he is going to say to knowledge: do you know up to what point you can know? Reason as much as you want, but do you really know up to what point you can reason without it becoming dangerous? Critique will say, in short, that it is not so much a matter of what we are undertaking, more or less courageously, than it is the idea we have of our knowledge and its limits. Our liberty is at stake and consequently, instead of let-ting someone else say "obey," it is at this point, once one has gotten an adequate idea of one's own knowledge and its limits, that the principle of autonomy can be discovered. One will then no longer have to hear the *obey;* or rather, the *obey* will be founded on autonomy itself.

I am not attempting to show the opposition there may be between Kant's analysis of the *Aufklärung* and his critical project. I think it would be easy to show that for Kant himself, this true courage to know which was put forward by the *Aufklärung,* this same courage to know involved recognizing the limits of knowledge. It would also be easy to show that, for Kant, autonomy is not at all opposed to obeying the sovereign. Nevertheless, in his attempt to desubjugate the subject in the context of power and truth, as a prolegomena to the whole present and future *Aufklärung,* Kant set forth critique's primordial responsibil-ity, to know knowledge.

I would not like to insist any further on the implications of this kind of gap be-tween *Aufklärung* and critique that Kant wanted to indicate. I would simply like to insist on this historical aspect of the problem which is suggested to us by what happened in the nineteenth century. The history of the nineteenth century of-fered a greater opportunity to pursue the critical enterprise that Kant had in some way situated at a distance from the *Aufklärung,* than it did for something like the *Aufklärung* itself. In other words, nineteenth-century history—and, of course, twentieth-century history, even more so—seem to have to side with Kant or at least provide a concrete hold on this new critical attitude, this critical attitude set back from the *Aufklärung,* and which Kant had made possible.

This historical hold, seemingly afforded much more to Kantian critique than to the courage of the *Aufklärung,* was characterized very simply by the follow-ing three basic features: first, positivist science, that is to say, it basically had confidence in itself, even when it remained carefully critical of each one of its results; second, the development of a state or a state system which justified itself as the reason and deep rationality of history and which, moreover, selected as its instruments procedures to rationalize the economy and society; and hence, the third feature, this stitching together of scientific positivism and the develop-ment of states, a science of the state, or a statism, if you like, A fabric of tight re-lationships is woven between them such that science is going to play an increasingly determinant part in the development of productive forces and, such that, in addition, state-type powers are going to be increasingly exercised through refined techniques. Thus, the fact that the 1784 question, *What is Auf-klärung?,* or rather the way in which Kant, in terms of this question and the an-swer he gave it, tried to situate his critical enterprise, this questioning about the relationships between *Aufklärung* and *Critique* is going to legitimately arouse suspicion or, in any case, more and more skeptical questioning: for what excesses of power, for what governmentalization, all the more impossible to evade as it is reasonably justified, is reason not itself historically responsible?

Moreover, I think that the future of this question was not exactly the same in Germany and in France for historical reasons which should be analyzed because they are complex.

Roughly, one can say this: it is less perhaps because of the recent development of the beautiful, all-new and rational State in Germany than due to a very old attachment of the Universities to the *Wissenschaft* and to administrative and state structures, that there is this suspicion that something in rationalization and maybe even in reason itself is responsible for excesses of power, well, then!: it seems to me that this suspicion was especially well-developed in Germany and let us say to make it short, that it was especially developed within what we could call the German Left. In any case, from the Hegelian Left to the Frankfurt School, there has been a complete critique of positivism, objectivism, rationalization, of *technè* and technicalization, a whole critique of the relationships between the fundamental project of science and techniques whose objective was to show the connections between science's naive presumptions, on one hand, and the forms of domination characteristic of contemporary society, on the other. To cite the example presumably the most distant from what could be called a Leftist critique, we should recall that Husserl, in 1936, referred the contemporary crisis of European humanity to something that involved the relationships between knowledge and technique, from *épistèmè* to *technè*.

In France, the conditions for the exercise of philosophy and political reflection were very different. And because of this, the critique of presumptuous reason and its specific effects of power do not seem to have been directed in the same way. And it would be, I think, aligned with a certain kind of thinking on the Right, during the nineteenth and twentieth centuries, where one can again find this same historical indictment of reason or rationalization in the name of the effects of power that it carries along with it. In any case, the block constituted by the Enlightenment and the Revolution has no doubt prevented us in a general way from truly and profoundly questioning this relationship between rationalization and power. Perhaps it is also because the Reformation, that is to say, what I believe was a very deeply rooted, first critical movement of the art of not being governed, the fact that the Reformation did not have the same degree of expansion and success in France as it had in Germany, clearly shows that in France this notion of the *Aufklärung*, with all the problems it posed, was not as widely accepted, and moreover, never became as influential a historical reference as it did in Germany. Let us say that in France, we were satisfied with a certain political valorization of the eighteenth-century philosophers even though Enlightenment thought was disqualified as a minor episode in the history of philosophy. In

Germany, on the contrary, the *Aufklärung* was certainly understood, for better or worse, it doesn't matter, as an important episode, a sort of brilliant manifestation of the profound destination of Western reason. In the *Aufklärung* and in the whole period that runs from the sixteenth to the eighteenth century and serves as the reference for this notion of *Aufklärung*, an attempt was being made to decipher and recognize the most accentuated slope of this line of Western reason whereas it was the politics to which it was linked that became the object of suspicious examination. This is, if you will, roughly the chasm between France and Germany in terms of the way the problem of the *Aufklärung* was posed during the nineteenth and the first half of the twentieth century.

I do believe that the situation in France has changed in recent years. It seems to me that in France, in fact (just as the problem of the *Aufklärung* had been so important in German thought since Mendelssohn, Kant, through Hegel, Nietzsche, Husserl, the Frankfurt School, etc., an era has arrived where precisely this problem of the *Aufklärung* can be re-approached in significant proximity to the work of the Frankfurt School. Let us say, once again to be brief—and it comes as no surprise—that the question of what the *Aufklärung* is has returned to us through phenomenology and the problems it raised. Actually, it has come back to us through the question of meaning and what can constitute meaning. How it is that meaning could be had out of nonsense? How does meaning occur? This is a question which clearly is the complement to another: how is it that the great movement of rationalization has led us to so much noise, so much furor, so much silence and so many sad mechanisms? After all, we shouldn't forget that *La Nausée* is more or less contemporaneous with the *Krisis*. And it is through the analysis, after the war, of the following, that meaning is being solely constituted by systems of constraints characteristic of the signifying machinery. It seems to me that it is through the analysis of this fact whereby meaning only exists through the effects of coercion which are specific to these structures that, by a strange short-cut, the problem between *ratio* and *power* was rediscovered. I also think (and this would definitely be a study to do) that—analyzing the history of science, this whole problematization of the history of the sciences (no doubt also rooted in phenomenology which, in France, by way of Cavaillès, via Bachelard and through Georges Canguilhem, belongs to another history altogether)—the historical problem of the historicity of the sciences has some relationships to and analogies with and echoes, to some degree, this problem of the constitution of meaning. How is this rationality born? How is it formed from something which is totally different from it? There we have the reciprocal and inverse problem of that of the *Aufklärung*: how is it that rationalization leads to the furor of power?

So it seems that whether it be the research on the constitution of meaning with the discovery that meaning is only constituted by the coercive structures of the signifier or analyses done on the history of scientific rationality with the effects of constraint linked to its institutionalization and the constitution of models, all this, all this historical research has done, I believe, is break in like a ray of morning light through a kind of narrow academic window to merge into what was, after all, the deep undertow of our history for the past century. For all the claim that our social and economic organization lacked rationality, we found ourselves facing I don't know if it's too much or too little reason, but in any case surely facing too much power. For all the praises we lavished on the promises of the revolution, I don't know if it is a good or a bad thing where it actually occurred, but we found ourselves faced with the inertia of a power which was maintaining itself indefinitely. And for all our vindication of the opposition between ideologies of violence and the veritable scientific theory of society, that of the proletariat and of history, we found ourselves with two forms of power that resembled each other like two brothers: Fascism and Stalinism. Hence, the question returns: what is the *Aufklärung?* Consequently, the series of problems which distinguished the analyses of Max Weber is reactivated: where are we with this rationalization which can be said to characterize not only Western thought and science since the 16th century, but also social relationships, state organizations, economic practices and perhaps even individual behaviors? What about this rationalization with its effects of constraint and maybe of obnubilation, of the never radically contested but still all massive and ever-growing establishment of a vast technical and scientific system?

This problem, for which in France we must now shoulder the responsibility, is this problem of what is the *Aufklärung?* We can approach it in different ways. And the way in which I would like to approach this—you should trust me about it—is absolutely not evoked here to be critical or polemical. For these two reasons I am seeking nothing else than to point out differences and somehow see up to what point we can multiply them, disseminate them, and distinguish them in terms of each other, displacing, if you will, the forms of analyses of this *Aufklärung* problem, which is perhaps, after all, the problem of modern philosophy.

In tackling this problem which shows our fellowship with the Frankfurt School, I would like, in any case, to immediately note that making the *Aufklärung* the central question definitely means a number of things. First, it means that we are engaging a certain historical and philosophical practice which has nothing to do with the philosophy of history or the history of philosophy. It is a certain historical-philosophical practice, and by that I mean that the domain of experience referred to by this philosophical work in no way excludes any other. It is neither inner experience, nor the fundamental structures of scientific knowledge. It is also not a group of historical contents elaborated elsewhere, treated by historians and received as ready-made facts. Actually, in this historical-philosophical practice, one has to make one's own history, fabricate history, as if through fiction, in terms of how it would be traversed by the question of the relationships between structures of rationality which articulate true discourse and the mechanisms of subjugation which are linked to it. This is evidently a question which displaces the historical objects familiar to historians towards the problem of the subject and the truth about which historians are not usually concerned. We also see that this question invests philosophical work, philosophical thought and the philosophical analysis in empirical contents designed by it. It follows, if you will, that historians faced with this historical or philosophical work are going to say: "yes, of course, yes, maybe." In any case, it is never exactly right, given the effect of interference due to the displacement toward the subject and the truth about which I was speaking. And even if they don't take on an air of offended guinea-fowls, philosophers generally think: "philosophy, in spite of everything, is something else altogether." And this is due to the effect of falling, of returning to an empiricity which is not even grounded in inner experience.

Let us grant these sideline voices all the importance they deserve, and it is indeed a great deal of importance. They indicate at least negatively that we are on the right path, and by this I mean that through the historical contents that we elaborate and to which we adhere because they are true or because they are valued as true, the question is being raised: "what, therefore, am I," I who belong to this humanity, perhaps to this piece of it, at this point in time, at this instant of humanity which is subjected to the power of truth in general and truths in particular? The first characteristic of this historical-philosophical practice, if you will, is to desubjectify the philosophical question by way of historical contents, to liberate historical contents by examining the effects of power whose truth affects them and from which they supposedly derive. In addition, this historical-philosophical practice is clearly found in the privileged relationship to a certain period which can be determined empirically. Even if it is relatively and necessarily vague, the Enlightenment period is certainly designated as a formative stage for modern humanity. This is the *Aufklärung* in the wide sense of the term to which Kant, Weber, etc. referred, a period without fixed dates, with multiple points of entry since one can also define it by the formation of capitalism, the constitution of the bourgeois world, the establishment of state systems, the foundation of modern science with all its correlative techniques, the organization of a confrontation between the art of being governed and that of not being quite so governed. Consequently, this is a privileged period for historical-philosophical work, since these relationships between power, truth and the subject appear live on the surface of visible transformations. Yet it is also a privilege in the sense that one has to form a matrix from it in order to transit through a whole series of other possible domains. Let us say, if you will, that it is not because we privilege the eighteenth century, because we are interested in it, that we encounter the problem of the *Aufklärung*. I would say instead that it is because we fundamentally want to ask the question, *What is Aufklärung?* that we encounter the historical scheme of our modernity. The point is not to say that the Greeks of the fifth century are a little like the philosophers of the eighteenth or that the twelfth century was already a kind of Renaissance, but rather to try to see under what conditions, at the cost of which modifications or generalizations we can apply this question of the *Aufklärung* to any moment in history, that is, the question of the relationships between power, truth and the subject.

Such is the general framework of this research I would call historical-philosophical. Now we will see how we can conduct it.

I was saying before that I wanted in any case to very vaguely trace possible tracks other than those which seemed to have been up till now most willingly cleared. This in no way accuses the latter of leading nowhere or of not providing any valid results. I would simply like to say and suggest the following: it seems to me that this question of the *Aufklärung*, since Kant, because of Kant, and presumably because of this separation he introduced between *Aufklärung* and *critique*, was essentially raised in terms of knowledge *(connaissance)*, that is, by starting with what was the historical destiny of knowledge at the time of the constitution of modern science. Also, by looking for what in this destiny already indicated the indefinite effects of power to which this question was necessarily going to be linked through objectivism, positivism, technicism, etc., by connecting this knowledge with the conditions of the constitution and legitimacy of all possible knowledge, and finally, by seeing how the exit from legitimacy (illusion, error, forgetting, recovery, etc.) occurred in history. In a word, this is the procedure of analysis that seems to me to have been deeply mobilized by the gap between *critique* and *Aufklärung* engineered by Kant. I believe that from this point on, we see a procedure of analysis which is basically the one most often followed, an analytical procedure which could be called an investigation into the legitimacy of historical modes of knowing *(connaître)*. It is in this way, in any case, that many eighteenth-century philosophers understood it, it is also how Dilthey, Habermas, etc., understood it. Still, more simply put: what false idea has knowledge gotten of itself and what excessive use has it exposed itself to, to what domination is it therefore linked?

Well, now! Rather than this procedure which takes shape as an investigation into the legitimacy of historical modes of knowing, we can perhaps envision a different procedure. It may take the question of the *Aufklärung* as its way of gaining access, not to the problem of knowledge, but to that of power. It would proceed not as an investigation into legitimacy, but as something I would call an examination of *"eventalization" (événementialisation)*. Forgive me for this horrible word! And, right away, what does it mean? What I understand by the pro-

cedure of eventalization, whilst historians cry out in grief, would be the following: first, one takes groups of elements where, in a totally empirical and temporary way, connections between mechanisms of coercion and contents of
knowledge can be identified. Mechanisms of different types of coercion, maybe
also legislative elements, rules, material set-ups, authoritative phenomena, etc.
One would also consider the contents of knowledge in terms of their diversity
and heterogeneity, view them in the context of the effects of power they generate in as much as they are validated by their belonging to a system of knowledge. We are therefore not attempting to find out what is true or false, founded
or unfounded, real or illusory, scientific or ideological, legitimate or abusive.
What we are trying to find out is what are the links, what are the connections
that can be identified between mechanisms of coercion and elements of knowledge, what is the interplay of relay and support developed between them, such
that a given element of knowledge takes on the effects of power in a given system where it is allocated to a true, probable, uncertain or false element, such that
a procedure of coercion acquires the very form and justifications of a rational,
calculated, technically efficient element, etc.

Therefore, on this first level, there is no case made here for the attribution of
legitimacy, no assigning points of error and illusion.

And this is why, at this level, it seems to me that one can use two words whose
function is not to designate entities, powers *(puissances)* or something like transcendentals, but rather to perform a systematic reduction of value for the domains to which they refer, let us say, a neutralization concerning the effects of
legitimacy and an elucidation of what makes them at some point acceptable and
in fact, had them accepted. Hence, the use of the word knowledge *(savoir)* that
refers to all procedures and all effects of knowledge *(connaissance)* which are
acceptable at a given point in time and in a specific domain; and secondly, the
term power *(pouvoir)* which merely covers a whole series of particular mechanisms, definable and defined, which seem likely to induce behaviors or discourses. We see right away that these two terms only have a methodological
function. It is not a matter of identifying general principles of reality through
them, but of somehow pinpointing the analytical front, the type of element that
must be pertinent for the analysis. It is furthermore a matter of preventing the
perspective of legitimation from coming into play as it does when the terms
knowledge *(connaissance)* or domination are used. It is also important, at every
stage in the analysis, to be able to give knowledge and power a precise and determined content: such and such an element of knowledge, such and such a
mechanism of power. No one should ever think that there exists *one* knowledge
or *one* power, or worse, *knowledge* or *power* which would operate in and of themselves. Knowledge and power are only an analytical grid. We also see that this
grid is not made up of two categories with elements which are foreign to one an-

other, with what would be from knowledge on one side and what would be from power, on the other—and what I was saying before about them made them exterior to one another—for nothing can exist as an element of knowledge if, on one hand, it does not conform to a set of rules and constraints characteristic, for example, of a given type of scientific discourse in a given period, and if, on the other hand, it does not possess the effects of coercion or simply the incentives peculiar to what is scientifically validated or simply rational or simply generally accepted, etc. Conversely, nothing can function as a mechanism of power if it is not deployed according to procedures, instruments, means, and objectives which can be validated in more or less coherent systems of knowledge. It is therefore not a matter of describing what knowledge is and what power is and how one would repress the other or how the other would abuse the one, but rather, a nexus of knowledge-power has to be described so that we can grasp what constitutes the acceptability of a system, be it the mental health system, the penal system, delinquency, sexuality, etc.

In short, it seems that from the empirical observability for us of an ensemble to its historical acceptability, to the very period of time during which it is actually observable, the route goes by way of an analysis of the knowledge-power nexus supporting it, recouping it at the point where it is accepted, moving toward what makes it acceptable, of course, not in general, but only where it is accepted. This is what can be characterized as recouping it in its positivity. Here, then, is a type of procedure which, unconcerned with legitimizing and consequently, excluding the fundamental point of view of the law, runs through the cycle of positivity by proceeding from the fact of acceptance to the system of acceptability analyzed through the knowledge-power interplay. Let us say that this is, approximately, the *archeological* level.

Secondly, one sees right away from this type of analysis that there are several dangers which cannot fail to appear as its negative and costly consequences.

These positivities are ensembles which are not at all obvious in the sense that whatever habits or routines may have made them familiar to us, whatever the blinding force of the power mechanisms they call into play or whatever justifications they may have developed, they were not made acceptable by any originally existing right. And what must be extracted in order to fathom what could have made them acceptable is precisely that they were not at all obvious, that they were not inscribed in any *a priori,* nor contained in any precedent. There are two correlative operations to perform: bring out the conditions of acceptability of a system and follow the breaking points which indicate its emergence. It was not at all obvious that madness and mental illness were superimposed in the institutional and scientific system of psychiatry. It was not a given either that punishment, imprisonment and penitentiary discipline had come to be articulated in the penal system. It was also not a given that desire, concupiscence and individuals' sexual behavior had to actually be articulated one upon the other in a system of knowledge and normality called sexuality. The identification of the acceptability of a system cannot be dissociated from identifying what made it difficult to accept: its arbitrary nature in terms of knowledge, its violence in terms of power, in short, its energy. Hence, it is necessary to take responsibility for this structure in order to better account for its artifices.

The second consequence is also costly and negative, for these ensembles are not analyzed as universals to which history, with its particular circumstances, would add a number of modifications. Of course, many accepted elements, many conditions of acceptability may have a long history, but what has to be recovered in some way through the analysis of these positivities are not incarnations of an essence, or individualizations of a species, but rather, pure singularities: the singularity of madness in the modern Western world, the absolute singularity of sexuality, the absolute singularity of our moral-legal system of punishment.

There is no foundational recourse, no escape within a pure form. This is, without a doubt, one of the most important and debatable aspects of this historical-philosophical approach. If it neither wants to swing toward the philosophy of history, nor toward historical analysis, then it has to keep itself within the field of immanence of pure singularities. Then what? Rupture, discontinuity, singularity, pure description, still tableau, no explanation, dead-end, you know all that. One may say that the analysis of positivities does not partake in these so-called explicative procedures to which are attributed causal value according to three conditions:

1. causal value is only recognized in explanations targeting a final authority, valorized as a profound and unique agency; for some, it is economics; for others, demography;
2. causal value is only recognized for that which obeys a pyramid formation pointing towards the cause or causal focus, the unitary origin;
3. and, finally, causal value is only recognized for that which establishes a certain unavoidability, or at least, that which approaches necessity.

The analysis of positivities, to the degree that these are pure singularities which are assigned not to a species or an essence, but to simple conditions of acceptability, well then, this analysis requires the deployment of a complex and tight causal network, but presumably of another kind, the kind which would not obey this requirement of being saturated by a deep, unitary, pyramidal and necessary principle. We have to establish a network which accounts for this singularity as an effect. Hence there is a need for a multiplicity of relationships, a differentiation between different types of relationships, between different forms of necessity among connections, a deciphering of circular interactions and actions taking into account the intersection of heterogeneous processes. There is, therefore, nothing more foreign to such an analysis than the rejection of causality. Nevertheless, what is very important is not that such analyses bring a whole group of derived phenomena back to a cause, but rather that they are capable of making a singular positivity intelligible precisely in terms of that which makes it singular.

Let us say, roughly, that as opposed to a genesis oriented towards the unity of some principial cause burdened with multiple descendants, what is proposed instead is a *genealogy*, that is, something that attempts to restore the conditions for the appearance of a singularity born out of multiple determining elements of which it is not the product, but rather the effect. A process of making it intelligible but with the clear understanding that this does not function according to any principle of closure. There is no principle of closure for several reasons.

The first is that this singular effect can be accounted for in terms of relationships which are, if not totally, at least predominantly, relationships of interactions between individuals or groups. In other words, these relationships involve subjects, types of behavior, decisions and choices. It is not in the nature of things that we are likely to find support. Support for this network of intelligible relationships is in the logic inherent to the context of interactions with its always variable margins of non-certainty.

There is also no closure because the relationships we are attempting to establish to account for a singularity as an effect, this network of relationships must not make up one plane only. These relationships are in perpetual slippage from one another. At a given level, the logic of interactions operates between individuals who are able to respect its singular effects, both its specificity and its rules, while managing along with other elements interactions operating at another level, such that, in a way, none of these interactions appears to be primary or absolutely totalizing. Each interaction can be re-situated in a context that exceeds it and conversely, however local it may be, each has an effect or possible effect on the interaction to which it belongs and by which it is enveloped. Therefore, schematically speaking, we have perpetual mobility, essential fragility or rather the complex interplay between what replicates the same process and what transforms it. In short, here we would have to bring out a whole form of analyses which could be called *strategics*.

In speaking of archeology, strategy and genealogy, I am not thinking of three successive levels which would be derived, one from the other, but of characterizing three necessarily contemporaneous dimensions in the same analysis. These three dimensions, by their very simultaneity, should allow us to recoup whatever positivities there are, that is, those conditions which make acceptable a singularity whose intelligibility is established by identifying interactions and strategies within which it is integrated. It is such research accounting for . . . [*a few sentences are missing here where the tape was turned over*] . . . produced as an effect, and finally *eventalization* in that we have to deal with something whose stability, deep rootedness and foundation is never such that we cannot in one way or another envisage, if not its disappearance then at least, identifying by what and from what its disappearance is possible.

I was saying before that instead of defining the problem in terms of knowledge and legitimation, it was necessary to approach the question in terms of power and eventualization. As you see, one does not have to work with power understood as domination, as mastery, as a fundamental given, a unique principle, explanation or irreducible law. On the contrary, it always has to be considered in relation to a field of interactions, contemplated in a relationship which cannot be dissociated from forms of knowledge. One always has to think about it in such a way as to see how it is associated with a domain of possibility and consequently, of reversibility, of possible reversal.

Thus you see that the question is no longer through what error, illusion, oversight, or illegitimacy has knowledge come to induce effects of domination manifested in the modern world by the hegemony of [*inaudible*]. The question instead would be: how can the indivisibility of knowledge and power in the context of interactions and multiple strategies induce both singularities, fixed according to their conditions of acceptability, and a field of possibles, of openings, indecisions, reversals and possible dislocations which make them fragile, temporary, and which turn these effects into events, nothing more, nothing less than events? In what way can the effects of coercion characteristic of these positivities not be dissipated by a return to the legitimate destination of knowledge and by a reflection on the transcendental or semi-transcendental that fixes knowledge, but how can they instead be reversed or released from within a concrete strategic field, this concrete strategic field that induced them, starting with this decision not to be governed?

In conclusion, given the movement which swung critical attitude over into the question of critique or better yet, the movement responsible for reassessing the *Aufklärung* enterprise within the critical project whose intent was to allow knowledge to acquire an adequate idea of itself—given this swinging movement, this slippage, this way of deporting the question of the *Aufklärung* into critique—might it not now be necessary to follow the opposite route? Might we not try to travel this road, but in the opposite direction? And if it is necessary to ask the question about knowledge in its relationship to domination, it would be, first and foremost, from a certain decision-making will not to be governed, the decision-making will, both an individual and collective attitude which meant, as Kant said, to get out of one's minority. A question of attitude. You see now why I could not, did not dare, give a title to my conference since if I had, it would have been: "What is the *Aufklärung*?"

LIVES OF INFAMOUS MEN

This is not a book of history. The selection found here was guided by nothing more substantial than my taste, my pleasure, an emotion, laughter, surprise, a certain dread, or some other feeling whose intensity I might have trouble justifying, now that the first moment of discovery has passed.

It's an anthology of existences. Lives of a few lines or a few pages, nameless misfortunes and adventures gathered into a handful of words. Brief lives, encountered by chance in books and documents. *Exempla,* but unlike those collected by the sages in the course of their reading, they are examples that convey not so much lessons to ponder as brief effects whose force fades almost at once. The term "news" would fit them rather well, I think, because of the double reference it suggests: to the rapid pace of the narrative and to the reality of the events that are related. For the things said in these texts are so compressed that one isn't sure whether the intensity that sparks through them is due more to the vividness of the words or to the jostling violence of the facts they tell. Singular lives, transformed into strange poems through who knows what twists of fate—that is what I decided to gather into a kind of herbarium.

As I recall, the idea came to me one day when I was reading, at the Bibliothèque Nationale, a record of Internment written at the very beginning of the eighteenth century. If I'm not mistaken, it occurred to me as I read these two notices:

Mathurin Milan, placed in the hospital of Charenton, 31 August 1707: "His madness was always to hide from his family, to lead an obscure life in the country, to have actions at law, to lend usuriously and without security, to lead

---

This essay is the introduction to an anthology of the prison archives of the Hôpital général and the Bastille, part of a series that Foucault compiled and presented under the collective title *Parallel Lives* (Gallimard). The series includes the memoir of Herculine Barbin and the still untranslated *Le Désordre des familles (The Disorder of Families)*, a volume of "poison pen letters" that Foucault compiled with the historian Arlette Farge.—Eds.

his feeble mind down unknown paths, and to believe himself capable of the greatest employments."

Jean Antoine Touzard, placed in the castle of Bicêtre, 21 April 1701: "Seditious apostate friar, capable of the greatest crimes, sodomite, atheist if that were possible; this individual is a veritable monster of abomination whom it would be better to stifle than to leave at large."

It would be hard to say exactly what I felt when I read these fragments and many others that were similar. No doubt, one of these impressions that are called "physical," as if there could be any other kind. I admit that these "short stories," suddenly emerging from two and a half centuries of silence, stirred more fibers within me than what is ordinarily called "literature," without my being able to say even now if I was more moved by the beauty of that Classical style, draped in a few sentences around characters that were plainly wretched, or by the excesses, the blend of dark stubbornness and rascality, of these lives whose disarray and relentless energy one senses beneath the stone-smooth words.

A long time ago I made use of documents like these for a book. If I did so back then, it was doubtless because of the resonance I still experience today when I happen to encounter these lowly lives reduced to ashes in the few sentences that struck them down. The dream would have been to restore their intensity in an analysis. Lacking the necessary talent, I brooded over the analysis alone. I considered the texts in their dryness, trying to determine their reason for being, what institutions or what political practice they referred to, seeking to understand why it had suddenly been so important in a society like ours to "stifle" (as one stifles a cry, smothers a fire, or strangles an animal) a scandalous monk or a peculiar and inconsequential usurer. I looked for the reason why people were so zealous to prevent the feebleminded from walking down unknown paths. But the first intensities that had motivated me remained excluded. And since there was a good chance that they wouldn't enter into the order of reasons at all, seeing that my discourse was incapable of conveying them in the necessary way, wouldn't it be better to leave them in the very form that had caused me to first feel them?

Whence the idea of this collection, done more or less as the occasion arose. A collection compiled without haste and without a clear purpose. For a long time I thought of presenting it in a systematic order, with a few rudiments of explanation, and in such a way that it would exhibit a minimum of historical significance. I decided against this, for reasons that I will come back to later. I resolved simply to assemble a certain number of texts, for the intensity they seem to me to have. I have appended a few preliminary remarks to them, and I have distributed them so as to preserve, as best I could, the effect of each.

So this book will not answer the purpose of historians, even less than it will others'. A mood-based and purely subjective book? I would say rather—but it may come to the same thing—that it's a rule- and game-based book, the book of a little obsession that found its system. I think that the poem of the oddball usurer or that of the sodomite monk served as a model throughout. It was in order to recapture something like those flash existences, those poem-lives, that I laid down a certain number of simple rules for myself:

- The persons included must have actually existed.
- These existences must have been both obscure and ill-fated.
- They must have been recounted in a few pages or, better, a few sentences, as brief as possible.
- These tales must not just constitute strange or pathetic anecdotes; but, in one way or another (because they were complaints, denunciations, orders, or reports), they must have truly formed part of the minuscule history of these existences, of their misfortune, their wildness, or their dubious madness.
- And for us still, the shock of these words must give rise to a certain effect of beauty mixed with dread.

But I should say a little more about these rules that may appear arbitrary.

I wanted it always to be a matter of real existences: that one might be able to give them a place and a date; that behind these names that no longer say anything, behind these quick words which may well have been false, mendacious, unjust, exaggerated, there were men who lived and died, with sufferings, meannesses, jealousies, vociferations. So I excluded everything in the way of imagination or literature: none of the dark heroes that the latter have invented appeared as intense to me as these cobblers, these army deserters, these garment-sellers, these scriveners, these vagabond monks, all of them rabid, scandalous, or pitiful. And this was owing, no doubt, to the mere fact that they are known to have lived. I likewise ruled out all the texts that might be memoirs, recollections, tableaus, all those recounting a slice of reality but keeping the distance of observation, of memory, of curiosity, or of amusement. I was determined that these texts always be in a relation or, rather, in the greatest possible number of relations with reality: not only that they refer to it, but they be operative within it; that they form part of the dramaturgy of the real; that they constitute the instrument of a retaliation, the weapon of a hatred, an episode in a battle, the gesticulation of a despair or a jealousy, an entreaty or an order. I didn't try to bring together texts that would be more faithful to reality than others, that would merit inclusion for their representative value, but, rather, texts that played a part in the reality they speak of—and that, in return, whatever their inaccuracy, their exaggeration, or

their hypocrisy, are traversed by it: fragments of discourse trailing the fragments of a reality they are part of. One won't see a collection of verbal portraits
here, but traps, weapons, cries, gestures, attitudes, ruses, intrigues for which
words were the instruments. Real lives were "enacted" [*"jouées"*] in these few
sentences: by this I don't mean that they were represented but that their liberty,
their misfortune, often their death, in any case their fate, were actually decided
therein, at least in part. These discourses really crossed lives; existences were
actually risked and lost in these words.

Another requirement of mine was that these personages themselves be obscure; that nothing would have prepared them for any notoriety; that they
would not have been endowed with any of the established and recognized no-
bilities—those of birth, fortune, saintliness, heroism, or genius; that they would
have belonged to those billions of existences destined to pass away without a
trace; that in their misfortunes, their passions, in those loves and hatreds there
would be something gray and ordinary in comparison with what is usually
deemed worthy of being recounted; that, nevertheless, they be propelled by a
violence, an energy, an excess expressed in the malice, vileness, baseness, obstinacy, or ill-fortune this gave them in the eyes of their fellows—and in proportion to its very mediocrity, a sort of appalling or pitiful grandeur. I had gone in
search of these sorts of particles endowed with an energy all the greater for their
being small and difficult to discern.

But in order for some part of them to reach us, a beam of light had to illuminate them, for a moment at least. A light coming from elsewhere. What
snatched them from the darkness in which they could, perhaps should, have remained was the encounter with power; without that collision, it's very unlikely
that any word would be there to recall their fleeting trajectory. The power that
watched these lives, that pursued them, that lent its attention, if only for a moment, to their complaints and their little racket, and marked them with its claw
was what gave rise to the few words about them that remain for us—either because someone decided to appeal to it in order to denounce, complain, solicit,
entreat, or because he chose to intervene and in a few words to judge and decide.
All those lives destined to pass beneath any discourse and disappear without
ever having been told were able to leave traces—brief, incisive, often enigmatic—only at the point of their instantaneous contact with power. So that it is
doubtless impossible to ever grasp them again in themselves, as they might have
been "in a free state"; they can no longer be separated out from the declama-
tions, the tactical biases, the obligatory lies that power games and power relations presuppose.

I will be told: "That's so like you, always with the same inability to cross the
line, to pass to the other side, to listen and convey the language that comes from

elsewhere or from below; always the same choice, on the side of power, of what it says or causes to be said. Why not go listen to these lives where they speak in their own voice?" But, first of all, would anything at all remain of what they were in their violence or in their singular misfortune had they not, at a given moment, met up with power and provoked its forces? Is it not one of the fundamental traits of our society, after all, that destiny takes the form of a relation with power, of a struggle with or against it? Indeed, the most intense point of a life, the point where its energy is concentrated, is where it comes up against power, struggles with it, attempts to use its forces and to evade its traps. The brief and strident words that went back and forth between power and the most inessential existences doubtless constitute, for the latter, the only monument they have ever been granted: it is what gives them, for the passage through time, the bit of brilliance, the brief flash that carries them to us.

In short, I wanted to assemble a few rudiments for a legend of obscure men, out of the discourses that, in sorrow or in rage, they exchanged with power.

A "legend" because, as in all legends, there is a certain ambiguity between the fictional and the real—but it occurs for opposite reasons. Whatever its kernel of reality, the legendary is nothing else, finally, but the sum of what is said about it. It is indifferent to the existence or nonexistence of the persons whose glory it transmits. If they existed, the legend covers them with so many wonders, embellishing them with so many impossibilities, that it's almost as if they had never lived. And if they are purely imaginary, the legend reports so many insistent tales about them that they take on the historical thickness of someone who existed. In the texts that follow, the existence of these men and women comes down to exactly what was said about them: nothing subsists of what they were or what they did, other than what is found in a few sentences. Here it is rarity and not prolixity that makes reality equivalent to fiction. Having been nothing in history, having played no appreciable role in events or among important people, having left no identifiable trace around them, they don't have and never will have any existence outside the precarious domicile of these words. And through those texts which tell about them, they come down to us bearing no more of the markings of reality than if they had come from *La Légende dorée* or from an adventure novel.[1] This purely verbal existence, which makes these forlorn or villainous individuals into quasi-fictional beings, is due to their nearly complete disappearance, and to that luck or mischance which resulted in the survival, through the peradventure of rediscovered documents, of a scarce few words that speak of them or that are pronounced by them. A dark but, above all, a dry legend, reduced to what was said one day and preserved down to our day by improbable encounters.

That is another trait of this dark legend. It has not been transmitted like one that was gilded by some deep necessity, following continuous paths. By nature, it is bereft of any tradition; discontinuities, effacement, oblivion, convergences, reappearances: this is the only way it can reach us. Chance carries it from the beginning. It first required a combination of circumstances that, contrary to all expectations, focused the attention of power and the outburst of its anger on the most obscure individual, on his mediocre life, on his (after all, rather ordinary) faults: a stroke of misfortune that caused the vigilance of officials or of institutions, aimed no doubt at suppressing all disorder, to pick on this person rather than that, this scandalous monk, this beaten woman, this inveterate and furious drunkard, this quarrelsome merchant, and not so many others who were making just as much of a ruckus. And then it had to be just this document, among so many others scattered and lost, which came down to us and be rediscovered and read. So that between these people of no importance and us who have no more importance than they, there is no necessary connection. Nothing made it likely for them to emerge from the shadows, they instead of others, with their lives and their sorrows. We may amuse ourselves, if we wish, by seeing a revenge in this: the chance that enabled these absolutely undistinguished people to emerge from their place amid the dead multitudes, to gesticulate again, to manifest their rage, their affliction, or their invincible determination to err—perhaps it makes up for the bad luck that brought power's lightning bolt down upon them, in spite of their modesty and anonymity.

Lives that are as though they hadn't been, that survive only from the clash with a power that wished only to annihilate them or at least to obliterate them, lives that come back to us only through the effect of multiple accidents—these are the infamies that I wanted to assemble here in the form of a few remains. There exists a false infamy, the kind with which those men of terror or scandal, Gilles de Rais, Guillery or Cartouche, Sade and Lacenaire,[2] are blessed. Apparently infamous, because of the abominable memories they have left, the misdeeds attributed to them, the respectful horror they have inspired, they are actually men of glorious legend, even if the reasons for that renown are the opposite of those that constitute or ought to constitute the greatness of men. Their infamy is only a modality of the universal *fama*. But the apostate friar, the feeble minds lost on unknown paths, those are infamous in the strict sense: they no longer exist except through the terrible words that were destined to render them forever unworthy of the memory of men. And chance determined that these words, these words alone, would subsist. The return of these lives to reality occurs in the very form in which they were driven out of the world. Useless to look for another face for them, or to suspect a different greatness in them; they are no longer anything but that which was meant to crush them—neither more nor less. Such is infamy in the strict sense, the infamy that, being unmixed with ambiguous scandal or unspoken admiration, has nothing to do with any sort of glory.

In comparison with infamy's great collection, which would gather its traces from everywhere and all times, I'm well aware that the selection here is paltry, narrow, a bit monotonous. It comprises documents that all date approximately from the same hundred years, 1660–1760, and come from the same source: archives of confinement, of the police, of petitions to the King, and of *lettres de cachet*. Let us suppose that this may be a first volume and that *Lives of Infamous Men* will be extended to other times and other places.

I chose this period and this type of texts because of an old familiarity. But if the taste I've had for them for years has not diminished, and if I come back to them now, it's because I suspect they manifest a beginning, or at any rate an important event, in which political mechanisms and discursive effects intersected.

These texts from the seventeenth and eighteenth centuries (especially when compared with the flatness of later administrative and police documents) display a brilliance, reveal a splendor of phrasing, a vehemence that belies, in our judgment at least, the pettiness of the affair or the rather shameful meanness of intent. The most pitiful lives are described with the imprecations or emphasis that would seem to suit the most tragic. A comical effect, no doubt: there is something ludicrous in summoning all the power of words, and through them the supreme power of heaven and earth, around insignificant disorders or such ordinary woes. "Unable to bear the weight of the most excessive sorrow, the clerk Duschene ventures, with a humble and respectful confidence, to throw himself at the feet of Your Majesty to implore his justice against the cruelest of all women. . . . What hope must not rise in the breast of this unfortunate one who, reduced to the last extremity, today appeals to Your Majesty after having exhausted all the ways of gentleness, remonstrance, and consideration to bring back to her duty a wife who lacks all sentiment of religion, honor, probity, and even humanity? Such is, Sire, the state of this poor wretch who dares to voice his plaintive appeal to the ears of Your Majesty." Or that abandoned wetnurse who asks for the arrest of her husband on behalf of her four children "who may have nothing to expect from their father but a terrible example of the effects of disorder. Your justice, my Lord, will surely spare them such a degrading lesson, will prevent opprobrium and infamy for me and my family, by rendering incapable of doing any injury to society a bad citizen who will not fail to bring it harm." We may laugh at this, but it should be kept in mind that to this rhetoric, grandiloquent only because of the smallness of the things to which it is applied, power responds in terms that appear no less excessive—with the difference that its words convey the fulguration of its decisions—and their solemnity may be warranted, if not by the importance of what they punish, then by the harshness of the penalty they impose. If some caster of horoscopes is locked up, this is because "there are few crimes she has not committed, and none of which she is not capable. So there is as much charity as justice in immediately ridding the public of so dangerous a woman, who has robbed it, duped it, and scandalized it with impunity for so many years." And about a young addlebrain, a bad son and a ne'er-do-well: "He is a monster of libertinage and impiety. . . . Practices all the vices: knavish, disobedient, impetuous, violent, capable of deliberate attacks on the life of his own father . . . always in the company of the worst prostitutes. Nothing that is said about his knaveries and profligacies makes any impression on his heart; he responds only with a scoundrel's smile that communicates his callousness and gives no reason to think he is anything short of incurable." With the least peccadillo, one is always in the abominable, or at least in the discourse of invective and execration. These loose women and these unruly children do not pale next to Nero or Rodogune. The discourse of power in the Classical age, like the discourses addressed to it, produces monsters. Why this emphatic theater of the quotidian?

Christianity had in large part organized power's hold on the ordinary preoccupations of life: an obligation to run the minuscule everyday world regularly through the mill of language, revealing the common faults, the imperceptible failings even, and down to the murky interplay of thoughts, intentions, and desires; a ritual of confession in which the one speaking is at the same the one spoken about; an effacement of the thing said by its very utterance, but also with an augmentation of the confession itself, which must remain secret, and not leave any other trace behind it but repentance and acts of contrition. The Christian West invented that astonishing constraint, which it imposed on everyone, to tell everything in order to efface everything, to express even the most minor faults in an unbroken, relentless, exhaustive murmur which nothing must elude, but which must not outlive itself even for a moment. For hundreds of millions of men and over a period of centuries, evil had to be confessed in the first person, in an obligatory and ephemeral whisper.

But, from the end of the seventeenth century, this mechanism was encircled and outreached by another one whose operation was very different. An administrative and no longer a religious apparatus; a recording mechanism instead of a pardoning mechanism. The objective was the same, however, at least in part: to bring the quotidian into discourse, to survey the tiny universe of irregularities and unimportant disorders. In this system, though, confession does not play the eminent role that Christianity had reserved for it. For this social mapping and control, long-standing procedures are used, but ones that had been localized up to then: the denunciation, the complaint, the inquiry, the report, spying, the interrogation. And everything that is said in this way is noted down in writing, is accumulated, is gathered into dossiers and archives. The single, instantaneous, and traceless voice of the penitential confession that effaced evil as it effaced itself would now be supplanted by multiple voices, which were to be deposited in an enormous documentary mass and thus constitute, through time, a sort of constantly growing record of all the world's woes. The minuscule trouble of misery and transgression is no longer sent to heaven through the scarcely audible confidence of the confession: it accumulates on earth in the form of written traces. An entirely different type of relations is established between power, discourse, and the quotidian, an altogether different way of governing the latter and of formulating it. For ordinary life, a new mise-en-scène is born.

We are familiar with its first instruments, archaic but already complex: they are the petitions, the *lettres de cachet* or king's orders, the various internments, the police reports and decisions. I won't go back over these things, which are already well known; I'll just recall certain aspects that may account for the strange intensity, and for a kind of beauty that sometimes emanates from these hastily drawn images in which unfortunate men assume, for us who perceive them from such a great distance, the guise of infamy. The *lettre de cachet*, internment, the generalized presence of the police—all that usually evokes only the despotism of an absolute monarchy. But one cannot help but see that this "arbitrariness" was a kind of public service. Except in the rarest of cases, the "king's orders" did not strike without warning, crashing down from above as signs of the monarch's anger. More often than not, they were requested against someone by his entourage—his father and mother, one of his relatives, his family, his sons or daughters, his neighbors, the local priest on occasion, or some notable. They were solicited for some obscure family trouble, as if it involved a great crime meriting the sovereign's wrath: rejected or abused spouses, a squandered fortune, conflicts of interest, disobedient young people, knavery or carousing, and all the little disorders of conduct. The *lettre de cachet* that was presented as the express and particular will of the king to have one of his subjects confined, outside the channels of regular justice, was nothing more than the response to such petitions coming from below. But it was not freely granted to anyone requesting it: an inquiry must precede it, for the purpose of substantiating the claims made in the petition. It needed to establish whether the debauchery or drunken spree, the violence or the libertinage, called for an internment, and under what conditions and for how long—a job for the police, who would collect statements by witnesses, information from spies, and all the haze of doubtful rumor that forms around each individual.

The system of *lettre de cachet* and internment was only a rather brief episode, lasting for little more than a century and limited to France. But it is nonetheless important in the history of power mechanisms. It did not bring about the uninvited intrusion of royal arbitrariness in the most everyday dimension of life. It ensured, rather, the distribution of that power through complex circuits and a whole interplay of petitions and responses. An absolutist abuse? Maybe so, yet not in the sense that the absolute monarch purely and simply abused his own power; rather, in the sense that each individual could avail himself, for his own ends and against others, of absolute power in its enormity—a sort of placing of the mechanisms of sovereignty at one's disposal, an opportunity to divert its effects to one's own benefit, for anyone clever enough to capture them. A certain number of consequences followed from this: political sovereignty penetrated into the most elementary dimension of the social body; the resources of an absolutist political power, beyond the traditional weapons of authority and submission, could be brought into play between subject and subject, sometimes the most humble of them, between family members and between neighbors, and in relations of interests, of profession, of rivalry, of love and hate. Providing one knew how to play the game, every individual could become for the other a terrible and lawless monarch: *homo homini rex*. A whole political network became interwoven with the fabric of everyday life. But it was still necessary, at least for a moment, to appropriate this power, channel it, capture it, and bend it in the direction one wanted; if one meant to take advantage of it, it was necessary to "seduce" it. It became both an object of covetousness and an object of seduction; it was desirable, then, precisely insofar as it was dreadful. The intervention of a limitless political power in everyday relations thus became not only acceptable and familiar but deeply condoned—not without becoming, from that very fact, the theme of a generalized fear. We should not be surprised at this inclination which, little by little, opened up the relations of appurtenance or dependence that traditionally connect the family to administrative and political controls. Nor should we be surprised that the king's boundless power, thus operating in the midst of passions, rages, miseries, and mischiefs, was able to become—despite or perhaps even because of its utility—an object of execration. Those who resorted to the *lettres de cachet* and the king who granted them were caught in the trap of their complicity: the first lost more and more of their traditional prerogatives to an administrative authority. As for the king, he became detestable from having meddled on a daily basis in so many hatreds and intrigues. As I recall, it was the Duke de Chaulieu who said, in the *Mémoires de deux jeunes mariées,* that by cutting off the king's head, the French Revolution decapitated all family men.[3]

For the moment, I would like to single out one element from all the foregoing: with this apparatus comprising petitions, *lettres de cachets,* internment, and police, there would issue an endless number of discourses that would pervade daily life and take charge of the minuscule ills of insignificant lives, but in a completely different manner from the confession. Neighborhood disputes, the quarrels of parents and children, misunderstandings between couples, the excesses of wine and sex, public altercations, and many secret passions would all be caught in the nets of power which stretched through rather complex circuits. There was a kind of immense and omnipresent call for the processing of these disturbances and these petty sufferings into discourse. An unending hum began to be heard, the sound of the discourse that delivered individual variations of behavior, shames, and secrets into the grip of power. The commonplace ceased to belong to silence, to the passing rumor or the fleeting confession. All those ingredients of the ordinary, the unimportant detail, obscurity, unexceptional days, community life, could and must be told—better still, written down. They became describable and transcribable, precisely insofar as they were traversed by the mechanisms of a political power. For a long time, only the actions of great men had merited being told without mockery: only blood, birth, and exploit gave a right to history. And if it sometimes happened that the lowliest men acceded to a kind of glory, this was by virtue of some extraordinary fact—the distinction of a saintliness or the enormity of a crime. There was never a thought that there might be, in the everyday run of things, something like a secret to raise, that the inessential might be, in a certain way, important, until the blank gaze of power came to rest on these minuscule commotions.

The birth, consequently, of an immense possibility for discourse. A certain knowledge of the quotidian had a part at least in its origin, together with a grid of intelligibility that the West undertook to extend over our actions, our ways of being and of behaving. But the birth in question depended also on the real and virtual omnipresence of the monarch; one had to imagine him sufficiently near to all those miseries, sufficiently attentive to the least of those disorders, before one could attempt to invoke him: he had to seem endowed with a kind of physical ubiquity himself. In its first form, this discourse concerning the quotidian was turned entirely toward the king; it was addressed to him; it had to slip into the great ceremonious rituals of power; it had to adopt their form and take on their signs. The commonplace could be told, described, observed, categorized, and indexed only within a power relation that was haunted by the figure of the king—by his real power or by the specter of his might. Hence the peculiar form of that discourse: it required a decorative, imprecatory, or supplicating language. All those little everyday squabbles had to be told with the emphasis of rare events worthy of royal attention; these inconsequential affairs had to be dressed up in grand rhetoric. In subsequent periods, neither the dreary reports of police administration nor the case histories of medicine or psychiatry would ever recapture such effects of language. At times, a sumptuous verbal edifice for relating an obscure piece of meanness or a minor intrigue; at others, a few brief sentences that strike down a poor wretch and plunge him back into his darkness; or the long tale of sorrows recounted in the form of supplication and humility. The political discourse of banality could not be anything but solemn.

But these texts also manifested another effect of incongruity. It often happened that the petitions for internment were lodged by illiterate or semiliterate persons of humble circumstance; they themselves, with their meager skills, or an underqualified scribe in their place, would compose as best they could the formulas or turns of phrase they believed to be required when one addressed the king or high officials, and they would stir in words that were awkward and violent, loutish expressions by which they hoped no doubt to give their petitions more force and truthfulness. In this way, crude, clumsy, and jarring expressions would suddenly appear in the midst of solemn and disjointed sentences, alongside nonsensical words; the obligatory and ritualistic language would be interspersed with outbursts of impatience, anger, rage, passion, rancor, and rebellion. The rules of this stilted discourse were thus upset by a vibration, by wild intensities muscling in with their own ways of saying things. This is how the wife of Nicolas Bienfait speaks: she "takes the liberty of representing very humbly to your Lordship that said Nicolas Bienfait, coachman, is a highly debauched man who is killing her with blows, and who is selling everything having already caused the deaths of his two wives, the first of whom he killed her child in the body, the second of whom after having sold and eaten what was hers, by his bad treatment caused her to die from languishment, even trying to strangle her on the eve of her death. . . . The third, he wishes to eat her heart on the grill, not to mention many other murders he did. My Lord, I throw myself at the feet of Your Highness to beseech Your Mercy. I hope that from your goodness you will render me justice, because my life being risked at every moment, I shall not cease praying to God for the preservation of your health. . . ."

The texts that I've brought together here are homogeneous, and they may well appear monotonous. Yet they function in the element of disparity. A disparity between the things recounted and the manner of telling them; a disparity between those who complain and those who have every power over them; a disparity between the minuscule order of the problems raised and the enormity of the power brought into play; a disparity between the language of ceremony and power and that of rage or helplessness. These are texts that nod in the direction of Racine, or Bossuet, or Crébillon; but they convey a whole stock of popular turbulence, of misery, and violence, of "baseness" as it was called, that no literature in that period could have accommodated. They bring tramps, poor wretches, or simply mediocre individuals onto a strange stage where they strike poses, speechify, and declaim, where they drape themselves in the bits of cloth they need if they wish to draw attention in the theater of power. At times they remind one of a poor troupe of jugglers and clowns who deck themselves out in makeshift scraps of old finery to play before an audience of aristocrats who will make fun of them. Except that they are staking their whole life on the performance: they are playing before powerful men who can decide their fate. Characters out of Céline, trying to make themselves heard at Versailles.

One day, all this incongruity would be swept away. Power exercised at the level of everyday life would no longer be that of a near and distant, omnipotent, and capricious monarch, the source of all justice and an object of every sort of enticement, both a political principle and a magical authority; it would be made up of a fine, differentiated, continuous network, in which the various institutions of the judiciary, the police, medicine, and psychiatry would operate hand in hand. And the discourse that would then take form would no longer have that old artificial and clumsy theatricality: it would develop in a language that would claim to be that of observation and neutrality. The commonplace would be analyzed through the efficient but colorless categories of administration, journalism, and science—unless one goes a little further to seek out its splendors in the domain of literature. In the seventeenth and eighteenth centuries, we are still in the rough and barbarous age when all these mediations don't exist: the body of the *misérables* is brought into almost direct contact with that of the king, their agitation with his ceremonies. There, not even a shared language but, rather, a clash between the cries and the rituals, between the disorders to be told and the rigor of the forms that must be followed. Whence, for us who look from afar at that first upsurge of the everyday into the code of the political, the strange fulgurations that appear, something gaudy and intense that will later be lost, when these things and these men will be made into "matters," into incidents or cases.

An important moment, this one, when a society lent words, turns of phrase, and sentences, language rituals to the anonymous mass of people so that they might speak of themselves—speak publicly and on the triple condition that their discourse be uttered and put in circulation within a well-defined apparatus of power; that it reveal the hitherto barely perceptible lower depths of social existence, and through the access provided by that diminutive war of passions and interests, it offer power the possibility of a sovereign intervention. Dionysius' ear was a small, rudimentary machine by comparison. How light power would be, and easy to dismantle no doubt, if all it did was to observe, spy, detect, prohibit, and punish; but it incites, provokes, produces. It is not simply eye and ear: it makes people act and speak.

This machinery was doubtless important for the constitution of new knowledges [*savoirs*]. It was not unconnected, moreover, with a whole new regime of literature. I don't mean to say that the *lettre de cachet* was at the point of origin of new literary forms; rather, that at the turn of the seventeenth and eighteenth centuries relations of discourse, power, everyday life, and truth were knotted together in a new way, one in which literature was also entangled.

The fable, in the proper sense of the word, is that which deserves to be told. For a long time in Western society, everyday life could accede to discourse only if it was traversed and transfigured by the legendary: it had to be drawn out of itself by heroism, the exploit, adventures, Providence and grace, or occasionally the heinous crime. It needed to be marked with a touch of impossibility—only then did it become expressible. What made it inaccessible enabled it to function as lesson and example. The more extraordinary the tale, the more capable it was of casting a spell or of persuading. In this game of the "exemplary fabulous," indifference to truth and untruth was therefore fundamental. If someone happened to describe the shabby side of reality, this was mainly to produce a comical effect: the mere fact of talking about it made people laugh.

Starting in the seventeenth century, the West saw the emergence of a whole "fable" of obscure life, from which the fabulous was banished. The impossible or the ridiculous ceased to be the condition under which the ordinary could be recounted. An art of language was born whose task was no longer to tell of the improbable but to bring into view that which doesn't, which can't and mustn't, appear—to tell the last and most tenuous degrees of the real. Just as an apparatus was being installed for forcing people to tell the "insignificant" ["*l'infime*"]—that which isn't told, which doesn't merit any glory, therefore, the "infamous"—a new imperative was forming that would constitute what could be called the "immanent ethic" of Western literary discourse. Its ceremonial functions would gradually fade; it would no longer have the task of manifesting in a tangible way the all too visible radiance of force, grace, heroism, and might but, rather, of searching for the things hardest to perceive—the most hidden, hardest to tell and to show, and lastly most forbidden and scandalous. A kind of injunction to ferret out the most nocturnal and most quotidian elements of existence (even if this sometimes meant discovering the solemn figures of fate) would mark out the course that literature would follow from the seventeenth century onward, from the time it began to be literature in the modern sense of the word. More than a specific form, more than an essential connection with form, it was this constraint—I was about to say "principle"—that characterized literature and carried its immense movement all the way to us: an obligation to tell the most common of secrets. Literature does not epitomize this great policy, this great discursive ethic by itself; and, certainly, there is more to literature than that; but that is where it has its locus and its conditions of existence.

Whence its dual relation to truth and to power. Whereas the fabulous could function only in a suspension between true and false, literature based itself, rather, on a decision of nontruth: it explicitly presented itself as artifice while promising to produce effects of truth that were recognizable as such. The importance that was given, in the Classical period, to naturalness and imitation was doubtless one of the first ways of formulating this functioning of literature "in truth." Fiction thus replaced fable, the novel broke free of the fantastical and was able to develop only by freeing itself from it ever more completely. Hence, literature belongs to the great system of constraint by which the West obliged the quotidian to enter into discourse. But literature occupies a special place within that system: determined to seek out the quotidian beneath the quotidian itself, to cross boundaries, to ruthlessly or insidiously bring our secrets out in the open, to displace rules and codes, to compel the unmentionable to be told, it will thus tend to place itself outside the law, or at least to take on the burden of scandal, transgression, or revolt. More than any other form of language, it remains the discourse of "infamy": it has the duty of saying what is most resistant to being said—the worst, the most secret, the most insufferable, the shameless. The fascination that psychoanalysis and literature have exerted on each other for years is significant in this connection. But it should not be forgotten that this singular position of literature is only the effect of a certain system [*dispositif*] of power that traverses the economy of discourses and strategies of truth in the West.

I began by saying that these texts might be read as so many "short stories." That was saying too much, no doubt; none of them will ever measure up to the least tale by Chekhov, Maupassant, or James. Neither "quasi-" nor "subliterature," they are not even the first sketch of a genre; they are the action, in disorder, noise, and pain, of power on lives, and the discourse that comes of it. *Manon Lescaut* tells one of the stories that are presented here.[4]

Notes

1. This is the name given to the collection of lives of saints that was compiled in the eighteenth century by the Dominican Jacques de Voragine, *La Légende dorée* (Paris: Garnier-Flammarion, nos. 132–133, 1967), 2 vols.—Eds.

2. Gilles de Rais was the original Bluebeard (he killed six of his wives, and was discovered by his seventh); Cartouche was a famous highwayman; Sade is the Marquis de, after whom "sadism" is named; Lacenaire was a serial murderer condemned to death during Louis-Bonaparte's tenure (1840s), and also the author of a notorious memoir of his exploits.—Eds.

3. This is an allusion to remarks by the Duke de Chaulieu, reported in the *Lettre de Mademoiselle de Chaulieu à Madame de L'Estorade*, in Honoré de Balzac, *Mémoires de deux jeunes mariées* (Paris: Librairie nouvelle, 1856), p. 59: "En coupant la tête à Louis XVI, la Révolution a coupé la tête à tous les pères de famille."—Eds.

4. A. F. Prévost, *Les Aventures du chevalier Des Grieux et de Manon Lescaut* (Amsterdam, 1733).

SOCIETY MUST BE DEFENDED

In order to conduct a concrete analysis of power relations, one would have to abandon the juridical notion of sovereignty. That model pre-supposes the individual as a subject of natural rights or original powers; it aims to account for the ideal genesis of the state; and it makes law the fundamental manifestation of power. One would have to study power not on the basis of the primitive terms of the relation but starting from the relation itself, inasmuch as the relation is what determines the elements on which it bears: instead of asking ideal subjects what part of themselves or what powers of theirs they have surrendered, allowing themselves to be subjectified [*se laisser assujettir*], one would need to inquire how relations of subjectivation can manufacture subjects. Similarly, rather than looking for the single form, the central point from which all the forms of power would be derived by way of consequence or development, one must first let them stand forth in their multiplicity, their differences, their specificity, their reversibility: study them therefore as relations of force that intersect, interrelate, converge, or, on the contrary, oppose one another or tend to cancel each other out. Finally, instead of privileging law as a manifestation of power, it would be better to try and identify the different techniques of constraint that it brings into play.

If it is necessary to avoid reducing the analysis of power to the scheme suggested by the juridical constitution of sovereignty, if it is necessary to think about power in terms of force relations, must it be deciphered, then, according to the general form of war? Can war serve as an effective analyzer of power relations?

This question overlays several others:

- Should war be considered as a primary and fundamental state of things in relation to which all the phenomena of social domination, differentiation, and hierarchization are considered as secondary?

- Do the processes of antagonism, confrontation, and struggle between individuals, groups, or classes belong, in the last instance, to the general processes of warfare?
- Can the set of notions derived from strategy or tactics constitute a valid and adequate instrument for analyzing power relations?
- Are military and war-related institutions and, in a general way, the methods utilized for waging war, immediately or remotely, directly or indirectly, the nucleus of political institutions?
- But perhaps the question that needs to be asked first of all is this one: How, since when and how, did people begin to imagine that it is war that functions in power relations, that an uninterrupted combat undermines peace, and that the civil order is basically an order of battle?

That is the question that was posed in this year's course. How was war perceived in the background of peace? Who looked in the din and confusion of war, in the mud of battles, for the principle of intelligibility of order, institutions, and history? Who first thought that politics was war pursued by other means?

A paradox appears at a glance. With the evolution of states since the beginning of the Middle Ages, it seems that the practices and institutions of war pursued a visible development. Moreover, they tended to be concentrated in the hands of a central power that alone had the right and the means of war; owing to that very fact, they withdrew, albeit slowly, from the person-to-person, group-to-group relationship, and a line of development led them increasingly to be a state privilege. Furthermore and as a result, war tends to become the professional and technical prerogative of a carefully defined and controlled military apparatus. In short, a society pervaded by warlike relations was slowly replaced by a state equipped with military institutions.

Now, this transformation had scarcely been completed when there appeared a certain type of discourse on the relations of society and war. A historico-political discourse—very different from the philosophico-juridical discourse organized around the problem of sovereignty—makes war the permanent basis of all the institutions of power. This discourse appeared shortly after the end of the wars of religion and at the beginning of the great English political struggles of the seventeenth century. According to this discourse, which was illustrated in England by Coke or Lilburne, in France by Boulainvilliers and later by Du Buat-Nançay,[1] it was war that presided over the birth of states: not the ideal war imagined by the philosophers of the state of nature but real wars and actual battles; laws are born in the middle of expeditions, conquests, and burning cities; but war also continues to rage within the mechanisms of power—or, at least, to constitute the secret driving force of institutions, laws, and order. Beneath the omissions, illusions, and lies that make us believe in the necessities of nature or the functional requirements of order, we are bound to reencounter war: it is the cipher of peace. It continuously divides the entire social body; it places each of us in one camp or the other. And it is not enough to find this war again as an explanatory principle; we must reactivate it, make it leave the mute, larval forms in which it goes about its business almost without our being aware of it, and lead it to a decisive battle that we must prepare for it we intend to be victorious.

Through this thematic, which I have characterized loosely thus far, one can understand the importance of this form of analysis.

1. The subject who speaks in this discourse cannot occupy the position of the universal subject. In that general struggle of which he speaks, he is necessarily on one side or the other; he is in the battle, he has adversaries, he fights for a victory. No doubt, he tries to make right prevail, but the right in question is his particular right, marked by a relation of conquest, domination, or antiquity: rights of triumphant invasions or millennial occupations. And if he also speaks of truth, it is that perspectival and strategic truth that enables him to win the victory. So, in this case, we have a political and historical discourse that lays claim to truth and right, while explicitly excluding itself from juridico-philosophical universality. Its role is not the one that lawmakers and philosophers dreamed of, from Solon to Kant: to take a position between the adversaries, at the center of and above the conflict, and impose an armistice, establish an order that brings reconciliation. It is a matter of positing a right stamped with dissymmetry and functioning as a privilege to be maintained or reestablished, of asserting a truth that functions as a weapon. For the subject who speaks this sort of discourse, universal truth and general right are illusions and traps.

2. We are dealing, moreover, with a discourse that turns the traditional values of intelligibility upside down. An explanation from below, which is not the simplest, the most elementary, the clearest explanation but, rather, the most confused, the murkiest, the most disorderly, the most haphazard. What is meant to serve as a principle of decipherment is the confusion of violence, passions, enmities, revenges; it is also the web of petty circumstances that decide defeats and victories. The dark, elliptical god of battles must illuminate the long days of order, labor, and peace. Fury must account for harmonies. Thus, at the beginning of history and law one will posit a series of brute facts (physical vigor, force, character traits), a series of chance happenings (defeats, victories, successes or failures of conspiracy, rebellions or alliances). And only above this tangle will a growing rationality take shape, that of calculations and strategies—a rationality that, as one rises and it develops, becomes increasingly fragile, more and more spiteful, more closely tied to illusion, to fancy, to mystification. So we have the complete opposite of those traditional analyses

which attempt to rediscover, beneath the visible brutality of bodies and passions, a fundamental, abiding rationality, linked by nature to the just and the good.

This type of discourse develops entirely within the historical dimension. It undertakes not to measure history, unjust governments, abuses, and acts of violence with the ideal principle of a reason or a law but, rather, to awaken, beneath the form of institutions or laws, the forgotten past of real struggles, of masked victories or defeats, the dried blood in the codes. It takes as its field of reference the undefined movement of history. But at the same time it is possible for it to draw support from the traditional mythical forms (the lost age of great ancestors, the imminence of new times and millennial revenge, the coming of a new kingdom that will wipe out the ancient defeats): it is a discourse that will be able to carry both the nostalgia of decaying aristocracies and the ardor of popular revenges.

In summary, as against the philosophico-juridical discourse organized in terms of the problem of sovereignty and law, this discourse which deciphers the continued existence of war in society is essentially a historico-political discourse, a discourse in which truth functions as a weapon for a partisan victory, a discourse at once darkly critical and intensely mythical.

This year's course was devoted to the emergence of that form of analysis: how was war (and its different aspects—invasion, battle, conquest, victory, relations of victors and vanquished, pillage and appropriation, uprisings) used as an analyzer of history and, in a general way, of social relations?

1. One must first set aside some false paternities—that of Hobbes, in particular. What Hobbes calls the "war of all against all" is not in any way a real historical war but a game of representations by which each measures the danger that each represents for him, estimates the others' will to fight, and calculates the risk he himself would be taking if he resorted to force. Sovereignty—whether it involves a "commonwealth by institution" or a "commonwealth by acquisition"—is established not by an act of bellicose domination but, rather, by a calculation that allows war to be avoided. For Hobbes it is nonwar that founds the state and gives it its form.[2]

2. The history of wars as wombs of states was doubtless outlined in the sixteenth century at the end of the wars of religion (in France, for example, in the work of Hotman[3]). But it was mostly in the seventeenth century that this type of analysis was developed. In England, first, in the parliamentary opposition and among the Puritans, with the idea that English society, since the eleventh century, was a society of conquest: monarchy and aristocracy, with their characteristic institutions, were seen as Norman imports, while the Saxon people preserved, not without difficulty, a few traces of their original freedoms.

Against this background of martial domination. English historians such as Coke or Selden[4] restored the chief episodes of England's history; each of these is analyzed either as a consequence or as a resumption of that historically primary state of war between two hostile races with different institutions and interests. The revolution of which these historians are the contemporaries and sometimes the protagonists would thus be the last battle and the revenge of that ancient war.

An analysis of the same type is also found in France, but at a later date and, above all, in the aristocratic circles of the end of the reign of Louis XIV. Boulainvilliers will give it the most rigorous formulation; but this time the story is told, and the rights are asserted, in the name of the victor. By giving itself a Germanic origin, the French aristocracy lays claim to the right of conquest, hence of eminent possession, upon all the lands of the realm and of absolute dominion over all the Gallic or Roman inhabitants; but it also claims prerogatives with respect to royal power, which would have been established originally only by its consent, and which should always be kept within the limits established back then. The history written in this way is no longer, as in England, that of the perpetual confrontation of the vanquished and the victors, with uprising and extracted concessions as a basic category; it will be the history of the king's usurpations or betrayals with regard to the nobility from which he descended, and of his unnatural collusions with a bourgeoisie of Gallo-Roman origin. This scheme of analysis, taken up again by Freret[5] and especially Du Buat-Nançay, was the object of a whole series of polemical exchanges and the occasion of substantial historical research up to the Revolution.

The important point is that the principle of historical analysis was sought in the duality and the war of races. Starting from there and going via the works of Augustin[6] and Amédée Thierry,[7] two types of decipherment of history will develop in the nineteenth century: one will be linked to class struggle, the other to biological confrontation.

This year's seminar was devoted to a study of the category of "the dangerous individual" in criminal psychiatry. The notions connected with the theme of "social defense" were compared with the notions connected with the new theories of civil responsibility, as they appeared at the end of the nineteenth century.

Notes

1. Sir E. Coke, *Argumentum Anti-Normannicum, or an Argument Proving, from Ancient Stories and Records, that William, Duke of Normandy, Made No Absolute Conquest of England by the Word* (London: Derby, 1682); J. Lilburne, *English Birth Right Justified Against All Arbitrary Usurpation* (London, 1645); *An*

Anatomy of the Lord's Tiranny and Injustice (London, 1646); Count H. de Boulainvilliers, *Mémoire pour la noblesse de France contre les ducs et pairs* (n.p., 1717); *Histoire de l'ancien gouvernement de la France, avec XIV lettres historiques sur les parlements ou états généraux* (The Hague: Gesse et Neaulne, 1727), 3 vols.; *Essai sur la noblesse de France, contenant une dissertation sur son origine et son abaissement* (Amsterdam, 1732). Count L.-G. Du Buat-Nançay, *Les Origines ou l'Ancien Gouvernement de la France, de l'Italie, de l'Allemagne* (Paris: Didot, 1757), 4 vols.; *Histoire ancienne des peuples de l'Europe* (Paris: Desaint, 1772), 12 vols.

2. T. Hobbes, *Leviathan, or the Matter, Form and Power of a Commonwealth Ecclesiastical and Civil* (London: Crooke, 1651): *Léviathan: Traité de la matière, de la forme et du pouvoir de la république ecclésiastique et civile*, trans. F. Tricaud (Paris: Sirey, 1971).

3. F. Hotman, *Discours simple et véritable des rages exercés par la France, des horribles et indignes meurtres commis es personnes de Gaspar de Coligny et de plusieurs grands seigneurs* (Basel: Vaullemand, 1573); *La Gaule françoise* (Cologne: Bertulphe, 1574).

4. J. Selden, *England's epinomis* (1610), in *Opera omnia* (London: Walthoe, 1726), vol. 3: *De Jure naturali et gentium juxta disciplinam Ebraerorum libri septem* (London: Bishopius, 1640); *An Historical Discourse of the Uniformity of the Government of England* (London: Walbancke, 1647).

5. N. Freret, *Recherches historiques sur les moeurs et le gouvernement des Français, dans les divers temps de la monarchie: De l'origine des Francs et de leur établissement dans les Gaules*, in *Oeuvres complètes*, vols. 5–6 (Paris: Moutardier, 1796); *Vues générales sur l'origine et le mélange des anciennes nations et sur la manière d'en étudier l'histoire*, ibid., vol. 18.

6. A. J. Thierry, *Histoire de la conquête de l'Angleterre par les Normands, de ses causes et de ses suites jusqu'à nos jours* (Paris: Tessier, 1825), 2 vols.; *Récits des temps mérovingiens, précédés de considérations sur l'histoire de France* (Paris: Tessier, 1840), 2 vols.

7. A. J. Thierry, *Histoire des Gaulois, depuis les temps les plus reculés jusqu'a l'entière soumission de la Gaulle à la domination romaine* (Paris: Sautelet, 1828), 3 vols.

TRUTH AND POWER

Q: *Could you briefly outline the route that led you from your work on madness in the Classical age to the study of criminality and delinquency?*

A: When I was studying during the early fifties, one of the great problems that arose was that of the political status of science and the ideological functions it could serve. It wasn't exactly the Lysenko business that dominated everything, but I believe that around that sordid affair—which had long remained buried and carefully hidden—a whole number of interesting questions were provoked. These can all be summed up in two words: power and knowledge. I believe I wrote *Madness and Civilization* to some extent within the horizon of these questions. For me, it was a matter of saying this: If, concerning a science like theoretical physics or organic chemistry, one poses the problem of its relations with the political and economic structures of society, isn't one posing an excessively complicated question? Doesn't this set the threshold of possible explanations impossibly high? But, on the other hand, if one takes a form of knowledge [*savoir*] like psychiatry, won't the question be much easier to resolve, since the epistemological profile of psychiatry is a low one and psychiatric practice is linked with a whole range of institutions, economic requirements, and political issues of social regulation? Couldn't the interweaving of effects of power and knowledge be grasped with greater certainty in the case of a science as "dubious" as psychiatry? It was this same question which I wanted to pose concerning medicine in *The Birth of the Clinic:* medicine certainly has a much more solid scientific armature than psychiatry, but it too is profoundly enmeshed in social structures. What rather threw me at the time was the fact that the question I was posing totally failed to interest those to whom I addressed it. They regarded it as a problem that was politically unimportant and epistemologically vulgar.

The interview was conducted in June 1976; published in Alessandro Fontana and Pasquale Pasquino, eds., *Microfisica del potere: interventi politici*, trans. C. Lazzeri (Turin: Einaudi, 1977) pp. 3–28.—Eds.

I think there were three reasons for this. The first is that, for Marxist intellectuals in France (and there they were playing the role prescribed for them by the PCF), the problem consisted in gaining for themselves the recognition of the university institutions and establishment. Consequently, they found it necessary to pose the same theoretical questions as the academic establishment, to deal with the same problems and topics: "We may be Marxists, but for all that we are not strangers to your preoccupations, rather, we are the only ones able to provide new solutions for your old concerns." Marxism sought to win acceptance as a renewal of the liberal university tradition—just as, more broadly, during the same period the communists presented themselves as the only people capable of taking over and reinvigorating the nationalist tradition. Hence, in the field we are concerned with here, it followed that they wanted to take up the "noblest," most academic problems in the history of the sciences: mathematics and physics, in short the themes valorized by Pierre Maurice Marie Duhem, Edmund Husserl, and Alexandre Koyré. Medicine and psychiatry didn't seem to them to be very noble or serious matters, nor to stand on the same level as the great forms of classical rationalism.

The second reason is that post-Stalinist Stalinism, by excluding from Marxist discourse everything that wasn't a frightened repetition of the already said, would not permit the broaching of uncharted domains. There were no ready-made concepts, no approved terms of vocabulary available for questions like the power-effects of psychiatry or the political function of medicine, whereas on the contrary innumerable exchanges between Marxists and academics, from Marx via Engels and Lenin down to the present, had nourished a whole tradition of discourse on "science," in the nineteenth-century sense of that term. The price Marxists paid for their fidelity to the old positivism was a radical deafness to a whole series of questions posed by science.

Finally, there is perhaps a third reason, but I can't be absolutely sure that it played a part. I wonder nevertheless whether, among intellectuals in or close to the PCF, there wasn't a refusal to pose the problem of internment, of the political use of psychiatry, and, in more general sense, of the disciplinary grid of society. No doubt, little was then known in 1955–60 of the real extent of the Gulag, but I believe that many sensed it, in any case many had a feeling that it was better not to talk about those things—it was a danger zone, marked by warning signs. Of course, it's difficult in retrospect to judge people's degree of awareness. But, in any case, you well know how easily the Party leadership—which knew everything, of course—could circulate instructions preventing people from speaking about this or that, or precluding this or that line of research. At any rate, if the question of Pavlovian psychiatry did get discussed among a few doctors close to the PCF, psychiatric politics and psychiatry as politics were hardly considered to be respectable topics.

What I myself tried to do in this domain was met with a great silence among the French intellectual Left. And it was only around 1968, and in spite of the Marxist tradition and the PCF, that all these questions came to assume their political significance, with a sharpness I had never envisaged, showing how timid and hesitant those early books of mine had still been. Without the political opening created during those years, I would surely never have had the courage to take up these problems again and pursue my research in the direction of penal theory, prisons, and disciplines.

Q: *So there is a certain "discontinuity" in your theoretical trajectory. Incidentally, what do you think today about this concept of discontinuity, on the basis of which you have been all too rapidly and readily labeled as a "structuralist" historian?*
A: This business about discontinuity has always rather bewildered me. In the new edition of the *Petit Larousse* it says: "Foucault: a philosopher who founds his theory of history on discontinuity." That leaves me flabbergasted. No doubt, I didn't make myself sufficiently clear in *The Order of Things*, though I said a good deal there about this question. It seemed to me that in certain empirical forms of knowledge like biology, political economy, psychiatry, medicine, and so on, the rhythm of transformation doesn't follow the smooth, continuist schemas of development which are normally accepted. The great biological image of a progressive maturation of science still underpins a good many historical analyses; it does not seem to me to be pertinent to history. In a science like medicine, for example, up to the end of the eighteenth century one has a certain type of discourse whose gradual transformation, within a period of twenty-five or thirty years, broke not only with the "true" propositions it had hitherto been possible to formulate but also, more profoundly, with the ways of speaking and seeing, the whole ensemble of practices which served as supports for medical knowledge. These are not simply new discoveries, there is a whole new "regime" in discourse and forms of knowledge. And all this happens in the space of a few years. This is something that is undeniable, once one has looked at the texts with sufficient attention. My problem was not at all to say "*Voilà*, long live discontinuity, we are in the discontinuous and a good thing too," but to pose the question "How is it that at certain moments and in certain orders of knowledge, there are these sudden take-offs, these hastenings of evolution, these transformations which fail to correspond to the calm, continuist image that is normally accredited?" But the important thing here is not that such changes can be rapid and extensive or, rather, it is that this extent and rapidity are only the sign of something else—a modification in the rules of formation of statements which are accepted as scientifically true. Thus, it is not a change of content (refutation of old errors, recovery of old truths), nor is it a change of theoretical form (renewal of a paradigm, modification of systematic ensem-

bles). It is a question of what *governs* statements, and the way in which they *govern* each other so as to constitute a set of propositions that are scientifically acceptable and, hence, capable of being verified or falsified by scientific procedures. In short, there is a problem of the regime, the politics of the scientific statement. At this level, it's not so much a matter of knowing what external power imposes itself on science as of what effects of power circulate among scientific statements, what constitutes, as it were, their internal regime of power, and how and why at certain moments that regime undergoes a global modification.

It was these different regimes that I tried to identify and describe in *The Order of Things*, all the while making it clear that I wasn't trying for the moment to explain them, and that it would be necessary to try and do this in a subsequent work. But what was lacking here was this problem of the "discursive regime," of the effects of power peculiar to the play of statements. I confused this too much with systematicity, theoretical form, or something like a paradigm. This same central problem of power, which at that time I had not yet properly isolated, emerges in two very different aspects at the point of junction of *Madness and Civilization* and *The Order of Things*.

Q: *We need, then, to locate the notion of discontinuity in its proper context. And perhaps there is another concept that is both more difficult and more central to your thought, the concept of an event. For, in relation to the event, a whole generation was long trapped in an* impasse, *in that following the works of ethnologists—some of them great ethnologists—a dichotomy was established between structures (the think-able) and the event considered as the site of the irrational, the unthinkable, that which does not and cannot enter into the mechanism and play of analysis, at least in the form which this took in structuralism. In a recent discussion published in the journal* L'Homme, *three eminent anthropologists posed this question once again about the concept of event, and said: The event is what always escapes our rational grasp, the domain of "absolute contingency"; we are thinkers who analyze structures, history is no concern of ours, what could we be expected to have to say about it, and so forth. This opposition, then, between event and structure is the site and the product of a certain anthropology. I would say this has had devastating effects among historians who have finally reached the point of trying to dismiss the event and the "événementiel" as an inferior order of history dealing with trivial facts, chance occurrences, and so on. Whereas it is a fact that there are nodal problems in history which are neither a matter of trivial circumstances nor of those beautiful structures that are so orderly, intelligible, and transparent to analysis. For instance, the "great internment" you described in* Madness and Civilization *perhaps represents one of these nodes which elude the dichotomy of structure and event. Could you elaborate from our present standpoint on this renewal and reformulation of the concept of event?*

A: One can agree that structuralism formed the most systematic effort to evacuate the concept of the event, not only from ethnology but from a whole series of other sciences and in the extreme case from history. In that sense, I don't see who could be more of an antistructuralist than myself. But the important thing is to avoid trying to do for the event what was previously done with the concept of structure. It's not a matter of locating everything on one level, that of the event, but of realizing that there are actually a whole order of levels of different types of events differing in amplitude, chronological breadth, and capacity to produce effects.

The problem is at once to distinguish among events, to differentiate the networks and levels to which they belong, and to reconstitute the lines along which they are connected and engender one another. From this follows a refusal of analyses couched in terms of the symbolic field or the domain of signifying structures, and a recourse to analyses in terms of the genealogy of relations of force, strategic developments, and tactics. Here I believe one's point of reference should not be to the great model of language [*langue*] and signs but, rather, to that of war and battle. The history that bears and determines us has the form of a war rather than that of a language—relations of power, not relations of meaning. History has no "meaning," though this is not to say that it is absurd or incoherent. On the contrary, it is intelligible and should be susceptible of analysis down to the smallest detail—but this in accordance with the intelligibility of struggles, of strategies and tactics. Neither the dialectic, as the logic of contradictions, nor semiotics, as the structure of communication, can account for the intrinsic intelligibility of conflicts. "Dialectic" is a way of evading the always open and hazardous reality of conflict by reducing it to a Hegelian skeleton, and "semiology" is a way of avoiding its violent, bloody, and lethal character by reducing it to the calm Platonic form of language and dialogue.

Q: *In the context of this problem of discursivity, I think one can be confident in saying that you were the first person to pose the question of power regarding discourse, and that at a time when analyses in terms of the concept or object of the "text," along with the accompanying methodology of semiology, structuralism, and so on, were the prevailing fashion. Posing for discourse the question of power means basically to ask whom discourse serves. It isn't so much a matter of analyzing discourse into its unsaid, its implicit meaning, because (as you have often repeated) discourses are transparent, they need no interpretation, no one to assign them a meaning. If one reads "texts" in a certain way, one perceives that they speak clearly to us and require no further supplementary sense or interpretation. This question of power that you have addressed to discourse naturally has particular effects and implications in relation to methodology and contemporary historical researches. Could you briefly situate within your work this question you have posed—if indeed it's true that you have posed it?*

A: I don't think I was the first to pose the question. On the contrary, I'm struck by the difficulty I had in formulating it. When I think back now, I ask myself what else it was that I was talking about in *Madness and Civilization* or *The Birth of the Clinic*, but power? Yet I'm perfectly aware that I scarcely ever used the word and never had such a field of analyses at my disposal. I can say that this was an incapacity linked undoubtedly with the political situation in which we found ourselves. It is hard to see where, either on the Right or the Left, this problem of power could then have been posed. On the Right, it was posed only in terms of constitution, sovereignty, and so on, that is, in juridical terms; on the Marxist side, it was posed only in terms of the state apparatus. The way power was exercised—concretely, and in detail—with its specificity, its techniques and tactics, was something that no one attempted to ascertain; they contented themselves with denouncing it in a polemical and global fashion as it existed among the "other," in the adversary camp. Where Soviet socialist power was in question, its opponents called it totalitarianism; power in Western capitalism was denounced by the Marxists as class domination; but the mechanics of power in themselves were never analyzed. This task could only begin after 1968, that is to say, on the basis of daily struggles at grass-roots level, among those whose fight was located in the fine meshes of the web of power. This was where the concrete nature of power became visible, along with the prospect that these analyses of power would prove fruitful in accounting for all that had hitherto remained outside the field of political analysis. To put it very simply, psychiatric internment, the mental normalization of individuals, and penal institutions have no doubt a fairly limited importance if one is only looking for their economic significance. On the other hand, they are undoubtedly essential to the general functioning of the wheels of power. So long as the posing of the question of power was kept subordinate to the economic instance and the system of interests this served, there was a tendency to regard these problems as of small importance.

Q: *So a certain kind of Marxism and a certain kind of phenomenology constituted an objective obstacle to the formulation of this problematic?*
A: Yes, if you like, to the extent that it's true that, in our student days, people of my generation were brought up on these two forms of analysis, one in terms of the constituent subject, the other in terms of the economic in the last instance, ideology and the play of superstructures and infrastructures.

Q: *Still within this methodological context, how would you situate the genealogical approach? As a questioning of the conditions of possibility, modalities, and constitution of the "objects" and domains you have successively analyzed, what makes it necessary?*
A: I wanted to see how these problems of constitution could be resolved within

a historical framework, instead of referring them back to a constituent object (madness, criminality, or whatever). But this historical contextualization needed to be something more than the simple relativization of the phenomenological subject. I don't believe the problem can be solved by historicizing the subject as posited by the phenomenologists, fabricating a subject that evolves through the course of history. One has to dispense with the constituent subject, to get rid of the subject itself, that's to say, to arrive at an analysis that can account for the constitution of the subject within a historical framework. And this is what I would call genealogy, that is, a form of history that can account for the constitution of knowledges, discourses, domains of objects, and so on, without having to make reference to a subject that is either transcendental in relation to the field of events or runs in its empty sameness throughout the course of history.

Q: *Marxist phenomenology and a certain kind of Marxism have clearly acted as a screen and an obstacle; there are two further concepts that continue today to act as a screen and an obstacle—ideology, on the one hand, and repression, on the other.*

All history comes to be thought of within these categories, which serve to assign a meaning to such diverse phenomena as normalization, sexuality, and power. And, regardless of whether these two concepts are explicitly utilized, in the end one always comes back, on the one hand, to ideology—where it is easy to make the reference back to Marx—and, on the other, to repression, which is a concept often and readily employed by Freud throughout the course of his career. Hence, I would like to put forward the following suggestion: Behind these concepts and among those who (properly or improperly) employ them, there is a kind of nostalgia. Behind the concept of ideology lies the nostalgia for a quasi-transparent form of knowledge, free from all error and illusion, and behind the concept of repression is the longing for a form of power innocent of all coercion, discipline, and normalization. On the one hand, a power without a bludgeon, and, on the other, knowledge without deception. You have called these two concepts, ideology and repression, negative, "psychological," insufficiently analytical. This is particularly the case in Discipline and Punish *where, even if there isn't an extended discussion of these concepts, there is nevertheless a kind of analysis that allows one to go beyond the traditional forms of explanation and intelligibility, which in the last (and not only the last) instance rest on the concepts of ideology and repression. Could you perhaps use this occasion to specify more explicitly your thoughts on these matters? With* Discipline and Punish, *a kind of positive history seems to be emerging, free of all the negativity and psychologism implicit in those two universal skeleton keys.*

A: The notion of ideology appears to me to be difficult to make use of, for three reasons. The first is that, like it or not, it always stands in virtual opposition to something else that is supposed to count as truth. Now, I believe that the problem does not consist in drawing the line between that which, in a discourse, falls under the category of scientificity or truth, and that which comes under some other category; rather, it consists in seeing historically how effects of truth are produced within discourses that, in themselves, are neither true nor false. The second drawback is that the concept of ideology refers, I think necessarily, to something of the order of a subject. Thirdly, ideology stands in a secondary position relative to something that functions as its infrastructure, as its material, economic determinant, and so on. For these three reasons, I think that this is a notion that cannot be used without circumspection.

The notion of repression is a more insidious one, or, in any event, I myself have had much more trouble in freeing myself of it insofar as it does indeed appear to correspond so well with a whole range of phenomena that belong among the effects of power. When I wrote *Madness and Civilization*, I made at least an implicit use of this notion of repression. I think indeed that I was positing the existence of a sort of living, voluble, and anxious madness that the mechanisms of power and psychiatry were supposed to have come to repress and reduce to silence. But it seems to me now that the notion of repression is quite inadequate for capturing what is precisely the productive aspect of power. In defining the effects of power as repression, one adopts a purely juridical conception of such power, one identifies power with a law that says no—power is taken, above all, as carrying the force of a prohibition. Now, I believe that this is a wholly negative, narrow, skeletal conception of power, one that has been curiously widespread. If power were never anything but repressive, if it never did anything but to say no, do you really think one would be brought to obey it? What makes power hold good, what makes it accepted, is simply the fact that it doesn't only weigh on us as a force that says no; it also traverses and produces things, it induces pleasure, forms knowledge, produces discourse. It needs to be considered as a productive network that runs through the whole social body, much more than as a negative instance whose function is repression. In *Discipline and Punish*, what I wanted to show was how, from the seventeenth and eighteenth centuries onward, there was a veritable technological take-off in the productivity of power. Not only did the monarchies of the Classical period develop great state apparatuses (the army, the police, and fiscal administration) but, above all, in this period what one might call a new "economy" of power was established, that is to say, procedures that allowed the effects of power to circulate in a manner at once continuous, uninterrupted, adapted, and "individualized" throughout the entire social body. These new techniques are both much more efficient and much less wasteful (less costly economically, less risky in their results, less open to loopholes and resistances) than the techniques previously employed, which were based on a mixture of more or less forced tolerances (from recognized privileges to endemic criminality) and costly ostentation (spectacular and discontinuous interventions of power, the most violent form of which was the "exemplary," because exceptional, punishment).

Q: *Repression is a concept used, above all, in relation to sexuality. It was held that bourgeois society represses sexuality, stifles sexual desire, and so forth. And when one considers for example the campaign launched against masturbation in the eighteenth century, or the medical discourse on homosexuality in the second half of the nineteenth century, or discourse on sexuality in general, one does seem to be faced with a discourse of repression. In reality, though, this discourse serves to make possible a whole series of interventions, tactical and positive interventions of surveillance, circulation, control, and so forth, which seem to have been intimately linked with techniques that give the appearance of repression or are at least liable to be interpreted as such. I believe the crusade against masturbation is a typical example of this.*

A: Certainly. It is customary to say that bourgeois society repressed infantile sexuality to the point where it refused even to speak of it or acknowledge its existence. It was necessary to wait until Freud for the discovery at last to be made that children have a sexuality. Now, if you read all the books on pedagogy and child medicine—all the manuals for parents that were published in the eighteenth century—you find that children's sex is spoken of constantly and in every possible context. One might argue that the purpose of these discourses was precisely to prevent children from having a sexuality. But their *effect* was to din it into parents' heads that their children's sex constituted a fundamental problem in terms of their parental educational responsibilities, and to din it into children's heads that their relationship with their own body and their own sex was to be a fundamental problem as far as *they* were concerned; and this had the consequence of sexually exciting the bodies of children while at the same time fixing the parental gaze and vigilance on the peril of infantile sexuality. The result was a sexualizing of the infantile body, a sexualizing of the bodily relationship between parent and child, a sexualizing of the familial domain. "Sexuality" is far more one of the positive products of power than power was ever repressive of sex. I believe that it is precisely these positive mechanisms that need to be investigated, and here one must free oneself of the juridical schematism of all previous characterizations of the nature of power. Hence, a historical problem arises, namely that of discovering why the West has insisted for so long on seeing the power it exercises as juridical and negative rather than as technical and positive.

Q: *Perhaps this is because it has always been thought that power is mediated through the forms prescribed in the great juridical and philosophical theories, and that there is a fundamental, immutable gulf between those who exercise power and those who undergo it.*

A: I wonder if this isn't bound up with the institution of monarchy. This developed during the Middle Ages against the backdrop of the previously endemic struggles between feudal power agencies. The monarchy presented itself as a referee, a power capable of putting an end to war, violence, and pillage and saying no to these struggles and private feuds. It made itself acceptable by allocating itself a juridical and negative function, albeit one whose limits it naturally began at once to overstep. Sovereign, law, and prohibition formed a system of representation of power which was extended during the subsequent era by the theories of right: political theory has never ceased to be obsessed with the person of the sovereign. Such theories still continue today to busy themselves with the problem of sovereignty. What we need, however, is a political philosophy that isn't erected around the problem of sovereignty or, therefore, around the problems of law and prohibition. We need to cut off the king's head. In political theory that has still to be done.

Q: *The king's head still hasn't been cut off, yet already people are trying to replace it with discipline, that vast system instituted in the seventeenth century comprising the functions of surveillance, normalization, and control, and, a little later, those of punishment, correction, education, and so on. One wonders where this system comes from, why it emerges and what its use is. And today there is rather a tendency to attribute a subject to it, a great, molar, totalitarian subject, namely the modern state, constituted in the sixteenth and seventeenth centuries and bringing with it (according to the classical theories) the professional army, the police, and the administrative bureaucracy.*

A: To pose the problem in terms of the state means to continue posing it in terms of sovereign and sovereignty, that is to say, in terms of law. If one describes all these phenomena of power as dependent on the state apparatus, this means grasping them as essentially repressive: the army as a power of death, police and justice as punitive instances, and so on. I don't want to say that the state isn't important; what I want to say is that relations of power, and hence the analysis that must be made of them, necessarily extend beyond the limits of the state—in two senses. First of all, because the state, for all the omnipotence of its apparatuses, is far from being able to occupy the whole field of actual power relations; and, further, because the state can only operate on the basis of other, already-existing power relations. The state is superstructural in relation to a whole series of power networks that invest the body, sexuality, the family, kinship, knowledge, technology, and so forth. True, these networks stand in a conditioning-conditioned relationship to a kind of "metapower" structured essentially around a certain number of great prohibition functions; but this metapower with its prohibitions can only take hold and secure its footing where it is rooted in a whole series of multiple and indefinite power relations that supply the necessary basis for the great negative forms of power. That is just what I was trying to make apparent in my book.

Q: *Doesn't this open up the possibility of overcoming the dualism of political struggles that eternally feed on the opposition between the state, on the one hand, and revolution, on the other? Doesn't it indicate a wider field of conflicts than that where the adversary is the state?*

A: I would say that the state consists in the codification of a whole number of power relations that render its functioning possible, and that revolution is a different type of codification of the same relations. This implies that there are many different kinds of revolution, roughly speaking, as many kinds as there are possible subversive recodifications of power relations—and, further, that one can perfectly well conceive of revolutions that leave essentially untouched the power relations that form the basis for the functioning of the state.

Q: *You have said about power as an object of research that one has to invert Clausewitz's formula so as to arrive at the idea that politics is the continuation of war by other means. Does the military model seem to you on the basis of your most recent researches to be the best one for describing power; is war here simply a metaphorical model, or is it the literal, regular, everyday mode of operation of power?*

A: This is the problem I now find myself confronting. As soon as one endeavors to detach power with its techniques and procedures from the form of law within which it has been theoretically confined up until now, one is driven to ask this basic question: Isn't power simply a form of warlike domination? Shouldn't one therefore conceive of all problems of power in terms of relations of war? Isn't power a sort of generalized war that, at particular moments, assumes the forms of peace and the state? Peace would then be a form of war, and the state a means of waging it.

A whole range of problems emerge here. Who wages war against whom? Is it between two classes, or more? Is it a war of all against all? What is the role of the army and military institutions in this civil society where permanent war is waged? What is the relevance of concepts of tactics and strategy for analyzing structures and political processes? What is the essence and mode of transformation of power relations? All these questions need to be explored. In any case, it's astonishing to see how easily and self-evidently people talk of warlike relations of power or of class struggle without ever making it clear whether some form of war is meant, and if so what form.

Q: *We have already talked about this disciplinary power whose effects, rules, and mode of constitution you describe in* Discipline and Punish. *One might ask here, why surveillance? What is the use of surveillance? Now, there is a phenomenon that*

emerges during the eighteenth century, namely the discovery of population as an ob-
ject of scientific investigation; people begin to inquire into birth rates, death rates,
and changes in population, and to say for the first time that it is impossible to govern
a state without knowing its population. M. Moheau for example, who was one of the
first to organize this kind of research on an administrative basis, seems to see its goal
as lying in the problems of political control of a population. Does this disciplinary
power then act alone and of itself, or rather, doesn't it draw support from something
more general, namely, this fixed conception of a population that reproduces itself in
the proper way, composed of people who marry in the proper way and behave in the
proper way, according to precisely determined norms? One would then have, on the
one hand, a sort of global, molar body, the body of the population, together with a
whole series of discourses concerning it, and then, on the other hand, down below, the
small bodies, the docile, individual bodies, the microbodies of discipline. Even if
you are only perhaps at the beginning of your researches here, could you say how you
see the nature of the relationships—if any—engendered between these different
bodies: the molar body of the population and the microbodies of individuals?

A: Your question is exactly on target. I find it difficult to reply because I am
working on this problem right now. I believe one must keep in view the fact that,
along with all the fundamental technical inventions and discoveries of the seventeenth and eighteenth centuries, a new technology of the exercise of power
also emerged which was probably even more important than the constitutional
reforms and new forms of government established at the end of the eighteenth
century. In the camp of the Left, one often hears people saying that power is that
which abstracts, which negates the body, represses, suppresses, and so forth. I
would say instead that what I find most striking about these new technologies of
power introduced since the seventeenth and eighteenth centuries is their concrete and precise character, their grasp of a multiple and differentiated reality.
In feudal societies, power functioned essentially through signs and levies. Signs
of loyalty to the feudal lords, rituals, ceremonies, and so forth, and levies in the
form of taxes, pillage, hunting, war, and so on. In the seventeenth and eighteenth centuries, a form of power comes into being that begins to exercise itself
through social production and social service. It becomes a matter of obtaining
productive service from individuals in their concrete lives. And, in consequence, a real and effective "incorporation" of power was necessary, in the
sense that power had to be able to gain access to the bodies of individuals, to
their acts, attitudes, and modes of everyday behavior. Hence the significance of
methods such as school discipline, which succeeded in making children's bodies
the object of highly complex systems of manipulation and conditioning. At the
same time, though, these new techniques of power needed to grapple with the
phenomena of population, in short to undertake the administration, control,
and direction of the accumulation of men (the economic system that promotes

the accumulation of capital and the system of power that ordains the accumulation of men are, from the seventeenth century on, correlated and inseparable phenomena): hence there arise the problems of demography, public health, hygiene, housing conditions, longevity, and fertility. And I believe that the political significance of the problem of sex is due to the fact that sex is located at the point of intersection of the discipline of the body and the control of the population.

Q: *Finally, a question you have been asked before: The work you do, these preoccupations of yours, the results you arrive at, what use can one finally make of all this in everyday political struggles? You have spoken previously of local struggles as the specific site of confrontation with power, outside and beyond all such global, general instances as parties or classes. What does this imply about the role of intellectuals? If one isn't an "organic" intellectual acting as the spokesman for a global organization, if one doesn't purport to function as the bringer, the master of truth, what position is the intellectual to assume?*

A: For a long period, the "left" intellectual spoke, and was acknowledged the right of speaking, in the capacity of master of truth and justice.[1] He was heard, or purported to make himself heard, as the spokesman of the universal. To be an intellectual meant something like being the consciousness/conscience of us all. I think we have here an idea transposed from Marxism, from a faded Marxism indeed. Just as the proletariat, by the necessity of its historical situation, is the bearer of the universal (but its immediate, unreflected bearer, barely conscious of itself as such), so the intellectual, through his moral, theoretical, and political choice, aspires to be the bearer of this universality in its conscious, elaborated form. The intellectual is thus taken as the clear, individual figure of a universality whose obscure, collective form is embodied in the proletariat.

Some years have now passed since the intellectual was called upon to play this role. A new mode of the "connection between theory and practice" has been established. Intellectuals have become used to working not in the modality of the "universal," the "exemplary," the "just-and-true-for-all," but within specific sectors, at the precise points where their own conditions of life or work situate them (housing, the hospital, the asylum, the laboratory, the university, family and sexual relations). This has undoubtedly given them a much more immediate and concrete awareness of struggles. And they have met here with problems that are specific, "nonuniversal," and often different from those of the proletariat or the masses. And yet I believe intellectuals have actually been drawn closer to the proletariat and the masses, for two reasons. First, because it has been a question of real, material, everyday struggles; and second, because they have often been confronted, albeit in a different form, by the same adversary as the proletariat, namely, the multinational corporations, the judicial and police apparatuses, the property speculators, and so on. This is what I would call the "specific" intellectual as opposed to the "universal" intellectual.

This new configuration has a further political significance. It makes it possible if not to integrate them at least to rearticulate categories that were previously kept separate. The intellectual par excellence used to be the writer: as a universal consciousness, a free subject, he was counterposed to those intellectuals who were merely *competent instances* in the service of the state or capital—technicians, magistrates, teachers. Since the time when each individual's specific activity began to serve as the basis for politicization, the threshold of *writing*, as the sacralizing mark of the intellectual, has disappeared. And it has become possible to develop lateral connections across different forms of knowledge and from one focus of politicization to another. Magistrates and psychiatrists, doctors and social workers, laboratory technicians and sociologists have become able to participate—both within their own fields and through mutual exchange and support—in a global process of politicization of intellectuals. This process explains how, even as the writer tends to disappear as a figurehead, the university and the academic emerge if not as principal elements then at least as "exchangers," privileged points of intersection. If the universities and education have become politically ultrasensitive areas, this is no doubt the reason why. And what is called the "crisis of the universities" should be interpreted not as a loss of power but, on the contrary, as a multiplication and reinforcement of their power effects as centers in a polymorphous ensemble of intellectuals who virtually all pass through and relate themselves to the academic system. The whole relentless theorization of writing we saw in the sixties was doubtless only a swan song. Through it, the writer was fighting for the preservation of his political privilege. But the fact that it was precisely a matter of theory, that he needed scientific credentials (founded in linguistics, semiology, psychoanalysis), that this theory took its references from the direction of Saussure, or Chomsky, and so on, and that it gave rise to such mediocre literary products—all this proves that the activity of the writer was no longer at the focus of things.

It seems to me that this figure of the "specific" intellectual has emerged since World War II. Perhaps it was the atomic scientist (in a word or, rather, a name: Oppenheimer) who acted as the point of transition between the universal and the specific intellectual. It's because he had a direct and localized relation to scientific knowledge and institutions that the atomic scientist could make his intervention; but, since the nuclear threat affected the whole human race and the fate of the world, his discourse could at the same time be the discourse of the universal. Under the rubric of this protest, which concerned the entire world, the atomic expert brought into play his specific position in the order of knowledge. And for the first time, I think, the intellectual was hounded by political powers, no longer on account of a general discourse he conducted but because of the knowledge at his disposal: it was at this level that he constituted a political threat. I am only speaking here of Western intellectuals. What happened in the Soviet Union is analogous with this on a number of points, but different on many others. There is certainly a whole study that needs to be made of scientific dissidence in the West and the socialist countries since 1945.

It is possible to suppose that the "universal" intellectual, as he functioned in the nineteenth and early twentieth centuries, was in fact derived from a quite specific historical figure—the man of justice, the man of law, who counterposes to power, despotism, and the abuses and arrogance of wealth the universality of justice and the equity of an ideal law. The great political struggles of the eighteenth century were fought over law, right, the constitution, the just in reason and law, that which can and must apply universally. What we call today "the intellectual" (I mean the intellectual in the political not the sociological sense of the word, in other words, the person who uses his knowledge, his competence, and his relation to truth in the field of political struggles) was, I think, an offspring of the jurist, or at any rate of the man who invoked the universality of a just law, if necessary against the legal professions themselves (Voltaire, in France, is the prototype of such intellectuals). The "universal" intellectual derives from the jurist or notable, and finds his fullest manifestation in the writer, the bearer of values and significations in which all can recognize themselves. The "specific" intellectual derives from quite another figure, not the jurist or notable, but the savant or expert. I said just now that it's with the atomic scientists that this latter figure comes to the forefront. In fact, it was preparing in the wings for some time before and was even present on at least a corner of the stage from about the end of the nineteenth century. No doubt it's with Darwin or, rather, with the post-Darwinian evolutionists that this figure begins to appear clearly. The stormy relationship between evolutionism and the socialists, as well as the highly ambiguous effects of evolutionism (on sociology, criminology, psychiatry, and eugenics, for example) mark the important moment when the savant begins to intervene in contemporary political struggles in the name of a "local" scientific truth—however important the latter may be. Historically, Darwin represents this point of inflection in the history of the Western intellectual. (Zola is very significant from this point of view: he is the type of the "universal" intellectual, bearer of law and militant of equity, but he ballasts his discourse with a whole invocation of nosology and evolutionism, which he believes to be scientific, though he grasps them very poorly in any case, and whose political effects on his own discourse are very equivocal.) If one were to study this closely, one would have to follow how the physicists, at the turn of the century, reentered the field of political debate. The debates between the theorists of socialism and the theorists of relativity are of capital importance in this history.

At all events, biology and physics were to a privileged degree the zones of formation of this new personage, the specific intellectual. The extension of technico-scientific structures in the economic and strategic domain was what gave him his real importance. The figure in which the functions and prestige of this new intellectual are concentrated is no longer that of the "writer of genius" but that of the "absolute savant," no longer he who bears the values of all, opposes the unjust sovereign or his ministers and makes his cry resound even beyond the grave. It is, rather, he who, along with a handful of others, has at his disposal—whether in the service of the state or against it—powers that can either benefit or irrevocably destroy life. He is no longer the rhapsodist of the eternal but the strategist of life and death. Meanwhile, we are at present experiencing the disappearance of the figure of the "great writer."

Now let's come back to more precise details. We accept, alongside the development of technico-scientific structures in contemporary society, the importance gained by the specific intellectual in recent decades, as well as the acceleration of this process since around 1960. Now, the "specific" intellectual encounters certain obstacles and faces certain dangers. The danger of remaining at the level of conjunctural struggles, pressing demands restricted to particular sectors. The risk of letting himself be manipulated by the political parties or trade union apparatuses that control these local struggles. Above all, the risk of being unable to develop these struggles for lack of a global strategy or outside support—the risk, too, of not being followed, or only by very limited groups. In France, we can see at the moment an example of this. The struggle around the prisons, the penal system, and the police-judicial system, because it has developed "in solitary," among social workers and exprisoners, has tended increasingly to separate itself from the forces that would have enabled it to grow. It has allowed itself to be penetrated by a whole naive, archaic ideology that makes the criminal at once into the innocent victim and the pure rebel—society's scapegoat—and the young wolf of future revolutions. This return to anarchist themes of the late nineteenth century was possible only because of a failure of integration of current strategies. And the result has been a deep split between this campaign with its monotonous, lyrical little chant, heard only among a few small groups, and the masses who have good reason not to accept it as valid political currency, but who also—thanks to the studiously cultivated fear of criminals—tolerate the maintenance or, rather, the reinforcement of the judicial and police apparatuses.

It seems to me that we are now at a point where the function of the specific intellectual needs to be reconsidered. Reconsidered but not abandoned, despite the nostalgia of some for the great "universal" intellectuals and the desire for a new philosophy, a new worldview. Suffice it to consider the important results that have been achieved in psychiatry: they prove that these local, specific struggles haven't been a mistake and haven't led to a dead end. One may even say that the role of the specific intellectual must become more and more important in proportion to the political responsibilities which he is obliged willy-nilly to accept, as a nuclear scientist, computer expert, pharmacologist, and so on. It would be a dangerous error to discount him politically in his specific relation to a local form of power, either on the grounds that this is a specialist matter that doesn't concern the masses (which is doubly wrong: they are already aware of it, and in any case implicated in it), or that the specific intellectual serves the interests of state or capital (which is true, but at the same time shows the strategic position he occupies); or, again, on the grounds that he propagates a scientific ideology (which isn't always true, and is anyway certainly a secondary matter compared with the fundamental point: the effects proper to true discourses).

The important thing here, I believe, is that truth isn't outside power or lacking in power: contrary to a myth whose history and functions would repay further study, truth isn't the reward of free spirits, the child of protracted solitude, nor the privilege of those who have succeeded in liberating themselves. Truth is a thing of this world: it is produced only by virtue of multiple forms of constraint. And it induces regular effects of power. Each society has its regime of truth, its "general politics" of truth—that is, the types of discourse it accepts and makes function as true; the mechanisms and instances that enable one to distinguish true and false statements; the means by which each is sanctioned; the techniques and procedures accorded value in the acquisition of truth; the status of those who are charged with saying what counts as true.

In societies like ours, the "political economy" of truth is characterized by five important traits. "Truth" is centered on the form of scientific discourse and the institutions that produce it; it is subject to constant economic and political incitement (the demand for truth, as much for economic production as for political power); it is the object, under diverse forms, of immense diffusion and consumption (circulating through apparatuses of education and information whose extent is relatively broad in the social body, notwithstanding certain strict limitations); it is produced and transmitted under the control, dominant if not exclusive, of a few great political and economic apparatuses (university, army, writing, media); finally, it is the issue of a whole political debate and social confrontation ("ideological" struggles).

It seems to me that what must now be taken into account in the intellectual is not the "bearer of universal values." Rather, it's the person occupying a specific position—but whose specificity is linked, in a society like ours, to the general functioning of an apparatus of truth. In other words, the intellectual has a threefold specificity: that of his class position (whether as petty-bourgeois in the service of capitalism or "organic" intellectual of the proletariat); that of his conditions of life and work, linked to his condition as an intellectual (his field of research, his place in a laboratory, the political and economic demands to which he submits or against which he rebels, in the university, the hospital, and so on); finally, the specificity of the politics of truth in our societies. And it's with this last factor that his position can take on a general significance, and that his local, specific struggle can have effects and implications that are not simply professional or sectoral. The intellectual can operate and struggle at the general level of that regime of truth so essential to the structure and functioning of our society. There is a battle "for truth," or at least "around truth"—it being understood once again that by truth I mean not "the ensemble of truths to be discovered and accepted" but, rather, "the ensemble of rules according to which the true and the false are separated and specific effects of power attached to the true," it being understood also that it's not a matter of a battle "on behalf" of the truth but of a battle about the status of truth and the economic and political role it plays. It is necessary to think of the political problems of intellectuals not in terms of "science" and "ideology" but in terms of "truth" and "power." And thus the question of the professionalization of intellectuals and the division between intellectual and manual labor can be envisaged in a new way.

All this must seem very confused and uncertain. Uncertain indeed, and what I am saying here is, above all, to be taken as a hypothesis. In order for it to be a little less confused, however, I would like to put forward a few "propositions"—not firm assertions but simply suggestions to be further tested and evaluated.

"Truth" is to be understood as a system of ordered procedures for the production, regulation, distribution, circulation, and operation of statements.

"Truth" is linked in a circular relation with systems of power that produce and sustain it, and to effects of power which it induces and which extend it—a "regime" of truth.

This regime is not merely ideological or superstructural; it was a condition of the formation and development of capitalism. And it's this same regime which, subject to certain modifications, operates in the socialist countries (I leave open here the question of China, about which I know little).

The essential political problem for the intellectual is not to criticize the ideological contents supposedly linked to science, or to ensure that his own scientific practice is accompanied by a correct ideology, but that of ascertaining the possibility of constituting a new politics of truth. The problem is not changing people's consciousnesses—or what's in their heads—but the political, economic, institutional regime of the production of truth.

It's not a matter of emancipating truth from every system of power (which would be a chimera, for truth is already power) but of detaching the power of truth from the forms of hegemony, social, economic, and cultural, within which it operates at the present time.

The political question, to sum up, is not error, illusion, alienated consciousness, or ideology; it is truth itself. Hence the importance of Nietzsche.

Notes

1. Foucault's response to this final question was given in writing.

THE BIRTH OF SOCIAL MEDICINE

In my first lecture, I tried to demonstrate that the basic problem did not lie in the opposition of antimedicine to medicine but, rather, in the development of the medical system and the model followed for the "take-off" in medicine and sanitation that occurred in the West from the eighteenth century onward. I emphasized three points that I consider important.

First: Biohistory—that is, the effect of medical intervention at the biological level, the imprint left on human history, one may assume, by the strong medical intervention that began in the eighteenth century. It is clear that humanity did not remain immune to medicalization. This points to a first field of study that has not really been cultivated yet, though it is well marked out.

We know that various infectious diseases disappeared from the West even before the introduction of the twentieth century's great chemical therapy. The plaque—or the set of diseases given that name by chroniclers, historians, and doctors—faded away in the course of the eighteenth and nineteenth centuries, without our really knowing either the reasons for, or the mechanisms of, that phenomenon, which deserves to be studied.

Another notorious case, that of tuberculosis: compared with 700 patients who died of tuberculosis in 1812, only 350 suffered the same fate in 1882, when Koch discovered the bacillus that was to make him famous; and when chemical therapy was introduced in 1945, the number had shrunk to 50. How and for what reason did this retreat of the disease come about? What were the mechanisms that intervened at the level of biohistory? There is no doubt that the change of socio-economic conditions, the organism's phenomena of adaptation and resistance, the weakening of the bacillus itself, as well as the measures of

---

This is the second of two lectures that Foucault delivered at the State University of Rio de Janeiro in October of 1974, both of them on the emergence of what is known as "public health." The first lecture, titled "Crisis of Medicine or Crisis of Anti-medicine?" was published in a Portuguese translation in 1976. This essay appeared in Portuguese in 1977.—Eds.

hygiene and isolation played an important role. Knowledge concerning this subject is far from complete, but it would be interesting to study the evolution of relations between humanity, the bacillary or viral field, and the interventions of hygiene, medicine, and the different therapeutic techniques.

In France a group of historians—including Emmanuel Le Roy Ladurie and Jean-Pierre Peter[1]—has begun to analyze these phenomena. Using conscription statistics from the nineteenth century, they have examined certain somatic developments of the human species.

Second: Medicalization—that is, the fact that starting in the eighteenth century human existence, human behavior, and the human body were brought into an increasingly dense and important network of medicalization that allowed fewer and fewer things to escape.

Medical research, more and more penetrating and meticulous, and the development of health institutions would also merit being studied. That is what we are trying to do at the Collège de France. Some of us are studying the growth of hospitalization and its mechanisms from the eighteenth century to the beginning of the nineteenth century, while others are focusing on hospitals and are planning to carry out a study of the habitat and all that surrounds it: the roads system, transport routes, and mass infrastructure [*équipements collectifs*] that ensure the functioning of everyday life, especially in urban environments.

Third: The economy of health—that is, the integration and improvement of health, health services, and health consumption in the economic development of privileged societies. This is a difficult and complex problem whose antecedents are not very well known. In France, there exists a group devoting itself to this task, the Centre d'Etudes et de Recherches du Bien-être (CEREBRE), which includes Alain Letourmy, Serge Karenty, and Charles Dupuy. It is mainly studying the problems of health consumption over the last thirty years.

THE HISTORY OF MEDICALIZATION

Given that I am mainly concerned with retracing the history of medicalization, I will proceed by analyzing some of the aspects of the medicalization of societies and the population starting in the nineteenth century, taking the French example as my reference since I am more familiar with it. Concretely, I will refer to the birth of social medicine.

It is often remarked that certain criticisms of current medical practice hold that ancient—Greek and Egyptian—medicine or the forms of medicine of primitive societies are social, collective medicines that are not centered on the individual. My ignorance in ethnology and Egyptology prevents me from having an opinion about the issue; but from what I know of Greek history, the idea leaves me puzzled and I don't see how Greek medicine can be characterized as collective or social.

But these are not important problems. The question is whether the modern—that is, scientific—medicine born at the end of the eighteenth century between Giambattista Morgagni and Xavier Bichat, with the introduction of pathological anatomy, is or is not individual. Can we affirm, as some people do, that modern medicine is individual because it has worked its way into market relations? That modern medicine, being linked to a capitalist economy, is an individual or individualistic medicine amenable only to the market relation joining the doctor to the patient, and that it is impervious to the global, collective dimension of society?

One could show that this is not the case. Modern medicine is a social medicine whose basis is a certain technology of the social body; medicine is a social practice, and only one of its aspects is individualistic and valorizes the relations between the doctor and the patient.

In this connection, I would like to refer you to the work of Varn L. Bullough, *The Development of Medicine as a Profession: The Contribution of the Medieval University to Modern Medicine*,[2] in which the individualistic character of medieval medicine becomes evident while the collective dimension of medical activity is shown to be extremely inconspicuous and limited.

What I maintain is that, with capitalism, we did not go from a collective medicine to a private medicine. Exactly the opposite occurred: capitalism, which developed from the end of the eighteenth century to the beginning of the nineteenth century, started by socializing a first object, the body, as a factor of productive force, of labor power. Society's control over individuals was accomplished not only through consciousness or ideology but also in the body and with the body. For capitalist society, it was biopolitics, the biological, the somatic, the corporal, that mattered more than anything else. The body is a biopolitical reality; medicine is a biopolitical strategy.

How was this socialization brought about? I would like to explain my position in terms of certain generally accepted hypotheses. There is no doubt that the human body was politically and socially recognized as a labor force. Yet it seems to be characteristic of the development of social medicine, or of Western medicine itself, that medical power did not concern itself at the start with the human body as labor power. Medicine was not interested in the proletarian's body, the human body, as an instrument of labor. That was not the case before the second half of the nineteenth century, when the problem of the body, health, and the level of productive force of individuals was raised.

The three stages of the formation of social medicine could be reconstructed in this way: first, state medicine, then urban medicine, and, finally, labor force medicine.

STATE MEDICINE

"State medicine" developed primarily in Germany, at the beginning of the eighteenth century. Thinking of this specific problem, one is reminded of Marx's statement that economics was English, politics French, and philosophy German. But, as a matter of fact, it was in Germany in the seventeenth century—long before France and England—that what can be called the science of the state was formed. The concept of *Staatswissenschaft* is a product of Germany. Under the term "science of the state," we can group together two aspects that appeared in that country during that era. First, a field of study [*un savoir*] whose object was the state—not only the natural resources of a society or the living conditions of its population but also the general operation of the political machine. Research concerning the resources and the functioning of states constituted an eighteenth-century German discipline. And second, the expression also denotes the methods by which the state produces and accumulates the knowledge that enable it to guarantee its operation.

The state, as an object of study, as an instrument and locus of acquisition of a specific body of knowledge, developed more rapidly in Germany than in France and England. It isn't easy to determine the reasons for this phenomenon, and historians have not yet given much attention to this question nor to the problem of the birth of a science of the state or of a state-oriented science in Germany. In my opinion, this is explained by the fact that Germany was converted to a unitary state only in the nineteenth century, after having been a mere juxtaposition of quasi-states, pseudo-states, small entities that fell short of "statehood." But it so happened that, as states were forming, state-centered technologies [*savoirs étatiques*] and interest in the very functioning of the state were developing. The small size of the states, their close proximity, their perpetual conflicts and confrontations, the always-unbalanced and changeable relation of force, obliged them to weigh and compare themselves against the others, to imitate their methods and try to replace force with other types of relations.

Large states like France or England, on the other hand, managed to function relatively well, equipped with powerful machines such as the army or the police. In Germany the smallness of the states made this discursive consciousness of the state-directed functioning of society necessary and possible.

There is another explanation for this evolution of the science of the state: the slow development or stagnation of the German economy in the eighteenth century, after the Thirty Years' War and the great treaties of France and Austria.

After the first burst of development in Germany during the Renaissance, a limited form of bourgeoisie appeared, a bourgeoisie whose economic advance was blocked in the seventeenth century, preventing it from finding an occupa-

tion and making a living in commerce and the nascent manufacture and industry. So it sought refuge in service to the sovereigns, forming a corps of func-
tionaries available for the state machine the princes wanted to construct in order
to alter the force relations with their neighbors.

This economically inactive bourgeoisie lined up beside sovereigns confronted with a situation of continuous struggle, and offered them its men, its
competence, its wealth, and so on, for the organization of states. In this way, the
modern concept of the state, with its apparatus, its civil servants, its knowledge,
was to develop in Germany long before in other, politically more powerful countries such as France, or economically more developed ones such as England.

The modern state appeared where there was neither political power nor economic development. It was precisely for these negative reasons that Prussia,
economically less developed and politically more unstable, was that first modern state, born in the heart of Europe. While France and England clung to the
old structures, Prussia became the first modern state.

The only purpose of these historical remarks on the birth, in the eighteenth
century, of a science of the state and of reflection concerning the state, is to try
to explain why and how state medicine was able to appear first in Germany.

At the end of the sixteenth century and the beginning of the seventeenth century, in a political, economic, and scientific climate characteristic of the epoch
dominated by mercantilism, all the nations of Europe began to take an interest
in the health of their populations. Mercantilism was not simply an economic
theory, then, but also a political practice that aimed at regulating international
monetary currents, the corresponding flows of goods, and the productive activity of the population. Mercantilist policy was based essentially on the growth of
production and of the active population—the overall object being to establish
commercial exchanges that would enable Europe to achieve the greatest possible monetary influence and, thereby, to finance the maintenance of armies and
of the whole apparatus that endows a state with real strength in its relations with
others.

With this in view, France, England, and Austria began to evaluate the active
strength of their populations. Thus, birth and death rate statistics appeared in
France and, in England, the great census surveys that began in the seventeenth
century. But at the time, in both France and England, the only health interest
shown by the state had to do with drawing up of tables of birthrate and mortality, which were true indications of the population's health and growth, without
any organized intervention to raise the level of health.

In Germany, on the other hand, a medical practice developed that was actually devoted to the improvement of public health. Frank and Daniel, for example, proposed, between 1750 and 1770, a program aimed in that direction; it was
what was called for the first time a state "medical police." The concept of *Medi-*

zinischepolizei, medical police, which appeared in 1764, implied much more than a simple mortality and birth census.

Programmed in Germany in the middle of the seventeenth century and set up at the end of that century and the beginning of the next, the medical police consisted of:

- A system of observation of sickness, based on information gathered from the hospitals and doctors of different towns and regions, and, at the state level, recording of the different epidemic and endemic phenomena that were observed.

- Another very important aspect that should be noted: the standardization of medical practice and medical knowledge. Up to that point, authority in the matter of medical education and the awarding of diplomas had been left in the hands of the university and, more particularly, the medical guild. Then there emerged the idea of a standardization of medical instruction and, more specifically, of a public supervision of training programs and the granting of degrees. Medicine and doctors were thus the first object of standardization. This concept began by being applied to the doctor before being applied to the patient. The doctor was the first standardized individual in Germany. This movement, which spread to all of Europe, should be studied by anyone interested in the history of the sciences. In Germany, the phenomenon affected doctors, but in France, for example, standardization of activities at the state level concerned the military industry at the start: the production of cannons and rifles was standardized first, in the middle of the eighteenth century, to ensure that any type of rifle could be used by any soldier, any cannon could be repaired in any repair shop, and so on. After standardizing cannons, France went on to "normalize" its professors. The first *écoles normales* designed to offer all professors the same type of training and, consequently, the same level of competence, were created in about 1775 and were institutionalized in 1790–91. France standardized its cannons and its professors; Germany standardized its doctors.

- An administrative organization for overseeing the activity of doctors. In Prussia and the other states of Germany, at the level of the ministry or the central administration, a special office was assigned the task of collecting the data the doctors conveyed; observing how medical investigations were carried out; verifying which treatments were administered: describing the reactions after the appearance of an epidemic disease, and so on; and, finally, issuing directives based on these centralized data. All of this presupposed, of course, a subordination of medical practice to a higher administrative authority.

- The creation of medical officers, appointed by the government, who would take responsibility for a region. They derived their power from the authority they possessed or from the exercise of the authority conferred on them by their knowledge.

Such was the plan adopted by Prussia at the beginning of the nineteenth century, a sort of pyramid going from the district doctor responsible for a population of 6,000 to 10,000 inhabitants, to officers in charge of a much larger region whose population comprised between 35,000 and 50,000 inhabitants. This was when the doctor appeared as a health administrator.

The organization of a state medical knowledge, the standardization of the medical profession, the subordination of doctors to a general administration, and, finally, the incorporation of the different doctors into a state-controlled medical organization produced a series of completely new phenomena that characterized what could be called a "state medicine."

This state medicine, which appeared somewhat precociously, since it existed before the creation of the great scientific medicine of Morgagni and Bichat, did not have the objective of forming a labor force adapted to the needs of the industries that were then developing. It was not the workers' bodies that interested this public health administration but the bodies of individuals insofar as they combined to constitute the state. It was a matter not of labor power but of the strength of the state in those conflicts that set it against its neighbors— economic conflicts, no doubt, but also political ones. Thus, medicine was obliged to perfect and develop that state strength, and this concern on the part of state medicine implied a certain economico-political solidarity. It would be a mistake, therefore, to try to link it to an immediate interest in obtaining a vigorous and available reserve of labor power.

The example of Germany is also important because it shows how, paradoxically, modern medicine appeared at statism's zenith. After these projects were introduced—for the most part at the end of the eighteenth century and the beginning of the nineteenth, after state medicine was established in Germany— no state ventured to propose a medicine that was as clearly bureaucratized, collectivized, and "statized." Consequently, there was no gradual transformation of an increasingly state-administered and socialized medicine. In a very different way, the great clinical medicine of the nineteenth century was immediately preceded by an extremely statized medicine. The other systems of social medicine in the eighteenth and nineteenth centuries were scaled-down variations of this state-dominated administrative model introduced in Germany in those years.

That is a first series of phenomena to which I wish to refer. It has not drawn the attention of historians of medicine, but it was very closely analyzed by George Rosen in his studies on the relationships between cameralism, mercantilism, and the concept of medical police. In 1953 he published in the *Bulletin of the History of Medicine* an article devoted to this problem, titled "Cameralism and the Concept of Medical Police."[3] He also studied it later in his book, *A History of Public Health.*[4]

URBAN MEDICINE

The second form of the development of social medicine is represented by the example of France, where at the end of the eighteenth century a social medicine appeared, seemingly not based on the state structure, as in Germany, but on an entirely different phenomenon—urbanization. Social medicine developed in France in conjunction with the expansion of urban structures.

To find out why and how such a phenomenon occurred, let us do a bit of history. We have to imagine a large French city between 1750 and 1780 as a jumbled multitude of heterogeneous territories and rival powers. Paris, for example, did not form a territorial unit, a region where a single authority was exercised; rather, it was made up of a set of seignorial authorities held by the laity, the Church, the religious communities, and the guilds, authorities with their own autonomy and jurisdiction. And representatives of the state existed as well: the representatives of the crown, the chief of police, the representatives of the high judicial court.

In the second half of the eighteenth century, the problem of the unification of urban authority was raised. At this time, the need was felt—at least in the large conglomerates—to unify the city, to organize the urban corporate body in a coherent and homogeneous way, to govern it by a single, well-regulated authority.

Different factors played a part in this. In the first place, there were undoubtedly economic considerations. As the city was transformed into an important market hub that centralized commercial activities—not only at the regional but also at the national and even international level—the multiplicity of jurisdictions and authorities became more intolerable for the budding industry. The fact that the city was not only a market center but also a place of production made it necessary to resort to homogeneous and coherent mechanisms of regulation.

The second reason was political. The development of cities, the appearance of a poor, laboring population that was transformed during the nineteenth century into a proletariat, was bound to increase the tensions inside the cities. The coexistence of different small groups—guilds, professions, associations, and so on—that were mutually opposed but balanced and neutralized one another, began to reduce down to a sort of confrontation between rich and poor, commoners and bourgeoisie; this resulted in more frequent urban disturbances and insurrections involving more and more people. Although the so-called subsistence revolts—that is, the fact that on the occasion of a price hike or wage cut, the poorest people, no longer able to feed themselves, would pillage the silos, markets, and granaries—were not an entirely new phenomenon in the eighteenth century, they became more and more violent and led to the great disturbances during the time of the French Revolution.

In summary, we may affirm that in Europe, up through the seventeenth century, the major social threat came from the countryside. Poor peasants, who paid more and more taxes, would grab their sickles and set out to storm the castles and towns. The revolts of the seventeenth century were peasant revolts, subsequent to which the cities were unified. In contrast, at the end of the eighteenth century, peasant revolts started to disappear thanks to the raising of the peasants' standard of living—but urban conflicts became more frequent with the formation of an underclass [*plèbe*] undergoing proletarianization. Hence the need for a real political authority capable of dealing with the problem of this urban population.

It was during this period that a feeling of fear, of anxiety, about cities emerged and grew. For example, in reference to cities, the late eighteenth-century philosopher Pierre Jean George Cabanis said that whenever men came together their morals changed for the worse; whenever they came together in closed places their morals and their health deteriorated. So there arose what could be called an urban fear, a fear of the city, a very characteristic uneasiness: a fear of the workshops and factories being constructed, the crowding together of the population, the excessive height of the buildings, the urban epidemics, the rumors that invaded the city; a fear of the sinks and pits on which were constructed houses that threatened to collapse at any moment.

The life of the big eighteenth-century cities, especially Paris, provoked a series of panics. One might mention here the example of the Cemetery of the Innocents, in the center of Paris, into which the cadavers of those who lacked the resources or the social stature to buy or to merit an individual grave were thrown, one on top of the other. Urban panic was characteristic of the politico-sanitary anxiety, the uneasiness that appeared as the urban machine developed. Measures had to be taken to control these medical and political phenomena, which caused the population of the cities to experience such intense anxiety.

At this moment a new mechanism intervened, one that, though it could be predicted, does not enter into the usual scheme of historians of medicine. What was the reaction of the bourgeois class that, while not exercising power, held back by the traditional authorities, laid claim to it? A well-known but rarely employed model of intervention was appealed to—the model of the quarantine.

Since the end of the Middle Ages, there was, not just in France but in all European countries, what would now be called an "emergency plan." It was to be applied when the plague or another serious epidemic disease appeared in a city.

1. All people must stay in their dwelling in order to be localized in a single place. Every family in its home and, if possible, every person in his or her own room. Everyone was to stay put.
2. The city was to be divided into four districts placed under the responsibility of a specially designated person. This district head supervised inspectors whose job it was to patrol all the streets by day or stand watch to verify that no one left his house. So this amounted to a generalized system of surveillance that compartmentalized and controlled the city.
3. These street or district monitors were supposed to present to the mayor a detailed daily report on everything they had observed. Thus, not only was a generalized system of surveillance employed but also a centralized system of information.
4. The inspectors were to check on all the cities' dwellings every day. In all the streets they walked through, they asked every inhabitant to show himself at the window in order to verify that he still lived there and to note this down in the register. The fact that a person did not appear at the window meant that he was sick, that he had contracted the plague and consequently needed to be transported to a special infirmary, outside the city. Thus, an exhaustive record of the number of living and dead would be compiled, with daily updating.
5. A house by house disinfection, with the help of perfumes and incense, would be carried out.

The quarantine plan represented the politico-medical ideal of a good sanitary organization of eighteenth-century cities. There were basically two great models of medical organization in Western history: one that was engendered by leprosy, the other by the plague.

In the Middle Ages, when a leprosy case was discovered he was immediately expelled from the common space, the city, exiled to a gloomy, ambiguous place where his illness would blend with that of others. The mechanism of expulsion was that of purification of the urban environment. In that era, medicalizing an individual meant separating him and, in this way, purifying the others. It was a medicine of exclusion. At the beginning of the seventeenth century, even the internment of individuals who were demented, misshapen, and so on, was still mandated by this concept.

In contrast, there was another great politico-medical system established, not against leprosy but against the plague. In this case, medicine did not exclude the afflicted person or remove him to a dismal and turbid region. Medicine's political power consisted in distributing individuals side by side, isolating them, individualizing them, observing them one by one, monitoring their state of health, checking to see whether they were still alive or had died, and, in this way, main-

taining society in a compartmentalized space that was closely watched and controlled by means of a painstaking record of all the events that occurred.

So there was a medical schema of reaction against leprosy—that of a religious type of exclusion, and of purification of the city. There was also the one
motivated by the plague, a strategy that did not practice internment and reloca-
tion outside the urban center; rather, it depended on a meticulous analysis of the
city, on a continuous recording. The religious model was replaced, therefore, by
the military model. It was military inspection, basically, that served as a model
for this politico-medical organization.

Urban medicine, in the second half of the eighteenth century, with its methods of observation, hospitalization, and so on, was nothing but an improvement
on the politico-medical schema of the quarantine that appeared at the end of the
Middle Ages, that is, in the sixteenth and seventeenth centuries. Public hygiene
was a refined variation of the quarantine, the beginnings of the great urban
medicine that appeared in the second half of the eighteenth century and developed especially in France from that time on.

The main objectives of urban medicine were the following:

First: Study the accumulation and piling-up of refuse that might cause illnesses in the urban space, the places that generated and propagated epidemic or
endemic phenomena. Graveyards were the main concern here. Thus, protests
against cemeteries appeared between 1740 and 1750. The first great removals to
the city's periphery began around 1750. It was during this period that the individualized cemetery came into existence, that is, the individual coffin and the
tomb reserved for the members of a family, where each of their names was inscribed.

It is often thought that, in modern society, the cult of the dead comes to us
from Christianity. I don't share that opinion. There is nothing in Christian theology that urges respect for the corpse as such. The omnipotent Christian god
can raise the dead even when they have been mixed together in the ossuary.

The individualization of the corpse, the coffin, and the grave appeared at the
end of the eighteenth century not for the theologico-religious reasons having to
do with respect for dead bodies but, rather, for politico-sanitary reasons having
to do with respect for living ones. To protect the living from the harmful influence of the dead, the latter must be just as well indexed as the former—even better, if possible.

Thus, in the outskirts of the cities, at the end of the eighteenth century, what
appeared was a veritable army of dead people, as perfectly aligned as a regiment
being passed in review. It was necessary therefore to monitor, analyze, and reduce this constant threat which the dead represented. So they were transported
to the country and placed side by side in the great flatlands that surrounded the
cities.

This was not a Christian idea but a medical and political one. The best proof of this is that when the notion of moving the Cemetery of the Innocents in Paris was conceived, Antoine-François de Fourcroy, one of the greatest chemists of the end of the eighteenth century, was consulted about combating its influence. It was he who asked that it be moved; it was he who, in studying the relations between the living organism and the ambient air, took charge of that first medical and urban policing sanctioned by the banishment of the cemeteries.

Another example is furnished by the case of the slaughterhouses, also located in the center of Paris. It was decided, after consultation with the Academy of Sciences, to install them on the city's western fringe, at La Villette.

Medicine's first objective consisted therefore in analyzing the zones of congestion, disorder, and danger within the urban precincts.

Second: Urban medicine had a new objective—controlling circulation. Not the circulation of individuals but of things and elements, mainly water and air.

It was an old eighteenth-century belief that air had a direct influence on the organism because it carried miasmas; or because its excess chilliness, hotness, dryness, or wetness would be transmitted to the organism; and, finally, because the air exerted a direct pressure on the body through mechanical action. The air was considered to be one of the great pathogenic factors.

But how to maintain air quality in a city? How to obtain healthy air when the latter was blocked and kept from circulating between the walls, houses, enclosures, and so on? Thus, the need arose to open up the avenues of the urban space in order to preserve the health of the population. The opinion of commissions from the Academy of Sciences, doctors, chemists, and so on, was also solicited in an effort to find the best methods for ventilating the city. One of the best-known cases was demolition. Due to overcrowding and the high price of land during the Middle Ages, some houses were built on the gradients. So it was thought that these houses were preventing air circulation above the streams and retaining the humid air on the slopes: they were systematically torn down. In addition, calculations were performed showing the number of deaths avoided thanks to the demolition of three houses built on the Pont-Neuf—four hundred persons per year, twenty thousand in fifty years, and so on.

In this way, aeration corridors and air currents were organized, the same as had been done with water. In Paris, in 1767, the architect Moreau had the precocious idea of organizing the banks and islands of the Seine so that the river current itself would cleanse the city of its miasmas.

Thus, the second objective of urban medicine was the establishment and control of a good circulation of water and air.

Third: Another major goal of urban medicine was the organization of what could be called distributions and sequences. Where to place the different elements necessary to the shared life of the city? The problem of the respective position of the fountains and sewers, the pumps and river washhouses was raised. How to prevent the infiltration of dirty water into the drinking water fountains? How to keep the population's clean water supply from being mixed with the waste water from the nearby washhouses?

In the second half of the eighteenth century, this organization was thought to be the cause of the main urban epidemic diseases. This led to the first hydrographic plan of Paris, in 1742. It was the first survey of the places where water that wasn't contaminated by the sewers could be drawn, and the first attempt at defining a policy for river life. When the French Revolution broke out in 1789, Paris had already been carefully studied by an urban medical police that had established directives for bringing about a veritable sanitary organization of the city.

And yet, up to the end of the eighteenth century, there had not been any conflict between medicine and the other forms of authority such as private property, for example. Official policy relating to private property, to the private dwelling, was not sketched out before the eighteenth century, except for one of its aspects—the subsurface. Underground spaces belonging to the house owner remained subject to certain rules concerning their use and the construction of tunnels.

This was the problem of subsurface ownership that was raised in the eighteenth century with the advent of mining technology. When the capability for digging deep mines developed, the problem of their ownership appeared. In the middle of the eighteenth century, a binding legislation relating to the subsoil was formulated: it provided that the state and the king were the sole owners of the subsoil, and not disposers of the ground. In this way, the Paris subsoil was controlled by the authorities, whereas the surface was not, at least as concerned private property. Public spaces, such as places of circulation, cemeteries, ossuaries, and slaughterhouses, were controlled starting in the eighteenth century, which was not the case with private property before the nineteenth century.

Medicalization of the city in the eighteenth century is important for several reasons:

First: Through urban social medicine, the medical profession came directly in contact with other related sciences, mainly chemistry. Since that period of confusion during which Paracelsus and Vahelmont tried to establish the relationships between medicine and chemistry, nothing more had been learned on the subject. It was precisely the analysis of water, of air currents, of the conditions of life and respiration which brought medicine and chemistry into contact. Fourcroy and Antoine-Laurent Lavosier became interested in the problem of the organism in connection with control of the urban air.

The entry of medical practice into a corpus of physico-chemical science was brought about through urbanization. Scientific medicine did not grow out of private, individualized medicine, nor was it inspired by greater interest in the individual. The introduction of medicine into the general functioning of scientific discourse and knowledge occurred through medicine's socialization, the establishment of a collective, social, urban medicine. It is by all this that the importance of urban medicine is measured.

Second: Urban medicine is not really a medicine of man, the body, and the organism but a medicine of things—air, water, decompositions, fermentations. It is a medicine of the living conditions of the existential milieu.

Although the term "environment" did not appear, this medicine of things already outlined the concept, and the naturalists of the end of the eighteenth century, such as Cuvier, would develop it. The relationship between the organism and the environment was established simultaneously in the field of natural sciences and of medicine via urban medicine. The progression was not from analysis of the organism to analysis of the environment. Medicine went from analysis of the environment to that of the effects of the environment on the organism and, finally, to analysis of the organism itself. The organization of urban medicine was important for the formation of scientific medicine.

Third: With urban medicine there appeared, shortly before the French Revolution, the notion of salubrity. One of the decisions made by the Constituent Assembly between 1790 and 1791 was, for example, the creation of salubrity committees in the departments and main cities.

It should be pointed out that salubrity did not mean the same thing as health; rather, it referred to the state of the environment and those factors of it which made the improvement of health possible. Salubrity was the material and social basis capable of ensuring the best possible health for individuals. In connection with this, the concept of public health [*hygiène publique*] appeared, as a technique for controlling and modifying those elements of the environment which might promote that health or, on the contrary, harm it.

Salubrity and insalubrity designated the state of things and of the environment insofar as they affected health: public health was the politico-scientific control of that environment.

Thus, the concept of salubrity appeared at the beginning of the French Revolution. The concept of public health was to be, in nineteenth-century France, the one that brought together the essential components of social medicine. One of the major journals of this period, the *Annales d'hygiène publique et de médecine légale*, which began to appear in 1829, would become the organ of French social medicine.

This medicine remained far removed from state medicine of the sort that could be found in Germany; it was much closer to small communities, such as towns and districts. At the same time, it could not count on any specific instrument of power. The problem of private property, a sacred principle, kept this medicine from being endowed with a strong authority. But while *Staatsmediẓin* surpassed it in the authority at its disposal, there is no doubt that its keenness of observation and its scientific character were superior.

A large part of nineteenth-century scientific medicine originated in the experience of this urban medicine which developed at the end of the eighteenth century.

LABOR FORCE MEDICINE

The third direction of social medicine can be examined through the English example. Poor people's medicine, labor force or worker's medicine, was not the first but the last objective of social medicine. First the state, then the city, and finally poor people and workers were the object of medicalization.

What characterized French urban medicine was respect for the private sphere and the rule of not having to regard the poor, the underclass, or the people as an element that threatened public health. Consequently, the poor or the workers were not thought of in the same way as cemeteries, ossuaries, slaughterhouses, and so on.

Why didn't the problem of the poor as a source of medical danger arise in the course of the eighteenth century? There are several reasons for this. One is quantitative in nature: the number of poor people in the cities was not large enough for poverty to represent a real danger. But there was a more important reason: urban activity depended on the poor. A city's poor people accomplished a certain number of tasks: they delivered the mail, collected the garbage, picked up old furniture, used clothing, redistributed or resold scrap materials, and so on. They thus formed part of urban life. In this era, the houses didn't have numbers and there was no postal service either. No one knew the city and all its nooks better than the poor; they carried out a series of basic functions such as water hauling or refuse disposal.

Insofar as the poor formed part of the urban system, like the sewers or pipes, they performed an indisputable function and could not be considered as a danger. At the level where they were placed, they were useful. But starting in the second third of the nineteenth century, the problem of poverty was raised in terms of menace, of danger. The reasons are diverse:

1. Political reasons, first of all: during the French Revolution and in England during the great social unrest of the beginning of the nineteenth century, the destitute population transformed itself into a political force capable of revolting or at least of participating in revolts.
2. In the nineteenth century, means were found for partly replacing the services

offered by the underclass, such as the setting up of a postal service and a transport system. These reforms were at the origin of a wave of popular disturbances launched against these systems, which deprived the most needy of bread and of the very possibility of living.

3. With the cholera epidemic of 1832, which began in Paris, then spread throughout Europe, a set of political and health fears occasioned by the proletarian or plebeian population crystallized.

It was in this period that the decision was first made to divide the urban space into rich areas and poor areas. The feeling was that cohabitation between rich and poor in an undifferentiated urban environment constituted a health and political hazard for the city. The establishment of rich districts and poor districts dates from this time. Political authority thus began to intervene in property and private dwelling rights. This was the time of the great reshaping, under the Second Empire, of the urban zone of Paris.

These are the reasons for which, up until the nineteenth century, the urban population was not regarded as a medical danger.

In England—where industrial development was being experienced, and where, consequently, the formation of a proletariat was faster and more extensive—a new form of social medicine appeared. This doesn't mean that state medicine projects of the German type did not exist as well. For example, in about 1840, John Chadwick was largely inspired by German methods in formulating his plans. Moreover, in 1846 Rumsay wrote a work titled *Health and Sickness of Town Populations*[5] which reflects the content of French urban medicine.

It was essentially the Poor Law[6] that made English medicine a social medicine insofar as this law implied a medical control of the destitute. Since the poor benefited from the welfare system, it became obligatory to subject them to various medical controls.

With the Poor Law, an important factor in the history of social medicine made an ambiguous appearance: the idea of a tax-supported welfare, of a medical intervention that would constitute a means of helping the poorest individuals to meet their health needs, something that poverty placed beyond their hope. At the same time, it made it possible to maintain a control by which the wealthy classes, or their government representatives, would guarantee the health of the needy classes and, consequently, protect the privileged population. In this way, an officially sanctioned sanitary cordon between the rich and the poor was set in place within the cities. To that end, the latter were offered the possibility of receiving free or low-cost treatment. Thus, the wealthy freed themselves of the risk of being victims of epidemic phenomena issuing from the disadvantaged class.

The transposition of the major problem of that period's bourgeoisie is clearly visible in the medical legislation: At what cost? Under what conditions?

How to guarantee its political security? The medical legislation contained in the Poor Law was consistent with that process. But that law—and the protection assistance, together with the control assistance it entailed—was only the first component of a complex system whose other components appeared later, around 1870, with the great founders of English social medicine. Chief among them was John Simon, who completed the medical legislation with an official service organizing not medical treatment but medical control of the population. I am referring to the systems of the Health Service, the Health Offices, which appeared in England in 1875, and were estimated to number a thousand toward the end of the nineteenth century. Their functions were the following:

- Control of vaccination, obliging the different elements of the population to be immunized.
- Organizing the record of epidemics and diseases capable of turning into an epidemic, making the reporting of dangerous illnesses mandatory.
- Localization of unhealthy places and, if necessary, destruction of those seedbeds of insalubrity.

The Health Service developed out of the same thinking that produced the Poor Law. The Poor Law provided for a medical service expressly intended for the poor. The Health Service, on the other hand, was characterized by protection of the entire population without distinction, and by the fact that it was comprised of doctors offering nonindividualized care extending to the whole population, preventive measures to be taken, and, just like French urban medicine, objects, places, social environment, and so on.

However, analysis of the Health Service's operation shows that it was a means of completing at the collective level the same controls that were guaranteed by the Poor Law. Intervention in unhealthy places, verification of vaccinations, and disease records were really aimed at controlling the needy social classes.

It was precisely for these reasons that, in the second half of the nineteenth century, English medical control administered by the Health Offices provoked violent popular reactions and resistances, small-scale antimedical insurrections. R. M. Macleod drew attention to these cases of medical resistance in a series of articles published by the journal *Public Law* in 1967.[7] I think it would be interesting to analyze how this medicine, organized in the form of a control of the needy population, incurred such reactions—not only in England but in various countries of the world. For example, it is curious to observe that the dissident religious groups, so numerous in the English-speaking Protestant countries, had the primary goal during the seventeenth and eighteenth centuries of opposing state religion and interference by the state in religious affairs, whereas those

groups which reappeared in the course of the nineteenth century were concerned with combating medicalization, with asserting the right to life, the right
to get sick, to care for oneself and to die in the manner one wished. This desire
to escape from compulsory medicalization was one of the characteristics of
these numerous apparently religious groups that were intensely active at the
end of the nineteenth century, as they still are today.

In Catholic countries the situation was different. What meaning would the
pilgrimage to Lourdes have, from the end of the nineteenth century to our time,
for the millions of poor pilgrims who arrive there every year, if not that of
being a sort of muddled resistance to the obligatory medicalization of their
bodies and their illnesses?

Instead of seeing in these religious practices a present-day residue of archaic
beliefs, shouldn't they be seen as the contemporary form of a political struggle
against politically authoritarian medicine, the socialization of medicine, the
medical control that presses mainly on the poor population? The strength of
these continuing practices resides in the fact that they constitute a reaction
against this poor people's medicine, in the service of a class, English social medicine being an example.

In a general way, we may affirm that, in contrast to German state medicine of
the eighteenth century, there appeared in the nineteenth century—above all, in
England—a medicine that consisted mainly in a control of the health and the
bodies of the needy classes, to make them more fit for labor and less dangerous
to the wealthy classes.

Unlike urban medicine and especially state medicine, this English approach
to medicine was to have a future. The English system of Simon and his successors enabled three things to be established: medical assistance of the poor, control of the health of the labor force, and a general surveying of public health,
whereby the wealthy classes would be protected from the greatest dangers. Further—and this is where its originality lies—it enabled the creation of three superimposed and coexisting medical systems: a welfare medicine designed for
the poorest people; an administrative medicine responsible for general problems such as vaccination, epidemics, and so on; and a private medicine benefit-
ing those who could afford it.

The German system of state medicine was burdensome, and French urban
medicine was a general plan of control without any specific instrument of authority; but the English system made possible the organization of a medicine
with different features and forms of authority—depending on whether it was a
question of welfare, administrative, or private medicine—and the establishment of well-defined sectors that allowed a fairly complete medical survey to be
constituted in the last years of the nineteenth century. With the Beveridge Plan[8]
and the medical systems of today's richest and most industrialized countries, it

is always a matter of bringing these three sectors of medicine into play, although they are linked together in different ways.

Notes

1. Emmanuel Le Roy Ladurie, Jean-Pierre Peter, Paul Dumont, *Anthropologie du conscrit français d'après les comptes numériques et sommaires du recrutement de l'armée (1819–1826)* (Paris: Mouton "Civilisations et Sociétés," no. 28, 1972).

2. Varn L. Bullough, *The Development of Medicine as a Profession: The Contribution of the Medieval University to Modern Medicine* (New York: Hafner, 1965).

3. George Rosen, "Cameralism and the Concept of Medical Police," *Bulletin of the History of Medicine* 27 (1953), pp. 21–42.

4. Rosen, *A History of Public Health* (New York: MD Publications, 1958).

5. Rumsay, *Health and Sickness of Town Populations* (London: William Ridgway, 1846).

6. A law instituted in the nineteenth century stipulating assistance for the poor at public expense.—Eds.

7. R. M. Macleod, "Law, Medicine and Public Opinion: The Resistance to Compulsory Health Legislation, 1870–1907," in *Public Law: The Constitutional and Administrative Law of the Commonwealth* (London), no. 2 (Summer 1967), pt. 1. pp. 107–128; no. 3 (Autumn 1967), pt. 2, pp. 189–211.

8. The Beveridge Plan was instituted in Great Britain in 1942. Its measures were designed to ensure that every British citizen would enjoy adequate health and medical care.—Eds.

THE POLITICS OF HEALTH IN
THE EIGHTEENTH CENTURY

To begin with, two preliminary remarks:

    First: It is, no doubt, not very fruitful to look for a relation of anteriority or dependence between the two terms of, on the one hand, a private, "liberal" medicine that was subject to the mechanisms of individual initiative and to the laws of the market, and, on the other, a medical politics drawing support from structures of power and concerning itself with the health of a collectivity. It is somewhat mythical to suppose that Western medicine originated as a collective practice, endowed by magico-religious institutions with its social character and gradually dismantled through the subsequent organization of private clienteles.[1] But it is equally inadequate to posit, at the historical threshold of modern medicine, the existence of a singular, private, individual medical relation, "clinical" in its economic functioning and epistemological form, and to imagine that a series of corrections, adjustments, and constraints gradually came to socialize this relation, causing it, to some extent, to be taken charge of by the collectivity.

    What the eighteenth century shows, in any case, is a double-sided process. The development of a medical market in the form of private clienteles, the extension of a network of personnel offering qualified medical attention, the growth of individual and family demand for health care, the emergence of a clinical medicine strongly centered on individual examination, diagnosis, and therapy, the explicitly moral and scientific (and secretly economic) exaltation of "private consultation"—in short, the progressive emplacement of what was to become the great medical edifice of the nineteenth century: these things cannot be divorced from the concurrent organization of a politics of health, the consideration of disease as a political and economic problem for social collectivities which they must seek to resolve as a matter of overall policy. "Private" and "socialized" medicine, in their reciprocal support and opposition, both derive from a common global strategy. No doubt, there is no society that does not practice some kind of "noso-politics": the eighteenth century didn't invent it. But it prescribed new rules, and above all transposed the practice onto an explicit, concerted level of analysis such as had been previously unknown. At this point, the age entered is one not so much of social medicine as of a considered noso-politics.

Second: The center of initiative, organization, and control for this politics should not be located only in the apparatuses of the state. In fact, there were a number of distinct health policies, and various different methods for taking charge of medical problems: those of religious groups (the considerable importance, for example, of the Quakers and the various dissenting movements in England); those of charitable and benevolent associations, ranging from the parish *bureaux* to the philanthropic societies, which operated rather like organs of the surveillance of one class over those others which, precisely because they are less able to defend themselves, are sources of collective danger; those of the learned societies, the eighteenth-century academies and the early nineteenth-century statistics societies, which endeavor to organize a global, quantifiable knowledge of morbid phenomena. Health and sickness, as characteristics of a group, a population, are problematized in the eighteenth century through the initiatives of multiple social instances, in relation to which the state itself plays various different roles. On occasion, it intervenes directly: a policy of free distributions of medicines is pursued in France on a varying scale from Louis XIV to Louis XVI. From time to time it also establishes bodies for purposes of consultation and information (the Prussian Sanitary Collegium dates from 1685; the Royal Society of Medicine is founded in France in 1776). Sometimes the state's projects for authoritarian medical organization are thwarted: the Code of Health elaborated by Mai and accepted by the Elector Palatine in 1800 was never put into effect. Occasionally, the state is also the object of solicitations, which it resists.

Thus the eighteenth-century problematization of noso-politics correlates not with a uniform trend of state intervention in the practice of medicine but, rather, with the emergence at a multitude of sites in the social body of health and disease as problems requiring some form or other of collective control measures. Rather than being the product of a vertical initiative coming from above, noso-politics in the eighteenth century figures as a problem with a number of different origins and orientations, being the problem of the health of all as a priority for all, the state of health of a population as a general objective of policy.

The most striking trait of this noso-politics, concern with which extends throughout French, and indeed European society in the eighteenth century, certainly consists in the displacement of health problems relative to problems of

assistance. Schematically, one can say that up to the end of the seventeenth century, institutions for assistance to the poor serve as the collective means of dealing with disease. Certainly, there are exceptions to this: the regulations for times
of epidemic, measures taken in plague towns, and the quarantines enforced in
certain large ports all constituted forms of authoritarian medicalization not or-
ganically linked to techniques of assistance. But outside these limit cases, medicine understood and practiced as a "service" operated simply as one of the
components of "assistance." It was addressed to the category, so important despite the vagueness of its boundaries, of the "sick poor." In economic terms,
this medical service was provided mainly thanks to charitable foundations. Institutionally, it was exercised within the framework of lay and religious organizations devoted to a number of ends: distribution of food and clothing, care for
abandoned children, projects of elementary education and moral proselytism,
provision of workshops and workrooms, and in some cases the surveillance of
"unstable" or "troublesome" elements (in the cities, the hospital *bureaux* had a
jurisdiction over vagabonds and beggars, and the parish *bureaux* and charitable
societies also very explicitly adopted the role of denouncing "bad subjects").
From a technical point of view, the role of therapeutics in the working of the
hospitals in the Classical age was limited in extent when compared with the scale
of provision of material assistance or with the administrative structure. Sickness is only one among a range of factors—including infirmity, old age, inability to find work, and destitution—that compose the figure of the "needy
pauper" who deserves hospitalization.

The first phenomenon in the eighteenth century we should note is the progressive dislocation of these mixed and polyvalent procedures of assistance.
This dismantling is carried out or, rather, is called for (since it only begins to become effective late in the century) as the upshot of a general reexamination of
modes of investment and capitalization. The system of "foundations," which
immobilize substantial sums of money and whose revenues serve to support the
idle and thus allow them to remain outside the circuits of production, is criticized by economists and administrators. The process of dismemberment is also
carried out as a result of a finer grid of observation of the population and the
distinctions this observation aims to draw between the different categories of
unfortunates to which charity confusedly addresses itself. In this process of the
gradual attenuation of traditional social statuses, the "pauper" is one of the first
to be effaced, giving way to a whole series of functional discriminations (the
good poor and the bad poor, the willfully idle and the involuntarily unemployed, those who can do some kind of work and those who cannot). An analysis of idleness—and its conditions and effects—tends to replace the somewhat
global charitable sacralization of "the poor." This analysis has as its practical
objective at best to make poverty useful by fixing it to the apparatus of produc-

tion, at worst to lighten as much as possible the burden it imposes on the rest of society. The problem is to set the "able-bodied" poor to work and transform them into a useful labor force; but it is also to assure the self-financing by the poor themselves of the cost of their sickness and temporary or permanent incapacitation, and further to make profitable in the short or long term the education of orphans and foundlings. Thus, a complete utilitarian decomposition of poverty is marked out, and the specific problem of the sickness of the poor begins to figure in the relationship of the imperatives of labor to the needs of production.

But one must also note another process more general than the first, and more than its simple elaboration: this is the emergence of the health and physical well-being of the population in general as one of the essential objectives of political power. Here it is not a matter of offering support to a particularly fragile, troubled, and troublesome margin of the population but of how to raise the level of health of the social body as a whole. Different power apparatuses are called upon to take charge of "bodies," not simply so as to exact blood service from them or levy dues but to help and if necessary constrain them to ensure their own good health. The imperative of health—at once the duty of each and the objective of all.

Taking a longer perspective, one could say that from the heart of the Middle Ages power traditionally exercised two great functions, that of war and peace. It exercised them through the hard-won monopoly of arms, and that of the arbitration of lawsuits and punishments of crimes, which it ensured through its control of judicial functions. *Pax et justitia*. To these functions were added—from the end of the Middle Ages—those of the maintenance of order and the organization of enrichment. Now, in the eighteenth century we find a further function emerging, that of the disposition of society as a milieu of physical well-being, health, and optimal longevity. The exercise of these three latter functions—order, enrichment, and health—is assured less through a single apparatus than by an ensemble of multiple regulations and institutions which in the eighteenth century take the generic name of "police." Down to the end of the ancien régime, the term "police" does not signify (at least not exclusively) the institution of police in the modern sense; "police" is the ensemble of mechanisms serving to ensure order, the properly channeled growth of wealth, and the conditions of preservation of health "in general." N. De Lamare's *Treatise* on police, the great charter of police functions in the Classical period, is significant in this respect. The eleven headings under which it classifies police activities can readily be distinguished in terms of three main sets of aims: economic regulation (the circulation of commodities, manufacturing processes, the obligations of tradespeople both to one another and to their clientele), measures of public order (surveillance of dangerous individuals, expulsion of vagabonds and, if necessary, beggars, and the pursuit of criminals), and general rules of hygiene (checks on the quality of foodstuffs sold, the water supply, and the cleanliness of streets).

At the point when the mixed procedures of police are being broken down into these elements and the problem of sickness among the poor is identified in its economic specificity, the health and physical well-being of populations comes to figure as a political objective that the "police" of the social body must ensure along with those of economic regulation and the needs of order. The sudden importance assumed by medicine in the eighteenth century originates at the point of intersection of a new, "analytical" economy of assistance with the emergence of a general "police" of health. The new noso-politics inscribes the specific question of the sickness of the poor within the general problem of the health of populations, and makes the shift from the narrow context of charitable aid to the more general form of a "medical police," imposing its constraints and dispensing its services. The texts of Th. Rau (the *Medizinische Polizei Ordnung* of 1764), and above all the great work of J. P. Frank, *System einer medizinischen Polizei*, give this transformation its most coherent expression.

What is the basis for this transformation? Broadly, one can say it has to do with the preservation, upkeep, and conservation of the "labor force." No doubt, though, the problem is a wider one. It arguably concerns the economico-political effects of the accumulation of men. The great eighteenth-century demographic upswing in Western Europe, the necessity for coordinating and integrating it into the apparatus of production, and the urgency of controlling it with finer and more adequate power mechanisms cause "population," with its numerical variables of space and chronology, longevity and health, to emerge not only as a problem but as an object of surveillance, analysis, intervention, modifications, and so on. The project of a technology of population begins to be sketched: demographic estimates, the calculation of the pyramid of ages, different life expectancies and levels of mortality, studies of the reciprocal relations of growth of wealth and growth of population, various measures of incitement to marriage and procreation, the development of forms of education and professional training. Within this set of problems, the "body"—the body of individuals and the body of populations—appears as the bearer of new variables, not merely as between the scarce and the numerous, the submissive and the restive, rich and poor, healthy and sick, strong and weak, but also as between the more or less utilizable, more or less amenable to profitable investment, those with greater or lesser prospects of survival, death and illness, and with more or less capacity for being usefully trained. The biological traits of a population become relevant factors for economic management, and it becomes necessary to organize around them an apparatus that will ensure not only their subjection [*asujettissement*] but the constant increase of their utility.

This enables us to understand the main characteristics of eighteenth-century noso-politics as follows:

(1) *The privilege of the child and the medicalization of the family.* The problem of "children" (that is, of their number at birth and the relation of births to mortalities) is now joined by the problem of "childhood" (that is, of survival to adulthood, the physical and economic conditions for this survival, the necessary and sufficient amount of investment for the period of child development to become useful—in brief, the organization of this "phase" perceived as being both specific and finalized). It is no longer just a matter of producing an optimum number of children, but one of the correct management of this age of life.

New and highly detailed rules serve to codify relations between adults and children. The relations of filial submission and the system of signs these entail certainly persist, with few changes. But they are to be henceforth invested by a whole series of obligations imposed on parents and children alike: obligations of a physical kind (care, contact, hygiene, cleanliness, attentive proximity), suckling of children by their mothers, clean clothing, physical exercise to ensure the proper development of the organism—the permanent and exacting corporal relation between adults and their children. The family is no longer to be just a system of relations inscribed in a social status, a kinship system, a mechanism for the transmission of property; it is to become a dense, saturated, permanent, continuous physical environment that envelops, maintains, and develops the child's body. Hence, it assumes a material figure defined within a narrower compass; it organizes itself as the child's immediate environment, tending increasingly to become its basic framework for survival and growth. This leads to an effect of tightening, or at least intensification, of the elements and relations constituting the restricted family (the group of parents and children). It also leads to a certain inversion of axes: the conjugal bond serves no longer only, nor even perhaps primarily, to establish the junction of two lines of descent, but also to organize the matrix of the new adult individual. No doubt, it still serves to give rise to two lineages and hence to produce a descent; but it serves also to produce—under the best possible conditions—a human being who will live to the state of adulthood. The new "conjugality" lies, rather, in the link between parents and children. The family, seen as a narrow, localized pedagogical apparatus, consolidates itself within the interior of the great traditional family-as-alliance. And at the same time health—and principally the health of children—becomes one of the family's most demanding objectives. The rectangle of parents and children must become a sort of homeostasis of health. At all events, from the eighteenth century onward the healthy, clean, fit body, a purified, cleansed, aerated domestic space, the medically optimal siting of individuals, places, beds, and utensils, and the interplay of the "caring" and the "cared for" figure among the family's essential laws. And from this period the family becomes the most constant agent of medicalization. From the second half of the eighteenth century, the family is the target for a great enterprise of medical acculturation. The first wave of this offensive bears on care of children, especially babies. Among the principal texts are Audrey's *L'Orthopédie* (1749), Vandermonde's *Essai sur la manière de perfectionner l'espèce humaine* (1756), Cadogan's *An Essay upon Nursing, and the Management of Children, from Their Birth to Three Years of Age* (1748; French trans., 1752), des Essartz's *Traité de l'éducation corporelle en bas age* (1760), Ballexserd's *Dissertation sur l'éducation physique des enfants* (1762), Raulin's *De la Conservation des enfants* (1768), Nicolas' *Le Cri de la nature en faveur des enfants nouveaunés* (1775), Daignan's *Tableau des sociétés de la vie humaine* (1786), Saucerotte's *De la Conservation des enfants* (year IV), W. Buchan's *Advice to Mothers on the Subject of Their Own Health; and on the Means of Promoting the Health, Strength and Beauty of Their Off-spring* (1803; French trans., 1804), J. A. Millot's *Le Nestor français* (1807), Laplace-Chanvre's *Dissertation sur quelques points de l'éducation physique et morale des enfants* (1813), Leretz's *Hygiène des enfants* (1814), and Prévost-Leygonie's *Essai sur l'éducation physique des enfants* (1813). This literature gains even further in extension in the nineteenth century with the appearance of a whole series of journals that address themselves directly to the lower classes.

The long campaign of inoculation and vaccination has its place in this movement to organize around the child a system of medical care for which the family is to bear the moral responsibility and at least part of the economic cost. Via different routes, the policy for orphans follows an analogous strategy. Special institutions are opened: the Foundling Hospital, the Enfants Trouvés in Paris; but there is also a system organized for placing children with nurses or in families where they can make themselves useful by taking at least a minimal part in domestic life, and where, moreover, they will find a more favorable milieu of development at less cost than in a hospital where they would be barracked until adolescence.

The medical politics outlined in the eighteenth century in all European countries has as its first effect the organization of the family or, rather, the familychildren complex, as the first and most important instance for the medicalization of individuals. The family is assigned a linking role between general objectives regarding the good health of the social body and individuals' desire or need for care. This enables a "private" ethic of good health as the reciprocal duty of parents and children to be articulated onto a collective system of hygiene and scientific technics of cure made available to individual and family demand by a professional corps of doctors qualified and, as it were, recommended by the state. The rights and duties of individuals respecting their health and that of others, the market where supply and demand for medical care meet, authoritarian interventions of power in the order of hygiene and illness accompanied at the same time by the institutionalizing and protection of the private doctor-patient relation—all these features in their multiplicity and coherence characterize the global functioning of the politics of health in the nineteenth century. Yet they cannot be properly understood if one abstracts them from this central element formed in the eighteenth century, the medicalized and medicalizing family.

(2) *The privilege of hygiene and the function of medicine as an instance of social control.* The old notion of the regime, understood at once as a rule of life and a form of preventive medicine, tends to become enlarged into that of the collective "regime" of a population in general, with the disappearance of the great epidemic tempests, the reduction of the death rate, and the extension of the average lifespan and life expectancy for every age group as its triple objective. This program of hygiene as a regime of health for populations entails a certain number of authoritarian medical interventions and controls.

First of all, control of the urban space in general: it is this space that constitutes perhaps the most dangerous environment for the population. The disposition of various quarters, their humidity and exposure, the ventilation of the city as a whole, its sewage and drainage systems, the siting of abattoirs and cemeteries, the density of population—all these are decisive factors for the mortality and morbidity of the inhabitants. The city with its principal spatial variables appears as a medicalizable object. Whereas the medical topographies of regions analyze climatic and geological conditions outside human control, and can only recommend measures of correction and compensation, the urban topographies outline, in negative at least, the general principles of a concerted urban policy. During the eighteenth century the idea of the pathogenic city inspires a whole mythology and very real states of popular panic (the Charnel House of the Innocents in Paris was one of these high places of fear); it also gave rise to a medical discourse on urban morbidity and the placing under surveillance of a whole range of urban developments, constructions, and institutions.[2]

In a more precise and localized fashion, the needs of hygiene demand an authoritarian medical intervention in what are regarded as the privileged breeding grounds of disease: prisons, ships, harbor installations, the *hôpitaux généraux* where vagabonds, beggars, and invalids mingle together; the hospitals themselves—whose medical staffing is usually inadequate—aggravate or complicate the diseases of their patients, to say nothing of their diffusing of pathological germs into the outside world. Thus, priority areas of medicalization in the urban environment are isolated and are destined to constitute so many points for the exercise and application of an intensified medical power. Doctors will, moreover, have the task of teaching individuals the basic rules of hygiene, which they must respect for the sake of their own health and that of others: hygiene of food and habitat, exhortations to seek treatment in case of illness.

Medicine, as a general technique of health even more than as a service to the sick or an art of cures, assumes an increasingly important place in the administrative system and the machinery of power, a role constantly widened and strengthened throughout the eighteenth century. The doctor wins a footing within the different instances of social power. The administration acts as a point of support and sometimes a point of departure for the great medical inquiries into the health of populations; and, conversely, doctors devote an increasing amount of their activity to tasks, both general and administrative, assigned to them by power. A "medico-administrative" knowledge begins to develop concerning society, its health and sickness, its conditions of life, housing and habits; this serves as the basic core for the "social economy" and sociology of the nineteenth century. And there is likewise constituted a politico-medical hold on a population hedged in by a whole series of prescriptions relating not only to disease but to general forms of existence and behavior (food and drink, sexuality and fecundity, clothing and the layout of living space).

A number of phenomena dating from the eighteenth century testify to this hygienist interpretation of political and medical questions and the "surplus of power" it bestows on the doctor: the increasing presence of doctors in the academies and learned societies, the very substantial medical participation in the production of the Encyclopedias, their presence as counselors to representatives of power, the organization of medical societies officially charged with a certain number of administrative responsibilities and qualified to adopt or recommend authoritarian measures, the frequent role of doctors as programmers of a well-ordered society (the doctor as social or political reformer is a frequent figure in the second half of the eighteenth century), and the superabundance of doctors in the Revolutionary Assemblies. The doctor becomes the great adviser and expert, if not in the art of governing at least in that of observing, correcting, and improving the social "body" and maintaining it in a permanent state of health. And it is the doctor's function as hygienist rather than his prestige as a therapist that assures him this politically privileged position in the eighteenth century, prior to his accumulation of economic and social privileges in the nineteenth century.

The challenge to the hospital institution in the eighteenth century can be understood on the basis of these three major phenomena: the emergence of "population" with its biomedical variables of longevity and health; the organization of the narrowly parental family as a relay in a process of medicalization for which it acts both as the permanent source and the ultimate instrument; and the inter-

lacing of medical and administrative instances in organizing the control of collective hygiene.

The point is that, in relation to these new problems, the hospital appears as an
obsolete structure in many respects. A fragment of space closed in on itself, a
place of internment of men and diseases, its ceremonious but inept architecture
multiplying the ills in its interior without preventing their outward diffusion,
the hospital is more the seat of death for the cities where it is sited than a therapeutic agent for the population as a whole. Not only the difficulty of admission
and the stringent conditions imposed on those seeking to enter, but also the incessant disorder of comings and goings, inefficient medical surveillance, and
the difficulty of effective treatment cause the hospital to be regarded as an inadequate instrument from the moment the population in general is specified as the
object of medicalization and the overall improvement in its level of health as the
objective. The hospital is perceived as an area of darkness within the urban
space that medicine is called upon to purify. And it acts as a dead weight on the
economy since it provides a mode of assistance that can never make possible the
diminution of poverty, but at best the survival of certain paupers—and hence
their increase in number, the prolongation of their sicknesses, the consolidation
of their ill-health with all the consequent effects of contagion.

Hence there is the idea, which spreads during the eighteenth century, of a replacement of the hospital by three principal mechanisms. The first of these is
the organization of a domestic form of "hospitalization." No doubt, this has its
risks where epidemics are concerned, but it has economic advantages in that the
cost to society of the patient's upkeep is far less as he is fed and cared for at home
in the normal manner. The cost to the social body is hardly more than the loss
represented by his forced idleness, and then only where he had actually been
working. The method also offers medical advantages, in that the family—given
a little advice—can attend to the patient's needs in a constant and adjustable
manner impossible under hospital administration: each family will be enabled to
function as a small, temporary, individual, and inexpensive hospital. But such a
procedure requires the replacement of the hospital to be backed by a medical
corps dispersed throughout the social body and able to offer treatment either
free or as cheaply as possible. A medical staffing of the population, provided it
is permanent, flexible, and easy to make use of, should render unnecessary a
good many of the traditional hospitals. Finally, it is possible to envisage the
care, consultation, and distribution of medicaments already offered by certain
hospitals to outpatients being extended to a general basis, without the need to
hold or intern the patients: this is the method of the dispensaries that aim to retain the technical advantages of hospitalization without its medical and economic drawbacks.

These three methods gave rise, especially in the latter half of the eighteenth century, to a whole series of projects and programs. They inspired a number of experiments. In 1769, the Red Lion Square dispensary for poor children was opened in London. Thirty years later almost every district of the city had its dispensary, and the annual number of those receiving free treatment there was estimated at nearly 50,000. In France it seems that the main effort was toward the improvement, extension, and more or less homogeneous distribution of medical personnel in town and country. The reform of medical and surgical studies (in 1772 and 1784), the requirement of doctors to practice in boroughs and small towns before being admitted to certain of the large cities, the work of investigation and coordination performed by the Royal Society of Medicine, the increasing part occupied by control of health and hygiene in the responsibilities of the Intendants, the development of free distribution of medication under the authority of doctors designated by the administration, all these measures are related to a health policy resting on the extensive presence of medical personnel in the social body. At the extreme point of these criticisms of the hospital and this project for its replacement, one finds under the Revolution a marked tendency toward "dehospitalization"; this tendency is already perceptible in the reports of the *Comité de mendicité*, with the project to establish a doctor or surgeon in each rural district to care for the indigent, supervise children under assistance, and practice inoculation. It becomes more clearly formulated under the Convention, with the proposal for three doctors in each district to provide the main health care for the whole population. However, the disappearance of the hospital was never more than the vanishing point of a utopian perspective. The real work lay in the effort to elaborate a complex system of functions in which the hospital comes to have a specialized role relative to the family (now considered as the primary instance of health), to the extensive and continuous network of medical personnel, and to the administrative control of the population. It is within this complex framework of policies that the reform of the hospital is attempted.

The first problem concerns the spatial adaptation of the hospital, and in particular its adaptation to the urban space in which it is located. A series of discussions and conflicts arise between different schemes of implantation, respectively advocating massive hospitals capable of accommodating a sizable population, uniting and thus rendering more coherent the various forms of treatment—or, alternatively, smaller hospitals where patients will receive better attention and the risks of contagion will be less grave. There was another, connected problem: Should hospitals be sited outside the cities, where ventilation is better and there is no risk of hospital miasmas being diffused among the population?—a solution which in general was linked to the planning of large architectural installations; or should a multiplicity of small hospitals be built at scattered points where they can most easily be reached by the population that will use them?—a solution that often involves the coupling of hospital and dispensary. In either case, the hospital is intended to become a functional element in an urban space where its effects must be subject to measurement and control.

It is also necessary to organize the internal space of the hospital so as to make it medically efficacious, a place no longer of assistance but of therapeutic action. The hospital must function as a "curing machine." First, in a negative way: all the factors that make the hospital dangerous for its occupants must be suppressed, solving the problem of the circulation of air (which must be constantly renewed without its miasmas or mephitic qualities being carried from one patient to another), and solving as well the problem of the changing, transport, and laundering of bed linen. Second, in a positive way, the space of the hospital must be organized according to a concerted therapeutic strategy, through the uninterrupted presence and hierarchical prerogatives of doctors, through systems of observation, notation, and record-taking. These make it possible to fix the knowledge of different cases, to follow their particular evolution, and also to globalize the data that bear on the long-term life of a whole population, and, finally, the substitution of better-adapted medical and pharmaceutical cures for the somewhat indiscriminate curative regimes that formed the essential part of traditional nursing. The hospital tends toward becoming an essential element in medical technology, not simply as a place for curing, but as an instrument which, for a certain number of serious cases, makes curing possible.

Consequently, it becomes necessary in the hospital to articulate medical knowledge with therapeutic efficiency. In the eighteenth century, specialized hospitals emerge. If there existed certain establishments previously reserved for madmen or venereal patients, this was less for the sake of any specialized treatment than as a measure of exclusion or out of fear. The new "unifunctional" hospital, on the other hand, comes to be organized only from the moment when hospitalization becomes the basis, and sometimes the condition, for a more or less complex therapeutic approach. The Middlesex Hospital, intended for the treatment of smallpox and the practice of vaccination, was opened in London in 1745, the London Fever Hospital dates from 1802, and the Royal Ophthalmic Hospital from 1804. The first Maternity Hospital was opened in London in 1749. In Paris, the Enfants Malades was founded in 1802. One sees the gradual constitution of a hospital system whose therapeutic function is strongly emphasized—designed, on the one hand, to cover with sufficient continuity the urban or rural space whose population it has charge of, and, on the other, to articulate itself with medical knowledge and its classifications and techniques.

Finally, the hospital must serve as the supporting structure for the permanent staffing of the population by medical personnel. Both for economic and medical reasons, it must be possible to make the passage from treatment at home to a hospital regime. By their visiting rounds, country and city doctors must lighten the burden of the hospitals and prevent their overcrowding; in return the hospital must be accessible to patients on the advice and at the request of their doctors. Moreover, the hospital as a place of accumulation and development of knowledge must provide for the training of doctors for private practice. At the end of the eighteenth century, clinical teaching in the hospital—the first rudiments of which appear in Holland with Sylvius and then Boerhaave, at Vienna with Van Swieten, and at Edinburgh through the linking of the School of Medicine with the Edinburgh Infirmary—becomes the general principle around which the reorganization of medical studies is undertaken. The hospital, a therapeutic instrument for the patients who occupy it, contributes at the same time, through its clinical teaching and the quality of the medical knowledge acquired there, to the improvement of the population's health as a whole.

The return of the hospitals, and more particularly the projects for their architectural, institutional, and technical reorganization, owed its importance in the eighteenth century to this set of problems relating to urban space, the mass of the population with its biological characteristics, the close-knit family cell and the bodies of individuals. It is in the history of these materialities, which are at once political and economic, that the "physical" process of transformation of the hospitals is inscribed.

Notes

1. Cf. George Rosen, *A History of Public Health* (New York: MD Publications, 1958).

2. Cf., for example, J. P. L. Morel, *Dissertation sur les causes qui contribuent le plus à rendre cachectique et rachitique la constitution d'un grand nombre d'enfants de la ville de Lille* [A dissertation on the causes which most contribute to rendering the constitution of a great number of children in the city of Lille cachectic and rachitic], 1812.

NIETZSCHE, GENEALOGY, HISTORY

1.

Genealogy is gray, meticulous, and patiently documentary. It operates on a field of entangled and confused parchments, on documents that have been scratched over and recopied many times.

On this basis, it is obvious that Paul Ree was wrong to follow the English tendency in describing the history of morality in terms of a linear development—in reducing its entire history and genesis to an exclusive concern for utility. He assumed that words had kept their meaning, that desires still pointed in a single direction, and that ideas retained their logic; and he ignored the fact that the world of speech and desires has known invasions, struggles, plundering, disguises, ploys. From these elements, however, genealogy retrieves an indispensable restraint: it must record the singularity of events outside of any monotonous finality; it must seek them in the most unpromising places, in what we tend to feel is without history—in sentiments, love, conscience, instincts; it must be sensitive to their recurrence, not in order to trace the gradual curve of their evolution but to isolate the different scenes where they engaged in different roles. Finally, genealogy must define even those instances when they are absent, the moment when they remained unrealized (Plato, at Syracuse, did not become Muhammed).

Genealogy, consequently, requires patience and a knowledge of details, and it depends on a vast accumulation of source material. Its "cyclopean monuments" [1] are constructed from "discreet and apparently insignificant truths and according to a rigorous method"; they cannot be the product of "large and well-

This essay originally appeared in *Hommage à Jean Hyppolite* (Paris: Presses Universitaires de France, 1971), pp. 145–72. The translation, by Donald F. Brouchard and Sherry Simon, has been slightly amended.

meaning errors."² In short, genealogy demands relentless erudition. Genealogy does not oppose itself to history as the lofty and profound gaze of the philosopher might compare to the molelike perspective of the scholar; on the contrary, it rejects the metahistorical deployment of ideal significations and indefinite teleologies. It opposes itself to the search for "origins."

2.

In Nietzsche, we find two uses of the word *Ursprung*. The first is unstressed, and it is found alternately with other terms such as *Entstehung, Herkunft, Abkunft, Geburt.* In *The Genealogy of Morals,* for example, *Entstehung* or *Ursprung* serves equally well to denote the origin of duty or guilty conscience;³ and in the discussion of logic and knowledge in *The Gay Science,* their origin is indiscriminately referred to as *Ursprung, Entstehung,* or *Herkunft.*⁴

The other use of the word is stressed. On occasion, Nietzsche places the term in opposition to another: in the first paragraph of *Human, All Too Human* the miraculous origin [*Wunderursprung*] sought by metaphysics is set against the analyses of historical philosophy, which poses questions *über Herkunft und Anfang. Ursprung* is also used in an ironic and deceptive manner. In what, for instance, do we find the original basis [*Ursprung*] of morality, a foundation sought after since Plato? "In detestable, narrow-minded conclusions. *Pudenda origo.*"⁵ Or again, Where should we seek the origin of religion [*Ursprung*], which Schopenhauer located in a particular metaphysical sentiment of the hereafter? It belongs, very simply, to an invention [*Erfindung*], a sleight-of-hand, an artifice [*Kunststück*], a secret formula, in the rituals of black magic, in the work of the *Schwarzkünstler.*⁶

One of the most significant texts with respect to the use of all these terms and to the variations in the use of *Ursprung* is the preface to the *Genealogy*. At the beginning of the text its objective is defined as an examination of the origin of moral preconceptions and the term used is *Herkunft*. Then Nietzsche proceeds by retracing his personal involvement with this question: he recalls the period when he "calligraphied" philosophy, when he questioned if God must be held responsible for the origin of evil. He now finds this question amusing and properly characterizes it as a search for *Ursprung* (he will shortly use the same term to summarize Paul Ree's activity).⁷ Farther on he evokes the analyses that are characteristically Nietzschean and that begin with *Human, All Too Human.* Here he speaks of *Herkunfthypothesen.* This use of the word *Herkunft* cannot be arbitrary, since it serves to designate a number of texts, beginning with *Human, All Too Human,* which deal with the origin of morality, asceticism, justice, and punishment. And yet the word used in all these works had been *Ursprung.*⁸ It would seem that at this point in the *Genealogy* Nietzsche wished to validate an opposition between *Herkunft* and *Ursprung* that he had not put into play ten years earlier. But immediately following the use of the two terms in a specific sense, Nietzsche reverts, in the final paragraphs of the preface, to a usage that is neutral and equivalent.[9]

Why did Nietzsche challenge the pursuit of the origin [*Ursprung*], at least on those occasions when he is truly a genealogist? First, because it is an attempt to capture the exact essence of things, their purest possibilities, and their carefully protected identities; because this search assumes the existence of immobile forms that precede the external world of accident and succession. This search is directed to "that which was already there," the "very same" of an image of a primordial truth fully adequate to its nature, and it necessitates the removal of every mask to ultimately disclose an original identity. However, if the genealogist refuses to extend his faith in metaphysics, if he listens to history, he finds that there is "something altogether different" behind things: not a timeless and essential secret but the secret that they have no essence, or that their essence was fabricated in a piecemeal fashion from alien forms. Examining the history of reason, he learns that it was born in an altogether "reasonable" fashion—from chance;[10] devotion to truth and the precision of scientific methods arose from the passion of scholars, their reciprocal hatred, their fanatical and unending discussions, and their spirit of competition—the personal conflicts that slowly forged the weapons of reason.[11] Further, genealogical analysis shows that the concept of liberty is an "invention of the ruling classes"[12] and not fundamental to man's nature or at the root of his attachment to being and truth. What is found at the historical beginning of things is not the inviolable identity of their origin; it is the dissension of other things. It is disparity.

History also teaches us how to laugh at the solemnities of the origin. The lofty origin is no more than "a metaphysical extension which arises from the belief that things are most precious and essential at the moment of birth."[13] We tend to think that this is the moment of their greatest perfection, when they emerged dazzling from the hands of a creator or in the shadowless light of a first morning. The origin always precedes the Fall. It comes before the body, before the world and time; it is associated with the gods, and its story is always sung as a theogony. But historical beginnings are lowly: not in the sense of modest or discreet, like the steps of a dove, but derisive and ironic, capable of undoing every infatuation. "We wished to awaken the feeling of man's sovereignty by showing his divine birth: this path is now forbidden, since a monkey stands at the entrance."[14] Man began with a grimace at what he would become; and Zarathustra himself is plagued by a monkey who jumps along behind him, pulling on his coattails.

The final postulate of the origin is linked to the first two: it would be the site of truth. From the vantage point of an absolute distance, free from the restraints of positive knowledge [*connaissance*], the origin makes possible a field of knowledge [*savoir*] whose function is to recover it, but always in a false recognition due to the excesses of its own speech. The origin lies at a place of inevitable loss, the point where the truth of things is knotted to a truthful discourse, the site of a fleeting articulation that discourse has obscured and finally lost. It is a new cruelty of history that compels a reversal of this relationship and the abandonment of "adolescent" quests: behind the always recent, avaricious, and measured truth, it posits the ancient proliferation of errors. It is now impossible to believe that "in the rending of the veil, truth remains truthful; we have lived long enough not to be taken in." [15] Truth is undoubtedly the sort of error that cannot be refuted because it was hardened into an unalterable form in the long baking process of history. [16] Moreover, the very question of truth, the right it appropriates to refute error and oppose itself to appearance, the manner in which by turns it was initially made available to the wise, then was withdrawn by men of piety to an unattainable world where it was given the double role of consolation and imperative, finally rejected as a useless notion, superfluous and contradicted on all sides—does this not form a history, the history of an error we call truth? Truth, and its original reign, has had a history within history from which we are barely emerging "in the time of the shortest shadow," when light no longer seems to flow from the depths of the sky or to arise from the first moments of the day. [17]

A genealogy of values, morality, asceticism, and knowledge will never confuse itself with a quest for their "origins," will never neglect as inaccessible all the episodes of history. On the contrary, it will cultivate the details and accidents that accompany every beginning; it will be scrupulously attentive to their petty malice; it will await their emergence, once unmasked, as the face of the other. Wherever it is made to go, it will not be reticent—in "excavating the depths," in allowing time for these elements to escape from a labyrinth where no truth had ever detained them. The genealogist needs history to dispel the chimeras of the origin, somewhat in the manner of the pious philosopher who needs a doctor to exorcise the shadow of his soul. He must be able to recognize the events of history, its jolts, its surprises, its unsteady victories and unpalatable defeats—the basis of all beginnings, atavisms, and heredities. Similarly, he must be able to diagnose the illnesses of the body, its conditions of weakness and strength, its breakdowns and resistances, to be in a position to judge philosophical discourse. History is the concrete body of becoming; with its moments of intensity, its lapses, its extended periods of feverish agitation, its fainting spells; and only a metaphysician would seek its soul in the distant ideality of the origin.

3.

Entstehung and *Herkunft* are more exact than *Ursprung* in recording the true object of genealogy; and, though they are ordinarily translated as "origin," we must attempt to reestablish their proper use.

Herkunft is the equivalent of stock or *descent;* it is the ancient affiliation to a group, sustained by the bonds of blood, tradition, or social status. The analysis of *Herkunft* often involves a consideration of race or social type.[18] But the traits it attempts to identify are not the exclusive generic characteristics of an individual, a sentiment, or an idea, which permit us to qualify them as "Greek" or "English"; rather, it seeks the subtle, singular, and subindividual marks that might possibly intersect in them to form a network that is difficult to unravel. Far from being a category of resemblance, this origin allows the setting apart, the sorting out of different traits: the Germans imagined they had finally accounted for their complexity by saying they possessed a double soul; they were fooled by a simple computation, or rather, they were simply trying to master the racial disorder from which they had formed themselves.[19] Where the soul pretends unification or the Me fabricates a coherent identity, the genealogist sets out to study the beginning—numberless beginnings, whose faint traces and hints of color are readily seen by a historical eye. The analysis of descent permits the dissociation of the Me, its recognition and displacement as an empty synthesis, in liberating a profusion of lost events.

An examination of descent also permits the discovery, under the unique aspect of a trait or a concept, of the myriad events through which—thanks to which, against which—they were formed. Genealogy does not pretend to go back in time to restore an unbroken continuity that operates beyond the dispersion of oblivion; its task is not to demonstrate that the past actively exists in the present, that it continues secretly to animate the present, having imposed a predetermined form on all its vicissitudes. Genealogy does not resemble the evolution of a species and does not map the destiny of a people. On the contrary, to follow the complex course of descent is to maintain passing events in their proper dispersion; it is to identify the accidents, the minute deviations—or conversely, the complete reversals—the errors, the false appraisals, and the faulty calculations that gave birth to those things which continue to exist and have value for us; it is to discover that truth or being lies not at the root of what we know and what we are but the exteriority of accidents.[20] This is undoubtedly why every origin of morality from the moment it stops being pious—and *Herkunft* can never be—has value as a critique.[21]

Deriving from such a source is a dangerous legacy. In numerous instances, Nietzsche associates the terms *Herkunft* and *Erbschaft*. Nevertheless, we should not be deceived into thinking that this heritage is an acquisition, a possession that grows and solidifies; rather, it is an unstable assemblage of faults, fissures, and heterogeneous layers that threaten the fragile inheritor from within or from underneath: "injustice or instability in the minds of certain men, their disorder and lack of decorum, are the final consequences of their ancestors' numberless logical inaccuracies, hasty conclusions, and superficiality."[22] The search for descent is not the erecting of foundations: on the contrary, it disturbs what was previously considered immobile; it fragments what was thought unified; it shows the heterogeneity of what was imagined consistent with itself. What convictions and, far more decisively, what knowledge can resist it? If a genealogical analysis of a scholar were made—of one who collects facts and carefully accounts for them—his *Herkunft* would quickly divulge the official papers of the scribe and the pleadings of the lawyer—their father[23]—in their apparently disinterested attention, in their "pure" devotion to objectivity.

Finally, descent attaches itself to the body.[24] It inscribes itself in the nervous system, in temperament, in the digestive apparatus; it appears in faulty respiration, in improper diets, in the debilitated and prostrate bodies of those whose ancestors committed errors. Fathers have only to mistake effects for causes, believe in the reality of an "afterlife" or maintain the value of eternal truths, and the bodies of their children will suffer. Cowardice and hypocrisy, for their part, are the simple offshoots of error: not in a Socratic sense, not that evil is the result of a mistake, not because of a turning away from an original truth, but because the body maintains, in life as in death, through its strength or weakness, the sanction of every truth and error, as it sustains, in an inverse manner, the origin—descent. Why did men invent the contemplative life? Why give a supreme value to this form of existence? Why maintain the absolute truth of those fictions which sustain it? "During barbarous ages . . . if the strength of an individual declined, if he felt himself tired or sick, melancholy or satiated and, as a consequence, without desire or appetite for a short time, he became relatively a better man, that is, less dangerous. His pessimistic ideas only take form as words or reflections. In this frame of mind, he either became a thinker and prophet or used his imagination to feed his superstitions."[25] The body—and everything that touches it: diet, climate, and soil—is the domain of the *Herkunft*. The body manifests the stigmata of past experience and also gives rise to desires, failings, and errors. These elements may join in a body where they achieve a sudden expression, but just as often, their encounter is an engagement in which they efface each other, and pursue their insurmountable conflict.

The body is the surface of the inscription of events (traced by language and dissolved by ideas), the locus of the dissociation of the Me (to which it tries to impart the chimera of a substantial unity), and a volume in perpetual disintegration. Genealogy, as an analysis of descent, is thus situated within the articulation of the body and history. Its task is to expose a body totally imprinted by history and the process of history's destruction of the body.

4.

Entstehung designates *emergence,* the moment of arising. It stands as the principle and the singular law of an apparition. As it is wrong to search for descent in an uninterrupted continuity, we should avoid accounting for emergence by appeal to its final term; the eye was not always intended for contemplation, and punishment has had other purposes than setting an example. These developments may appear as a culmination, but they are merely the current episodes in a series of subjugations: the eye initially responded to the requirements of hunting and warfare; and punishment has been subjected by turns to a variety of needs—revenge, excluding an aggressor, compensating a victim, creating fear. In placing present needs at the origin, the metaphysician would convince us of an obscure purpose that seeks its realization at the moment it arises. Genealogy, however, seeks to reestablish the various systems of subjection: not the anticipatory power of meaning, but the hazardous play of dominations.

Emergence is always produced in a particular state of forces. The analysis of the *Entstehung* must delineate this interaction, the manner of the struggle that these forces wage against each other or against adverse circumstances, and the attempt to avoid degeneration and regain strength by dividing these forces against themselves. It is in this sense that the emergence of a species (animal or human) and its solidification are secured "in an extended battle against conditions which are essentially and constantly unfavorable." In fact, "the species must realize itself as a species, as something—characterized by the durability, uniformity, and simplicity of its form—which can prevail in the perpetual struggle against outsiders or the uprising of those it oppresses from within." On the other hand, individual differences emerge in another state of the relationship of forces, when the species has become victorious and when it is no longer threatened from outside. In this condition, we find a struggle "of egoisms turned against each other, each bursting forth in a splintering of forces and a general striving for the sun and for the light." [26] There are also times when force contends against itself, and not only in the intoxication of an abundance, which allows it to divide itself, but at the moment when it weakens. Force reacts against its growing lassitude and gains strength; it imposes limits, inflicts torments and mortifications; it masks these actions as a higher morality and, in exchange, regains its strength. In this manner, the ascetic ideal was born, "in the instinct of a decadent life which . . . struggles for its own existence." [27] This also describes the movement in which the Reformation arose, precisely where the Church was least corrupt;[28] German Catholicism, in the sixteenth century, retained enough strength to turn against itself, to mortify its own body and history, and to spiritualize itself into a pure religion of conscience.

Emergence is thus the entry of forces; it is their eruption, the leap from the wings to center stage, each in its youthful strength. When Nietzsche calls the *Entstehungsherd* of the concept of goodness is not specifically the energy of the strong or the reaction of the weak, but precisely this scene where they are displayed superimposed or face to face.[29] It is nothing but the space that divides them, the void through which they exchange their threatening gestures and speeches. As descent qualifies the strength or weakness of an instinct and its inscription on a body, emergence designates a place of confrontation, but not as a closed field offering the spectacle of a struggle among equals. Rather, as Nietzsche demonstrates in his analysis of good and evil, it is a "nonplace," a pure distance, which indicates that the adversaries do not belong to a common space. Consequently, no one is responsible for an emergence; no one can glory in it, since it always occurs in the interstice.

In a sense, only a single drama is ever staged in this "nonplace," the endlessly repeated play of dominations. The domination of certain men over others leads to the differentiation of values;[30] class domination generates the idea of liberty;[31] and the forceful appropriation of things necessary to survival and the imposition of a duration not intrinsic to them account for the origin of logic.[32] This relationship of domination is no more a "relationship" than the place where it occurs is a place; and, precisely for this reason, it is fixed, throughout its history, in rituals, in meticulous procedures that impose rights and obligations. It establishes marks of its power and engraves memories on things and even within bodies. It makes itself accountable for debts and gives rise to the universe of rules, which is by no means designed to temper violence, but rather to satisfy it. It would be wrong to follow traditional beliefs in thinking that total war exhausts itself in its own contradictions and ends by renouncing violence and submitting to civil laws. On the contrary, the law is the calculated pleasure of relentlessness. It is the promised blood, which permits the perpetual instigation of new dominations and the staging of meticulously repeated scenes of violence. The desire for peace, the serenity of compromise, and the tacit acceptance of the law, far from representing a major moral conversion or a utilitarian calculation that gave rise to the law, are but its result and, in point of fact, its perversion: "guilt, conscience, and duty had their threshold of emergence in the right to secure obligations; and their inception, like that of any major event on earth, was saturated in blood."[33] Humanity does not gradually progress from combat to combat until it arrives at universal reciprocity, where the rule of law finally replaces warfare; humanity installs each of its violences in a system of rules and thus proceeds from domination to domination.

And it is these rules which allow violence to be inflicted on violence and the resurgence of new forces that are sufficiently strong to dominate those in power. Rules are empty in themselves, violent and unfinalized; they are made to serve this or that, and can be bent to any purpose. The successes of history belong to those who are capable of seizing these rules, to replace those who had used them, to disguise themselves so as to pervert them, invert their meaning, and redirect them against those who had initially imposed them; introducing themselves into this complex mechanism, they will make it function in such a way that the dominators find themselves dominated by their own rules. The isolation of different points of emergence does not conform to the successive configurations of an identical meaning; rather, they result from substitutions, displacements, disguised conquests, and systematic reversals. If interpretation were the slow exposure of the meaning hidden in an origin, then only metaphysics could interpret the development of humanity. But if interpretation is the violent or surreptitious appropriation of a system of rules, which in itself has no essential meaning, in order to impose a direction, to bend it to a new will, to force its participation in a different game, and to subject it to secondary rules, then the development of humanity is a series of interpretations. The role of genealogy is to record its history: the history of morals, ideals, and metaphysical concepts, the history of the concept of liberty or of the ascetic life; as they stand for the emergence of different interpretations, they must be made to appear as events in the theater of procedures.

5.

What is the relationship between genealogy, seen as the examination of *Herkunft* and *Entstehung,* and history in the traditional sense? We could, of course, examine Nietzsche's celebrated apostrophes against history, but we will put these aside for the moment and consider those instances when he conceives of genealogy as *wirkliche Historie,* or its more frequent characterization as historical "spirit" or "sense." [34] In fact, Nietzsche's criticism, beginning with the second of the *Untimely Meditations,* always questioned the form of history that reintroduces (and always assumes) a suprahistorical perspective: a history whose function is to compose the finally reduced diversity of time into a totality fully closed upon itself; a history that always encourages subjective recognitions and attributes a form of reconciliation to all the displacements of the past; a history whose perspective on all that precedes it implies the end of time, a completed development. The historian's history finds its support outside of time and claims to base its judgments on an apocalyptic objectivity. This is only possible, however, because of its belief in eternal truth, the immortality of the soul, and the nature of consciousness as always identical to itself. Once the historical sense is mastered by a suprahistorical perspective, metaphysics can bend it to its own purpose, and, by aligning it to the demands of objective science, it can impose its own "Egyptianism." On the other hand, the historical sense can evade metaphysics and become a privileged instrument of genealogy if it refuses the certainty of absolutes. Given this, it corresponds to the acuity of a glance that distinguishes, separates, and disperses; that is capable of liberating divergence and marginal elements—the kind of dissociating view that is capable of decomposing itself, capable of shattering the unity of man's being through which it was thought that he could extend his sovereignty to the events of his past.

Historical sense reintroduces into the realm of becoming everything considered immortal in man, and just so does it practice *wirkliche Historie*. We believe that feelings are immutable, but every sentiment, particularly the noblest and most disinterested, has a history. We believe in the dull constancy of instinctual life and imagine that it continues to exert its force indiscriminately in the present as it did in the past. But historical knowledge easily disintegrates this unity, points out its avatars, depicts its wavering course, locates its moments of strength and weakness, and defines its oscillating reign. It easily seizes the slow elaboration of instincts and those movements where, in turning upon themselves, they relentlessly set about their self-destruction.[35] We believe, in any event, that the body obeys the exclusive laws of physiology, and that it escapes the influence of history, but this too is false. The body is molded by a great many distinct regimes; it is broken down by the rhythms of work, rest, and holidays; it is poisoned by food or values, through eating habits or moral laws; it constructs resistances.[36] "Effective" history differs from the history of historians in being without constants. Nothing in man—not even his body—is sufficiently stable to serve as the basis for self-recognition or for understanding other men. The traditional devices for constructing a comprehensive view of history and for retracing the past as a patient and continuous development must be systematically dismantled. Necessarily, we must dismiss those tendencies which encourage the consoling play of recognitions. Knowledge [*savoir*], even under the banner of history, does not depend on "rediscovery," and it emphatically excludes the "rediscovery of ourselves." History becomes "effective" to the degree that it introduces discontinuity into our very being—as it divides our emotions, dramatizes our instincts, multiplies our body and sets it against itself. "Effective" history leaves nothing around the self, deprives the self of the reassuring stability of life and nature, and it will not permit itself to be transported by a voiceless obstinacy toward a millennial ending. It will uproot its traditional foundations and relentlessly disrupt its pretended continuity. This is because knowledge is not made for understanding; it is made for cutting.

From these observations, we can grasp the particular traits of the historical sense as Nietzsche understood it—the sense which opposes *wirkliche Historie* to traditional history. The former inverts the relationship ordinarily established between the eruption of an event and necessary continuity. An entire historical tradition (theological or rationalistic) aims at dissolving the singular event into an ideal continuity—as a theological movement or a natural process. "Effective" history, however, deals with events in terms of their most unique characteristics, their most acute manifestations. An event, consequently, is not a decision, a treaty, a reign, or a battle, but the reversal of a relationship of forces, the usurpation of power, the appropriation of a vocabulary turned against those who had once used it, a domination that grows feeble, poisons itself, grows slack, the entry of a masked "other." The forces operating in history do not obey destiny or regulative mechanisms, but the luck of the battle.[37] They do not manifest the successive forms of a primordial intention and their attention is not that of a conclusion, for they always appear through the singular randomness of events. The inverse of the Christian world, spun entirely by a divine spider, and different from the world of the Greeks, divided between the realm of will and the great cosmic folly, the world of effective history knows only one kingdom, without providence or final cause, where there is only "the iron hand of necessity shaking the dice-box of chance."[38] Chance is not simply the drawing of lots but raising the stakes in every attempt to master chance through the will to power, and giving rise to the risk of an even greater chance.[39] The world such as we are acquainted with it is not this ultimately simple configuration where events are reduced to accentuate their essential traits, their final meaning, or their initial and final value. On the contrary, it is a profusion of entangled events. If it appears as a "marvelous motley, profound and totally meaningful," this is because it began and continues its secret existence through a "host of errors and phantasms."[40] We want historians to confirm our belief that the present rests upon profound intentions and immutable necessities. But the true historical sense confirms our existence among countless lost events, without a landmark or a point of reference.

The historical sense can also invert the relationship that traditional history, in its dependence on metaphysics, establishes between proximity and distance. The latter is given to a contemplation of distances and heights: the noblest periods, the highest forms, the most abstract ideas, the purest individualities. It accomplishes this by getting as near as possible, placing itself at the foot of its mountain peaks, at the risk of adopting the famous perspective of frogs. Effective history, on the other hand, shortens its vision to those things nearest to it—the body, the nervous system, nutrition, digestion, and energies; it unearths decadence, and if it chances upon lofty epochs, it is with the suspicion—not vindictive but joyous—of finding a barbarous and shameful confusion. It has no fear of looking down, but it looks from above and descends to seize the various perspectives, to disclose dispersions and differences, to leave things undisturbed in their own dimension and intensity. It reverses the surreptitious practice of historians, their pretension to examine things farthest from themselves, the groveling manner in which they approach this promising distance (like the metaphysicians who proclaim the existence of an afterlife, situated at a distance from this world, as a promise of their reward). Effective history studies what is closest, but in an abrupt dispossession, so as to seize it at a distance (an approach similar to that of a doctor who looks closely, who plunges to make a diagnosis and to state its difference). Historical sense has more in common with medicine than philosophy; and it should not surprise us that Nietzsche occasionally employs the phrase "historically and physiologically," [41] since among the philosopher's idiosyncracies is a complete denial of the body. This includes, as well, "the absence of historical sense, a hatred for the idea of development, Egyptianism," the obstinate "placing of conclusions at the beginning," of "making last things first." [42] History has a more important task than to be a handmaiden to philosophy, to recount the necessary birth of truth and values; it should become a differential knowledge [*connaissance*] of energies and failings, heights and degenerations, poisons and antidotes. Its task is to become a curative science. [43]

The final trait of effective history is its affirmation of a perspectival knowledge [*savoir*]. Historians take unusual pains to erase the elements in their work which reveal their grounding in a particular time and place, their preferences in a controversy—the unavoidable obstacles of their passion. Nietzsche's version of historical sense is explicit in its perspective and acknowledges its system of injustice. Its perception is slanted, being a deliberate appraisal, affirmation, or negation; it follows the lingering and poisonous traces, prescribes the best antidote. It is not given to a discreet effacement before the objects it observes and does not submit itself to their processes; nor does it seek laws, since it gives equal weight to its own sight and to its objects. Through this historical sense, knowledge is allowed to create its own genealogy in the act of cognition; and *wirkliche Historie* composes a genealogy of history as the vertical projection of its position.

6.

In that genealogy of history he sketches in several versions, Nietzsche links historical sense to the historian's history. They share a beginning that is similarly impure and confused, share the same sign in which the symptoms of sickness can be recognized as well as the seed of an exquisite flower. [44] They arose simultaneously to follow their separate ways, but our task is to trace their common genealogy.

The descent [*Herkunft*] of the historian is unequivocal: he is of humble birth.

A characteristic of history is to be without choice: it is prepared to acquaint itself with everything, without any hierarchy of importance; to understand everything, without regard to eminence; to accept everything, without making any distinctions. Nothing must escape it and, more important, nothing must be excluded. Historians argue that this proves their tact and discretion. After all, what right have they to impose their tastes and preferences when they seek to determine what actually occurred in the past? What they in fact exhibit is a total lack of taste, a certain crudity that tries to take liberties with what is most exalted, a satisfaction in meeting up with what is base. The historian is insensitive to all disgusting things; or rather, he especially enjoys those things which should be repugnant to him. His apparent serenity follows from his concerted avoidance of the exceptional and his reduction of all things to the lowest common denominator. Nothing is allowed to stand above him; and underlying his desire for total knowledge is his search for the secrets that belittle everything: "base curiosity." What is the source of history? It comes from the plebs. To whom is it addressed? To the plebs. And its discourse strongly resembles the demagogue's refrain: "No one is greater than you and anyone who presumes to get the better of you—you who are good—is evil." The historian, who functions as his double, can be heard to echo: "No past is greater than your present, and, through my meticulous erudition, I will rid you of your infatuations and transform the grandeur of history into pettiness, evil, and misfortune." The historian's ancestry goes back to Socrates.

This demagoguery, of course, must be masked. It must hide its singular malice under the cloak of universals. As the demagogue is obliged to invoke truth, laws of essences, and eternal necessity, the historian must invoke objectivity, the accuracy of facts, and the permanence of the past. The demagogue denies the body to secure the sovereignty of a timeless idea, and the historian effaces his proper individuality so that others may enter the stage and reclaim their own speech. He is divided against himself: forced to silence his preferences and overcome his distaste, to blur his own perspective and replace it with the fiction of a universal geometry, to mimic death in order to enter the kingdom of the dead, to adopt a faceless anonymity. In this world where he has conquered his individual will, he becomes a guide to the inevitable law of a superior will. Having curbed the demands of his individual will in his knowledge, he will disclose the form of an eternal will in his object of study. The objectivity of historians inverts the relationships of will and knowledge, and it is, in the same stroke, a necessary belief in providence, in final causes and teleology. The historian belongs to the family of ascetics. "I can't stand these lustful eunuchs of history, all the seductions of an ascetic ideal; I can't stand these blanched tombs producing life or those tired and indifferent beings who dress up in the part of wisdom and adopt an objective point of view." [45]

The *Entstehung* of history is found in nineteenth-century Europe: the land of interminglings and bastardy, the period of the "man-of-mixture." We have become barbarians with respect to those rare moments of high civilization: cities in ruin and enigmatic monuments are spread out before us; we stop before gaping walls; we ask what gods inhabited these empty temples. Great epochs lacked this curiosity, lacked our excessive deference; they ignored their predecessors: the Classical period ignored Shakespeare. The decadence of Europe presents an immense spectacle (while stronger periods refrained from such exhibitions), and the nature of this scene is to represent a theater; lacking monuments of our own making, which properly belong to us, we live among a crowd of scenery. But there is more. Europeans no longer know themselves; they ignore their mixed ancestries and seek a proper role. They lack individuality. We can begin to understand the spontaneous historical bent of the nineteenth century: the anemia of its forces and those mixtures that effaced all its individual traits produced the same results as the mortifications of asceticism; its inability to create, its absence of artistic works, and its need to rely on past achievements forced it to adopt the base curiosity of plebs.

If this fully represents the genealogy of history, how could it become, in its own right, a genealogical analysis? Why did it not continue as a form of demagogic or religious knowledge? How could it change roles on the same stage? Only by being seized, dominated, and turned against its birth. And it is this movement which properly describes the specific nature of the *Entstehung:* it is not the unavoidable conclusion of a long preparation but a scene where forces are risked and confront one another where they emerge triumphant, where they can also be confiscated. The locus of emergence for metaphysics was surely Athenian demogoguery, the vulgar spite of Socrates and his belief in immortality, and Plato could have seized this Socratic philosophy to turn it against itself. Undoubtedly, he was often tempted to do so, but his defeat lies in its consecration. The problem was similar in the nineteenth century—to avoid doing for the popular asceticism of historians what Plato did for Socrates. This historical trait should not be founded on a philosophy of history, but dismantled, beginning with the things it produced. It is necessary to master history so as to turn it to genealogical uses, that is, strictly anti-Platonic purposes. Only then will the historical sense free itself from the demands of a suprahistorical history.

7.

The historical sense gives rise to three uses that oppose and correspond to the three Platonic modalities of history. The first is parodic, directed against reality, and opposes the theme of history as reminiscence or recognition; the second is dissociative, directed against identity, and opposes history given as continuity or representative of a tradition; the third is sacrificial, directed against truth, and opposes history as knowledge [*connaissance*]. They imply a use of history that severs its connection to memory, its metaphysical and anthropological model, and constructs a countermemory—a transformation of history into a totally different form of time.

First, the parodic and farcical use. The historian offers this confused and anonymous European, who no longer knows himself or what name he should adopt, the possibility of alternative identities, more individualized and real than his own. But the man with historical sense will see that this substitution is simply a disguise. Historians supplied the Revolution with Roman prototypes, Romanticism with knight's armor, and the Wagnerian era was given the sword of a German hero—emphemeral props whose unreality points to our own. No one kept them from venerating these religions, from going to Bayreuth to commemorate a new afterlife; they were free, as well, to be transformed into street vendors of empty identities. The good historian, the genealogist, will know what to make of this masquerade. He will not be too serious to enjoy it; on the contrary, he will push the masquerade to its limit and prepare the great carnival of time where masks are constantly reappearing. No longer the identification of our faint individuality with the solid identities of the past, but our "unrealization" through the excessive choice of identities—Frederick of Hohenstaufen, Caesar, Jesus, Dionysus, and possibly Zarathustra. Taking up these masks, revitalizing the buffoonery of history, we adopt an identity whose unreality surpasses that of God, who started the charade. "Perhaps, we can discover a realm where originality is again possible as parodists of history and buffoons of God." [46] In this, we recognize the parodic double of what the second of the *Untimely Meditations* called "monumental history": a history given to reestablishing the high points of historical development and their maintenance in a perpetual presence, given to the recovery of works, actions, and creations through the monogram of their personal essence. But in 1874 Nietzsche accused this history, one totally devoted to veneration, of barring access to the actual intensities and creations of life. The parody of his last texts serves to emphasize that "monumental history" is itself a parody. Genealogy is history in the form of a concerted carnival.

The second use of history is the systematic dissociation of our identity. For this rather weak identity, which we attempt to support and to unify under a mask, is in itself only a parody: it is plural; countless souls dispute its possession; numerous systems intersect and dominate one another. The study of history makes one "happy, unlike the metaphysicians, to possess in oneself not an immortal soul but many mortal ones." [47] And in each of these souls, history will discover not a forgotten identity, eager to be reborn, but a complex system of distinct and multiple elements, unable to be mastered by the powers of synthesis: "It is a sign of superior culture to maintain, in a fully conscious way, certain phases of its evolution which lesser men pass through without thought. The initial result is that we can understand those who resemble us as a completely determined system and as representative of diverse cultures, that is to say, as necessary and capable of modification. And, in return, we are able to separate the phases of our own evolution and consider them individually." [48] The purpose of history, guided by genealogy, is not to discover the roots of our identity, but to commit itself to its dissipation. It does not seek to define our unique threshold of emergence, the homeland to which metaphysicians promise a return; it seeks to make visible all of those discontinuities that cross us. "Antiquarian history," according to the *Untimely Meditations,* pursues opposite goals. It seeks the continuities of soil, language, and urban life in which our present is rooted, and, "by cultivating in a delicate manner that which existed for all time, it tries to conserve for posterity the conditions under which we were born." [49] This type of history was objected to in the *Meditations* because it tended to block creativity in support of the laws of fidelity. Somewhat later—and already in *Human, All Too Human*—Nietzsche reconsiders the task of the antiquarian, but with an altogether different emphasis. If genealogy in its own right gives rise to questions concerning our native land, native language, or the laws that govern us, its intention is to reveal the heterogeneous systems that, masked by the self, inhibit the formation of any form of identity.

The third use of history is the sacrifice of the subject of knowledge [*connaissance*]. In appearance or, rather, according to the mask it bears, historical consciousness is neutral, devoid of passions, and committed solely to truth. But if it examines itself and if, more generally, it interrogates the various forms of scientific consciousness in its history, it finds that all these forms and transformations are aspects of the will to knowledge [*savoir*]: instinct, passion, the inquisitor's devotion, cruel subtlety, and malice. It discovers the violence of a position that sides against those who are happy in their ignorance, against the effective illusions by which humanity protects itself, a position that encourages the dangers of research and delights in disturbing discoveries. [50] The historical analysis of this rancorous will to knowledge[a] [*vouloir-savoir*] reveals that all knowledge [*connaissance*] rests upon injustice (that there is no right, not even in the act of knowing, to truth or a foundation for truth), and that the instinct for knowledge is malicious (something murderous, opposed to the happiness of mankind). Even in the greatly expanded form it assumes today, the will to knowledge does not achieve a universal truth; man is not given an exact and serene mastery of nature. On the contrary, it ceaselessly multiplies the risks, creates dangers in every area; it breaks down illusory defenses; it dissolves the unity of the subject; it releases those elements of itself that are devoted to its subversion and destruction. Knowledge [*savoir*] does not slowly detach itself from its empirical roots, the initial needs from which it arose, to become pure speculation subject only to the demands of reason; its development is not tied to the constitution and affirmation of a free subject; rather, it creates a progressive enslavement to its instinctive violence. Where religions once demanded the sacrifice of bodies, knowledge now calls for experimentation on ourselves,[51] calls us to the sacrifice of the subject of knowledge [*connaissance*]. "Knowledge [*connaissance*] has been transformed among us into a passion which fears no sacrifice, which fears nothing but its own extinction. It may be that mankind will eventually perish from this passion for knowledge. If not through passion, then through weakness. We must be prepared to state our choice: do we wish humanity to end in fire and light or to end on the sands?"[52] We should now replace the two great problems of nineteenth-century philosophy, passed on by Fichte and Hegel (the reciprocal basis of truth and liberty and the possibility of absolute knowledge [*savoir*]), with the theme that "to perish through absolute knowledge [*connaissance*] may well form a part of the basis of being."[53] This does not mean, in terms of a critical procedure, that the will to truth is limited by the intrinsic finitude of cognition [*connaissance*], but that it loses all sense of limitations and all claim to truth in its unavoidable sacrifice of the subject of knowledge [*connaissance*]. "It may be that there remains one prodigious idea which might be made to prevail over every other aspiration, which might overcome the most victorious: the idea of humanity sacrificing itself. It seems indisputable that if this new constellation appeared on the horizon, only the desire to know truth, with its enormous prerogatives, could direct and sustain such a sacrifice. For to knowledge [*connaissance*], no sacrifice is too great. Of course, this problem has never been posed."[54]

The *Untimely Meditations* discussed the critical use of history: its just treatment of the past, its decisive cutting of the roots, its rejection of traditional attitudes of reverence, its liberation of man by presenting him with other origins than those in which he prefers to see himself. Nietzsche, however, reproached critical history for detaching us from every real source and for sacrificing the very movement of life to the exclusive concern for truth. Somewhat later, as we have seen, Nietzsche reconsiders this line of thought he had at first refused, but he directs it to altogether different ends. It is no longer a question of judging the past in the name of a truth that only we can possess in the present, but of risking the destruction of the subject who seeks knowledge [*connaissance*], in the endless deployment of the will to knowledge [*savoir*].

In a sense, genealogy returns to the three modalities of history that Nietzsche recognized in 1874. It returns to them in spite of the objections that Nietzsche raised in the name of the affirmative and creative powers of life. But they are metamorphosed: the veneration of monuments becomes parody; the respect for ancient continuities becomes systematic dissociation; the critique of the injustices of the past by a truth held by men in the present becomes the destruction of the man who maintains knowledge [*connaissance*] by the injustice proper to the will to knowledge.

Notes

1. Nietzsche, *The Gay Science* [1882], trans. Walter Kaufmann (New York: Random House, 1974), no. 7.

2. Nietzsche, *Human, All Too Human* [1878], in *Complete Works* (New York: Gordon, 1974), no. 3.

3. Nietzsche, *On the Genealogy of Morals* [1887], in *Basic Writings of Nietzsche*, ed. and trans. Walter Kaufmann (New York: Modern Library, 1968), pt. 2, secs. 6, 8.

4. *Gay Science*, nos. 110, 111, 300.

5. Nietzsche, *The Dawn of Day* [1881], in *Complete Works* (New York: Gordon, 1974), no. 102. *Pudenda origo* is "shameful origin."—Ed.

6. *Gay Science*, nos. 151, 353; also *Dawn*, no. 62; *Genealogy*, pt. 1, sec. 14; Nietzsche, "The Four Great Errors," in *Twilight of the Idols* [1888], in *The Portable Nietzsche*, ed. and trans. Walter Kaufmann (New York: Viking, 1954), sec. 7. *Schwarzkünstler* is a black magician.—Ed.

7. Paul Ree's text was entitled *Ursprung der Moralischen Empfindungen*.

8. In *Human, All Too Human*, aphorism 92 was entitled *Ursprung der Gerechtigkeit*.

9. In the main body of the *Genealogy*, *Ursprung* and *Herkunft* are used interchangeably in numerous instances (pt. 1, sec. 2; pt. 2, secs. 8, 11, 12, 16, 17).

10. *Dawn*, no. 123.

11. *Human, All Too Human*, no. 34.

12. Nietzsche, *The Wanderer and His Shadow* [1880], in *Complete Works* (New York: Gordon, 1974), no. 9.

13. Ibid., no. 3.

14. *Dawn*, no. 49.

15. Nietzsche, *Nietzsche Contra Wagner* [1888], in *Portable Nietzsche*, pp. 661–68.

16. *Gay Science*, nos. 110, 265.

17. Nietzsche, "How the True World Finally Became a Fable," *Twilight of Idols*, pp. 485–86.

18. For example, on race, see Nietzsche's *Gay Science*, no. 135; *Beyond Good and Evil* [1886], in *Basic Writings*, nos. 200, 242, 244; *Genealogy*, pt. 1, sec. 5; on social type see *Gay Science*, nos. 348–9; *Beyond Good and Evil*, no. 260.

19. *Beyond Good and Evil*, no. 244.

20. *Genealogy*, pt. 3, sec. 17. The *Abkunft* of feelings of depression.

21. Nietzsche, " 'Reason' in Philosophy," *Twilight of Idols*, pp. 479–84.

22. *Dawn*, no. 247.

23. *Gay Science*, nos. 348–49.

24. Ibid.

25. *Dawn*, no. 42.

26. *Beyond Good and Evil*, no. 262.

27. *Genealogy*, pt. 3, no. 13.

28. *Gay Science*, no. 148. It is also to an anemia of the will that one must attribute the *Entstehung* of Buddhism and Christianity.

29. *Genealogy*, pt. 1, sec. 2.

30. *Beyond Good and Evil*, no. 260; see also *Genealogy*, pt. 2, sec. 12.

31. *Wanderer*, no. 9.

32. *Gay Science*, no. 111.

33. *Genealogy*, pt. 2, no. 6.

34. *Genealogy*, preface, sec. 7, and pt. 1, sec. 2; *Beyond Good and Evil*, no. 224.

35. *Gay Science*, no. 7.

36. Ibid.

37. *Genealogy*, pt. 2, sec. 12.

38. *Dawn*, no. 130.

39. *Genealogy*, pt. 2, sec. 12.

40. *Human, All Too Human*, no. 16.

41. *Twilight of Idols*, no. 44.

42. " 'Reason' in Philosophy, " *Twilight of Idols*, nos. 1, 4.

43. *Wanderer*, no. 188.

44. *Gay Science*, no. 337.

45. *Genealogy*, pt. 3, sec. 25.

46. *Beyond Good and Evil*, no. 223.

47. *Wanderer*, "Opinions and Mixed Statements," no. 17.

48. *Human, All Too Human*, no. 274.

49. Nietzsche, *Untimely Meditations* [1873–74] in *Complete Works*, pt. 2, no. 3.

50. See *Dawn*, nos. 429, 432; *Gay Science*, no. 333; *Beyond Good and Evil*, nos. 229–30.

 a. The French phrase *vouloir-savoir* means both the will to knowledge and knowledge as revenge.

51. *Dawn*, no. 501.

52. Ibid., no. 429.

53. *Beyond Good and Evil*, no. 39.

54. *Dawn*, no. 45.

MADNESS AND SOCIETY

In the West the traditional approach to the study of systems of thought has consisted in focusing only on positive phenomena. During the past few years, however, in ethnology, Lévi-Strauss has explored a method that makes it possible to reveal the negative structure in any society or culture. For example, he has demonstrated that if incest is prohibited within a culture this is not due to the affirmation of a certain type of values; it is because there is a checkerboard, as it were, with barely perceptible gray or light blue squares that define a culture's mode of existence. It is the weave [*trame*] of these squares that I wanted to apply to the study of systems of thought. Thus for me it was a matter not of knowing what is affirmed and valorized in a society or a system of thought but of studying what is rejected and excluded. I merely used a method of working that was already recognized in ethnology.

Madness has always been excluded. Now, during the last fifty years in what are called the "advanced countries," comparative ethnologists and psychiatrists have attempted, first of all, to determine whether the madness that was encountered in their countries—that is, mental disorders such as obsessional neurosis, paranoia, schizophrenia—also existed in so-called primitive societies. They have tried to find out, second, whether those primitive societies did not assign a different status to the mentally disturbed than the one seen in their own countries. Whereas in their society the mad were excluded, didn't primitive societies attribute a positive value to them? For example, aren't the shamans in Siberia or North America mental cases? Third, they asked themselves whether certain societies were not ill themselves. For example, Ruth Benedict concluded that the entire Kwakiutl tribe exhibited a paranoiac character.

In speaking to you today, I would like to take an opposite approach to the one

This text, a lecture given 29 September 1970 at the Franco-Japanese Institute in Kyoto, first appeared in Japanese translation in *Misuzu* (Dec. 1970), pp. 16–22. Robert Hurley's translation.

taken by these researchers. I would like first to look at the status of the mentally disturbed in primitive societies; second, to see how the matter stands in our industrial societies; third, to reflect on the mutation that occurred in the nineteenth century; and finally, by way of conclusion, to demonstrate that the position the madman is in has not fundamentally changed in modern industrial society.

Roughly, the areas of human activity can be divided into these four categories:

- labor, or economic production;
- sexuality, family; that is, reproduction of society;
- language, speech;
- ludic activities such as games and festivals.

In all societies there are persons who have behaviors different from others that do not conform to the commonly defined rules in these four areas—in short, what are called "marginal individuals." Already in the ordinary population, the relationship to labor varies according to gender and age. In many societies, if the political and ecclesiastical leaders happen to control the labor of others or serve as intermediaries with supernatural power, they do not work directly themselves and are not involved in the production cycle.

There are also persons who are outside the second cycle of social reproduction. Celibates constitute an example, and one sees many of these, among religious devotees in particular. Moreover, among the Indians of North America, we know that there exist homosexuals and transvestites: it has to be said that they occupy a marginal position in social reproduction.

Third, in discourse as well, there are persons who escape the norm. The words they employ have different meanings. In the case of a prophet, words with a symbolic meaning could one day reveal their hidden truth. The words that poets use are of an aesthetic order and also escape the norm.

Fourth, in all societies there are persons excluded from the games and festivals. Sometimes they are excluded because they are considered dangerous; other times they are themselves the object of a festival. Like the scapegoat among the Hebrews, it may happen that someone is sacrificed after taking responsibility for the others' crime; while the ceremony of his exclusion takes place, the people stage a festival.

In all these cases, those who are excluded differ from one area to another, but it may happen that the same person is excluded in every area. I am thinking of the madman. In every society, or almost, the madman is excluded in all things and, depending on the case, he is given a religious, magical, ludic, or pathological status.

For example, in a primitive tribe of Australia, the madman is regarded as an individual to be feared by the society, a man endowed with a supernatural force. In other instances, certain madmen become victims of society. In any case, they are people who have behaviors that are different from the others, in labor, in the family, in discourse, and in games.

What I would now like to address is the fact that in our industrial societies madmen are similarly excluded from ordinary society by an isomorphic system of exclusion and are assigned a marginal condition.

First, as far as labor is concerned, even in our day the first criterion for determining madness in an individual consists in showing that he is unfit for work. Freud said correctly that the madman (he was talking mainly about neurotics) was a person who could neither work nor love. I will come back to the verb "love," but there is a profound truth in this idea of Freud's. In Europe in the Middle Ages, the existence of madmen was accepted. Sometimes they would get excited and unstable, or they would turn out to be lazy, but they were allowed to wander around. Now, beginning in the seventeenth century, roughly, industrial society was formed and the existence of such persons was no longer tolerated. In response to the requirements of industrial society, large establishments for confining them were created almost simultaneously in France and in England. It was not just madmen who were put there, but also the unemployed, sick people, old people, all those who were unable to work.

According to the traditional account of historians, it was at the end of the eighteenth century—that is in 1793 in France—that Philippe Pinel freed madmen from their chains, and it was at about the same time in England that Samuel Tuke, a Quaker, created a psychiatric hospital. It is thought that madmen were treated as criminals until then, and that Pinel and Tuke labeled them "ill" for the first time. But I am obliged to say that this account is erroneous. In the first place, it is not true that before the Revolution madmen were regarded as criminals; second, it is a misconception to think that madmen were freed of their former status.

This second idea probably constitutes a greater misconception than the first. In general, in primitive society and modern society alike, in the Middle Ages as well as in the twentieth century, what might be called a "universal status" was given to madmen. The only difference is that, from the seventeenth century to the nineteenth century, the right to demand the confinement of a madman belonged to the family: it was the family, first of all, that excluded madmen. Now, starting in the nineteenth century, this prerogative was gradually lost to the family and granted to physicians. In order to confine a madman, a medical certificate was required; once confined, the madman was deprived of all responsibility and any rights as a family member—he even lost his citizenship and was the object of a judicial interdiction. It could be said that law prevailed over medicine in endowing madmen with a marginal status.

Second, there is one fact to note in regard to sexuality and the family system. When one consults European documents up to the beginning of the nineteenth century, sexual practices such as masturbation, homosexuality, and nymphomania are not at all treated as belonging to the domain of psychiatry. It was from the beginning of the nineteenth century that these sexual anomalies were identified with madness and considered as disturbances manifested by an individual who was incapable of adapting to the European bourgeois family. The idea that the main cause of madness resided in sexual anomaly was reinforced when Beyle described creeping paralysis and demonstrated that it was due to syphilis. When Freud considered disturbance of the libido as a cause or an expression of madness, this exerted the same type of influence.

Third, the madman's status with respect to language was curious in Europe. On the one hand, the speech of madmen was rejected as being worthless, and, on the other, it was never completely nullified. We may say that the fool was, in a sense, the institutionalization of the speech of madness. Without any relation to morality and politics, and, moreover, under the cover of irresponsibility, he told, in a symbolic form, the truth that ordinary men could not state.

To take a second example, up to the nineteenth century, literature was highly institutionalized for buttressing the social ethic and for entertaining people. Now, in our day, literature has completely rid itself of all that and has become totally anarchic. This suggests a curious affinity between literature and madness. Literary language is not constrained by the rules of everyday language. For example, it is not subject to the severe rule of constant truth-telling, any more than the teller is under the obligation to always remain sincere in what he thinks and feels. In short, unlike the words of politics or the sciences, those of literature occupy a marginal position with respect to everyday language.

As regards European literature, literary language became especially marginal during these three periods:

1. In the sixteenth century it became more marginal than it was in the Middle Ages: the epics and the chivalrous novels were destructive and contentious with respect to society. That is true of Erasmus' *The Praise of Folly*, the work of Tasso, or Elizabethan drama. In France, there is even a literature of madness that appeared. The Duke de Bouillon went so far as to have the text of a madman printed at his own expense, and the French took pleasure in reading it.

2. The second period goes from the end of the eighteenth century to the beginning of the nineteenth century. As to literature by madmen, one notes the publication of the poetry of Hölderlin and Blake, and, later, the work of Raymond Roussel. This last writer entered a psychiatric hospital for obsessional neurosis in order to be treated by the eminent psychiatrist Pierre Janet, but he ended up committing suicide. It is significant that a contemporary author such as Alain Robbe-Grillet took Raymond Roussel as his starting point, dedicating

his first book to him.[1] For his part, Antonin Artaud was a schizophrenic: it was he who, after the weakening of surrealism, created a break-through in the poetic world, opening up new vistas. For that matter, one has only to consider Nietzsche or Baudelaire to affirm that one must imitate madness or actually become mad in order to establish new fields in literature.

3. These days, people are paying more and more attention to the relationship between literature and madness. All things considered, madness and literature are marginal in relation to everyday language, and they are looking for the secret of general literary production in a model which is madness.

Finally, let us reflect on the situation the madman is in with respect to games in an industrial society. In the traditional European theater—I imagine the same thing is true in Japan—the fool assumed a central role, from the Middle Ages to the eighteenth century. The madman made the spectators laugh, for he saw what the other actors did not see, and he revealed the ending of the plot before they did. That is, he is an individual who reveals the truth with spirit. Shakespeare's *King Lear* is a good example. The king is a victim of his own fantasy, but at the same time he is someone who tells the truth. In other words, in the theater the madman is a character who expresses with his body the truth that the other actors and spectators are not aware of, a character through whom the truth appears.

Further, in the Middle Ages there were many festivals, but among them there was only one that was not religious. It is called the Festival of Folly. In this festival, the social and traditional roles were completely reversed: a poor man played the role of a rich man, a weak man that of a powerful one. The sexes were inverted, the sexual prohibitions nullified. On the occasion of this holiday, the lower class had the right to say what they wanted to the bishop or the mayor. In general, it was insults . . . In short, during this festival all the social, linguistic, and familial institutions were overturned and called back in question. In church, an irreverent layman celebrated mass, after which he would bring in a donkey whose braying was perceived as a mockery of the litany of mass. In sum, it was a counterholiday in relation to Sunday, Christmas or Easter, one that escaped from the habitual circuit of ordinary festivals.

In our time, the politico-religious meaning of festivals has been lost; instead, we resort to alcohol or drugs as a way of contesting the social order, and we have thus created a kind of artificial madness. Basically, it is an imitation of madness, and it can be seen as an attempt to set society ablaze by creating the same state as madness.

I am absolutely not a structuralist. Structuralism is only a means of analysis. For example, how have the conditions under which the madman lives changed from

Middle Ages to the present day? What were the conditions necessary for that change? I merely make use of the structuralist method to analyze all that.

In the Middle Ages and during the Renaissance madmen were permitted to exist in the midst of society. What is called the "village idiot" did not get married, did not participate in games, and he was fed and supported by others. He would roam from town to town, sometimes he would enter the army, he would become a peddler; but when he became too worked up and dangerous, the others would construct a little house outside town where they would temporarily confine him. Arab society is still tolerant toward madmen. In the seventeenth century European society became intolerant toward them. The cause of this, as I said, is that industrial society began to take form. I also told how, from before 1650 to 1750, in cities such as Hamburg, Lyon, and Paris, large-sized institutions were created for interning not only madmen but old people, the sick, the unemployed, idlers, prostitutes—all those who found themselves outside the social order. Capitalist industrial society could not tolerate the existence of groups of vagabonds. Out of a Parisian population numbering a half-million inhabitants, six thousand were confined. In these establishments there was no therapeutic intention; everyone was subjected to forced labor. In 1665 the police were reorganized in Paris; it was then that a grid of squares for social conditioning [*formation*] was constituted. The police kept constant watch over the confined vagabonds.

The irony is that work therapy is frequently practiced in modern psychiatric hospitals. The logic underlying this practice is obvious. If incapacity for work is the first criterion of madness, one has only to teach the patients to work in the hospital to cure them of their madness.

Now, why did the situation of madmen change from the end of the eighteenth century to the beginning of the nineteenth century? It is said that Pinel liberated the madmen in 1793, but those he liberated were only sick people, old people, idlers, prostitutes; he left the madmen in the institutions. This took place when it did because, at the beginning of the nineteenth century, the speed of industrial development accelerated, and, in accordance with the first principle of capitalism, the hordes of unemployed proletarians were regarded as a reserve army of labor power. For that reason, those who did not work but were able to work were let out of the establishments. But there, too, a second process of selection took effect: not only those who were unwilling to work, but those who did not have the ability to work, namely the mad, were left in the establishments and regarded as patients whose troubles had characterological or psychological causes.

Thus what had previously been a confinement institution became a psychiatric hospital, a treatment organization. In the years that followed, hospitals were set in place: (1) to confine those who were unable to work for physical reasons; (2) to confine those who could not work for nonphysical reasons. In this way, mental disorders had become the object of medicine and a social category called "psychiatry" was born.

I am not trying to deny the validity of psychiatry, but this medicalization of the madman occurred quite late historically, and it does not seem to me that this result exerted a profound influence on his status. Furthermore, if this medicalization occurred, it was, as I said earlier, essentially for economic and social reasons: that was how the madman was made identical to the mentally ill individual and an entity called "mental illness" was discovered and developed. Psychiatric hospitals were created as something symmetrical to hospitals for physical illnesses. It could be said that the madman is an avatar of our capitalist societies, and it seems that, at bottom, the status of the madman does not vary at all between primitive societies and advanced societies. This only demonstrates the primitivism of our societies.

Today, in sum, I wanted to show the traumatizing quality that our societies still possess. If something has slightly revalorized the status of the madman, it would be the emergence of psychoanalysis and the psychotropic drugs. But that breakthrough has only just begun; our society still excludes madmen. As to whether this is the case only in capitalist societies, and as to how things are in socialist societies, my sociological knowledge is not adequate for making a judgment.

Note

1. Alain Robbe-Grillet, *Un Régicide* (Paris: Minuit, 1948).

WHAT IS AN AUTHOR?

The coming into being of the notion of "author" constitutes the privileged moment of individualization in the history of ideas, knowledge, literature, philosophy, and the sciences. Even today, when we reconstruct the history of a concept, literary genre, or school of philosophy, such categories seem relatively weak, secondary, and superimposed scansions in comparison with the solid and fundamental unit of the author and the work.

I shall not offer here a sociohistorical analysis of the author's persona. Certainly, it would be worth examining how the author became individualized in a culture like ours, what status he has been given, at what moment studies of authenticity and attribution began, in what kind of system of valorization the author was involved, at what point we began to recount the lives of authors rather than of heroes, and how this fundamental category of "the-man-and-his-work criticism" began. For the moment, however, I want to deal solely with the relationship between text and author and with the manner in which the text points to this figure that, at least in appearance, is outside it and antecedes it.

Beckett nicely formulates the theme with which I would like to begin: " 'What does it matter who is speaking,' someone said, 'what does it matter who is speaking.' " In this indifference appears one of the fundamental ethical principles of contemporary writing [*écriture*]. I say "ethical" because this indifference is really not a trait characterizing the manner in which one speaks and writes but, rather, a kind of immanent rule, taken up over and over again, never fully applied, not designating writing as something completed, but dominating it as a practice. Since it is too familiar to require a lengthy analysis, this immanent rule can be adequately illustrated here by tracing two of its major themes.

First of all, we can say that today's writing has freed itself from the theme of

This essay is the text of a lecture presented to the Société Française de philosophie on 22 February 1969 (Foucault gave a modified form of the lecture in the United States in 1970). This translation, by Josué V. Harari, has been slightly modified.

expression. Referring only to itself, but without being restricted to the confines of its interiority, writing is identified with its own unfolded exteriority. This means that it is an interplay of signs arranged less according to its signified content than according to the very nature of the signifier. Writing unfolds like a game [*jeu*] that invariably goes beyond its own rules and transgresses its limits. In writing, the point is not to manifest or exalt the act of writing, nor is it to pin a subject within language; it is, rather, a question of creating a space into which the writing subject constantly disappears.

The second theme, writing's relationship with death, is even more familiar. This link subverts an old tradition exemplified by the Greek epic, which was intended to perpetuate the immortality of the hero: if he was willing to die young, it was so that his life, consecrated and magnified by death, might pass into immortality; the narrative then redeemed this accepted death. In another way, the motivation, as well as the theme and the pretext of Arabian narratives—such as *The Thousand and One Nights*—was also the eluding of death: one spoke, telling stories into the early morning, in order to forestall death, to postpone the day of reckoning that would silence the narrator. Scheherazade's narrative is an effort, renewed each night, to keep death outside the circle of life.

Our culture has metamorphosed this idea of narrative, or writing, as something designed to ward off death. Writing has become linked to sacrifice, even to the sacrifice of life: it is now a voluntary effacement that does not need to be represented in books, since it is brought about in the writer's very existence. The work, which once had the duty of providing immortality, now possesses the right to kill, to be its author's murderer, as in the cases of Flaubert, Proust, and Kafka. That is not all, however: this relationship between writing and death is also manifested in the effacement of the writing subject's individual characteristics. Using all the contrivances that he sets up between himself and what he writes, the writing subject cancels out the signs of his particular individuality. As a result, the mark of the writer is reduced to nothing more than the singularity of his absence; he must assume the role of the dead man in the game of writing.

None of this is recent; criticism and philosophy took note of the disappearance—or death—of the author some time ago. But the consequences of their discovery of it have not been sufficiently examined, nor has its import been accurately measured. A certain number of notions that are intended to replace the privileged position of the author actually seem to preserve that privilege and suppress the real meaning of his disappearance. I shall examine two of these notions, both of great importance today.

The first is the idea of the work [*oeuvre*]. It is a very familiar thesis that the task of criticism is not to bring out the work's relationships with the author, nor to reconstruct through the text a thought or experience, but rather to analyze the work through its structure, its architecture, its intrinsic form, and the play of its internal relationships. At this point, however, a problem arises: What is a work? What is this curious unity which we designate as a work? Of what elements is it composed? Is it not what an author has written? Difficulties appear immediately. If an individual were not an author, could we say that what he wrote, said, left behind in his papers, or what has been collected of his remarks, could be called a "work"? When Sade was not considered an author, what was the status of his papers? Simply rolls of paper onto which he ceaselessly uncoiled his fantasies during his imprisonment.

Even when an individual has been accepted as an author, we must still ask whether everything that he wrote, said, or left behind is part of his work. The problem is both theoretical and technical. When undertaking the publication of Nietzsche's works, for example, where should one stop? Surely everything must be published, but what is "everything"? Everything that Nietzsche himself published, certainly. And what about the rough drafts for his works? Obviously. The plans for his aphorisms? Yes. The deleted passages and the notes at the bottom of the page? Yes. What if, within a workbook filled with aphorisms, one finds a reference, the notation of a meeting or of an address, or a laundry list: is it a work, or not? Why not? And so on, ad infinitum. How can one define a work amid the millions of traces left by someone after his death? A theory of the work does not exist, and the empirical task of those who naively undertake the editing of works often suffers in the absence of such a theory.

We could go even further: Does *The Thousand and One Nights* constitute a work? What about Clement of Alexandria's *Miscellanies* or Diogenes Laërtes' *Lives?* A multitude of questions arises with regard to this notion of the work. Consequently, it is not enough to declare that we should do without the writer (the author) and study the work itself. The word *work* and the unity that it designates are probably as problematic as the status of the author's individuality.

Another notion which has hindered us from taking full measure of the author's disappearance, blurring and concealing the moment of this effacement and subtly preserving the author's existence, is the notion of writing [*écriture*]. When rigorously applied, this notion should allow us not only to circumvent references to the author, but also to situate his recent absence. The notion of writing, as currently employed, is concerned with neither the act of writing nor the indication—be it symptom or sign—of a meaning that someone might have wanted to express. We try, with great effort, to imagine the general condition of each text, the condition of both the space in which it is dispersed and the time in which it unfolds.

In current usage, however, the notion of writing seems to transpose the empirical characteristics of the author into a transcendental anonymity. We are content to efface the more visible marks of the author's empiricity by playing off, one against the other, two ways of characterizing writing, namely, the critical and the religious approaches. Giving writing a primal status seems to be a way of retranslating, in transcendental terms, both the theological affirmation of its sacred character and the critical affirmation of its creative character. To admit that writing is, because of the very history that it made possible, subject to the test of oblivion and repression, seems to represent, in transcendental terms, the religious principle of the hidden meaning (which requires interpretation) and the critical principle of implicit significations, silent determinations, and obscured contents (which give rise to commentary). To imagine writing as absence seems to be a simple repetition, in transcendental terms, of both the religious principle of inalterable and yet never fulfilled tradition, and the aesthetic principle of the work's survival, its perpetuation beyond the author's death, and its enigmatic excess in relation to him.

This usage of the notion of writing runs the risk of maintaining the author's privileges under the protection of the a priori: it keeps alive, in the gray light of neutralization, the interplay of those representations that formed a particular image of the author. The author's disappearance, which, since Mallarmé, has been a constantly recurring event, is subject to a series of transcendental barriers. There seems to be an important dividing line between those who believe that they can still locate today's discontinuities [*ruptures*] in the historicotranscendental tradition of the nineteenth century and those who try to free themselves once and for all from that tradition.

It is not enough, however, to repeat the empty affirmation that the author has disappeared. For the same reason, it is not enough to keep repeating that God and man have died a common death. Instead, we must locate the space left empty by the author's disappearance, follow the distribution of gaps and breaches, and watch for the openings this disappearance uncovers.

First, we need to clarify briefly the problems arising from the use of the author's name. What is an author's name? How does it function? Far from offering a solution, I shall only indicate some of the difficulties that it presents.

The author's name is a proper name, and therefore it raises the problems common to all proper names. (Here I refer to Searle's analyses, among others.[1]) Obviously, one cannot turn a proper name into a pure and simple reference. It has other than indicative functions: more than an indication, a gesture, a finger pointed at someone, it is the equivalent of a description. When one says "Aristotle," one employs a word that is the equivalent of one, or a series, of definite descriptions, such as "the author of the *Analytics*," "the founder of ontology," and so forth. One cannot stop there, however, because a proper name does not have just one signification. When we discover that Arthur Rimbaud did not write *La Chasse spirituelle*, we cannot pretend that the meaning of this proper name, or that of the author, has been altered. The proper name and the author's name are situated between the two poles of description and designation: they must have a certain link with what they name, but one that is neither entirely in the mode of designation nor in that description; it must be a specific link. However—and it is here that the particular difficulties of the author's name arise—the links between the proper name and the individual named and between the author's name and what it names are not isomorphic and do not function in the same way. There are several differences.

If, for example, Pierre Dupont does not have blue eyes, or was not born in Paris, or is not a doctor, the name Pierre Dupont will still always refer to the same person; such things do not modify the link of designation. The problems raised by the author's name are much more complex, however. If I discover that Shakespeare was not born in the house we visit today, this is a modification that, obviously, will not alter the functioning of the author's name. But if we proved that Shakespeare did not write those sonnets which pass for his, that would constitute a significant change and affect the manner in which the author's name functions. If we proved that Shakespeare wrote Bacon's *Organon* by showing that the same author wrote both the works of Bacon and those of Shakespeare, that would be a third type of change that would entirely modify the functioning of the author's name. The author's name is not, therefore, just a proper name like the rest.

Many other facts point out the paradoxical singularity of the author's name. To say that Pierre Dupont does not exist is not at all the same as saying that Homer or Hermes Trismegistus did not exist. In the first case, it means that no one has the name Pierre Dupont; in the second, it means that several people were mixed together under one name, or that the true author had none of the traits traditionally ascribed to the personae of Homer or Hermes. To say that X's real name is actually Jacques Durand instead of Pierre Dupont is not the same as saying that Stendhal's name was Henri Beyle. One could also question the meaning and functioning of propositions like "Bourbaki is so-and-so, so-and-so, and so forth," and "Victor Eremita, Climacus, Anticlimacus, Frater Taciturnus, Constantine Constantius, all of these are Kierkegaard."

These differences may result from the fact that an author's name is not simply an element in a discourse (capable of being either subject or object, of being replaced by a pronoun, and the like); it performs a certain role with regard to narrative discourse, assuring a classificatory function. Such a name permits one to group together a certain number of texts, define them, differentiate them from and contrast them to others. In addition, it establishes a relationship among the texts. Hermes Trismegistus did not exist, nor did Hippocrates—in the sense that Balzac existed—but the fact that several texts have been placed under the same name indicates that there has been established among them a relationship of homogeneity, filiation, authentication of some texts by the use of others, re-

382 THE ESSENTIAL FOUCAULT

ciprocal explication, or concomitant utilization. The author's name serves to characterize a certain mode of being of discourse: the fact that the discourse has an author's name, that one can say "this was written by so-and-so" or "so-and-so is its author," shows that this discourse is not ordinary everyday speech that merely comes and goes, not something that is immediately consumable. On the contrary, it is a speech that must be received in a certain mode and that, in a given culture, must receive a certain status.

It would seem that the author's name, unlike other proper names, does not pass from the interior of a discourse to the real and exterior individual who produced it; instead, the name seems always to be present, marking off the edges of the text, revealing, or at least characterizing, its mode of being. The author's name manifests the appearance of a certain discursive set and indicates the status of this discourse within a society and a culture. It has no legal status, nor is it located in the fiction of the work; rather, it is located in the break that founds a certain discursive construct and its very particular mode of being. As a result, we could say that in a civilization like our own there are a certain number of discourses endowed with the "author function" while others are deprived of it. A private letter may well have a signer—it does not have an author; a contract may well have a guarantor—it does not have an author. An anonymous text posted on a wall probably has an editor—but not an author. The author function is therefore characteristic of the mode of existence, circulation, and functioning of certain discourses within a society.

Let us analyze this "author function" as we have just described it. In our culture, how does one characterize a discourse containing the author function? In what way is this discourse different from other discourses? If we limit our remarks to the author of a book or a text, we can isolate four different characteristics.

First of all, discourses are objects of appropriation. The form of ownership from which they spring is of a rather particular type, one that has been codified for many years. We should note that, historically, this type of ownership has always been subsequent to what one might call penal appropriation. Texts, books, and discourses really began to have authors (other than mythical, sacralized and sacralizing figures) to the extent that authors became subject to punishment, that is, to the extent that discourses could be transgressive. In our culture (and doubtless in many others), discourse was not originally a product, a thing, a kind of goods; it was essentially an act—an act placed in the bipolar field of the sacred and the profane, the licit and the illicit, the religious and the blasphemous. Historically, it was a gesture fraught with risks before becoming goods caught up in a circuit of ownership.

Once a system of ownership for texts came into being, once strict rules concerning author's rights, author—publisher relations, rights of reproduction,

and related matters were enacted—at the end of the eighteenth and the beginning of the nineteenth century—the possibility of transgression attached to the
act of writing took on, more and more, the form of an imperative peculiar to literature. It is as if the author, beginning with the moment at which he was placed
in the system of property that characterizes our society, compensated for the
status that he thus acquired by rediscovering the old bipolar field of discourse,
systematically practicing transgression and thereby restoring danger to a writing that was now guaranteed the benefits of ownership.

The author function does not affect all discourses in a universal and constant
way, however. In our civilization, it has not always been the same types of texts
that have required attribution to an author. There was a time when the texts we
today call "literary" (narratives, stories, epics, tragedies, comedies) were accepted, put into circulation, and valorized without any question about the identity of their author; their anonymity caused no difficulties since their
ancientness, whether real or imagined, was regarded as a sufficient guarantee of
their status. On the other hand, those texts we now would call scientific—those
dealing with cosmology and the heavens, medicine and illnesses, natural sciences and geography—were accepted in the Middle Ages, and accepted as
"true," only when marked with the name of their author. "Hippocrates said,"
"Pliny recounts," were not really formulas of an argument based on authority;
they were the markers inserted in discourses that were supposed to be received
as statements of demonstrated truth.

A switch takes place in the seventeenth or eighteenth century. Scientific discourses began to be received for themselves, in the anonymity of an established
or always redemonstrable truth; their membership in a systematic ensemble,
and not the reference to the individual who produced them, stood as their guarantee. The author function faded away, and the inventor's name served only to
christen a theorem, proposition, particular effect, property, body, group of elements, or pathological syndrome. By the same token, literary discourses came
to be accepted only when endowed with the author function. We now ask of
each poetic or fictional text: From where does it come, who wrote it, when,
under what circumstances, or beginning with what design? The meaning ascribed to it and the status or value accorded it depend on the manner in which
we answer these questions. And if a text should be discovered in a state of
anonymity—whether as a consequence of an accident or the author's explicit
wish—the game becomes one of rediscovering the author. Since literary
anonymity is not tolerable, we can accept it only in the guise of an enigma. As a
result, the author function today plays an important role in our view of literary
works. (These are obviously generalizations that would have to be refined insofar as recent critical practice is concerned. Criticism began some time ago to
treat works according to their genre and type, following the recurrent elements

that are enfigured in them, as proper variations around an invariant that is no longer the individual creator. Even so, if in mathematics reference to the author is barely anything any longer but a manner of naming theorems or sets of propositions, in biology and medicine the indication of the author and the date of his work play a rather different role. It is not simply a manner of indicating the source, but of providing a certain index of "reality" in relation to the techniques and objects of experience made use of in a particular period and in such-and-such a laboratory.)

The third characteristic of this author function is that it does not develop spontaneously as the attribution of a discourse to an individual. It is, rather, the result of a complex operation that constructs a certain being of reason that we call "author." Critics doubtless try to give this being of reason a realistic status, by discerning, in the individual, a "deep" motive, a "creative" power, or a "design," the milieu in which writing originates. Nevertheless, these aspects of an individual which we designate as making him an author are only a projection, in more or less psychologizing terms, of the operations we force texts to undergo, the connections we make, the traits we establish as pertinent, the continuities we recognize, or the exclusions we practice. All these operations vary according to periods and types of discourse. We do not construct a "philosophical author" as we do a "poet," just as in the eighteenth century one did not construct a novelist as we do today. Still, we can find through the ages certain constants in the rules of author construction.

It seems, for example, that the manner in which literary criticism once defined the author—or, rather, constructed the figure of the author beginning with existing texts and discourses—is directly derived from the manner in which Christian tradition authenticated (or rejected) the texts at its disposal. In order to "rediscover" an author in a work, modern criticism uses methods similar to those that Christian exegesis employed when trying to prove the value of a text by its author's saintliness. In *De Viris illustribus*, Saint Jerome explains that homonymy is not sufficient to identify legitimately authors of more than one work: different individuals could have had the same name, or one man could have, illegitimately, borrowed another's patronymic. The name as an individual trademark is not enough when one works within a textual tradition.

How, then, can one attribute several discourses to one and the same author? How can one use the author function to determine if one is dealing with one or several individuals? Saint Jerome proposes four criteria: (1) if among several books attributed to an author one is inferior to the others, it must be withdrawn from the list of the author's works (the author is therefore defined as a constant level of value); (2) the same should be done if certain texts contradict the doctrine expounded in the author's other works (the author is thus defined as a field of conceptual or theoretical coherence); (3) one must also exclude works that are written in a different style, containing words and expressions not ordinarily found in the writer's production (the author is here conceived as a stylistic unity); (4) finally, passages quoting statements made or mentioning events that occurred after the author's death must be regarded as interpolated texts (the author is here seen as a historical figure at the crossroads of a certain number of events).

Modern literary criticism, even when—as is now customary—it is not concerned with questions of authentication, still defines the author in much the same way; the author provides the basis for explaining not only the presence of certain events in a work, but also their transformations, distortions, and diverse modifications (through his biography, the determination of his individual perspective, the analysis of his social position, and the revelation of his basic design). The author is also the principle of a certain unity of writing—all differences having to be resolved, at least in part, by the principles of evolution, maturation, or influence. The author also serves to neutralize the contradictions that may emerge in a series of texts: there must be—at a certain level of his thought or desire, of his consciousness or unconscious—a point where contradictions are resolved, where incompatible elements are at last tied together or organized around a fundamental or originating contradiction. Finally, the author is a particular source of expression that, in more or less completed forms, is manifested equally well, and with similar validity, in works, sketches, letters, fragments, and so on. Clearly, Saint Jerome's four criteria of authenticity (criteria that seem totally insufficient for today's exegetes) do define the four modalities according to which modern criticism brings the author function into play.

But the author function is not a pure and simple reconstruction made second-hand from a text given as inert material. The text always contains a certain number of signs referring to the author. These signs, well known to grammarians, are personal pronouns, adverbs of time and place, and verb conjugation. Such elements do not play the same role in discourses provided with the author function as in those lacking it. In the latter, such "shifters" refer to the real speaker and to the spatio-temporal coordinates of his discourse (although certain modifications can occur, as in the operation of relating discourses in the first person). In the former, however, their role is more complex and variable. Everyone knows that, in a novel offered as a narrator's account, neither the first-person pronoun nor the present indicative refers exactly to the writer or to the moment in which he writes but, rather, to an alter ego whose distance from the author varies, often changing in the course of the work. It would be just as wrong to equate the author with the real writer as to equate him with the fictitious speaker; the author function is carried out and operates in the scission itself, in this division and this distance.

One might object that this is a characteristic peculiar to novelistic or poetic discourse, a game in which only "quasi discourses" participate. In fact, however, all discourses endowed with the author function possess this plurality of self. The self that speaks in the preface to a treatise on mathematics—and that indicates the circumstances of the treatise's composition—is identical neither in its position nor in its functioning to the self that speaks in the course of a demonstration, and that appears in the form of "I conclude" or "I suppose." In the first case, the "I" refers to an individual without an equivalent who, in a determined place and time, completed a certain task; in the second, the "I" indicates an instance and a level of demonstration which any individual could perform provided that he accepted the same system of symbols, play of axioms, and set of previous demonstrations. We could also, in the same treatise, locate a third self, one that speaks to tell the work's meaning, the obstacles encountered, the results obtained, and the remaining problems; this self is situated in the field of already existing or yet-to-appear mathematical discourses. The author function is not assumed by the first of these selves at the expense of the other two, which would then be nothing more than a fictitious splitting in two of the first one. On the contrary, in these discourses the author function operates so as to effect the dispersion of these three simultaneous selves.

No doubt, analysis could discover still more characteristic traits of the author function. I will limit myself to these four, however, because they seem both the most visible and the most important. They can be summarized as follows: (1) the author function is linked to the juridical and institutional system that encompasses, determines, and articulates the universe of discourses; (2) it does not affect all discourses in the same way at all times and in all types of civilization; (3) it is not defined by the spontaneous attribution of a discourse to its producer but, rather, by a series of specific and complex operations; (4) it does not refer purely and simply to a real individual, since it can give rise simultaneously to several selves, to several subjects—positions that can be occupied by different classes of individuals.

Up to this point I have unjustifiably limited my subject. Certainly the author function in painting, music, and other arts should have been discussed; but even supposing that we remain within the world of discourse, as I want to do, I seem to have given the term "author" much too narrow a meaning. I have discussed the author only in the limited sense of a person to whom the production of a text, a book, or a work can be legitimately attributed. It is easy to see that in the sphere of discourse one can be the author of much more than a book—one can be the author of a theory, tradition, or discipline in which other books and authors will in their turn find a place. These authors are in a position that I will call "transdiscursive." This is a recurring phenomenon—certainly as old as our civilization. Homer, Aristotle, and the Church Fathers, as well as the first mathematicians and the originators of the Hippocratic tradition, all played this role. Furthermore, in the course of the nineteenth century, there appeared in Europe another, more uncommon, kind of author, whom one should confuse with neither the "great" literary authors, nor the authors of religious texts, nor the founders of science. In a somewhat arbitrary way we shall call those who belong in this last group "founders of discursivity."

They are unique in that they are not just the authors of their own works. They have produced something else: the possibilities and the rules for the formation of other texts. In this sense they are very different, for example, from a novelist, who is, in fact, nothing more than the author of his own text. Freud is not just the author of *The Interpretation of Dreams* or *Jokes and Their Relation to the Unconscious;* Marx is not just the author of the *Communist Manifesto* or *Das Kapital:* they both have established an endless possibility of discourse. Obviously, it is easy to object. One might say that it is not true that the author of a novel is only the author of his own text; in a sense, he also, provided that he acquires some "importance," governs and commands more than that. To take a very simple example, one could say that Ann Radcliffe not only wrote *The Castles of Athlin and Dunbayne* and several other novels but also made possible the appearance of the Gothic horror novel at the beginning of the nineteenth century; in that respect, her author function exceeds her own work. But I think there is an answer to this objection. These founders of discursivity (I use Marx and Freud as examples, because I believe them to be both the first and the most important cases) make possible something altogether different from what a novelist makes possible. Ann Radcliffe's texts opened the way for a certain number of resemblances and analogies which have their model or principle in her work. The latter contains characteristic signs, figures, relationships, and structures that could be reused by others. In other words, to say that Ann Radcliffe founded the Gothic horror novel means that in the nineteenth-century Gothic novel one will find, as in Ann Radcliffe's works, the theme of the heroine caught in the trap of her own innocence, the hidden castle, the character of the black, cursed hero devoted to making the world expiate the evil done to him, and all the rest of it. On the other hand, when I speak of Marx or Freud as founders of discursivity, I mean that they made possible not only a certain number of analogies but also (and equally important) a certain number of differences. They have created a possibility for something other than their discourse, yet something belonging to what they founded. To say that Freud founded psychoanalysis does not (simply) mean that we find the concept of the libido or the technique of dream analysis in the works of Karl Abraham or Melanie Klein; it means that Freud made possible a certain number of divergences—with respect to his own texts, concepts, and hypotheses—that all arise from the psychoanalytic discourse itself.

This would seem to present a new difficulty, however, or at least a new problem: is the above not true, after all, of any founder of a science, or of any author who has introduced some transformation into a science that might be called fecund? After all, Galileo made possible not only those discourses which repeated the laws he had formulated, but also statements very different from what he himself had said. If Georges Cuvier is the founder of biology, or Ferdinand de Saussure the founder of linguistics, it is not because they were imitated, nor because people have since taken up again the concept of organism or sign; it is because Cuvier made possible, to a certain extent, a theory of evolution diametrically opposed to his own fixism; it is because Saussure made possible a generative grammar radically different from his structural analyses. Superficially, then, the initiation of discursive practices appears similar to the founding of any scientific endeavor.

Still, there is a difference, and a notable one. In the case of a science, the act that founds it is on an equal footing with its future transformations; this act becomes in some respects part of the set of modifications that it makes possible. Of course, this belonging can take several forms. In the future development of a science, the founding act may appear as little more than a particular instance of a more general phenomenon that unveils itself in the process. It can also turn out to be marred by intuition and empirical bias; one must then reformulate it, making it the object of a certain number of supplementary theoretical operations that establish it more rigorously, and so on. Finally, it can seem to be a hasty generalization that must be retraced. In other words, the founding act of a science can always be reintroduced within the machinery of those transformations which derive from it.

In contrast, the initiation of a discursive practice is heterogeneous to its subsequent transformations. To expand a type of discursivity, such as psychoanalysis as founded by Freud, is not to give it a formal generality it would not have permitted at the outset but, rather, to open it up to a certain number of possible applications. To limit psychoanalysis as a type of discursivity is, in reality, to try to isolate in the founding act an eventually restricted number of propositions or statements to which, alone, one grants a founding value, and in relation to which certain concepts or theories accepted by Freud might be considered as derived, secondary, and accessory. In addition, one does not declare certain propositions in the work of these founders to be false: instead, when trying to seize the act of founding, one sets aside those statements that are not pertinent, either because they are deemed inessential, or because they are considered "prehistoric" and derived from another type of discursivity. In other words, unlike the founding of a science, the initiation of a discursive practice does not participate in its later transformations. As a result, one defines a proposition's theoretical validity in relation to the work of the founders—while, in the case of Galileo and Newton, it is in relation to what physics or cosmology is in its intrinsic structure and normativity that one affirms the validity of any proposition those men may have put forth. To phrase it very schematically: the work of initiators of discursivity is not situated in the space that science defines; rather, it is the science or the discursivity which refers back to their work as primary coordinates.

In this way we can understand the inevitable necessity, within these fields of discursivity, for a "return to the origin." This return, which is part of the discursive field itself, never stops modifying it. The return is not a historical supplement that would be added to the discursivity, or merely an ornament; on the contrary, it constitutes an effective and necessary task of transforming the discursive practice itself. Reexamination of Galileo's text may well change our understanding of the history of mechanics, but it will never be able to change mechanics itself. On the other hand, reexamining Freud's texts modifies psychoanalysis itself, just as a reexamination of Marx's would modify Marxism.

What I have just outlined regarding these "discursive instaurations" is, of course, very schematic; this is true, in particular, of the opposition I have tried to draw between discursive initiation and scientific founding. It is not always easy to distinguish between the two; moreover, nothing proves that they are two mutually exclusive procedures. I have attempted the distinction for only one reason: to show that the author function, which is complex enough when one tries to situate it at the level of a book or a series of texts that carry a given signature, involves still more determining factors when one tries to analyze it in larger units, such as groups of works or entire disciplines.

To conclude, I would like to review the reasons why I attach a certain importance to what I have said.

On the one hand, an analysis in the direction that I have outlined might provide for an approach to a typology of discourse. It seems to me, at least at first glance, that such a typology cannot be constructed solely from the grammatical features, formal structures, and objects of discourse: more likely, there exist properties or relationships peculiar to discourse (not reducible to the rules of grammar and logic), and one must use these to distinguish the major categories of discourse. The relationship (or nonrelationship) with an author, and the different forms this relationship takes, constitute—in a quite visible manner—one of these discursive properties.

On the other hand, I believe that one could find here an introduction to the historical analysis of discourse. Perhaps it is time to study discourses not only in terms of their expressive value or formal transformations but according to their modes of existence. The modes of circulation, valorization, attribution, and appropriation of discourses vary with each culture and are modified within each. The manner in which they are articulated according to social relationships can be more readily understood, I believe, in the activity of the author function and in its modifications than in the themes or concepts that discourses set in motion.

It would seem that one could also, beginning with analyses of this type, reexamine the privileges of the subject. I realize that in undertaking the internal and architectonic analysis of a work (be it a literary text, philosophical system, or scientific work), in setting aside biographical and psychological references, one has already called back into question the absolute character and founding role of the subject. Still, perhaps one must return to this question, not in order to reestablish the theme of an originating subject but to grasp the subject's points of insertion, modes of functioning, and system of dependencies. Doing so means overturning the traditional problem, no longer raising the questions: How can a free subject penetrate the density of things and give it meaning? How can it activate the rules of a language from within and thus give rise to the designs that are properly its own? Instead, these questions will be raised: How, under what conditions, and in what forms can something like a subject appear in the order of discourse? What place can it occupy in each type of discourse, what functions can it assume, and by obeying what rules? In short, it is a matter of depriving the subject (or its substitute) of its role as originator, and of analyzing the subject as a variable and complex function of discourse.

Second, there are reasons dealing with the "ideological" status of the author. The question then becomes: How can one reduce the great peril, the great danger with which fiction threatens our world? The answer is: One can reduce it with the author. The author allows a limitation of the cancerous and dangerous proliferation of significations within a world where one is thrifty not only with one's resources and riches but also with one's discourses and their significations. The author is the principle of thrift in the proliferation of meaning. As a result, we must entirely reverse the traditional idea of the author. We are accustomed, as we have seen earlier, to saying that the author is the genial creator of a work in which he deposits, with infinite wealth and generosity, an inexhaustible world of significations. We are used to thinking that the author is so different from all other men, and so transcendent with regard to all languages that, as soon as he speaks, meaning begins to proliferate, to proliferate indefinitely.

The truth is quite the contrary: the author is not an indefinite source of significations that fill a work; the author does not precede the works; he is a certain functional principle by which, in our culture, one limits, excludes, and chooses; in short, by which one impedes the free circulation, the free manipulation, the free composition, decomposition, and recomposition of fiction. In fact, if we are accustomed to presenting the author as a genius, as a perpetual surging of invention, it is because, in reality, we make him function in exactly the opposite fashion. One can say that the author is an ideological product, since we represent him as the opposite of his historically real function. When a historically given function is represented in a figure that inverts it, one has an ideological production. The author is therefore the ideological figure by which one marks the manner in which we fear the proliferation of meaning.

In saying this, I seem to call for a form of culture in which fiction would not be limited by the figure of the author. It would be pure romanticism, however, to imagine a culture in which the fictive would operate in an absolutely free state, in which fiction would be put at the disposal of everyone and would develop without passing through something like a necessary or constraining figure. Although, since the eighteenth century, the author has played the role of the regulator of the fictive, a role quite characteristic of our era of industrial and bourgeois society, of individualism and private property, still, given the historical modifications that are taking place, it does not seem necessary that the author function remain constant in form, complexity, and even in existence. I think that, as our society changes, at the very moment when it is in the process of changing, the author function will disappear, and in such a manner that fiction and its polysemous texts will once again function according to another mode, but still with a system of constraint—one that will no longer be the author but will have to be determined or, perhaps, experienced [*expérimenter*].

All discourses, whatever their status, form, value, and whatever the treatment to which they will be subjected, would then develop in the anonymity of a murmur. We would no longer hear the questions that have been rehashed for so long: Who really spoke? Is it really he and not someone else? With what authenticity or originality? And what part of his deepest self did he express in his discourse? Instead, there would be other questions, like these: What are the modes of existence of this discourse? Where has it been used, how can it circulate, and who can appropriate it for himself? What are the places in it where there is room for possible subjects? Who can assume these various subject functions? And behind all these questions, we would hear hardly anything but the stirring of an indifference: What difference does it make who is speaking?

Notes

1. John Searle, *Speech Acts: An Essay in the Philosophy of Language* (Cambridge, Eng.: Cambridge University Press, 1969), pp. 162–74—Ed.

ON THE ARCHAEOLOGY OF THE SCIENCES: RESPONSE TO THE EPISTEMOLOGY CIRCLE

O ur sole intention in asking these questions of the author of *Madness and Civilization*, *Birth of the Clinic*, and *The Order of Things*, was to get him to state the critical propositions on which the possibility of his theory and the implications of his method are founded. The Circle[1] proceeded by requesting him to define his replies in relation to the status, the history, and the concept of science.

ON THE EPISTEME AND EPISTEMOLOGICAL RUPTURE

Since the work of Gaston Bachelard the notion of epistemological rupture has served to designate the discontinuity, which the history and philosophy of the sciences claim to detect, between the birth of every science and the "tissue of tenacious positive, solidary errors" which in retrospect is recognized to have preceded it. The prototypical examples of Galileo, Newton, and Lavoisier, but also those of Einstein and Mendeleev, illustrate the horizontal perpetuation of that rupture.

The author of *The Order of Things* detects a vertical discontinuity between the epistemic configuration of one epoch and the next.

We ask him: What relations are maintained between that horizontality and that vertically?[2]

This "response" to the Paris Epistemology Circle originally appeared in *Cahiers pour l'analyse* 9 (Summer 1968): *Genealogy of the Sciences*, pp. 9–40. The translation has been extensively amended.

The archaeological periodization delimits within the continuum synchronic sets which group learnings together in the pattern of unitary systems. Would he accept the alternative that was proposed to him between a radical historicism (archaeology could predict its own reinscription into a new discourse) and a sort of absolute knowledge (of which some authors could have had the presentment independently of epistemic constraints)?

FOUCAULT'S REPLY

A curious intersection. For decades now historians have preferred to devote their attention to long periods of time. As if, beneath the political peripeties and their episodes, historians undertook to bring to light the stable and resilient equilibria, the imperceptible processes, constant readjustments, the tendential phenomena that culminate, then reverse after secular continuities, the movements of accumulation and slow saturations, the great immobile and mute bases that the tangle of traditional narratives had hidden beneath a thick coating of events. To conduct this analysis, historians deploy the instruments they have partly fashioned and partly received: models of economic growth, quantitative analysis of the flows of exchange, profiles of demographic growth and regression, and the study of climatic fluctuations. These tools have enabled them to distinguish, in the field of history, various sedimentary strata; the linear successions, which until then had been the object of research, were replaced by a set of deeper uncouplings. From political instability to the dilatoriness proper to "material civilization," the levels of analysis have multiplied; each level has its specific ruptures; each contains a periodicity that belongs only to itself. And the units become broader the further one descends toward the deeper strata. The old historical question (what link to establish between discontinuous events) is replaced, from now on, by a series of difficult interrogations: Which layers should be isolated from each other? What type and criteria of periodization need to be adopted for each of them? What system of relations, (hierarchy, dominance, tier-arrangement, univocal determination, circular causality), can be established between them.

Now, in about the same period, in those disciplines which are called the history of ideas, of the sciences, of philosophy, of thought and also literature (their specificity can be left aside for the moment), in those disciplines which, in spite of their titles, on the whole escape the work of the historian and his methods, attention was displaced from the vast units forming an "epoch" or "century" toward phenomena of rupture. Beneath the great continuities of thought, beneath the massive and homogeneous manifestations of the mind, and beneath the stubborn development of a science struggling from its beginnings to exist and complete itself, attempts have been made to detect the occurrence of interruptions. Gaston Bachelard has charted out the epistemological thresholds that interrupt the indefinite accumulation of knowledges [*connaissances*]; Martial Geroult has described the enclosed systems, the closed conceptual architectures that partition the space of philosophical discourse; Georges Canguilhem has analyzed the mutations, displacements, and transformations in the field of validity and the rules for the use of concepts. As for literary analysis, it is the internal structure of the oeuvre—on a still smaller scale the text—that it examines.

But this intersection should not give us any illusions. We should not accept on trust the appearance that certain historical disciplines have moved from continuity to discontinuity, while others—really history as such—were moving from the swarm of discontinuities to broad and uninterrupted units. In fact, what has happened is that the notion of discontinuity has changed in status. For history in its classical form, discontinuity was both the given and the unthinkable: it was both what presented itself in the form of scattered events, institutions, ideas, or practices; and what had to be evaded, reduced, effaced by the historian's discourse in order to reveal the continuity of the concatenations. Discontinuity was that stigma of temporal dispersion which it was the historian's duty to suppress from history.

It has now become one of the fundamental elements of historical analysis. It appears in this analysis with a triple role. First it constitutes a deliberate operation of the historian (and no longer what he receives willy-nilly from the material he has to deal with): for he must, at least as a systematic hypothesis, distinguish between the possible levels of his analysis, and establish the periodizations that suit them. It is also the result of his description (and no longer what has to be eliminated by the action of his analysis): for what he undertakes to discover is the limits of a process, the point of change of a curve, the reversal of a regulatory movement, the bounds of an oscillation, the threshold of a function, the emergence of a mechanism, the moment a circular causality is upset. Finally, it is a concept that his work constantly specifies. It is no longer a pure and uniform void interposing a single blank between two positive patterns; it has a different form and function, according to the domain and level to which it is assigned. A notion that cannot but be rather paradoxical: since it is both instrument and object of the investigation, since it delimits the field of an analysis of which it is itself an effect; since it makes it possible to individualize the domains but can only be established by comparing them; since it only breaks down units in order to establish new ones; since it punctuates series and duplicates levels; and, in the last analysis, since it is not just a concept present in the historian's discourse but one that he secretly presupposes. On what basis could he speak if not on that of this rupture which offers him history as an object—and its own history?

To be schematic, we could say that history and, in a general way, historical disciplines have ceased to be the reconstitution of the concatenations behind the apparent sequences; they now practice the systematic introduction of discontinuity. The great change that characterizes them in our epoch is not the extension of their domain to economic mechanisms with which they have long been familiar nor is it the integration of ideological phenomena, forms of thought, or types of mentality: they were already being analyzed in the nineteenth century. It is, rather, the transformation of discontinuity: its transition from obstacle to practice; an internalization into the discourse of the historian which means it need no longer be an external fatality that has to be reduced but, rather, an operational concept to be utilized; an inversion of signs thanks to which it is no longer the negative of historical reading (its underside, its failure, the limits of its power) but the positive element that determines its object and validates its analysis. We must be prepared to understand what has become history in the real work of the historians: a certain controlled use of discontinuity for the analysis of temporal series.

It is clear that many remain blind to this fact which is contemporaneous with us and yet which historical knowledge has born witness to for nearly half a century. Indeed, if history could remain the chain of uninterrupted continuities, if it ceaselessly linked together concatenations that no analysis could undo without abstraction, if it wove obscure syntheses always in the process of reconstitution around men, their words and their deeds, it would be a privileged shelter for consciousness: what it takes away from the latter by bringing to light material determinations, inert practices, unconscious processes, forgotten intentions in the silence of institutions and things, it would restore in the form of a spontaneous synthesis; or rather, it would allow it to pick up once again all the threads that had escaped it, to reanimate all those dead activities, and to become again the sovereign subject in a new or restored light. Continuous history is the correlate of consciousness: the guarantee that what escapes from it can be restored to it; the promise that it will some day be able to appropriate outright all those things which surround it and weigh down on it, to restore its mastery over them, and to find in them what really must be called—leaving the word all its overload of meaning—its home. The desire to make historical analysis the discourse of continuity, and make human consciousness the originating subject of all knowledge and all practice, are the two faces of one and the same system of thought. Time is conceived in terms of totalization, and revolution never as anything but a coming to consciousness.

However, since the beginning of this century, psychoanalytical, linguistic, and then ethnological research has dispossessed the subject of the laws of its desire, the forms of its speech, the rules of its action, and the systems of its mythical discourses. Those in France who are securely in control, constantly reply:

"Yes, but history . . . history, which is not a structure, but becoming; not simultaneity, but succession; not a system but a practice; not a form, but a never-ending effort of a consciousness coming back to itself, and attempting to regain control of itself right down to the most basic of its conditions; history, which is not discontinuity but long and uninterrupted patience." But in order to chant this contestatory litany, it was essential to divert attention from the work of historians, that is, refuse to see what is actually happening in their practice and discourse; close one's eyes to the great mutation of their discipline; remain obstinately blind to the fact that perhaps history is not a better shelter for the sovereignty of consciousness, less perilous than that of myths, language or sexuality; in short, for the sake of salvation, it was essential to reconstitute a history that is no longer being done. And if this history could not offer enough security, the development of thought, knowledges [*connaissances*], knowledge [*savoir*], and the development of a consciousness forever close to itself, indefinitely bound to its past and present in all its moment, was asked to save what had to be saved: Who dares strip the subject of its recent history? Every time the use of discontinuity becomes too visible in an historical analysis (particularly if it is concerned with knowledge) the cry goes up: History murdered! But do not make a mistake here: what is mourned for so loudly is in no sense the obliteration of history but the disappearance of that form of history which was secretly, but in its entirely, transferred to the synthetic activity of the subject. All the treasure of the past had been hoarded in the ancient citadel of this history. It was believed to be strong, because it was sanctified, and it was the last bastion of philosophical anthropology [*de la pensée anthropologique*]. But historians went elsewhere long ago. They can no longer be counted on to protect the privileges or to reaffirm once again—however necessary it might be in the present troubles—that history at least is living and continuous.

THE FIELD OF DISCURSIVE EVENTS

If one wants to apply the concept of discontinuity systematically (that is, to define it, to use it in as general a way as possible and to validate it) to these domains—so uncertain of their frontiers and so indecisive in their content—which are called the history of ideas, thought, science, knowledges [*connaissances*], a certain number of problems arise.

First, the negative tasks. It is essential to break free of a set of notions connected with the postulate of continuity. Doubtless, they do not have a very rigorous structure, but their function is very precise. Such is the notion of tradition, which makes it possible both to register all innovations with respect to a system of permanent coordinates and to give a status to an ensemble of constant phenomena. Such is the notion of influence, which gives a more mystical than substantial support to the facts of transmission and communication. Such is the notion of development, which makes it possible to describe a sequence of events as the manifestation of one and the same organizing principle. Such is the symmetrical and inverse notion of teleology or evolution toward a normative stage. Such are the notions of the mentality or spirit of an age, which make it possible to establish a community of meanings, of symbolic ties or a play of resemblances and mirrors between simultaneous or successive phenomena. It is necessary to abandon those readymade syntheses, those groupings which are admitted before any examination, those links of which the validity is accepted at the outset; to drive out the obscure forms and forces by which it is customary to link together the thoughts of men and their discourses; to accept having no other business in the first instance than with a population of dispersed events.

There is no longer any need to consider as valid the lines of demarcation between disciplines or the groups with which we have become familiar. As they stand, one cannot accept either the distinction between the broad types of discourse, or that between forms of genres (science literature, philosophy, religion, history, fiction, and so on). The reasons are blindingly obvious. We are ourselves uncertain of the use of these distinctions in the world of our own discourse. This is true a fortiori when one is concerned to analyze sets of statements which were distributed, scattered, and generally characterized in a completely different manner; after all, "literature" and "politics" are recent categories that can only be applied to medieval or even Classical culture by means of a retrospective hypothesis and by a play of new analogies or semantic resemblances. Neither literature nor politics nor, consequently, philosophy and the sciences were articulated in the field of discourse in the seventeenth and eighteenth centuries as they were in the nineteenth century. Anyway, it is clearly necessary to recognize that these divisions—those which we accept today, or those which are contemporary to the discourses studied—are always themselves reflexive categories, principles of classification, normative rules and institutionalized types; they are, in turn, facts of discourse which merit analysis alongside other facts, which certainly have complex relations with them, but do not have intrinsic characteristics that are autonomous and universally recognizable.

But, above all, the unities that must be questioned are those which appear most immediately—those of the book and the oeuvre. At first sight they cannot be removed without extreme artificiality; they are given in a most certain manner, either by a material individualization (a book is a thing that occupies a determinate space, has its economic value, and itself marks the limits of its beginning and end with a number) or by an assignable relation (even if in certain cases it is rather problematic) between discourses and the individual who has put them forward. And yet, as soon as one looks at them more closely, the difficulties begin. They are no less than those that the linguist encounters when he seeks to define the unity of a sentence, or the historian encounters when he seeks to define the unity of literature or science. The unity of a book is not a homogeneous unity: the relations that exist between different mathematical treatises are not the same as those existing between different philosophical texts. The difference between one of Stendahl's novels and one of Dostoyevsky's novels cannot be superposed upon that which separates two volumes of The Human Comedy; and the latter, in its turn, cannot be superposed upon that which separates *Ulysses* from *The Portrait of the Artist as a Young Man*. Further, the edges of a book are neither clear nor rigorously delineated. No book exists by itself, it is always in a relation of support and dependence vis-à-vis other books; it is a point in a network—it contains a system of indications that point, explicitly or implicitly, to other books, other texts, or other sentences. If one is concerned with a book of physics, or with a collection of political speeches, or with a science fiction novel, the system of indications and consequently the complex relations of autonomy and heteronomy will differ. However much the book is given as an object one might have in hand, however much it is constrained within the little paralleliped that encloses it, its unity is variable and relative; the latter is neither constructed nor indicated, and consequently cannot be described except from out of a discursive field.

As for the oeuvre, the problems it raises are still more difficult. On the face of it, the oeuvre is merely the sum of the texts that can be designated by the sign of a proper name. But the designation (even if one leaves aside the problems of attribution) is not a homogeneous function: an author's name does not designate a text that he published himself under his own name, another that he presented under a pseudonym, another that might be discovered after his death in crude form, still another that is no more than scribbling, a notebook of jottings, a "paper," in the same fashion. The constitution of a complete oeuvre or an opus presumes a number of theoretical choices that are easy neither to justify nor even to formulate. Is it enough to add to the texts published by an author those he projected putting into print but which remained incomplete only by the fact of his death? Must one add abandoned outlines? And what status to give to letters, to notes, to reported conversations, to remarks recorded by auditors—in short, to the immense swarm of verbal traces that an individual leaves around him at the moment of death, which speak so many different languages in an indefinite intersection, and which will linger for centuries, perhaps for millennia, before being effaced? In any case, the designation of a text by the name "Mallarmé" is doubtless not of the same type if it is a matter of English themes, translations of Edgar Allan Poe, poems, or responses to inquiries. The same relation does not exist between the name of Nietzsche, on the one hand, and the youthful autobiographies, the scholarly dissertations, the philological articles,

Zarathustra, Ecce homo, the letters, the last postcards signed by Dionysos or Kaiser Nietzsche, the innumerable notebooks in which laundry lists are entangled with sketches of aphorisms, on the other.

In fact, the only unity that can be recognized in the "oeuvre" of an author is a certain function of expression. The presumption is that there must be a level (as deep as it is necessary to presume it to be) at which the oeuvre reveals itself, in all its fragments, even the most minuscule and inessential, as the expression of the thought, or the experience, or the imagination, or the unconscious of the author, or of historical determinations in which he was caught. But one soon sees that the unity of the opus, far from being immediately given, is constituted by an operation; that this operation is interpretative (in the sense that it deciphers, in the text, the expression or transcription of something at once hidden and manifest); that, in the end, the operation that determines the opus, in its unity—and consequently the oeuvre itself as the result of that operation—will not be the same for the author of *Theater and Its Double* or for the author of the *Tractatus Logico-philosophicus.* The oeuvre cannot be considered either an immediate unity, or a certain unity, or a homogeneous unity.

Finally, as a last measure to put out of circulation the unreflected continuities by means of which the discourse that one seeks to analyze is half-secretly organized in advance, it is crucial to renounce two postulates that are bound together, facing one another. The one assumes that it is never possible to find the irruption of a genuine event in the order of discourse; that, beyond every apparent beginning, there is always a secret origin—so secret and primordial that it can never be entirely recaptured in itself. So much so that one is led fatefully through the naïveté of chronologies, toward an indefinitely distant point, never present in any history. The point itself could only be its own emptiness; all beginnings from that point could only be recommencements or occultations (strictly speaking both, in one and the same gesture.) Linked to this is the thesis that every manifest discourse secretly rests on an "already said"; but that this "already said" is not just a phrase already pronounced, a text already written, but a "never said"—a disembodied discourse, a voice as silent as a breath, a writing that is only the void left by its own trace. It is thus presumed that all that discourse happens to put into words is already found articulated in that half silence which precedes it, which continues to run obstinately underneath it, but which it uncovers and renders quiet. In the final account, manifest discourse would only be the depressive presence of what it does not say; and the nonsaid would be a hollow that animates from the interior all that is said. The first motif dedicates the historical analysis of discourse to being a quest for and repetition of an origin that escapes all determination of origin. The second dedicates it to being an interpretation or monitoring of an already-said that would at the same time be a nonsaid. These two themes, which function to guarantee the infinite continuity of discourse and its secret presence to itself in the action of an absence that is always one stage farther back, must be renounced. Each moment of discourse must be welcomed in its irruption as an event; in the punctuation where it appears; and in the temporal dispersion that allows it to be repeated, known, forgotten, transformed, wiped out down to its slightest traces, and buried far from every eye in the dust of books. There is no need to retrace the discourse to the remote presence of its origin; it must be treated in the play of its immediacy.

Once these preliminary forms of continuity, these unregulated syntheses of discourse are set aside, a whole domain is set free. An immense domain, but one that can be defined; it is constituted by the set of all effective statements (whether spoken or written) in their dispersion as events and in the immediacy that is proper to each. Before it is dealt with as a science, a novel, a political discourse, or the work of an author, or even a book, the material to be handled in its initial neutrality is a population of events in the space of discourse in general. Hence the project of a *pure description of the facts of discourse*. This description is easily distinguished from a linguistic analysis. Of course, one can establish a linguistic system (if one does not construct it artificially) only by utilizing a corpus of statements [*énoncés*], or a collection of discursive acts. But it is then an issue of defining, on the basis of an ensemble that has the value of a sample, rules that permit the eventual construction of different statements. Even if it disappeared a long time ago, even if no one speaks it anymore and it is reestablished on rare fragments, a language always constitutes a system for possible statements. It is a finite ensemble of rules which authorizes an infinite number of performances. Discourse, in contrast, is the always-finite and temporally limited ensemble of those statements alone which were formulated. They might be innumerable; they might, by their mass, exceed any capacity for registration; they nevertheless constitute a finite ensemble. The question asked by linguistic analysis, concerning a discursive act, is always: According to what rules has this statement been constituted and consequently, according to what rules could other similar statements be constructed? The description of discourse asks a different question: How is it that this statement appeared, rather than some other one in its place?

Similarly, it is clear why this description of discourse is opposed to the analysis of thought. There, too, a system of thought can only be reconstituted from a definite ensemble of discourses. But this ensemble is treated in such a manner that one attempts to rediscover, beyond the statements themselves, the intention of the speaking subject, his conscious activity, what he meant, or even the unconscious pattern that emerges against his will in what he says or in the hardly discernible cracks in his explicit utterances. At any rate, it is a matter of reconstituting another discourse, rediscovering the barely audible, murmuring, endless utterance that animates the voice heard from within and reestablishing the tenuous and invisible text that skims through the interstices of the written lines and occasionally jostles them. The analysis of thought is always *allegorical* in relation to the discourse which it uses. Its question is invariably: What, then, was being said in what was said? But the analysis of discourse is directed to another end: it is concerned to grasp the statement in the narrowness and singularity of its event; to determine the conditions of its existence, to fix its limits as accurately as possible, to establish its correlations with the other statements with which it may be linked, and to show what other forms of articulation it excludes. It does not look beneath what is manifest for the barely heard mutterings of another discourse. It must show why the discourse could not be other than it was, what makes it exclusive of other discourses, and how it takes up a position among other discourses and in relation to them which no other could occupy. The real question of the analysis of discourse could, therefore, be formulated as follows: What is this regular existence that comes to the fore in what is said— and nowhere else?

One might ask what is the ultimate purpose of this suspension of all accepted units, this obstinate pursuit of discontinuity, if it is no more than a matter of releasing a cloud of discursive events, of collecting them and preserving them in their absolute dispersion. In fact, the systematic effacement of merely given units makes it possible, first, to restore to the statement its singularity as an event. It is no longer regarded merely as the intervention of a linguistic structure, nor as the epoisodic manifestation of a deeper significance than itself; it is dealt with at the level of its historical irruption; an attempt is made to direct attention at the incision it constitutes, this irreducible—and often minute—emergence. However banal it is, however unimportant its consequences may seem, however quickly it is forgotten after its appearance, however little understood or badly deciphered one would think it, however quickly it may be devoured by the night, a statement is always an event that neither language nor meaning can completely exhaust. A strange event, certainly: first, because, on the one hand, it is linked to an act of writing or to the articulation of a speech but, on the other hand, opens for itself a residual existence in the field of a memory or in the materiality of manuscripts, books, and any other form of record; then because it is unique like every other event, but is open to repetition, transformation, and reactivation; finally, because it is linked both to the situations that give rise to it, and to the consequences it gives rise to, but also at the same time and in quite another modality, to the statements that precede it and follow it.

But the instance of the enunciative event has been isolated with respect to language and thought not in order to deal with it in itself as if it were independent, solitary, and sovereign. On the contrary, the aim is to grasp how these statements, as events and in their so peculiar specificity, can be articulated to events that are not discursive in nature, but may be of a technical, practical, economic, social, political, or other variety. To reveal in its purity the space through which discursive events are scattered is not to undertake to establish it inside a break [*coupure*] that nothing could cross; it is not to close it in on itself; nor, a fortiori, to open it to a transcendence; on the contrary, it is to acquire the freedom to describe a series of relations between it and other systems outside it. Relations that have to be established—without recourse to the general form of language or to the individual consciousness of the speaking subjects—in the field of events.

The third advantage of such a description of discursive acts is that releasing them from all the groupings that present themselves as natural, immediate, and universal unities makes it possible to describe other unities, but this time by a set of controlled decisions. Given that the conditions are clearly defined, it might be legitimate, on the basis of correctly described relations, to constitute discursive ensembles that would not be new but would, however, have remained invisible. Those ensembles would not be at all new, because they would be made up of already-formulated statements, between which a certain number of well-determined relations could be recognized. But these relations would never have been formulated for themselves in the statements in question (unlike, for example, those explicit relations which are posed and pronounced by the discourse itself when it adopts the form of the novel, or is inscribed in a series of mathematical theorems). But these invisible relations would in no way constitute a kind of secret discourse animating the manifest discourses from within; it is not therefore an interpretation that could make them come to light but, rather, the analysis of their coexistence, of their succession, of their mutual dependence, of their reciprocal determination, of their independent or correlative transformation. All together (though they can never be analyzed exhaustively), they form what might be called, by a kind of play on words—for consciousness is never present in such a description—the "unconscious," not of the speaking subject, but of the thing said.

Finally, a more general theme might be outlined on the horizon of all these investigations—the theme of the mode of existence of discursive events in a culture. What has to be brought out is the set of conditions which, at a given moment and in a determinate society, govern the appearance of statements, their preservation, the links established between them, the way they are grouped in statutory sets, the role they play, the action of values or consecrations by which they are affected, the way they are invested in practices or attitudes, the principles according to which they come into circulation, are repressed, forgotten, destroyed or reactivated. In short, it is a matter of the discourse in the system of its institutionalization. I shall call an *archive*, not the totality of texts that have been preserved by a civilization or the set of traces that could be salvaged from its downfall, but the series of rules which determine in a culture the appearance and disappearance of statements, their retention and their destruction, their pradoxical existence as *events* and *things*. To analyze the facts of discourse in the general element of the archive is to consider them, not at all as *documents* (of a concealed significance or a rule of construction), but as *monuments;*[3] it is—leaving aside every geological metaphor, without assigning any origin, without the least gesture toward the beginnings of an *archē*—to do what the rules of the etymological game allow us to call something like an *archaeology.*

Such, more or less, is the problematic of *Madness and Civilization,* of *The Birth of the Clinic,* and of *The Order of Things.* None of these texts is autonomous or sufficient by itself; they all depend upon one another, to the extent that each involves the very partial exploration of a limited region. They should be read as an ensemble of descriptive experiments still in basic outline. However, if it is not necessary to apologize for their being quite so partial and full of gaps, the choices to which they are obedient must be explained. For if the general field of discursive events permits of no a priori parceling, it is nevertheless out of the question that all the relations characteristic of the archive might be described in one block. As a first approximation, a provisional parceling must be accepted; an initial region, which analysis will overturn and reorganize once it has been able to define an ensemble of relations. How to delimit that region? On the one hand, it is necessary to choose a domain empirically in which the relations have a chance of being numerous, dense, and relatively easy to describe. And in what other region do discursive events seem most linked to one another, and in the most decipherable relations, than what is generally designated by the term "science"? But, on the other hand, how to have the greatest chance of capturing in a statment not the moment of its formal structure and its laws of construction but, rather, that of its existence and its rules of manifestation, except by addressing oneself to little formalized groups of discourses in which the statements do not appear to be engendered according to the rules of pure syntax? Finally, how to be sure that one will not fall prey to all those unreflective unities or syntheses which refer to the speaking subject, the subject of discourse, the author of a text—in short, to all these anthropological categories? If not perhaps by considering precisely the ensemble of the statements through which these categories are constituted—the ensemble of the statements that have chosen the subject of discourses (their proper subject) as "object," and have undertaken to deploy it as a field of knowledges [*connaissances*]?

Hence the privilege accorded de facto to that discourse set which might, very schematically, be said to define the "sciences of man." But this privilege is only one of a point of departure. One must keep two facts well in mind: that the analysis of discursive events and the description of the archive are not in any way limited to the same domain; and that the dividing-up of the domain itself can be considered neither definitive nor absolutely valid. It is a matter of a first approximation, which should permit relations to be made apparent that have a chance of effacing the limits of that first sketch. Now, I should indeed acknowledge that such a project of description as I am trying at present to circumscribe is itself caught up in that region that I am trying, by way of an initial approach, to analyze, and that it runs the risk of being dissociated under the effect of analysis. I am investigating that strange and quite problematic configuration of human sciences to which my own discourse is tied. I am analyzing the space in which I speak. I am laying myself open to undoing and recomposing that space which indicates to me the first indices of my discourse. I am seeking to disassociate its visible coordinates and shake up its surface immobility. I thus risk raising, at each instant and beneath each of my resolutions, the question of knowing whence it can arise, for everything I say could well have the effect of displacing the place from which I am saying it. So though I might have responded to the question of whence I claimed to be speaking—I, who want, from such a height and from so far away, to describe the discourses of others—simply by saying that I believed myself to have been speaking from the same place as those discourses, I must now acknowledge that I can myself no longer speak from where I showed them to be speaking without saying it, but instead only from that difference, that infinitesimal discontinuity which my discourse already left in its wake.

DISCURSIVE FORMATIONS AND POSITIVITIES

I thus undertook to describe relations of coexistence among statements. I took care not to pay heed to any of those unities that could be presumed of them, and that tradition placed at my disposal—whether the work of an author, the cohesion of an epoch, or the evolution of a science. I did not go beyond the presence of events close to my own discourse—certain to be dealing with a coherent system from that point forward if I managed to describe a system of relations among them.

Initially, it seemed to me that certain statements could form a set insofar as they referred to one and the same object. After all, statements concerning madness, for example, are not all on the same formal level (they are far from all obeying the criteria required for a scientific statement): they do not all belong to the same semantic field (some come from medical semantics, others from legal or administrative semantics; others use a literary vocabulary), but they are all related to that object outlined in different ways in individual or social experience which can be designated as madness. Yet it is easy to see that the unity of the object does not allow the individualization of a set of statements and the establishment of a descriptive and constant relation between them. This for two reasons. First, the object, far from being that in relation to which it is possible to define a set of statements is, rather, constituted by the set of those formulations; it would be wrong to look for the unity of the discourse of psychopathology or psychiatry in "mental illness"; it would certainly be wrong to ask of the very being of this illness, of its hidden content, of its truth, dumb and shut in on itself, what it has been possible to say of it at any given moment: rather, mental illness has been constituted by the set of what it has been possible to say in the group of all the statements that named it, delineated it, described and explained it, gave account of its developments, indicated its diverse correlations, judged it, and eventually allowed it to speak by articulating, in its name, discourses which were to pass for its speech. But there is more: That ensemble of statements which concern madness, and in truth constitute it, is far from being related only to a single object, from having formed it once and for all and conserved it indefinitely as its inexhaustible horizon of ideality. The object that the medical statements of the seventeenth or eighteenth century posed as their correlate is not identical to the object that takes form through juridical sentences or police measures. So, too, all the objects of psychopathological discourse were modified from Phillipe Pinel or Etienne Esquirol to Eugen Bleuler; the same illnesses are not at all in question for the former and the latter—at once because the code of perceiving and the techniques of description changed, because the designation of madness and its general parceling no longer follow the same criteria, and because the function and role of medical discourse, the practices it sanctions and in which it is invested, and the distance at which it keeps the patient, were profoundly modified.

One could, perhaps should, conclude of this multiplicity of objects that it is not possible to admit, as a unity that would validly constitute an ensemble of statements, the "discourse concerning madness." It would perhaps be necessary to restrict oneself only to those groups which have one and the same object—the discourse on melancholy, or on neurosis. But one would soon become aware that each of these discourses, in turn, constituted its object and worked on it up to the point of transforming it entirely. So much so that the problem arises of knowing whether the unity of a discourse is wrought not by the permanence and singularity of an object but, rather, by the common space in which diverse objects stand out and are continuously transformed. The characteristic relation that permits the individualization of a general unity of statements concerning madness would therefore be the rule of the simultaneous or successive appearance of the various objects that are named, described, analyzed, valued, or judged in it; the law of their exclusion or mutual implication; the system that governs their transformation. The unity of the discourses on madness is not founded on the existence of the object "madness," or on the constitution of a unique horizon of objectivity; it is the series of rules which make possible, during a given period, the appearance of medical descriptions (with their object), the appearance of a series of discriminatory and repressive measures (with their particular object), and the appearance of a set of practices codified in prescriptions or medical treatments (with their specific objects). It is thus the set of rules which takes account of the object's noncoincidence with itself, its perpetual difference, its deviation and dispersion rather than of the object itself in its identity. Over and above the unity of discourses on madness, it is the pattern of the rules which define the transformations of these different objects, their nonidentity through time, the break that is produced in them, and the internal discontinuity that suspends their permanence. Paradoxically, to define the individuality of a set of statements does not consist of individualizing its object, fixing its identity, or describing the characteristics that it permanently retains; on the contrary, it is to describe the dispersion of these objects, to grasp all the interstices that separate them, to measure the distances reigning between them—in other words, to formulate their law of distribution. I will not call this system the "domain" of objects (since that word implies unity, closure, close proximity rather than scattering and dispersion). A bit arbitrarily, I will give it the name "referential"; and I will say, for example, that "madness" is not the object (or referent) common to a group of propositions but is, rather, the referential or law of dispersion of different objects or referents put into play by an ensemble of statements whose unity this law defines precisely.

The second criterion that could be used to constitute discursive sets is the type of enunciation used. It had seemed to me, for example, that from the beginning of the nineteenth century medical science was characterized less by its objects or concepts (of which the former remained the same while the latter were entirely transformed) than by a certain *style*, a certain constant form of enunciation: a descriptive science could be seen coming into existence. For the first time, medicine is constituted no longer by an ensemble of traditions, of observations, of heterogeneous recipes but by a corpus of knowledge which assumes that but one way of seeing is brought to the same things, that there is but one graphing of the perceptual field, one analysis of the pathological phenomenon in accord with the visible space of the body, one system of transcribing what is seen into what is said (one vocabulary, one set of metaphors). In short, medicine seemed to be formalizing itself as a series of descriptive statements. But here, too, it proved necessary to abandon this initial hypothesis. I had to admit that clinical medicine was just as much a set of political prescriptions, economic decisions, institutional settlements and educational models as it was a set of descriptions; that, at any rate, the latter could not be abstracted from the former, and that descriptive enunciation was only one of the formulations present in clinical discourse as a whole. Recognize that this description has not ceased to be displaced: whether because, from Xavier Bichat to cellular pathology, the same things stopped being described; or because, from visual examination, auscultation, and palpation to the use of the microscope and biological tests, the system of information was modified; or yet because, from simple anatomo-clinical correlation to the minute analysis of physiopathological processes, the lexicon of signs and their decipherment was entirely reconstituted; or finally, because the doctor had little by little ceased himself to be the site of recording and interpretation, and because beside him, outside of him, masses of documentation, instruments of correlation, and techniques of analysis came to be constituted, of which he of course had to make use, but which modified his position as inspecting subject with respect to the patient.

All these alterations, which perhaps today take us out of clinical medicine, were put into place slowly, in the course of the nineteenth century, in the interior of clinical discourse and in the space that it outlined. If one wanted to define that discourse by a codified form of enunciation (for example, the description of a certain number of determinate elements on the surface of the body, inspected by the eye, the ear, and the fingers of the doctor; the identification of descriptive unities and of complex signs; the estimation of their probable significance; the prescription of the corresponding course of therapy), it would be necessary to acknowledge that clinical medicine was unmade as soon as it appeared, and that it had hardly been formulated except with Bichat and René Laënnec. In fact, the unity of the clinical discourse is not a determinate form of statements, but the set of rules which simultaneously or successively made possible not only purely perceptual descriptions but also observations mediated through instruments, protocols of laboratory experiments, statistical calculations, epidemiological or demographic observations, institutional settlements, and political decisions. This whole set cannot be subject to a unique model of linear concatenation. It is, rather, a question of a group of diverse enunciations which are far from obeying the same formal rules, from having the same exigencies of proof, from maintaining a constant relation to truth, and from having the same operational function. What must be characterized as clinical medicine is the coexistence of those dispersed and heterogeneous statements; it is the system that governs their distribution, the support they give to each other, the way in which they imply or exclude each other, the transformation they undergo, and the pattern of their arisal, disposition, and replacement. A temporal coincidence can be established between the appearance of the discourse and the introduction of a privileged type of enunciation in medicine; but the latter does not have a constituent or normative role. A set of diverse enunciative forms are unfolded beside and around this phenomenon; and it is the general ordering of this unfolding that constitutes, in its individuality, clinical discourse. The rule of formation of

these statements in their heterogencity, in the very impossibility of their integration into a single syntactic chain, is what I shall term enunciative divergence
[*l'écarténonciatif*]. And I shall say that clinical medicine is characterized, as an individualized discursive set, by the divergence or the law of dispersion which
governs the diversity of its statements.

The third criterion by which unitary groups of statements could be established is the existence of a series of permanent and internally consistent concepts. It might be supposed, for example, that the analysis of language and of
grammatical facts made from Lancelot to the end of the eighteenth century depended on a definite number of concepts whose content and use were established
once and for all: the concept of judgment defined as the general and normative
form of every sentence, the concepts of subject and attribute grouped together
in the more general category of the noun, the concept of the verb used as the
equivalent of the logical copula, the concept of the word defined as the sign of a
representation. In this way it would seem possible to reconstitute the conceptual
architecture of Classical grammar. But here again limitations appear immediately. One could hardly make use of such elements in describing the analyses
done by the authors of Port Royal. One has to admit that new concepts appear,
some of which may be derived from the ones I have listed, but others of which
are heterogeneous, and some even incompatible with them. The notions of natural or inverted syntactic order, of the complement (introduced at the beginning
of the eighteenth century by Beauzée), can no doubt be integrated into the conceptual system of the Port Royal grammar. But neither the idea of a value originally expressive of sounds, nor that of a primitive knowledge enveloped in
words and obscurely transmitted by them, nor that of a regularity of the historical evolution of consonants, can be deduced from the set of concepts used by the
grammarians of the eighteenth century. Even more; the conception of the verb
as a simple name allowing the designation of an action or an operation; the definition of the sentence no longer as an attributive proposition but as a series of
designative elements the ensemble of which produced a representation—all of
this is rigorously incompatible with the collection of concepts of which Claude
Lancelot or Nicolas Beauzée could make use. Must we then admit that grammar
only apparently constitutes a consistent set; and that this set of statements,
analyses, descriptions, principles and consequences, and deductions is a false
unity, though it survived under this name for more than a century?

In fact, it is possible to define a common system beneath all the more or less
heterogeneous concepts of Classical grammar, which explains not only their
emergence but also their dispersion and, eventually, their incompatibility. This
system is not constituted by concepts any more general and abstract than those
which appear on the surface and are openly manipulated there; it is constituted,
rather, by a set of rules of formation of concepts. This set is itself divided into

four subordinate groups. There is the group that governs the formation of those concepts which permit the description and analysis of the sentence as a unit in which the elements (the words) are not merely juxtaposed but related to one another. This set of rules may be called the theory of *attribution;* and without it itself being modified, this theory was able to make a place for the concepts of the verb-copula, or the verb-name specific to an action, or the verb-tie of the elements of representation. There is also the group that governs the formation of those concepts which permit a description of the relations between the different signifying elements of the sentence and the different elements of what is represented by these signs. This is the theory of *articulation,* which can, in its specific unity, render an account of concepts as different as that of the word as the result of an analysis of thought and that of the word as an instrument by which such an analysis can be made. The theory of *designation* governs the emergence not only of such concepts as that of the arbitrary and conventional sign but also that of the spontaneous and natural sign, immediately charged with expressive value (thus permitting the reintroduction of the action of language in the real or ideal becoming of humanity). Finally, the theory of *derivation* accounts for the formation of a very dispersed and heterogeneous series of notions; the idea of an immobility of language which is only subject to change as a result of external accidents; the idea of a historical correlation between the development of language and the individual's capacities for analysis, reflection, and understanding [*connaissance*] the idea of a circular determination between the forms of language, those of writing, knowledge and science, those of social organization, and, finally, those of historical progress; the idea of poetry understood not only as a particular use of vocabulary and grammar but as the spontaneous movement of language shifting in the space of human imagination, which is, by its very nature, metaphorical. These four "theories"—which are four formative schemata of concepts—have describable relations between them: they assume each other; they oppose each other in pairs; they derive one from the other and, in elaborating their logical sequence, they link up the discourses, which can neither be unified nor superposable, into a single pattern. They form what may be called a *theoretical network*. This term must not be understood to mean a group of fundamental concepts which could regroup all the others and permit their replacement in the unity of a deductive architecture but, rather, the general law of their dispersion, heterogenity, and incompatibility (whether simultaneous or successive)—the rule of their insurmountable plurality. And it is only permissible to recognize an individualizable set of statements in general grammar insofar as all the concepts that appear are interconnected, intersect, interfere with and follow each other, are hidden and scattered in it, are formed from one and the same theoretical network.

Finally, one might attempt to constitute units of discourse on the basis of an identity of opinions. The "human sciences" are so condemned to polemic, so open to the play of preferences or interests, so permeable by philosophical or ethical themes, so apt in certain cases to political utilization, also so near to certain religious dogmas that it is legitimate in the first instance to suppose that a certain thematic might be capable of binding together a set of discourses, of balancing it like an organism that has its needs, its internal power and its survival capacities. For example, might not one constitute everything that belonged to evolutionist discourse from Buffon to Darwin as a unit? First, this theme is more philosophical than scientific, closer to cosmology than to biology; it has, rather, guided investigations from afar than named, discovered and explained results; it always presupposed more than was known, but on the basis of this fundamental choice, it made obligatory the transformation into discursive knowledge [*savoir*] what was outlined as a hypothesis or as an exigency. Might one not speak in the same way of the physiocratic idea? An idea that postulated the natural character of the three ground rents beyond any proof and before any analysis; which therefore presupposed the political and economic primacy of landed property; which ruled out any analysis of the mechanisms of industrial production; which implied, in return, the description of the circulation of money inside a state, of its distribution between different social categories, and of the channels whereby it returned to production; which finally led Ricardo to consider the cases in which this triple rent did not appear, the conditions in which its formation was possible, and therefore to denounce the arbitrary character of the physiocratic theme?

But such an attempt leads one to make two opposing but complementary observations. In one case, the same fact of opinion, the same thematic, the same choice is articulated on the basis of two completely different series of concepts, two completely different types of discourse and two completely different fields of objects: the evolutionist idea, in its most general formulation, is perhaps the same in Benoît de Maillet, Théophile de Bordeau or Diderot, and in Darwin; but in fact what makes it possible and consistent is not at all of the same order in both cases. In the eighteenth century the evolutionist idea is a choice made on the basis of two well-determined possibilities: either it is admitted that the common ancestry of species forms a completely pregiven continuity interrupted and in some sense torn apart only by natural catastrophes, by the dramatic history of the earth, by the upheavals of an extrinsic time (in which case it is this time which creates the discontinuity, ruling out evolutionism); or, on the other hand, it is admitted that it is time that creates the continuity, the changes in nature that compel species to take characters different from those which were pregiven—such that the more or less continous table of the species is like the outcrop of a whole stratum of time beneath the eyes of the naturalist. In the nineteenth century, the evolutionist idea is a choice that no longer involves the constitution of a table of species but, rather, the modalities of the interaction between an organism, all of whose elements are solidary, and an environment that provides it with its real conditions of life. One "idea" only, but based on two systems of choices.

On the other hand, in the case of physiocracy, one can say Quesnay's choice depends on exactly the same system of concepts as the contrary opinion upheld by those who might be called the "utilitarians." In this period, the analysis of wealth contained a relatively limited series of concepts, and one that was generally agreed upon (everyone defined money in the same way, as a mere sign without any value except through the practically necessary materiality of that sign; everyone explained price in the same way, by the mechanism of barter and by the quantity of labor necessary to obtain the commodity; everyone determined the price of a given labor in the same way, by the cost of the upkeep of a worker and his family while the work was being done). But on the basis of this single conceptual system, there were two methods of explaining the formation of value, depending on whether the analysis was made on the basis of exchange or on that of the remuneration of the working day. These two possibilities inscribed in economic theory and in the rules of its conceptual system gave rise to two different opinions on the basis of the same elements.

It would finally be quite incorrect to look for the principles of the individualization of a discourse in matters of opinion. What defines the unity of natural history, for example, is not the permanence of particular ideas such as that of evolution; what defines the unity of economic discourse in the eighteenth century is not the conflict between the physiocrats and the utilitarians, or between the owners of landed property and the partisans of commerce and industry. What permits the individualization of a discourse and gives it an independent existence is the system of points of choice which it offers from a field of given objects, from a determinate enunciative scale; and from a series of concepts defined in their content and use. Therefore, it would be inadequate to look for the general foundations of a discourse and the overall form of its historical identity in a theoretical option; for a similar option can reappear in two types of discourse, and a single discourse can give rise to several different options. Neither the permanence of opinions through time nor the dialectic of their conflicts is sufficient to individualize a set of statements. To do that, one must be able to register the distribution of points of choice, and define, behind every option, a *field of strategic possibilities*. If the physiocrats' analysis is a part of the same discourse as the utilitarians' analysis, it is not because they lived during the same period, nor because they confronted one another in the same society, nor because their interests were entangled in the same economy, but because their two options derive from one and the same distribution of points of choice, in one and the same strategic field. This field is not the total of all the conflicting elements, nor is it an obscure unity divided against itself and refusing to recognize itself in the mask of each of its opponents; it is the law of formation and dispersion of all possible options.

To sum up, we have here four criteria enabling us to recognize discursive units that are not at all the traditional unities (whether "text," "work," "science"; whatever the domain or form of the discourse, whatever the concepts it uses or the choices it manifests). These four criteria are not only not incompatible, they demand one another: the first defines the unity of a discourse by the rule of formation of all its *objects;* the next by the rule of formation of all its *syntactic* types; the third by the rule of formation of all its *semantic* elements; the fourth by the rule of formation of all its *operational* eventualities. All the aspects of discourse are thus covered. And when it is possible, in a group of statements, to register and describe *one* referential, *one* type of enunciative divergence, *one* theoretical network, *one* field of strategic possibilities, then one can be sure that they belong to what can be called a *discursive formation*. This formation groups together a whole population of statement-events. Obviously, neither in its criteria, in its limits, nor in its internal relations, does it coincide with the immediate and visible unities into which statements are conventionally grouped. It brings to light relations between the phenomena of enunciation which had hitherto remained in darkness and were not immediately transcribed on the surface of discourses. But what it brings to light is not a secret, the unity of a hidden meaning, nor a general and unique form; it is a controlled system of differences and dispersions. This four-level system which governs a discursive formation and has to explain, not its common elements but the play of its divergences, its interstices, its distances—in some sense its blanks rather than its full surfaces—that is what I propose to call its *positivity*.

KNOWLEDGE

At the outset the problem was to define unities that could be legitimately installed in such a disproportionate domain as that of statement-events other than the hastily admitted forms of synthesis. I tried to give an answer to this question which would be empirical (and articulated in precise inquiries) and critical (since it concerned the place from which I was posing the question, the region which situated it, the spontaneous unity within which I could believe I was talking). Hence the investigations into the domain of the discourses which installed, or claimed to install, a "scientific" knowledge [*connaissance*] of living, speaking, and working men. These investigations have brought to light sets of statements which I have called "discursive formations" and systems that should explain these sets called "positivities." But have I not purely and simply produced a history of the human "sciences"—or, if you will, of the inexact knowledges [*connaissances*] whose accumulation has not yet managed to constitute a science? Am I not still caught in their apparent divisions and in the system they pretend to adopt for themselves? Have I not made a kind of critical epistemology of these patterns which cannot firmly be said really to deserve the name of sciences?

In fact, the discursive formations I have separated or described do not precisely coincide with the delimitation of these sciences (or pseudo-sciences). Undoubtedly I opened my inquiry into the history of madness on the basis of the existence at present of a discourse that calls itself psychopathology (which some may regard as having pretentions to be scientific); undoubtedly I undertook to analyze what it was possible to say about wealth, money, exchange, about linguistic signs and the functioning of words, in the seventeenth and eighteenth centuries on the basis of the existence of an economics and a linguistics (whose criteria of scientific rigor may well be contested by some). But the positivities obtained at the end of the analysis and the discursive formations that they group together do not cover the same space as these disciplines, and are not articulated as they are; to go further, they cannot be superimposed on what it was possible to regard as a science or as an autonomous form of discourse in the period under study. Thus the system of positivity analyzed in *Madness and Civilization* does not explain, either exclusively or in a privileged way, what doctors were able to say about mental disease at the time; rather, it defines the referential, the enunciative scale, the theoretical network, the points of choice which made possible the very dispersion of medical statements, institutional controls, administrative measures, literary expressions, and philosophical formulations. The discursive formation constituted and described by the analysis goes far beyond the account that might have been given of the prehistory of psychopathology or of the genesis of its concepts.

In *The Order of Things* this situation is inverted. The positivities obtained by description isolate discursive formations which are narrower than the scientific domains recognised in the first instance. The system of natural history permits the explanation of a certain number of statements about the resemblances and differences between beings, the constitutions of specific and generic characteristics, the distribution of relationship in the general space of the table; but it does not govern the analysis of involuntary movement, nor the theory of genera, nor the chemical explanations of growth. The existence, the autonomy, the internal consistency and the limitation of this discursive formation precisely constitute one of the reasons why a general science of life was not formulated in the Classical age. Similarly, the positivity that governed the analysis of wealth in the same period did not determine every statement about exchange, commercial transactions and prices: it left out "political arithmetic," which did not enter the field of economic theory until much later, when a new system of positivity had made the introduction of that kind of discourse into economic analysis both possible and necessary. Nor does general grammar explain all that it was possible to say about language in the Classical age (whether by exegetes of religious texts, by philosophers, or by theoreticians of literary works). In none of those three cases was it a matter of discovering what men could have thought about language, wealth or life at a time when a biology, an economics, and a philology were slowly and stealthily constituting themselves; nor was it a matter of finding out the errors, prejudices, confusions, or even fantasies still mixed up with the concepts on their way to formation; nor was it a matter of knowing the price in breaks and repressions which a science, or at least a discipline with scientific pretensions, had to pay in order to constitute itself at last on such impure ground. It was a matter of bringing out the system of that "impurity"—or rather, for the word can have no meaning in this analysis, of explaining the simultaneous appearance of a certain number of statements whose level of scientificity, form, and degree of elaboration may well seem heterogeneous to us in retrospect.

The discursive formation analyzed in *The Birth of the Clinic* represents a third case. It is much broader than medical discourse, in the strict sense of the term (the scientific theory of illness, of its forms, of its determinations and of therapeutic instruments): it encompasses a whole series of political reflections, reform programs, legislative measures, administrative settlements, and ethical considerations; but, on the other hand, it does not include everything it was possible to know in the period studied about the human body, about its workings, its anatomico-physiological correlations, and about the disturbances that may occur in it. The unity of clinical discourse is in no sense the unity of a science or of a set of knowledges attempting to acquire a scientific status. It is a complex unity: the criteria by which we can—or think we can—distinguish one science from another (for example, physiology from pathology), a more developed science from one which is less so (for example, biochemistry from neurology), a really scientific discourse (such as hormonology) from a mere condification of experience (such as semiology), a real science (such as microbiology) from a science that was not a science (such as phrenology), could not be applied to it. Clinical medicine constitutes neither a false science nor a true one, although in the name of present-day criteria we may assume the right to recognize the truth of certain of its statements and the falsity of certain others. It is an enunciative ensemble both theoretical and practical, descriptive and institutional, analytical and prescriptive, made up of inferences as well as decisions, of assertions as well as degrees.

Discursive formations are neither current sciences in gestation, nor sciences formerly recognized as such, then fallen into desuetude and abandoned as a result of the new requirements of our criteria. They are unities of a different kind and on a different level from what is called today (or was once called) a "science." In order to characterize them, the distinction between scientific and non-scientific is not pertinent: they are epistemologically neutral. As for the systems of positivity which ensure unitary grouping, they are not rational structures, nor are they forces, equilibria, oppositions or dialectics between forms of rationality and irrational constraints; the distinction between the rational and its opposite is not pertinent in describing these unities; they are not the laws of intelligibility but the laws of the formation of a whole set of objects, types of formulation, concepts, and theoretical options which are invested in institutions, techniques, collective and individual behavior, political operations, scientific activities, literary fictions and theoretical speculations. The set thus formulated from the system of positivity, and manifested in the unity of a discursive formation, is what might be called a knowledge [*savoir*]. Knowledge is not the sum of scientific knowledges [*connaissances*], since it should always be possible to say whether the latter are true or false, accurate or not, approximate or definite, contradictory or consistent; none of these distinctions is pertinent in describing knowledge, which is the set of the elements (objects, types of formulation, concepts and theoretical choices) formed from one and the same positivity in a field of a unitary discursive formation.

We are now dealing with a complex pattern. It can and must be analyzed both as a formation of statements (when considering the population of discursive events that are part of it); as a positivity (when considering the system that governs the dispersion of the objects, the types of formulation, the concepts and the opinions that come into play in these statements); as a knowledge (when considering these objects, types of formulation, concepts and opinions as they are invested in a science, a technical recipe, an institution, a fictional narrative, a legal or political practice, and so on). *Knowledge* cannot be analyzed in terms of knowledges; nor can positivity in terms of rationality; nor can the discursive formation in terms of science. And one cannot ask that their description be equivalent to a history of knowledges, a genesis of rationality or the epistemology of a science.

It remains true, nonetheless, that it is possible to describe a certain number of relations between the sciences (with their structures of rationality and the sum of their knowledges) and the discursive formations (with their system of positivity and the field of their knowledge). For it is true that only formal criteria can decide about the scientificity of a science, that is, can define the conditions that make it possible as a science; but they can never account for its factual existence, that is, its historical appearance, the events, episodes, obstacles, dissensions, expectations, delays, and facilitations that have been able to stamp its actual destiny. If, for example, it was necessary to wait for the end of the eighteenth century for the concept of life to become fundamental in the analysis of

living beings, or if the registering of the resemblances between Latin and San-
skrit could not have given birth before Franz Bopp to a comparative and historical grammar, or again, if the established fact of intestinal lesions in "feverous"
ailments could not give rise before the beginning of the nineteenth century to an
anatomo-pathological medicine, the reason is to be sought neither in the epistemological structure of biology in general, nor of grammatical science, nor of
medical science; nor, moreover, in the error that would sustain men's blindness
for so long. It resides instead in the morphology of knowledge, in the system of
positivities, in the internal disposition of discursive formations. Even more, it is
in the element of knowledge that the conditions of the appearance of a science,
or at least of a discursive ensemble that acquires or claims the models of scientificity, are determined. If, toward the beginning of the nineteenth century, one
witnesses the formation, under the name of political economy, of a discursive
ensemble that gives itself the signs of scientificity, and imposes a certain number
of formal rules; if, at about the same period, certain discourses are organized on
the model of medical, clinical, and semiological discourses in order to be constituted as psychopathology, the cause of these "sciences"—whether for their
actual equilibrium, or for the ideal form toward which they supposedly aim—
cannot be demanded retrospectively. Nor can cause be demanded for a project
of rationalization that would take form then in the minds of men but be unable
to take charge of what these discourses had in the way of specificity. It is in the
field of knowledge that the analysis of these conditions of appearance must be
undertaken—at the level of discursive ensembles and the play of positivities.

Under the general term of the "conditions of possibility" of a science, two
heteromorphous systems must be distinguished. The first defines the conditions
of the science as a science: it is relative to its domain of objects, to the type of
language it uses, to the concepts it has at its disposal or it is seeking to establish;
it defines the formal and semantic rules required for a statement to belong to the
science; it is instituted either by the science in question, insofar as it poses its
own norms for itself, or by another science, insofar it imposes itself on the former as a model of formalization; at any rate, these conditions of scientificity are
internal to scientific discourse in general and cannot be defined other than
through it. The other system is concerned with the possibility of a science in its
historical existence. It is external to the former system, and the two cannot be
superposed. It is constituted by a field of discursive sets which have neither the
same status, units, organization, nor the same functioning as the sciences to
which they give rise. These discursive sets should not be seen as a rhapsody of
false knowledges, archaic themes, and irrational figures which the sciences, in
their sovereignty, definitively thrust aside into the night of a prehistory. Nor
should they be imagined as the outline of future sciences that are still confusedly
wrapped around their futures, vegetating for a time in the half sleep of silent

germination. Finally, they should not be conceived as the only epistemological system to which those supposedly false, quasi- or pseudo-sciences, the human sciences, are susceptible. In fact, the system is concerned with patterns that have their own consistency, laws of formation and autonomous disposition. To analyze discursive formations, positivities, and the knowledge which corresponds to them is not to assign forms of scientificity but, rather, to run through a field of historical determination which must account for the appearance, retention, transformation, and, in the last analysis, the erasure of discourses, some of which are still recognized today as scientific, some of which have lost that status, some have never pretended to acquire it, and finally, others have never attempted to acquire it. In a word, knowledge is not science in the successive displacement of its internal structures; it is the field of its actual history.

SEVERAL REMARKS

The analysis of discursive formations and of their system of positivity in the element of knowledge concerns only certain determinations of discursive events. There can be no question of constituting a unitary discipline replacing all other descriptions of discourses and invalidating them *en bloc*. Rather, it is a question of giving a place to different, already-familiar, and often long-practiced types of analyses: of determining their level of functioning and effectivity; of defining their points of application, and, finally, of avoiding the illusions to which they can give rise. To bring into existence the dimension of knowledge as a specific dimension is not to reject the various analyses of science; it is to unfold as broadly as possible the space in which they can come to rest. Above all, it is to give free rein to two forms of extrapolation which have symmetrical and inverse reductive roles: epistemological extrapolation and genetic extrapolation.

Epistemological extrapolation should not be confused with the (always-legitimate and possible) analysis of the formal structures that may characterize a scientific discourse. But it does suggest that these structures are enough to define for a science the historical law of its appearance and unfolding. *Genetic* extrapolation should not be confused with the (always-legitimate and possible) description of the context—whether discursive, technical, economic, or institutional—in which a science appeared. But it does suggest that the internal organization of a science and its formal norms can be described on the basis of its external conditions. In one case, the science is given the responsibility of explaining its own historicity; in the other, various historical determinations are required to explain a scientificity. But this is to ignore the fact that the place in which a science appears and unfolds is neither this science itself distributed according to a teleological sequence, nor a set of mute practices or extrinsic determinations, but the field of knowledge, with the set of relations which traverse it. This misconstrual can, in fact, be explained by the privilege granted to two types of sciences, which serve in general as models whereas they are surely limit cases. There are indeed sciences of such a type that every episode of their historical development can be taken up again in the interior of their deductive system; their history can, in fact, be described as a movement of lateral extension, then of repetition and generalization at a higher level, such that each moment appears either as a special region, or as a definite degree of formalization; sequences are abolished in favor of proximities that do not reproduce them; and dates are removed in order to reveal synchronies that know no calendar. This is clearly the case with mathematics, in which Cartesian algebra defines a special region in a field that was generalized by Joseph-Louis Lagrange, Niels Henrik Abel, and Evariste Galois; in which the Greek method of exhaustion seems to be contemporary with the calculus of definite integrals. On the other hand, there are sciences that can only secure their unity through time by the narration or critical repetition of their own history: if there has been one and only one psychology since Gustave Fechner, if there has been only one sociology since Auguste Comte, or even since Emile Durkheim, it is not insofar as it is possible to assign a single epistemological structure (as tenuous as is conceivable) to so many diverse discourses; it is insofar as sociology or psychology have at each moment located their discourse in a historical field they themselves had traversed in the critical mode of confirmation or invalidation. The history of mathematics is always on the point of crossing the boundary of epistemological description; the epistemology of "sciences" such as psychology or sociology is always on the edge of a genetic description.

That is why, far from constituting privileged examples for the analysis of all other scientific domains, these two extreme cases instead threaten to lead to an error: the failure to reveal, at once in their specificity and in their relations, the level of epistemological structures and the level of determinations of knowledge; the fact that all sciences (even ones as highly formalized as mathematics) presuppose a space of historicity that does not coincide with the interaction of its forms; but that all sciences (even ones as heavy with empiricity as psychology and as far from the norms required to constitute a science) exist in the field of a knowledge which does not merely prescribe the sequence of their episodes, but which determines their laws of formation according to a describable system. On the other hand, there are "intermediate" sciences—such as biology, physiology, political economy, linguistics, philology—that ought to provide the models: for with them it is impossible to fuse the instance of knowledge and the form of science into a false unity, or to elide the moment of knowledge.

It is possible, on this basis, to situate a certain number of legitimate descriptions of scientific discourse in their possibility, but also to define them in their limits. Descriptions that are directed not toward knowledge as an instance of formation but to the objects, forms of enunciation, concepts, and, finally, to the opinions to which they give rise; descriptions that will, nevertheless, only remain legitimate on the condition that they do not pretend to discover the conditions of existence of something as a scientific discourse. It is thus perfectly legitimate to describe the series of opinions or theoretical options which emerge in a science and à propos a science: one should be able to define, for a historical period or determinate domain, what the principles of choice are, in what way (by what rhetoric or dialectic) they are manifested, hidden, or justified, how the field of the polemic is organized and institutionalized, what the motivations that may characterize the individuals are; in short, there is room for a *doxology*, the description (sociological or linguistic, statical or interpretative) of the facts of opinion. But there is also *doxological illusion* each time one sets forth description as the analysis of the conditions of the existence of a science. This illusion has two aspects. It admits that the actuality of opinions, instead of being determined by the strategic possibilities of conceptual games, refers directly to the divergences of interests or mental habits among individuals; opinion would be the irruption of the nonscientific (of the psychological, of the political, of the social, of the religious) in the specific domain of science. But, on the other hand, it presumes that opinion constitutes the central nucleus, the fulcrum from which the entire ensemble of scientific statements is deployed; opinion would manifest the impact of fundamental choices (metaphysical, religious, political) of which the diverse concepts of biology, or of economics, or of linguistics, would only be the positive, superficial version, the transcription into a determinate vocabulary, the mask blind to itself. The doxological illusion is one manner of eliding the field of a mode of knowledge as the site and law of formation of theoretical opinions.

Similarly, it is perfectly legitimate to describe, for a given science, certain of its concepts or its conceptual ensembles: the definition given them, the use made of them, the field in which the attempt is made to validate them, the transformations to which they are made subject, the way in which they are generalized or transferred from one domain to another. It is equally legitimate to describe, in connection with a science, the forms of propositions that it recognizes as valid, the types of inference to which it has recourse, the rules to which it appeals in order to link statements to one another or to render them equivalent, the laws that it lays down in order to govern their transformations or their substitutions. In short, one can always establish the semantics and the syntax of a scientific discourse. But it is necessary to protect oneself from what one would call the *formalist illusion:* that is, from imagining that these laws of construction are at the same time and with full title the conditions of existence; that valid concepts and propositions are nothing more than the giving of form to an undomesticated experience, or the result of reworking concepts and propositions already in place.

One must guard against imagining that science is launched into existence out of a certain degree of conceptualization and a certain way of proceeding in the construction and the concatenation of propositions; that it is enough, in describing its emergence within the field of discourses, to register the linguistic level that characterizes it. The formalist illusion elides knowledge (the theoretical network and enunciative repartition) as the site and law of formation of concepts and propositions.

Finally, it is possible and legitimate to define, by a regional analysis, the domain of objects to which a science addresses itself. And to analyze it either on the horizon of ideality which the science constitutes (by a code of abstraction, by rules of manipulation, by a system of presentation and potential representation) or in the world of things to which those objects refer. For if it is true that the object of biology or of political economy is indeed defined by a particular struture of ideality peculiar to these two sciences, and if these objects are not purely and simply the life in which individual human beings participate, or the industrialization they have fashioned, nevertheless, these objects refer to experience or to a definite phase of capitalist evolution. But it would be incorrect to believe (through an *illusion of experience*) that there are regions or domains of things which present themselves spontaneously to an activity of idealization and to the work of scientific language; that these things unfurl themselves in the order in which history, technology, discoveries, institutions, and human instruments have managed to constitute them or bring them to light; that all scientific elaboration is only a certain way of reading, deciphering, abstracting, decomposing, and recomposing what is given either in a natural (and consequently generally valid) experience or in a cultural (and consequently relative and historical) experience. There is an illusion that consists of the supposition that science is grounded in the plenitude of a concrete and lived experience; that geometry elaborates a perceived space, that biology gives form to the intimate experience of life, or that political economy translates the processes of industrialization at the level of theoretical discourse; therefore, that the referent itself contains the law of the scientific object. But it is equally illusory to imagine that science is established by an act of rupture and decision, that it frees itself at one stroke from the qualitative field and from all the murmurings of the imaginary by the violence (serene or polemical) of a reason that founds itself by its own assertions—that is, that the scientific object brings itself into existence of itself in its own identity.

If there are, at the same time, both relations and a break between the analysis of life and the familiarity of the body, suffering, sickness, and death; if there are ties and separations between political economy and a particular form of production; if, in a general way, science refers to experience and yet detaches itself from it, it is not a matter of univocal determination, nor of a sovereign, constant, and definitive break. In fact, these relations of reference and separation are specific to each scientific discourse, and their form varies through history. This is because they are themselves determined by the specific instance of knowledge. The latter defines the laws of formation of scientific objects and by the same action specifies the connections or oppositions between science and experience. Their extreme proximity and their unbridgeable distance is never given at the outset; it finds its principle in the morphology of the referential; this is what defines the reciprocal disposition—the confrontation, opposition, their system of communication—of the referent and the object. Between science and experience, there is knowledge no longer as an invisible mediation, or as a secret complicit pander between two distances so difficult to reconcile and unravel at the same time. In fact, knowledge determines the space in which science and experience can be separated and situated one in relation to the other.

What the archaeology of knowledge places out of bounds is thus not the possibility of diverse descriptions to which scientific discourse can give rise; it is, rather, the general thematic of "understanding" [*connaissance*]. Understanding is the continuity of science and experience, their indissociable interlinkage, their indefinite reversibility. It is a play of forms that anticipate all contents insofar as they have already rendered them possible. It is a field of originary contents that silently outline the forms through which they can be read. It is the peculiar instauration of the formal within a successive order, that of psychological or historical geneses; but it is the ordering of the empirical by a form whose teleology is imposed upon it. Understanding confers upon experience the charge of giving an account of the effective existence of science; it confers upon scientificity the charge of giving an account of the historical emergence of the forms and of the system it follows. The thematic of understanding is tantamount to the denegation of knowledge.

To this major thematic, several others are linked. One, that of a constituent activity that would assure—by a series of fundamental operations anterior to all explicit acts, to all concrete manipulations, to all given contents—the unity of a science defined by a system of formal requisites and a world defined as the horizon of all possible experiences. Another, that of a subject who assures, in its reflexive unity, the synthesis of the successive diversity of the given with the ideality that profiles itself, in its identity, through the course of time. Finally, and above all, the great historico-transcendental thematic that ran through the nineteenth century and barely exhausts itself even today in the tireless repetition of these two questions: What should history be, what absolutely archaic project did it need to have traversed, what fundamental telos established it from its first moment forward (or rather, from whatever it was that made its first moment possible) and directs it, in shadow, toward a conclusion yet withheld in order that the truth might see the light of day, or that it might recognize, in that always-remote brightness, the return of what its origin had already obscured? And the other question immediately arises: What must this truth, or perhaps this more than originary opening be in order that history might not unfold without covering it over, hiding it, plunging it into an oblivion by whose repetition, whose recall, and so whose ever-incomplete memory history would always be marked? One can do whatever one likes to make these questions as radical as possible. They would still remain tied, in spite of every effort to effect a separation, to an analytics of the subject and to a problematics of understanding.

In opposition to all these themes, it might be said that knowledge, as the field of historicity in which the sciences appear, is free of any constituent activity, disengaged from any reference to an origin or to a historico-transcendental teleology, detached from any reliance upon a foundational subjectivity. Of all the previous forms of synthesis by which the discontinuous events of discourse were hoped to be unified, these latter were for more than a century the most insistent and most redoubtable; they animated the thematic of a continuous history perceptually linked to itself and put indefinitely to the tasks of reprise and totalization. History had to be continuous in order for the sovereignty of the subject to be safeguarded; but, reciprocally, a constituent subjectivity and a transcendental teleology had to run through history in order that the latter could be thought in its unity. Thus the anonymous discontinuity of knowledge was excluded from discourse and thrown out into the unthinkable.

Notes

1. The Epistemology Circle consisted of Alain Badiou, Jacques Bouveresse, Yves Duroux, Alain Grosrichard, Thomas Herbert, Patrick Hochart, Jean Malthoit, Jacques-Alain Miller, Jean-Claude Milner, Jean Mosconi, Jacques Nassif, Bernard Pautrat, François Regnault, and Michel Torto—Ed.

2. We refer, in this question, to the following passage from Georges Canguilhem's article on Foucault's book (*Critique* 242 [July 1967], pp. 612–13): "Concerning a theoretical knowledge [*savoir*], is it possible to think of it in the specificity of its concept without reference to some norm? Among the theoretical discourses conducted in conformity with the epistemic systems of the seventeenth and eighteenth centuries, some, such as natural history, were discarded by the episteme of the nineteenth century, but others were integrated into it. Newtonian physics did not pass away with the physiology of animal economy, even though the former served the latter as a model. Georges Buffon was refuted by Darwin, if not by Etienne Geoffrey Saint-Hilaire. But Newton is no more refuted by Einstein than by Maxwell; Darwin was not refuted by Mendel and Morgan. The sequence Galileo-Newton-Einstein does not contain ruptures similar to those in the sequence Tournefort-Linnaeus-Engler in botanical taxonomy."

3. I am indebted to Georges Canguilhem for the idea of using the word in this sense.

THE THOUGHT OF THE OUTSIDE

I LIE, I SPEAK

In ancient times, this simple assertion was enough to shake the foundations of Greek truth: "I lie, I speak," on the other hand, puts the whole of modern fiction to the test.

The force of these assertions is not in fact the same. As we know, Epimenides' argument can be mastered if, discourse having been slyly folded back upon itself, a distinction is made between two propositions, the first of which is the object of the second. The grammatical configuration of the paradox cannot suppress this essential duality, try as it might to dodge it (particularly if the paradox is locked into "I lie" in its simple form). Every proposition must be of a higher "type" than that which serves as its object. That the object-proposition recurs in the proposition that designates it; that the Cretan's sincerity is compromised the instant he speaks by the content of his assertion; that he may indeed be lying about lying—all this is less an insurmountable logical obstacle than the result of a plain and simple fact—the speaking subject is also the subject about which it speaks.

In forthrightly saying "I speak" I am exposed to none of these perils; the two propositions hidden in the statement ("I speak" and "I say that I speak") in no way compromise each other. I am protected by the impenetrable fortress of the assertion's self-assertion, by the way it coincides exactly with itself, leaving no jagged edges, averting all danger of error by saying no more than that I am speaking. Neither in the words in question nor in the subject that pronounces them is there an obstacle or insinuation to come between the object-proposition and the proposition that states it. It is therefore true, undeniably true, that I am speaking when I say that I am speaking.

This essay originally appeared in *Critique* 229 (June 1966), pp. 523–46. The translation, by Brian Massumi, has been slightly amended.

But things may not be that simple. Although the formal position of "I speak" does not raise problems of its own, its meaning opens a potentially unlimited realm of questions, in spite of its apparent clarity. "I speak" refers to a supporting discourse that provides it with an object. That discourse, however, is missing; the sovereignty of "I speak" can only reside in the absence of any other language; the discourse about which I speak does not preexist the nakedness articulated the moment I say, "I speak"; it disappears the instant I fall silent. Any possibility of language dries up in the transitivity of its execution. The desert surrounds it. In what extreme delicacy, at what slight and singular point, could a language come together in an attempt to recapture itself in the stripped-down form, "I speak"? Unless, of course, the void in which the contentless slimness of "I speak" is manifested were an absolute opening through which language endlessly spreads forth, while the subject—the "I" who speaks—fragments, disperses, scatters, disappearing in that naked space. If the only site for language is indeed the solitary sovereignty of "I speak," then in principle nothing can limit it—not the one to whom it is addressed, not the truth of what it says, not the values or systems of representation it utilizes. In short, it is no longer discourse and the communication of meaning, but a spreading forth of language in its raw state, an unfolding of pure exteriority. And the subject that speaks is less the responsible agent of a discourse (what holds it, what uses it to assert and judge, what sometimes represents itself in it by means of a grammatical form designed to have that effect) than a nonexistence in whose emptiness the unending outpouring of language uninterruptedly continues.

It is a widely held belief that modern literature is characterized by a doubling-back that enables it to designate itself; this self-reference supposedly allows it both to interiorize to the extreme (to state nothing but itself) and to manifest itself in the shimmering sign of its distant existence. In fact, the event that gave rise to what we call "literature" in the strict sense is only superficially an interiorization; it is far more a question of a passage to the "outside": language escapes the mode of being of discourse—in other words, the dynasty of representation—and literary speech develops from itself, forming a network in which each point is distinct, distant from even its closest neighbors, and has a position in relation to every other point in a space that simultaneously holds and separates them all. Literature is not language approaching itself until it reaches the point of its fiery manifestation; it is, rather, language getting as far away from itself as possible. And if, in this setting "outside of itself," it unveils its own being, the sudden clarity reveals not a folding-back but a gap, not a turning back of signs upon themselves but a dispersion. The "subject" of literature (what speaks in it and what it speaks about) is less language in its positivity than the void that language takes as its space when it articulates itself in the nakedness of "I speak."

This neutral space is what characterizes contemporary Western fiction (which is why it is no longer mythology or rhetoric). The reason it is now so necessary to think through this fiction—while in the past it was a matter of thinking the truth—is that "I speak" runs counter to "I think." "I think" led to the indubitable certainty of the "I" and its existence; "I speak," on the other hand, distances, disperses, effaces that existence and lets only its empty emplacement appear. Thought about thought, an entire tradition wider than philosophy, has taught us that thought leads us to the deepest interiority. Speech about speech leads us, by way of literature as well as perhaps by other paths, to the outside in which the speaking subject disappears. No doubt, that is why Western thought took so long to think the being of language: as if it had a premonition of the danger that the naked experience of language poses for the self-evidence of "I think."

THE EXPERIENCE OF THE OUTSIDE

The breakthrough to a language from which the subject is excluded, the bringing to light of a perhaps irremediable incompatibility between the appearing of language in its being and consciousness of the self in its identity, is an experience now being heralded at diverse points in culture: in the simple gesture of writing as in attempts to formalize language; in the study of myths as in psychoanalysis; in the search for a Logos that would be like the birthplace of all of Western reason. We are standing on the edge of an abyss that had long been invisible: the being of language only appears for itself with the disappearance of the subject. How can we gain access to this strange relation? Perhaps through a form of thought whose still vague possibility was sketched by Western culture in its margins. A thought that stands outside subjectivity, setting its limits as though from without, articulating its end, making its dispersion shine forth, taking in only its invincible absence; and that, at the same time, stands at the threshold of all positivity, not in order to grasp its foundation or justification but in order to regain the space of its unfolding, the void serving as its site, the distance in which it is constituted and into which its immediate certainties slip the moment they are glimpsed—a thought that, in relation to the interiority of our philosophical reflection and the positivity of our knowledge, constitutes what in a phrase we might call "the thought of the outside."

It will one day be necessary to try to define the fundamental forms and categories of this "thought of the outside." It will also be necessary to try to retrace its path, to find out where it comes to us from and in what direction it is moving. One might assume that it was born of the mystical thinking that has prowled the confines of Christianity since the texts of the Pseudo-Dionysus: perhaps it survived for a millennium or so in the various forms of negative theology. Yet nothing is less certain: although this experience involves going "outside of one-self," this is done ultimately in order to find oneself, to wrap and gather oneself in the dazzling interiority of a thought that is rightfully Being and Speech, in other words, Discourse, even if it is the silence beyond all language and the nothingness beyond all being.

It is less rash to suppose that the first rending to expose the thought of the outside was, paradoxically, the recursive monologue of the Marquis de Sade. In the age of Kant and Hegel, at a time when the interiorization of the law of his-tory and the world was being imperiously demanded by Western consciousness as never before, Sade never ceases speaking of the nakedness of desire as the lawless law of the world. In the same period Hölderlin's poetry manifested the shimmering absence of the gods and pronounced the new law of the obligation to wait, infinitely long no doubt, for the enigmatic succor of "God's failing." Can it be said without stretching things that Sade and Hölderlin simultaneously introduced into our thinking, for the coming century, but in some way crypti-cally, the experience of the outside—the former by laying desire bare in the in-finite murmur of discourse, the latter by discovering that the gods had wandered off through a rift in language as it was in the process of losing its bearings? That experience was afterward to remain not exactly hidden, because it had not penetrated the thickness of our culture, but afloat, foreign, exterior to our interiority, for the entire time the demand was being formulated, most im-periously, to interiorize the world, to erase alienation, to move beyond the false moment of alienation [*Entäusserung*], to humanize nature, to naturalize man, and to recover on earth the treasures that had been spent in heaven.

The same experience resurfaced in the second half of the nineteenth century at the very core of language, which had become—even though our culture was still seeking to mirror itself in it as if it held the secret of its interiority—the sparkle of the outside. It resurfaces in Nietzsche's discovery that all of Western metaphysics is tied not only to its grammar (that had been largely suspected since Schlegel) but to those who, in holding discourse, have a hold over the right to speak; and in Mallarmé when language appears as a leave-taking from that which it names, but especially—beginning with *Igitur* and continuing through the aleatory and autonomous theatricality of *Le Livre*—as the movement of the speaker's disappearance; and in Artaud, when all of discursive language is con-strained to come undone in the violence of the body and the cry, and when thought, forsaking the wordy interiority of consciousness, becomes a material energy, the suffering of the flesh, the persecution and rending of the subject it-self; and in Bataille, when thought ceases to be the discourse of contradiction or the unconscious, becoming the discourse of the limit, of ruptured subjectivity, transgression; and in Klossowski, with the experience of the double, of the ex-teriority of simulacra, of the insane theatrical multiplication of the Me.

Blanchot is perhaps more than just another witness to this thought. So far, has he withdrawn into the manifestation of his work, so completely is he, not hidden by his texts, but absent from their existence and absent by virtue of the marvelous force of their existence, that for us he is that thought itself—its real, absolutely distant, shimmering, invisible presence, its necessary destiny, its inevitable law, its calm, infinite, measured strength.

REFLECTION, FICTION

It is extremely difficult to find a language faithful to this thought. Any purely reflexive discourse runs the risk of leading the experience of the outside back to the dimension of interiority; reflection tends irresistibly to repatriate it to the side of consciousness and to develop it into a description of living that depicts the "outside" as the experience of the body, space, the limits of the will, and the ineffaceable presence of the other. The vocabulary of fiction is equally perilous: due to the thickness of its images, sometimes merely by virtue of the transparency of the most neutral or hastiest figures, it risks setting down readymade meanings that stitch the old fabric of interiority back together in the form of an imagined outside.

Hence the necessity of converting reflexive language. It must be directed not toward any inner confirmation—not toward a kind of central, unshakable certitude—but toward an outer bound where it must continually content itself. When language arrives at its own edge, what it finds is not a positivity that contradicts it but the void that will efface it. Into that void it must go, consenting to come undone in the rumbling, in the immediate negation of what it says, in a silence that is not the intimacy of a secret but a pure outside where words endlessly unravel. That is why Blanchot's language does not use negation dialectically. To negate dialectically brings what one negates into the troubled interiority of the mind. To negate one's own discourse, as Blanchot does, is to cast it ceaselessly outside of itself, to deprive it at every moment not only of what it has just said, but of the very ability to speak. It is to leave it where it lies, far behind one, in order to be free for a new beginning—a beginning that is a pure origin because its only principles are itself and the void, but that is also a rebeginning because what freed that void was the language of the past in the act of hollowing itself out. Not reflection, but forgetting; not contradiction, but a contestation that effaces; not reconciliation, but droning on and on; not mind in laborious conquest of its unity, but the endless erosion of the outside; not truth finally shedding light on itself, but the streaming and distress of a language that has always already begun. "Not speech, barely a murmur, barely a tremor, less than silence, less than the abyss of the void; the fullness of the void, something one cannot silence, occupying all of space, the uninterrupted, the incessant, a tremor and already a murmur, not a murmur but speech, and not just any speech, distinct speech, precise speech, within my reach." [1]

This kind of symmetrical conversion is required of the language of fiction. It must no longer be a power that tirelessly produces images and makes them shine but, rather, a power that undoes them, that lessens their overload, that infuses them with an inner transparency that illuminates them little by little until they burst and scatter in the lightness of the unimaginable. Blanchot's fictions are, rather than the images themselves, their transformation, displacement, and neutral interstices. They are precise; the only figures they outline are in the gray tones of everyday life and the anonymous. And when wonder overtakes them, it is never in themselves but in the void surrounding them, in the space in which they are set, rootless and without foundation. The fictitious is never in things or in people but in the impossible verisimilitude of what lies between them—encounters, the proximity of what is most distant, the absolute dissimulation in our very midst. Therefore, fiction consists not in showing the invisible, but in showing the extent to which the invisibility of the visible is invisible. Thus, it bears a profound relation to space; understood in this way, space is to fiction what the negative is to reflection (whereas dialectical negation is tied to the fable of time). No doubt, this is the role that houses, hallways, doors, and rooms play in almost all of Blanchot's narratives: placeless places, beckoning thresholds, closed, forbidden spaces that are nevertheless exposed to the winds, hallways fanned by doors that open rooms for unbearable encounters and create gulfs between them, across which voices cannot carry, and that even muffle cries; corridors leading to more corridors where the night resounds, beyond sleep, with the smothered voices of those who speak, with the cough of the sick, with the death rattle of the dying, with the suspended breath of those who ceaselessly cease living; a long and narrow room, like a tunnel, in which approach and distance—the approach of forgetting, the distance of the wait—draw near to one another and unendingly move apart.

Thus reflexive patience, always directed outside itself, and a fiction that cancels itself out in the void where it undoes its forms intersect to form a discourse appearing with no conclusion and no image, with no truth and no theater, with no proof, no mask, no affirmation, free of any center, unfettered to any native soil; a discourse that constitutes its own space as the outside toward which, and outside of which, it speaks. This discourse, as speech of the outside whose words welcome the outside it addresses, has the openness of a commentary: the repetition of what continually murmurs outside. But this discourse, as a speech that is always outside what it says, is an incessant advance toward that whose absolutely fine-spun light has never received language. This singular mode of being of discourse—a return to the ambiguous hollowness of undoing and origin—no doubt defines the common ground of Blanchot's "novels" and "narra-tives," and of his "criticism." From the moment discourse ceases to follow the slope of self-interiorizing thought and, addressing the very being of language, returns thought to the outside; from that moment, in a single stroke, it becomes a meticulous narration of experiences, encounters, and improbable signs—language about the outside of all language, speech about the invisible side of words. And it becomes attentiveness to what in language already exists, has al-ready been said, imprinted, manifested—a listening less to what is articulated in language than to the void circulating between its words, to the murmur that is forever taking it apart; a discourse on the nondiscourse of all language; the fic-tion of the invisible space in which it appears. That is why the distinction be-tween "novels," "narratives," and "criticism" is progressively weakened in Blanchot until, in *L'Attente l'oubli*, language alone is allowed to speak—what is no one's, is neither fiction nor reflection, neither already said nor never yet said, but is instead "between them, this place with its fixed open expanse, the reten-tion of things in their latent state." [2]

BEING ATTRACTED AND NEGLIGENT

Attraction is no doubt for Blanchot what desire is for Sade, force for Nietzsche, the materiality of thought for Antonin Artaud, and transgression for Georges Bataille: the pure, most naked, experience of the outside. It is necessary to be clear about what the word designates: "attraction," as Blanchot means it, does not depend on any charm. Nor does it break one's solitude or found any posi-tive communication. To be attracted is not to be beckoned by the allure of the exterior, rather, it is to suffer—in emptiness and destitution—the presence of the outside and, tied to that presence, the fact that one is irremediably outside the outside. Far from calling on one interiority to draw close to another, attrac-tion makes it imperiously manifest that the outside is there, open, without depth, without protection or reserve (how could it have any when it had no interiority, and, instead, infinitely unfolds outside any enclosure?), but that one cannot gain access to that opening because the outside never yields its essence. The outside cannot offer itself as a positive presence—as something inwardly illuminated by the certainty of its own existence—but only as an absence that pulls as far away from itself as possible, receding into the sign it makes to draw one toward it, as though it were possible to reach it. Attraction, the marvelous simplicity of opening, has nothing to offer but the infinite void that opens beneath the feet of the person it attracts, the indifference that greets him as if he were not there, a si-lence too insistent to be resisted and too ambiguous to be deciphered and defin-itively interpreted—nothing to offer but a woman's gesture in a window, a door left ajar, the smile of a guard before a forbidden threshold, a gaze condemned to death.

Negligence is the necessary correlate of attraction. The relations between them are complex. To be susceptible to attraction a person must be negligent—essentially negligent, with total disregard for what one is doing (in *Aminadab*, Thomas enters the fabulous boardinghouse only because he neglects to enter the house across the street) and with the attitude that one's past and kin and whole other life is nonexistent, thus relegating them to the outside (neither in the boardinghouse in *Aminadab* nor in the city in *Le Très-haut*, nor in the "sanatorium" of *Le Dernier homme*, nor in the apartment in *Le Moment voulu* does one know what is going on outside, or care to know: one is outside the outside, which is never figured, only incessantly hinted at by the whiteness of its absence, the pallor of an abstract memory, or at most by the glint of snow through a window). This kind of negligence is in fact the flip side of a zealousness—a mute, unjustified, obstinate diligence in surrendering oneself, against all odds, to being attracted by attraction, or more precisely (since attraction has no positivity) to being, in the void, the aimless movement without a moving body of attraction itself. Pierre Klossowski was so right to emphasize that in *Le Très-haut* Henri's last name is "Sorge" (Care) although it is mentioned only once or twice in the text.

But is this zeal always alert? Does it not commit an oversight that may seem trifling but is in fact more crucial than that massive forgetting of an entire life, of all prior attachments and relations? Is not the stride that tirelessly carries the attracted person forward precisely distraction and error? Was it not necessary to "hold back, stay put," as is suggested several times in *Celui qui ne m'accompagnait pas* and in *Le Moment voulu?* Is it not in the nature of zeal to weigh itself down with its own solicitude, to hold it too far, to multiply steps, to grow dizzy with stubbornness, to advance toward the attraction, when attraction speaks imperiously from the depths of its withdrawal only to what is itself withdrawn? It is of the essence of zeal to be negligent, to believe that what is concealed lies elsewhere, that the past will repeat itself, that the law applies to it, that it is awaited, watched over, spied upon. Who will ever know if Thomas—perhaps "Doubting Thomas" should come to mind—had more faith than the others in his questioning of his own belief and in his demands to see and touch? And is what he touched on a body of flesh really what he was after when he asked for a resurrected presence? And was not the illumination suffusing him as much shadow as light? Perhaps Lucie was not who he was looking for; perhaps he should have questioned the person who was thrust on him for a companion; perhaps, instead of trying to get to the upper stories to find the implausible woman who had smiled at him, he should have followed the simple path, taken the gentlest slope, and abandoned himself to the vegetal powers below. Perhaps it was not he who had been called, perhaps someone else was awaited.

All this uncertainty, which makes zeal and negligence two indefinitely reversible figures, undoubtedly has as its principle "the carelessness ruling the
house."[3] This negligence is more visible, more concealed, more ambiguous yet
more fundamental than any other. Everything in it can be deciphered as an intentional sign, as secret diligence, as spying or entrapment: perhaps the lazy servants are hidden powers; perhaps the wheel of fortune dispenses fates recorded
long ago in books. But now zeal does not envelop negligence as its necessary al-
lotment of shadow; rather, negligence remains so indifferent to what can manifest or conceal it that any gesture pertaining to it takes on the value of a sign. It
was out of negligence that Thomas was called: the opening of attraction and the
negligence welcoming the person who is attracted are one and the same. The constraint it creates is not simply blind (which is why it is absolute, and absolutely
nonreciprocal). It is illusory; it binds no one because it itself is bound to that bond
and can no longer be pure and open attraction. How could attraction not be essentially negligent—leaving things what they are, letting time pass and repeat,
letting people advance toward it? For it is the infinite outside, for it is nothing that
does not fall outside it, for it undoes every figure of interiority in pure dispersion.

One is attracted precisely to the extent that one is neglected. This is why zeal
can only consist in neglecting that negligence, in oneself becoming a courageously negligent solicitude, in going toward the light in negligence of shadow,
until it is discovered that the light itself is only negligence, a pure outside equivalent to a darkness that disperses, like a blown-out candle, the negligent zeal it
had attracted.

WHERE IS THE LAW, AND
WHAT DOES THE LAW DO?

Being negligent, being attracted, is a way of manifesting and concealing the
law—of manifesting the withdrawal with which it conceals itself, of consequently attracting it in a light that hides it.

If it were self-evident and in the heart, the law would no longer be the law,
but the sweet interiority of consciousness. If, on the other hand, it were present
in a text, if it were possible to decipher it between the lines of a book, if it were
in a register that could be consulted, then it would have the solidity of external
things: it would be possible to follow or disobey it. Where then would its power
reside, by what force or prestige would it command respect? In fact, the presence of the law is its concealment. Sovereignly, the law haunts cities, institutions, conduct, and gestures; whatever one does, however great the disorder and
carelessness, it has already applied its might: "The house is always, at every in-

stant, in proper order." [4] Taking liberties is not enough to interrupt it; you might think that you have detached yourself from it and can observe its exercise from without. The moment you believe that you can read its decrees from afar, and that they apply only to other people, is the moment you are closest to the law; you make it circulate, you "contribute to the enforcement of a public decree." [5] Yet this perpetual manifestation never illuminates what the law says or wants: the law is not the principle or inner rule of conduct. It is the outside that envelops actions, thereby removing them from all interiority; it is the darkness beyond their borders; it is the void that surrounds them, converting, unknown to anyone, their singularity into the gray monotony of the universal and opening around them a space of uneasiness, of dissatisfaction, of multiplied zeal.

And of transgression. How could one know the law and truly experience it, how could one force it to come into view, to exercise its powers clearly, to speak, without provoking it, without pursuing it into its recesses, without resolutely going even farther into the outside into which it is always receding? How can one see its invisibility unless it has turned into its opposite, punishment, which, after all, is only the law overstepped, irritated, beside itself? But, if punishment could be provoked merely by the arbitrary actions of those who violate the law, then the law would be in their control: they would be able to touch it and make it appear at will; they would be masters of its shadow and light. That is why transgression endeavors to overstep prohibition in an attempt to attract the law to itself; it always surrenders to the attraction of the essential withdrawal of the law; it obstinately advances into the opening of an invisibility over which it will never triumph; insanely, it endeavors to make the law appear in order to be able to venerate it and dazzle it with its own luminous face; all it ends up doing is reinforcing the law in its weakness—the lightness of the night that is its invincible, impalpable substance. The law is the shadow toward which every gesture necessarily advances; it is itself the shadow of the advancing gesture.

Aminadab and *Le Très-haut* form a diptych, one on each side of the invisibility of the law. In the first novel, the strange boardinghouse Thomas enters (attracted, called, perhaps elected, although not without being constrained to cross many forbidden thresholds) seems subject to an unknown law: its nearness and absence are continually recalled by doors open and prohibited, by the great wheel handing out blank or undecipherable fates, by the overhang of an upper-story from which the appeal originates, from which anonymous orders fall, but to which no one can gain access. The day some people decide to track the law into its lair is the day they encounter the monotony of the place where they are already, as well as violence, blood, death, and collapse, and finally resignation, despair, and a voluntary, fatal disappearance into the outside: for the outside of the law is so inaccessible that anyone who tries to conquer and penetrate it is consigned not to punishment which would be the law finally placed under restraint; but to the outside of that outside—to the profoundest forgetting of all. What it is that is served by the "domestics"—those *guards* and *servants* who, unlike the "boarders," "belong to the house" and must represent the law, enforcing it and submitting silently to it—is known to no one, not even to themselves (do they serve the house or the will of the guests?). As far as anyone knows, they could even be former boarders who became servants. They are simultaneously zeal and indifference, drunkenness and attentiveness, slumber and tireless activity, the twin figures of wickedness and solicitude: what conceals concealment and what makes it manifest.

In *Le Très-haut* the law itself (somewhat like the upper story in *Aminadab*, in its monotonous resemblance and exact identity with every other law) is manifested in its essential concealment. Sorge ("care" for and of the law: the solicitude one feels for the law, and the solicitude of the law for those to whom it is applied, even, especially, if they wish to escape it), Henri Sorge, is a bureaucrat: he works at City Hall, in the office of vital statistics; he is only a tiny cog in a strange machine that turns individual existences into an institution; he is the first form of the law, because he transforms every birth into an archive. But then he abandons his duty (but is it really an abandonment? He takes a vacation and extends it—unofficially, it is true, but with the complicity of the administration, which tacitly arranges this essential idleness). This quasi retirement—is it a cause or an effect?—is enough to throw everyone's existence into disarray, and for death to inaugurate a reign that is no longer the classifying reign of the municipal register but the dishonored, contagious, anonymous reign of the epidemic; not the real death of decease and its certification, but a hazy charnel house where no one knows who is a patient and who is a doctor, who is a guard and who is a victim, whether it is a prison or a hospital, a safe house or a fortress of evil. All dams have burst, everything overflows its bounds: the dynasty of rising waters, the kingdom of dubious dampness, oozing, abscesses, and vomiting: individualities dissolve; sweating bodies melt into the walls; endless screams blare through the fingers that muffle them. Yet when Sorge leaves state service, where he was responsible for ordering other people's existence, he does not go outside the law; quite the opposite, he forces it to manifest itself at the empty place he just abandoned. The movement by which he effaces his singular existence and removes it from the universality of the law in fact exalts the law; through that movement he serves the law, shows its perfection, "obliges" it, while at the same time linking it to its own disappearance (which is, in a sense, the opposite of transgressive existence exemplified by Bouxx and Dorte); he has become one with the law.

The law can only respond to this provocation by withdrawing: not by retreating into a still deeper silence, but by remaining immobile in its identity. One can, of course, plunge into the open void: plots can hatch, rumors of sabotage can spread, arson and murder can replace the most ceremonious order; the order of the law was never so sovereign than at this moment, when it envelops precisely what had tried to overturn it. Anyone who attempts to oppose the law in order to found a new order, to organize a second police force, to institute a new state, will only encounter the silent and infinitely accommodating welcome of the law. The law does not change: it subsided into the grave once and for all, and each of its forms is only a metamorphosis of that never-ending death. Sorge wears a mask from Greek tragedy—he has a threatening and pitiful mother like Clytemnestra, a dead father, a sister relentless in her mourning, an all-powerful and insidious father-in-law. He is Orestes in submission, an Orestes whose concern is to escape the law in order better to submit himself to it. In that he insists on living in the plague quarter, he is also a god who consents to die among humans, but who cannot succeed in dying and therefore leaves the promise of the law empty, creating a silence rent by the profoundest of screams: where is the law, what does the law do? And when, by virtue of a new metamorphosis or a new sinking into his own identity, he is recognized, named, denounced, venerated, ridiculed by a woman bearing a strange resemblance to his sister, at that moment, he, the possessor of every name, is transformed into something unnameable, an absent absence, the amorphous presence of the void and the mute horror of that presence. But perhaps this death of God is the opposite of death (the ignominy of a limp and slimy thing twitching for all eternity); and the gesture with which he kills her finally liberates his language—a language that has nothing more to say than the "I speak, I am speaking now" of the law, indefinitely prolonged by the simple fact of that language's proclamation in the outside of its muteness.

EURYDICE AND THE SIRENS

The law averts its face and returns to the shadows the instant one looks at it; when one tries to hear its words, what one catches is a song that is no more than the fatal promise of a future song.

The Sirens are the elusive and forbidden form of the alluring voice. They are nothing but song. Only a silvery wake in the sea, the hollow of a wave, a cave in the rocks, the whiteness of the beach—what are they in their very being if not a pure appeal, if not the mirthful void of listening, if not attentiveness, if not an invitation to pause? Their music is the opposite of a hymn: no presence shimmers in their immortal words; only the promise of a future song accompanies their melody. What makes them seductive is less what they make it possible to hear than what sparkles in the remoteness of their words, the future of what they say. Their fascination is due not to their current song but to what it promises to be. What the Sirens promise to sing to Ulysses is his own past exploits, transformed into a poem for the future: "We know all the suffering, all the suffering

inflicted by the gods on the people of Argos and Troy on the fields of Troad."
Presented as though in negative outline, the song is but the attraction of song;
yet what it promises the hero is nothing other than a duplicate of what he has
lived through, known, and suffered, precisely what he himself is. A promise at
once deceptive and truthful. It lies because all those who surrender to seduction
and steer their ships toward the beach will only meet death. But it speaks the truth
in that it is death that enables the song to sound and endlessly recount the heroes'
adventure. Yet one must refuse to hear this song so pure—so pure that it says
nothing more than its own devouring withdrawal—that one must plug one's
ears, pass by it as if one were deaf, in order to live and thus begin to sing. Or,
rather, in order for the narrative that will never die to be born, one must listen but
remain at the mast, wrists and ankles tied; one must vanquish all desire by a trick
that does violence to itself; one must experience all suffering by remaining at the
threshold of the alluring abyss; one must finally find oneself beyond song, as if
one had crossed death while still alive only to restore it in a second language.

   Then there is the figure of Eurydice. She would seem to be the exact opposite,
since she must be summoned back from the shadows by the melody of a song capable of seducing and lulling death, and since the hero is unable to resist Eurydice's power of enchantment, of which she herself is the saddest victim. Yet she
is a close relative of the Sirens: just as they sing only the future of a song, she
shows only the promise of a face. Orpheus may have succeeded in quieting barking dogs and beguiling sinister forces, but on the return trip he should have been
chained like Ulysses or as unperceiving as his sailors. In fact, he was the hero and
his crew combined in a single character: he was seized by the forbidden desire
and untied himself with his own hands, letting the invisible face disappear into
the shadows, just as Ulysses let the song he did not hear vanish in the waves. Each
of their voices is then freed: Ulysses' with his salvation and the possibility of
telling the tale of his marvelous adventure; Orpheus's with his absolute loss and
never-ending lament. But it is possible that behind Ulysses' triumphant narrative there prevails the inaudible lament of not having listened better and longer,
of not having ventured as close as possible to the wondrous voice that might
have finished the song. And that behind Orpheus's laments shines the glory of
having seen, however fleetingly, the unattainable face at the very instant it
turned away and returned to darkness—a nameless, placeless hymn to the light.

   These two figures are profoundly interwoven in Blanchot's work.[6] Some of
his narratives, for example *L'Arrêt de mort*, are dedicated to the gaze of Orpheus: the gaze that at the wavering threshold of death goes in search of the sub-
merged presence and tries to bring its image back to the light of day, but secures
only the nothingness in which the poem can subsequently appear. In Blanchot,
however, Orpheus does not see Eurydice's face in a movement that conceals it
and makes it visible: he is able to contemplate it face to face; he sees with his own

eyes the open gaze of death, "the most terrible gaze a living thing can encounter." It is that gaze, or rather the narrator's gaze into that gaze, that exerts
an extraordinary power of attraction; it is what makes a second woman appear
in the middle of the night in an already-captive state of stupefaction and forces
her to wear the plaster mask allowing one to contemplate "face to face that
which lives eternally." The gaze of Orpheus acquires the fatal power that sang
in the voice of the Sirens. Similarly, the narrator of *Au Moment voulu* goes in
search of Judith in the forbidden place where she is imprisoned; against all expectations, he easily finds her, like an overly close Eurydice who offers herself
in an impossible, happy return. But the figure lurking in the background who
guards her, and from which Orpheus comes to wrest her, is less a dark and in-
flexible goddess than a pure voice: "Indifferent and neutral, withdrawn into a
vocal realm where she is so completely stripped of superfluous perfections that
she seems deprived of herself: just, but in a way reminiscent of justice ruled by
every negative destiny."[7] Is not this voice—which "sings blankly" and offers so
little to be heard—the voice of the Sirens, whose seductiveness resides in the
void they open, in the fascinated immobility seizing all who listen?

THE COMPANION

At the first signs of attraction, when the withdrawal of the desired face remains
sketchy, when the firmness of the solitary voice is just beginning to stand out
against the blur of the murmur, something like a sweet and violent movement intrudes on interiority, drawing it out of itself, turning it around, bringing forth
next to it—or rather right behind it—the background figure of a companion
who always remains hidden but always makes it patently obvious that he is there;
a double that keeps his distance, an accosting resemblance. The instant that interiority is lured out of itself, an outside empties the place into which interiority
customarily retreats and deprives it of the possibility of retreat: a form arises—
less than a form, a kind of stubborn, amorphous anonymity—that divests interiority of its identity, hollows it out, divides it into noncoincident twin figures,
divests it of its unmediated right to say *I,* and pits against its discourse a speech
that is indissociably echo and denial. To lend an ear to the silvery voice of the
Sirens, to turn toward the forbidden face that has already concealed itself, is not
simply to abandon the world and the distraction of appearance; it is suddenly to
feel grow within oneself a desert at the other end of which (but this immeasura-
ble distance is also as thin as a line) gleams a language without an assignable
subject, a godless law, a personal pronoun without a person, an eyeless expres-
sionless face, an other that is the same. Does the principle of attraction secretly
reside in this tear and this bond? When one thought that one was being drawn

out of oneself by an inaccessible remoteness, was it not simply that this mute presence was bearing down in the shadows with all its inevitable weight? The empty outside of attraction is perhaps identical to the nearby outside of the double. That would make the companion attraction at the height of its dissimulation: it is dissimulated because it presents itself as a pure, close, stubborn, redundant presence, as one figure too many; and because it repels more than it attracts, because one must keep it at a distance, because there is always the danger that one will be absorbed by it and compromised by it in boundless confusion. This means that the companion acts both as a demand to which one is never equal and a weight of which one would like to rid oneself. One is irretrievably bound to the companion with a familiarity that is hard to bear; yet one must draw still closer to him and create a bond with him different from the absence of ties that attaches one to him through the faceless form of absence.

This figure is infinitely reversible. Is the companion an unacknowledged guide? Is he a law that is manifest but is not visible as law? Or does he constitute a heavy mass, an encumbering inertia, a slumber threatening to engulf all vigilance? No sooner does Thomas enter the house to which he has been attracted by a half-made gesture and an ambiguous smile than he receives a strange double (is this what, according to the meaning of the title, is "God-given"?): the double's apparently wounded face is only the outline of a face tattooed over his, and in spite of hideous flaws, he retains something like "a reflection of former beauty." Does he know the secrets of the house better than anyone else, as he will boast at the end of the novel? Is not his apparent fatuousness but a silent awaiting of the question? Is he a guide or a prisoner? Does he count among the inaccessible powers that dominate the house, or is he only a domestic? His name is *Dom*. He is invisible and falls silent whenever Thomas addresses a third party, and soon disappears entirely; but when Thomas seems to have finally gained entry to the house, when he thinks he has found the face and voice he was seeking, when he is being treated as a domestic, Dom reappears in possession of, or claiming to be in possession of, the law and speech: Thomas had been wrong to have had so little faith, to have failed to question him who was there to respond, to have squandered his zeal on his wish to gain access to the upper stories, when it would have been enough for him to allow himself to go down. The more choked Thomas's voice becomes, the more Dom speaks, assuming the right to speak and to speak for him. All of language totters; when Dom uses the first person, it is actually Thomas's language that is speaking, without him, in the void that the wake of his visible absence leaves in a darkness connected to dazzling light.

The companion is also indissociably what is closest and farthest away. In *Le Très-haut* he is represented by Dorte, the man from "down there"; he is a stranger to the law and stands outside the order of the city; he is illness in its raw state, disseminated death infusing life; by contrast to the "Most High" of the

title he is "Most Low"; and yet he is obsessively close; he is unreservedly familiar; he freely confides; he is inexhaustibly and multiply present; he is the eternal
neighbor; the sound of his cough carries across doors and walls; his death throes
resound through the house; and in this world oozing moisture, water rising on
all sides, Dorte's flesh itself, his fever and sweat, cross the partition to stain
Sorge's room next door. When he finally dies, howling in one last transgression
that he is not dead, his scream goes out into the hand that muffles it, forever vi-
brating in Sorge's fingers. Sorge's flesh and bones, his body, will long remain
that death, and the cry that contests and confirms it.

It is in this movement which is the pivot of language that the essence of the
stubborn companion is most clearly manifested. The companion is not a privileged interlocutor, some other speaking subject; he is the nameless limit language reaches. That limit, however, is in no way positive; it is instead the deep
into which language is forever disappearing only to return identical to itself, the
echo of a different discourse that says the same thing, of the same discourse saying something else. *"Celui qui ne m'accompagnait pas"* ("he who did not accompany me") has no name (and wishes to be kept in that essential anonymity); he is
a faceless, gazeless *he* who can only see through the language of another whom
he submits to the order of his own night; he edges as close as can be to the *I* that
speaks in the first person, and whose words and phrases he repeats in an infinite
void. Yet there is no bond between them; an immeasurable distance separates
them. That is why he who says *I* must continually approach him in order finally
to meet the companion who does not accompany him and who forms no bond
with him that is positive enough to be manifested by being untied. There is no
pact to tie them to each other; yet they are powerfully linked by a constant questioning (describe what you see, are you writing now?) and by the uninterrupted
discourse manifesting the impossibility of responding. It is as if this withdrawal, this hollowness that is perhaps nothing more than the inexorable erosion of the person who speaks, cleared a neutral space of language. The
narrative plunges into the space between the narrator and the inseparable companion who does not accompany him; it runs the full length of the straight line
separating the speaking *I* from the *he* he is in his spoken being; it unfolds a placeless place that is the outside of all speech and writing, that brings them forth and
dispossesses them, that imposes its law on them, that manifests through its infinite unraveling their momentary gleaming and sparkling disappearance.

NEITHER ONE NOR THE OTHER

Despite several consonances, we are quite far from the experience through
which some are wont to lose themselves in order to find themselves. The char-

acteristic movement of mysticism is to attempt to join—even if it means cross-ing the night—the positivity of an existence by opening a difficult line of com-munication with it. Even when that existence contents itself, hollows itself out in the labor of its own negativity, infinitely withdrawing into a lightless day, a shadowless night, a visibility devoid of shape, it is still a shelter in which experi-ence can rest. The shelter is created as much by the law of a Word as by the open expanse of silence. For in the form of the experience, silence is the immeasura-ble, inaudible, primal breath from which all manifest discourse issues; or speech is a reign with the power to hold itself in silent suspense.

The experience of the outside has nothing to do with that. The movement of attraction and the withdrawal of the companion lay bare what precedes all speech, what underlies all silence: the continuous streaming of language. A lan-guage spoken by no one: any subject it may have is no more than a grammatical fold. A language not resolved by any silence: any interruption is only a white stain on its seamless sheet. It opens a neutral space in which no existence can take root. Mallarmé taught us that the word is the manifest nonexistence of what it designates; we now know that the being of language is the visible effacement of the one who speaks: "Saying that I hear these words would not explain for me the dangerous strangeness of my relations with them. . . . They do not speak, they are not inside; on the contrary, they lack all intimacy and lie entirely out-side. What they designate consigns me to this outside of all speech, seemingly more secret and more inward than the inner voice of conscience. But that out-side is empty, the secret has no depth, what is repeated is the emptiness of repe-tition, it does not speak and yet has always been said."[8] The experiences Blanchot narrates lead to this anonymity of language liberated and opened to its own boundlessness. What they find in that murmuring space is less an endpoint than the site without geography of their possible rebeginning: hence the direct and luminous, at last serene, question Thomas asks at the end of *Aminadab* when all speech seems to be denied him; and the pure flash of the empty prom-ise—"now I am speaking"—in *Le Très-haut;* and the appearance in the final pages of *Celui qui ne m'accompagnait pas* of a smile that has no face but is worn at last by a silent name; or the first contact with the words of the subsequent re-beginning at the end of *Le Dernier homme.*

Language is then freed from all of the old myths by which our awareness of words, discourse, and literature has been shaped. For a long time it was thought that language had mastery over time, that it acted both as the future bond of the promise and as memory and narrative; it was thought to be prophecy and his-tory; it was also thought that in its sovereignty it could bring to light the eternal and visible body of truth; it was thought that its essence resided in the form of words or in the breath that made them vibrate. In fact, it is only a formless rum-bling, a streaming; its power resides in dissimulation. That is why it is one with the erosion of time; it is depthless forgetting and the transparent emptiness of waiting.

Language, its every word, is indeed directed at contents that preexist it; but in its own being, provided that it holds as close to its being as possible, it only unfolds in the pureness of the wait. Waiting is directed at nothing: any object that could gratify it would only efface it. Still, it is not confined to one place, it is not a resigned immobility; it has the endurance of a movement that will never end and would never promise itself the reward of rest; it does not wrap itself in interiority; all of it falls irremediably outside. Waiting cannot wait for itself at the end of its own past, nor rejoice in its own patience, nor steel itself once and for all, for it was never lacking in courage. What takes it up is not memory but forgetting. This forgetting, however, should not be confused with the scatteredness of distraction or the slumber of vigilance; it is a wakefulness so alert, so lucid, so new that it is a goodbye to night and a pure opening onto a day to come. In this respect forgetting is extreme attentiveness—so extreme that it effaces any singular face that might present itself to it. Once defined, a form is simultaneously too old and too new, too strange and too familiar, not to be instantly rejected by the purity of the wait, and thereby condemned to the immediacy of forgetting. It is in forgetting that the wait remains a waiting: an acute attention to what is radically new, with no bond of resemblance or continuity with anything else (the newness of the wait drawn outside of itself and freed from any past); attention to what is most profoundly old (for deep down the wait has never stopped waiting).

Language—in its attentive and forgetful being, with its power of dissimulation that effaces every determinate meaning and even the existence of the speaker, in the gray neutrality that constitutes the essential hiding place of all being and thereby frees the space of the image—is neither truth nor time, neither eternity nor man; it is instead the always undone form of the outside. It places the origin in contact with death, or rather brings them both to light in the flash of their infinite oscillation—a momentary contact in a boundless space. The pure outside of the origin, if that is indeed what language is eager to greet, never solidifies into a penetrable and immobile positivity; and the perpetually rebegun outside of death, although carried toward the light by the essential forgetting of language, never sets the limit at which truth would finally begin to take shape. They immediately flip sides. The origin takes on the transparency of the endless; death opens interminably onto the repetition of the beginning. And what language *is* (not what it means, not the form in which it says what it means), what language is in its being, is that softest of voices, that nearly imperceptible retreat, that weakness deep inside and surrounding every thing and every face—what bathes the belated effort of the origin and the dawnlike erosion of death in the same neutral light, at once day and night. Orpheus's murderous forgetting, Ulysses' wait in chains, are the very being of language.

At a time when language was defined as the place of truth and the bond of time, it was placed in absolute peril by the Cretan Epimenides' assertion that all Cretans were liars: the way in which that discourse was bound to itself undid any possibility of truth. On the other hand, when language is revealed to be the reciprocal transparency of the origin and death, every single existence receives, through the simple assertion "I speak," the threatening promise of its own disappearance, its future appearance.

Notes

1. Maurice Blanchot, *Celui qui ne m'accompagnait pas* (Paris: Gallimard, 1953), p. 125 [*The One Who Was Standing Apart From Me*, trans. Lydia Davis (Barrytown, N.Y.: Station Hill, 1993), pp. 66–67].

2. Blanchot, *L'Attente l'oubli* (Paris: Gallimard, 1962), p. 162.

3. Blanchot, *Aminadab* (Paris: Gallimard, 1942), p. 235.

4. Ibid, p. 122.

5. Blanchot, *Le Très-haut* (Paris: Gallimard, 1948), p. 81.

6. See Blanchot, *L'Espace littéraire* (Paris: Gallimard, 1955), pp. 179–184; and *Le Livre à venir* (Paris: Gallimard, 1955), pp. 9–17 [cf. "The Gaze of Orpheus" and "The Song of the Sirens," in Blanchot, *The Gaze of Orpheus*, trans. Lydia Davis (Barrytown, N.Y.: Station Hill, 1981), pp. 99–104 and 105–113].

7. Blanchot, *Au moment voulu* (Paris: Gallimard, 1951), pp. 68–69.

8. Blanchot, *Celui qui ne m'accompagnait pas*, pp. 136–37 [*The One Who Was Standing Apart From Me*, p. 72].

A PREFACE TO TRANSGRESSION

W e like to believe that sexuality has regained, in contemporary experience, its truth as a process of nature, a truth that has long been lingering
in the shadows and hiding under various disguises—until now, that is, when our
positive awareness allows us to decipher it so that it may at last emerge in the
clear light of language. Yet never did sexuality enjoy a more immediately natural understanding, and never did it know a greater "felicity of expression," than
in the Christian world of fallen bodies and of sin. The proof is its whole tradition of mysticism and spirituality, which was incapable of dividing the continuous forms of desire, of rapture, of penetration, of ecstasy, of that outpouring
which leaves us spent: all of these experiences seemed to lead, without interruption or limit, right to the heart of a divine love of which they were both the outpouring and the source returning upon itself. What characterizes modern
sexuality from Sade to Freud is not its having found the language of its logic or
of its nature, but, rather, through the violence done by such languages, its having been "denatured"—cast into an empty zone in which it achieves whatever
meager form is bestowed upon it by the establishment of its limits, and in which
it points to nothing beyond itself, no prolongation, except the frenzy that dis-
rupts it. We have not in the least liberated sexuality, though we have, to be exact,
carried it to its limits: the limit of consciousness, because it ultimately dictates
the only possible reading of our unconscious; the limit of the law, since it seems
the sole substance of universal taboos; the limit of language, since it traces that
line of foam showing just how far speech may advance upon the sands of silence. Thus, it is not through sexuality that we communicate with the orderly
and pleasingly profane world of animals; rather, sexuality is a fissure—not one

This essay first appeared in a special issue of *Critique* (195–96 [Aug.—Sept. 1963], pp. 751–69] devoted to Georges
Bataille. This translation, by Donald F. Bouchard and Sherry Simon, has been slightly amended.

that surrounds us as the basis of our isolation or individuality but one that marks the limit within us and designates us as a limit.

Perhaps we could say that it has become the only division possible in a world now emptied of objects, beings, and spaces to desecrate. Not that it proffers any new content for our millenary exploit, rather, it permits a profanation without object, a profanation that is empty and turned inward upon itself, whose instruments are brought to bear on nothing but each other. Profanation in a world that no longer recognizes any positive meaning in the sacred—is this not more or less what we may call transgression? In that zone which our culture affords for our gestures and speech, transgression prescribes not only the sole manner of discovering the sacred in its unmediated substance, but also a way of recomposing its empty form, its absence, through which it becomes all the more scintillating. A rigorous language, as it arises from sexuality, will not reveal the secret of man's natural being, nor will it express the serenity of anthropological truths, but rather, it will say that he exists without God; the speech given to sexuality is contemporaneous, both in time and in structure, with that through which we announced to ourselves that God is dead. From the moment that Sade delivered its first words and marked out, in a single discourse, the boundaries of what suddenly became its kingdom, the language of sexuality has lifted us into the night where God is absent, and where all of our actions are addressed to this absence in a profanation that at once identifies it, dissipates it, exhausts itself in it, and restores it to the empty purity of its transgression.

There indeed exists a modern form of sexuality: it is that which offers itself in the superficial discourse of a solid and natural animality, while obscurely addressing itself to Absence, to this high region where Bataille placed, in a night not soon to be ended, the characters of *Eponine:*

In this strained stillness, through the haze of my intoxication, I seemed to sense that the wind was dying down; a long silence flowed from the immensity of the sky. The priest knelt down softly. He began to sing in a despondent key, slowly as if at someone's death: *Miserere mei Deus, secondum misericordiam magnam tuam.* The way he moaned this sensuous melody was highly suspicious. He was strangely confessing his anguish before the delights of the flesh. A priest should conquer us by his denials but his efforts to humble himself only made him stand out more insistently; the loveliness of his chant, set against the silent sky, enveloped him in a solitude of morose pleasures. My reverie was shattered by a felicitous acclamation, an infinite acclamation already on the edge of oblivion. Seeing the priest as she emerged from the dream which still visibly dazed her senses, Eponine began to laugh and with such intensity that she was completely shaken; she turned her body and, leaning against the railing, trembled like a child. She was laughing with her head in her hands and the priest, barely stifling a clucking noise, raised his head, his arms uplifted, only to see a naked behind: the wind had lifted her coat and, made defenseless by the laughter, she had been unable to close it.[1]

Perhaps the importance of sexuality in our culture, the fact that since Sade it has persistently been linked to the most profound decisions of our language, derives from nothing else than this correspondence which connects it to the death of God. Not that this death should be understood as the end of his historical reign, or as the finally delivered judgment of his nonexistence, but as the now-constant space of our experience. By denying us the limit of the Limitless, the death of God leads to an experience in which nothing may again announce the exteriority of being, and consequently to an experience that is *interior* and *sovereign*. But such an experience, for which the death of God is an explosive reality, discloses as its own secret and clarification, its intrinsic finitude, the limitless reign of the Limit, and the emptiness of those excesses in which it spends itself and where it is found wanting. In this sense, the inner experience is, throughout, an experience of the *impossible* (the impossible being both that which we experience and that which constitutes the experience). The death of God is not merely an "event" that gave shape to contemporary experience as we now know it: it continues indefinitely tracing its great skeletal outline.

Bataille was perfectly conscious of the possibilities of thought that could be released by this death, and of the impossibilities in which it entangled thought. What, indeed, is the meaning of the death of God, if not a strange solidarity between the stunning realization of his non-existence and the act that kills him? But what does it mean to kill God if he does not exist, to kill God *who has never existed?* Perhaps it means to kill God both because he does not exist and to guarantee that he will not exist—certainly a cause for laughter: to kill God to liberate life from this existence that limits it, but also to bring it back to those limits that are annulled by this limitless existence—as a sacrifice; to kill God to return him to this nothingness he is and to manifest his existence at the center of a light that blazes like a presence—for the ecstasy; to kill God in order to lose language in a deafening night and because this would must make him bleed until there springs forth "an immense alleluia lost in the interminable silence"—and this is communication. The death of God restores us not to a limited and positivistic world but to a world exposed by the experience of its limits, made and unmade by that excess which transgresses it.

Undoubtedly it is excess that discovers that sexuality and the death of God are bound to the same experience; or that again shows us, as if in "the most incongruous book of all," that "God is a whore." And from this perspective the thought that relates to God and the thought that relates to sexuality are linked in a common form, since Sade to be sure, but never in our day with as much insistence and difficulty as in Bataille. And if it were necessary to give, in opposition to sexuality, a precise definition of eroticism, it would have to be the following: an experience of sexuality which links, for its own ends, an overcoming of limits to the death of God. "Eroticism can say what mysticism never could (its strength failed when it tried): God is nothing if not the surpassing of God in every sense of vulgar being, in that of horror or impurity; and ultimately in the sense of nothing." [2]

Thus, at the root of sexuality, of the movement that nothing can ever limit (because it is, from its origin and in its totality, constantly involved with the limit), and at the root of this discourse on God which Western culture has maintained for so long—without any sense of the impropriety of "thoughtlessly adding to language a word which surpasses all words" or any clear sense that it places us at the limits of all possible languages—a singular experience is shaped: that of transgression. Perhaps one day it will seem as decisive for our culture, as much a part of its soil, as the experience of contradiction was at an earlier time for dialectical thought. But in spite of so many scattered signs, the language in which transgression will find its space and the illumination of its being lies almost entirely in the future.

It is surely possible, however, to find in Bataille its calcinated roots, its promising ashes.

Transgression is an action that involves the limit, that narrow zone of a line where it displays the flash of its passage, but perhaps also its entire trajectory, even its origin; it is likely that transgression has its entire space in the line it crosses. The play of limits and transgression seems to be regulated by a simple obstinacy: transgression incessantly crosses and recrosses a line that closes up behind it in a wave of extremely short duration, and thus it is made to return once more right to the horizon of the uncrossable. But this play is considerably more complex: these elements are situated in an uncertain context, in certainties that are immediately upset so that thought is ineffectual as soon as it attempts to seize them.

The limit and transgression depend on each other for whatever density of being they possess: a limit could not exist if it were absolutely uncrossable and, reciprocally, transgression would be pointless if it merely crossed a limit composed of illusions and shadows. But can the limit have a life of its own outside of the act that gloriously passes through it and negates it? What becomes of it after this act and what might it have been before? For its part, does transgression not exhaust its nature when it violates the limit, being nothing beyond this point in time? And this point, this curious intersection of beings that do not exist outside it but totally exchange what they are within it—is it not also everything that overflows from it on all sides? It serves as a glorification of what it excludes: the limit opens violently onto the limitless, finds itself suddenly carried away by the content it had rejected and fulfilled by this alien plenitude that invades it to the core of its being. Transgression carries the limit right to the limit of its being; transgression forces the limit to face the fact of its imminent disappearance, to find itself in what it excludes (perhaps, to be more exact, to recognize itself for the first time), to experience its positive truth in its downward fall. And yet, toward what is transgression unleashed in its movement of pure violence, if not that which imprisons it, toward the limit and those elements it contains? What bears the brunt of its aggression, and to what void does it owe the unrestrained fullness of its being, if not that which it crosses in its violent act and which, as its destiny, it crosses out in the line it effaces?

Transgression, then, is not related to the limit as black to white, the prohibited to the lawful, the outside to the inside, or as the open area of a building to its enclosed spaces. Rather, their relationship takes the form of a spiral that no simple infraction can exhaust. Perhaps it is like a flash of lightning in the night which, from the beginning of time, gives a dense and black intensity to the night it denies; which lights up the night from the inside, from top to bottom, and yet owes to the dark the stark clarity of its manifestation, its harrowing and poised singularity. The flash loses itself in this space it marks with its sovereignty and becomes silent now that it has given a name to obscurity.

Since this existence is both so pure and so complicated, it must be detached from its questionable association to ethics if we want to understand it and to begin thinking from it and in the space it denotes; it must be liberated from the scandalous or subversive, that is, from anything aroused by negative associations. Transgression does not seek to oppose one thing to another, nor does it achieve its purpose through mockery or by upsetting the solidity of foundations; it does not transform the other side of the mirror, beyond an invisible and uncrossable line, into a glittering expanse. Transgression is neither violence in a divided world (in an ethical world) nor a victory over limits (in a dialectical or revolutionary world); and, exactly for this reason, its role is to measure the excessive distance that it opens at the heart of the limit and to trace the flashing line that causes the limit to arise. Transgression contains nothing negative, but affirms limited being—affirms the limitlessness into which it leaps as it opens this zone to existence for the first time. But, correspondingly, this affirmation contains nothing positive: no content can bind it, since, by definition, no limit can possibly restrict it. Perhaps it is simply an affirmation of division; but only insofar as division is not understood to mean a cutting gesture, or the establishment of a separation or the measuring of a distance, only retaining that in it which may designate the existence of difference.

Perhaps when contemporary philosophy discovered the possibility of nonpositive affirmation, it began a process of reorientation whose only equivalent is the shift instituted by Kant when he distinguished the *nihil negativum* and the *nihil privativum*—a distinction known to have opened the way for the advance of critical thought.[3] This philosophy of nonpositive affirmation, in other words of the testing of the limit, is, I believe, what Blanchot was defining through his principle of "contestation." Contestation does not imply a generalized negation, but an affirmation that affirms nothing, a radical break of transitivity. Rather than being a process of thought for denying existences or values, contestation is the act that carries them all to their limits and, from there, to the Limit where an ontological decision achieves its end; to contest is to proceed until one reaches the empty core where being achieves its limit and where the limit defines being. There, at the transgressed limit, the "yes" of contestation reverberates, leaving without echo the hee-haw of Nietzsche's braying ass.

Thus, contestation shapes an experience that Bataille wanted to circumscribe through every detour and repetition of his work, an experience that has the power "to implicate (and to question) everything without possible respite" and to indicate, in the place where it occurs and in its most essential form, "the immediacy of being." Nothing is more alien to this experience than the demonic character who, true to his nature, "denies everything." Transgression opens onto a scintillating and constantly affirmed world, a world without shadow or twilight, without that serpentine "no" that bites into fruits and lodges their contradictions at their core. It is the solar inversion of satanic denial. It was originally linked to the divine, or rather, from this limit marked by the sacred it opens the space where the divine functions. The discovery of such a category by a philosophy that questions itself about the existence of the limit is evidently one of the countless signs that our path is a path of return and that, with each day, we are becoming more Greek. Yet this motion should not be understood as the promised return to a homeland or the recovery of an original soil that produced and will naturally resolve every opposition. In reintroducing the experience of the divine at the center of thought, philosophy has been well aware since Nietzsche (or it should very well know) that it questions an origin without positivity and an opening indifferent to the patience of the negative. No form of dialectical movement, no analysis of constitutions and of their transcendental ground can serve as support for thinking about such an experience or even as access to this experience. In our day, would not the instantaneous play of the limit and of transgression be the essential test for a thought that centers on the "origin," for that form of thought to which Nietzsche dedicated us from the beginning of his works and one that would be, absolutely and in the same motion, a Critique and an Ontology, an understanding that comprehends both finitude and being?

What possibilities generated this thought from which everything, up until our time, has seemingly diverted us, but as if to lead us to the point of its returning? From what impossibilities does it derive its hold on us? Undoubtedly, it can be said that it comes to us through that opening made by Kant in Western philosophy when he articulated, in a manner that is still enigmatic, metaphysical discourse and reflection on the limits of our reason. However, Kant ended by closing this opening when he ultimately relegated all critical investigations to an anthropological question; and undoubtedly, we have subsequently interpreted Kant's actions as the granting of an indefinite respite to metaphysics, because dialectics substituted for the questioning of being and limits the play of contradiction and totality. To awaken us from the confused sleep of dialectics and of anthropology, we required the Nietzschean figures of tragedy, of Dionysus, of the death of God, of the philosopher's hammer, of the Superman approaching with the steps of a dove, of the Return. But why, in our day, is discursive language so ineffectual when asked to maintain the presence of these figures and to maintain itself through them? Why is it so nearly silent before them, as if it were forced to yield its voice so that they may continue to find their words, to yield to these extreme forms of language in which Bataille, Maurice Blanchot, and Pierre Klossowski have made their home, which they have made the summits of thought?

The sovereignty of these experiences must surely be recognized some day, and we must try to assimilate them: not to reveal their truth—a ridiculous pretension with respect to words that form our limits—but to serve as the basis for finally liberating our language. But our task for today is to direct our attention to this nondiscursive language, this language which, for almost two centuries, has stubbornly maintained its disruptive existence in our culture; it will be enough to examine its nature, to explore the source of this language which is neither complete nor fully in control of itself, even though it is sovereign for us and hangs above us, this language which is sometimes immobilized in scenes we customarily call "erotic" and suddenly volatized in a philosophical turbulence, when it seems to lose its very basis.

The parcelling out of philosophical discourse and descriptive scenes in Sade's books is undoubtedly the product of complex architectural laws. It is quite probable that the simple rules of alternation, of continuity, or of thematic contrast are inadequate for defining the space of the language where descriptions and demonstrations are articulated, where a rational order is linked to an order of pleasures, and where, especially, subjects are located both in the movement of various discourses and in a constellation of bodies. Let us simply say that this space is completely covered by a language that is discursive (even when it involves a narrative), explicit (even when it denotes nothing), and continuous (especially at the moment the thread passes from one character to another): a language that nevertheless does not have an absolute subject, that never discovers the one who ultimately speaks and incessantly maintains its *hold* on speech from the announcement of the "triumph of philosophy" in Justine's first adventure to Juliette's corpseless disappearance into eternity. Bataille's language, on the other hand, continually breaks down at the center of its space, exposing in his nakedness, in the inertia of ecstasy, a visible and insistent subject who had tried to keep language at arms length, but who now finds himself thrown by it, exhausted, upon the sands of that which he can no longer say.

How is it possible to discover, under all these different figures, that form of thought we carelessly call "the philosophy of eroticism," but in which it would be necessary to recognize (which is no less, but also much more) an essential experience for our culture since Kant and Sade—the experience of finitude and being, of the limit and transgression? What is the proper space of this form of thought and what language can it adopt? Undoubtedly, no form of reflection, yet developed, no established discourse, can supply its model, its foundation, or even the riches of its vocabulary. Would it be of help, in any case, to argue by analogy that we must find a language for the transgressive which would be what dialectics was, in an earlier time, for contradiction? Our efforts are undoubtedly better spent in trying to speak of this experience and in making it speak from the depths where its language fails, from precisely the place where words escape it, where the subject who speaks has just vanished, where the spectacle topples over before an upturned eye—from where Bataille's death has recently placed his language. We can only hope, now that his death has sent us to the pure transgression of his texts, that they will protect those who seek a language for the thought of the limit, that they will serve as a dwelling place for what may already be a ruined project. In effect, do we not grasp the possibility of such thought in a language that necessarily strips it of any semblance of thought and leads it to the very impossibility of language? Right to this limit where the existence of language becomes problematic? The reason is that philosophical language is linked beyond all memory (or nearly so) to dialectics; and the dialectic was able to become the form and interior movement of philosophy from the time of Kant only through a redoubling of the millenary space from which philosophy had always spoken. We know full well that reference to Kant has invariably addressed us to the most formative elements of Greek thought: not to recapture a lost experience but to bring us closer to the possibility of nondialectical language. This age of commentary in which we live, this historical redoubling from which there seems no escape, does not indicate the velocity of our language in a field now devoid of new philosophical objects, which must be constantly recrossed in a forgetful and always rejuvenated glance. But far more to the point, it indicates the inadequacy, the profound silence, of a philosophical language that has been chased from its natural element, from its original dialectics, by the novelists found in its domain. If philosophy is now experienced as a multiple desert, it is not because it has lost its proper object or the freshness of its experience but because it has been suddenly divested of that language which is

historically "natural" to it. We experience not the end of philosophy but a philosophy that regains its speech and finds itself again only in the marginal region
that borders its limits—that is, one that finds itself either in a purified metalan-
guage or in the thickness of words enclosed by their darkness, by their blind
truth. The prodigious distance that separates these alternatives and manifests
our philosophical dispersion marks, more than a disarray, a profound coherence. This separation and real incompatibility is the actual distance from whose
depths philosophy addresses us. It is here that we must focus our attention.

But what language can arise from such an absence? And, above all, who is the
philosopher who will now begin to speak? "What of us when, having become
sobered, we learn what we are? Lost among idlers in the night, where we can
only hate the semblance of light coming from their small talk." [4] In a language
stripped of dialectics, at the heart of what it says but also at the root of its possibility, the philosopher is aware that "we are not everything"; he learns as well
that even the philosopher does not inhabit the whole of his language like a secret
and perfectly fluent god. Next to himself, he discovers the existence of another
language that also speaks and of which he is not the master, one that strives,
fails, and falls silent, one that he cannot manipulate, the language he spoke at
one time and has now separated itself from him, now gravitating in a space increasingly silent. Most of all, he discovers that he is not always lodged in his
language in the same fashion, and that in the location from which a subject had
traditionally spoken in philosophy—one whose obvious and garrulous identity
has remained unexamined from Plato to Nietzsche—a void has been hollowed
out in which a multiplicity of speaking subjects are joined and severed, combined and excluded. From the lessons on Homer to the cries of a madman in the
streets of Turin, who can be said to have spoken this continuous language, so
obstinately the same? Was it the Wanderer or his shadow? The philosopher or
the first of the nonphilosophers? Zarathustra, his monkey, or already the Superman? Dionysus, Christ, their reconciled figures, or finally this man right here?
The breakdown of philosophical subjectivity and its dispersion in a language
that dispossesses it while multiplying it within the space created by its absence is
probably one of the fundamental structures of contemporary thought. Again,
this is not the end of philosophy but, rather, the end of the philosopher as the
sovereign and primary form of philosophical language. And perhaps to all
those who strive above all to maintain the unity of the philosopher's grammatical function—at the price of the coherence, even of the existence of philosophical language—we could oppose Bataille's exemplary enterprise: his desperate
and relentless attack on the preeminence of the philosophical subject as it confronted him in his own work, in his experience and his language that became his
private torment, in the first reflected torture of that which speaks in philosophical language—in the dispersion of stars that encircle a median night, allowing

voiceless words to be born. "Like a flock chased by an infinite shepherd, we, the bleating wave, would flee, endlessly flee from the horror of reducing being to totality." [5]

It is not only the juxtaposition of reflective and novelistic texts in the language of thought that makes us aware of the shattering of the philosophical [*philosophant*] subject. The words of Bataille define the situation in far greater detail: in the constant movement to different levels of speech and a systematic disengagement from the "I" who has begun to speak and is already on the verge of deploying his language and installing himself in it; temporal disengagements ("I was writing this," or similarly, "in retrospect, if I return to this matter"); shifts in the distance separating a speaker from his words (in a diary, notebooks, poems, stories, meditations, or discourses intended for demonstration); an inner detachment from the assumed sovereignty of thought or writing (through books, anonymous texts, prefaces to his books, footnotes). And it is at the center of the philosophical subject's disappearance that philosophical language proceeds as if through a labyrinth, not to recapture him, but to test (and through language itself) the extremity of its loss. That is, it proceeds to the limit and to this opening where its being surges forth, but where it is already lost, completely overflowing itself, emptied of itself to the point where it becomes an absolute void—an opening which is communication: "at this point there is no need to elaborate; as my rapture escapes me, I immediately reenter the night of a lost child, anguished in his desire to prolong his ravishment, with no other end than exhaustion, no way of stopping short of fainting. It is such excruciating bliss." [6]

This experience forms the exact reversal of the movement that has sustained the wisdom of the West at least since the time of Socrates, that is, the wisdom to which philosophical language promised the serene unity of a subjectivity that would triumph in it, having been fully constituted by it and through it. But if the language of philosophy is one in which the philosopher's torments are tirelessly repeated and his subjectivity is discarded, then not only is wisdom meaningless as the philosopher's form of composition and reward, but in the expiration of philosophical language a possibility inevitably arises (that upon which it falls—the face of the die; and the place into which it falls—the void into which the die is cast): the possibility of the mad philosopher. In short, the experience of the philosopher who finds, not outside his language (the result of an external accident or imaginary exercise) but at the inner core of its possibilities, the transgression of his philosophical being; and thus, the nondialectical language of the limit that only arises in transgressing the one who speaks. This play of transgression and being is fundamental for the constitution of philosophical language, which reproduces and undoubtedly produces it.

Essentially the product of fissures, abrupt descents, and broken contours, this misshapen and craglike language describes a circle; it refers to itself and is folded back on a questioning of its limits—as if it were nothing more than a small night lamp that flashes with a strange light, signaling the void from which it arises and to which it addresses everything it illuminates and touches. Perhaps, it is this curious configuration that explains why Bataille attributed such obstinate prestige to the Eye. Throughout his career (from his first novel to *Larmes d'Eros*), the eye was to keep its value as a figure of inner experience: "When at the height of anguish, I gently solicit a strange absurdity, an eye opens at the summit, in the middle of my skull." [7] This is because the eye, a small white globe that encloses its darkness, traces a limiting circle that only sight can cross. And the darkness within, the somber core of the eye, pours out into the world like a fountain which sees, that is, which lights up the world; but the eye also gathers up all the light of the world in the pupil, that small black spot, where it is transformed into the bright night of an image. The eye is mirror and lamp: it discharges its light into the world around it, while in a movement that is not necessarily contradictory, it precipitates this same light into the transparency of its well. Its globe has the expansive quality of a marvelous seed—like an egg imploding toward the center of night and extreme light, which it is and which it has just ceased to be. It is the figure of being in the act of transgressing its own limit.

The eye, in a philosophy of reflection, derives from its capacity to observe the power of becoming always more interior to itself. Lying behind each eye that sees, there exists a more tenuous one, an eye so discreet and yet so agile that its all-powerful glance can be said to eat away at the flesh of its white globe; behind this particular eye, there exists another and, then, still others, each progressively more subtle until we arrive at an eye whose entire substance is nothing but the pure transparency of a vision. This inner movement is finally resolved in a nonmaterial center where the intangible forms of truth are created and combined, in this heart of things which is the sovereign subject. Bataille reverses this entire direction: sight, crossing the globular limit of the eye, constitutes the eye in its instantaneous being; sight carries it away in this luminous stream (an outpouring fountain, streaming tears and, shortly, blood), hurls the eye outside of itself, conducts it to the limit where it bursts out in the immediately extinguished flame of its being. Only a small white ball, veined with blood, is left behind, only an exorbitated eye to which all sight is now denied. And in the place from which sight had once passed, only a cranial cavity remains, only this black globe which the uprooted eye has made to close upon its sphere, depriving it of vision but offering to this absence the spectacle of that indestructible core which now imprisons the dead glance. In the distance created by this violence and uprooting, the eye is seen absolutely but denied any possibility of sight: the philosophizing subject has been dispossessed and pursued to its limit, and the sovereignty of philosophical language can now be heard from the distance, in the measureless void left behind by the exorbitated subject.

But perhaps the eye accomplishes the most essential aspect of its play when forced from its ordinary position, it is made to turn upward in a movement that leads it back to the nocturnal and starred interior of the skull and it is made to show us its usually concealed surface, white and unseeing: it shuts out the day in a movement that manifests its own whiteness (whiteness being undoubtedly the image of clarity, its surface reflection, but for this very reason it cannot communicate with it or communicate it); and the circular night of the pupil is made to address the central absence that it illuminates with a flash, revealing it as night. The upturned orb suggests both the most open and the most impenetrable eye: causing its sphere to pivot, while remaining exactly the same and in the same place, it overturns day and night, crosses their limit, but only to find it again on the same line and from the other side; and the white hemisphere that appears momentarily at the place where the pupil once opened is like the being of the eye as it crosses the limit of its vision—when it transgresses this opening to the light of day which defined the transgression of every sight. "If man did not imperiously close his eyes, he would finally be unable to see the things worth seeing." [8]

But what we need to see does not involve any interior secret or the discovery of a more nocturnal world. Torn from its ordinary position and made to turn inward in its orbit, the eye now only pours its light into a bony cavern. This turning up of its globe may seem a betrayal of "la petite mort," but more exactly, it simply indicates the death that it experiences right where it is, in this springing up in place that causes the eye to rotate. Death, for the eye, is not the always elevated line of the horizon, but the limit it ceaselessly transgresses in its natural location, in the hollow where every vision originates, and where this limit is elevated into an absolute limit by an ecstatic movement that allows the eye to spring up from the other side. The upturned eye discovers the bond that links language and death at the moment it acts out this relationship of the limit and being; and it is perhaps from this that it derives its prestige, in permitting the possibility of a language for this play. Thus, the great scenes that interrupt Bataille's stories invariably concern the spectacle of erotic deaths, where upturned eyes display their white limits and rotate inward in gigantic and empty orbits. *Le Bleu du ciel* gives a singularly precise outline of this movement: early in November, when the earth of German cemeteries is alive with the twinkling light of candles and candle stubs, the narrator is lying with Dorothy among the tombstones; making love among the dead, the earth around him appears like the sky on a bright night. And the sky above forms a great hollow orbit, a death mask, in which he recognizes his inevitable end at the moment that pleasure overturns the four globes of flesh, causing the revolution of his sight. "The earth under Dorothy's body was open like a tomb, her belly opened itself to me like a fresh grave. We were struck with stupor, making love on a starred cemetery. Each light marked a skeleton in a grave and formed a wavering sky as perturbed as our mingled bodies. I unfastened Dorothy's dress, I dirtied her clothes and her breast with the fresh earth which was stuck to my fingers. Our bodies trembled like two rows of chattering teeth."[9]

But what might this mean at the heart of a system of thought? What significance has this insistent eye which appears to encompass what Bataille successively designated *the inner experience, the extreme possibility, the cosmic process,* or simply *meditation?* It is certainly no more metaphoric than Descartes's phrasing of the "clear perception of sight" or this sharp point of the mind which he called *acies mentis.* In point of fact, the upturned eye has no meaning in Bataille's language, can have no meaning, since it marks its limit. It indicates the moment when language, arriving at its confines, overleaps itself, explodes and radically challenges itself in laughter, tears, the eyes rolled back in ecstasy, the mute and exorbitated horror of sacrifice, and where it remains fixed in this way at the limit of its void, speaking of itself in a second language in which the absence of a sovereign subject outlines its essential emptiness and incessantly fractures the unity of its discourse. The enucleated or rolled-back eye marks the zone of Bataille's philosophical language, the void into which it pours and loses itself, but in which it never stops talking—somewhat like the interior, diaphanous, and illuminated eye of mystics and spiritualists that marks the point at which the secret language of prayer is embedded and choked by a marvellous communication that silences it. Similarly, but in an inverted manner, the eye in Bataille delineates the zone shared by language and death, the place where language discovers its being in the crossing of its limits—the nondialectical form of philosophical language.

This eye, as the fundamental figure of the place from which Bataille speaks and in which his broken language finds its uninterrupted domain, establishes the connection, prior to any form of discourse, that exists between the death of God (a sun that rotates and the great eyelid that closes upon the world), the experience of finitude (springing up in death twisting the light that is extinguished as it discovers that the interior is an empty skull, a central absence), and the turning-back of language upon itself at the moment that it fails—a conjunction that undoubtedly has no other equivalent than the association, well known in other philosophies, of sight to truth or of contemplation to the absolute. Revealed to this eye, which in its pivoting conceals itself for all time, is the being of the limit: "I will never forget the violent and marvellous experience that comes from the will to open one's eyes, facing what exists, what happens."

Perhaps in the movement that carries it to a total night, the experience of transgression brings to light this relationship of finitude to being, this moment of the limit that anthropological thought, since Kant, could only designate from the distance and from the exterior through the language of dialectics.

The twentieth century will undoubtedly have discovered the related categories of exhaustion, excess, the limit, and transgression—the strange and unyielding form of these irrevocable movements that consume and consummate us. In a form of thought that considers man as worker and producer—that of European culture since the end of the eighteenth century—consumption was based entirely on need, and need based itself exclusively on the model of hunger. When this element was introduced into an investigation of profit (the appetite of those who have satisfied their hunger), it inserted man into a dialectic of production which had a simple anthropological meaning: if man was alienated from his real nature and immediate needs through his labor and the production of objects with his hands, it was nevertheless through its agency that he recaptured his essence and achieved the indefinite gratification of his needs. But it would undoubtedly be misguided to conceive of hunger as that irreducible anthropological factor in the definition of work, production, and profit; and similarly, need has an altogether different status, or it responds at the very least to a code whose laws cannot be confined to a dialectic of production. The discovery of sexuality—the discovery of that firmament of indefinite unreality where Sade placed it from the beginning, the discovery of those systematic forms of prohibition we now know imprison it, the discovery of the universal nature of transgression in which it is both object and instrument—indicates in a sufficiently forceful way the impossibility of attributing the millenary language of dialectics to the major experience that sexuality forms for us.

Perhaps the emergence of sexuality in our culture is an event of multiple values: it is tied to the death of God and to the ontological void that His death fixed at the limit of our thought; it is also tied to the still-silent and groping apparition of a form of thought in which the interrogation of the limit replaces the search for totality, and the act of transgression replaces the movement of contradictions. Finally, it involves the questioning of language by language in a circularity that the "scandalous" violence of erotic literature, far from ending, displays from its first use of words. Sexuality is only decisive for our culture as spoken, and to the degree it is spoken. Not that it is our language that has been eroticized now for nearly two centuries; rather, since Sade and the death of God, the universe of language has absorbed our sexuality, denatured it, placed it in a void where it establishes its sovereignty and where it incessantly sets up as the Law the limits it transgresses. In this sense, the appearance of sexuality as a fundamental problem marks the slippage of a philosophy of man as worker to a philosophy based on a being who speaks; and insofar as philosophy has traditionally maintained a secondary role to knowledge and work, it must be admitted, not as a sign of crisis but of essential structure, that it is now secondary to language. Not that philosophy is now fated to a role of repetition or commentary, but that it experiences itself and its limits in language and in this transgression of language which carries it, as it did Bataille, to the faltering of the speaking subject. On the day that sexuality began to speak and to be spoken, language no longer served as a veil for the infinite; and in the density it acquired on that day, we now experience finitude and being. In its dark domain, we now encounter the absence of God, our death, limits, and their transgression. But perhaps it is also a source of light for those who have liberated their thought from all forms of dialectical language, as it became for Bataille, on more than one occasion, when he experienced the loss of his language in the dead of night. "What I call night differs from the darkness of thoughts: night possesses the violence of light. Yes, night: the youth and the intoxication of thinking." [10]

Perhaps this "difficulty with words" that now hampers philosophy, a condition fully explored by Bataille, should not be identified with the loss of language that the closure of dialectics seemed to indicate. Rather, it follows from the actual penetration of philosophical experience in language and the discovery that the experience of the limit, and the manner in which philosophy must now understand it, is realized in language and in the movement where it says what cannot be said.

Perhaps this "difficulty with words" also defines the space given over to an experience in which the speaking subject, instead of expressing himself, is exposed, goes to encounter his finitude and, under each of his words, is brought back to the reality of his own death: that zone, in short, which transforms every work into the sort of "tauromachy" suggested by Michel Leiris, who was thinking of his own actions as a writer but undoubtedly also of Bataille.[11] In any event, it is on the white beach of an arena (a gigantic eye) where Bataille experienced the fact—crucial for his thought and characteristic of all his language—that death *communicated with communication*, and that the uprooted eye, a white and silent sphere, could become a violent seed in the night of the body, that it could render present this absence of which sexuality has never stopped speaking and from which it is made to speak incessantly. When the horn of the bull (a glittering knife that carries the threat of night, and an exact reversal of the image of light that emerges from the night of the eye) penetrates the eyeball of the toreador, who is blinded and killed, Simone performs an act we have come to expect: she swallows a pale and skinless seed and returns to its original night the luminous virility that has just committed murder. The eye is returned back to its night, the globe of the arena turns upward and rotates; but it is the moment in which being necessarily appears in its immediacy and in which *the act that crosses the limit touches absence itself:* "Two globes of the same color and consistency were simultaneously activated in opposite directions. A bull's white testicle had penetrated Simone's black and pink flesh; an eye had emerged from the head of the young man. This coincidence, linked until death to a sort of urinary lique-faction of the sky, gave me Marcelle for a moment. I seemed, in this ungraspable instant, to touch her." [12]

Notes

1. Georges Bataille, *L'Abbé C.*, part two: "Récit de Charles" [1950], in *Oeuvres complètes* (Paris: Galli-mard, 1971), vol. 3, pp. 263–64.

2. Bataille, *L'Erotisme*, part two: "Etudes diverses," VII: "Préface to *Madame Edwards*" [1957], in *Oeu-vres complètes*, vol. 3, pp. 263–64 (*Eroticism*, trans. M. Dalwood [San Francisco: City Lights, 1986], p. 269).

3. See Immanuel Kant's *Critique of Pure Reason* [1781], trans. and ed. Norman Kemp Smith (London: MacMillan, 1933), p. 295–Ed.

4. Bataille, *Somme athéologique*, part one: *L'Expérience intérieure* [1943] (6th ed., Paris: Gallimard, 1954), Preface, p. 10.

5. Bataille, *L'Expérience intérieure*, part two: *Le Supplice*, p. 54.

6. Ibid., p. 74.

7. Bataille, *L'Expérience intérieure*, part three: *Le Bleu du ciel*, p. 101.

8. Bataille, *La Littérature et le mal: Boudelaire* [1957], in *Oeuvres complètes* [*Literature and Evil*, trans. Alastair Hamilton (London: Martin Boyars, 1973), p. 40].

9. Bataille, *Le Bleu de ciel* [1957], in *Oeuvres complètes*, vol. 3 (1971), pp. 481–82.

10. Bataille, *Le Coupable: la divinité du rire* [1961], in *Oeuvres complètes*, vol. 5 (1973), p. 354 [*Guilty*, trans. B. Boone (San Francisco: Lapis, 1988), p. 108].

11. Michel Leiris, *De la Littérature considérée comme une tauromachie* (Paris: Gallimard, 1946) [*Manhood*, trans. Richard Howard (London: Jonathan Cape, 1968)].

12. Bataille, *Histoire de l'oeil: sous le soleil de Saville*, new version, in *Oeuvres complètes*, vol. 1 (1970), ap-pendix, p. 598 [*Story of the Eye*, trans. Joachim Neugroschel (San Francisco: City Lights, 1987), pp. 65–66].

PERMISSIONS